ASPECTS of WESTERN CIVILIZATION

ASPECTS of WESTERN CIVILIZATION

Problems and Sources in History

Volume II

Second Edition

Edited by

PERRY M. ROGERS

The Ohio State University

Prentice Hall, Englewood Cliffs, New Jersey 07632

Library of Congress Cataloging-in-Publication Data

Aspects of Western civilization : problems and sources in history /
  edited by Perry M. Rogers. — 2nd ed.
    p.   cm.
  Includes bibliographical references.
  ISBN 0–13–050758–X (v. 1). — ISBN 0–13–051897–2 (v. 2)
  1. Civilization, Western—History. 2. Civilization, Western—
History—Sources.   I. Rogers, Perry McAdow.
CB245.A86 1992
909′.09821—dc20   91–32035
                                            CIP

Acquisitions editor: Stephen Dalphin
Copy editor: Bobbie Reitt
Editorial assistant: Caffie Risher
Editorial/production supervision: Joan Powers
Interior design: Karen Buck
Cover design: George Cornell
Cover art: "The Proportions of Man" by Leonardo da Vinci, courtesy of
  Accademia, Venice.
Prepress buyer: Kelly Behr
Manufacturing buyer: Mary Ann Gloriande

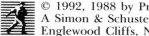

© 1992, 1988 by Prentice-Hall, Inc.
A Simon & Schuster Company
Englewood Cliffs, New Jersey 07632

Printed in the United States of America
10 9 8 7 6 5 4 3 2 1

ISBN 0-13-051897-2

Prentice-Hall International (UK) Limited, *London*
Prentice-Hall of Australia Pty. Limited, *Sydney*
Prentice-Hall Canada Inc., *Toronto*
Prentice-Hall Hispanoamericana, S.A., *Mexico*
Prentice-Hall of India Private Limited, *New Delhi*
Prentice-Hall of Japan, Inc., *Tokyo*
Simon & Schuster Asia Pte. Ltd., *Singapore*
Editora Prentice-Hall do Brasil, Ltda., *Rio de Janeiro*

For Ann
Elisa, Kit, and Tyler

Brief Contents

VOLUME II

Contents

4 The Industrial Revolution   *183*

5 Nationalism and Imperialism: The Motives and Methods of Expansion   *221*

Nationalism   *224*

Motives for Imperialism   *231*

Preface

The Roman orator Cicero once remarked that "History is the witness of the times, the torch of truth, the life of memory, the teacher of life, the messenger of antiquity." In spite of these noble words, historians have often labored under the burden of justifying the study of events that are over and done. Human beings are practical, more concerned with their present and future than with their past. And yet the study of history provides us with unique opportunities for self-knowledge. It teaches us what we have done and therefore helps define what we are. On a less abstract level, the study of history enables us to judge present circumstances by drawing on the laboratory of the past. Those who have lived and died, through their recorded attitudes, actions, and ideas, have left a legacy of experience.

One of the best ways to travel through time and perceive the very "humanness" of history is through the study of primary sources. These are the documents, coins, letters, inscriptions, and monuments of past ages. The task of historians is to evaluate this evidence with a critical eye and then construct a narrative that is consistent with the "facts" as they have been established. Such interpretations are inherently subjective and open to dispute. History is thus filled with controversy as historians argue their way toward the truth. The only effective way to understand the past is through personal examination of the primary sources.

Yet, for the beginning student, this poses some difficulties. Such inquiry casts the student adrift from the security of accepting the "truth" as revealed in a textbook. In fact, history is too often presented in a deceptively objective manner; one learns facts and dates in an effort to obtain the right answers for multiple-choice tests. But the student who has wrestled with primary sources and has experienced voices from the past on a more intimate level accepts the responsibility of evaluation and judgment. He or she understands that history does not easily lend itself to right answers, but demands reflection on the problems that have confronted past societies and are at play even in our contemporary world.

Aspects of Western Civilization offers the student an opportunity to evaluate the primary sources of the past in a structured and organized format. The documents provided include state papers, secret dispatches, letters, diary accounts, poems, newspaper articles, papal encyclicals, propaganda fliers, and even wall graffiti. Occasionally, the assessments of modern historians are included. Yet this two-volume book has been conceived as more than a simple compilation of sources. The subtitle of the work, *Problems and Sources in History*, gives true indication of the nature of its premise. Students learn from the past most effectively when faced with problems that have meaning for their own lives. In evaluating the material from *Aspects of Western Civilization*, the student will discover that issues are not nearly as simple as they may appear at first glance. Historical sources often contradict each other, and truth then depends upon logic and upon one's own experience and outlook on life. Throughout these volumes, the student is confronted with basic questions regarding historical development, human nature, moral action, and practical necessity. The text is therefore broad in its scope, incorporating a wide variety of political, social, economic, religious, intellectual, and scientific issues. It is internally organized around seven major themes that provide direction and cohesion while allowing for originality of thought in both written and oral analysis:

1. *Imperialism.* How has imperialism been justified throughout Western history, and what are the moral implications of gaining and maintaining empire? Is defensive imperialism a practical foreign policy option? This theme is often juxtaposed with subtopics of nationalism, war, altruism, and human nature.

2. *Church/State Relationships.* Is there a natural competition between these two controlling units in society? Which is more influential, which legacy more enduring? How has religion been used as a means of securing political power or of instituting social change? The Judeo-Christian heritage of Western Civilization forms the basis of this theme.

3. *Systems of Government.* The student is introduced to the various systems of rule that have shaped Western Civilization: classical democracy, representative democracy (republican government), oligarchy, constitutional monarchy, divine-right monarchy, theocracy, and dictatorship (especially fascism and totalitarian rule). What are the advantages and drawbacks to each? This rubric also includes the concepts of balance of power and containment, principles of succession, geopolitics, and so-

cial and economic theories such as capitalism, communism, and socialism.

4. *Revolution.* The text examines the varieties of revolution: political, intellectual, economic, and social. What are the underlying and precipitating causes of political revolution? How essential is the intellectual foundation? Are social demands and spontaneity more important elements in radical action?

5. *Propaganda.* What is the role of propaganda in history? Many sections examine the use and abuse of information, often in connection with absolute government, revolution, imperialism, or genocide. How are art and architecture, as well as the written word, used in the "creation of belief"? This theme emphasizes the relativity of truth and stresses the responsibility of the individual in assessing the validity of evidence.

6. *Women in History.* The text intends to help remedy the omission of women from the history of Western society and to develop an appreciation of their contributions to the intellectual and political framework of Western Civilization. At issue is how women have been viewed—or rendered invisible—throughout history and how individually and collectively their presence is inextricably linked with the development and progress of civilization. This inclusive approach stresses the importance of achieving a perspective that lends value and practical application to history.

7. *Historical Change and Transition.* What are the main determinants of change in history? How important is the individual in effecting change, or is society regulated by unseen social and economic forces? What role does chance play? What are the components of civilization and how do we assess progress or decline? Are civilizations biological in nature? Is a crisis/response theory of change valid? This theme works toward providing the student with a philosophy of history and against the tendency to divide history into strict periods. It stresses the close connection between the past and the present.

Structure of the Book

Each chapter begins with a series of quotations from various historians, statesmen, philosophers, literary figures, or religious spokespersons who offer insight on the subject matter of the chapter. These quotations may well be used in conjunction with the study questions at the end of the unit. After the quotations, an introduction provides a brief historical background and identifies the themes or questions to be discussed in the chapter.

Following this general introduction, the primary sources are presented with extensive direction for the student. A headnote explains in more detail the historical or biographical background for each primary source and focuses attention on themes or interrelationships with other sources. Each chapter concludes with a chronology designed to orient the student to the broader context of history, and a series of study questions that can form the basis of oral discussion or written analysis. The questions do not seek mere regurgitation of information, but demand a more thoughtful response based on reflective analysis of the primary sources.

Use of the Book

Aspects of Western Civilization offers the instructor a wide variety of didactic applications. The chapters fit into a more or less standard lecture format and are ordered chronologically. An entire chapter may be assigned for oral discussion, or sections from each chapter may satisfy particular interests or requirements. Some of the chapters provide extensive treatment of a broad historical topic ("The Medieval World: Dark Ages?"; " 'I Am the State': The Development of Absolutism in England and France"; " 'Dare to Know!': The Revolution of the Mind in the Seventeenth and Eighteenth Centuries"; " 'Liberty, Equality, Fraternity!': The French Revolution and the Rise of Napoleon"; "Our Contemporary World: The Progress of Civilization"). In order to make them manageable and effective, I have grouped them into topical sections (with correspondingly labeled study questions) that can be utilized separately, if so desired.

The chapters may also be assigned for written analysis. One of the most important concerns of both instructor and student in an introductory class is the written assignment. *Aspects of Western Civilization* has been designed to provide self-contained topics that are problem-oriented, promote reflection and analysis, and encourage responsible citation of particular primary sources. The study questions for each chapter should generally produce an eight- to ten-page paper.

Acknowledgments

I would particularly like to thank friends and colleagues who contributed their expertise and enthusiasm to this book. Professors Alan Beyerchen and Kenneth Andrien of The Ohio State University advised me on particular matters in the initial phases of writing. Mary Alice Fite provided me with material and insight that added greatly to the accuracy of the text, and Jack Guy read drafts of some chapters, offering sterling commentary throughout. Sara Shriner typed a difficult manuscript time and again with unfailing determination and good cheer. Stephen Dalphin, Acquisitions Editor at Prentice Hall, afforded wise direction throughout the various phases of production. Special thanks to Diana Livesey, who proofread the entire manuscript and offered several suggestions and ideas that improved the second edition substantially. Thanks also to the students of Columbus School for Girls, who "tested" the chapters in this book with their typical diligence and hard work; the final product has benefited greatly from their suggestions and ideas. Finally, I owe an immeasurable debt to my wife, Ann, who suffered all the outrageous fortune and disruption that goes into writing a book of this kind over a period of years—she did it with me.

P. M. R.

ASPECTS of WESTERN CIVILIZATION

1

"I Am the State": The Development of Absolutism in England and France

It is atheism and blasphemy to dispute what God can do; so it is presumption and contempt to dispute what a king can do, or say that a king cannot do this or that.

—James I

It is in my person alone that ultimate power resides. It is from me alone that my courts derive their authority. It is to me alone that the power to make law belongs, without any dependence and without any division. The whole public order comes from me, and the rights and interests of the nation are necessarily joined with mine and rest only in my hands.

—Louis XIV

Resistance on the part of people to the supreme legislative power of the state is never legitimate; it is the duty of the people to bear any abuse of the supreme power.

—Immanuel Kant

Every subject's duty is the king's, but every subject's soul is his own.

—William Shakespeare

It has often been said that the primary purpose of government is to create and maintain a stable domestic environment. Only through such stability and domestic tranquility can a government establish a strong defense against threatening foes and also pursue a successful foreign policy.

When the state is divided against itself into several political, social, or economic factions, it is weak and thus susceptible to invasion or revolution. This is a rather conservative opinion, and others throughout the years have argued that a state based primarily on efficiency and security does not tolerate new ideas or respond quickly to the needs of its citizens; in essence, such a state is not progressive in outlook, but seeks only to maintain the status quo. At the root of these different ideas lies a basic problem: To what extent are citizens of a state able to rule themselves? Is democracy a "noble experiment" that errs by ascribing extraordinary possibilities to ordinary people? Indeed, is progress best served when a citizen body is directed and controlled by a monarch or even a dictator who uses all the resources of the state to achieve his goals? These questions form the basis of political theory in the Western world. How best should humans organize society in order to provide stability, security, and happiness?

During the fifteenth through the eighteenth centuries, these questions were of fundamental importance. As the Middle Ages blended into the Renaissance, decentralized feudalism gave way to more structured monarchies in France, England, and Spain. The modern state was forming under the control of kings who had relatively few restrictions on their authority. The major exception to this was England, whose monarch had coexisted since the thirteenth century with a developing parliament, or representative body, and was beholden to certain laws and decrees (such as the Magna Carta of 1215), which guaranteed basic civil rights for Englishmen. It is perhaps because of this long tradition of more or less shared power and responsibilities that England was the first major state to experience the conflicts that inevitably resulted from such an arrangement.

Between 1603 and 1715, England experienced the most tumultuous years of its long history. The glorious reign of Queen Elizabeth I (1558–1603) gave way to increasing religious dissension under her successor, James I (1603–1625). The new king, who hailed from Scotland, lacked tact and was ignorant of English institutions. More seriously, he was an advocate of absolute, divine-right monarchy. According to this theory, the authority of a king was unlimited and could not be challenged because it was sanctioned by God. The reign of James I began a breach between the monarchy and Parliament that was eventually to result in a civil war (1642–1646) between supporters of the Parliament (Roundheads) and those of the king (Cavaliers). The victory of Parliament was crowned with the beheading of King Charles I (1649), an act without precedent in English history. After this, the government was controlled first by Parliament alone and then under the direction of Oliver Cromwell, who was determined to give England efficient rule as Lord Protector (1653–1658). On Cromwell's death the monarchy was restored under Charles II (1660–1685), but it was conciliatory to the will of Parliament. The final breach occurred when

King James II (1685–1688) once again tried to assert authority as an absolute monarch. Parliament deposed him, banned his Catholic relatives from succession, and invited the popular Dutch Protestant leader William of Orange and his wife Mary to rule as monarchs (1688). This "Glorious Revolution" was bloodless and resulted in a Bill of Rights that limited the powers of the monarchy; henceforward the king would rule with the consent of Parliament.

Seventeenth-century France, in contrast to England, saw representative government crushed by the success of absolute monarchy. It was Henry IV (1589–1610) who began the process of establishing a strong centralized state by curtailing the privileges of the nobility and restricting provincial governors and regional councils called *parlements*. Henry and his finance minister, the Duke of Sully (1560–1641), also sought to control the finances of the state by establishing government monopolies on gunpowder, mines, and salt. When Henry IV was assassinated in 1610, he was succeeded by his son, Louis XIII (1610–1643). Since Louis was only nine years old at the time of his father's death, France was ruled by his mother, Marie de Medici, who sought internal security by promoting Cardinal Richelieu (1585–1642) as chief advisor to the king. Richelieu, an efficient and shrewd counselor, was determined to make France the dominant European power by consolidating the domestic authority of the king. There was to be but one law—that of the king. To this end, Richelieu imprisoned and executed recalcitrant nobles; indeed, the French nobility eventually became docile in their subservience at court. Richelieu was succeeded in 1642 by another cardinal named Mazarin (1602–1661), who acted as regent for the young monarch, Louis XIV. It is because of the strict policies of Richelieu and Mazarin that Louis XIV inherited a basic foundation for absolute rule.

The reign of Louis XIV (1643–1714) was of fundamental importance for the establishment of France both as the supreme political power on the Continent and as the dominant cultural influence throughout Europe. The sun shone brightly on the fortunes of France in the seventeenth and eighteenth centuries, and Louis, or the "Sun King" as he was called, became the model of stable, secure rule. His control over his subjects was absolute, subject to no authority except that of God. God had appointed Louis, and God alone could judge his actions. Thus, all political, social, economic, and military decisions were made by the king and his various advisors without interference or input from the people of France. Collectively, his subjects were Louis' children and as such were expected to follow the policies of their "father." Louis' famous comment, "I am the state," was the essence of French divine-right monarchy.

This period of history, however, was not in any sense tranquil. For over half a century before Louis' accession, France had been disrupted by religious wars between Catholics, whom the French monarchy supported, and the Huguenots, or French Protestants. The wars had secured certain political and military privileges for the Huguenots that were scarcely compatible with the ideal of a strong, centralized monarchy. When Louis assumed control of the government in 1661 after his eighteen-year minority, the Huguenots were still an independent religious group, officially tolerated by the crown, but an embarrassment nonetheless. Finally, in 1685, Louis demanded conformity to Catholic doctrine and revoked the Edict of Nantes (1598), which had decreed religious tolerance toward the Huguenots.

Another major threat to the tranquility of the state and the supremacy of royal power came from the nobility. During the minority of Louis XIV, France had lapsed into civil war, fomented by nobles who were jealous of the increasing power of the monarchy and particularly its close financial support from an active middle class. To many, the chaos of such disturbances was a greater fear than the existence of a strong, centralized monarchy that could ensure domestic tranquility and external security. This fear of chaos and desire for order probably lay behind popular support of Louis' divine-right monarchy. The longevity and relative harmony of his reign demonstrates Louis' successful disarming of the nobility. His magnificent palace at Versailles, testimony to his pursuit of order, not only was an enduring artistic legacy of his reign, but also served a practical purpose: Louis could house all his important nobles at the palace and thus maintain close control over their activities. Louis reserved high government positions for hand-picked members of the aristocracy and aspiring middle class, who thus owed their success to him; this in turn assured their loyalty.

In the late seventeenth and early eighteenth centuries, France was the envy and terror of Europe, its most powerful state and cultural center. Other monarchs imitated Louis' court at Versailles and even the palace itself. His army was perhaps the best-trained and best-supplied military force of its day, and his diplomatic service proved to be a model of excellence. The French language became accepted as the common tongue among diplomats. French dominance of European affairs was cultural as well as political.

The purpose of this chapter is to examine the theory and practice of absolute rule, especially as it was experienced in England, and as applied quite differently in France under Louis XIV. Is absolute monarchy a natural form of government, in keeping with the human desire to follow, and to be taken care of? Or do you resist this idea? To what extent is absolutism, whether justified by God or by force of arms, different from tyranny? Is a competent, even enlightened despot more attractive than divisive democracy? Charles I, Oliver Cromwell, and Louis XIV were all aggressive rulers who struggled to define and maintain their dominant positions. Indeed, Louis sought glory in foreign wars and domestic stability under the motto "one King, one law, one faith." The formula is simplistic, yet the policy was effective. To his admirers, Louis represented the quintessential monarch. Yet, the Sun King was certainly not without his critics. And Oliver Cromwell, in the fluid political environment of seventeenth-century England, can be seen variously as the "caretaker of democracy," as well as the "scourge of freedom." Each would have you believe that his actions were in accordance with the preference of his particular political community and required by necessities of state. But voices of dissent must also be heard for a balanced assessment of absolutism.

SECTION I: THE ENGLISH REVOLUTION

James I and the Origins of Confrontation (1603–1625)

When Queen Elizabeth died in 1603, she was succeeded by her nephew, James I (1603–1625), who was already king of Scotland. He was a leader of ability and assertive personality who inherited an ambiguous political position in England. It was never very clear to James, who had no experience with parliamentary institutions in Scotland, just where the authority of the king left off and where that of the Parliament began. Since England had no written constitution, the country was governed through traditions and laws that had developed since Magna Carta in 1215. During the sixteenth century, Parliament grew into a powerful representative institution fully confirmed in its authority to offer advice to the monarch on questions of policy and especially in its control over taxation. James thus was looking to rule England with the kind of dominant authority he had exercised in Scotland, while the English Parliament had adopted an aggressive attitude designed to uphold their traditional rights and privileges.

Some of James' ideas on the nature of absolute rule and the position of kings were presented in the following speech to Parliament in 1610.

Speech to Parliament (1610)

KING JAMES I

The state of Monarchy is the supremest thing upon earth; for kings are not only God's lieutenants upon earth and sit upon God's throne, but even by God himself they are called gods. There be three principal similitudes that illustrate the state of Monarchy; one taken out of the Word of God and the two other out of the grounds of policy and philosophy. In the Scriptures kings are called gods, and so their power after a certain relation compared to the Divine power. Kings are also compared to the fathers of families, for a king is truly *parens patriae*, the politic father of his people. And lastly, kings are compared to the head of this microcosm of the body of man.

Kings are justly called gods for that they exercise a manner or resemblance of Divine power upon earth; for if you will consider the attributes to God you shall see how they agree in the person of a king. God hath power to create or destroy, make or unmake, at his pleasure; to give life or send death; to judge all, and to be judged nor accountable to none; to raise low things and to make high things low at his pleasure; and to God are both soul and body due. And the like power have kings: they make and unmake their subjects; they have power of raising and casting down; of life and of

"Speech to Parliament" is from James I, *Works* (1616), pp. 528–531.

death; judges over all their subjects and in all causes, and yet accountable to none but God only. They have power to exalt low things and abase high things, and make of their subjects like men at the chess, a pawn to take a bishop or a knight, and to cry up or down any of their subjects as they do their money. And to the King is due both the affection of the soul and the service of the body of his subjects.

As for the father of a family, . . . a father may dispose of his inheritance to his children at his pleasure, yea, even disinherit the eldest upon just occasions and prefer the youngest, according to his liking; make them beggars or rich at his pleasure; restrain or banish out of his presence, as he finds them give cause of offence, or restore them in favour again with the penitent sinner. So may the King deal with his subjects.

And lastly, as for the head of the natural body, the head has the power of directing all the members of the body to that use which the judgment in the head thinks most convenient. It may apply sharp cures or cut off corrupt members, let blood in what proportion it thinks fit and as the body may spare; but yet is all this power ordained by God *ad aedificationem, non ad destructionem* [for the benefit of the body, not for its destruction]. For although God have power as well of destruction as of creation or maintenance, yet will it not agree with the wisdom of God to exercise his power in the destruction of nature and overturning the whole frame of things, since his creatures were made that his glory might thereby be the better expressed; so were he a foolish father that would disinherit or destroy his children without a cause or leave off the careful education of them; and it were an idle head that would in place of physic so poison or phlebotomize the body as might breed a dangerous distemper or destruction thereof.

But now in these our times we are to distinguish between the state of kings in their first original and between the state of settled kings and monarchs that do at this time govern in civil kingdoms. . . . Every just king in a settled kingdom is bound to observe that paction made to his people by his laws in framing his government. . . . And therefore a king governing in a settled kingdom leaves to be a king and degenerates into a tyrant as soon as he leaves off to rule according to his laws. . . . And though no Christian man ought to allow any rebellion of people against their Prince, yet doth God never leave kings unpunished when they transgress these limits. . . . Therefore all kings that are not tyrants or perjured will be glad to bound themselves within the limits of their laws, and they that persuade them the contrary are vipers and pests, both against them and the commonwealth. For it is a great difference between a king's government in a settled State and what kings in their original power might do. . . . As for my part, I thank God I have ever given good proof that I never had intention to the contrary. And I am sure to go to my grave with that reputation and comfort, that never king was in all his time more careful to have his laws duly observed, and himself to govern thereafter, than I.

I conclude then this point touching the power of kings with this axiom of Divinity: That as to dispute what God may do is blasphemy, . . . so is it sedition in subjects to dispute what a king may do in the height of power; but just kings will ever be willing to declare what they will do, if they will not incur the curse of God. I will not be content that my power be disputed upon, but I shall ever be willing to make the reason appear of all my doings, and rule my actions according to my laws.

Charles I and the Struggle for Constitutional Government (1625–1649)

Although James I succeeded in avoiding a sharp break with Parliament over the limits of royal authority and the supremacy of the Anglican Church, events moved to a crisis under his son, Charles I (1625–1649). Charles seemed to have none of the qualifications of a successful ruler. In 1624, he advised his dying father into a war with Spain and then one with France. Both fared poorly and, although at peace again by 1630, the monarchy was in severe financial straits. When Parliament failed to grant him customary revenues, Charles collected them away through "forced loans" from the people, imprisoning those who refused to pay. Troops in transit to war zones were often quartered in private English homes. Politically, the king's authoritarianism was blatant and alienated many of those who could have helped him.

Religiously, tensions also increased under Charles. He was a devout Anglican, who looked to the maintenance of the Church of England as the moderate and stable force that had been so ably directed by his predecessor, Elizabeth I. But the Church of England was in turmoil, split into two factions. The Puritans wanted to modify the rites and doctrines of the Anglican Church in accordance with the Calvinist creed of predestination and by preaching as an integral part of worship. The other faction, known as the Arminians, emphasized human free will and a conservative definition of the sacraments and rituals of the church. Charles had difficulty maintaining his political position in the realm since his enemies in Parliament denounced him as an Arminian and accused him of even being a "papist" in support of Catholicism and the supremacy of the pope. Although Charles was quite willing to tolerate Catholics, these charges were untrue. Nevertheless, Charles was saddled with a majority in the House of Commons, who actively pursued their own policies in religion and foreign affairs by withholding the appropriation of taxes. As a result, Charles was compelled to negotiate and compromise as evidenced by the Petition of Right.

The Petition of Right (1628)

To the King's Most Excellent Majesty:

Whereas it is declared and enacted by a statute made in the time of the reign of King Edward the First [1272–1307] . . . that no tallage or aid shall be laid or levied by the King or his heirs in this realm, without the will and assent of the Archbishops, Bishops, Earls, Barons, Knights, Burgesses, and other freemen of the commonalty of this realm: and by authority of Parliament held in the five and twentieth year of the reign of King Edward the Third [1352], it is declared and enacted, that from thenceforth no person shall be compelled to make any loans to the King against his will, because such loans were against reason and the franchise of the land; and by other laws of this realm it is provided, that . . . [your subjects] should not be compelled to contribute any tax, tallage, aid, or other like charge, not set by common consent in Parliament:

2. Yet nevertheless, . . . your people have been required to lend certain sums of money unto your Majesty, and many of them upon their refusal so to do . . . have been therefore imprisoned, confined, and in sundry other ways molested and disquieted:

3. And where also by the statute called, "The Great Charter of the Liberties of England" [Magna Carta, 1215], it is declared and enacted, that no freeman may be taken or imprisoned or be disseised of his freehold or liberties, or his free customs, or be outlawed or exiled, or in any manner destroyed, but by the lawful judgment of his peers, or by the law of the land:

4. And in the eight and twentieth year of the reign of King Edward the Third [1355], it was declared and enacted by authority of Parliament, that no man of what estate or condition . . . be put out of his lands or tenements, nor taken, nor imprisoned, nor disinherited, nor put to death, without being brought to answer by due process of law:

5. Nevertheless, against the tenor of the said statutes, and the other good laws and statutes of your realm, . . . divers of your subjects have of late been imprisoned without any cause showed, and when for their deliverance they were brought before your Justices . . . and yet were returned back to several prisons, without being charged with anything to which they might make answer according to the law.

6. And whereas of late great companies of soldiers and mariners have been dispersed into divers counties of the realm, and the inhabitants against their wills have been compelled to receive them into their houses, and there to suffer them to stay, against the laws and customs of this realm, and to the great grievance and vexation of the people. . . .

9. And also sundry grievous offenders . . . have escaped the punishments due to them by the laws and statutes of this your realm, by reason that divers of your officers and ministers of justice have unjustly refused . . . to proceed against such offenders according to the same laws and statutes.

10. They do therefore humbly pray your Most Excellent Majesty, that

no man hereafter be compelled to make or yield any gift, loan, benevolence, tax, or such like charge, without common consent by Act of Parliament; and that none be called to make answer, or take such oath, or to give attendance, or be confined, or otherwise molested or disquieted concerning the same, or for refusal thereof; and that no freeman . . . be imprisoned or detained; and that your Majesty will be pleased to remove the said soldiers and mariners, and that your people may not be so burdened in time to come; and that the aforesaid commissions for proceeding by martial law, may be revoked and annulled; and that hereafter no commissions of like nature may issue forth to any person or persons whatsoever, to be executed . . . destroyed or put to death, contrary to the laws and franchise of the land.

11. All which they most humbly pray of your Most Excellent Majesty, as their rights and liberties according to the laws and statutes of this realm.

[Which Petition being read . . . the King's answer was thus delivered unto it]:

The King wills that right be done according to the laws and customs of the realm; and that the statutes be put in due execution, that his subjects may have no cause to complain of any wrong or oppressions, contrary to their just rights and liberties. . . .

The Grand Remonstrance (December 12, 1641)

Although it is true that Charles accepted the Petition of Right, he did not intend to deprive himself of income that could be obtained through reviving ancient rights of the crown that had fallen into disuse. After a serious parliamentary attempt to limit royal prerogative in 1629, Charles dismissed Parliament and did not call it into session for eleven years. To conserve his limited resources, Charles and his ministers instituted a policy called thorough, *whereby strict efficiency and administrative centralization would contribute to the king's ability to operate independently of Parliament. Charles handled the finances of the country by enforcing neglected laws and relying on impositions such as "ship money"(1634) that the courts determined could be garnered as personal income without the approval of Parliament. These issues were disputed throughout the decade, but since Parliament could not be called into session by anyone but the king, there was no official confrontation.*

The situation changed in 1640 when Charles was compelled to summon Parliament in order to provide funds to quell a rebellion in Scotland that had been provoked when Charles imposed an episcopal system and an Anglican prayer book on the Calvinist Scots. The Parliament reacted quickly by passing a series of acts that were designed to curtail royal power: Parliament in the

"The Petition of Right" is from George Burton Adams and H. Morse Stephens, eds., *Select Documents of English Constitutional History* (New York: The Macmillan Company, 1916), pp. 339–342.

"The Grand Remonstrance" is from Samuel Gardiner, ed., *The Constitutional Documents of the Puritan Revolution* (Oxford: Clarendon Press, 1889), pp. 127–154.

future was to meet at least every three years; the king's chief minister, the Earl of Strafford, was accused of high treason and executed; Parliament resolved that it could not be dissolved without its own consent and abolished the king's personally controlled court (Star Chamber) and the "ship money" tax, which the king had used for financial support in lieu of parliamentary taxation. Because Charles was faced with the crisis of a Scottish rebellion, he signed all of these acts, thus making them valid statutes.

Royal authority had thus been limited by large majorities in Parliament. In 1641, the more radical members of the House of Commons drafted the Grand Remonstrance, which detailed the grievances lodged against the monarchy during the preceding twenty years. Charles' reply makes it clear that he refused to assent to Parliament's assertion of authority.

Most Gracious Sovereign,

Your Majesty's most humble and faithful subjects the Commons in this present Parliament assembled, do with much thankfulness and joy acknowledge the great mercy and favour of God, in giving your Majesty a safe and peaceable return out of Scotland into your kingdom of England, where the pressing dangers and distempers of the State have caused us with much earnestness to desire the comfort of your royal authority, to give more life and power to the dutiful and loyal counsels and endeavours of your Parliament, for the prevention of that eminent ruin and destruction wherein your kingdoms of England and Scotland are threatened. The duty which we owe to your Majesty and our country, cannot but make us very sensible and apprehensive, that the multiplicity, sharpness and malignity of those evils under which we have now many years suffered, are fomented and cherished by a corrupt and ill affected party, who . . . have sought by many false scandals and imputations, cunningly insinuated and dispersed amongst the people, to blemish and disgrace our proceedings in this Parliament, and to get themselves a party and faction among your subjects, for the better strengthening themselves in their wicked courses, and hindering those provisions and remedies which might, by the wisdom of your Majesty and counsel of your Parliament, be opposed against them.

For preventing thereof, and the better information of your Majesty, your Peers and all your other loyal subjects, we have been necessitated to make a declaration of the state of the kingdom, . . . which we do humbly present to your Majesty, without the least intention to lay any blemish upon your royal person, but only to represent how your royal authority and trust have been abused, to the great prejudice and danger of your Majesty, and of all your good subjects. . . .

The Grand Remonstrance

The root of this mischief we find to be a malignant and pernicious design of subverting the fundamental laws and principles of government, upon which the religion and justice of this kingdom are firmly established . . .:

12. The privilege of Parliament [was] broken by imprisoning divers members of the House, detaining them close prisoners for many months together, without the liberty of using books, pen, ink or paper; denying them all the comforts of life, all means of preservation of health, not permitting their wives to come unto them even in the time of their sickness.

13. And for the completing of that cruelty, after years spent in such miserable durance, depriving them of the necessary means of spiritual consolation, not suffering them to [travel] abroad to enjoy God's ordinances in God's House, or God's ministers to come to them to minister comfort to them in their private chambers.

14. And to keep them still in this oppressed condition, not admitting them to be bailed according to law, . . . sentencing and fining some of them for matters done in Parliament; and extorting the payments of those fines from them, enforcing others to put in security of good behaviour before they could be released.

16. Upon the dissolution of both these Parliaments, untrue and scandalous declarations were published to asperse their proceedings, and some of their members unjustly; to make them odious, and [legitimate] the violence which was used against them; proclamations set out to the same purpose; and to the great dejecting of the hearts of the people, forbidding them even to speak of Parliaments.

17. After the breach of the Parliament [its dissolution in 1629 on order of Charles], injustice, oppression and violence broke in upon us without any restraint or moderation, and yet the first project was the great sums exacted through the whole kingdom . . . against all rules of justice. . . .

24. The desperate design of engrossing all the gunpowder into one hand, keeping it in the Tower of London, and setting so high a rate upon it that the poorer sort were not able to buy it, nor could any have it without license, thereby to leave the several parts of the kingdom destitute of their necessary defence, and by selling so dear that which was sold to make an unlawful advantage of it to the great charge and detriment of the subject.

33. And not only private interest, but also public faith, have been broken in seizing of the money and bullion in the mint, and the whole kingdom like to be robbed at once.

34. Great numbers of His Majesty's subjects for refusing those unlawful charges, have been vexed with long and expensive [law] suits, some fined and censured, other committed to long and hard imprisonments and confinements, to the loss of health in many, of life in some, and others have had their houses broken up, their goods seized, some have been restrained from their lawful callings.

37. The Court of Star Chamber has abounded in extravagant censures, not only for the maintenance and improvement of monopolies and other unlawful taxes, but for divers other causes where there has been no offence, or very small; whereby His Majesty's subjects have been oppressed by grievous fines, imprisonments, stigmatisings, mutilations, whippings, pillories, gags, confinements, [and] banishments.

48. Titles of honour, judicial places, sergeantships at law, and other offices have been sold for great sums of money, whereby the common justice of the kingdom has been much endangered . . . by giving occasion to bribery, extortion, partiality, it seldom happening that places ill-gotten are well used.

51. The Bishops, and the rest of the Clergy did triumph in the suspensions, excommunications, deprivations, and degradations of divers painful, learned and pious ministers, in the vexation and grievous oppression of great numbers of His Majesty's good subjects.

59. Many noble personages were councillors in name, but the power and authority remained in a few of such as were most addicted to this party [Papists], whose resolutions and determinations were brought to the table for countenance and execution, and not for debate and deliberation, and no man could offer to oppose them without disgrace and hazard to himself.

79. After the Parliament ended the 5th of May, 1640, this party grew so bold as to counsel the King to supply himself out of his subjects' estates by his own power, at his own will, without their consent.

80. The very next day some members of both Houses had their studies and cabinets, yea, their pockets searched: another of them not long after was committed close prisoner for not delivering some petitions which he received by authority of that House.

88. The Popish party enjoyed such exemptions from penal laws as amounted to a toleration, besides many other encouragements and Court favours.

169. [The king's counselors] have sought by many subtle practices to cause jealousies and divisions betwixt us and our brethren of Scotland, by slandering their proceedings and intentions towards us, and by secret endeavours to instigate and incense them and us one against another.

171. They have laboured to seduce and corrupt some of the Commons' House to draw them into conspiracies and combinations against the liberty of the Parliament.

172. And by their instruments and agents they have attempted to disaffect and discontent His Majesty's army, and to engage it for the maintenance of their wicked and traitorous designs. . . .

182. [The king's counselors] infuse into the people that we mean to abolish all Church government, and leave every man to his own fancy for the service and worship of God, absolving him of that obedience which he owes under God unto His Majesty, whom we know to be entrusted with the ecclesiastical law as well as with the temporal, to regulate all the members of the Church of England, by such rules of order and discipline as are established by Parliament, which is his great council, in all affairs both in Church and State.

186. They have maliciously charged us that we intend to destroy and discourage learning, whereas it is our chiefest care and desire to advance it.

187. And we intended likewise to reform and purge the fountains of learning, the two Universities, that the streams flowing from thence may be clear and pure, and an honour and comfort to the whole land.

202. That all Councillors of State may be sworn to observe those laws which concern the subject in his liberty, that they may likewise take an oath not to receive or give reward of pension from any foreign prince.

204. That His Majesty may have cause to be in love with good counsel and good men, by showing him in an humble and dutiful manner how full of advantage it would be to himself, to see his own estate settled in a plentiful condition to support his honour; to see his people united in ways of duty to him, and endeavours of the public good; to see happiness, wealth, peace and safety derived to his own kingdom, and procured to his allies by the influence of his own power and government.

The King's Response to the Grand Remonstrance (December 23, 1641)

KING CHARLES I

We having received from you, soon after our return out of Scotland, a long petition consisting of many desires of great moment, together with a declaration of a very unusual nature annexed thereunto, we had taken some time to consider of it . . . being confident that your own reason and regard to us . . . would have restrained you from the publishing of it till such time as you should have received our answer to it; but, much against our expectation, finding the contrary, that the said declaration is already abroad in print, . . . we must let you know that we are very sensible of the disrespect. Notwithstanding, it is our intention that no failing on your part shall make us fail in ours of giving all due satisfaction to the desires of our people in a parliamentary way; and therefore we send you this answer to your petition. . . .

We say that although there are divers things in the preamble of it which we are so far from admitting that we profess we cannot at all understand them, as of 'a wicked and malignant party prevalent in the government'; of 'some of that party admitted to our Privy Council and to other employments of trust, and nearest to us and our children'; of 'endeavours to sow among the people false scandals and imputations, to blemish and disgrace the proceedings of the Parliament'; all, or any of them, did we know of, we should be as ready to remedy and punish as you to complain of, so that the prayers of your petition are grounded upon such premises as we must in no way admit; yet, notwithstanding, we are pleased to give this answer to you. . . .

To the second prayer of the petition, concerning the removal and choice of councillors, we know not any of our Council to whom the character set forth in the petition can belong; that by those whom we had exposed to trial, we have already given you sufficient testimony that there is no man so

"The King's Response" is from Samuel Gardiner, ed., *The Constitutional Documents of the Puritan Revolution* (Oxford: Clarendon Press, 1889), pp. 155–158.

near unto us in place or affection, whom we will not leave to the justice of the law, if you shall bring a particular charge and sufficient proofs against him; and of this we do again assure you, but in the meantime we wish you to forbear such general aspersions as may reflect upon all our Council, since you name none in particular.

That for the choice of our councillors and ministers of state, it were to debar us that natural liberty all freeman have; and as it is the undoubted right of the Crown of England to call such persons to our secret counsels to public employment and our particular service as we shall think fit, so we are, and ever shall be, very careful to make election of such persons in those places of trust as shall have given good testimonies of their abilities and integrity, and against whom there can be no just cause of exception . . . ; and to choices of this nature, we assure you that the mediation of the nearest unto us hath always concurred.

For conclusion, your promise to apply yourselves to such courses as may support our royal estate with honour and plenty at home, and with power and reputation abroad, is that which we have ever promised ourself, both from your loyalties and affections and also for what we have already done . . . for the comfort and happiness of our people.

The Articles of High Treason (January 3, 1642)

The Grand Remonstrance was approved by the slim margin of 159–148, with nearly half of the House of Commons refusing to vote. It was by no means clear that the real majority in Commons wanted to limit the king's prerogatives and authority so drastically. At this point, Charles made a fatal political mistake. He denounced six members of Parliament as traitors and entered the House of Commons in order to arrest them. The warrant for their arrest is first presented, followed by an eyewitness account of the king's presence in the House.

Articles of high treason and other high misdemeanours against the Lord Kimbolton, Mr. Denzil Holles, Sir Arthur Haslerigg, Mr. John Pym, Mr. John Hampden and Mr. William Strode.

1. That they have traitorously endeavoured to subvert the fundamental laws and government of the kingdom of England, to deprive the King of his regal power, and to place in subjects an arbitrary and tyrannical power over the lives, liberties and estates of His Majesty's liege people.
2. That they have traitorously endeavoured, by many foul aspersions upon His Majesty and his government, to alienate the affections of his people, and to make His Majesty odious unto them.
3. That they have endeavoured to draw His Majesty's late army to

"The Articles of High Treason" is from Samuel Gardiner, ed., *The Constitutional Documents of the Puritan Revolution* (Oxford: Clarendon Press, 1889), pp. 158–159.

disobedience to His Majesty's commands, and to side with them in their traitorous designs.

4. That they have traitorously invited and encouraged a foreign power [Scotland] to invade His Majesty's kingdom of England.

5. That they have traitorously endeavoured to subvert the rights and the very being of Parliaments.

6. That for the completing of their traitorous designs they have endeavoured . . . by force and terror, to compel the Parliament to join with them in their traitorous designs, and to that end have actually raised and countenanced tumults against the King and Parliament.

7. And that they have traitorously conspired to levy, and actually have levied war against the King.

"Privilege! Privilege!"

JOHN RUSHWORTH

And as His Majesty . . . entered the House [of Commons] and passed up toward the Chair, he cast his eye on the right hand near the Bar of the House, where Mr. Pym used to sit; but his Majesty not seeing him there (knowing him well) went up to the Chair, and said, "By your leave, Mr. Speaker, I must borrow your chair a little." Whereupon the Speaker came out of the Chair and his Majesty stepped up into it; after he had stood in the Chair a while, casting his eye upon the members as they stood up uncovered, but could not discern any of the five members [accused of treason] to be there . . . Then his Majesty made this speech.

"Gentlemen, I am sorry for this occasion of coming unto you. Yesterday I sent a Sergeant at Arms upon a very important occasion, to apprehend some that by my command were accused of high treason; whereunto I did expect obedience and not a message. And I must declare unto you here that, albeit no king that ever was in England shall be more careful of your privileges, to maintain them to the uttermost of his power, than I shall be; yet you must know that in cases of treason no person has a privilege. And therefore I am come to know if any of these persons that were accused are here. For I must tell you, Gentlemen, that so long as these persons that I have accused (for no light crime, but for treason) are here, I cannot expect that this House will be in the right way that I do heartily wish it. Therefore I am come to tell you that I must have them wheresoever I find them. Well, since I see all the birds are flown, I do expect from you that you shall send them unto me as soon as they return hither. But I assure you, on the word of a king, I never did intend any force, but shall proceed against them in a legal and fair way, for I never did intend any other.

"And now, since I cannot do what I came for, I think this no unfit

" 'Privilege! Privilege!' " is from John Rushworth, *Historical Collections* (London, 1721), vol. 4 pp. 477–478.

occasion to repeat what I have said formerly that whatsoever I have done in favor and to the good of my subjects, I do mean to maintain it.

"I will trouble you no more, but tell you I do expect as soon as they come to the House you will send them to me; otherwise I must take my own course to find them."

When the king was looking about the House, the Speaker standing below by the Chair, his Majesty asked him whether any of these persons were in the House. Whether he saw any of them? And where they were? To which the Speaker, falling on his knee, thus answered, "May it please your Majesty, I have neither eyes to see, nor tongue to speak in this place but as the House is pleased to direct me, whose servant I am here; and humbly beg your Majesty's pardon, that I cannot give any other answer than this to what your Majesty is pleased to demand of me."

The king, having concluded his speech, went out of the House again, which was in great disorder, and many members cried out aloud, so as he might hear them, "Privilege! Privilege!" and forthwith adjourned till the next day at one of the clock.

The Militia Ordinance (March 5, 1642)

Stung by his failure to arrest the ringleaders of his parliamentary opposition, Charles withdrew from London. In his absence, both houses of Parliament raised an army without royal consent to suppress a rebellion in Ireland. The king's reply bitterly recounts his ancient right to command the forces of the realm.

Whereas there has been of late a most dangerous and desperate design upon the House of Commons, which we have just cause to believe to be an effect of the bloody counsels of Papists and other ill-affected persons, who have already raised a rebellion in the kingdom of Ireland; and by reason of many discoveries we cannot but fear they will proceed not only to stir up the like rebellion and insurrections in this kingdom of England, but also to back them with forces from abroad.

For the safety therefore of His Majesty's person, the Parliament and kingdom in this time of imminent danger:

It is ordained by the Lords and Commons now in Parliament assembled, that Henry Earl of Holland shall be Lieutenant of the County of Berks, Oliver Earl of Bolingbroke shall be Lieutenant of the County of Bedford, &c.

And shall severally and respectively have power to assemble and call together all and singular His Majesty's subjects, within the said several and respective counties and places, as well within liberties as without, that are meet and fit for the wars, and them to train and exercise and put in

"The Militia Ordinance" is from Samuel Gardiner, ed., *The Constitutional Documents of the Puritan Revolution* (Oxford: Clarendon Press, 1889), pp. 166–167.

readiness, and them after their abilities and faculties well and sufficiently, from time to time to cause to be arrayed and weaponed, and to take the muster of them in places most fit for that purpose.

The King's Reply to the Militia Ordinance (May 27, 1642)

KING CHARLES I

Whereas, by the statute made in the seventh year of King Edward the First [1279], the Prelates, Earls, Barons and Commonalty of the realm affirmed in Parliament, that to the King it belongs . . . to defend wearing of armour and all other force against the peace, at all times when it shall please him, and to punish them which do the contrary according to the laws and usages of the realm; and . . . all subjects are bound to aid the King as their sovereign lord, at all seasons when need shall be; and whereas we understand that, expressly contrary to the said statute and other good laws of this our kingdom, under [legitimacy] and pretence of an Ordinance of Parliament, without our consent, or any commission or warrant from us, the trained bands and militia of this kingdom have been lately, and are intended to be put in arms, and drawn into companies in a warlike manner, whereby the peace and quiet of our subjects is, or may be, disturbed; we being desirous, by all gracious and fair admonitions, to prevent that some malignant persons in this our kingdom do not by degrees seduce our good subjects from their due obedience to us and the laws of this our kingdom . . . do therefore, by this our Proclamation, expressly charge and command all our sheriffs, and all colonels, lieutenant-colonels, sergeant-majors, captains, officers and soldiers, belonging to the trained bands of this our kingdom, and like-wise all high and petty constables, and other our officers and subjects whatsoever, upon their allegiance, and as they tender the peace of this our kingdom, not to muster, levy raise or march, or to summon or warn, upon any warrant, order or ordinance from one or both of our Houses of Parliament.

The Supremacy of the "Rump Parliament" (December 6, 1648)

Relations between the king and Parliament deteriorated quickly, and in June of 1642, Charles raised an army in recognition of "an urgent and inevitable necessity of putting our subjects into a posture of defense for the safeguard both

"The King's Reply" is from Samuel Gardiner, ed., *The Constitutional Documents of the Puritan Revolution* (Oxford: Clarendon Press, 1889), pp. 169–170.

"The Supremacy of the 'Rump Parliament' " is from W. Cobbett, *Parliamentary History of England* (London, 1868), vol. 3, col. 1257.

of our person and people." In response, Parliament a month later raised an army "for the safety of the King's person, defence of both Houses of Parliament, and those who have obeyed their orders and commands, and preserving of the true religion, the laws, the liberty and peace of the kingdom."

A bloody civil war ensued that ended in the defeat of the royal forces (Cavaliers) and Scots with whom the king had allied in 1647. But in 1648, Parliament was divided between a majority who wanted to negotiate with the king for the reestablishment of the monarchy (although with limited powers) and the army, which sought the death of the king. Under the direction of Oliver Cromwell, a fiery member of Parliament and primary architect of the New Model Army that was responsible for the Roundhead victory over the king, the Parliament was purged of all members opposed to the army's policies. The surviving remnant called the "rump Parliament" declared their supremacy and established a High Court of Justice in order to try the king on charges of high treason. This act was passed by the Commons, but not by the Lords.

The following documents present the establishment of the radicalized "rump Parliament," the charges leveled against the king by the High Court, and his response to those charges, which he was not allowed to deliver at the trial.

RESOLVED:

That the commons of England, in parliament assembled, do declare that the people are, under God, the original of all just power. And do also declare, that the commons of England, in parliament assembled, being chosen by and representing the people have the supreme power in this nation. And do also declare, that whatsoever is enacted, or declared for law, by the commons in parliament assembled has the force of a law; and all the people of this nation are concluded thereby, although the consent of king, or house of peers, be not had thereunto.

Charges against the King (January 20, 1649)

That the said Charles Stuart, being admitted King of England, and therein trusted with a limited power to govern by, and according to the laws of the land, and not otherwise; and by his trust, oath, and office, being obliged to use the power committed to him for the good and benefit of the people, and for the preservation of their rights and liberties; yet, nevertheless, out of a wicked design to erect and uphold in himself an unlimited and tyrannical power to rule according to his will, and to overthrow the rights and liberties of the people, yea, to take away and make void the foundations thereof, and of all redress and remedy of misgovernment, which by

"Charges against the King" is from Samuel Gardiner, ed., *The Constitutional Documents of the Puritan Revolution* (Oxford: Clarendon Press, 1889), pp. 283–285.

the fundamental constitutions of this kingdom were reserved on the peoples' behalf in the right and power of frequent and successive Parliaments, or national meetings in Council; he, the said Charles Stuart, for accomplishment of such his designs, and for the protecting of himself and his adherents in his and their wicked practices, to the same ends has traitorously and maliciously levied war against the present Parliament, and the people therein represented. . . .

He, the said Charles Stuart, has caused and procured many thousands of the free people of this nation to be slain; and by divisions, parties, and insurrections within this land, by invasions from foreign parts, endeavoured and procured by him, and by many other evil ways and means, he, the said Charles Stuart, has . . . carried on the said war both by land and sea . . . by which . . . much innocent blood of the free people of this nation has been split, many families have been undone, the public treasure wasted and exhausted, trade obstructed and miserably decayed, vast expense and damage to the nation incurred, and many parts of this land spoiled, some of them even to desolation. . . .

All which wicked designs, wars, and evil practices of him, the said Charles Stuart, have been, and are carried on for the advancement and upholding of a personal interest of will, power, and pretended prerogative to himself and his family, against the public interest, common right, liberty, justice, and peace of the people of this nation, by and from whom he was entrusted as aforesaid.

By all which it appears that the said Charles Stuart has been, and is the occasioner, author, and continuer of the said unnatural, cruel and bloody wars; and therein guilty of all the treasons, murders, rapines, burnings, spoils, desolations, damages and mischiefs to this nation, acted and committed in the said wars, or occasioned thereby.

"The True Liberty of All My Subjects"
(January 21, 1649)

KING CHARLES I

Having already made my protestations, not only against the illegality of this pretended Court, but also, that no earthly power can justly call (who am your King) in question as a delinquent, I would not any more open my mouth upon this occasion, more than to refer myself to what I have spoken, were I in this case alone concerned: but the duty I owe to God in the preservation of the true liberty of my people will not suffer me at this

" 'The True Liberty of All My Subjects' " is from Samuel Gardiner, ed., *The Constitutional Documents of the Puritan Revolution* (Oxford: Clarendon Press, 1889), pp. 284–286.

time to be silent: for, how can any free-born subject of England call life or anything he possesses his own, if power without right daily make new, and abrogate the old fundamental laws of the land which I now take to be the present case? . . . Yet I will show you the reason why I am confident you cannot judge me, nor indeed the meanest man in England: for I will not (like you) without showing a reason, seek to impose a belief upon my subjects.

There is no proceeding just against any man, but what is warranted, either by God's laws or the municipal laws of the country where he lives. Now I am most confident this day's proceeding cannot be warranted by God's laws; for, on the contrary, the authority of obedience unto Kings is clearly warranted, and strictly commanded in both the Old and New Testament, which, if denied, I am ready instantly to prove. . . .

Then for the law of this land, I am no less confident, that no learned lawyer will affirm that an impeachment can lie against the King, they all going in his name: and one of their maxims is, that the King can do no wrong. . . . But how the House of Commons can erect a Court of Judicature, . . . I leave to God and the world to judge. And it were full as strange, that they should pretend to make laws without King or Lords' House, to any that have heard speak of the laws of England.

And admitting, but not granting, that the people of England's commission could grant you pretended power, I see nothing you can show for that; for certainly you never asked the question of the tenth man in the kingdom, and in this way you manifestly wrong even the poorest ploughman, if you demand not his free consent: nor can you pretend any [legitimacy] for this your pretended commission, without the consent at least of the major part of every man in England of whatsoever quality or condition, which I am sure you never went about to seek, so far are you from having it. Thus you see that I speak not for my own right alone, as I am your King, but also for the true liberty of all my subjects, which consists not in the power of government, but in living under such laws, such a government, as may give themselves the best assurance of their lives, and property of their goods. . . .

Besides all this, the peace of the kingdom is not least in my thoughts; and what hope of settlement is there, so long as power reigns without rule or law, changing the whole frame of that government under which this kingdom has flourished for many hundred years? . . . By this time, it will be too sensibly evident, that the arms I took up were only to defend the fundamental laws of this kingdom against those who have supposed my power has totally changed the ancient government.

Thus, having showed you briefly the reasons why I cannot submit to your pretended authority, without violating the trust which I have from God for the welfare and liberty of my people, I expect from you either clear reasons to [refute] my judgment, showing me that I am in an error . . . or that you will withdraw your proceedings.

Death Warrant for the King (January 29, 1649)

The following death warrant was issued for the king on order of the High Court, whose legitimacy he had called into question. On the scaffold, Charles gave a last defense of his reign.

Whereas Charles Stuart, King of England, is, and stands convicted, attainted, and condemned of high treason, and other high crimes; and sentence upon Saturday last was pronounced against him by this Court, to be put to death by the severing of his head from his body; of which sentence, execution yet remains to be done; these are therefore to will and require you to see the said sentence executed in the open street before Whitehall, upon the morrow, being the thirtieth day of this instant month of January, between the hours of ten in the morning and five in the afternoon of the same day, with full effect. And for so doing this shall be your sufficient warrant. And these are to require all officers, soldiers, and others, the good people of this nation of England, to be assisting unto you in this service.

To Col. Francis Hacker, Col. Huncks, and Lieut.-Col. Phayre, and to every of them.

> Given under our hands and seals,
> John Bradshaw
> Thomas Grey
> Oliver Cromwell &c. &c.

The Execution of Charles I: "I Am the Martyr of the People" (January 30, 1649)

NATHANIEL CROUCH

The scaffold was hung round with black, the floor covered with black baize, and the ax and block laid in the middle of the scaffold. . . . The multitudes of people that came to be spectators [was] very great. [The king spoke]:

"I shall be very little heard of anybody here. . . . Indeed, I could hold my peace very well, if I did not think that holding my peace would make some men think that I did submit to the guilt as well as to the punishment; but I think it is my duty to God first, and to my country, for to clear myself both as an honest man, a good King, and a good Christian. I shall begin with my innocence; in truth, . . . I never did begin a war with the two Houses of Parliament, and I call God to witness, to whom I must shortly make an account, that I never did intend to encroach upon their privileges, they

"Death Warrant for the King" is from G. Adams and H. Stephens, eds., *Select Documents of English Constitutional History* (New York: The Macmillan Company, 1916), pp. 290.
"The Execution of Charles I" is from *England's Black Tribunal*, 5th ed., pp. 42–47.

began upon me; it is the militia they began upon—they confessed that the militia was mine, but they thought it fit to have it from me; and if anybody will look, . . . he will clearly see that they began these unhappy troubles, not I. So that as to the guilt of these enormous crimes that are laid against me, I hope . . . that God will clear me of it; . . . God forbid that I should lay it upon the two Houses of Parliament; [since] there is no necessity of either, I hope they are free of this guilt. For I do believe that ill instruments between them and me has been the chief cause of all this bloodshed.

"For the people: and truly I desire their liberty and freedom as much as anybody whatsoever, but I must tell you that their liberty and freedom consists in having of government, those laws by which their life and their goods may be most their own. It is not for having share in government, Sirs; that is nothing pertaining to them. A subject and a sovereign are clear different things, and therefore until they do that, I mean, that you do put the people in that liberty, . . . certainly they will never enjoy themselves.

"Sirs, it was for this that now I am come here. If I would have given way to an arbitrary way, for to have all laws changed according to the power of the sword, I needed not to have come here. And therefore I tell you . . . that I am the martyr of the people."

Then the King speaking to the executioner said, "I shall say but very short prayers, and when I thrust out my hands—."

Then he called to the bishop for his cap, and having put it on, asked the executioner, "Does my hair trouble you?" who desired him to put it all under his cap; which, as he was doing by the help of the bishop and the executioner, he turned to the bishop, and said, "I have a good cause, and a gracious God on my side."

Bishop: There is but one stage more, which, though turbulent and troublesome, yet is a very short one. You may consider it will soon carry you a very great way; it will carry you from earth to heaven; and there you shall find to your great joy the prize you hasten to, a crown of glory."

King: "I go from a corruptible to an incorruptible crown; where no disturbance can be, no disturbance in the world."

Bishop: "You are exchanged from a temporal to an eternal crown—a good exchange."

Then the king asked the executioner, "Is my hair well?" Then taking off his doublet . . . and looking upon the block, said to the executioner, "You must set it fast."

Executioner: "It is fast, sir."

King: "It might have been a little higher."

Executioner: "It can be no higher, sir."

King: "When I put out my hands this way, then—"

Then having said a few words to himself, as he stood, with hands and eyes lifted up, immediately stooping down he laid his neck upon the block; and the executioner, again putting his hair under his cap, his Majesty, thinking he had been going to strike, bade him, "Stay for the sign."

Executioner: "Yes, I will, an it please your Majesty."

After a very short pause, his Majesty stretching forth his hands, the executioner at one blow severed his head from his body; which, being held up and shown to the people, was with his body put into a coffin covered with black velvet and carried into his lodging.

His blood was taken up by diverse persons for different ends; by some as trophies of their villainy; by others as relics of a martyr; and in some has had the same effect, by the blessing of God, which was often found in his sacred touch when living.

Consolidation of the Commonwealth (1649–1653)

Parliament immediately established its supremacy in the new political environment by passing a series of acts which abolished the office of king (March 17, 1649) and the House of Lords (March 19, 1649), and instituted the Commonwealth of England "for the good of the people." The crime of high treason was thus appropriately defined in order to bolster and protect the new regime, as the next document attests.

Treason and the Commonwealth (July 17, 1650)

Whereas the Parliament has abolished the kingly office in England and Ireland, and in the dominions and territories thereunto belonging; and having resolved and declared, that the people shall for the future be governed by its own Representatives or national meetings in Council, chosen and entrusted by them for that purpose, has settled the Government in the way of a Commonwealth and Free State, without King or House of Lords: be it enacted by this present Parliament, and by the authority of the same, that if any person shall maliciously or advisedly publish, by writing, printing, or openly declaring, that the said Government is tyrannical, usurped, or unlawful; or that the Commons in Parliament assembled are not the supreme authority of this nation; or shall plot,

"Treason and the Commonwealth" is from G. Adams and H. Stephens, eds., *Select Documents of English Constitutional History* (New York: The Macmillan Company, 1916), pp. 400–401.

contrive, or endeavour to stir up, or raise force against the present Government, or for the subversion or alteration of the same, and shall declare the same by any open deed, that then every such offence shall be taken, deemed, and adjudged by authority of this Parliament to be high treason.

And whereas the Keepers of the liberty of England, and the Council of State, constituted . . . by authority of Parliament, are to be under the said representatives in Parliament entrusted for the maintenance of the said Government with several powers and authorities limited, given, and appointed unto them by the Parliament: be it likewise enacted by the authority aforesaid, that if any person shall maliciously and advisedly plot or endeavour the subversion of the said Keepers of the liberty of England, or the Council of State, . . . then every such offence and offenses shall be taken, deemed, and declared to be high treason.

Leviathan (1651)

THOMAS HOBBES

The establishment of a commonwealth without a king was uncharted political territory for England. The institution of monarchy could arguably trace its national origins to the ninth-century warrior king Alfred the Great, and its consolidation under the Norman king, William the Conqueror, in 1066. Rule by Parliament without prescribed executive leadership beyond a Council of State contributed to a fluid political environment with factional infighting and corruption. Some doubted the benefits of "unregulated" democracy.

Thomas Hobbes was one of the great political philosophers of the seventeenth century. His major work, entitled Leviathan, *was published in 1651 and reflects the insecurity and fear of the English Revolution that had resulted in civil war (1642–1646) and had just seen the decapitation of a sovereign monarch in 1649. Hobbes himself, because of his aristocratic associations, had been forced to flee England. Not surprisingly,* Leviathan *is a treatise that advocates political absolutism. Its theme is power, and it justifies absolute rule as necessary in order to subdue the violence of human nature and promote a reasonable existence. For Hobbes, the authority of the absolute monarch did not lie in hereditary right or in divine sanction, but only in his ability to achieve power and maintain it. In this sense, Hobbes borrowed much from the Renaissance political philosopher Niccolò Machiavelli. But Hobbes went much further by providing an integrated social and political philosophy of government.*

Nature has made men so equal, in the faculties of the body and mind; as that though there be found one man sometimes manifestly stronger in body, or of quicker mind than another; yet when all is reckoned together, the differences between man and man, is not so considerable. . . . For as to

"Leviathan" is from W. Molesworth, ed., *The English Works of Thomas Hobbes*, vol. 3 (London: John Bohn, 1839), from chapters 13 and 17,pp. 110–113, 153, 157–158. Text modernized by the editor.

the strength of body, the weakest has strength enough to kill the strongest, either by secret machination, or by confederacy with others, that are in the same danger with himself.

And as to the faculties of the mind . . . I find yet a greater equality among men, than that of strength. . . . Such is the nature of men, that howsoever they may acknowledge many others to be more witty, or more eloquent, or more learned; yet they will hardly believe there are many so wise as themselves; for they see their own wit at hand, and other men's at a distance. . . .

From this equality of ability, arises equality of hope in the attaining of our ends. And therefore if any two men desire the same thing, which nevertheless they cannot both enjoy, they become enemies; and in the way to their end, which is principally their own conservation . . . endeavour to destroy, or subdue one another. And from hence it comes to pass, that . . . an invader has no more to fear than another man's single power; if one plant, sow, build, and possess a convenient seat, others may probably be expected to come prepared with forces united, to dispossess, and deprive him, not only of the fruit of his labour, but also of his life, or liberty. And the invader again is in the like danger of another . . . [Thus], men have no pleasure, but on the contrary a great deal of grief, in keeping company, where there is no power able to over-awe them all. . . .

So that in the nature of man, we find three principal causes of quarrel. First, competition; secondly, insecurity; thirdly, glory.

The first, makes men invade for gain; the second, for safety; and the third, for reputation. The first use violence, to make themselves master of other men's persons, wives, children, and cattle; the second, to defend them; the third, for trifles, as a word, a smile, a different opinion, and any other sign of undervalue, either direct in their persons, or by reflection in their kindred, their friends, their nation, their profession, or their name.

[Therefore, it is clear] that during the time men live without a common power to keep them all in awe, they are in that condition which is called war; and such a war is of every man, against every man. . . . In such condition, there is no place for industry; because the fruit thereof is uncertain: and consequently no culture of the earth; no navigation, nor use of the commodities that may be imported by sea; no commodious building; no instruments of moving, and removing, such things as require much force; no knowledge of the face of the earth; no account of time; no arts; no letters; no society; and which is worst of all, continual fear, and danger of violent death; and the life of man, solitary, poor, nasty, brutish, and short. . . .

The final cause, end, or design of men, who naturally love liberty, and dominion over others, [is] the introduction of that restraint upon themselves, [by] which we see them live in commonwealths. . . . The only way to erect such a common power, as may be able to defend them from the invasion of foreigners, and the injuries of one another, and thereby to secure them in such sort, as that by their own industry, and by the fruits of the earth, they may nourish themselves and live contentedly; is, to confer all their power and strength upon one man, or upon one assembly of men, that may reduce all their wills, by plurality of voices, unto one will. . . . [All men shall] submit their wills . . . to his will, and their judgments, to his judgment. This is more than consent, or concord; it is a real unity of them all, in one and the same person, made by covenant of every man with every man, in such manner, as if every man should say to every man, *I authorize and give up my right of governing myself, to this man, or to this assembly of men, on this condition, that you give up your right to him, and authorize all his actions in like manner.* This done, the multitude so united in one person, is called a COMMONWEALTH. . . . This is the generation of that great LEVIATHAN, or rather, to speak more reverently, of that *mortal god,* to which we own under the *immortal God,* our peace and defence. For by this authority, given him by every particular man in the commonwealth, he hath the use of so much power and strength conferred on him, that by terror thereof, he is enabled to perform the wills of them all, to peace at home, and mutual aid against their enemies abroad. And in him consists the essence of the commonwealth; which, to define it, is *one person of whose acts a great multitude, by mutual covenants one with another, have made themselves every one the author, to the end he may use the strength and means of them all, as he shall think expedient, for their peace and common defence.*

And . . . this person, is called SOVEREIGN, and said to have *sovereign power;* and every one besides, his SUBJECT.

The Lord Protector: Oliver Cromwell (1653–1658)

The central figure in the period from the English civil wars to the end of the Commonwealth in 1660 was Oliver Cromwell. He was born in 1599 to a family of solid, though not distinguished reputation. In 1628, he became a member of Parliament and played an active, if not a leading role in the controversies of the time. Presumably he voted for the Grand Remonstrance, for he once declared that he would have sold all his possessions and left the country if it had not been passed. When war came, he was a primary architect of the New Model Army that rebounded to defeat the king's forces at Marsten Moor (1644) and at Naseby (1645). Cromwell's military skill and political talents assured him a position of prominence, though he was never supreme commander of the parliamentary forces during the wars.

When the Commonwealth was established in 1649, Cromwell was sent to reconquer and pacify Ireland, which had broken away from English control during the civil wars. His brutality in reducing the Irish shocked even his contemporaries, but Cromwell in a letter of 1649 noted that their destruction was "a righteous judgment of God" and that extreme measures "tend to prevent the effusion of blood for the future, which are satisfactory grounds to such actions."

When Charles II, son of the executed monarch, landed in Scotland in 1650, Cromwell was dispatched to deal with this threat to the new Commonwealth. After two smashing victories, Cromwell entered London in triumph and was granted an annual income and the royal palace of Hampton Court as a residence. When the "rump Parliament" seemed on the verge of making itself perpetual in April 1653, Cromwell felt constrained to dismiss it, so disillusioned was he with the moral fabric of its membership. His strict Puritan standards are evident in the following account.

Cromwell's Dismissal of the "Rump Parliament" (April 22, 1653)

EDMUND LUDLOW

Calling to Major-General Harrison, who was on the other side of the House, to come to him, [Cromwell] told him, that he judged the Parliament ripe for a dissolution, and this to be the time of doing it. The Major-General answered, . . . "Sir, the work is very great and dangerous, therefore I desire you seriously to consider of it before you engage in it." "You say well," replied General [Cromwell], and thereupon sat still for about a quarter of an hour; and then . . . he said again to Major-General Harrison, "this is the time I must do it"; and suddenly standing up, made a speech, wherein he loaded the Parliament with the vilest reproaches, charging them not to have a heart to do any thing for the public good, to have espoused the corrupt interest of . . . lawyers who were the supporters of tyranny and oppression, accusing them of an intention to perpetuate themselves in power, . . . and thereupon told them, that the Lord had done with them, and had chosen other instruments for the carrying on his work that were more worthy. This he spoke with so much passion and discomposure of mind, as if he had been distracted.

Sir Peter Wentworth stood up to answer him, and said, that this was the first time that ever he had heard such unbecoming language given to the Parliament, and that it was the more horrid in that it came from their servant . . . whom they had so highly trusted and obliged: but as he was going on, the General stepped into the midst of the House, where continuing his distracted language, he said, "Come, come, I will put an end to your prating"; then walking up and down the House like a madman, and kicking the ground with his feet, he cried out, "You are no Parliament, I say you are no Parliament; I will put an end to your sitting; call them in"; whereupon the sergeant attending the Parliament opened the doors, and . . . two files of musketeers entered the House; which Sir Henry Vane observing from his place, said aloud, "This is not honest, yea it is against morality and common honesty." Then Cromwell fell a railing at him, crying out with a

"Cromwell's Dismissal of the 'Rump Parliament' " is from C. H. Firth, *The Memoirs of Edmund Ludlow* (Oxford: Oxford University Press, 1894), vol. 1, pp. 352–354.

loud voice, "O Sir Henry Vane, Sir Henry Vane, the lord deliver me from Sir Henry Vane." Then looking upon one of the members, he said, "There sits a drunkard"; and giving much reviling language to others, he commanded the mace [symbolic of Parliament's authority] to be taken away, saying "What shall we do with this bauble here, take it away." Having brought all into this disorder, Major-General Harrison went to the Speaker [of the House] as he sat in the chair, and told him, that seeing things were reduced to this pass, it would not be convenient for him to remain there. The Speaker answered, that he would not come down unless he were forced. "Sir," said Harrison, "I will lend you my hand"; and thereupon putting his hand within his, the Speaker came down. Then Cromwell applied himself to the members of the House, who were in number between 80 and 100, and said to them, "It's you that have forced me to this, for I have sought the Lord night and day, that he would rather slay me than put me upon the doing of this work."

The Instrument of Government (December 16, 1653)

In December of 1653, Cromwell finalized his political solution for the stability of the Commonwealth. The Instrument of Government established Cromwell as Lord Protector of the Commonwealth, a misleading title, which some have suggested was created to mask his military despotism. In a speech dated 1657, a year before his death, Cromwell denied the crown that would have formalized his position as king of England.

The government of the Commonwealth of England, Scotland, and Ireland, and the dominions thereunto belonging:

1. That the supreme legislative authority of the Commonwealth of England, Scotland, and Ireland, shall be and reside in one person, and the people assembled in Parliament; the style of which person shall be the Lord Protector of the Commonwealth of England, or Ireland.
2. That the exercise of the chief magistracy and the administration of the government over the said countries and the dominions, and the people thereof, shall be in the Lord Protector, assisted with a council. . . .
4. That the Lord Protector, the Parliament sitting, shall dispose and order the militia and forces, both by sea and land, for the peace and good of the three nations, by consent of the Parliament.

"The Instrument of Government" is from George Adams and H. Stephens, eds., *Select Documents of English Constitutional History* (New York: the Macmillan Company, 1916), pp. 407–416.

6. That the laws shall not be altered, suspended, abrogated, or repealed, nor any new law made, nor any tax, charge, or imposition laid upon the people, but by common consent in Parliament. . . .

7. That there shall be a Parliament summoned to meet at Westminster upon the third day of September, 1654, and that successively a Parliament shall be summoned once in every third year, to be accounted from the dissolution of the present Parliament.

14. That all and every person and persons, who have aided, advised, assisted, or abetted in any war against the Parliament, since the first day of January, 1641 . . . shall be disabled and incapable to be elected, or to give any vote in the election of any members to serve in the next Parliament, or in the three succeeding Triennial Parliaments.

15. That all such, who have advised, assisted, or abetted the rebellion of Ireland, shall be disabled and incapable for ever to be elected, or give any vote in the election of any member to serve in Parliament; as also all such who do or shall profess the Roman Catholic religion.

17. That the persons who shall be elected to serve in Parliament, shall be such as are persons of known integrity, fearing God, and of good conversation. . . .

23. That the Lord Protector, with the advice of the major part of the Council, shall . . . when the necessities of the State require it, summon Parliaments, which shall not be . . . dissolved without their own consent, during the first three months of their sitting.

24. That all Bills agreed unto by the Parliament, shall be presented to the Lord Protector for his consent; and in case he shall not give his consent thereto within twenty days after they shall be presented to him . . . then . . . such Bills shall pass into and become laws, although he shall not give his consent thereunto.

32. That the office of Lord Protector over these nations shall be elective and not hereditary; and upon the death of the Lord Protector, another fit person shall be forthwith elected to succeed him in the Government; which election shall be by the Council. . . .

33. That Oliver Cromwell, Captain-General of the forces of England, Scotland and Ireland, shall be, and is hereby declared to be, Lord Protector of the Commonwealth. . . .

36. That such as profess faith in God by Jesus Christ (though differing in judgment from the doctrine, worship or discipline publicly held forth) shall not be restrained from, but shall be protected in, the profession of the faith and exercise of their religion . . . provided this liberty be not extended to Popery. . . .

51. That every successive Lord Protector over these nations shall take and subscribe a solemn oath . . . that he will seek the peace, quiet and welfare of these nations, cause law and justice to be equally administered, and . . . will govern these nations according to the laws, statutes and customs thereof.

Cromwell Denies the Crown (May 8, 1657)

OLIVER CROMWELL

Mr. Speaker,

I have, the best I can, resolved the whole business in my thoughts. . . . I think [this] is a government that, in the aims of it, seeks the settling the nation on a good foot, in relation to civil rights and liberties, which are the rights of the nation. And I hope I shall never be found to be one of them that go about to rob the nation of those rights, but shall ever be found to serve them, what I can, to the attaining of them. It is also exceeding well provided there for the safety and security of honest men, in the great, natural, and religious liberty, which is liberty of conscience. These are the great fundamentals; and I must bear my testimony to them . . . so long as God lets me live in this world, that the intentions of the thing are very honorable and honest, and the product worthy of a Parliament.

I have only had the unhappiness . . . not to be convinced of the necessity of that thing, that has been so often insisted on by you, to wit, the title of King, as in itself so necessary, as it seems to apprehended by yourselves. . . . And, while you are granting other liberties, surely you will not deny me this? It being not only a liberty, but a duty . . . to examine mine own heart, and thoughts, and judgment, in every work which I am to set my hand to, or to appear in, or for . . . I have truly thought, and do still think, that if I should at the best do anything on this account, to answer your expectation, at the best I should do it doubtingly. And certainly what is so done, is not of faith, —is sin to him that does it. I should not be an honest man if I should not tell you, that I cannot accept of the government, nor undertake the trouble and charge of it. . . . I say, I am persuaded therefore to return this answer to you, that I cannot undertake this government with that title of King. And that is my answer to this great weighty business.

The Character of Oliver Cromwell

Oliver Cromwell, like many other individuals who have played a major role in the determination of historical events, was a complex and controversial figure. The two accounts of his career that follow were written from very different perspectives.

John Milton (1608–1674) has achieved a place of literary distinction as one of the greatest poets of the English language. Concerned with the Puritan cause, Milton spent many of the years from 1641 to 1660 pamphleteering for

"Cromwell Denies the Crown" is from Charles Stainer, ed., *Speeches of Oliver Cromwell* (London: Henry Frowde, 1901), pp. 350–353.

This portrait of Oliver Cromwell portrays a stern resolution and omniscience that saw England through civil war and constitutional chaos. Did the English Parliament substitute one king (Charles I) for another in the guise of "Lord Protector"?

civil and religious liberty and serving as the secretary for foreign languages in the Cromwell government. After the Restoration of the Stuart monarchy in 1660, he was arrested but soon released.

Edward Hyde (1609–1674), on the other hand, championed Parliament's cause in judiciously limiting the royal prerogative, but he remained a close advisor to Charles I and even served as guardian to his son, Charles II, and later chancellor. His strict morality and acerbic temper eventually led to exile in France, where he finished a history of the civil wars.

The following excerpts are from these two important and influential ministers of state, nearly the same age, writing about the most dramatic and controversial personality of their time.

"To You Our Country Owes Its Liberties" (1654)

JOHN MILTON

The whole surface of the British empire has been the scene of [Cromwell's] exploits, and the theatre of his triumphs. . . . He collected an army as numerous and as well equipped as any one ever did in so short a time; which was uniformly obedient to his orders, and dear to the affections of the citizens; which was formidable to the enemy in the field, but never cruel to those who laid down their arms; which committed no lawless ravages on the persons or the property of the inhabitants; who, when they compared their conduct with the turbulence, the intemperance, the impiety and the debauchery of the royalists, were wont to salute them as friends and to consider them as guests. They were a stay to the good, a terror to the evil, and the warmest advocates for every exertion of piety and virtue.

[Here Milton addresses himself directly to Cromwell regarding the dismissal of the "rump Parliament."]

But when you saw that the business [of governing the realm] was artfully procrastinated, that every one was more intent on his own selfish interest than on the public good, that the people complained of the disappointments which they had experienced, and the fallacious promises by which they had been gulled, that they were the dupes of a few overbearing individuals, you put an end to their domination.

In this state of desolation to which we were reduced, you, O Cromwell! alone remained to conduct the government and to save the country. We all willingly yield the palm of sovereignty to your unrivalled ability and virtue, except the few among us who, either ambitious of honors which they have not the capacity to sustain, or who envy those which are conferred on one more worthy than themselves, or else who do not know that nothing in the world is more pleasing to God, more agreeable to reason, more politically just, or more generally useful, than that the supreme power should be vested in the best and the wisest of men. Such, O Cromwell, all acknowledge you to be. . . . Other names you neither have nor could endure; and you deservedly reject that pomp of title which attracts the gaze and admiration of the multitude.

Do you then, sir, continue your course with the same unrivalled magnanimity; it sits well upon you;—to you our country owes its liberties. . . . And, after having endured so many sufferings and encountered so many perils for the sake of liberty, do not suffer it, now it is obtained, either to be violated by yourself, or in any one instance impaired by others. You cannot be truly free unless we are free too; for such is the nature of things, that he who entrenches on the liberty of others is the first to lose his own and become a slave.

" 'To You Our Country Owes Its Liberties' " is from John Milton, *Second Defense of the People of England* (1654).

But if you, who have hitherto been the patron and tutelary genius of liberty, if you, who are exceeded by no one in justice, in piety and goodness, should hereafter invade that liberty which you have defended, your conduct must be fatally operative, not only against the cause of liberty, but the general interests of piety and virtue. Your integrity and virtue will appear to have evaporated, your faith in religion to have been small; your character with posterity will dwindle into insignificance, by which a most destructive blow will be leveled against the happiness of mankind.

At once wisely and discreetly to hold the sceptre over three powerful nations, to persuade people to relinquish inveterate and corrupt for new and more beneficial maxims and institutions, to penetrate into the remotest parts of the country, to have the mind present and operative in every quarter, to watch against surprise, to provide against danger, to reject the blandishments of pleasure and pomp of power—these are exertions compared with which the labor of war is mere pastime; which will require every energy and employ every faculty that you possess; which demand a man supported from above and almost instructed by immediate inspiration.

"Guilty of Crimes for Which Hell-Fire Is Prepared" (1704)

EDWARD HYDE, EARL OF CLARENDON

He was one of those men [whom his very enemies could not condemn without commending him at the same time], for he could never have done half that mischief without great parts of courage, industry and judgment. He must have had a wonderful understanding in the natures and humors of men, and as great a dexterity in applying them, who, from a private and obscure birth (though of a good family) without interest or estate, alliance or friendship, could raise himself to such a height and compound and knead such opposite and contradictory tempers, humors and interests into a consistence that contributed to his designs and to their own destruction. . . . Without doubt, no man with more wickedness ever attempted any thing, or brought to pass what he desired more wickedly, more in the face and contempt of religion and moral honesty; yet wickedness as great as his could never have accomplished those designs without the assistance of a great spirit, an admirable circumspection and sagacity, and a most magnanimous resolution. . . .

After he was confirmed and invested Protector . . . he consulted with very few upon any action of importance. . . . What he once resolved, in which he was not rash, he would not be dissuaded from, nor endure any

" 'Guilty of Crimes for Which Hell-Fire Is Prepared' " is from Edward Hyde, *The True Historical Narrative of the Rebellion and the Civil Wars in England,* vol. 3 (1704), pp. 862–864.

contradiction of his power and authority; but extorted obedience from them who were not willing to yield it. . . .

To conclude his character, Cromwell was not so far a man of blood as to follow Machiavelli's method, which prescribes upon a total alteration of government, as a thing absolutely necessary, to cut off all the heads of those, and extirpate their families, who are friends to the old one. It was confidently reported that in the Council of Officers it was more than once proposed that there might be a general massacre of all the royal party, as the only expedient to secure the government, but that Cromwell would never consent to it; it may be, out of too much contempt of his enemies. In a word, as he was guilty of many crimes against which damnation is denounced and for which hell-fire is prepared, so he had some good qualities, which have caused the memory of some men in all ages to be celebrated; and he will be looked upon by posterity as a brave wicked man.

The Glorious Revolution (1688–1689)

Oliver Cromwell died in 1658 and his son, Richard, was elected Lord Protector. He was simply not able to accumulate the support or achieve the authority that had maintained his father in power. The army soon seized control and some of its leaders promoted the restoration of the Stuart monarchy as the only way to end the chronic political turbulence. The "rump Parliament" was called back into session by one of the commanders, and it summoned Charles Stuart from exile and installed him as Charles II. After the bloodshed of a civil war, the execution of a king, and the struggle of creating the Commonwealth, the Stuart monarchy had been restored to power.

But England had been politically changed in the process. The Restoration of 1660 left Parliament essentially supreme but allowed the king to lead the nation with authority. What really undid the later Stuart monarchs was their inability to handle the Catholic problem. Charles II ruled an officially Anglican nation but personally harbored a sympathy for Catholicism. Since he left no legitimate children, the crown passed to his brother James II (1685–1688). James was an avowed Catholic, and when he fathered a son by his Catholic second wife, Parliament was threatened with the reality of a Catholic heir to the throne. Some of the Parliamentary leadership opened negotiations with William of Orange, a Protestant leader who had made his reputation on the Continent as the container of Catholic France. He accepted the invitation to take the English crown and ruled jointly with his wife (a Protestant daughter of James II) as William III and Mary II. After an initial attempt to rally support, James fled to France, giving William a nearly bloodless victory.

Parliament quickly enacted a Bill of Rights in 1689 that laid down the principles of parliamentary supremacy that had been in dispute since the Petition of Right in 1628.

The Bill of Rights (1689)

Whereas the said late King James II having abdicated the government, and the throne being thereby vacant, his Highness the prince of Orange (whom it has pleased Almighty God to make the glorious instrument of delivering this kingdom from popery and arbitrary power) did . . . cause letters to be written . . . for the choosing of such persons to represent them, as were of right to be sent to parliament . . . being now assembled in a full and free representative of this nation . . . do in the first place . . . for the vindicating and asserting their ancient rights and liberties, declare:

1. That the pretended power of suspending of laws, or the execution of laws, by regal authority, without the consent of parliament, is illegal.

2. That the pretended power of dispensing with laws, or the execution of laws, by regal authority, as it has been assumed and exercised of late [by James II], is illegal.

4. That levying of money for or to the use of the crown . . . without the grant of parliament . . . is illegal.

5. That it is the right of the subjects to petition the king. . . .

6. That the raising or keeping of a standing army within the kingdom in time of peace, unless it be with the consent of parliament is against the law. . . .

8. That election of members of parliament ought to be free.

9. That the freedom of speech, and debates or proceedings in parliament, ought not to be impeached or questioned in any court or place out of parliament.

10. That excessive bail ought not to be required, nor excessive fines imposed; nor cruel and unusual punishments inflicted.

13. And that for redress of all grievances, and for the amending, strengthening, and preserving of the laws, parliament ought to be held frequently. . . .

SECTION II: THE ABSOLUTISM OF LOUIS XIV

The Theory of Divine-Right Monarchy

The stable monarchy that Louis XIV inherited was largely the product of two master political craftsmen, cardinals Richelieu and Mazarin. These statesmen actually ran the day-to-day affairs of the French state under Louis XIII and

"The Bill of Rights" is from *Statutes of the Realm*, 6:142.

during Louis XIV's minority, respectively. *Under their strict control, the French nobility was subdued and made to realize that the king was absolute in his authority and would tolerate no defiance. It was under their direction from 1610 to 1661 that absolutism was advanced out of the realm of theory and made a part of the political life of France.*

The practical rule of any government must be justified through some doctrine, whether it be a devotion to the principles of democracy or to the more blatant dictum "might makes right." Louis XIV justified his absolutism through the belief that God so willed it. Such a "divine-right" monarch ruled with the authority of God and was beholden to no power except that of God. For his part, the king was accountable to God and was expected to rule with the best interests of his people at heart.

The following selections explain the theoretical basis of Louis' absolutism. The first is by Jean Domat (1624–1696), one of the most renown jurists and legal scholars of his age. He was responsible for a codification of French law that was sponsored by the king himself. The selection presented is from his treatment of French public law and may be regarded as the official statement of divine-right absolutism. The second excerpt is from a treatise by Jacques Benique Bossuet (1627–1704), bishop and tutor to Louis XIV's heir. An eloquent political writer, Bossuet justified divine-right monarchy by basing his support on direct evidence from the Bible. The treatise, entitled Politics Drawn from the Very Words of Scripture, *was directed specifically at Louis' son and successor, the Dauphin.*

The Ideal Absolute State (1697)

JEAN DOMAT

All men being equal by nature because of the humanity that is their essence, nature does not cause some to be inferior to others. But in this natural equality, they are separated by other principles that render their conditions unequal and give rise to relationships and dependencies that determine their varying duties toward others and render government necessary. . . .

The first distinction that subjects some persons to others is that which birth introduces between parents and children. . . . The second distinction among persons is that which requires different employments in society and unites all in the body of which each is a member. . . . And it is these varying occupations and dependencies that create the ties that form society among men, as those of its members form a body. This renders it necessary that a head coerce and rule the body of society and maintain order among those who should give the public the benefit of the different contributions that their stations require of them. . . .

Since government is necessary for the common good and God himself established it, it follows that those who are its subjects must be submissive and obedient. For otherwise they would resist God, and the government which should be the source of the peace and unity that make possible the public good would suffer from dissension and trouble that would destroy it. . . .

As obedience is necessary to preserve the order and peace that unite the head and members of the body of the state, it is the universal obligation of all subjects in all cases to obey the ruler's orders without assuming the liberty of judging them. For otherwise each man would be master because of his right to examine what might be just or unjust, and this liberty would favor sedition. Thus every man owes obedience even to unjust laws and orders, provided that he may execute and obey them without injustice. And the only exception that may exempt him from this obligation is limited to cases in which he may not obey without violating divine law. . . .

According to these principles, which are the natural foundations of the authority of those who govern, their power should have two essential attributes: first, to cause justice to rule without exception and, second, to be as absolute as the rule of justice, that is, as absolute as the rule of God Himself who is justice, rules according to its principles, and desires rulers to do likewise. . . .

Since the power of princes comes to them from God and is placed in their hands as an instrument of his providence and his guidance of the states that He commits to their rule, it is clear that princes should use their power in proportion to the objectives that providence and divine guidance seek . . . and that power is confided to them to this end. This is without doubt the foundation and first principle of all the duties of sovereigns that consist of causing God Himself to rule, that is, regulating all things according to His will, which is nothing more than justice. The rule of justice should be the glory of the rule of princes. . . .

The power of sovereigns includes the authority to exercise the functions of government and to use the force that is necessary to their ministry. For authority without force would be despised and almost useless, while force without legitimate authority would be mere tyranny. . . .

There are two uses of sovereign power that are necessary to the public tranquillity. One consists of constraining the subjects to obey and repressing violence and injustice, the other of defending the state against the aggressions of its enemies. Power should be accompanied by the force that is required for these two functions.

The use of force for the maintenance of public tranquillity within the state includes all that is required to protect the sovereign himself from rebellions that would be frequent if authority and force were not united, and all that is required to keep order among the subjects, repress violence against individuals and the general public, execute the orders of the sovereign, and effect all that is required for the administration of justice. Since the use of force and the occasions that require it are never-ending, the government of the sovereign must maintain the force that is needed for the rule of justice. This requires officials and ministers in various functions and the use of arms whenever necessary. . . .

One should include among the rights that the law gives the sovereign that of acquiring all the evidences of grandeur and majesty that are needed to bring renown to the authority and dignity of such great power and to instill awe in the minds of the subjects. For although the latter should view royal power as from God and submit to it regardless of tangible indications of grandeur, God accompanies his own power with a visible majesty that extends over land and sea. . . . When He wishes to exercise his august power as lawgiver, He proclaims his laws with prodigies that inspire reverence and unspeakable terror. He is therefore willing that sovereigns enhance the dignity of their power . . . in such manner as to win the respect of the people. . . .

The general duties . . . of those who have sovereign authority include all that concern the administration of justice, the general polity of the state, public order, tranquillity of the subjects, security of families, attention to all that may contribute to the general good, the choice of skillful ministers who love justice and truth . . . discrimination between justice and clemency whenever justice might suffer from relaxation of its rigor, wise distribution of benefits, rewards, exemptions, privileges and other concessions, wise administration of the public funds, prudence regarding foreigners, and all that may render government agreeable to the good, terrible to the wicked, and entirely worthy of the divine function of ruling men by wielding power that comes only from God and is a participation in his own.

As the final duty of the sovereign, one may add the following which stems from the administration of justice and includes all others. Although his power seems to place him above the law, since no man has the right to call him to account for his conduct, he should observe the laws that concern himself not only because he should be an example to his subjects and render their duty pleasant but because he is not dispensed from his own duty by his sovereign power. On the contrary, his rank obliges him to subordinate his personal interests to the general good of the state, which it is his glory to regard as his own.

Politics and Scripture (1679)

JACQUES BENIQUE BOSSUET

Monarchical government is the best form: If it is the most natural, it is therefore the most enduring, and in consequence the strongest form of government. It is also the best defense against division, which is the deadliest disease of states, and the most certain cause of their downfall. "Every kingdom divided against itself is brought to desolation; and every city or house divided against itself shall not stand." . . . [Matt. 12:25]

The purpose of founding states is unity, and there is no greater unity than being under one ruler. There is also no greater strength, for all [the wills] concur. . . .

Kings should respect their powers and only employ them for the general good: Since their power comes from above, as has been stated, they should not believe that they are masters of it and may use it just as they please; they should exercise it with fear and restraint, as a thing conferred on them by God, for which they are answerable to Him. "Hear therefore, O ye Kings, and understand; learn, ye that be judges of the ends of the earth. Give ear, ye that rule the people, and glory in the multitude of nations. For power is given you of the Lord, and sovereignty from the Highest, who shall try your works and search out your counsels. Because, being ministers of His kingdom, ye have not judged aright, not kept the law, nor walked after the counsel of God. Horribly and speedily shall He come upon you: for a sharp judgment shall be to them that are in high places. . . ." [Wis. 6]

Kings should therefore tremble to exercise the power which God has given to them, and remember how terrible a sacrilege it is to abuse the power which comes from God.

We have seen kings seated on the throne of the Lord, holding in their hand the sword which He has committed to their charge. What blasphemy and presumption it is for an unjust ruler to occupy the throne of God and give judgments contrary to His law, to wield the sword which He has placed in their hands to oppress and destroy His children!

There is no higher judgment than that of the prince: Kings are gods, and partake in some measure of the independence of God: "I have said, Ye are gods; and all of you are children of the most High." [Ps. 82:6]

From this we conclude that he who refuses obedience to the prince is not to be referred to another judgment, but condemned to death without appeal, as an enemy of the public peace and of human society. . . .

The prince can correct himself, when he knows that he has erred; but against his authority there can be no redress save in that authority itself.

Kings are not therefore above the law: Kings are therefore, as others, subject to the equity of the laws, both because they are bound to act justly, and because they owe it to the people to set an example of fairness. But they are not liable to the penalties of the law: or, in the language of theology, princes are subject to the laws in their directive, but not in their coercive function.

Definition of majesty: Nothing is more majestic than all-embracing goodness: and there is no greater debasement of majesty than misery brought upon subjects by the prince. . . .

God is the essence of holiness, goodness, power, reason. In these consists the divine majesty. In their reflection consists the majesty of the prince.

So great is this majesty that its source cannot be found to reside in the prince: it is borrowed from God, who entrusts it to the prince for the good of his people, to which end it is well that it be restrained by a higher power. . . .

O kings, be bold therefore in the exercise of your power; for it is divine and beneficial to the human race; but wield it with humility. It is conferred on you from without. It leaves you in the end weak and mortal, it leaves you still sinners: and it lays upon you a heavier charge to render to God.

On arbitrary government which is not found among us in well-ordered states: It is one thing for a government to be absolute, and quite another for it to be arbitrary. It is absolute in that it is not liable to constraint, there being no other power capable of coercing the sovereign, who is in this sense independent of all human authority. But it does not follow from this that the government is arbitrary, for besides the fact that all is subject to the judgment of God (which is also true of those governments we have just called arbitrary), there are also [fundamental] laws, in such empires, so that whatever is done contrary to them is null in a legal sense: moreover, there is always an opportunity for redress, either at other times or in other conditions. Thus each man remains the legitimate owner of his property. . . .

This is what is termed legitimate government, by its very nature the opposite of arbitrary government.

The Practice of Absolute Rule

Letters to His Heirs: "Allow Good Sense to Act"
KING LOUIS XIV

In this selection, drawn from Louis' memoirs, the king himself gives practical advice to his heirs concerning the demands and duties of absolute monarchy.

Two things without doubt were absolutely necessary: very hard work on my part, and a wise choice of persons capable of seconding it.

As for work, it may be, my son, that you will begin to read these Memoirs at an age when one is far more in the habit of dreading than loving it, only too happy to have escaped subjection to tutors and to have your hours regulated no longer, nor lengthy and prescribed study laid down for you.

On this heading I will not warn you solely that it is none the less toil *by which* one reigns, and *for which* one reigns, and that the conditions of royalty, which may seem to you sometimes hard and vexatious in so lofty a position, would appear pleasant and easy if there was any doubt of your reaching it.

There is something more, my son, and I hope that your own experience

"Letters to His Heirs" is from Jean Longnon, ed., *A King's Lessons in Statecraft: Louis XIV*, trans. H. Wilson (London: T. Fisher Unwin Ltd., 1924), pp. 48–53, 149.

Louis XIV, ''The Sun King''; Gian Lorenzo Bernini, after; *National Gallery of Art, Washington; Samuel H. Kress Collection*

will never teach it to you: nothing could be more laborious to you than a great amount of idleness if you were to have the misfortune to fall into it through beginning by being disgusted with public affairs, then with pleasure, then with idleness itself, seeking everywhere fruitlessly for what can never be found, that is to say, the sweetness of repose and leisure without having the preceding fatigue and occupation.

I laid a rule on myself to work regularly twice every day, and for two or three hours each time with different persons, without counting the hours which I passed privately and alone, nor the time which I was able to give on particular occasions to any special affairs that might arise. There was no moment when I did not permit people to talk to me about them, provided that they were urgent; with the exception of foreign ministers who sometimes find too favourable moments in the familiarity allowed to them, either to obtain or to discover something, and whom one should not hear without being previously prepared.

I cannot tell you what fruit I gathered immediately I had taken this resolution. I felt myself, as it were, uplifted in thought and courage; I found myself quite another man, and with joy reproached myself for having been too long unaware of it. This first timidity, which a little self-judgment always produces and which at the beginning gave me pain, especially on occasions when I had to speak in public, disappeared in less than no time. The only thing I felt then was that I was King, and born to be one. I experienced next a delicious feeling, hard to express, and which you will not know yourself except by tasting it as I have done. For you must not imagine, my son, that the affairs of State are like some obscure and thorny path of learning which may possibly have already wearied you, wherein the mind strives to raise itself with effort above its purview, more often to arrive at no conclusion, and whose utility or apparent utility is repugnant to us as much as its difficulty. The function of Kings consists principally in allowing good sense to act, which always acts naturally and without effort. What we apply ourselves to is sometimes less difficult that what we do only for our amusement. Its usefulness always follows. A King, however skillful and enlightened be his ministers, cannot put his own hand to the work without its effects being seen. Success, which is agreeable in everything, even in the smallest matters, gratifies us in these as well as in the greatest, and there is no satisfaction to equal that of noting every day some progress in glorious and lofty enterprises, and in the happiness of the people which has been planned and thought out by oneself. All that is most necessary to this work is at the same time agreeable, for; in a word, my son, it is to have one's eyes open to the whole earth; to learn each hour the news concerning every province and every nation, the secrets of every court, the mood and the weaknesses of each Prince and of every foreign minister; to be well-informed on an infinite number of matters about which we are supposed to know nothing; to elicit from our subjects what they hide from us with the greatest care; to discover the most remote opinions of our own courtiers and the most hidden interests of those who come to us with quite contrary professions. I do not know of any other pleasure we would not renounce for that, even if curiosity alone gave us the opportunity. . . .

• • •

I gave orders to the four Secretaries of State no longer to sign anything whatsoever without speaking to me; likewise to the Controller, and that he should authorise nothing as regards finance without its being registered in a book which must remain with me, and being noted down in a very abridged abstract form in which at any moment, and at a glance, I could see the state of the funds, and past and future expenditure. . . .

• • •

Regarding the persons whose duty it was to second my labours, I resolved at all costs to have no prime minister; and if you will believe me, my son, and all your successors after you, the name shall be banished for ever from France, for there is nothing more undignified than to see all the administration on one side, and on the other, the mere title of King.

To effect this, it was necessary to divide my confidence and the execution of my orders without giving it entirely to one single person, applying these different people to different spheres according to their diverse talents, which is perhaps the first and greatest gift that Princes can possess.

I also made a resolution on a further matter. With a view the better to unite in myself alone all the authority of a master, although there must be in all affairs a certain amount of detail to which our occupations and also our dignity do not permit us to descend as a rule, I conceived the plan, after I should have made choice of my ministers, of entering sometimes into matters with each one of them, and when they least expected it, in order that they might understand that I could do the same upon other subjects and at any moment. Besides, a knowledge of some small detail acquired only occasionally, and for amusement rather than as a regular rule, is instructive little by little and without fatigue, on a thousand things which are not without their use in general resolutions, and which we ought to know and do ourselves were it possible that a single man could know and do everything.

• • •

I have never failed, when an occasion has presented itself, to impress upon you the great respect we should have for religion, and the deference we should show to its ministers in matters specially connected with their mission, that is to say, with the celebration of the Sacred Mysteries and the preaching of the doctrine of the Gospels. But because people connected with the Church are liable to presume a little too much on the advantages attaching to their profession, and are willing sometimes to make use of them in order to whittle down their most rightful duties, I feel obliged to explain to you certain points on this question which may be of importance.

The first is that Kings are absolute *seigneurs,* and from their nature have full and free disposal of all property both secular and ecclesiastical, to use it as wise dispensers, that is to say, in accordance with the requirements of their State. . . .

The Revocation of the Edict of Nantes (1685)

KING LOUIS XIV

On October 22, 1685, Louis XIV annulled the Edict of Nantes, which had provided political and religious freedom for the French Protestants, or Huguenots, since 1598. Louis was determined to control a nation that was unified politically under his rule and religiously under his faith; Catholicism was to be the only accepted religion for the French people. The revocation was hailed by Catholics but was not without its critics even at court, as reflected in the opinion of the duke of Saint-Simon, which follows the text of the treaty.

I. Be it known that [with] . . . our certain knowledge, full power, and royal authority, we have, by this present perpetual and irrevocable edict, suppressed and revoked . . . the edict of our said grandfather, [Henry IV], null and void, together with all concessions . . . in favor of the said persons of the [Reformed religion], . . . and it is our pleasure, that all the temples of those of the said [Reformed religion] situate in our kingdom, countries, territories, and the lordships under our crown, shall be demolished without delay.

II. We forbid our subjects of the [Reformed religion] to meet any more for the exercise of the said religion in any place or private house, under any pretext whatever. . . .

III. We likewise forbid all noblemen . . . to hold such religious exercises in their houses or fiefs, under penalty . . . of imprisonment and confiscation.

IV. We enjoin all ministers of the said [Reformed religion], who do not choose to become converts and to embrace the Catholic, apostolic, and Roman religion, to leave our kingdom and the territories subject to us within a fortnight of the publication of our present edict . . . on pain of being sent to the galleys. . . .

VII. We forbid private schools for the instruction of children of the said [Reformed religion], and in general all things whatever which can be regarded as a concession of any kind in favor of the said religion.

VIII. As for children who may be born of persons of the said [Reformed religion], we desire that from henceforth they be baptized by the parish priests. We enjoin parents to send them to the churches for that purpose, under penalty of five hundred livres fine . . . and thereafter the children shall be brought up in the Catholic, apostolic, and Roman religion, which we expressly enjoin the local magistrates to see done.

X. We repeat our most express prohibition to all our subjects of the said [Reformed religion], together with their wives and children, against leaving our kingdom, lands, and territories subject to us, or transporting their goods and effect therefrom under penalty, as respects the men, of

"The Revocation of the Edict of Nantes" is from James H. Robinson, ed., *Readings in European History*, vol. 2 (Boston: Ginn and Company, 1906), pp. 288–291.

being sent to the galleys, and as respects the women, of imprisonment and confiscation.

XII. As for the rest, liberty is granted to the said persons of the [Reformed religion], pending the time when it shall please God to enlighten them as well as others to remain in the cities and places of our kingdom, lands, and territories subject to us, and there to continue their commerce, and to enjoy their possessions, without being subjected to molestation . . . on condition of not engaging in the exercise of the said religion. . . .

"A Frightful Plot": Results of the Revocation
THE DUKE OF SAINT-SIMON

The revocation of the Edict of Nantes, without the slightest pretext of necessity, and the various proscriptions that followed it, were the fruits of a frightful plot, in which the new spouse was one of the chief conspirators, and which depopulated a quarter of the realm; ruined its commerce; weakened it in every direction; gave it up for a long time to the public and avowed pillage of the dragoons; authorized torments and punishments by which many innocent people of both sexes were killed by thousands; ruined a numerous class; tore in pieces a world of families; armed relatives against relatives, so as to seize their property and leave them to die in hunger; banished our manufactures to foreign lands; made those lands flourish and overflow at the expense of France, and enabled them to build new cities; gave to the world the spectacle of a prodigious population proscribed without crime, stripped, fugitive, wandering, and seeking shelter far from their country; sent to the galleys nobles, rich old men, people carefully nurtured, weak, and delicate;—and all solely on account of religion. . . .

The king congratulated himself on his power and his piety. He believed himself to have brought back the days of the apostles, and attributed to himself all the honor. The bishops wrote panegyrics of him; the Jesuits made the pulpit resound with his praise. All France was filled with horror and confusion; and yet there was never such triumph and joy, such boundless laudation of the king.

The Sighs of Enslaved France (1690)
PIERRE JURIEU

As a result of the revocation of the Edict of Nantes, the persecution of Huguenots began in earnest. The author of the following memoirs cannot be

" 'A Frightful Plot' " is from James H. Robinson, ed., *Readings in European History*, vol. 2 (Boston: Ginn and Company, 1906), pp. 291–293.

"The Sighs of Enslaved France" is from William F. Church, ed. and trans., *The Impact of Absolutism in France: National Experience under Richelieu, Mazarin and Louis XIV* (New York: John Wiley & Sons, 1969), pp. 102–105. Copyright © 1969 John Wiley & Sons, Inc. Reprinted by permission of John Wiley & Sons, Inc.

positively identified, but they are probably from the pen of Pierre Jurieu, a Calvinist pastor who had fled to Holland. Louis endured much criticism from such dissidents in exile. Jurieu's memoirs are among the most provocative because they characterize Louis' absolutism as oppressive and responsible for many of the ills of France.

The oppression of the people is caused primarily by the prodigious number of taxes and excessive levies of money that are everywhere taken in France. Taxes and finance are a science today, and one must be skilled to speak knowledgeably of them, but it suffices for us to relate what we all feel and what the people know of the matter. There are the personal and [land taxes]. There are taxes on salt, wine, merchandise, principal, and revenue. This miserable century has produced a flood of names [of taxes], most of which were unknown to our ancestors or, if some were known, they were not odious because of the moderation with which they were imposed and levied. . . . It does not serve my purpose to acquaint you with the details of these taxes so that you may feel their weight and injustice. It will suffice to enable you to understand the horrible oppression of these taxes by showing (1) the immense sums that are collected, (2) the violence and abuses that are committed in levying them, (3) the bad use that is made of them, and (4) the misery to which the people are reduced.

First, dear unfortunate compatriots, you should realize that the taxes that are taken from you comprise a sum perhaps greater than that which all the other princes of Europe together draw from their states. One thing is certain, that France pays two hundred million in taxes of which about three-fourths go into the coffers of the king and the rest to expenses of collection, tax-farmers, officials, keepers, receivers, the profits of financiers, and new fortunes that are created in almost a single day. For the collection of the salt tax alone, there is a great army of officers and constables. . . .

If tyranny is clear and evident in the immense sums that are levied in France, it is not less so in the manner of collecting them. Kings were established by the people to preserve their persons, lives, liberty, and properties. But the government of France has risen to such excessive tyranny that the prince today regards everything as belonging to him alone. He imposes taxes at will without consulting the people, the nobles, the Estates, or the Parlements. I shall tell you something that is true and that thousands know but most Frenchmen do not. During Colbert's ministry [supervisor of the royal finances] it was discussed whether the king should take immediate possession of all real and personal property in France and reduce it to royal domain, to be used and assigned to whomever the court judged appropriate without regard for former possession, heredity, or other rights. . . .

How much abuse and violence is committed in the collection of taxes? The meanest agent is a sacred person who has absolute power over gentlemen, the judiciary, and all the people. A single blow is capable of ruining the most powerful subject. They confiscate houses, furnishings, cattle, money, grain, wine, and everything in sight. The prisons are full of wretches who are responsible for sums that they impose upon other wretches who cannot pay what is demanded of them. Is there anything more harsh and cruel than the salt tax? They make you buy for ten or twelve *sous* per pound something that nature, the sun, and the sea provide for nothing and may be had for two farthings. Under pretext of exercising this royal right, the realm is flooded with a great army of scoundrels called constables of the gabelle [salt tax] who enter houses, penetrate the most secret places with impunity, and do not fail to find unauthorized salt wherever they think there is money. They condemn wretches to pay huge fines, cause them to rot in prison, and ruin families. They force salt upon people everywhere and give each family more than three times as much as they can consume. In the provinces by the sea, they will not permit a poor peasant to bring home salt water; they break jugs, beat people, and imprison them. In a word, every abuse is committed in levying this and other taxes which is done with horrible expense, seizures, imprisonments, and legal cases before the collectors and courts with costs far above the sums involved. . . .

This is how all of France is reduced to the greatest poverty. In earlier reigns, that is, during the ministries of Cardinal Richelieu and Cardinal Mazarin, France was already burdened with heavy taxes. But the manner of collecting them, although not entirely just, nevertheless exhausted the realm much less than the way in which they are collected today. . . . The government of today has changed all of this. M. de Colbert made a plan to reform the finances and applied it to the letter. But what was this reformation? It was not the diminution of taxes in order to relieve the people. . . . He increased the king's revenue by one half. . . .

After this, if we examine the use that is made of these immense sums that are collected with such abuses and extortion, we shall find all the characteristics of oppression and tyranny. It sometimes happens that princes and sovereigns exact levies that appear excessive and greatly inconvenience individuals, but are required by what are called the needs and necessities of the state. In France there is no such thing. There are neither *needs* nor *state*. As for the *state*, earlier it entered into everything; one spoke only of the interests of the *state*, the needs of the *state*, the preservation of the *state*, and the service of the *state*. To speak this way today would literally be a crime of *lese majesty* [treason]. The king has taken the place of the state. It is the service of the *king*, the interest of the *king*, the preservation of the provinces and wealth of the *king*. Therefore the king is all and the state nothing. And these are no mere figures of speech but realities. At the French court, no interest is considered but the personal interest of the king, that is, his grandeur and glory. He is the idol to which are sacrificed princes, great men and small, families, provinces, cities, finances and generally everything. Therefore, it is not for the good of the state that these horrible exactions are made, since there is no more state. . . .

This money is used solely to nourish and serve the greatest self-pride and arrogance that ever existed. It is so deep an abyss that it would have swallowed not only the wealth of the whole realm but that of all other states if the king had been able to take possession of it as he attempted to do. The king has caused himself to receive more false flattery than all the pagan demi-gods did with true flattery. Never before was flattery pushed to this point. Never has man loved praise and vainglory to the extent that this prince has sought them. In his court and around himself he supports a multitude of flatterers who constantly seek to outdo each other. He not only permits the erection of statues to himself, on which are inscribed blasphemies in his honor and below which all the nations of the earth are shown in chains; he causes himself to be represented in gold, silver, bronze, copper, marble, silk, in paintings, arches of triumph, and inscriptions. He fills all Paris, all his palaces, and the whole realm with his name and his exploits, as though he far surpasses the Alexanders, the Caesars, and all the heroes of antiquity.

Louis XIV: The Sun King

"Vanity Was His Ruin"

THE DUKE OF SAINT-SIMON

The duke of Saint-Simon (1675–1755) was a rather indifferent soldier and diplomat, but he was a passionate observer of affairs at Louis' court and has provided us with our most vivid account of the king and his activities. Saint-Simon was typical of the feudal nobility that Louis was trying to control, and thus this account, from his memoirs was by no means free from prejudice.

Portrait of the King

Louis XIV was made for a brilliant Court. In the midst of other men, his figure, his courage, his grace, his beauty, his grand mien, even the tone of his voice and the majestic and natural charm of all his person, distinguished him till his death as the King Bee, and showed that if he had only been born a simple private gentleman, he would equally have excelled in fetes, pleasures, and gallantry, and would have had the greatest success in love. . . . Vanity, this unmeasured and unreasonable love of admiration, was his ruin. His ministers, his generals, his mistresses, his courtiers, soon perceived his weakness. They praised him with emulation and spoiled him. Praises, or to say the truth, flattery, pleased him to such an extent, that the

" 'Vanity Was His Ruin' " is from Bayle St. John, ed., *The Memoirs of the Duke of Saint-Simon*, vol. 2 (New York: James Pott and Co., 1901), pp. 202–203, 214–219, 226–227, 231–232, 273–276.

coarsest was well received, the vilest even better relished. It was the sole means by which you could approach him. Those whom he liked owed his affection for them, to their untiring flatteries. This is what gave his ministers so much authority, and the opportunities they had for adulating him, of attributing everything to him, and of pretending to learn everything from him. Suppleness, meanness, an admiring, dependent, cringing manner—above all, an air of nothingness—were the sole means of pleasing him. . . .

Though his intellect, as I have said, was beneath mediocrity, it was capable of being formed. He loved glory, was fond of order and regularity; was by disposition prudent, moderate, discreet, master of his movements and his tongue. Will it be believed? He was also by disposition good and just! God had sufficiently gifted him to enable him to be a good King; perhaps even *a tolerably great King!* All the evil came to him from elsewhere. His early education was so neglected that nobody dared approach his apartment. He has often been heard to speak of those times with bitterness, and even to relate that, one evening he was found in the basin of the Palais Royale garden fountain, into which he had fallen! He was scarcely taught how to read or write, and remained so ignorant, that the most familiar historical and other facts were utterly unknown to him! He fell, accordingly, and sometimes even in public, into the grossest absurdities. . . .

Louis XIV took great pains to be well informed of all that passed everywhere; in the public places, in the private homes, in society and familiar intercourse. His spies and tell-tales were infinite. He had them of all species; many who were ignorant that their information reached him; others who knew it; others who wrote to him direct, sending their letters through channels he indicated; and all these letters were seen by him alone, and always before everything else; others who sometimes spoke to him secretly in his cabinet, entering by the back stairs. These unknown means ruined an infinite number of people of all classes, who never could discover the cause; often ruined them very unjustly; for the King, once prejudiced, never altered his opinion, or so rarely, that nothing was more rare. He had, too, another fault, very dangerous for others and often for himself, since it deprived him of good subjects. He had an excellent memory; in this way, that if he saw a man who, twenty years before, perhaps, had in some manner offended him, he did not forget the man, though he might forget the offence. This was enough, however, to exclude the person from all favour. The representations of a minister, of a general, of his confessor even, could not move the King. He would not yield.

The most cruel means by which the King was informed of what was passing—for many years before anybody knew it—was that of opening letters. The promptitude and dexterity with which they were opened passes understanding. He saw extracts from all the letters in which there were passages that the chiefs of the post-office, and then the minister who governed it, thought ought to go before him; entire letters, too, were sent to him, when their contents seemed to justify the sending. Thus the chiefs of the post, nay, the principal clerks were in a position to suppose what they pleased and against whom they pleased. A word of contempt against the King or the government, a joke, a detached phrase, was enough. It is incredible how many people, justly or unjustly, were more or less ruined, always without resource, without trial, and without knowing why. The secret was impenetrable; for nothing ever cost the King less than profound silence and dissimulation. . . .

The King loved air and exercise very much, as long as he could make use of them. He had excelled in dancing, and at tennis and mall. On horseback he was admirable, even at a late age. He liked to see everything done with grace and address. To acquit yourself well or ill before him was a merit or fault. He said that with things not necessary it was best not to meddle, unless they were done well. He was fond of shooting, and there was not a better or more graceful shot than he. . . .

He liked splendour, magnificence, and profusion in everything: you pleased him if you shone through the brilliancy of your houses, your clothes, your table, your equipages. Thus a taste for extravagance and luxury was disseminated through all classes of society; causing infinite harm, and leading to general confusion of rank and to ruin.

The King's Day

At eight o'clock the chief *valet de chambre* on duty, who alone had slept in the royal chamber, and who had dressed himself, awoke the King. The chief physician, the chief surgeon, and the nurse (as long as she lived), entered at the same time. The latter kissed the King; the others rubbed and often changed his shirt, because he was in the habit of sweating a great deal. At the quarter, the grand chamberlain was called (or, in the absence, the first gentleman of the chamber), and those who had what was called the *grandes entrées*. The chamberlain (or chief gentleman) drew back the curtains which had been closed again, and presented the holy-water from the vase, at the head of the bed. . . . Then all passed into the cabinet of the council. A very short religious service being over, the King called, they re-entered. The same officer gave him his dressing-gown; immediately after, other privileged courtiers entered, and then everybody, in time to find the King putting on his shoes and stockings, for he did almost everything himself and with address and grace. Every other day we saw him shave himself; and he had a little short wig in which he always appeared, even in bed, and on medicine days. He often spoke of the chase, and sometimes said a word to somebody. No toilette table was near him; he had simply a mirror held before him.

As soon as he was dressed, he prayed to God, at the side of his bed, where all the clergy present knelt, the cardinals without cushions, all the laity remaining standing; and the captain of the guards came to the balustrade during the prayer, after which the King passed into his cabinet.

He found there, or was followed by all who had the *entrée*, a very numerous company, for it included everybody in any office. He gave orders to each for the day; thus within a half a quarter of an hour it was known what he meant to do; and then all this crowd left directly. The bastards, a few favorites, and the valets alone were left. It was then a good opportunity for talking with the King; for example, about plans of gardens and buildings; and conversation lasted more or less according to the person engaged in it. . . .

On Sunday, and often on Monday, there was a council of state; on Tuesday a finance council; on Wednesday council of state; on Saturday finance council. Rarely were two held in one day or any on Thursday or Friday. Once or twice a month there was a council of despatches on Monday morning. . . .

The dinner was always *au petit couvert*, that is the King ate by himself in his chamber upon a square table in front of the middle window. It was more or less abundant, for he ordered in the morning whether it was to be "a little," or "very little" service. But even at this last, there were always many dishes, and three courses without counting the fruit.

The King's Diet

As during the last year of his life the King became more and more costive, Fagon [the court physician] made him eat at the commencement of his repasts many iced fruits, that is to say, mulberries, melons, and figs rotten from ripeness; and at his dessert many other fruits, finishing with a surprising quantity of sweetmeats. All the year round he ate at supper a prodigious quantity of salad. His soups, several of which he partook of morning and evening, were full of gravy, and were of exceeding strength, and everything that was served to him was full of spice, to double the usual extent, and very strong also. . . .

This summer he redoubled his regime of fruits and drinks. At last the former clogged his stomach, taken after soup, weakened the digestive organs and took away his appetite, which until then had never failed him all his life, though however late dinner might be delayed he never was hunger or wanted to eat. But after the first spoonfuls of soup, his appetite came, as I have several times heard him say, and he ate so prodigiously and so solidly morning and evening that no one could get accustomed to see it. So much water and so much fruit unconnected by anything spirituous, turned his blood into gangrene; while those forced night sweats diminished its strength and impoverished it; and thus his death was caused, as was seen by the opening of his body. The organs were found in such good and healthy condition that there is reason to believe he would have lived beyond his hundredth year. His stomach above all astonished, and also his bowels by their volume and extent, double that of the ordinary, whence it came that he was such a great yet uniform eater.

The King's Death

Friday, August the 30th, was a bad day preceded by a bad night. The King continually lost his reason. About five o'clock in the evening Madame de Maintenon left him, gave away her furniture to the domestics, and went to Saint-Cyr never to leave it.

On Saturday, the 31st of August, everything went from bad to worse. The gangrene had reached the knee and all the thigh. Towards eleven o'clock at night the King was found to be so ill that the prayers for the dying were said. This restored him to himself. He repeated the prayers in a voice so strong that it rose above all the other voices. At the end he recognised Cardinal de Rohan, and said to him, "These are the last favours of the Church." This was the last man to whom he spoke. He repeated several times, *Nunc et in hora mortis*, then said, "Oh, my God, come to my aid: hasten to succour me."

These were his last words. All the night he was without consciousness and in a long agony, which finished on Sunday, the 1st September, 1715, at a quarter past eight in the morning, three days before he had accomplished his seventy-seventh year, and in the seventy-second of his reign. He had survived all his sons and grandsons, except the King of Spain. Europe never saw so long a reign or France a King so old.

Impressions of the Palace at Versailles

In 1661, Louis XIV began construction of his famous palace at Versailles, about twenty miles from Paris. By 1668, two shifts of laborers were working constantly, and by 1682, enough of the palace had been completed to warrant Louis' move from Paris. Amid the construction that continued until 1710, Louis lived, along with most of the French aristocracy, entertaining lavishly and administering the affairs of state. The palace of Versailles were both admired and reviled, as is noted in the following excerpts, but it served its purpose as a monument to the glory of the Sun King.

"A Fine Chateau" (1664)

SEBASTIANO LOCATELLI

Sebastiano Locatelli was an Italian priest who visited France in 1664 and described the palace in these terms:

Versailles is a fine chateau begun by Louis XIII and completed by the reigning king. There is plentiful game in the vicinity. An aviary constructed of copper wire contains, I think, an example of every bird known

" 'A Fine Chateau' " is from Gilette Ziegler, ed., *The Court of Versailles in the Reign of Louis XIV*, trans. Simon Watson Taylor (London: George Allen and Unwin, Ltd., 1966), p. 25. Reprinted by permission of the publisher.

A full view of Versailles as it appeared after its expansion from a hunting lodge to the royal residence and seat of government (ca. 1682). A center of culture, the palace also served as propaganda, being symbolic of the absolute authority of the Sun King. (*The New York Public Library, Art and Architecture Room*)

to man. Indeed, I was shown more than forty species which I had never yet seen or even heard of. As regards the buildings, hunting facilities, comfort and pleasure, Versailles excels all the King's other chateaux, even Fountainbleau.

Three great roadways leading from the Cours la Reine in Paris to Versailles have already been started and will gradually be improved. They will be twenty-one miles in a straight line, planted with four lines of trees and divided into three pathways: the central pathway, to be paved for the use of carriages, will be four perches wide; the two flanking pathways, each a perch wide, will be raised, so forming a sort of levee. All this will cost the King a great sum of money, for this region is very hilly, and these hills must be levelled out over a distance of seven miles; it is true that they are not very high, and contain no stones. If these roadways are ever completed they will surely be unparalleled throughout the world.

A Celebration of Greatness (1665)

JEAN COLBERT

The expense of the palace was indeed a concern, especially to Jean Colbert, who supervised the royal finances. Still, in 1665, Colbert did not doubt that such a venture was an essential component of Louis' monarchy. In the second selection, Louis himself reveals the necessity of a palace on such a scale as Versailles. Other impressions of the palace follow.

If Your Majesty desires to discover where in Versailles are the more than 500,000 ecus spent there in two years, he will have great difficulty in finding them. Will he also deign to reflect that the Accounts of the Royal Buildings will always record the evidence that, during the time he has lavished such vast sums on this mansion, he has neglected the Louvre, which is assuredly the most superb palace in the world and the one worthiest of Your Majesty's greatness. . . . And God forbid that those many occasions which may impel him to go to war, and thus deprive him of the financial means to complete this superb building, should give him lasting occasion for regret at having lost the time and opportunity.

Your Majesty knows that, apart from glorious actions of war, nothing celebrates so advantageously the greatness and genius of princes than buildings, and all posterity measures them by the yardstick of these superb edifices which they have erected during their life. O what pity were the greatest and most virtuous of kings, of that real virtue which makes the greatest princes, to be measured by the scale of Versailles!

"A Celebration of Greatness" is from Gilette Ziegler, ed., *The Court of Versailles in the Reign of Louis XIV*, trans. Simon Watson Taylor (London: George Allen and Unwin, Ltd., 1966), p. 26. Reprinted by permission of the publisher.

Visible Majesty
KING LOUIS XIV

Those who imagine that these are merely matters of ceremony are gravely mistaken. The peoples over whom we reign, being able to apprehend the basic reality of things, usually derive their opinion from that they can see with their eyes.

Glory Secured (1684)
SIEUR DES COMBES

Italy must now yield to France the prize and garland which it has borne away hitherto from all the nations of the earth, in what regards the excellency of architecture, the beauty of the carving, the magnificence of painting, and the invention of aqueducts. . . . Versailles alone suffices to secure forever to France the glory it has at present, in surpassing all other kingdoms in the science of building: and it is beholding for this high esteem to the grandeur and magnificence of Louis the Great.

The Bad Taste of Versailles
THE DUKE OF SAINT-SIMON

As for the King himself, nobody ever approached his magnificence. His buildings, who could number them? At the same time, who was there who did not deplore the pride, the caprice, the bad taste seen in them? He built nothing useful or ornamental in Paris, except the Pont Royal, and that simply by necessity; so that despite its incomparable extent, Paris is inferior to many cities of Europe. Saint-Germains, a lovely spot, with a marvelous view, rich forest, terraces, gardens, and water he abandoned for Versailles; the dullest and most ungrateful of all places, without prospect, without wood, without water, without soil; for the ground is all shifting sand or swamp, the air accordingly bad.

But he liked to subjugate nature by art and treasure. He built at Versailles, on and on, without any general design, the beautiful and the ugly, the vast and the mean, all jumbled together. His own apartments and those

---

"Visible Majesty" is from Gilette Ziegler, ed., *The Court of Versailles in the Reign of Louis XIV*, trans. Simon Watson Taylor (London: George Allen and Unwin, Ltd., 1966), p. 26. Reprinted by permission of the publisher.

"Glory Secured" is from Sieur des Combes (Laurent Morellet), *An Historical Explication of What There Is Most Remarkable in That Wonder of the World, the French King's House at Versailles* (London, 1684).

"The Bad Taste of Versailles" is from Bayle St. John, ed., *The Memoirs of the Duke of Saint-Simon*, vol. 2 (New York: James Pott and Co., 1901), pp. 232–233.

of the Queen, are inconvenient to the last degree, dull, close, stinking. The gardens astonish by their magnificence, but cause regret by their bad taste. You are introduced to the freshness of the shade only by a vast torrid zone, at the end of which there is nothing for you but to mount or descend; and with the hill, which is very short, terminate the gardens. The violence everywhere done to nature repels and wearies us despite ourselves. The abundance of water, forced up and gathered together from all parts, is rendered green, thick, muddy; it disseminates humidity, unhealthy and evident; and an odour still more so. I might never finish upon the monstrous defects of a palace so immense and so immensely dear, with its accomplishments,which are still more so.

But the supply of water for the fountains was all defective at all moments, in spite of those seas of reservoirs which had cost so many millions to establish and to form upon the shifting sands and marsh. Who could have believed it? This defect became the ruin of the infantry which was turned out to do the work. . . . How many men were years in recovering from the effects of the contagion! How many never regained their health at all!

CHRONOLOGY: "I Am the State": The Development of Absolutism in England and France

1558–1603	Reign of Queen Elizabeth of England, last Tudor monarch.
1589–1610	Foundations of centralized monarchy in France established by King Henry IV and his finance minister, the Duke of Sully, through royal monopolies.
1603–1625	Reign of James I of England, first Stuart monarch. Conflict begins over kingly authority and the traditional rights and privileges of Parliament.
1610–1643	Reign of Louis XIII of France. The crown is managed by the king's advisor, Cardinal Richelieu, who further secures the foundation of French absolutism by indoctrinating the French with propaganda and spectacle.
1625–1649	Reign of Charles I of England. Confrontation with Parliament over specific power of king to raise funds by his own authority.
1628	Charles signs the Petition of Right: no forced loans or taxation without the consent of Parliament, no imprisonment without due cause, and no billeting of troops in private homes.
1628–1641	Charles rules without Parliament and runs the kingdom with his personal income until invasion of Scots in 1640.

1642–1646	Civil War between royal forces led by Charles (Cavaliers) and Parliamentary forces (Roundheads) ultimately led by Oliver Cromwell.
1643–1715	Reign of the "Sun King," Louis XIV. Construction begins on the royal palace at Versailles in 1661.
1649–1652	Outbreak of the Fronde in France: a series of widespread rebellions by segments of the French nobility and townspeople to stop the drift toward absolute monarchy in France. Young Louis XIV flees until the revolt collapses for lack of organization. Louis XIV convinced never to be a "king of straw" and is confirmed in the rightness of absolute rule.
1649	Execution of Charles I on charges of high treason.
1649–1653	The Commonwealth of England is established "for the good of the people."
1653–1658	Oliver Cromwell dismisses Parliament and rules England as Lord Protector.
1660–1685	Restoration of the monarchy under the rule of Charles II.
1685	Louis XIV revokes the Edict of Nantes, which had protected the religious freedoms and civil rights of French Protestants since 1598.
1688–1689	Parliament deposes James II and invites Protestant leader, William of Orange and his wife, Mary, to rule England jointly in what is termed, the Glorious Revolution.
1680–1700	Theory of absolute monarchy in France refined by Jean Domat and Jacques Benique Bossuet.

STUDY QUESTIONS

Section I: The English Revolution

1. Read James I's speech to Parliament (1610). Did James concede any authority to Parliament? Did his son, Charles I, rule in accordance with the principles of governance that James outlined? What in particular were Charles' views concerning the "rule of law"?
2. In the Petition of Right (1628), it was stated that no one could be "executed, destroyed or put to death, contrary to the laws and franchise of the land." The petition was promulgated as a check on the power of the monarch. How would James I have reacted to this petition, given the ideas contained in his speech to Parliament in 1610?
3. Analyze the concerns of Parliament as expressed in the Petition of Right (1628) and the Grand Remonstrance (1641). Organize these concerns into

categories of abuse (corruption, abuse of law, etc.). Which appears to be the category of most frequent abuse? Of most serious abuse? How did matters worsen between 1628 and 1641? Why? Note the reply of the king with regard to the charges made against his counselors in the Grand Remonstrance. Is his argument valid? Finally, was the king treated with dignity in these parliamentary documents? Or was Parliament overasserting its traditional authority?

4. Note that James I said kings, like gods, had the power of life and death, as judges over all their subjects, accountable to God only. After the execution of Charles I in 1649, this power seemed to reside in Parliament. How was this transformation achieved? What were the crucial decisions and circumstances, as evidenced by the documents, that resulted in the impotence of the monarchy and the execution of the king? Charles signed the Petition of Right in 1628 to uphold the laws and customs of the realm. How did Charles invoke this very idea in his defense entitled "The True Liberty of All My Subjects" (January 21, 1649)?

5. Analyze the "Articles of High Treason" directed against the six members of Parliament. Do you find any evidence in the Grand Remonstrance that might legitimize the king's aggressive stance against specific members of Parliament? Or was the king overreacting? Is the Grand Remonstrance a document respectful to the dignity and authority of the king?

6. King Charles I noted, in trying to arrest several members of Parliament in 1642, that "in cases of treason, no person has a privilege." Yet, it was upon this very charge that he was executed on authority of the "rump Parliament" and the High Court they established. How would you define the charge of "high treason?" How would you assess the guilt or innocence of Charles and the proscribed members of Parliament according to your definition?

7. Why did the Militia Ordinance of March 1642 pose such a threat to Charles I? Note the hostility to Catholics (papists) contained in the document. How was this a criticism of the king, and do you see evidence of similar criticism regarding the charge of "papism" in other decrees of Parliament? What is the expressed justification in the Militia Ordinance for Parliament's raising of an army on this occasion? Did Charles defend his ancient prerogatives effectively?

8. What were the main charges leveled against Charles I by the High Court on January 20, 1649? How does the tenor of this document differ from that of the Petition of Right or Grand Remonstrance? How effective was Charles in refuting Parliament's charges in defense of "the true liberty of my subjects." Both the king and Parliament asserted that they were upholding the laws and liberties of the English people. Whom do you believe?

9. Read carefully the death warrant and account of the execution of Charles I. Note the particular passages designed to appeal to your emotions. Are you sympathetic to the king's ordeal? To what extent is this

account propaganda? The king claimed to be the "martyr of the people." Did he succeed? Was Charles more influential dead than alive?

10. Discuss the ideas of Thomas Hobbes contained in the excerpt entitled *Leviathan*. What is his view of human nature, and how does he justify absolute monarchy? Be specific in your assessment. How does Hobbes' *Leviathan* reflect the uncertainty of the time?

11. Why did Oliver Cromwell dismiss the "rump Parliament" in 1653? Compare the reasons given by John Milton in his assessment of the character of Cromwell entitled "To You Our Country Owes Its Liberties." By dismissing Parliament, was Cromwell guilty of restricting the democratic bases of Parliament which had been so threatened by Charles I and so heartily promoted by Cromwell himself? On what principles did Cromwell justify his actions?

12. How would you define the position of Lord Protector as created by the Instrument of Government (1653)? Was he an absolute monarch? A constitutional monarch? Or simply the leader of a free commonwealth? Did the English Parliament substitute one king (Charles I) for another (Oliver Cromwell)? Why, then, did Cromwell refuse the title of "king?"

13. In Cromwell's letter refusing to accept the crown and the position of king of England (1657), he stated that he hoped he would never be found to be guilty of robbing the nation of civil rights and liberties, "but shall ever be found to serve them . . . to the attaining of them." He hoped to provide for security for the "great, natural and religious liberty, which is the liberty of conscience." After reading the document entitled "Treason and The Commonwealth" (1650) and the "The Instrument of Government" (1653), do you think he succeeded? Is freedom of speech central to freedom of conscience, or do the requirements of establishing political order preclude religious tolerance and open expression?

14. Compare the two evaluations of the character and career of Oliver Cromwell by John Milton and Edward Hyde, Earl of Clarendon. Note the elements of propaganda and overstatement in each. Which account do you find more in keeping with the evidence of the sources? What appears to be Milton's purpose in writing his account in 1654?

15. The Bill of Rights was formulated in 1689 after nearly seventy-five years of confrontation and accommodation between king and Parliament. Compare the principles stated in that document with those enunciated by James I in his speech to Parliament in 1610. How far had the English come in establishing constitutional rule and a restricted monarchy?

Section II: The Absolutism of Louis XIV

16. Louis XIV was a divine-right monarch. What does this mean, and how did Louis use religion to strengthen his political position in the state? How compelling in support of absolutism are the arguments of Jean Domat in "The Ideal Absolute State" and Jacques Benique Bossuet in "Politics and

Scripture"? What are the responsibilities of the king and the political advantages of absolute rule?

17. What is the difference between tyranny and the absolutism of Louis XIV's monarchy? What were the advantages and disadvantages of absolute rule for the different classes of French society? Who profited the most?

18. Analyze the Edict of Nantes. Why was it invoked in 1598 and why did Louis XIV revoke it? Was this a wise move politically? Are you persuaded by the duke of Saint-Simon's criticism? If you accept his criticism as valid, then how would you characterize the absolute rule of Louis XIV? Was he a tyrant—or a wise monarch?

19. Was Louis XIV a responsible monarch? From the accounts in his own memoirs and those of the duke of Saint-Simon, do you think that Louis worked hard at his job? How did he view his duties as king? Do the criticisms of Pierre Jurieu in "The Sighs of Enslaved France" seem valid to you? Why should a historian be somewhat careful in the judgments drawn from this evidence?

20. Look closely at the picture of Louis' palace at Versailles. In what ways did this structure reflect the character of Louis' monarchy? According to the comments contained in the section on Versailles, was the palace an effective propaganda medium? Why?

21. To what extent do you think absolute rule is a "natural" form of government, generally acceptable to most people, especially if it is benign or even enlightened so that the best interests of citizens are promoted? Do people want a government that provides for their security and happiness but prevents the participation and personal responsibility that a democracy demands? What are your own opinions on the subject?

2

"Dare to Know!": The Revolution of the Mind in the Seventeenth and Eighteenth Centuries

Intellect does not attain its full force unless it attacks power.

—Madame de Staël

Reason is the greatest enemy that faith has. It never comes to the aid of spiritual things, but . . . struggles against the divine Word, treating with contempt all that emanates from God.

—Martin Luther

I respect faith, but doubt is what gets you an education.

—Wilson Mizner

He who desires to have understanding must be free in mind.

—Alcinous

The real and legitimate goal of the sciences, is the endowment of human life with new inventions and riches.

—Francis Bacon

Science has done more for the development of western civilization in one hundred years than Christianity has done in eighteen hundred years.

—John Burroughs

When the great eighteenth-century thinker Immanuel Kant challenged his contemporaries to "Dare to Know!" he was also voicing a classic intellectual defiance of authority. The origin of the phrase can be traced to the Roman poet Horace, but nearly every era has possessed those individuals who are not satisfied with maintaining adherence to the "established doctrine" as defined by those in positions of authority. One must be bold in seeking knowledge, for there are many impediments to its attainment. Ideas have power. If successfully transmitted and accepted by the general population, they threaten the status quo, whatever its nature. This makes the pursuit of ideas a risky business that requires an intangible confidence, a willingness to gamble on the potential of an uncertain future. Curiosity and determination, therefore, coupled with a measure of defiance, are the essential components of progress.

Just as the individual in our modern society struggles to define and seek personal knowledge in order to make rational judgments independent of advertisers, politicians, and television preachers, so too did individuals in the seventeenth and eighteenth centuries struggle against similar constraints imposed on them by secular and spiritual institutions. Despite the condemnation of the Catholic Church and the intimidation of the Inquisition, people gradually changed the way they viewed the world around them. The long religious wars between Catholics and Protestants had ended by 1648, leaving people disillusioned and repulsed. Their belief had been shaken by the mindless fighting of the Thirty Years' War. Instead, many invested their confidence in a new association between Protestantism and monarchy. The compatibility between the Calvinists and commerce allowed the developing middle class to seek godly profit and at the same time build the economic foundations of a strong, centralized state. Contemporary with these political and economic developments was the rising influence of philosophers and writers whose primary concern lay within the realm of science and letters. With the aid of hindsight that only history can afford, we can now ascertain that most of the intellectual, political, economic, and social characteristics associated with the modern world came into being during the seventeenth and eighteenth centuries.

The human experience in Europe was indeed transformed. In the *salons* of Paris, in the coffee houses of London, the talk was of machines and the heavens, of natural laws and moral responsibility, of education and the purpose of religion. The ideals of reform captured the imagination and directed the energy of many writers, who exported great advancements in science and political thought throughout the world.

In the interest of understanding more fully the broad dimensions of this complex period, the chapter has been divided into two sections: the Scientific Revolution of the sixteenth and seventeenth centuries, and the Enlightenment of the eighteenth century. Although the study of ideas does not so easily lend itself to chronological arrangement as does political history, it is still possible to see intellectual development over time. The Enlightenment movement drew confidence from the scientific worldview that had developed as a result of the efforts and sacrifices of the pioneers of modern science.

Juxtaposed with the chaos of religious warfare and its attendant human destruction during the seventeenth century was an intellectual attempt to foster progress in the realm of science. Sweeping changes took place in human-ity's conception of the universe and of one's place in it. Although the movement has been called the Scientific Revolution, the changes were not rapid, nor did they involve large numbers of people. On the contrary, the revolution evolved slowly, through experimentation, often in makeshift laboratories. Yet great thinkers such as Sir Isaac Newton, René Descartes, and Francis Bacon at-tempted to discover the physical and natural laws of the universe and to organize and criticize that diverse body of knowledge. Thus did Descartes champion the principles of deduction and invent analytical geometry; so too did Newton seek to explain motion in the universe through observation, experimentation, and induction. Others, like John Locke, even endeavored to explain human relationships through such rational thought.

The eighteenth century has been called the Age of Reason, or the Enlight-enment. The writers and thinkers of this time, following precedents set in the preceding century, were convinced that natural laws governed the universe and that a human, being essentially a rational creature, could further discover and apply those laws in the world. These intellectuals, called *philosophes*, exam-ined and challenged the economic theories and political and religious assump-tions of the day. The *philosophes* were diverse in their thought and often contended among themselves, but they were united by the conviction that one had natural rights (defined by political philosopher John Locke as life, liberty, and property) and that one must control one's own destiny for the sole purpose of a better life on earth. Thus the political divine-right absolutism of King Louis XIV (1643–1715), although providing security, could not be tolerated by many *philosophes* because it curtailed individual liberty. Similarly, the *philosophes* were generally opposed to the accepted economic theory of mercantilism, which sought complete government control of the national economy and especially promoted the establishment of foreign trading monopolies. The production and distribution of goods in colonial markets were therefore regu-lated for the benefit of the mother country. The theory of capitalism was born as a reaction to this strict economic regulation by the state. Adam Smith, in his treatise *The Wealth of Nations* (1776), argued that such a rigid monopolistic policy restricted individual initiative and the natural pursuit of profit. In spiritual matters as well, the *philosophes* regarded religion, especially Chris-tianity, as fantasy that drew humanity away from the rational world into a realm of hope and belief in a nonexistent life beyond. The spiritual world was not subject to reason or proof and therefore drew scorn from the *philosophes*. Indeed, they contended that organized religion sought to control thought and was therefore anathema to true intellectual freedom.

But the rationalists of the Enlightenment were also adamant that knowledge must have practical purpose and inquiry must yield useful knowledge. Perhaps the best-known and most influential *philosophe* of them all, Voltaire, exclaimed: "What light has burst over Europe within the last few years! It is the light of common sense." Reason was synonymous with common sense. To the intellec-tuals of the time, anyone who could rid the mind of the chains of thought and social constraints established by the political and religious institutions of the day could possess reason.

Yet there is a certain naïveté in this relationship between reason and common sense that also characterized the *philosophes*. This naïveté appears most clearly in their conception of "progress." They professed a profound faith in the future and some even predicted a united era of peace and prosperity by the dawn of the twenty-first century. When one compares George Orwell's dire predictions in his novel *1984*, the contrast between the cockiness of the Age of Reason and the brutal realities of the twentieth century is staggering. The *philosophes* had none of the fear and distrust of human nature and technology that has been reflected in our experience with poisonous gas and nuclear destruction. For the Enlightened thinker, education in the simple laws of nature, technological progress, and increased production could only bring increased happiness. And for the eighteenth century, that was enough. Humankind was breaking its medieval chains, discarding archaic attitudes, and taking the risks requisite of a new era where religion was but a personal choice, and monarchs seemingly embodied Plato's ideal of philosopher-kings. It was therefore reasonable to think that happiness was in the offing.

This chapter introduces some of the most important personalities, ideas, and attitudes of this remarkable period. In so many ways, by "daring to know," the scientists and philosophers of the seventeenth and eighteenth centuries picked up the gauntlet laid down by the thinkers of the Renaissance and provided the intellectual challenge for future generations.

SECTION I: THE SCIENTIFIC REVOLUTION

The New Scientific Method

Sir Francis Bacon (1561–1626)

Sir Francis Bacon was born in London in 1561. Educated at Cambridge in law and science, he was an Englishman of almost universal accomplishment. He rose quickly as a lawyer during the reign of Queen Elizabeth I and was knighted in 1603 before being named chancellor by King James I in 1618. His career took a tragic turn in 1621 when he was charged with financial corruption, expelled from Parliament, and briefly imprisoned before his death in 1626. Throughout his career as a royal official, he wrote histories, moral essays, and philosophical treatises. But he never lost his interest in scientific studies, and, although not a scientist except in an amateur sense, he has traditionally been regarded as the father of scientific empiricism, the doctrine that all knowledge is derived from sense experience, observation, and experi-

mentation. In books such as The Advancement of Learning *(1605) and* Novum Organum *(1620), he set the tone for a new standard of scientific inquiry and attacked the medieval Scholastic belief that most truth had already been discovered by calling into question the traditional reverence for the authority of the ancient authors. Bacon urged his contemporaries to have confidence in their own abilities and see change as desirable.*

The following excerpts focus on the goals of Bacon's new methods of scientific inquiry and offer some of his thoughts on the relationship between religion and science.

"I Have Made a Beginning of the Work": *Novum Organum* (1620)

SIR FRANCIS BACON

For my own part at least, in obedience to the everlasting love of truth, I have committed myself to the uncertainties and difficulties and solitudes of the ways, and relying on the divine assistance have upheld my mind both against the shocks and embattled ranks of opinion, and against my own private and inward hesitations and scruples, and against the fogs and clouds of nature, and the phantoms flitting about on every side; in the hope of providing at last for the present and future generations guidance more faithful and secure. Wherein if I have made any progress, the way has been opened to me by no other means than the true and legitimate humiliation of the human spirit. For all those who before me have applied themselves to the invention of arts have but cast a glance or two upon facts and examples and experience, and straightway proceeded . . . to invoke their own spirits to give them oracles. I on the contrary, dwelling purely and constantly among the facts of nature, withdraw my intellect from them no further than may suffice to let the images and rays of natural objects meet in a point, as they do in the sense of vision. . . . And by these means I suppose that I have established for ever a true and lawful marriage between the empirical and the rational faculty, the unkind and ill-starred divorce and separation of which has thrown into confusion all the affairs of the human family. . . . I have sought on all sides diligently and faithfully to provide helps for the sense—substitutes to supply its failures, rectifications to correct its errors; and this I endeavour to accomplish not so much by instruments as by experiments. For the subtlety of experiments is far greater than that of the sense itself, even when assisted by exquisite instruments; such experiments, I mean, as are skilfully and artificially devised for the express purpose of determining the point in question. To the immediate and proper perception of the sense therefore I do not give much weight; but I contrive that the office of the sense shall be only to

" 'I Have Made a Beginning' " is from J. Spedding et al., *The Works of Francis Bacon* (Boston: Taggard and Thompson, 1863), vol. 8, pp. 31–34, 44–47, 53.

judge of the experiment, and that the experiment itself shall judge of the thing.

But I design not only to indicate and mark out the ways, but also to enter them. And therefore the third part of the work embraces the Phenomena of the Universe; that is to say, experience of every kind. . . . Those who aspire not to guess and divine, but to discover and know; who propose not to devise mimic and fabulous worlds of their own, but to examine and dissect the nature of this very world itself; must go to facts themselves for everything. . . . This therefore we must have, or the business must be forever abandoned. But up to this day such has been the condition of men in this matter, that it is no wonder if nature will not give herself into their hands. . . .

I have made a beginning of the work—a beginning, as I hope, not unimportant. . . . For the matter in hand is no mere felicity of speculation, but the real business and fortunes of the human race, and all power of operation. For man is but the servant and interpreter of nature: what he does and what he knows is only what he has observed of nature's order in fact or in thought; beyond this he knows nothing and can do nothing. For the chain of causes cannot by any force be loosed or broken, nor can nature be commanded except by being obeyed. And so those twin objects, human Knowledge and human Power, do really meet in one; and it is from ignorance of causes that operation fails.

The Advancement of Learning (1605)

SIR FRANCIS BACON

Lastly, some are weakly afraid lest a deeper search into nature should transgress the permitted limits of sober-mindedness, wrongfully wresting and transferring what is said in Holy Writ against those who pry into sacred mysteries to the hidden things of nature, which are barred by no prohibition. Others, with more subtlety, surmise and reflect that if the secondary causes are unknown, everything can be more readily referred to divine hand and rod—a point in which they think religion greatly concerned; which is, in fact, nothing else but to seek to gratify God with a lie. Others fear from past example that movements and changes in philosophy will end in assaults on religion; and others again appear apprehensive that in the investigation of nature something may be found to subvert, or at least shake, the authority of religion, especially with the unlearned.

But these two last fears seem to me to savor utterly of carnal wisdom; as if men in the recesses and secret thoughts of their hearts doubted and distrusted the strength of religion, and the empire of faith over the senses, and therefore feared that the investigation of truth in nature might be dangerous to them. But if the matter be truly considered, natural philosophy is, after the word of God, at once the surest medicine against supersti-

"The Advancement of Learning" is from James H. Robinson and Charles A. Beard, eds., *Readings in Modern European History*, vol. 1 (Boston: Ginn and Company, 1908), p. 176.

Sir Francis Bacon. The great *philosophe* Voltaire called him "the father of experimental philosophy." Bacon pioneered the method of inductive reasoning, thus providing an important intellectual foundation for the Scientific Revolution. (*New York Public Library Photograph Collection*)

tion and the most approved nourishment for faith; and therefore she is rightly given to religion as her most faithful handmaid, since the one displays the will of God, the other his power.

"He Is the Father of Experimental Philosophy"

VOLTAIRE

I shall confine myself to those things which so justly gained Lord Bacon the esteem of all Europe. The most singular and the best of all his pieces is

" 'He Is the Father of Experimental Philosophy' " is from Charles W. Eliot, ed. *The Harvard Classics*, vol. 34 (New York: P. F. Collier & Son Corporation, 1910), pp. 99–101.

that which, at this time, is the most useless and the least read, I mean his *Novum Scientiarum Organum*. This is the scaffold with which the new philosophy was raised; and when the edifice was built, part of it at least, the scaffold was no longer of use. . . . He is [thus] the father of experimental philosophy. . . .

No one before Lord Bacon was acquainted with experimental philosophy, nor with the several physical experiments which have been made since his time. . . . In a little while, experimental philosophy began to be cultivated in most parts of Europe. It was a hidden treasure which Lord Bacon had some notion of, and which all the philosophers, encouraged by his promises, endeavoured to dig up.

René Descartes (1596–1650)

René Descartes was born in 1596 in western France but lived primarily in Holland for the last twenty years of his life. He attended Jesuit schools and graduated in law from the university in Poitiers. He was not attracted to a legal career, however, and became a soldier in the German wars of the time. It was while he was billeted in a German town that he had an intellectual revelation akin, as he later maintained, to a religious conversion. He had a vision of the great potential for progress, if mathematical method were to be applied to all fields of knowledge. He thus pursued a career devoted to the propagation of a strict method, best exemplified by his invention of analytical geometry. Descartes believed that human beings were endowed by God with the ability to reason and that God served as the guarantor of the correctness of clear ideas. The material world could thus be understood through adherence to mathematical laws and methods of inquiry. Descartes championed the process of deductive reasoning whereby specific information could be logically deduced from general information. His method was influential well into the eighteenth century, when it was supplanted by the method of scientific induction, whereby generalizations could be drawn from the observation of specific data.

The following selection is drawn from Descartes' most famous work, Discourse on the Method of Rightly Conducting the Reason *(1636).*

"I Think, Therefore I Am": *Discourse on Method* (1636)
RENÉ DESCARTES

As a multitude of laws often furnishes excuses for vice, so that a state is much better governed when it has but few, and those few strictly observed, so in place of the great number of precepts of which logic is composed, I

"'I Think, Therefore I Am'" is from René Descartes, *The Discourse on Method and Metaphysical Meditations*, trans. G. B. Rawlings (London: Walter Scott, 1901), pp. 32–35, 60–61, 75–76.

René Descartes. The great champion of deductive reasoning, Descartes believed that because the world operated according to mathematical laws, it could be understood by the human mind. (*Réunion des Musées Nationaux*)

believed that I should find the following four sufficient, provided that I made a firm and constant resolve not once to omit to observe them.

The first was, never to accept anything as true when I did not recognize it clearly to be so, that is to say, to carefully avoid precipitation and prejudice, and to include in my opinions nothing beyond that which should present itself so clearly and so distinctly to my mind that I might have no occasion to doubt it.

The second was, to divide each of the difficulties which I should examine into as many parts as were possible, and as should be required for its better solution.

The third was, to conduct my thoughts in order, by beginning with the simplest objects, and those most easy to know, so as to mount little by little, as if by steps, to the most complex knowledge, and even assuming an order among those which do not naturally precede one another.

And the last was, to make everywhere enumerations so complete, and reviews so wide, that I should be sure of omitting nothing. . . .

I had long remarked that, in conduct, it is sometimes necessary to follow opinions known to be very uncertain, just as if they were indisputable, as has been said above; but then, because I desired to devote myself only to the research of truth, I thought it necessary to do exactly the contrary, and reject as absolutely false all in which I could conceive the least doubt, in order to see if afterwards there did not remain in my belief something which was entirely indisputable. Thus, because our senses sometimes deceive us, I wanted to suppose that nothing is such as they make us imagine it; and because some men err in reasoning . . . and judging that I was as liable to fail as any other, I rejected as false all the reasons which I had formerly accepted as [true]; . . . I resolved that everything which had ever entered into my mind was no more true than the illusions of my dreams. But immediately afterwards I observed that while I thus desired everything to be false, I, who thought, must of necessity [exist]; and remarking that this truth, *I think, therefore I am*, was so firm and so assured that all the most extravagant suppositions of the skeptics were unable to shake it, I judged that I could unhesitatingly accept it as the first principle of the philosophy I was seeking. . . .

After this, and reflecting upon the fact that I doubted, and that in consequence my being was not quite perfect (for I saw clearly that to know was a greater perfection than to doubt), I [wondered where] I had learned to think of something more perfect than I; and I knew for certain that it must be from some nature which was in reality more perfect. [And I clearly recognized that] this idea . . . had been put in me by a nature truly more perfect than I, which had in itself all perfections of which I could have any idea; that is, to explain myself in one word, God. . . .

Finally, whether awake or asleep, we ought never to allow ourselves to be persuaded of the truth of anything unless on the evidence of our Reason. And it must be noted that I say of our *Reason*, and not of our imagination or of our senses: thus, for example, although we very clearly see the sun, we ought not therefore to determine that it is only of the size which our sense of sight presents; and we may very distinctly imagine the head of a lion joined to the body of a goat, without being therefore shut up to the conclusion that a chimaera exists; for it is not a dictate of Reason that what we thus see or imagine is in reality existent; but it plainly tells us that all our ideas or notions contain in them some truth; for otherwise it could not be that God, who is wholly perfect and veracious, should have placed them in us.

Science and the Church

Nicolaus Copernicus (1473–1543)

One of the most important and fundamental areas of investigation during the Scientific Revolution was astronomy. For centuries, humans had subscribed to a geocentric theory that placed earth at the center of the universe with all the planets orbiting around it. This theory, ascribed to the Egyptian astronomer Ptolemy (fl. A.D. 150) and supported by Aristotelian physics, maintained that the earth had to be the center of the universe because of its heaviness and that the stars and other planets existed in surrounding crystalline spheres. Beyond these crystalline spheres lay the realm of God and the angels. This view was supported by the Catholic Church, which saw humanity as the central focus of God's creation and therefore at the epicenter of all existence. Biblical support for the geocentric theory included Psalm 104: "Thou didst set the earth on its foundation, so that it should never be shaken." Still, there were mathematical problems associated with this theory. For one, it was difficult to explain the motion of the planets, which seemed to be moving in noncircular patterns around the earth. At times the planets actually appeared to be going backward. This was explained by epicycles. Ptolemy maintained that planets make a second revolution in an orbit tangent to the first. It was therefore difficult to predict the location of a planet at any given time. A Polish astronomer named Nicolaus Copernicus (1473–1543) attempted to eliminate many of the mathematical inconsistencies by proposing that the sun, not the earth, was the center of the universe. In most other ways, including the acceptance of epicycles and the circular orbit of planets, Copernicus' system was still Ptolemaic. Yet Copernicus freed scientists from a rigid conception of cosmic structure and in essence proposed the empirical evidence of mathematics as the cornerstone of scientific thought. The first selection is the simple statement by Copernicus proposing the heliocentric theory; it is excerpted from a letter entitled Commentariolus, *written sometime after 1520. In 1543, Copernicus published* On the Revolutions of the Heavenly Spheres. *The second excerpt is from the preface of that work and was addressed to Pope Paul III. In it, Copernicus explains why he questioned the geocentric theory.*

The Heliocentric Statement (ca. 1520)
COPERNICUS

What appears to us as motions of the sun arise not from its motion but from the motion of the earth and our sphere, with which we revolve about the sun like any other planet. The earth has, then, more than one motion.

On the Movement of the Earth (1543)
COPERNICUS

I may well presume, most Holy Father, that certain people, as soon as they hear that in this book about the Revolutions of the Spheres of the Universe

---

"The Heliocentric Statement" is from Copernicus, *Three Copernican Treatises*, trans. Edward Rosen (New York: Columbia University Press, 1939), p. 58. © 1939, Columbia University Press. Reprinted by permission.

"On the Movement of the Earth" is from Copernicus, *De Revolutionibus Orbium Caelestium* (1543), trans. John F. Dobson and Selig Brodetsky, published in *Occasional Notes of the Royal Astronomical Society*, vol. 2, no. 1 (London: Royal Astronomical Society, 1947), excerpts from the preface and Book I.

I ascribe movement to the earthly globe, will cry out that, holding such views, I should at once be hissed off the stage. . . .

So I should like your Holiness to know that I was induced to think of a method of computing the motions of the spheres by nothing else than the knowledge that the mathematicians [who had previously considered the problem] are inconsistent in these investigations.

For, first, the mathematicians are so unsure of the movements of the Sun and Moon that they cannot even explain or observe the constant length of the seasonal year. Secondly, in determining the motions of these and of the other five planets, they use neither the same principles and hypotheses nor the same demonstrations of the apparent motions and revolutions. . . . Nor have they been able thereby to discern or deduce the principal thing—namely the shape of the Universe and the unchangeable symmetry of its parts. . . .

I pondered long upon this uncertainty of mathematical tradition in establishing the motions of the system of the spheres. At last I began to chafe that philosophers could by no means agree on any one certain theory of the mechanism of the Universe, wrought for us by a supremely good and orderly Creator. . . . I therefore took pains to read again the works of all the philosophers on whom I could lay hand to seek out whether any of them had even supposed that the motions of the spheres were other than those demanded by the [Ptolemaic] mathematical schools. I found first in Cicero that Hicetas [of Syracuse, fifth century B.C.] had realized that the Earth moved. Afterwards I found in Plutarch that certain others had held the like opinion. . . .

Thus assuming motions, which in my work I ascribe to the Earth, by long and frequent observations I have at last discovered that, if the motions of the rest of the planets be brought into relation with the circulation of the Earth and be reckoned in proportion to the circles of each planets, . . . the orders and magnitudes of all stars and spheres, nay the heavens themselves, become so bound together that nothing in any part thereof could be moved from its place without producing confusion of all the other parts of the Universe as a whole.

Galileo Galilei (1564–1642)

After Copernicus, the quest for rational truth was continued by Tycho Brahe, who compiled accurate tables of astronomical observations, and Johannes Kepler, who analyzed these tables and posited the elliptical orbits of planets. And yet this progress in scientific thought was to encounter various roadblocks beyond the difficulties of gathering and interpreting data. For the Catholic Church, the question was not one of empirical evidence and rational inquiry but rather of faith and authority.

During the sixteenth century, the Church established an organization that was designed to maintain purity of doctrine and authority over the faithful. The Inquisition, as it came to be called, was administered by Dominican friars, whose responsibilities had always involved the explanation of doctrine to those who had strayed from the path. Now they were actively to seek out those whose deeds and ideas seemed to contradict established Catholic doctrine. The Inquisition became a vehicle for reform through coercion, with allegiance being obtained through argument, intimidation, and torture if necessary.

During the seventeenth century, the Church found itself embroiled in events that again threatened its established authority. The attack was now centered on the new scientific theories that challenged Catholic doctrine and were being pursued and advocated independently of Church control. At the forefront of the controversy was one of the most influential scientists in history—Galileo Galilei.

Galileo was born in Pisa, Italy, in the year of Shakespeare's birth and Michelangelo's death (1564). He had much in common with these great men since he played the lute, painted, wrote poetry, and enjoyed polemics and satire. In 1592, Galileo was appointed professor of mathematics at the University of Padua, and he remained in this position for eighteen years, supporting a mistress, two daughters, a son, and a widowed mother on a small income supplemented by tutoring. During this time, Galileo came to doubt the teachings of Aristotle and other ancient philosophers and scientists which were accepted by the Church as being consistent with Catholic doctrine. Galileo had admired the mathematical aesthetics of the Copernican theory and became even more confirmed in his support of this thesis after viewing the heavens through a new instrument that he had recently improved—the telescope. Galileo considered himself a devout and obedient son of the Church, but he believed that the Bible conveyed truth figuratively as well as literally. He argued that scientific facts must first be discovered, then interpreted according to observation. As Galileo noted, "The Bible shows the way to go to Heaven, not the way the heavens go." No one, not even the pope, could alter the facts.

Galileo's response to charges that the ideas of Copernicus contradicted the Bible is contained in the following letter to the Grand Duchess of Tuscany in 1615. Nevertheless, the next year the heliocentric theory was condemned as formally heretical. For his impertinence and continuing adherence to the Copernican theory, Galileo was twice ordered to appear before the Inquisition, though he was a frail man of seventy. Under threat of torture, he finally recanted his position. Only in the late twentieth century has Galileo been formally absolved from his sin by Pope John Paul II.

Science and the Bible: Letter to the Grand Duchess of Tuscany (1615)

GALILEO GALILEI

Some years ago, as Your Serene Highness well knows, I discovered in the heavens many things that had not been seen before our own age. The

"Science and the Bible" is from *Discoveries and Opinions of Galileo* by Galileo Galilei, pp. 175, 177–179, 181–184, 189–190, 194–195. Copyright © 1957 by Stillman Drake. Used by permission of Doubleday, a division of Bantam, Doubleday, Dell Publishing Group, Inc.

novelty of these things, as well as some consequences which followed from them in contradiction to the physical notions commonly held among academic philosophers, stirred up against me no small number of professors—as if I had placed these things in the sky with my own hands in order to upset nature and overturn the sciences. . . .

Showing a greater fondness for their own opinions than for truth, they sought to deny and disprove the new things which, if they had cared to look for themselves, their own senses would have demonstrated to them. To this end they hurled various charges and published numerous writings filled with vain arguments, and they made the grave mistake of sprinkling these with passages taken from places in the Bible which they had failed to understand properly, and which were ill suited to their purposes. . . .

Persisting in their original resolve to destroy me and everything mine by any means they can think of, these men . . . know that as to the arrangement of the parts of the universe, I hold the sun to be situated motionless in the center of the revolution of the celestial orbs while the earth rotates on its axis and revolves about the sun. They know also that I support this position not only by refuting the arguments of Ptolemy and Aristotle, but by producing many counter-arguments; in particular, some which relate to physical effects whose causes can perhaps be assigned in no other way. In addition there are astronomical arguments derived from many things in my new celestial discoveries that plainly confute the Ptolemaic system while admirably agreeing with and confirming the contrary hypothesis. . . . These men have resolved to fabricate a shield for their fallacies out of the mantle of pretended religion and the authority of the Bible. These they apply, with little judgment, to the refutation of arguments that they do not understand and have not even listened to.

First they have endeavored to spread the opinion that such propositions in general are contrary to the Bible and are consequently damnable and heretical. . . . Next, becoming bolder, and hoping (though vainly) that this seed which first took root in their hypocritical minds would send out branches and ascend to heaven, they began scattering rumors among the people that before long this doctrine would be condemned by the supreme authority. . . .

They go about invoking the Bible, which they would have minister to their deceitful purposes. Contrary to the sense of the Bible and the intention of the holy Fathers, if I am not mistaken, they would extend such authorities until even in purely physical matters—where faith is not involved—they would have us altogether abandon reason and the evidence of our senses in favor of some biblical passage, though under the surface meaning of its words this passage may contain a different sense. . . .

I think in the first place that it is very pious to say and prudent to affirm that the holy Bible can never speak untruth—whenever its true meaning is understood. But I believe nobody will deny that it is often very abstruse, and may say things which are quite different from what its bare words signify. . . .

This being granted, I think that in discussion of physical problems we ought to begin not from the authority of scriptural passages, but from sense-experiences and necessary demonstrations; for the holy Bible and the phenomena of nature proceed alike from the divine Word, the former as the dictate of the Holy Ghost and the latter as the observant executrix of God's commands. It is necessary for the Bible, in order to be accommodated to the understanding of every man, to speak many things which appear to differ from the absolute truth so far as the bare meaning of the words is concerned. But Nature, on the other hand, is inexorable and immutable; she never transgresses the laws imposed upon her, or cares a whit whether her abstruse reasons and methods of operation are understandable to men. For that reason it appears that nothing physical which sense-experience sets before our eyes, or which necessary demonstrations prove to us, ought to be called in question (much less condemned) upon the testimony of biblical passages which may have some different meaning beneath their words. For the Bible is not chained in every expression to conditions as strict as those which govern all physical effects; nor is God any less excellently revealed in Nature's actions than in the sacred statements of the Bible. . . .

From this I do not mean to infer that we need not have an extraordinary esteem for the passages of holy Scripture. On the contrary, having arrived at any certainties in physics, we ought to utilize these as the most appropriate aids in the true exposition of the Bible and in the investigation of those meanings which are necessarily contained therein for these must be concordant with demonstrated truths. I should judge the authority of the Bible was designed to persuade men of those articles and propositions which, surpassing all human reasoning, could not be made credible by science, or by any other means than through the very mouth of the Holy Spirit. . . .

But I do not feel obliged to believe that the same God who had endowed us with senses, reason, and intellect has intended to forgo their use and by some other means to give us knowledge which we can attain by them.

The Foundations of Modern Science

Sir Isaac Newton (1642–1727)

Sir Isaac Newton was perhaps the most brilliant scientist in an age of genius. He drew on the work of his predecessors and his vast mental abilities to devise a system of physical laws that have endured for more than two hundred and fifty years. Newton reasoned that the planets and all other material objects in the universe moved in an orderly regimen, dictated by the principles of gravity and mutual attraction. Newton made no attempt to explain the nature of gravity itself, but he did demonstrate the principles mathematically. He adopted the methods of empirical observation established by Francis Bacon a half-century earlier and championed inductive reasoning as the primary method for scien-tific inquiry. With the work of Newton, the immense universe became rational and knowable, a realm of regularity, subject to immutable laws. Humankind no longer lived in a haphazard and chaotic universe, dependent on the intervention of spirits and angels for its regulation. And yet, Newton was no atheist. The new universe simply demanded a new conception of God. For Newton, science and faith could not only be reconciled but were mutually dependent. The following selection from his Optics *(1704) gives evidence of this important concept.*

Principles of Analysis—Induction and God: *Optics* (1704)

SIR ISAAC NEWTON

All these things being considered, it seems probable to me, that God in the Beginning formed Matter in solid, massy, hard, impenetrable, moveable Particles, of such Sizes and Figures, and with such other Properties, and in such Proportion to Space, as most conduced to the End for which he formed them; and that these primitive Particles being Solids, are incomparably harder than any porous Bodies compounded of them; even so very hard, as never to wear or break in pieces; no ordinary Power being able to divide what God himself made one in the first Creation. . . .

To derive two or three general Principles of Motion from Phaenomena, and afterwards to tell us how the Properties and Actions of all corporeal Things follow from those manifest Principles, would be a very great step in Philosophy, though the Causes of those Principles were not yet discovered: And therefore, I scruple not to propose the Principles of Motion . . . and leave their Causes to be found out.

Now by the help of these Principles, all material Things seem to have been composed of the hard and solid Particles above-mentioned, variously associated in the first Creation by the Counsel of an intelligent Agent. For it became him who created them to set them in order. And if he did so, it's unphilosophical to seek for any other Origin of the World, or to pretend that it might arise out of a Chaos by the mere Laws of Nature; though being once formed, it may continue by those Laws for many Ages. For while Comets move in very eccentric orbits in all manner of Positions, blind Fate could never make all the Planets move one and the same way in concentric orbits, some inconsiderable Irregularities excepted, which may have risen from the mutual Actions of Comets and Planets upon one another, and which will be apt to increase, till this System wants a Reformation. Such a wonderful Uniformity in the Planetary System must be allowed the Effect of Choice. And so must the Uniformity in the Bodies of Animals,

"Principles of Analysis" is from Sir Isaac Newton, *Optics* (London: W. & J. Innys, 1721), pp. 344–345, 375–381. Text modernized by the editor.

Sir Isaac Newton analyzing a ray of light: "If true greatness consists in having received from heaven a mighty genius, and in having employed it to enlighten our own mind and that of others, a man like Sir Isaac Newton, whose equal is hardly found in a thousand years, is the truly great man." Voltaire (*New York Public Library Picture Collection*)

they having generally a right and a left side shaped alike, and on either side of their Bodies two Legs behind, and either two Arms, or two legs, or two Wings before upon their Shoulders, and between their Shoulders a Neck running down into a Back-bone, and a Head upon it; and in the Head two Ears, two Eyes, a Nose, a Mouth, and a Tongue, alike situated . . . and the Instinct of Brutes and Insects, can be the effect of nothing else than the Wisdom and Skill of a powerful ever-living Agent, who being in all Places, is more able by his Will to move the Bodies within his boundless uniform Sensorium, and thereby to form and reform the Parts of the Universe, than we are by our Will to move the Parts of our own Bodies. And yet we are not to consider the World as the Body of God, or the several Parts thereof, as the Parts of God. He is a uniform Being, void of Organs, Members or Parts, and they are his Creatures subordinate to him, and subservient to his Will. . . .

And since Space is divisible *in infinitum*, and Matter is not necessarily in all places, it may be also allowed that God is able to create Particles of Matter of several Sizes and Figures, and in several Proportions to Space, and perhaps of different Densities and Forces, and thereby to vary the Laws of Nature, and make Worlds of several sorts in several Parts of the Universe. At least, I see nothing of Contradiction in all this.

As in Mathematics, so in Natural Philosophy, the Investigation of difficult Things by the Method of Analysis, ought ever to precede the Method of Composition. This Analysis consists in making Experiments and Observations, and in drawing general Conclusions from them by Induction, and admitting of no Objections against the Conclusions, but such as are taken from Experiments, or other certain Truths. For Hypotheses are not to be regarded in experimental Philosophy. And although the arguing from Experiments and Observations by Induction be no Demonstration of general Conclusions; yet it is the best way of arguing which the Nature of Things admits of. . . . By this way of Analysis, we may proceed from Compounds to Ingredients, and from Motions to the Forces producing them; and in general, from Effects to their Causes, and from particular Causes to more general ones, till the Argument end in the most general. This is the Method of Analysis: And the Synthesis consists in assuming the Causes discovered, and established as Principles, and by them explaining the Phaenomena proceeding from them, and proving the Explanations.

An Assessment of Newton and Descartes

VOLTAIRE

Not long ago, the following trite and frivolous question was debated in a very polite and learned company: Who was the greatest man, Caesar, Alexander, Tamerlane, Cromwell, etc.?

Somebody answered that Sir Isaac Newton excelled them all. The gentleman's assertion was very just; for if true greatness consists in having received from heaven a mighty genius, and in having employed it to enlighten our own mind and that of others, a man like Sir Isaac Newton, whose equal is hardly found in a thousand years, is the truly great man. And those politicians and conquerors (and all ages produce some) were generally so many illustrious wicked men. That man claims our respect who commands over the minds of the rest of the world by the force of truth, not those who enslave their fellow-creatures: he who is acquainted with the universe, not they who deface it. . . .

The progress of Sir Isaac Newton's life was quite different [from that of Descartes]. He lived happy, and very much honoured in his native country,

"An Assessment of Newton and Descartes" is from Charles W. Eliot, ed., *The Harvard Classics*, vol. 34 (New York: P. F. Collier & Son Corporation, 1910), pp. 99, 111–113.

to the age of eighty-five years. . . . We may admire Sir Isaac Newton on this occasion, but then we must not censure Descartes. The opinion that generally prevails in England with regard to these new philosophers is, that the latter [Descartes] was a dreamer, and the former [Newton] a sage.

Very few people in England read Descartes, whose works indeed are now useless. On the other side, but a small number peruse those of Sir Isaac, because to do this the student must be deeply skilled in mathematics, otherwise those works will be unintelligible to him. But notwithstanding this, these great men are the subject of everyone's discourse. . . . I indeed believe that very few will presume to compare Descartes's philosophy in any respect with that of Sir Isaac Newton. The former is an essay, the latter a masterpiece. But then the man who first brought us to the path of truth, was perhaps as great a genius as he who afterwards conducted us through it.

Descartes gave sight to the blind. These saw the errors of antiquity and of the sciences. The path he struck out has since become boundless.

William Harvey (1578–1657)

William Harvey has been termed the father of modern physiology. He was heir to a legacy of interest in the internal workings of the human body that had been most recently in evidence among artists during the Renaissance. But whereas Michelangelo studied the body to better represent the human form, Harvey sought to discover the internal workings on their own scientific merit. In this, he was more closely akin to the earlier scientific studies of Leonardo Da Vinci. Harvey built upon the work of the Greek physician, Galen (fl. A.D. 150), who demonstrated that the arteries carried blood instead of air. Harvey's exacting methods set the pattern of scientific research for generations. In the following selection, which was an address to the Royal College of Physicians in 1628, he gave the results of his methodical dissections and experiments.

"I Learn and Teach from the Fabric of Nature": On the Circulation of the Blood (1628)

WILLIAM HARVEY

As this book alone declares the blood to course and revolve by a new route, very different from the ancient and beaten pathway trodden for so many ages, and illustrated by such a host of learned and distinguished men, I was greatly afraid lest I might be charged with presumption did I lay my work before the public at home, or send it beyond seas for impression, unless I

" 'I Learn and Teach from the Fabric of Nature' " is from R. Willis, trans., *The Works of William Harvey* (London: Sydenham Society, 1847), pp. 5–7, 31–32, 45–47.

had first proposed its subject to you, had confirmed its conclusions by ocular demonstrations in your presence, had replied to your doubts and objections, and secured the assent and support of our distinguished President. For I was most intimately persuaded, that if I could make good by proposition before you and our College, . . . I had less to fear from others. . . . For true philosophers, who are only eager for truth and knowledge, never regard themselves as already so thoroughly informed, but that they welcome further information from whomsoever and from whencesoever it may come; nor are they so narrow-minded as to imagine any of the arts or sciences transmitted to us by the ancients, in such a state of forwardness or completeness, that nothing is left for the ingenuity and industry of others. . . . Neither do they swear such fealty to their mistress Antiquity, that they openly, and in sight of all, deny and desert their friend Truth. . . .

My dear colleagues . . . I profess both to learn and to teach anatomy, not from books, but from dissections; not from the positions of philosophers, but from the fabric of nature. . . .

From these and other observations of the like kind, I am persuaded it will be found that the motion of the heart is as follows:

First of all, the auricle contracts, and in the course of its contraction throws the blood, (which it contains in ample quantity as the head of the veins, the store-house and cistern of the blood,) into the ventricle, which being filled, the heart raises itself straightway, makes all its fibers tense, contracts the ventricles, and performs a beat, by which beat it immediately sends the blood supplied to it by the auricle into the arteries; the right ventricle sending its charge into the lungs by the vessel which is called vena arteriosi, but which, in structure and function, and all things else, is an artery; the left ventricle sending its charge into the aorta, and through this by the arteries to the body at large. . . .

Thus far I have spoken of the passage of the blood from the veins into the arteries, and of the manner in which it is transmitted and distributed by the action of the heart. . . . But what remains to be said upon the quantity and source of the blood which thus passes, is of so novel and unheard-of character, that I not only fear injury to myself from the envy of a few, but I tremble lest I have mankind at large for my enemies. . . . Still, the die is cast, and my trust is in my love of truth, and the candor that inheres in cultivated minds. And when I surveyed my mass of evidence, . . . I re-volved in my mind, what might be the quantity of blood which was trans-mitted, in how short a time its passage might be effected, and the like; . . . I began to think whether there might not be A MOTION, AS IT WERE, IN A CIRCLE. Now this I afterwards found to be true; and I finally saw that the blood, forced by the action of the left ventricle into the arteries, was distributed to the body at large . . . impelled by the right ventricle . . . through the veins, and so round to the left ventricle in the manner already indicated. . . .

The heart, consequently, is the beginning of life; the sun of the micro-cosm, even as the sun in his turn might well be designated the heart of the world; for it is the heart by whose virtue and pulse the blood is moved, perfected, made apt to nourish, and is preserved from corruption and coagulation; it is the household divinity which, discharging its function, nourishes, cherishes, quickens the whole body, and is indeed the foundation of life, the source of all action.

SECTION II: THE ENLIGHTENMENT

On the Human Condition and Human Progress

John Locke (1632–1704)

John Locke was one of the most important figures of this period of scientific discovery and reason. He initiated the Age of Enlightenment in England and France, was an inspirer of the U.S. Constitution, and remains a powerful influence on the life and thought of Western Civilization. Locke was educated at Oxford, where he was fascinated with experimental science. He became a physician but was particularly attracted to human relationships concerning how people learn, and how they are best governed. Well known in the academic circles of England and France, his political philosophy was to provide a confirmation of the Glorious Revolution of 1688 and a framework for the American and French revolutions of 1776 and 1789.

The following selection from one of his primary works investigates a seminal question debated in the Enlightenment: are children born with any innate ideas that have been inherited from parents, or are all ideas products of associations within society? This work extended empirical investigation into the realm of the human mind and reveals Locke's inquiring nature and intellectual depth.

The Blank Slate of the Mind: *An Essay Concerning Human Understanding* (1689)

JOHN LOCKE

It is established opinion among some men, that there are in the understanding certain *innate principles*; some primary notions, characters, as it were stamped upon the mind of man, which the soul receives in its very first being, and brings into the world with it. It would be sufficient to convince unprejudiced readers of the falseness of this supposition, if I

"The Blank Slate of the Mind" is from John Locke, *An Essay Concerning Human Understanding,* ed. A. D. Fraser (Oxford: Clarendon Press, 1894), vol. 1, pp. 37–38, 121–124.

should only show . . . how men, barely by the use of their natural faculties, may attain to all the knowledge they have, without the help of any innate impressions; and may arrive at certainty, without any such original notions or principles. . . .

Let us then suppose the mind to be, as we say, white paper, void of all characters, without any ideas:—How comes it to be furnished? Whence comes it by that vast store which the busy and boundless fancy of man has painted on it with an almost endless variety? Whence has it all the *materials* of reason and knowledge? To this I answer, in one word, EXPERIENCE. In that all our knowledge is founded; and from that it ultimately derives itself. Our observation employed either, about external sensible objects, or about the internal operations of our minds perceived and reflected on by ourselves, is that which supplies our understandings with all the *materials* of thinking. These two are the fountains of knowledge, from whence all the ideas we have, or can naturally have, do spring. . . .

The understanding seems to me not to have the least glimmering of any ideas which it does not receive from [sensation or reflection]. *External objects* furnish the mind with the ideas of sensible qualities, which are all those different perceptions they produce in us; and *the mind* furnishes the understanding with ideas of its own operations.

He that attentively considers the state of a child at his first coming into the world, will have little reason to think him stored with plenty of ideas that are to be the matter of his future knowledge. It is by degrees [that] he comes to be furnished with them. . . . But all that are born into the world being surrounded with bodies that perpetually and diversely affect them, variety of ideas, whether care be taken about it nor not, are imprinted on the minds of children. Light and colors are busy at hand everywhere when the eye is but open; sounds and some tangible qualities fail not to solicit their proper senses; but yet I think it will be granted easily, that if a child were kept in a place where he never saw any other but black and white till he were a man, he would have no more ideas of scarlet or green than he that from his childhood never tasted an oyster or a pineapple has of those particular relishes. . . .

"Mr. Locke Destroyed Innate Ideas"

VOLTAIRE

Descartes, born to discover the errors of antiquity, and at the same time to substitute his own, and hurried away by that systematic spirit which throws a cloud over the minds of the greatest men, thought he had demonstrated that the soul is the same thing as thought. . . . He asserted, that man thinks eternally, and that the soul, at its coming into the body, is informed with

" 'Mr. Locke Destroyed Innate Ideas' " is from Charles W. Eliot, ed. *The Harvard Classics*, vol. 34 (New York: P. F. Collier & Son Corporation, 1910), pp. 103–105.

the whole series of metaphysical notions: knowing God, infinite space, possessing all abstract ideas—in a word, completely endowed with the most sublime lights, which it unhappily forgets at its issuing from the womb.

Father Malebranche, in his sublime illusions, not only admitted innate ideas, but did not doubt of our living wholly in God, and that God is, as it were, our soul.

Such a multitude of reasoners having written the romance of the soul, a sage at last arose, who gave, with an air of the greatest modesty, the history of it. Mr. Locke has displayed the human soul in the same manner as an excellent anatomist explains the springs of the human body. He everywhere takes the light of physics for his guide. . . . He takes an infant at the instant of his birth; he traces, step by step, the progress of his understanding; examines what things he has in common with beasts, and what he possesses above them. . . .

No one shall ever [convince] me that I think always: and I am as little inclined as he could be to fancy that some weeks after I was conceived I was a very learned soul; knowing at that time a thousand things which I forgot at my birth; and possessing when in the womb (though to no manner of purpose) knowledge which I lost the instant I had occasion for it; and which I have never since been able to recover perfectly.

Mr. Locke, after having destroyed innate ideas; after having fully renounced the vanity of believing that we think always; after having laid down, from the most solid principles, that ideas enter the mind through the sense; having examined our simple and complex ideas; having traced the human mind through its several operations; having shown that all the languages in the world are imperfect, and the great abuse that is made of words every moment, he at last comes to consider the extent or rather the narrow limits of human knowledge.

Edward Gibbon (1737–1794)

One of the most enduring works of the Enlightenment came from the pen of Edward Gibbon. A rather frail individual, Gibbon was twenty-seven years old when he went to Rome to study antiquities. While musing amid the ruins of the Roman Capitol one evening, he was inspired to write a history of the decline and fall of the Roman Empire. This project gave his life direction, and he produced a work of exceptional historical perspective and incomparable literary style.

Gibbon moved in the elite circles of English society and associated with the brilliant lexicographer Samuel Johnson, the painter Sir Joshua Reynolds, and the Shakespearean actor David Garrick. He traveled widely in France and consulted philosophes *such as Denis Diderot, Jean Le Rond d'Alembert, and Voltaire. The following excerpt offers Gibbon's ideas on progress, a topic of continuing interest during the Age of Reason and for our contemporary world.*

The Progress of Mankind:
The Decline and Fall of the Roman Empire (1776)

EDWARD GIBBON

The discoveries of ancient and modern navigators, and the domestic history, or tradition, of the most enlightened nations, represent the *human savage*, naked both in mind and body, and destitute of laws, of arts, of ideas, and almost of language. From this abject condition, perhaps the primitive and universal state of man, he has gradually arisen to command the animals, to fertilise the earth, to traverse the ocean, and to measure the heavens. His progress in the improvement and exercise of his mental and corporeal faculties had been irregular and various; infinitely slow in the beginning, and increasing by degrees with redoubled velocity: ages of laborious ascent have been followed by a moment of rapid downfall; and the several climates of the globe have felt the vicissitudes of light and darkness. Yet the experience of four thousand years should enlarge our hopes, and diminish our apprehensions: we cannot determine to what height the human species may aspire in their advances towards perfection; but it may safely be presumed, that no people, unless the face of nature is changed, will relapse into their original barbarism. . . . Each village, each family, each individual, must always possess both ability and inclination, to perpetuate the use of fire and of metals; the propagation and service of domestic animals; the methods of hunting and fishing; the rudiments of navigation; the imperfect cultivation of corn, or other nutritive grain; and the simple practice of the mechanic trades. Private genius and public industry may be extirpated; but these hardy plants survive the tempest, and strike an everlasting root into the most unfavourable soil. The splendid days of Augustus and Trajan were eclipsed by a cloud of ignorance: and the Barbarians subverted the laws of palaces of Rome. But the scythe . . . still continued annually to mow the harvests of Italy. . . .

Since the first discovery of the arts, war, commerce, and religious zeal have diffused, among the savages of the Old and New World, these inestimable gifts; they have been successively propagated: they can never be lost. We may therefore acquiesce in the pleasing conclusion, that every age of the world has increased, and still increases, the real wealth, the happiness, the knowledge, and perhaps the virtue, of the human race.

Marquis de Condorcet (1743–1794)

Marie-Jean-Antoine-Nicolas de Caritat, best known by the rather imposing title Marquis de Condorcet, was descended from an ancient French family. He was educated at Rheims and Paris, where he showed ability in mathematics

---

"The Progress of Mankind" is from Edward Gibbon, *The History of the Decline and Fall of the Roman Empire*, ed. J. B. Bury (London: Methuen and Co., 1901), vol. 4, pp. 163–169.

under the tutelage of the famous philosophe *Jean Le Rond d'Alembert. A frequent contributor to the* Encyclopedia *of Diderot, Condorcet was a zealous propagator of the progressive views of the Enlightenment. He was one of the guiding minds behind the French Revolution in 1789, becoming secretary of the National Assembly and primary architect of the reform of the French educational system. His independent attitude flew in opposition to the radical policies of Robespierre, and he became a hunted man, hiding in thickets and quarries in the countryside of France before being captured and imprisoned. Two days later he was found dead in his cell, perhaps by poison.*

The following passage is from his most famous work, Sketch for a Historical Picture of the Progress of the Human Mind. *Its fundamental idea is that of the continual progress of the human race to an ultimate perfection. Wholly a man of the Enlightenment, an advocate of economic freedom, religious toleration, legal, and educational reform, Condorcet sought to apply reason to social affairs. In this, he became a precursor to the discipline of sociology.*

The Progress of the Human Mind (1795)

MARQUIS DE CONDORCET

All the causes which contribute to the improvement of the human species, all the means we have enumerated that insure its progress, must, from their very nature, exercise an influence always active, and acquire an extent forever increasing. . . .

And it cannot be doubted that the progress of the sanative art, that the use of more wholesome food and more comfortable habitations, . . . shall develop the physical powers by exercise, without at the same time impairing them by excess. . . . It is manifest that the improvement of the practice of medicine, become more efficacious in consequence of the progress of reason and the social order, must [put an end] to transmissible or contagious disorders as well to those general maladies resulting from climate, ailments, and the nature of certain occupations. Nor would it be difficult to prove that this hope might be extended to almost every other malady, of which it is probable we shall hereafter discover the most remote causes. Would it even be absurd to suppose this quality of melioration in the human species as susceptible of an indefinite advancement; to suppose that a period must one day arrive when death will be nothing more than the effect either of extraordinary accidents, or of the flow and gradual decay of the vital powers; and that the duration of the middle space, of the interval between the birth of man and this decay, will itself have no assignable limit? Certainly man will not become immortal; but may not the distance between the moment in which he draws his first breath and the common term when,

"The Progress of the Human Mind" is from Marquis de Condorcet, *Outlines of a Historical View of the Progress of the Human Mind* (Philadelphia: M. Carey, 1796), pp. 289–293.

in the course of nature, without malady, without accident, he finds it impossible any longer to exist, be necessarily protracted? . . .

May we not include in the same circle the intellectual and moral faculties? May not our parents, who transmit to us the advantages or defects of their conformation, and from whom we receive our features and shape, as well as our propensities to certain physical affections, transmit to us also that part of organization upon which intellect, strength of understanding, energy of soul or moral sensibility depend? Is it not probable that education by improving these qualities will at the same time have an influence upon, will modify and improve this organization itself? Analogy, an investigation of the human faculties, and even some facts, appear to authorize these conjectures, and thereby to enlarge the boundary of our hopes. . . .

And how admirably calculated is this view of the human race, emancipated from its chains, released alike from the dominion of chance, as well as from that of the enemies of its progress, and advancing with a firm and indeviate step in the parts of truth, to console the philosopher lamenting the errors, the flagrant acts of injustice, the crimes with which the earth is still polluted? It is the contemplation of this prospect that rewards him for all his efforts to assist the progress of reason and the establishment of liberty.

Cesare Beccaria (1738–1794)

Cesare Beccaria was the son of a Milanese aristocrat of modest means. He was educated initially at a Jesuit school, an experience that he later described as "fanatical" and stifling to "the development of human feelings." At the age of twenty-six, he became an international celebrity with the publication of his work on criminal law in 1764. Translated into several languages, it enjoyed a remarkable success in France, where it went through seven editions in six months. In it, Beccaria lashed out against the barbarities of the day, including the torture of prisoners in order to induce confession, the corruption of judges, and degrading and brutal punishments. Penalties, he concluded, should be scaled to the offense. Beccaria was the first modern writer to advocate the complete abolition of capital punishment, and his treatise remains the most important and influential volume written on criminal justice.

"The Greatest Happiness of the Greatest Number": *On Crimes and Punishments* (1764)
CESARE BECCARIA

If we look into history, we shall find that laws, which are, or ought to be, conventions between men in a state of freedom, have been, for the most part the work of the passions of a few, or the consequences of a fortuitous

" 'The Greatest Happiness of the Greatest Number' " is from Cesare Beccaria, *An Essay on Crimes and Punishments*, trans. E. D. Ingraham (Philadelphia: H. Nicklin, 1819), pp. xii, 18–19, 47, 59–60, 93–94, 104–105, 148–149.

or temporary necessity; not dictated by a cool examiner of human nature, who knew how to collect in one point the actions of a multitude, and had this only end in view, *the greatest happiness of the greatest number. . . .*

Observe that by *justice* I understand nothing more than that bond which is necessary to keep the interest of individuals united, without which men would return to their original state of barbarity. All punishments which exceed the necessity of preserving this bond are in their nature unjust. . . .

The end of punishment, therefore, is no other than to prevent the criminal from doing further injury to society, and to prevent others from committing the like offence. Such punishments, therefore, and such a mode of inflicting them ought to be chosen, as will make the strongest and most lasting impressions on the minds of others, with the least torment to the body of the criminal.

The torture of a criminal during the course of his trial is a cruelty consecrated by custom in most nations. It is used with an intent either to make him confess his crime, or to explain some contradiction into which he had been led during his examination, or discover his accomplices, or for some kind of metaphysical and incomprehensible purgation of infamy, or, finally, in order to discover other crimes of which he is not accused, but of which he may be guilty.

No man can be judged a criminal until he be found guilty; nor can society take from him the public protection until it have been proved that he has violated the conditions on which it was granted. What right, then, but that of power, can authorise the punishment of a citizen so long as there remains any doubt of his guilt? This dilemma is frequent. Either he is guilty, or not guilty. If guilty, he should only suffer the punishment ordained by the laws, and torture becomes useless, as his confession is unnecessary. If he be not guilty, you torture the innocent; for in the eye of the law, every man is innocent whose crime has not been proved. . . .

Crimes are more effectually prevented by the *certainty* than by the *severity* of punishment. . . . In proportion as punishments become more cruel, the minds of men, as a fluid rises to the same height with that which surrounds it, grow hardened and insensible; and the force of the passions still continuing, in the space of an hundred years the *wheel* [torture device] terrifies no more than formerly the *prison*. That a punishment may produce the effect required, it is sufficient that the evil it occasions should exceed the *good* expected from the crime, including in the calculation the certainty of the punishment, and the privation of the expected advantage. All severity beyond this is superfluous, and therefore tyrannical.

The punishment of death is pernicious to society, from the example of barbarity it affords. If the passions, or the necessity of war, have taught men to shed the blood of their fellow creatures, the laws, which are intended to moderate the ferocity of mankind, should not increase it by examples of barbarity, them more horrible as this punishment is usually attended with formal pageantry. Is it not absurd, that the laws, which detest and punish homicide, should, in order to prevent murder, publicly commit murder themselves? . . .

It is better to prevent crimes than to punish them. This is the fundamental principle of good legislation, which is the art of conducting men to the *maximum* of happiness, and to the *minimum* of misery, if we may apply this mathematical expression to the good and evil of life. . . .

Would you prevent crimes? Let the laws be clear and simple, let the entire force of the nation be united in their defence, let them be intended rather to favour every individual than any particular classes of men; let the laws be feared, and the laws only. The fear of the laws is salutary, but the fear of men is a fruitful and fatal source of crimes.

Adam Smith (1723–1790)

Adam Smith can rightly be considered one of the most influential thinkers of the Enlightenment. He studied moral philosophy at Oxford and in his mid-twenties conceived of an economic philosophy of "the obvious and simple system of natural liberty," which the world would come to know as capitalism. Prior to the appearance of his theory in 1776, mercantilism, with its emphasis on scarce goods, its strict government control of monopolies, exports, and colonies, was the dominant policy of European imperial governments. But Smith conceived of an expansive universe, full of opportunity for the individual or nation to exercise initiative, to accumulate wealth and serve others in the process.

The following excerpt from his major work, The Wealth of Nations, *focuses on Smith's view of human nature and the "invisible hand" of competition as guide to an economic system based on individual self-interest. If one views the Industrial Revolution of the early nineteenth century and the birth of Marxism in 1848 as being directly influenced by Smith's theories, then his impact on the history of the twentieth century is immeasurable.*

The Wealth of Nations (1776)

ADAM SMITH

Human Nature and the Division of Labor

This division of labour, from which so many advantages are derived, is not originally the effect of any human wisdom, which foresees and intends that general opulence to which it gives occasion. It is the necessary, though very slow and gradual, consequence of a certain propensity in human nature

"The Wealth of Nations" is from Adam Smith, *An Inquiry into the Nature and Causes of the Wealth of Nations*, ed. Edwin A. Seligman (London: J. M. Dent, 1901), pp. 12–15, 400–401, 436–437.

which has in view no such extensive utility; the propensity to truck, barter, and exchange one thing for another.

Whether this propensity be one of those original principles in human nature, of which no further account can be given; or whether, as seems more probable, it be the necessary consequence of the faculties of reason and speech, it belongs not to our present subject to enquire. It is common to all men, and to be found in no other race of animals, which seem to know neither this nor any other species of contracts. . . . In civilized society, [man] stands at all times in need of the cooperation and assistance of great multitudes, while his whole life is scarce sufficient to gain the friendship of a few persons. In almost every other race of animals each individual, when it is grown up to maturity, is entirely independent, and in its natural state has occasion for the assistance of no other living creature. But man has almost constant occasion for the help of his brethren, and it is in vain for him to expect it from their benevolence only. He will be more likely to prevail if he can interest their self-love in his favour, and show them that it is for their own advantage to do for him what he requires of them. Whoever offers to another a bargain of any kind, proposes to do this. Give me that which I want, and you shall have this which you want, is the meaning of every such offer; and it is in this manner that we obtain from one another the far greater part of those good offices which we stand in need of. It is not from the benevolence of the butcher, the brewer, or the baker, that we expect our dinner, but from their regard to their own interest. We address ourselves, not to their humanity but to their self-love, and never talk to them of our own necessities but of their advantages. . . .

The difference of natural talents in different men is, in reality, much less than we are aware of; and the very different genius which appears to distinguish men of different professions, when grown up to maturity, is not upon many occasions so much the cause, as the effect of the division of labour. The difference between the most dissimilar characters, between a philosopher and a common street porter, for example, seems to arise not so much from nature, as from habit, custom, and education. When they came into the world, and for the first six or eight years of their existence, they were, perhaps, very much alike, and neither their parents nor playfellows could perceive any remarkable difference. About that age, or soon after, they come to be employed in very different occupations. The difference of talents comes then to be taken notice of, and widens by degrees, till at last the vanity of the philosopher is willing to acknowledge scarce any resemblance. . . . By nature a philosopher is not in genius and disposition half so different from a street porter, as a mastiff is from a greyhound, or a greyhound from a spaniel, or this last from a shepherd's dog. . . . Among men, on the contrary, the most dissimilar geniuses are of use to one another; the different produces of their respective talents, by the general disposition to truck, barter, and exchange, being brought, as it were, into a common stock, where every man may purchase whatever part of the produce of other men's talents he has occasion for. . . .

The Invisible Hand

As every individual, therefore, endeavors as much as he can both to employ his capital in the support of domestic industry, and so to direct that industry that its produce may be of the greatest value; every individual necessarily labours to render the annual revenue of the society as great as he can. He generally, indeed, neither intends to promote the public interest, nor knows how much he is promoting it. . . . He intends only his own security; and by directing that industry in such a manner as its produce may be of the greatest value, he intends only his own gain, and he is in this, as in many other cases, led by an invisible hand to promote an end which was no part of his intention. Nor is it always the worse for the society that it was no part of it. By pursuing his own interest he frequently promotes that of the society more effectually than when he really intends to promote it. I have never known much good done by those who affected to trade for the public good. . . . The statesman, who should attempt to direct private people in what manner they ought to employ their capitals, would not only load himself with a most unnecessary attention, but assume an authority which could safely be trusted, not only to no single person, but to no council or senate whatever, and which would nowhere be so dangerous as in the hands of a man who had folly and presumption enough to fancy himself fit to exercise it.

Unreasonableness of Restraints

Each nation has been made to look with an invidious eye upon the prosperity of all nations with which it trades, and to consider their gain as its own loss. Commerce, which ought naturally to be, among nations, as among individuals, a bond of union and friendship, has become the most fertile source of discord and animosity. . . . The violence and injustice of the rulers of mankind is an ancient evil, for which, I am afraid, the nature of human affairs can scarce admit of a remedy. But the mean rapacity, the monopolising spirit of merchants and manufacturers, who neither are, nor ought to be, the rulers of mankind, though it cannot perhaps be corrected, may very easily be prevented from disturbing the tranquility of anybody but themselves.

That it was the spirit of monopoly which originally both invented and propagated this doctrine cannot be doubted; and they who first taught it were by no means such fools as they who believed it. In every country it always is and must be the interest of the great body of the people to buy whatever they want of those who sell it cheapest. The proposition is so very manifest that it seems ridiculous to take any pains to prove it; nor could it have ever been called in question had not the interested sophistry of merchants and manufacturers confounded the common sense of mankind. Their interest is, in this respect, directly opposite to that of the great body of the people. As it is the interest of the freemen of a [guild] to hinder the rest of the inhabitants from employing any workmen but themselves, so it is the interest of the merchants and manufacturers of every country to secure to themselves the monopoly of the home market. Hence in Great Britain, and in most other European countries, the extraordinary duties upon almost all goods imported by alien merchants. Hence the high duties and prohibitions upon all those foreign manufactures which can come into competition with our own. Hence, too, the extraordinary restraints upon the importation of almost all sorts of goods from those countries. . . . whom national animosity happens to be most violently inflamed. . . . This very competition, however, is advantageous to the great body of the people, who profit greatly besides by the good market which the great expense of such a nation affords them in every other way. . . .

Immanuel Kant (1724–1804)

Immanuel Kant was a German philosopher whose comprehensive and systematic work in the theory of knowledge, ethics, and aesthetics greatly influenced subsequent philosophy. Kant's entire life was spent in Königsberg, where he was educated and served as a popular teacher and lecturer at the local university. In his writings, he hoped to avoid the confusion of earlier thinkers by examining the possibilities and limitations of applied reason. He sought to accept the rationalism of the Enlightenment while still preserving a belief in human freedom, immortality, and the existence of God. In fact, Kant found the world open to pure reason to be quite limited and postulated a sphere of moral reality known only by "practical reason and conscience." Although he hoped to raise philosophy to the level of a science, he believed that all things could not be proved by discursive reasoning—God and eternal life among them.

In the following selection, Kant seeks to define the Enlightenment by empowering the individual to break away from a somnulent dependence, toward an active intellectual existence. Only through such personal initiative could one attain true enlightenment.

What Is Enlightenment? (1784)

IMMANUEL KANT

Enlightenment is man's release from his self-incurred tutelage. Tutelage is man's inability to make use of his understanding without direction from another. Self-incurred is this tutelage when its cause lies not in lack of

"What Is Enlightenment?" is from Immanuel Kant, *Foundations of the Metaphysics of Morals, What is Enlightenment?*, 2nd ed., trans. and ed. Lewis White Beck, (New York: Macmillan Publishing Company, 1990), pp. 83–85, 88. Copyright © 1990 by Macmillan Publishing Company. Reprinted by permission of the publisher.

reason but in lack of resolution and courage to use it without direction from another. *Dare to Know!* Have courage to use your own reason!—that is the motto of enlightenment.

Laziness and cowardice are the reasons why so great a portion of mankind, after nature has long since discharged them from external direction, nevertheless remains under lifelong tutelage, and why it is so easy for others to set themselves up as their guardians. It is so easy not to be of age. If I have a book which understands for me, a pastor who has a conscience for me, a physician who decides my diet, and so forth, I need not trouble myself. I need not think, if I can only pay—others will readily undertake the irksome work for me.

That the step to competence is held to be very dangerous by the far greater portion of mankind (and by the entire fair sex)—quite apart from its being arduous—is seen to by those guardians who have so kindly assumed superintendence over them. After the guardians have first made their domestic cattle dumb and have made sure that these placid creatures will not dare take a single step without the harness of the cart to which they are confined, the guardians then show them the danger which threatens if they try to go alone. Actually, however, this danger is not so great, for by falling a few times they would finally learn to walk alone. But an example of this failure makes them timid and ordinarily frightens them away from all further trials.

For any single individual to work himself out of the life under tutelage which has become almost his nature is very difficult. He has come to be fond of this state, and he is for the present really incapable of making use of his reason, for no one has ever let him try it out. Statutes and formulas, those mechanical tools of the rational employment or rather misemployment of his natural gifts, are the fetters of an everlasting tutelage. Whoever throws them off makes only an uncertain leap over the narrowest ditch because he is not accustomed to that kind of free motion. Therefore, there are only few who have succeeded by their own exercise of mind both in freeing themselves from incompetence and in achieving a steady pace.

But that the public should enlighten itself is more possible; indeed, if only freedom is granted, enlightenment is almost sure to follow. For there will always be some independent thinkers, even among the established guardians of the great masses, who, after throwing off the yoke of tutelage from their own shoulders, will disseminate the spirit of the rational appreciation of both their own worth and every man's vocation for thinking for himself. . . .

For this enlightenment, however, nothing is required but freedom, and indeed the most harmless among all the things to which this term can properly be applied. It is the freedom to make public use of one's reason at every point. But I hear on all sides, "Do not argue!" The officer says: "Do not argue but drill!" The tax collector: "Do not argue but pay!" The cleric: "Do not argue but believe!" Only one prince in the world [Frederick the

Great of Prussia] says, "Argue as much as you will, and about what you will, but obey!" Everywhere there is restriction on freedom. . . .

If we are asked, "Do we now live in an *enlightened* age?" the answer is, "No," but we do live in an *age of enlightenment*. As things now stand, much is lacking which prevents men from being, or easily becoming, capable of correctly using their own reason in religious matters with assurance and free from outside direction. But, on the other hand, we have clear indications that the field has now been opened wherein men may freely deal with these things and that the obstacles to general enlightenment or the release from self-imposed tutelage are gradually being reduced. In this respect, this is the age of enlightenment, or the century of Frederick.

Thoughts on Religion

Baron d'Holbach (1723–1789)

> *Paul-Henri Dietrich, Baron d'Holbach, was a naturalized French citizen who was best known for his radical atheism. Some of the most esteemed and even the more radicalized of the* philosophes, *including d'Alembert and Rousseau, reportedly withdrew from his gatherings, frightened by the audacity of their speculations. A major contributor of over 375 articles on chemistry and related topics to Diderot's* Encyclopedia, *Holbach's views on atheism represent an extreme in the critical analysis of the Age of Reason.*

God—"A Cause Contradicted by Its Effects": *Common Sense* (1770)

BARON D'HOLBACH

Morality and virtue are totally incompatible with the idea of a God, whose ministers and interpreters have painted him in all countries as the most fantastic, the most unjust, and the most cruel of tyrants, whose pretended wishes are to serve as rules and laws for the inhabitants of the earth? To discover the true principles of morality, men have no need of theology, of revelation, or of Gods; they need but common sense; they have only to look within themselves, to reflect upon their own nature, to consult their obvious interests, to consider the object of society and of each of the members

---

"God—'A Cause Contradicted by Its Effects' " is from Baron d'Holbach, *Common Sense*, trans. Anna Knoop (New York: Miss A. Knoop, 1884), pp. 43, 55–56, 63–65, 69–70.

who compose it, and they will easily understand that virtue is an advantage, and that vice is an injury to beings of their species.

By metaphysics, God is made a pure spirit, but has modern theology advanced one step further than the theology of the barbarians? They recognized a grand spirit as master of the world. The barbarians, like all ignorant men, attribute to spirits all the effects of which their inexperience prevents them from discovering the true causes. Ask a barbarian what causes your watch to move, he will answer, "a spirit!" Ask our philosophers what moves the universe, they will tell you "it is a spirit."

Is it not more natural and more intelligible to deduce all which exists, from the bosom of matter, whose existence is demonstrated by all our senses, whose effects we feel at every moment, which we see act, move, communicate, motion, and constantly bring living beings into existence, than to attribute the formation of things to an unknown force, to a spiritual being, who cannot draw from his ground that which he has not himself, and who, by the spiritual essence claimed for him, is incapable of making anything, and of putting anything in motion?

We are assured that the wonders of nature are sufficient to a belief in the existence of a God, and to convince us fully of this important truth. . . . The unprejudiced philosopher sees nothing in the wonders of nature but permanent and invariable law; nothing but the necessary effects of different combinations of diversified substance.

Whence comes man? What is his origin? Is he the result of the fortuitous meeting of atoms? Was the first man formed of the dust of the earth? I do not know! Man appears to me to be a production of nature like all others she embraces. I should be just as much embarrassed to tell you whence came the first stones, the first trees, the first elephants, the first ants, the first acorns, as to explain the origin of the human species. Recognize, we are told, the hand of God, of an infinitely intelligent and powerful workman, in a work so wonderful as the human machine. I would admit without question that the human machine appears to me surprising; but since man exists in nature, I do not believe it right to say that his formation is beyond the forces of nature. . . . I see that this admirable machine is subject to derangement; that at that time this wonderful intelligence is disordered, and sometimes totally disappears; from this I conclude that human intelligence depends upon a certain disposition of the material organs of the body, and that, because man is an intelligent being, it is not well to conclude that God must be an intelligent being, any more than because man is material, we are compelled to conclude that God is material. The intelligence of man no more proves the intelligence of God than the malice of men proves the malice of this God, of whom they pretend that man is the work. In whatever way theology is taken, God will always be a cause contradicted by its effects, or of whom it is impossible to judge by His works. We shall always see evil, imperfections, and follies resulting from a cause claimed to be full of goodness, or perfections, and of wisdom.

François Marie Arouet, Voltaire (1694–1778)

The Enlightenment is often characterized as an era of empirical reasoning and critical thought, of doubt and skepticism, of individual assertion at the expense of formal control by the state or church. For the most part, this is a fair assessment. God, if He existed, was prone to be antiseptic, the "great clock-winder," who created the universe and then sat back, uninvolved in the lives of His creations. This philosophy, called deism, generally prevailed among the philosophes. *It did not deny the existence of God, but it gave virtually no support to organized religion. The deists particularly denounced the mysteries of the Christian religion such as the Trinity, and miracles like the Virgin Birth, and the Eucharist. Since God was disinterested in the affairs of the world, formal prayers were useless. Deism enabled many of the* philosophes *to effect a reconciliation between a perfect God and an imperfect world.*

Voltaire was the quintessential personality of the Enlightenment. An author of dramas, histories, and scathing satires, his wit and intellectual power dominated the age. Voltaire was an adamant opponent of organized religion, but one of the most enthusiastic advocates of the deist viewpoint. In the following letter, Voltaire argues for the logic and necessity of a supreme deity. His ideas are generally representative of the enlightened thinkers of the age.

"If God Did Not Exist, He Would Have to Be Invented"

VOLTAIRE

To Frederick William, Prince of Prussia:

Monseigneur, the royal family of Prussia has excellent reasons for not wishing the annihilation of the soul. It has more right than anyone to immortality.

It is very true that we do not know any too well what the soul is: no one has ever seen it. All that we do know is that the eternal Lord of nature has given us the power of thinking, and of distinguishing virtue. It is not proved that this faculty survives our death: but the contrary is not proved either. It is possible, doubtless, that God has given thought to a particle to which, after we are no more, He will still give the power of thought: there is no inconsistency in this idea.

In the midst of all the doubts which we have discussed for four thousand years in four thousand ways, the safest course is to do nothing against one's

---

" 'If God Did Not Exist, He Would Have to Be Invented,' " is from S. G. Tallentyre, trans., *Voltaire in His Letters* (New York: G. P. Putnam's Sons, 1919).

conscience. With this secret, we can enjoy life and have nothing to fear from death.

There are some charlatans who admit no doubts. We know nothing of first principles. It is surely very presumptuous to define God, the angels, spirits, and to pretend to know precisely why God made the world, when we do not know why we can move our arms at our pleasure. Doubt is not a pleasant condition, but certainty is an absurd one.

What is most repellent in the *System of Nature* [by the Baron d'Holbach] . . . is the audacity with which it decides that there is no God, without even having tried to prove the impossibility. There is some eloquence in the book: but much more rant, and no sort of proof. It is a pernicious work, alike for princes and people: "*Si Dieu n'existait pas, il faudrait l'inventer.*" [If God did not exist, he would have to be invented].

But all nature cries aloud that He does exist: that there *is* a supreme intelligence, an immense power, an admirable order, and everything teaches us our own dependence on it.

From the depth of our profound ignorance, let us do our best: this is what I think, and what I have always thought, amid all the misery and follies inseparable from seventy-seven years of life. . . . I am, with deep respect,

Voltaire

Thoughts on Education

The Children's Hour

Education was a topic of great concern among the philosophes. *In an age where completeness of thought and range of education were often held at a premium, a secure and progressive education proved to be a great necessity among the aristocracy and middle class. With the advancements of the Scientific Revolution, the world was suddenly new again and parents sought advice not only on the method but also on the course of study that would prove most progressive in meeting the practical needs of a rapidly changing society. This process began early, for proper breeding and attitude had to be inculcated at a tender age.*

Once again, John Locke, with his interest in human development, led the way. In the first selection, he prioritizes the essential components of a progressive education for a friend who was looking for direction in the rearing of his children. In the next excerpt, note the criticism of Locke's views as offered by the great nonconformist of the age, Jean Jacques Rousseau. Rousseau in his treatise, Emile, *argued that experience was the best teacher and that one could learn more from nature than from books and tutors. His thoughts on the control of children, however, are rather astounding.*

The Requirements of a Progressive Education: *Some Thoughts Concerning Education* (1693)

JOHN LOCKE

To Edward Clarke, of Chipley, Esq.

SIR,

I myself have been consulted of late by so many who profess themselves at a loss how to breed their children, and the early corruption of youth is now become so general a complaint that he cannot be thought wholly impertinent who brings the consideration of this matter on the stage, and offers something, if it be but to excite others, or afford matter of correction: for errors in education should be less indulged than any. . . .

I imagine the minds of children as easily turned this or that way as water itself: and though this be the principal part, and our main care should be about the inside, yet the clay cottage is not to be neglected. I shall therefore . . . consider first the health of the body. . . .

One thing the mention of girls brings into my mind, which must not be forgot: let nature have scope to fashion the body as she thinks best. She works herself a great deal better and exacter than we can direct her. . . . Narrow breasts, short and stinking breath, ill lungs, and crookedness, are natural and almost constant effects of hard bodice, and clothes that pinch. That way of making slender waists and fine shapes serves but the more effectually to [ruin] them. . . . 'Tis generally known that the women of China . . . by bracing and binding them hard from their infancy, have very little feet. . . . Besides this, 'tis observed that their women are also very little and short-lived. . . . These defects in the female sex in that country are by some imputed to the unreasonable binding of their feet, whereby the free circulation of the blood is hindered, and the growth and health of the whole body suffers. . . . How much greater inconveniences may we expect, when the thorax, wherein is placed the heart and seat of life, is unnaturally compressed, and hindered from its due expansion? . . .

That which every gentleman . . . desires for his son, besides the estate he leaves him, is contained, I suppose, in these four things: *virtue, wisdom, breeding,* and *learning.*

I place *virtue* as the first and most necessary of those endowments that belong to a man or a gentleman; as absolutely requisite to make him valued and beloved by others, acceptable or tolerable to himself. Without that, I think, he will be happy neither in this nor the other world.

As the foundation of this, there ought very early to be imprinted on his mind a true notion of God, as of the independent Supreme Being, Author

"The Requirements of a Progressive Education" is from John Locke. *Some Thoughts Concerning Education*, 7th ed. (London, 1712).

and Maker of all things, from Whom we receive all our good, Who loves us, and gives us all things. And consequent to this, instill into him a love and reverence of this Supreme Being. . . .

Wisdom I take in the popular acceptation, for a man's managing his business ably and with foresight in this world. This is the product of a good natural temper, application of mind, and experience together, and [is initially] above the reach of children. . . . To accustom a child to have true notions of things, and not to be satisfied till he has them, to raise his mind to great and worthy thoughts, and to keep him at a distance from falsehood and cunning, which has always a broad mixture of falsehood in it, is the fittest preparation of a child for wisdom. The rest, which is to be learned from time, experience, and observation, and an acquaintance with men, their tempers, and designs, is not to be expected in the ignorance and inadvertency of childhood, or the inconsiderate heat and unweariness of youth. . . .

The next good quality belonging to a gentleman is *good breeding*. There are two sorts of ill breeding: the one a sheepish bashfulness, and the other a misbecoming negligence and disrespect in our carriage; both which are avoided by duly observing this one rule: *not to think meanly of ourselves, and not to think meanly of others.*

Keep them from vice and vicious dispositions, and such a kind of behavior in general will come with every degree of their age, as is suitable to that age and the company they ordinarily converse with; and as they grow in years, they will grow in attention and application. . . . But yet, I would have the father seldom interpose his authority and command in these cases, or in any other, but such as have a tendency to vicious habits. I think there are better ways of prevailing with them: and a gentle persuasion in reasoning, when the first point of submission to your will is got, will most times do much better.

It will perhaps be wondered that I mention *reasoning* with children; and yet I cannot but think that [is] the true way of dealing with them. They understand it as early as they do language; and . . . they love to be treated as rational creatures sooner than is imagined. 'Tis a pride should be cherished in them, and, as much as can be, made the greatest instrument to turn them by.

But when I talk of reasoning, I do not intend any other but such as is suited to the child's capacity and apprehension. Nobody can think a boy of three or seven years old should be argued with as a grown man. Long discourses and philosophical reasonings, at best, amaze and confound but do not instruct children. When I say, therefore, that they must be *treated as rational creatures*, I mean that you should make them sensible, by the mildness of your carriage, and the composure even in your correction of them, that what you do is reasonable in you, and useful and necessary for them. . . . This they are capable of understanding. . . .

You will wonder, perhaps, that I put *learning* last, especially if I tell you I think it the least part. This may seem strange in the mouth of a bookish man. . . . When I consider what ado is made about a little Latin and Greek, how many years are spent in it, and what a noise and business it makes to no purpose, I can hardly forbear thinking that the parents of children still live in fear of the schoolmaster's rod, which they look on as the only instrument of education; as a language or two to be its whole business. How else is it possible that a child should be chained to the oar seven, eight, or ten of the best years of his life, to get a language or two, which, I think, might be had at a great deal cheaper rate of pains and time, and be learned almost in playing?

"With Children Use Force, With Men Reason": *Emile* (1762)

JEAN JACQUES ROUSSEAU

Reasoning should not begin too soon—Locke's great maxim was that we ought to reason with children, and just now this maxim is much in fashion. I think, however, that its success does not warrant its reputation, and I find nothing more stupid than children who have been so much reasoned with. Reason, apparently a compound of all other faculties, that one latest developed, and with most difficulty, is the one proposed as agent in unfolding the faculties earliest used! The noblest work of education is to make a reasoning man, and we expect to train a young child by making him reason! This is beginning at the end; this is making an instrument of a result. If children understood how to reason they would not need to be educated. But by addressing them from their tenderest years in a language they cannot understand, you accustom them to be satisfied with words, to find fault with whatever is said to them, to think themselves as wise as their teachers, to wrangle and rebel. And what we mean they shall do from reasonable motives we are forced to obtain from them by adding the motive of avarice, or of fear, or of vanity.

Nature intends that children shall be children before they are men. If we insist on reversing this order we shall have fruit early indeed, but unripe and tasteless, and liable to early decay; we shall have young savants and old children. Childhood has its own methods of seeing, thinking, and feeling. Nothing shows less sense than to try to substitute our own methods for these. I would rather require a child ten years old to be five feet tall than to be judicious. Indeed, what use could he have at that age for the power to reason? It is a check upon physical strength, and the child needs none. . . .

In attempting to persuade your pupils to obedience you add to this alleged persuasion force and threats, or worse still, flattery and promises.

" 'With Children Use Force, With Men Reason' " is from Jean Jacques Rousseau, *Emile*, trans. Eleanor Worthington (Boston: Ginn, Heath & Co., 1883).

Bought over in this way by interest, or constrained by force, they pretend to be convinced by reason. . . .

What results from this? First of all that, by imposing upon them a duty they do not feel as such, you set them against your tyranny, and dissuade them from loving you; you teach them to be dissemblers, deceitful, wilfully untrue, for the sake of extorting rewards or of escaping punishments. Finally, by habituating them to cover a secret motive by an apparent motive, you give them the means of constantly misleading you, of concealing their true character from you, and of satisfying yourself and others with empty words when their occasion demands. You may say that the law, although binding on the conscience, uses constraint in dealing with grown men. I grant it; but what are these men but children spoiled by their education? This is precisely what ought to be prevented. With children use force, with men reason; such is the natural order of things. The wise man requires no laws.

The Organization of Knowledge

The scholars of the Enlightenment did not simply seek knowledge for their own personal joy, but rather planned for the aggrandizement of humankind in a larger sense. Perhaps the most laborious endeavor was the compilation of knowledge in comprehensive dictionaries or encyclopedias. Voltaire wrote a philosophical dictionary, as he termed it, wherein he defined certain concepts from faith and natural law to government and kissing, all with his inimitable flair and personal bias. Some excerpts appear in the first selection.

One of the most ambitious and dramatic accomplishments of the Enlightenment was the publication of the Encyclopedia, *a work of twenty-one volumes of text, twelve of plates illustrating the trades and mechanical arts, and two of index. The aim of the work was to provide a summary of human knowledge—a task that had been attempted before on a smaller scale, but with uneven and disappointing results.*

The mindset and guiding influence behind the Encyclopedia *was a young, little known journalist named Denis Diderot (1713–1784). Together with the renowned mathematician Jean le Rond d'Alembert, he directed the project from the publication of the first volume in 1745 to its completion forty years later in 1780. Diderot solicited the most accomplished scholars of the age to contribute articles on their research and to offer theories and opinions on a wide variety of topics. The task of distillation and compilation was formidable, and Diderot was constantly engaged in disputes with scholars, publishers, and the Catholic Church in bringing the project to its remarkable conclusion. Apart from the impressive body of knowledge contained in the* Encyclopedia, *it stands as the quintessential expression of the ideals and attitudes of the Enlightenment. The next two excerpts in this section are from the Preface and Introduction to the first volume. The last passage recounts the dedication of Diderot in overcoming opposition to his grand project.*

A Philosophical Dictionary (1764)

VOLTAIRE

Astrology

Astrology might rest on a better foundation than magic. For if no one has seen goblins, or lemurs, . . . or demons, the predictions of astrologers have often been found true. Let two astrologers be consulted on the life of an infant, and on the weather; if one of them says that the child shall live to manhood, the other that he shall not; if one foretells rain and the other fair weather, it is quite clear that [one of them] will be a prophet.

One of the most famous mathematicians of Europe, named Stöffler, who flourished in the fifteenth and sixteenth centuries, foretold a universal flood for the year 1524. The deluge was to happen in the month of February, and nothing can be more plausible, for Saturn, Jupiter, and Mars were in conjunction in the sign of Pisces. Every nation in Europe, Asia, and Africa that heard of the prediction was worried. The whole world expected the flood, in spite of the rainbow. . . . Each [person] provided himself with a boat to serve as an ark. . . . At last the month of February arrived, and not a drop of rain fell, never was a month more dry, never were the astrologers more embarrassed. However, we neither discouraged nor neglected them; almost all our princes continued to consult them.

I have not the honor to be a prince; nevertheless, the celebrated Count de Boulainvilliers and an Italian, named Colonna, who had great reputation at Paris, both foretold to me that I should assuredly die at the age of thirty-two. I have already been malicious enough to [outwit] them by thirty years in their calculation—for which I most humbly ask their pardon.

Authority

Miserable human beings, whether in green robes or in turbans, whether in black gowns or in [cloaks or clerical bands], never seek to use authority where nothing but reason will do, unless they wish to be [scorned] in all ages as the most impertinent of men, as well as to endure public hatred as the most unjust.

You have been told a hundred times of the insolent absurdity with which you condemned Galileo, and I speak to you of it for the hundred and first. I would have it inscribed over the door of your holy office.

Seven cardinals, assisted by certain minor friars, threw into prison the master of thinking in Italy, at the age of seventy; and made him live upon bread and water because he instructed mankind in that of which they were ignorant. . . .

"A Philosophical Dictionary" is from Tobias Smollett, ed., *The Works of Voltaire* (London: E. R. DuMont, 1901), vol. 6, pp. 93, 95–96, 178–179; vol. 8, pp. 260–266. Text modernized by the editor.

Further, a [university] Faculty, which possessed very small faculties, made a decree *against* innate ideas, and afterwards another *for* them, without the said Faculty being informed, except by its [officials] what an idea was.

In neighboring schools legal proceedings were commenced against the circulation of the blood. A process was issued against inoculation, and the parties [subpoenaed]. Twenty-one folio volumes were seized in which it was wickedly and falsely said that triangles have always three angles; that a father was older than his son; that Rhea Silvia lost her virginity before [giving birth to her child]; and that flour differs from oak leaves!

Democracy

There is ordinarily no comparison to be made between the crimes of the great, who are always ambitious, and those of the people, who never desire and who never can desire, anything but liberty and equality. These two sentiments, "liberty and equality," do not *necessarily* lead to slander, rapine, assassination, poisoning, and devastation of the lands of neighbors; but, the towering ambition and thirst for power of the great [plunge] them head-long into every kind of crime in all times and places. . . .

Popular government, therefore, is in itself . . . less abominable than monarchical despotism. The great vice of democracy is certainly not tyranny and cruelty. . . . [But] democracy seems to suit only a very small country and one that is fortunately situated. Small as it may be, it will commit many faults, because it will be composed of men. Discord will prevail in it, . . . but there will be no St. Bartholomews there, no Irish massacre, . . . no Inquisition, no condemnation to the galleys for having taken water from the ocean without paying for it—unless it be a republic of devils, established in some corner of hell. . . .

Every day we are asked which is better, a republic or a monarchy? The dispute always ends in agreeing that the government of men is exceedingly difficult. The Jews had God himself for their master; yet observe the events of their history. They have almost always been trampled upon and enslaved, and even today what a wretched figure they make!

Equality

Nothing can be clearer than that men, enjoying the faculties of their common nature, are in a state of equality; they are equal when they perform their animal functions, and exercise their understandings. . . . All animals of each species are on an equality with one another. . . .

It is impossible in our unhappy world to prevent men living in society from being divided into two classes, one of the rich who command, the other of the poor who obey, and these two are subdivided into various others, which have also their respective shades of difference. . . .

All the poor are not unhappy. The majority are born in that state, and constant labor prevents them from too sensibly feeling their situation; but when they do strongly feel it, then come wars such as those of the popular party against the senate at Rome, and those of the peasantry in Germany, England, and France. All these wars ended sooner or later with the subjection of the people, because the great have money, and money in a state commands everything; I say in a state, for the case is different between nation and nation. That nation which makes the best use of [the sword] will always subjugate another that has more gold but less courage.

Every man is born with an eager inclination for power, wealth, and pleasure, and also with a great taste for indolence. Every man, consequently, would wish to possess the fortunes and the wives or daughters of others, to be their master, to retain them in subjection to his whims, and to do nothing, or at least nothing but what is perfectly agreeable. You clearly perceive that with such amiable dispositions, it is as impossible for men to be equal as for two preachers or theology professors not to be jealous of each other.

The human race, constituted as it is, cannot exist unless there be an infinite number of useful individuals possessed of no property at all, for most certainly a man who is well off will not leave his own land to come and cultivate yours; and if you want a pair of shoes you will not get a lawyer to make them for you. Equality, then, is at the same time the most natural and the most implausible thing possible.

As men carry everything to excess if they have it in their power to do so, this inequality has been pushed too far; it has been maintained in many countries that no citizen has a right to [renounce the country of his birth]. The meaning of such a law must evidently be: "This country is so badly governed that we forbid every man from leaving for fear that everyone will leave it." Do better: excite in all your subjects a desire to stay with you, and in foreigners a desire to come and settle among you.

Every man has a right to [think himself equal] to other men, but it does not follow that a cardinal's cook should [order] his master to prepare his dinner. The cook, however, may say: "I am a man as well as my master; I was born like him crying, and shall like him die in anguish, attended by the same common ceremonies. We both perform the same animal functions. If the Turks get possession of Rome, and I then become a cardinal and my master a cook, I will take him into my service." This language is perfectly reasonable and just, but, while waiting for the Grand Turk to get possession of Rome, the cook is bound to do his duty, or all human society is subverted.

With respect to a man who is neither a cardinal's cook nor invested with any office whatever in the state—with respect to an individual who has no connections, and is disgusted at always being [patronized or scorned], who sees quite clearly that many men of quality and title have no more knowledge, wit, or virtue than himself, and is bored at waiting in their antechambers—what ought such a man to do? He ought to leave.

The *Encyclopedia* Is Announced (1750)

DENIS DIDEROT

It cannot be denied that, since the revival of letters among us, we owe partly to dictionaries the general enlightenment that has spread in society and the germ of science that is gradually preparing men's minds for more profound knowledge. How valuable would it not be, then, to have a book of this kind that one could consult on all subjects and that would serve as much to guide those who have the courage to work at the instruction of others as to enlighten those who only instruct themselves!

Up to now no one has conceived a work this large, or at least no one has carried one out. . . . The majority of [the earlier encyclopedias] appeared during the last century and were not completely scorned. It was found that if they did not show much talent, they at least bore the marks of labor and of knowledge. But what would these encyclopedias mean to us? What progress have we not made since then in the arts and sciences? How many truths discovered today, which were not foreseen then? True philosophy was in its cradle; the geometry of infinity did not yet exist; experimental physics was just appearing; there was no dialectic at all; the laws of sound criticism were entirely unknown. Descartes, Newton, Locke, Pascal, Racine, Bossuet, etc., either had not yet been born or had not yet written. The spirit of research and competition did not motivate the scholars: another spirit, . . . that of precision and method, had not yet conquered the various diversions of literature; and the academies, whose efforts have advanced the arts and sciences to such an extent, were not yet established. . . . At the end of this project you will find the tree of human knowledge, indicating the connection of ideas, which has directed us in this vast operation. If we come out of it with success, we will be primarily indebted to [Sir Francis] Bacon, who laid out the plan for a universal dictionary of the arts and sciences at a time when there were, so to speak, neither arts nor sciences. This extraordinary genius, faced with the impossibility of writing the history of what men knew, put down instead what they needed to learn. . . .

[In compiling this encyclopedia], we have consulted the most competent people in Paris and in the kingdom. We took the trouble of going to their workshops, to question them, to write from their dictation, to develop their thoughts, to obtain from them the terms peculiar to their professions, to draw up tables of these and define them, to talk with those from whom reports were obtained, and (an almost indispensable precaution) to correct, in long and frequent interviews with some people, what others had imperfectly, obscurely, and sometimes inaccurately explained.

"The *Encyclopedia* Is Announced" is from Nina B. Gunzenhauser, trans., in *Major Crises in Western Civilization*, vol. 2 (New York: Harcourt Brace and World, 1965), pp. 11–12.

Introduction to the *Encyclopedia* (1751)

JEAN LE ROND D'ALEMBERT

The *Encyclopedia* is, as its title proclaims, the work of a company of men of letters. Were we not one of them, we might venture to claim that they have, or are worthy of having, a good reputation. But without wishing to anticipate a judgment which scholars alone may form, it is at least our duty to set aside, before everything else, the objection most capable of prejudicing the success of such a vast enterprise. We declare, therefore, that we have by no means had the temerity to take upon ourselves alone a burden so far beyond our capabilities, and that our role as editors consists principally in putting in order materials of which the greater part was supplied to us. . . .

The work which we are beginning (and wish to complete) has two aims: as an *encyclopedia*, its purpose is to set forth, as well as possible, the order and continuity of human knowledge; as an *analytical dictionary of the arts, the sciences, and the professions*, its purpose is to contain, for each science and each art, whether liberal or mechanical, the general principles on which it is based and the most essential details which make up its body and substance. These two points of view, of *encyclopedia* and of *analytical dictionary*, will therefore dictate the outline and the division of this preliminary discourse. We will consider them, pursue them one after the other, and report on the means by which we have attempted to satisfy this double aim.

If one has ever reflected at all on the connections between discoveries, it is easy to realize that the arts and sciences lend each other mutual assistance that there is consequently a chain which joins them. But it is often difficult to reduce to a small number of rules or general ideas each particular science or art; it is no less difficult to enclose in a unified system the infinitely varied branches of human knowledge.

The first step we have to take in this research is to examine . . . the genealogy of our knowledge and the relationships within it, the causes which must have led to its birth and the nature that distinguishes it—in brief, to go back to the origin and generation of our ideas. Aside from the benefits we will reap from examining this encyclopedic enumeration of the arts and sciences, this will not be out of place at the head of an analytical dictionary of human knowledge.

We can divide all our knowledge into direct knowledge and reasoned knowledge. Direct knowledge is that which we receive immediately without an operation of our will, which finding open . . . all of the doors of our soul, enters it without resistance and without effort. Reasoned knowledge is that which the mind acquires in operating on direct knowledge, in uniting and combining it.

"Introduction to the *Encyclopedia*" is from Nina B. Gunzenhauser, trans., in *Major Crises in Western Civilization*, vol. 2 (New York: Harcourt Brace and World, 1965), pp. 13–14.

All of our direct knowledge can be reduced to that which we receive through the senses; from which it follows that we owe all our ideas to our sensations. The system of innate ideas, tempting in many respects . . . after having reigned for a long time [still] has some partisans; with such difficulty does truth [gain] its place. . . . At last, quite recently, there has been almost universal consensus that [innate ideas do not exist].

"We Did Not Live Entirely in Vain" (1764)
DENIS DIDEROT

The public has judged the first seven volumes; we ask for the current batch only the same indulgence. . . . From the point where we started to the point we have reached the distance was tremendous. . . . Thanks to our labor, those who come after us will be able to go further. Without declaring what they have yet to do, we will turn over to them at least the best book on tools and machines that ever existed . . . and an infinite number of precious morsels concerning all the sciences. O compatriots and contemporaries! With whatever severity you judge this work, remember that it was undertaken, continued, completed by a small number of isolated men, thwarted in their views, shown in the worst light, slandered and insulted in the most atrocious manner, having no other encouragement than the love of the good, no other support than several commendations, no other help but that which they found in the confidence of three or four tradesmen!

Our main purpose was to collect the discoveries of preceding centuries. . . . Should a revolution, the germ of which is forming perhaps in some unknown canton of the earth or incubating secretly in the very center of the civilized world, break out in time, destroy the cities, scatter the nations once again, and bring back ignorance and darkness; if one single complete set of this work survives, all will not be lost.

At least it cannot be contested, I think, that our work is on a level with our century, and that is something. The most enlightened man will find in it ideas that were unfamiliar to him and facts he did not know. If only general education could advance at such a rapid rate that twenty years from now there would be, out of a thousand of our pages, scarcely a single line that was not popular knowledge! It is up to the rulers of the world to hasten that happy revolution; it is they who expand or contract the sphere of enlightenment. Happy the time when they will all have understood that their security consists in commanding educated men! The major crimes have never been attempted by any except blinded fanatics. . . . [We hope that] we led our fellow men to love each other, to tolerate each other and to recognize at last the superiority of universal ethics over all the particular

" 'We Did Not Live Entirely in Vain' " is from Nina B. Gunzenhauser, trans., in *Major Crises in Western Civilization*, vol. 2 (New York: Harcourt Brace and World, 1965), pp. 35–37.

morals that inspire hatred and disorder and that break or relax the general and common bond. Such was our aim throughout. . . .

If one adds to the years of our life that had passed at the time we planned this work those we have given to its accomplishment, one will easily realize that we have lived more years than we have left. But we shall have received the compensation that we look for from our contemporaries and our descendants if we make them say one day that we did not live entirely in vain.

The Indispensable Woman

The Parisian salons during the Enlightenment brought writers together for elegant, stylized conversation. It was in the salon, a rather formal reception room of a private home, where the intellectual elite congregated to spend the evening engaged in disputation, storytelling, timely debate over the latest issues of the day, or relaxed musing about the potentials of the future. Good conversation flourished under the guidance of an elegant hostess, who often directed the debate, smoothed ruffled feathers, and generally maintained an atmosphere conducive to discovery and pleasant conversation. It was in this setting that women not only competed with men on an equal intellectual footing but assumed a leading role by organizing and conducting the proceedings. In the process, women often became the arbiters of good taste and the dispensers of merit.

The following selection gives testimony to one of the most remarkable women of the Age of Reason, Julie de Lespinasse. Note carefully why others regarded her as an indispensable woman.

The Parisian Salon of Julie de Lespinasse: "Her Imagination was the Mainspring, Her Reason the Regulator"

From *Memoir of Baron de Grimm*

Her circle met daily from five o'clock until nine in the evening. There we were sure to find choice men of all orders in the State, the Church, the Court,—military men, foreigners, and the most distinguished men of letters. Every one agrees that though the name of M. d'Alembert may have drawn them, it was she alone who kept them there. Devoted wholly to the

"The Parisian Salon of Julie de Lespinasse" is from Katherine P. Wormley, trans., *Letters of Julie de Lespinasse* (Boston: Hardy, Pratt and Co., 1903), pp. 34–35, 75.

care of preserving that society, of which she was the soul and the charm, she subordinated to this purpose all her tastes and all her personal intimacies. She seldom sent to the theatre or into the country, and when she did make an exception to this rule it was an event of which all Paris was notified in advance. . . . Politics, religion, philosophy, anecdotes, news, nothing was excluded from the conversation, and, thanks to her care, the most trivial little narrative gained, as naturally as possible, the place and notice it deserved. News of all kinds was gathered there in its first freshness.

From *Memoir of Marmontel*

The circle was formed of persons who were not bound together. She had taken them here and there in society, but so well assorted were they that once there they fell into harmony like the strings of an instrument touched by an able hand. Following out that comparison, I may say that she played the instrument with an art that came of genius; she seemed to know what tone each string would yield before she touched it; I mean to lay that our minds and our natures were so well known to her that in order to bring them into play she had but to say a word. Nowhere was conversation more lively, more brilliant, or better regulated than at her house. It was a rare phenomenon indeed, the degree of tempered, equable heat which she knew so well how to maintain, sometimes by moderating it, sometimes by quickening it. The continual activity of her soul was communicated to our souls, but measurably; her imagination was the mainspring, her reason the regulator. Remark that the brains she stirred at will were neither feeble nor frivolous: the Coudillacs and Turgots were among them; d'Alembert was like a simple, docile child beside her. Her talent for casting out a thought and giving it for discussion to men of that class, her own talent in discussing it with precision, sometimes with eloquence, her talent for bringing forward new ideas and varying the topic—always with the facility and ease of a fairy, who, with one touch of her wand, can change the scene of her enchantment—these talents, I say, were not those of an ordinary woman. It was not with the follies of fashion and vanity that daily, during four hours of conversation, without languor and without vacuum, she knew how to make herself interesting to a wide circle of strong minds.

CHRONOLOGY: "Dare to Know!": The Revolution of the Mind in the Seventeenth and Eighteenth Centuries

1543	Nicolaus Copernicus: *On the Revolutions of the Heavenly Spheres*
1605	Sir Francis Bacon: *The Advancement of Learning*
1609	Johannes Kepler: *On the Motion of Mars*

1620	Sir Francis Bacon: *Novum Organum*
1628	William Harvey: *On the Circulation of the Blood*
1632	Galileo Galilei: *Dialogues on the Two Chief Systems of the World*
1637	René Descartes: *Discourse on Method*
1682–1725	Reign of Peter the Great of Russia. In 1697, the Tsar visits western Europe to study the skills necessary to build Russia into a strong, modern state.
1687	Sir Isaac Newton: *Principia Mathematica*
1688–1689	Glorious Revolution in England
1690	John Locke: *Essay Concerning Human Understanding; Second Treatise of Civil Government*
1693	John Locke: *Some Thoughts Concerning Education*
1713–1740	Frederick William I builds up the military power of Prussia
1740–1748	Maria Theresa succeeds to the Austrian throne. War of the Austrian Succession: Frederick II of Prussia invades Austrian province of Silesia in violation of Pragmatic Sanction; Maria Theresa fights Frederick to a stalemate, but loses Silesia in the Treaty of Aix-la-Chapelle.
1748	The Baron de Montesquieu: *The Spirit of the Laws* David Hume: *Inquiry into Human Nature*
1751	Denis Diderot: First volume of the *Encyclopedia* appears
1756–1763	Seven Years War: France, Austria, Sweden, and Russia vs. Prussia (supported financially by Great Britain)
1762	Jean Jacques Rousseau: *The Social Contract*; and *Emile*
1763	Voltaire: *Treatise on Toleration*
1764	Voltaire: *Philosophical Dictionary* Cesare Beccaria: *On Crimes and Punishments*
1775–1783	American Revolution
1776	Edward Gibbon: *The Decline and Fall of the Roman Empire* Adam Smith: *The Wealth of Nations*

STUDY QUESTIONS

Section I: The Scientific Revolution

1. What was Sir Francis Bacon's contribution to the Scientific Revolution? What specific ideas does he offer about scientific method in *Novum*

Organum? Does Voltaire's statement that part of Bacon's seminal work on the new empirical method "was no longer of use" in the eighteenth century diminish Bacon's contributions to science?

2. How do some of Descarte's ideas on scientific method show the influence of Sir Francis Bacon? What did Descartes mean by the phrase "I think, therefore I am"? Why was this so fundamental to his method? Reconstruct his logic for the existence of God. Do you find it compelling?

3. Read Copernicus' statement on the movement of the sun and earth. What reasons does he give for supporting the heliocentric theory? Is he convincing? Why is it significant that Copernicus refers to ancient authors like Cicero and Plutarch?

4. What were Galileo's specific ideas regarding the relationship between science and the Bible? Be particular in your analysis. Why were Galileo's ideas considered dangerous by the Inquisition? Did the Inquisition do the Church more harm than good?

5. How would you define the process of induction as championed by Sir Isaac Newton? How does he specifically demonstrate this principle in his work on *Optics*? If Newton was such a methodical scientist, why did he accept the compatibility of science and God in the pursuit of empirical truth? What does Sir Francis Bacon say about this compatibility in his selection on the *Advancement of Learning* (1605)?

6. Consider the words of Martin Luther quoted at the beginning of this chapter: "Reason is the greatest enemy that faith has. It never comes to the aid of spiritual things, but . . . struggles against the divine Word, treating with contempt all that emanates from God." Does it surprise you that this statement comes from the leader of the Protestant Reformation? Discuss the compatibility of science and religion in light of this quotation.

7. What are some of the current areas of tension between science and religion? In our quest for knowledge and understanding about the world around us and our place in it, must one choose between the mind and the spirit?

8. Do you agree with Voltaire's assessment of Newton and Descartes? Why does he call Descartes a "dreamer" and his works, "now useless"? Most importantly, where does "greatness" lie? In the conquests of men like Julius Caesar or Alexander the Great, the political leadership of Augustus or Oliver Cromwell, or the intellectual influence of Isaac Newton? Do you agree with Voltaire on this?

9. Why did William Harvey want to present his findings in an address before the Royal College of Physicians? What was he afraid of? Why were his discoveries about the heart and circulation of blood so important and perhaps so threatening?

Section II: The Enlightenment

10. What do you think of Descartes' ideas (as noted by Voltaire) that the soul is the same thing as thought and that the human thinks eternally? Do you find Locke's assertion that the mind is a blank slate at birth and that there are no

innate ideas to be a compelling argument? What does Voltaire think? This still remains a disputed issue in modern psychology—can you solve it? What notions and actions are instinctive to human beings and what is learned through experience?

11. How do Edward Gibbon's ideas reflect the optimism of the Enlightenment? From a late-twentieth-century perspective, are you as confident as he was that "no people, unless the face of nature is changed, will relapse into their original barbarism"? Did the development of the atomic bomb "change the face of nature"? What did Marquis de Condorcet think about the progress of humankind? Have some of his predictions come true? Can they ever come true?

12. What mathematical equation did Cesare Beccaria apply to "the good and evil of life"? How do you think he might have reacted to our modern concern over capital punishment? Ultimately, how does a society prevent crime?

13. What was Adam Smith's view of human nature as expounded in the selection entitled "The Wealth of Nations"? Do you find his thoughts on self-interest to be compelling? Does his belief negate the sincerity of altruism? What are the primary ingredients of success in the world? How do you define the principle of the "invisible hand?" How do you interpret his phrase: "I have never known much good done by those who affected to trade for the public good"? Smith foresaw a "mean rapacity" of merchants and manufacturers that "perhaps cannot be corrected." Why was he so sure that it could "very easily be prevented from disturbing the tranquility of anybody but themselves"?

14. How does Immanuel Kant answer the question "What is Enlightenment?" In what ways do you see his views on freedom and risk in evidence throughout this chapter? Select *four* other thinkers and demonstrate specifically how Kant's attitude applies to the tenor of their writings.

15. Carefully scrutinize the arguments of Baron d'Holbach. Does his atheism seem well supported by his argument? What does he mean by denoting God as "a cause contradicted by its effects"? Why is deism a comfortable philosophy? Are you persuaded by Voltaire's arguments in opposition to the Baron d'Holbach as expressed in his letter to Frederick William of Prussia?

16. Compare the ideas of John Locke and Jean Jacques Rousseau on education. Do you agree with Locke's prioritization of the most important values to impart to children? What does he mean by "breeding"? Do you think his ideas on reasoning with children and the conduct of their education are sound and applicable even today? Compare Locke's ideas on children with those of Rousseau. Is there a certain, even compelling logic to Rousseau's arguments? Does Locke "begin at the end?" Will his advice produce "unripe fruit"?

17. Carefully read Voltaire's entries in his *Philosophical Dictionary*. Are any of his personal biases evident? Can you discern his view of human nature?

What does he mean when he says that equality "is the most natural and the most implausible thing possible"?

18. Why did Denis Diderot think a new encyclopedia not only useful but necessary in his age of Enlightenment? To whom does he attribute the greatest debt for the spirit of scholarship that permeated the time? What was the method that Diderot employed in obtaining articles for the *Encyclopedia*? According to d'Alembert, what were the aims of the *Encyclopedia*? What is the difference between reasoned knowledge and direct knowledge?

19. In the selection "We Did Not Live Entirely in Vain," Diderot expressed some of the general attitudes of the Enlightenment. He mentions the topics of toleration, education, progress, and ethics. Choose the specific writers and documents from this chapter that best represent Diderot's generalized comments. Defend your choices.

20. What talents did Julie de Lespinasse possess that made her indispensable to the success of her salon? How did women of her social class and education contribute to the progress of this age? Do you think that hers was an important function, or would this type of social/intellectual discussion have taken place without hostesses of such talent and ability? What does this say about the role of women during the Enlightenment?

3

"Liberty, Equality, Fraternity!": The French Revolution and the Rise of Napoleon

A time of revolution is not the season of true liberty. Alas! the obstinacy and perversion of men is such that she is too often obliged to borrow the very arms of despotism to overthrow him, and in order to reign in peace must establish herself by violence.

—William Wordsworth

The greatest dangers to liberty lurk in insidious encroachment by men of zeal—well-meaning, but without understanding.

—Justice Louis D. Brandeis

Extremism in the defense of liberty is no vice. And . . . moderation in the pursuit of justice is no virtue.

—Barry Goldwater

True tragedy arises when the idea of "justice" appears to be leading to the destruction of higher values.

—Max Scheler

What is the throne?—a bit of wood gilded and covered with velvet. I am the state—I alone am the representative of the people. . . . France has more need of me than I of France.

—Napoleon Bonaparte (1814)

Do you know what astounds me most about the world? It is the impotence of force to establish anything. In the end, the sword is always
conquered by the mind.

—Napoleon Bonaparte (1808)

Men of genius are meteors destined to be consumed in lighting up
their century.

—Napoleon Bonaparte (1791)

One of the most exciting periods of change and development in Western
Civilization occurred during the seventeenth and eighteenth centuries. The
attitudes and ideas that flourished during this time have formed the intellectual and political bases of our modern Western world.

Although the writers and thinkers of this period, often called *philosophes*,
generally advocated intellectual freedom and political equality, it should be
added that the eighteenth-century Enlightenment was not initially a concerted
effort, but took shape in individual minds over several generations; it did not
become a conscious movement until about 1750. Yet the ideas of such important figures as John Locke, the Baron de Montesquieu, Voltaire, Denis Diderot,
and Jean Jacques Rousseau were to be influential apart from the theoretical
and abstract world of thought. They were to give philosophical justification to
the notion that it was proper and desirable to remove a monarch who was
incompetent or inattentive to the needs of the people. Revolution often requires philosophical inspiration in order to succeed; without the underlying
attitude that revolution can be a proper and progressive act, perhaps the
French middle class would not have been motivated to lead a revolt against the
established order.

And yet the French Revolution in 1789 did not simply happen as a result of
intellectual commitment to abstract principles. In fact, there existed more
tangible evidence that revolution could succeed and produce desired results.
The precedents were clear. In 1649, the English executed their monarch,
Charles I, for his autocratic behavior, and in 1688, Parliament established itself
as the supreme depository of law and the "popular will" by restricting monarchical authority. It should be remembered, however, that the English had a
long tradition of representative government and monarchical limitation dating
back most importantly to the Magna Carta in 1215. The French lacked this
tradition, and their representative institution, the Estates-General, had not met
in 175 years. More recent precedent for French revolutionary action existed in
the American example. In 1776, the American colonies declared their independence from Britain and were supported in this venture by the French
government itself.

There were also economic problems that moved France toward revolution.
The wars and extravagance of Louis XIV had sent France to the brink of

bankruptcy by 1715—and Louis was a competent and diligent administrator. His heirs, on the other hand, were not particularly dedicated to the governance of France. Louis XV (1715–1774) was poorly educated and preferred to allow his mistresses (one of whom had been a Parisian prostitute) to control the politics of state. Louis XVI (1774–1792) was well educated but more interested in hunting than in administration. From 1715 to 1789, the French economy spiraled into chaos. With the nobility and church exempt from taxation, the burden fell upon the Third Estate.

The French Revolution drew much of its support from the Third Estate, a conglomeration of middle-class professionals, artisans, and peasants. As a group the middle class or *bourgeoisie* was ambitious, educated, and competent. Could they be expected to sit idly by while the nobility held offices that should have been theirs? Inspired by philosophical ideals as well as by potential economic and social advantages, they provided the leadership for the revolution. Lower members of the Third Estate, the artisans and peasants, generally could not read and were not concerned with philosophical justifications. It was the peasantry that labored under intolerable taxes, rents, and *corvées* (feudal services), which they were forced to undertake by the nobility without payment. What were their demands in 1789? Did their needs justify revolution?

The first part of this chapter will explore some of the ideological and social origins of the French Revolution, as well as some of its most important events, such as the storming of the Bastille, the execution of Louis XVI, and the Terror. Revolutions generally go through conservative and radical phases. Differences among revolutionaries often result in violence. The path toward freedom or despotism is littered with bodies and bloodshed. And in the power vacuum created by such chaos, the door is left open for a transfer of power. During the French Revolution, an individual seized the initiative, filled the power vacuum, and altered its course. His name was Napoleon Bonaparte.

The mere name of Napoleon (1769–1821) evokes a wide array of emotions. As is the case with most influential individuals, he inspires controversy. Some historians have described him as a force for good, a lawgiver and reformer who spread revolutionary ideals throughout Europe. Others have viewed him as an egomaniac whose lust for conquest overshadowed any other secondary achievements. Whatever final judgment one may make, it is clear that Napoleon Bonaparte had a brilliant mind, equally at home in the context of law and military strategy.

Napoleon was born in 1769 to a poor family of lesser nobility on the island of Corsica. The "little Corsican," as he was called, went to French schools and obtained a commission as a French artillery officer. He was enthusiastic about the revolution of 1789 and was rewarded for his military service against the British with a promotion to brigadier general. After the fall of Robespierre in 1794, Napoleon's radical political associations threatened his career, but he was able to convince the new government of his loyalty. This government was called the Directory, and it was composed of people who had benefited from the recent revolution and whose major goal was to perpetuate their own rule. Their chief opposition came from royalists who supported a monarch as head of France and who had won a majority of the seats in the legislature in 1797. With the aid of Napoleon, the Directory succeeded in overthrowing the elected officials and placed their own supporters in the legislature. Napoleon then received a command against the Austrians and Sardinians that resulted in a swift victory for the French and eventual annexation of Italy. Napoleon was hailed as a hero and decided to sail to Egypt, there to fight the British fleet and, it was hoped, cut off British contact and trade with her colonies in the East. However, the invasion of Egypt (1798) was a failure for the French; Napoleon abandoned his troops and returned to Paris, where he overthrew the Directory that he had once championed (November 10, 1799). Establishing a new government called the Consulate, he then issued the Constitution for the Year VIII (December 1799), which promoted liberal ideas such as universal manhood suffrage and a system of governmental checks and balances, but in reality granted Napoleon virtual dictatorial power as first consul. His position was confirmed by a plebiscite that approved the new constitution by a vote of 3,011,077 to 1,567. Both the middle and lower classes seemed satisfied to accept the security that Napoleon offered.

Napoleon then quickly consolidated his rule by achieving peace with Austria and Britain and by restoring order at home. In 1801, he concluded a concordat with the Catholic Church, which in fact resulted in the subordination of the Church to the state; there would be no controversy between secular and religious authority in Napoleonic France. So satisfied were French citizens that in 1802 they voted Napoleon consul for life. In 1804, there was simply no one with enough authority to grant him the final accolade, so Napoleon crowned himself Napoleon I, Emperor of the French. The pope sat nearby, watching the ceremony. Napoleon had achieved the ultimate authority, which had escaped even Charlemagne.

In his decade as emperor, Napoleon conquered most of Europe, spreading France's revolutionary ideals. It was at this time, too, that he paid great attention to domestic concerns and soon instituted reforms and programs, including a codification of laws known as the Napoleonic Code. His glory came to an end in 1814 when he was finally defeated by a coalition of European powers. Napoleon's brief return from exile was unsuccessful and resulted in his defeat by Lord Wellington at Waterloo. The victors agreed at the Congress of Vienna in 1815 that no single state should dominate Europe—power must be balanced. Another Napoleon would not be tolerated. The great general was ingloriously exiled to St. Helena, an isolated and inaccessible rock in the Atlantic. He died there in 1821 of stomach cancer or, as some modern researchers advocate, the victim of gradual poisoning. Even in death, Napoleon remains a controversial figure.

In the second part of this chapter, we will look at Napoleon's rise to power and especially his reforms and attempts to consolidate his position. Napoleon was certainly a military leader of genius, but his achievements often inspire philosophical rather than military analysis. His career raises questions about the nature of power and the ability of the individual to change the course of history. Is history motivated by social and economic forces over which individuals have no control? Or does the "hero" actually change history by force of personality and ability? Did Napoleon make France a great nation through his reforms and conquests? If so, does progress come about because of the imposition of reforms upon a people? Was Napoleon, who overthrew the legitimate, elected government of France and who installed a dictatorship, necessary for the progress of a revolution dedicated to liberty and equality? The French Revolution presents historians with complex problems of great importance. This chapter will focus on the components of revolution, the relationship between power and progress and factors of historical change. Finally, did the French Revolution succeed in realizing its ideals of liberty, equality, and fraternity?

SECTION I: THE FRENCH REVOLUTION

Justification for Revolution

The Political Framework

The following selections discuss the theoretical basis for revolution and present justification for the elimination of absolute monarchy. John Locke (1632–1704) was an English political philosopher whose Second Treatise of Civil Government *(1690) later influenced both the French and American revolutions. It is also the first philosophical statement of liberalism, a doctrine that sought the limitation of the arbitrary power of government and the establishment of legal equality, religious toleration, and freedom of the press. Baron de Montesquieu (1689–1755) was one of the most penetrating political analysts of his age. The selection from* The Spirit of the Laws *was published in 1748, about forty years before the French Revolution broke out. The third selection is from* The Social Contract *(1762) by Jean Jacques Rousseau (1712–1778). Although Rousseau spent much of his life in intimate contact with the* philosophes, *he rejected their attitude that the human being is a rational creature whose confidence in reason would result in liberty and equality. Rousseau advocated the elimination of political despotism and the introduction of a new social order in which only the authority of the "general will" of the governed placed limits on individual freedom. His ideas provided the most inspirational justification for revolutionary action during the eighteenth century.*

Second Treatise of Civil Government (1690)

JOHN LOCKE

Political power, then, I take to be a right of making laws with penalties of death, and consequently all less penalties, for the regulating and preserving of property, and of employing the force of the community, in the execution of such laws, and in the defence of the commonwealth from foreign injury; and all this only for the public good.

Chapter II: Of the State of Nature

To understand political power right, and derive it from its original, we must consider what state all men are naturally in, and that is, a state of perfect freedom to order their actions and dispose of their possessions and persons, as they think fit, within the bounds of the law of nature; without asking leave, or depending upon the will of any other man.

A state also of equality, wherein all the power and jurisdiction is reciprocal, no one having more than another; there being nothing more evident, than that creatures of the same species and rank, promiscuously born to all the same advantages of nature, and the use of the same faculties, should also be equal one amongst another without subordination or subjection; unless the lord and master of them all should, by any manifest declaration of his will, set one above another, and confer on him, by an evident and clear appointment, an undoubted right to dominion and sovereignty. . . .

But though this be a state of liberty, yet it is not a state of license: though man in that state has an uncontrollable liberty to dispose of his person or possessions, yet he has not liberty to destroy himself, or so much as any creature in his possession, but where some nobler use than its bare preservation call for it. The state of nature has a law of nature to govern it, which obliges every one: and reason, which is that law, teaches all mankind, who will but consult it, that being equal and independent, no one ought to harm another in his life, health, liberty, or possessions: for men being all the workmanship of one omnipotent and infinitely wise Maker; all the servants of one sovereign master, sent into the world by his order, and about his business; they are his property, whose workmanship they are, made to last during his, not another's pleasure: and being furnished with like faculties, sharing all in one community of nature, there cannot be supposed any such subordination among us, that may authorize us to destroy another, as if we were made for one another's uses, as the inferior ranks of creatures are for ours. Every one, as he is bound to preserve himself, . . . ought he, as much as he can, to preserve the rest of mankind, and may not, unless it be to do justice to an offender, take away or impair

---

"Second Treatise of Civil Government" is from John Locke, *The Treatises of Government* (London, 1694).

the life, or what tends to the preservation of life, the liberty, health, limb, or goods of another.

And that all men may be restrained from invading others' rights, and from doing hurt to one another, and the law of nature be observed, which willeth the peace and preservation of all mankind, the execution of the law of nature is, in that state, put into every man's hands, whereby every one has a right to punish the transgressors of that law to such a degree as may hinder its violation: for the law of nature would, as all other laws that concern men in this world, be in vain, if there were nobody that in the state of nature had a power to execute the law, and thereby preserve the innocent and restrain offenders. And if any one in the state of nature may punish another for any evil he has done, every one may do so: for in that state of perfect equality, where naturally there is no superiority or jurisdiction of one over another, what any may do in prosecution of that law, every one must needs have a right to do.

And thus, in the state of nature, "one man comes by a power over another"; but yet this is not an absolute or arbitrary power. . . .

Chapter III: Of the State of War

[It is reasonable and just that . . .] I should have a right to destroy that which threatens me with destruction; for, by the fundamental law of nature, man being to be preserved as much as possible, when all cannot be preserved, the safety of the innocent is to be preferred: and one may destroy a man who makes war upon him, or has discovered an enmity to his being, for the same reason that he may kill a wolf or a lion; because such men are not under the ties of the common law of reason, have no other rule, than that of force and violence, and so may be treated as beasts of prey, those dangerous and noxious creatures, that will be sure to destroy him whenever he falls into their power.

And hence it is, that he who attempts to get another man into his absolute power, does thereby put himself into a state of war with him; it being to be understood as a declaration of a design upon his life: for I have reason to conclude, that he who would get me into his power without my consent, would use me as he pleased when he got me there, and destroy me too when he had a fancy to it; for nobody can desire to have me in his absolute power, unless it be to compel me by force to that which is against the right of my freedom, i.e., make me a slave. To be free from such force is the only security of my preservation; and reason bids me look on him, as an enemy to my preservation, who would take away that freedom which is the fence to it; so that he who makes an attempt to enslave me, thereby puts himself into a state of war with me. He that, in the state of nature, would take away the freedom that belongs to any one in that state, must necessarily be supposed to have a design to take away everything else, that freedom being the foundation of all the rest; as he that, in the state of society, would take away the freedom belonging to those of that society or commonwealth, must be supposed to design to take away from them every thing else, and so be looked on as in a state of war. . . .

Chapter IV: Of Slavery

The natural liberty of man is to be free from any superior power on earth, and not to be under the will or legislative authority of man, but to have only the law of nature for his rule. The liberty of man, in society, is to be under no other legislative power, but that established, by consent, in the commonwealth; nor under the dominion of any will, or restraint of any law, but what that legislative shall enact, according to the trust put in it. Freedom then is not what Sir Robert Filmer tells us, "a liberty for every one to do what he lists, to live as he pleases, and not to be tied by any laws": but freedom of men under government is, to have a standing rule to live by, common to every one of that society, and made by the legislative power erected in it; a liberty to follow my own will in all things, where the rule prescribes not; and not to be subject to the inconstant, uncertain, unknown, arbitrary will of another man: as freedom of nature is, to be under any other restraint but the law of nature.

This freedom from absolute, arbitrary power, is so necessary to, and closely joined with a man's preservation, that he cannot part with it, but by what forfeits his preservation and life together.

Chapter VIII: Of the Beginning of Political Societies

Men being, as has been said by nature, all free, equal, and independent, no one can be put out of this estate, and subjected to the political power of another, without his own consent. The only way, whereby any one divests himself of his natural liberty, and puts on the bonds of civil society, is by agreeing with other men to join and unite into a community, for their comfortable, safe, and peaceable living one amongst another, in a secure enjoyment of their properties, and a greater security against any, that are not of it. This any number of men may do, because it injures not the freedom of the rest; they are left as they were in the liberty of the state of nature. When any number of men have so consented to make one community or government they are thereby presently incorporated, and make one body politic, wherein the majority have a right to act and conclude the rest.

For, when any number of men have, by the consent of every individual, made a community, they have thereby made that community one body, with a power to act as one body, which is only by the will and determination of the majority: . . . or else it is impossible that it should act or continue as one body, one community, which the consent of every individual that united into it, agreed that it should; and so every one is bound by that consent to be concluded by the majority. . . .

And thus every man, by consenting with others to make one body politic under one government, puts himself under an obligation, to every one of that society, to submit to the determination of the majority, and to be concluded by it; or else this original compact, whereby he with others incorporate into one society, would signify nothing, and be no compact, if he be left free, and under no other ties than he was in before in the state of nature.

Chapter IX: Of the Ends of Political Society and Government

If man in the state of nature be so free, as has been said: if he be absolute lord of his own person and possessions, equal to the greatest, and subject to nobody, why will he part with his freedom? why will he give up his empire, and subject himself to the dominion and control of any other power? To which it is obvious to answer, that though in the state of nature he hath such a right, yet the enjoyment of it is very uncertain, and constantly exposed to the invasion of others; for all being kings as much as he, every man his equal, and the greater part no strict observers of equity and justice, the enjoyment of the property he has in this state is very unsafe, very unsecure. This makes him willing to quit a condition, which however free, is full of fears and continual dangers: and it is not without reason, that he seeks out, and is willing to join in society with others, who are already united, or have a mind to unite, for the mutual preservation of their lives, liberties, and estates, which I call by the general name, property.

The great and chief end, therefore, of men's uniting into commonwealths, and putting themselves under government, is the preservation of their property. To which in the state of nature there are many things wanting. . . .

Chapter XV: Of Despotical Power

Despotical power is an absolute, arbitrary power one man has over another, to take away his life whenever he pleases; and this is a power which neither Nature gives, for it has made no such distinction between one man and another, nor compact can convey. . . . For having quitted reason, which God has given to be the rule betwixt man and man, and the peaceable ways which that teaches, and made use of force to compass his unjust ends upon another where he has no right, he renders himself liable to be destroyed by his adversary whenever he can, as any other noxious and brutish creature that is destructive to his being. . . .

Chapter XIX: Of the Dissolution of Government

The reason why men enter into society, is the preservation of their property; and the end why they choose and authorize a legislative, is, that there may be laws made, and rules set, as guards and fences to the properties of all the members of the society: to limit the power, and moderate the dominion, of every part and member of the society: for since it can never be supposed to be the will of the society, that the legislative should have a power to destroy that which every one designs to secure by entering into society, and for which the people submitted themselves to legislators of their own making; whenever the legislators endeavour to take away and destroy the property of the people, or to reduce them to slavery under arbitrary power, they put themselves into a state of war with the people, who are thereupon absolved from any farther obedience, and are left to the common refuge, which God hath provided for all men, against force and violence. Whensoever therefore the legislative shall transgress this fundamental rule of society; and either by ambition, fear, folly or corruption, endeavour to grasp themselves, or put into the hands of any other, an absolute power over the lives, liberties, and estates of the people, by this breach of trust they forfeit the power the people had put into their hands for quite contrary ends, and it devolves to the people, who have a right to resume their original liberty, and, by the establishment of a new legislative, (such as they shall think fit) provide for their own safety and security, which is the end for which they are in society. What I have said here, concerning the legislative in general holds true also concerning the supreme executor, who having a double trust put in him, both to have a part in the legislative, and the supreme execution of the law, acts against both, when he goes about to set up his own arbitrary will as the law of the society. . . .

Whosoever uses force without right, as every one does in society, who does it without law, puts himself into a state of war with those against whom he so used it; and in that state all former ties are cancelled, all other rights cease, and every one has a right to defend himself, and to resist the aggressor.

The Spirit of the Laws (1748)

BARON DE MONTESQUIEU

When the legislative and executive powers are united in the same person, or in the same body of magistrates, there can be no liberty; because apprehensions may arise lest the same monarch or senate should enact tyrannical laws to execute them in a tyrannical manner.

Again there is no liberty if the power of judging be not separated from the legislative and executive powers. Were it joined with the legislature, the life and liberty of the subject would be exposed to arbitrary control; for the judge would be then the legislator. Were it joined to the executive power, the judge might behave with all the violence of an oppressor.

There would be an end of everything were the same man or the same body, whether of the nobles or of the people, to exercise those three

---

"The Spirit of the Laws" is from Baron de Montesquieu (Charles de Secondat), *The Spirit of the Laws*, 2 vols. (London, 1758), pp. 216–217.

powers, that of enacting the laws, that of executing the public resolutions, and that of judging the crimes or differences of individuals.

Most kingdoms of Europe enjoy a moderate government because the prince who is invested with the two first powers leaves the third to his subjects. In Turkey, where these three powers are united in the sultan's person, the subjects groan under the weight of the most frightful oppression.

In the republics of Italy, where these three powers are united, there is less liberty than in our monarchies. Hence their government is obliged to have recourse to as violent methods for its support as even that of the Turks; witness the state inquisitors (at Venice), and the lion's mouth into which every informer may at all hours throw his written accusations.

What a situation must the poor subjects be in, under those republics! The same body of magistrates are possessed, as executors of the laws, of the whole power they have given themselves in quality of legislators. They may plunder the state by their general determination, and as they have likewise the judiciary power in their hands, every private citizen may be ruined by their particular decisions.

The whole power is here united in one body; and though there is no external pomp that indicates a despotic sway, yet the people feel the effects of it every moment.

Hence it is that many of the princes of Europe, whose aim has been levelled at arbitrary power, have constantly set out with uniting in their own persons all the branches of magistracy, and all the great offices of the state.

The Social Contract (1762)

JEAN JACQUES ROUSSEAU

Of the Social Compact

We will suppose that men in a state of nature are arrived at that crisis when the strength of each individual is insufficient to defend him from the attacks he is subject to. This primitive state can therefore subsist no longer; and the human race must perish, unless they change their manner of life.

As men cannot create for themselves new forces, but merely unite and direct those which already exist, the only means they can employ for the preservation is to form by aggregation an assemblage of forces that may be able to resist all assaults, be put in motion as one body, and act in concert upon all occasions.

This assemblage of forces must be produced by the concurrence of many: as the force and the liberty of a man are the chief instruments of his

"The Social Contract" is from Jean Jacques Rousseau, *An Inquiry into the Nature of the Social Contract* (London, 1791), pp. 33–49.

Jean Jacques Rousseau brilliantly challenged the established thought of his day and even alienated several *philosophes*. He outlined a political structure that he hoped would nurture human virtue.

preservation, how can he engage them without danger, and without neglect the care which is due to himself? This doubt, which leads directly to my subject, may be expressed in these words:

Where shall we find a form of association which will defend and protect with the whole aggregate force the person and the property of each individual; and by which every person, while united with ALL, shall obey only HIMSELF, and remain as free as before the union? Such is the fundamental problem, of which the Social Contract gives the solution.

The articles of this contract are so unalterably fixed by the nature of the act, that the least modification renders them vain and of no effect. They are the same everywhere, and are everywhere understood and admitted, even though they may never have been formally announced: so that, when once the social pact is violated in any instance, all obligations it created cease; and each individual is restored to his original rights, and resumes native liberty, as the consequence of losing that conventional liberty for which he exchanged them.

All the articles of the social contract will, when clearly understood, be found reducible to this single point—THE TOTAL ALIENATION OF EACH ASSOCIATE, AND ALL HIS RIGHTS, TO THE WHOLE COMMUNITY. For every individual gives himself up entirely—the condition of every person is alike; and being so, it would not be the interest of anyone to render himself offensive to others.

Moreover, the alienation is made without any reserve; the union is as complete as it can be, and no associate has a claim to anything; for if any individual was to retain rights not enjoyed in general by all, as there would be no common superior to decide between him and the public, each person being in some points his own proper judge, would soon pretend to be so in everything; and thus would the state of nature be revived, and the association become tyrannical or be annihilated.

Finally, each person gives himself to ALL, but not to any INDIVIDUAL: and as there is no one associate over whom the same right is not acquired which is ceded to him by others, each gains an equivalent for what he loses, and finds his force increased for preserving that which he possesses.

If, therefore, we exclude from the social compact all that is not essentially necessary, we shall find it reduced to the following terms:

"We each of us place, in common, his person, and all his power, under the supreme direction of the general will; and we receive into the body each member as an indivisible part of the whole."

From that moment, instead of so many separate persons as there are contractors, this act of association produces a moral collective body, composed of as many members as there are voices in the assembly; which from this act receives its unity, its common self, its life, and its will. This public person, which is thus formed by the union of all the private persons, took formerly the name of *city*, and now takes that of *republic* or *body politic*. It is called by its members *state* when it is passive, and *sovereign* when in activity: and whenever it is spoken of with other bodies of a similar kind, it is denominated *power*. The associates take collectively the name of *people*, and separately that *citizens*, as participating in the sovereign authority: they are also styled *subjects*, because they are subjected to the laws. But these terms are frequently confounded, and used one for the other; and a man must understand them well to distinguish when they are properly employed.

Of the Sovereign Power

It appears from this form that the act of association contains a reciprocal engagement between the public and individuals; and that each individual contracting as it were with himself, is engaged under a double character that is, as a part of the *sovereign power* engaging with individuals, and as a member of the *state* entering into a compact with the *sovereign power*. But we cannot apply here the maxim of civil right, that no person is bound by any engagement which he makes with himself; for there is a material difference between an obligation contracted towards *one's self* individually, and towards a collective body of *which one's self* constitutes a part.

It is necessary to observe here that the will of the public, expressed by a majority of votes—which can enforce obedience from the subjects to the sovereign power in consequence of the double character under which the members of that body appear—cannot bind the sovereign power to itself; and that it is against the nature of the body politic for the sovereign power to impose any one law which it cannot alter. Were they to consider themselves as acting under one character only, they would be in the situation of individuals forming each a contract with himself: but this is not the case; and therefore there can be no fundamental obligatory law established for the body of the people, not even the social contract. But this is of little moment, as that body could not very well engage itself to others in any manner which would not derogate from the contract. With respect to foreigners, it becomes a single being, an individual only.

But the body politic, or sovereign power, which derives its existence from the sacredness of the contract, can never bind itself, even towards others, in any thing that would derogate from the original act; such as alienating any portion of itself, or submitting to another sovereign; for by violating the contract its own existence would be at once annihilated, and by nothing nothing can be performed.

As soon as the multitude is thus united in one body, you cannot offend one of its members without attacking the whole; much less can you offend the whole without incurring the resentment of all the members. Thus duty and interest equally oblige the two contracting parties to lend their mutual aid to each other; and the same men must endeavour to unite under this double character all the advantages which attend it.

The sovereign power being formed only of the individuals which compose it, neither has, or can have, any interest contrary to theirs; consequently the sovereign power requires no guarantee towards its subjects, because it is impossible that the body should seek to injure all its members: and shall see presently that it can do no injury to any individual. The sovereign power by its nature must, while it exists, be everything it ought to be: it is not so with subjects towards the sovereign power; to which, notwithstanding the common interest subsisting between them, there is nothing to answer for the performance of their engagements, if some means is not found of ensuring their fidelity.

In fact, each individual may, as a man, have a private will, dissimilar contrary to the general will which he has as a citizen. His own particular interest may dictate to him very differently from the common interest; his mind, naturally and absolutely independent, may regard what he owes to the common cause as a gratuitous contribution, the omission of which would be less injurious to others than the payment would be burdensome to himself; and considering the moral person which constitutes the state as a creature of the imagination, because it is not a man, he may wish to enjoy the rights of a citizen, without being disposed to fulfill the duties of a subject: an injustice which would in its progress cause the ruin of the body politic.

In order therefore to prevent the social compact from becoming an empty formula, it tacitly includes this premise, which alone can give effect to the others—That whoever refuses to obey the general will, shall be compelled to it by the whole body, which is in fact only forcing him to be free; for this is the condition which guarantees his absolute personal independence to every citizen of the country: a condition which gives motion and effect to the political machine; which alone renders all civil engagements legal; and without which they would be absurd, tyrannical, and subject to the most enormous abuses.

Of the State

The passing from a state of nature to a civil state, produces in man a very remarkable change, by substituting justice for instinct, and giving to his actions a moral character which they wanted before.

It is at the moment of that transition that the voice of duty succeeds to physical impulse; and a sense of what is right, to the incitements of appetite. The man who had till then regarded none but himself, perceives that he must act on other principles, and learns to consult his reason before he listens to his propensities.

The Social Framework

Jean Jacques Rousseau's radical stance on nature and the establishment of the civil state was viewed as dangerous by many philosophes. *Voltaire, in a horrified state of mind, wrote to him: "Never has anyone employed so much genius to make us into beasts. When one reads your book, one is seized at once with a desire to go down on all fours." Indeed, under Rousseau, the social contract theory was limited in its application. Both Thomas Hobbes and John Locke advocated a government predicated on equality of human rights. Although Rousseau never mentioned women in his treatise* The Social Contract, *his many other works defined more exactly the particular role he assigned them in society. Rousseau's woman knew her place. He urged that women be "trained to bear the yoke from the first, so that they may not feel it." The first selection is from* Emile (1762), *his treatise on education.*

The events of 1789 were to bring into focus many of the philosophical arguments concerning natural rights presented in the previous section. But the emphasis was on the rights of male citizens. Many accepted the views of Rousseau that women were not rational creatures and lacked the capacity for understanding the abstract tenets of the Enlightenment. Mary Wollstonecraft, an English writer and early disciple of Rousseau's political views, nevertheless took him to task in the second selection. In her work A Vindication of the

Rights of Women *(1792), she extended the call for political liberty into the social realm. Her arguments gave justification to a different kind of revolution between the sexes.*

Woman: "Especially Constituted to Please Man"

JEAN JACQUES ROUSSEAU

A perfect man and a perfect woman ought no more to resemble each other in mind than in features. . . . In the union of the sexes each contributes equally toward the common end, but not in the same way. Hence arises the first assignable difference among their moral relations. One must be active and strong, the other passive and weak. One must needs have power and will, while it suffices that the other have little power of resistance.

This principle once established, it follows that woman is especially constituted to please man. If man ought to please her in turn, the necessity for it is less direct. His merit lies in his power; he pleases simply because he is strong. I grant that this is not the law of love, but it is the law of Nature, which is anterior even to love. . . .

The moment it is demonstrated that man and woman are not and ought not to be constituted in the same way, either in character or in constitution, it follows that they ought not to have the same education. In following the directions of Nature they ought to act in concert, but they ought not to do the same things; their duties have a common end, but the duties themselves are different, and consequently the tastes which direct them. After having tried to form the natural man, let us also see, in order not to leave our work incomplete, how the woman is to be formed who is befitting to this man. . . .

Woman is worth more as a woman, but less as a man; wherever she improves her rights she has the advantage, and wherever she attempts to usurp ours she remains inferior to us. Only exceptional cases can be urged against this general truth—the usual mode of argument adopted by the gallant partisans of the fair sex. . . .

Does it follow that she ought to be brought up in complete ignorance, and restricted solely to the duties of the household? . . . No, doubtless. . . . They ought to learn multitudes of things, but only those which it becomes them to know. . . . The whole education of women ought to be relative to men. To please them, to be useful to them, to make themselves loved and honored by them, to educate them when young, to care for them when grown, to counsel them, to console them, and to make life agreeable and sweet to them—these are the duties of women at all times, and what should be taught them from their infancy. . . .

The search for abstract and speculative truths, principles, and scientific axioms, whatever tends to generalize ideas, does not fall within the compass

"Woman: 'Especially Constituted to Please Man' " is from W. H. Payne, ed., *Rousseau's Emile* (New York: D. Appleton and Co., 1895), pp. 260–263, 281, 303.

of women; all their studies ought to have reference to the practical; it is for them to make the application of the principles which man has discovered. . . . She must therefore make a profound study of the mind of man, not the mind of man in general, through abstraction, but the mind of the men who surround her, the mind of the men to whom she is subject, either by law or by opinion. She must learn to penetrate their feelings through their conversation, their actions, their looks, and their gestures. Through her conversations, her actions, her looks, and her gestures she must know how to give them the feelings which are pleasing to her, without even seeming to think of them. . . .

A woman of wit is the scourge of her husband, her children, her friends, her servants, of everybody. . . . If all the men in the world were sensible, every girl of letters would remain unmarried all her life.

A Vindication of the Rights of Women (1792)

MARY WOLLSTONECRAFT

But what have women to do in society? . . . Women might certainly study the art of healing, and be physicians as well as nurses. . . . They might also study politics, and settle their benevolence on the broadest basis. . . . Business of various kinds, they might likewise pursue, if they were educated in a more orderly manner, which might save many from common and legal prostitution. Women would not then marry for a support . . . nor would an attempt to earn their own subsistence . . . sink them almost to the level of those poor abandoned creatures who live by prostitution. . . . The few employments open to women, so far from being liberal, are menial; and when a superior education enables them to take charge of the education of children as governesses, they are not treated like the tutors of sons. . . . But as women educated like gentlewomen, are never designed for the humiliating situation which necessity sometimes forces them to fill; these situations are considered in the light of a degradation; and they know little of the human heart, who need to be told, that nothing so painfully sharpens sensibility as such a fall in life.

How many women thus waste life away the prey of discontent, who might have practised as physicians, regulated a farm, managed a shop, and stood erect, supported by their own industry, instead of hanging their heads surcharged with the dew of sensibility, that consumes the beauty to which it at first gave lustre; nay, I . . . have seldom seen much compassion excited by the helplessness of females unless they were fair; then, perhaps pity was the soft handmaid of love, or the harbinger of lust. How much more respectable is the woman who earns her own bread by fulfilling any duty, than the most accomplished beauty!

"A Vindication of the Rights of Women" is from Mary Wollstonecraft, *A Vindication of the Rights of Women*, 2nd ed. (London: J. Johnson, 1792), chapter 9.

Proud of their weakness, however, [some women believe] they must always be protected, guarded from care, and all the rough toils that dignify the mind. If this be the fiat of fate, if they will make themselves insignificant and contemptible, sweetly to waste "life away," let them not expect to be valued when their beauty fades, for it is the fate of the fairest flowers to be admired and pulled to pieces by the careless hand that plucked them. In how many ways do I wish, from the purest benevolence, to impress this truth on my sex; yet I fear that they will not listen to a truth that dear bought experience has brought home to many an agitated bosom, nor willingly resign the privileges of rank and sex for the privileges of humanity, to which those have no claim who do not discharge its duties. . . .

Would men but generously snap our chains, and be content with rational fellowship instead of slavish obedience, they would find us more observant daughters, more affectionate sisters, more faithful wives, more reasonable mothers—in a word, better citizens. We should then love them with true affection, because we should learn to respect ourselves; and the peace of mind of a worthy man would not be interrupted by the idle vanity of his wife, nor the babes sent to nestle in a strange bosom, having never found a home in their mother's. . . .

It is time to effect a revolution in female manners—time to restore to them, as a part of the human species, labour by reforming themselves to reform the world. It is time to separate unchangeable morals from local manners. . . .

I wish to sum up what I have said in a few words, for I here throw down my gauntlet, and deny the existence of sexual virtues, not excepting modesty. For man and woman, truth, if I understand the meaning of the word, must be the same; yet the fanciful female character, so prettily drawn by poets an novelists, demanding the sacrifice of truth and sincerity, virtue becomes a relative idea, having no other foundation than utility, and of that utility men pretend arbitrarily to judge, shaping it to their own convenience.

Women, I allow, may have different duties to fulfill; but they are *human* duties, and the principles that should regulate the discharge of them, I sturdily maintain, must be the same.

To become respectable, the exercise of their understanding is necessary, there is no other foundation for independence of character; I mean explicitly to say that they must only bow to the authority of reason, instead of being the modest slaves of opinion.

In the superior ranks of life how seldom do we meet with a man of superior abilities, or even common acquirements? The reason appears to me clear: the state they are born in was an unnatural one. The human character has ever been formed by the employments the individual or class pursues; and if the faculties are not sharpened by necessity, they must remain obtuse. The argument may fairly be extended to women; for, seldom occupied by serious business, the pursuit of pleasure gives that insignificancy to their character which renders the society of the *great* so insipid. . . . Such are the blessings of civil governments, as they are at present organized, that wealth and female softness equally tend to debase mankind, and are produced by the same cause; but allowing women to be rational creatures, they should be incited to acquire virtues which they may call their own, for how can a rational being be ennobled by anything that is not obtained by its *own* exertions? . . .

There must be more equality established in society, or morality will never gain ground, and this virtuous equality will not rest firmly even when founded on a rock, if one half of mankind be chained to its bottom by fate, for they will be continually undermining it through ignorance or pride.

Conditions of Society on the Eve of Revolution

France was composed of three main classes, which were divided on the basis of occupation and ancient privilege. The First Estate consisted of the clergy, the Second Estate of the nobility, and the Third Estate of everyone else. Within the estates themselves there were also social divisions. The following selections relate many of the problems and criticisms of the time.

The Nobility

Corruption of the French Court

MARQUIS D'ARGENSON

Marquis d'Argenson was minister of foreign affairs under Louis XV. He claimed he "loved both royalty and the people."

The court! The court! In that single word lies all the nation's misfortune. . . . It is the court that corrupts the morals of the nation by its luxury, its extravagance, its artificial manners, its ignorance, and its intrigue in place of emulation. All places, positions, and grades in the army go to the courtiers through favoritism; hence there is no longer any attempt to rise by merit.

In the finances everything is sold; all the money of the provinces goes

"Corruption of the French Court" is from E. L. Higgins, ed., *The French Revolution as Told by Contemporaries* (Boston: Houghton Mifflin, 1966), p. 10. Copyright © 1938, renewed 1966 by Houghton Mifflin Company. Used by permission of the publisher.

to Paris never to return; all the people go there to make fortunes by intrigue . . . .

Justice cannot be administered with integrity; the judges fear the grandees, and base their hopes only upon favor. In short, the king no longer reigns, and disregards even the virtues that he has.

Those are the fruits of the establishment by Louis XIV of a capital at Versailles expressly for the court. He was still powerful and gave authority to his ministers. But these are not supported under Louis XV, who distrusts them and prefers his courtiers and favorites. There is, as a result, anarchy and an oligarchy of satraps. Favor means influence, and the possession of favor is more important than the rights of authority.

"Ancient Oaks Mutilated by Time"

MARQUIS DE BOUILLE

Marquis de Bouille was a noble, general, governor, and trusted advisor to Louis XVI.

The nobility had undergone still greater changes; it had lost, not only its ancient splendor, but almost its existence, and had entirely decayed. There had been in France nearly eighty thousand noble families. . . . Included in this numerous nobility were about a thousand families whose origin dated from the earliest times of the monarchy. Among these there were scarcely two or three hundred who had escaped poverty and misfortune. There could still be found at court a few great names which brought to mind the noted personages who had made them illustrious, but which too often were brought into disrepute by the vices of those who had inherited them. There were a few families in the provinces who had continued to exist and command respect. . . . The remainder of this ancient nobility languished in poverty, and resembled those ancient oaks mutilated by time, where nothing remains except the ravaged trunks. No longer convoked either for military service or for the provincial or national assemblies, they had lost their ancient hierarchy. If honorary titles remained to some illustrious or ancient families, they were also held by a multitude of newly created nobles who had acquired by their riches the right to assume them arbitrarily. . . . The nobility, in short, were not distinguishable from the other classes of citizens, except by the arbitrary favors of the court, and by the exemptions from imposts, less useful to them than onerous to the state and shocking to the people. They had conserved nothing of their ancient dignity and consideration; they retained only the hate and jealousy of the plebeians. Such was the situation of the nobility of the kingdom.

The Indifferent Nobility

COMPTE DE SÉGUR

Compte de Ségur was a liberal noble in favor at Louis XVI's court, a diplomatist, and a historian.

The heads of the old noble families, believing themselves as unshakable as the monarchy, slept without fear upon a volcano. The exercise of their charges; royal promotions, favors, or rebuffs; and the nomination or dismissal of ministers, were the sole objects of their attention, the motives of their movements, and the subjects of their conversations. Indifferent to the real affairs of state as to their own they allowed themselves to be governed, some by the intendants of the provinces, others by their own intendants; but they regarded with a chagrined and scornful eye the changes in costumes which were being introduced, the abandonment of liveries, the vogue of dress-coats and English styles.

The Superficial Education of the Nobility

MME. DE STAËL

Mme de Staël was an author and a liberal member of the nobility.

The great nobles in France were not very well informed, because they had nothing to gain by being so. Grace in conversation, which would please at court, was the surest means of arriving at honors. This superficial education was one cause of the downfall of the nobles: they could no longer fight against the intelligence of the third estate; they should have tried to surpass it. The great lords would have by degrees gained supremacy in the primary assemblies through their knowledge of administration, as formerly they had acquired it by their swords; and the public mind would have been prepared for the establishment of free institutions in France.

The Clergy

"Luxury, Debauchery, and Lavish Expenditure"
MARQUIS DE FERRIERÈS

Marquis de Ferrierès was a conservative noble, yet still a severe critic of the monarchy, the nobility, and revolutionaries.

There were dioceses which contained fifteen hundred square leagues, and others which contained only twenty; parishes which were ten leagues in circumference, and others which had scarcely fifteen families. Among the priests there were some whose allowances scarcely reached seven hundred livres; while in their neighborhood were benefices of ten and twelve thousand livres income, possessed of ecclesiastics who performed no function in the cult and who, residing elsewhere, carried away the revenue of these benefices, dissipating it in luxury, debauchery, and lavish expenditure. . . . Inasmuch as the appointment of bishops had been concentrated in the hands of the king, or rather in the hands of the ministers, too often the choice fell, not upon him who possessed the most apostolic virtues, but upon him whose family enjoyed the greatest influence. What evils have not resulted from this! Most of the bishops, incapable of fulfilling their duties, entered upon them with insuperable distaste. This distaste extended even to the places where they were to exercise their functions, and had become so general that the small number of prelates who remained were cited as models. The same abuses reigned in the selection of the grand vicars: all thought more of soliciting favors than of deserving them. Totally abandoned by those who were supposed to administer them, the dioceses remained in the hands of obscure secretaries.

The Peasantry

Beggars, Rags, and Misery
ARTHUR YOUNG

Arthur Young was an English writer on agricultural subjects who traveled through France before and during the revolution.

1787

The same wretched country continues to La Loge; the fields are scenes of pitiable management, as the houses are of misery. Yet all this country is

"Luxury, Debauchery, and Lavish Expenditure" is from E. L. Higgins, ed., *The French Revolution as Told by Contemporaries* (Boston: Houghton Mifflin, 1966), pp. 15–16. Copyright © 1938, renewed 1966 by Houghton Mifflin Company. Used by permission of the publisher.

"Beggars, Rags, and Misery" is from Arthur Young, *Travels in France during the Years 1781, 1788, 1789*, 3rd ed. (London: George Bell and Sons, 1889), pp. 19, 27.

highly improveable, if they knew what to do with it: the property, perhaps, of some of those glittering beings, who figured in the procession the other day at Versailles. Heaven grant me patience while I see a country thus neglected—and forgive me the oaths I swear at the absence and ignorance of the possessors. . . .

Pass Payrac, and meet many beggars, which we had not done before. All the country, girls and women, are without shoes or stockings; and the ploughmen at their work have neither sabots nor feet to their stockings. This is a poverty, that strikes at the root of national prosperity; a large consumption among the poor being of more consequence than among the rich the wealth of a nation lies in its circulation and consumption; and the case of poor people abstaining from the use of manufacturers of leather and wool ought to be considered as an evil of the first magnitude. It reminded me of the misery of Ireland.

1788

To Montauban. The poor people seem poor indeed; the children terribly ragged, if possible worse clad than if with no cloaths at all; as to shoes and stockings they are luxuries. A beautiful girl of six or seven years playing with a stick, and smiling under such a bundle of rags as made my heart ache to see her: they did not beg and when I gave them any thing seemed more surprized than obliged. One third of what I have seen of this province seems uncultivated, and nearly all of it in misery. What have kings, and ministers, and parliaments, and states, to answer for their prejudices, seeing millions of hands that would be industrious, idle and starving, through the execrable maxims of despotism, or the equally detestable prejudices of a feudal nobility. . . .

The Outbreak of Revolution (1789–1791)

Influence from Abroad

"A Philosophical Wind Is Blowing from England"
MARQUIS D'ARGENSON

In 1688, England was in the midst of political turmoil. The monarch, James II, had sought absolute control over the affairs of his realm, and Parliament reacted by deposing him. The monarchy was not eliminated, but Parliament took a more assertive role in the governance of the state. John Locke's Second Treatise on Government *(1690) was a reaction to and a commentary on these dynamic events. The "spirit of revolt" was spreading to Europe, as the following excerpts indicate. The first is from the* Memoirs *of Marquis d'Argenson (1694–1757), minister of foreign affairs under the French king Louis XV. The second offers commentary from a conservative Paris newspaper, dated June 12, 1778.*

A philosophical wind is blowing from England; one hears the murmur of the words *liberty* and *republicanism*; they are already in people's minds, and we know how public opinion rules the world. The times of adoration have passed; the name of master, so dear to our ancestors, sounds unpleasant to our ears. For all one knows, there is a new conception of government in certain heads that will emerge in battle array at the first occasion. Perhaps the revolution will be accomplished with less opposition than one thinks; there will be no need of princes of the blood, great lords, or religious fanaticism; all will be accomplished by acclamation, as in the election of popes at times. Today all classes are discontented: the military disbanded by the peace; the clergy offended in its privileges; the *parlements*, corporate bodies, provincial governments, debased in their functions; the lower classes crushed by taxes, and racked by misery; the financiers alone triumphant and reviving the reign of the Jews. Combustible matters everywhere. A riot might become a revolt, and a revolt a complete revolution; bringing real tribunes of the people, consuls, and commissaries; and depriving the king and his ministers of their excessive power for harm.

"The Origin of the Evil" (1778)

The origin of the evil must be looked for in the spirit of revolt and irreligion caused by the flood of infamous writings which circulate not only in the upper classes, but descend today even to the dwellings of the people.

From top to bottom of the social body, in the palace as in the cottage, imbecile ragamuffins, whom a wise government would do well to have whipped in the public square, set themselves up for philosophers and cultivate blasphemy. . . .

Elsewhere a flock of peddlers, unwatched by the police, disseminate in the country districts the infectious writings of Voltaire, of the materialist Diderot, of the dangerous misanthrope of Geneva [Rousseau], and those of Helvetius, the most fanatical of the unbelievers and the most ignoble apostle of pleasure.

All these books do not preach the disdain of religion and of right customs alone; they preach revolt against the royal authority and sap the base of all the conservative principles of the state.

The Domestic Crisis

"What Is the Third Estate?" (January 1789)

THE ABBÉ SIEYÈS

By August 1788, Louis XVI had decided to summon the Estates-General, a convocation of the three estates which had not met since 1614, in order to solve the government's financial problems. Louis was in debt and he wanted the Estates-General to raise new taxes. This pamphlet by the Abbé Sieyès (1748– 1836) was issued in January 1789, before the Estates-General met. It was intended to unite the various interests within the Third Estate toward a common cause: reform of the unequal voting procedure that gave advantage to the first two estates.

What Does the Third Estate Demand? To Become Something

The true petitions of this order may be appreciated only through the authentic claims directed to the government by the large municipalities of the kingdom. What is indicated therein? That the people wishes to be *something*, and, in truth, the very least that is possible. It wishes to have real representatives in the Estates General, that is to say, deputies *drawn from its order*, who are competent to be interpreters of its will and defenders of its interests. But what will it avail it to be present at the Estates General if the predominating interest there is contrary to its own! Its presence would only consecrate the oppression of which it would be the external victim. Thus, it is indeed certain that it cannot come to vote at the Estates General unless it is to have in that body *an influence at least equal to that of the privileged classes*; and it demands a number of representatives equal to that of the first two orders together. Finally, this equality of representation would become completely illusory if every chamber voted separately. The third estate demands, then, that votes be taken *by head and not by order*. This is the essence of those claims so alarming to the privileged classes, because they believed that thereby the reform of abuses would become inevitable. The real intention of the third estate is to have an influence in the Estates General equal to that of the privileged classes. I repeat, can it ask less?

What Remains to Be Done: Development of Some Principles

The time is past when the three orders, thinking only of defending themselves from ministerial despotism, were ready to unite against the common enemy. . . .

• • •

The third estate awaits, to no purpose, the meeting of all classes, the restitution of its political rights, and the plenitude of its civil rights; the fear of seeing abuses reformed alarms the first two orders far more than the desire for liberty inspires them. Between liberty and some odious privileges, they have chosen the latter. Their soul is identified with the favors of servitude. Today they dread this Estates General which but lately they invoked so ardently. All is well with them; they no longer complain, except of the spirit of innovation. They no longer lack anything; fear has given them a constitution.

The third estate must perceive in the trend of opinions and circumstances that it can hope for nothing except from its own enlightenment and courage. Reason and justice are in its favor; . . . there is no longer time to work for the conciliation of parties. What accord can be anticipated between the energy of the oppressed and the rage of the oppressors?

They have dared pronounce the word secession. They have menaced the King and the people. Well! Good God! How fortunate for the nation if this desirable secession might be made permanently! How easy it would be to dispense with the privileged classes! How difficult to induce them to be citizens!

• • •

In vain would they close their eyes to the revolution which time and force of circumstances have effected; it is none the less real. Formerly the third estate was serf, the noble order everything. Today the third estate is everything, the nobility but a word. . . .

In such a state of affairs, what must the third estate do if it wishes to gain possession of its political rights in a manner beneficial to the nation? There are two ways of attaining this objective. In following the first, the third estate must assemble apart: it will not meet with the nobility and the clergy at all; it will not remain with them, either by *order* or by *head*. I pray that they will keep in mind the enormous difference between the assembly of the third estate and that of the other two orders. The first represents 25,000,000 men, and deliberates concerning the interests of the nation. The two others, were they to unite, have the powers of only about 200,000 individuals, and think only of their privileges. The third estate alone, they say, cannot constitute the *Estates General*. Well! So much the better! It will form a *National Assembly*.

Women of the Third Estate (January 1789)

Juxtaposed with the famous document just presented is the little-known petition from the women of the Third Estate. The petitioners were women of humble orgin who sought not political equality, but dignity and the opportunity to

"Women of the Third Estate" is from Darline Gay Levy et al., eds., *Women in Revolutionary Paris 1789–1795* (Urbana: University of Illinois Press, 1979), pp. 18–20. Copyright © 1979 by the Board of Trustees of the University of Illinois. Reprinted by permission of the publisher.

improve themselves. It is important to note that they did not conceive of themselves as part of the political process but appealed directly to the king to improve the conditions of their lives.

Sire,

At a time when the various orders of the state are busy with their interests, when everyone is trying to assert his titles and his rights, when some people are worrying about recalling centuries of servitude and anarchy, when others are making every effort to shake off the last links which still bind them to the imperious remains of the feudal system, women— continual objects of the admiration and scorn of men—women, wouldn't it be possible for them also to make their voice heard amidst this general agitation?

Excluded from the national assemblies by laws too well consolidated for them to hope to break, they do not ask, Sire, for your permission to send their deputies to the Estates General. . . . We prefer, Sire, to place our cause at your feet; not wishing to obtain anything except from your heart, we address our complaints and confide our miseries to it.

The women of the Third Estate are almost all born without fortune; their education is very neglected or very defective. . . . If nature has refused them beauty, they get married without dowry to unfortunate artisans, lead aimless, difficult lives stuck away in the provinces, and give birth to children they are incapable of raising. If, on the contrary, they are born pretty, without culture, without principles, without any idea of morals, they become the prey of the first seducer, commit a first sin, come to Paris to bury their shame, end by losing it altogether, and die victims of licentious ways. . . .

Also, several, solely because they are born girls, are disdained by their parents, who refuse to set them up, preferring to concentrate their fortune on the head of a son whom they designate to carry on their name in the capital; for it is good that Your Majesty understands that we also have names to keep up. Or, if old age finds them spinsters, they spend it in tears and see themselves the object of the scorn of their nearest relatives. . . .

We ask to be enlightened, to have work, not in order to usurp men's authority, but in order to be better esteemed by them, so that we might have the means of living out of the way of misfortune and so that poverty does not force the weakest among us . . . to join the crowd of unfortunate beings who overpopulate the streets and whose debauched audacity is a disgrace to our sex and to the men who keep them company. . . .

We implore you, Sire, to set up free schools where we could learn our language on the basis of principles and religion and ethics. . . .

We ask to come out of the state of ignorance, to be able to give our children a sound and reasonable education so as to make of them subjects worthy of serving you. We will teach them to cherish the beautiful name of Frenchmen [and] we will transmit to them the love we have for Your Majesty.

The Tennis Court Oath (June 20, 1789)

From the outset, the Estates-General was hampered by organizational disputes. After several weeks of frustration, the Third Estate invited the clergy and nobility to join them in organizing a new legislative body. Only a few of the lower clergy accepted, but the National Assembly was thus formed on June 17, 1789. Three days later they were accidently locked out of their usual meeting place, and they marched to a nearby tennis court, where they took an oath to draft a new constitution for France. This is one of the most important documents of the revolution. The oath was taken orally and individually with but one vote in dissension. The president of the National Assembly was barely able to save the dissenter from bodily harm.

The National Assembly, considering that it has been summoned to establish the constitution of the kingdom, to effect the regeneration of public order, and to maintain the true principles of monarchy; that nothing can prevent it from continuing its deliberations in whatever place it may be forced to establish itself; and, finally, that wheresoever its members are assembled, *there* is the National Assembly;

Decrees that all members of this Assembly shall immediately take a solemn oath not to separate, and to reassemble wherever circumstances require, until the constitution of the kingdom is established and consolidated upon firm foundations; and that, the said oath taken, all members and each one of them individually shall ratify this steadfast resolution by signature.

The Fall of the Bastille (July 14, 1789)

The Bastille was a fortress built to protect the eastern gates of Paris. It had also been used as a prison for political offenders of the Old Regime. Hence, it served as a symbol of monarchical despotism. On July 14, 1789, a mob, irritated at the dismissal of a popular minister of the king, paraded through the streets of Paris, searching for arms and clashing with the military. They stormed the Bastille and slaughtered many of its small garrison. Although this act yielded few political prisoners of the king, the event would provide a catalyst to the revolution and is commemorated today in France with special reverence. Louis XVI, however, did not view it with such import. The entry in his diary for July 14, 1789, was "rien" (nothing), signifying that he failed to kill any game in his hunt that day. The following accounts of the fall of the Bastille are drawn from various witnesses and contemporaries of the event.

"The Tennis Court Oath" is reprinted with permission of Macmillan Publishing Company from *A Documentary Survey of the French Revolution*, edited by John Hall Stewart, p. 88. Copyright 1951 by Macmillan Publishing Company, renewed 1979 by John Hall Stewart.

"The Fall of the Bastille" is from E. L. Higgins, ed., *The French Revolution as Told by Contemporaries* (Boston: Houghton Mifflin, 1966), pp. 98–100. Copyright © 1938, renewed 1966 by Houghton Mifflin Company. Used by permission of the publisher.

The Oath of the Tennis Court by Jacques Louis David. Having pledged their cooperation in the establishment of the National Assembly, members from the different estates took the famous oath to write a new constitution for France. (*Giraudon/Art Resource, NY*)

The Surrender

It was then that M. de Launay [commander of the forces of the Bastille] asked the garrison what course should be followed, that he saw no other than to blow himself up rather than to expose himself to having his throat cut by the people, from the fury of which they could not escape; that they must remount the towers, continue to fight, and blow themselves up rather than surrender.

The soldiers replied that it was impossible to fight any longer, that they would resign themselves to everything rather than destroy such a great number of citizens, that it was best to put the drummer on the towers to beat the recall, hoist a white flag, and capitulate. The governor, having no flag, gave them a white handkerchief. An officer wrote out the capitulation and passed it through the hole, saying that they desired to render themselves and lay down their arms, on condition of a promise not to massacre the troop; there was a cry of, "Lower your bridge; nothing will happen to you!"

• • •

The little drawbridge of the fort being first opened, Elie [one of the leaders of the attacking force] entered with his companions, all brave and honorable men, and fully determined to keep his word. On seeing him the governor went up to him, embraced him, and presented him with his sword, with the keys of the Bastille.

"I refused his sword," said Elie to me, "and took only the keys." His companions received the staff and the officers of the garrison with the same cordiality, swearing to serve them as guard and defense; but they swore in vain.

As soon as the great bridge was let down (and it is not known by what hand that was done) the people rushed into the court of the castle and, full of fury, seized on the troop of Invalides. Elie and the honest men who had entered with him exerted all their efforts to tear from the hands of the people the victims which they themselves had delivered to it. Ferocity held obstinately attached to its prey. Several of these soldiers, whose lives had been promised them, were assassinated; others were dragged like slaves through the street of Paris. Twenty-two were brought to the Grève, and, after humiliations and inhuman treatment, they had the affliction of seeing two of their comrades hanged. When they were presented at the Hotel de Ville, a furious madman said to them: "You deserve to be hanged; and you shall be so presently." De Launay, torn from the arms of those who wished to save him, had his head cut off under the walls of the Hotel de Ville. In the midst of his assassins, he defended his life with the courage of despair; but he fell under their number. De Losme-Salbray, his major, was murdered in the same manner. The adjutant, Mirai, had been so, near the Bastille. Pernon, an old lieutenant of the Invalides, was assassinated on the wharf Saint-Paul, as he was going to the hall. Another lieutenant, Caron, was covered with wounds. The head of the Marquis de Launay was carried about Paris by this same populace that he would have crushed had he not been moved to pity. Such were the exploits of those who have since been called the heroes and conquerors of the Bastille.

The King Informed of the Fall of the Bastille

When M. de Liancourt had made known to the king the total defection of his guards, the taking of the Bastille, the massacres that had taken place, the rising of two hundred thousand men, after a few moments' silence the king said, "It is then a revolt." "No, Sire," replied the duke. "It is a revolution."

Declaration of the Rights of Man (August 27, 1789)

The Declaration of the Rights of Man, issued by the National Assembly on August 27, 1789, served as a preamble to the French constitution, which was as yet unwritten. Its articles detail abuses of the Old Regime and was imitative of American bills of rights that had been attached to state constitutions. The declaration in turn influenced several European constitutions in the nineteenth century.

The representatives of the French people, organized as a National Assembly, believing that the ignorance, neglect, or contempt of the rights of man are the sole causes of public calamities and of the corruption of governments, have determined to set forth in a solemn declaration the natural, inalienable, and sacred rights of man, in order that this declaration, being constantly before all the members of the social body, shall remind them continually of their rights and duties; in order that the acts of the legislative power, as well as those of the executive power, may be compared at any moment with the objects and purposes of all political institutions and may thus be more respected; and, lastly, in order that the grievances of the citizens, based hereafter upon simple and incontestable principles, shall tend to the maintenance of the constitution and redound to the happiness of all. Therefore the National Assembly recognizes and proclaims, in the presence and under the auspices of the Supreme Being, the following rights of man and of the citizen:

Article 1. Men are born and remain free and equal in rights. Social distinctions may be founded only upon the general good.

"Declaration of the Rights of Man" is from James H. Robinson and Charles A. Beard, eds., *Readings in Modern European History*, vol. 1 (Boston: Ginn and Company, 1908), pp. 260–262.

2. The aim of all political association is the preservation of the natural and imprescriptible rights of man. These rights are liberty, property, security, and resistance to oppression.

3. The principle of all sovereignty resides essentially in the nation. No body nor individual may exercise any authority which does not proceed directly from the nation.

4. Liberty consists in the freedom to do everything which injures no one else; hence the exercise of the natural rights of each man has no limits except those which assure to the other members of the society the enjoyment of the same rights. These limits can only be determined by law.

5. Law can only prohibit such actions as are hurtful to society. Nothing may be prevented which is not forbidden by law, and no one may be forced to do anything not provided for by law.

6. Law is the expression of the general will. Every citizen has a right to participate personally, or through his representative, in its formation. It must be the same for all, whether it protects or punishes. All citizens, being equal in the eyes of the law, are equally eligible to all dignities and to all public positions and occupations, according to their abilities, and without distinction except that of their virtues and talents.

7. No person shall be accused, arrested, or imprisoned, except in the cases and according to the forms prescribed by law. Any one soliciting, transmitting, executing, or causing to be executed, any arbitrary order, shall be punished. But any citizen summoned or arrested in virtue of the law shall submit without delay, as resistance constitutes an offense.

8. The law shall provide for such punishments only as are strictly and obviously necessary, and no one shall suffer punishment except it be legally inflicted in virtue of a law passed and promulgated before the commission of the offense.

9. As all persons are held innocent until they shall have been declared guilty, if arrest shall be deemed indispensable, all harshness not essential to the securing of the prisoner's person shall be severely repressed by law.

10. No one shall be disquieted on account of his opinions, including his religious views, provided their manifestation does not disturb the public order established by law.

11. The free communication of ideas and opinions is one of the most precious of the rights of man. Every citizen may, accordingly, speak, write, and print with freedom, but shall be responsible for such abuses of this freedom as shall be defined by law.

12. The security of the rights of man and of the citizen requires public military forces. These forces are, therefore, established for the good of all and not for the personal advantage of those to whom they shall be entrusted.

13. A common contribution is essential for the maintenance of the public forces and for the cost of administration. This should be equitably distributed among all the citizens in proportion to their means.

14. All the citizens have a right to decide, either personally or by their representatives, as to the necessity of the public contribution; to grant this freely; to know to what uses it is put; and to fix the proportion, the mode of assessment and of collection and the duration of the taxes.

15. Society has the right to require of every public agent an account of his administration.

16. A society in which the observance of the law is not assured, nor the separation of powers defined, has no constitution at all.

17. Since property is an inviolable and sacred right, no one shall be deprived thereof except where public necessity, legally determined, shall clearly demand it, and then only on condition that the owner shall have been previously and equitably indemnified.

Reflections on the Revolution (1790)

EDMUND BURKE

Edmund Burke (1729–1797) was a respected member of the English Parliament who gained extraordinary influence in public affairs through his writings. The following selection from his most famous work, Reflections on the Revolution in France *(1790), gives evidence of his regret concerning the changes that had taken place during the first year of the revolution. Burke left a legacy of conservative thought that proved a solace to many whose status was jeopardized by revolutionary action. Burke's contributions to conservative political theory would provide a serious challenge to liberalism in the nineteenth century.*

When I see the spirit of liberty in action, I see a strong principle at work; and this, for a while, is all I can possibly know of it. The wild *gas*, the fixed air is plainly broke loose: but we ought to suspend our judgment until the first effervescence is a little subsided, till the liquor is cleared, and until we see something deeper than the agitation of a troubled and frothy surface. I must be tolerably sure, before I venture publicly to congratulate men upon a blessing, that they have really received one. Flattery corrupts both the receiver and the giver; and adulation is not of more service to the people than to kings. I should therefore suspend my congratulations on the new liberty of France, until I was informed how it had been combined with government; with public force; with the discipline and obedience of armies; with the collection of an effective and well-distributed revenue; with morality and religion; with the solidity for property; with peace and order; with civil and social manners. All these (in their way) are good things too;

"Reflections on the Revolution" is from Edmund Burke, *Reflections on the Revolution in France*, in *The Works of the Right Honourable Edmund Burke*, vol. 2 (London: Henry G. Bohn, 1864), pp. 515–516.

and, without them, liberty is not a benefit while it lasts, and is not likely to continue long. The effect of liberty to individuals is, that they may do what they please: we ought to see what it will please them to do, before we risk congratulations, which may soon be turned into complaints. Prudence would dictate this in the case of separate insulated private men; but liberty, when men act in bodies, is *power*. Considerate people, before they declare themselves, will observe the use which is made of *power*; and particularly of so trying a thing as *new* power in *new* persons, of whose principles, tempers, and dispositions, they have little or no experience, and in situations where those who appear the most stirring in the scene may possibly not be the real movers. . . .

The age of chivalry is gone.—That of sophisters, economists, and calculators, has succeeded; and the glory of Europe is extinguished for ever. Never, never more, shall we behold that generous loyalty to rank and sex, that proud submission, that dignified obedience, that subordination of the heart, which kept alive, even in servitude itself, the spirit of an exalted freedom. The unbought grace of life, the cheap defence of nations, the nurse of manly sentiment and heroic enterprize is gone! It is gone, that sensibility of principle, that chastity of honour, which felt a stain like a wound, which inspired courage while it mitigated ferocity, which ennobled whatever it touched, and under which vice itself lost half its evil, by losing all its grossness. . . .

But now all is to be changed. All the pleasing illusions, which made power gentle, and obedience liberal, which harmonized the different shades of life, and which, by a bland assimilation, incorporated into politics the sentiments which beautify and soften private society, are to be dissolved by this new conquering empire of light and reason. All the decent drapery of life is to be rudely torn off. All the super-added ideas, furnished from the wardrobe of a moral imagination, which the heart owns, and the understanding ratifies, as necessary to cover the defects of our naked shivering nature, and to raise it to dignity in our own estimation, are to be exploded as a ridiculous, absurd, and antiquated fashion.

On this scheme of things, a king is but a man; a queen is but a woman; a woman is but an animal; and an animal not of the highest order. . . . On the scheme of this barbarous philosophy, which is the offspring of cold hearts and muddy understandings, and which is as void of solid wisdom, as it is destitute of all taste and elegance, laws are to be supported only by their own terrors, and by the concern, which each individual may find in them, from his own private speculations, or even spare to them from his own private interests. In the groves of *their* academy, at the end of every vista, you see nothing but the gallows. . . . When the old feudal and chivalrous spirit of *Fealty*, which, by freeing kings from fear, freed both kings and subjects from the precautions of tyranny, shall be extinct in the minds of men, plots and assassinations will be anticipated by preventive murder and preventive confiscation, and that long roll of grim and bloody maxims, which form the political code of all power, not standing on its own honour, and the honour of those who are to obey it. Kings will be tyrants from policy when subjects are rebels from principle. . . .

To make a government requires no great prudence. Settle the seat of power; teach obedience: and the work is done. To give Freedom is still more easy. It is not necessary to guide; it only requires to let go the rein. But to form a *free government*; that is, to temper together these opposite elements of liberty and restraint in one consistent work, requires much thought, deep reflection, a sagacious, powerful, and combining mind. This I do not find in those who take the lead in the National Assembly. Perhaps they are not so miserably deficient as they appear. I rather believe it. It would put them below the common level of human understanding. But when the leaders choose to make themselves bidders at an auction of popularity, their talents, in the construction of the state, will be of no service. They will become flatterers instead of legislators; the instruments, not the guides, of the people. If any of them should happen to propose a scheme of liberty, soberly limited, and defined with proper qualifications, he will be immediately outbid by his competitors, who will produce something more splendidly popular. Suspicions will be raised of his fidelity to his cause. Moderation will be stigmatized as the virtue of cowards; and compromise as the prudence of traitors; until, in hopes of preserving the credit which may enable him to temper, and moderate, on some occasions, the popular leader is obliged to become active in propagating doctrines, and establishing powers, that will afterwards defeat any sober purpose at which he ultimately might have aimed.

The improvements of the National Assembly are superficial, their errors fundamental.

The Clerical Oath of Loyalty (November 27, 1790)

The serious financial crisis that had existed before the revolution and had actually resulted in the calling of the Estates-General persisted. In order to pay off the national debt, the Assembly took decisive action and confiscated church lands. Such a radical act required an ecclesiastical reconstruction. In July 1790, the National Assembly issued the Civil Constitution of the Clergy. This placed the Roman Catholic Church under the direct control of the secular state. Bishops and priests were reduced in number and became salaried employees of the state. In this move, the Assembly consulted neither the pope nor the French clergy. It was a major blunder that divided the clergy and brought the condemnation of the pope; many devout Catholics were then forced to choose between their loyalty to the revolution and that to the Church. This domination of the French state over the Catholic Church was to continue under Napoleon and resulted in a papal offensive against liberalism throughout the nineteenth century. The following selection is a decree that was designed to test the loyalty of the clergy to the religious reorganization of the state.

Bishops and former archbishops and *curés* maintained in office, [directors of seminaries, . . . teachers in seminaries and colleges, and all other ecclesiastical public functionaries], shall be required to take, if they have not done so, the oath to which they are subject by article 39 of the decree . . . concerning the Civil Constitution of the Clergy. Accordingly, by virtue of this latter decree, they shall swear to watch carefully over the faithful of the diocese or parish entrusted to them, to be faithful to the nation, to the law, and to the King, and to maintain with all their power the Constitution decreed by the National Assembly and accepted by the King. . . .

In case the said bishops, former archbishops, *curés*, and other ecclesiastical public functionaries, after having taken their respective oaths, fail therein, either by refusing to obey the decrees of the National Assembly accepted or sanctioned by the King, or by constituting or instigating opposition to their execution, they shall be prosecuted in the district courts as rebels resisting the law, and punished by deprivation of their stipend, and, moreover, they shall be declared to have forfeited the rights of active citizenship and to be ineligible for any public office. Consequently, provision shall be made for their replacement, according to the said decree [Civil Constitution of the Clergy]. . . .

All ecclesiastical or lay persons who unite to contrive a refusal to obey the decrees of the National Assembly accepted or sanctioned by the King, or to constitute or instigate opposition to the execution thereof, likewise shall be prosecuted as disturbers of public order, and punished according to the rigor of the laws.

Letter from Louis XVI to Foreign Courts
(April 23, 1791)

The following selection is a letter issued by Louis XVI's minister of foreign affairs. It was designed to calm foreign monarchs who feared that the example of the French Revolution might jeopardize their own thrones. Its tacit purpose, however, was to conceal the king's preparations for leaving France. On June 20, 1791, the royal family managed to get out of Paris. Traveling in disguise with false passports, they were detained and arrested in Varennes, about 150 miles from Paris. The king was disgraced and the monarchy suffered a humiliating blow.

What is called the Revolution is only the destruction of a multitude of abuses accumulated over centuries through the errors of the people or the power of the ministers, which has never been the power of the kings. These abuses were no less calamitous to the nation than to the monarch; during happy reigns authority had not ceased to attack them without being able to destroy them. They no longer exist. The sovereign nation now has only citizens equal in rights, no despot but the law, no agencies but the public functionaries, and the King is the first of these functionaries. Such is the French Revolution.

It was bound to have as enemies all who, in a first moment of error, lamented the abuses of the former government because of self-interest. Hence the apparent division which has manifested itself within the kingdom, and which daily grows weaker; hence, perhaps, some severe laws and circumstances which time will correct. But the King, whose real force is indivisible from that of the nation, who has no other ambition than the welfare of the people, no other real power than that which is delegated to him, the King was obliged to adopt without hesitation a favorable constitution which would regenerate, at one and the same time, his authority, the nation, and the monarchy. All his power has been preserved, except the formidable power to make laws; he remains in charge of negotiations with foreign powers and of the task of defending the kingdom and repulsing its enemies; but henceforth the French nation will no longer have any external enemies save its aggressors. It no longer has internal enemies except those who, still nourishing themselves on foolish hopes, believe that the will of twenty-four million men, restored to their natural rights, after having organized the kingdom so that there remain only memories of the old forms and former abuses, is not an immutable, an irrevocable constitution.

The most dangerous of these enemies are those who have a predilection for spreading doubts concerning the intentions of the monarch. These men are entirely culpable or entirely blinded; they believe themselves the friends of the King—they are the only enemies of the monarchy. They would have deprived the monarch of the love and confidence of a great nation if his principles and integrity had not been so well known. Ah! What has the King not done to show that he counted the French Revolution and the Constitution also among his titles to glory? After having accepted and sanctioned all the laws, he has not neglected any means of having them put into effect. As early as the month of February of last year, in the midst of the National Assembly, he promised to maintain them; he took oath thereto in the midst of the universal federation of the kingdom. Honored with the title of Restorer of French Liberty, he will transmit more than a crown to his son; he will bequeath him a constitutional monarchy.

The enemies of the Constitution do not cease to repeat that the King is not happy; as if there might exist for a king any happiness other than that of the people! They say that his authority is debased; as if authority founded upon force were not less powerful and less certain than the authority of the law! Finally, that the King is not free: atrocious calumny, if it be supposed that his will might be forced; absurd one, if they take for default of liberty the consent His Majesty has several times expressed to remain among the citizens of Paris. . . .

Signed: Montmorin

The King's Declaration (June 20, 1791)

KING LOUIS XVI

Upon his flight from Paris to Varennes, Louis XVI left behind the following declaration, which reveals his true feelings about the French Revolution. After Louis' arrest, the declaration was read aloud to the National Assembly and firmly established the king's duplicity.

As long as the King could hope to see order and the welfare of the kingdom regenerated by the means employed by the National Assembly, and by his residence near that assembly in the capital of the kingdom, no sacrifice mattered to him; . . . but today, when his sole recompense for so many sacrifices consists of seeing the monarchy destroyed, all powers disregarded, property violated, personal security everywhere endangered, crimes unpunished, and total anarchy taking the place of law, while the semblance of authority provided by the new Constitution is insufficient to repair a single one of the ills afflicting the kingdom, the King, having solemnly protested against all the acts issued during his captivity, deems it his duty to place before Frenchmen and the entire universe the picture of his conduct and that of the government which has established itself in the kingdom. . . .

Let us, then, examine the several branches of the government.

Justice. The King has no share in making the laws; he has only the right to obstruct, until the third legislature, matters which are not regarded as constitutional, and to request the National Assembly to apply itself to such and such matters, without possessing the right to make a formal proposal thereon. Justice is rendered in the name of the King . . . ; but it is only a matter of form. . . .

Internal Administration. There is entirely too much authority in the hands of the departments, districts, and municipalities, which impede the working of the machine, and may often thwart one another. All these bodies are elected by the people, and are not under the jurisdiction of the government. . . .

Foreign Affairs. Appointment to ministerial posts at foreign courts and the conduct of negotiations have been reserved to the King; but the King's liberty in such appointments is as void as for those of officers in the army; . . . The revision and confirmation of treaties, which is reserved to the

National Assembly, and the nomination of a diplomatic committee absolutely nullify [this] provision. . . .

Finances. . . . There is still no exact statement of receipts and expenditures. . . . The ordinary taxes are at present greatly in arrears, and the extraordinary expedient of the first one billion, two hundred millions in *assignats* is almost exhausted. . . . The regulation of funds, the collection of taxes, the assessment among the departments, the rewards for services rendered, all have been removed from the King's supervision. . . .

The King does not think it possible to govern a kingdom of such great extent and importance as France through the means established by the National Assembly, as they exist at present. His Majesty, in granting to all decrees, without distinction, a sanction which he well knew could not be refused, was influenced by a desire to avoid all discussion, which experience has shown to be useless to say the least; he feared, moreover, that he would be suspected of wishing to retard or to bring about the failure of the efforts of the National Assembly, in the success of which the nation took so great an interest. . . .

Frenchmen, . . . would you want the anarchy and despotism of the clubs to supplant the monarchical government under which the nation has prospered for fourteen hundred years? Would you want to see your King overwhelmed with insults and deprived of his liberty, while he devotes himself entirely to the establishment of yours?

Love for their kings is one of the virtues of Frenchmen, and His Majesty has personally received too many touching proofs thereof ever to be able to forget them. The rebels are well aware that, so long as this love abides, their work can never succeed; they know, likewise, that in order to enfeeble it, it is necessary, if possible, to destroy the respect which has always accompanied it; and that is the source of the outrages which the King has experienced during the past two years, and of all the ills which he has suffered. . . .

In view of all these facts and the King's present inability to effect the good and prevent the evil that is perpetrated, is it astonishing that the King has sought to recover his liberty and to place himself and his family in safety?

Frenchmen, and especially you Parisians, you inhabitants of a city which the ancestors of His Majesty were pleased to call the good city of Paris, distrust the suggestions and lies of your false friends. Return to your king; he will always be your father, your best friend. What pleasure will he not take in forgetting all his personal injuries, and in beholding himself again in your midst, when a constitution, freely accepted by him, shall cause our holy religion to be respected, the government to be established upon a firm foundation and made useful by its functioning, the property and position of every person no longer to be disturbed, the laws no longer to be violated with impunity, and, finally, liberty to be established on firm and immovable foundations.

Signed, LOUIS

The Radicalization of the Revolution (1792–1794)

The Fall of Louis XVI

The months following the king's flight from Paris were tense and saw the eventual erosion of royalist support and the abolition of the monarchy in September 1792. Louis was indicted on December 11, 1792. The first selection indicates that he was being tried for treason. The king denied most of the charges and blamed the rest on others. Nevertheless, a small majority of votes in the Assembly sent him to the guillotine. The second excerpt is an eyewitness account of the execution by Henry Edgeworth de Firmont, the king's confessor, who accompanied Louis to the scaffold. Justification for regicide came two days later by way of a proclamation of the government to the French people. The last selection is from the memoirs of Mme. Roland, a guiding spirit of the revolutionary Girondist faction who was eventually imprisoned and sent to the guillotine herself.

The Indictment of Louis XVI (December 11, 1792)

Louis, the French people accuses you of having committed a multitude of crimes in order to establish your tyranny by destroying its liberty.

1. On 20 June, 1789, you attacked the sovereignty of the people by suspending the assemblies of its representatives and by driving them by violence from the place of their sessions. . . .

2. On 23 June you wished to dictate laws to the nation; you surrounded its representatives with troops; you presented them with two royal declarations, subversive of every liberty, and you ordered them to separate. Your declarations and the minutes of the Assembly establish these outrages undeniably.

3. You caused an army to march against the citizens of Paris; your satellites caused their blood to flow, and you withdrew this army only when the capture of the Bastille and the general insurrection apprised you that the people were victorious. . . .

6. For a long time you contemplated flight; . . . but on 21 June you made your escape with a false passport; you left a declaration against those same constitutional articles; you ordered the ministers not to sign any documents emanating from the National Assembly, and you forbade the

Minister of Justice to deliver the Seals of State. The people's money was wasted in achieving the success of this treason. . . .

7. On 14 September you apparently accepted the Constitution; your speeches announced a desire to maintain it, and you worked to overthrow it before it even was achieved.

15. Your brothers, enemies of the state, have rallied the *émigrés* [French nobility in self-imposed exile] under their colors; they have raised regiments, borrowed money, and contracted alliances in your name; you disavowed them only when you were quite certain that you could not harm their plans. . . .

30. You tried to bribe, with considerable sums, several members of the Constituent and Legislative Assemblies. . . .

31. You allowed the French nation to be disgraced in Germany, in Italy, and in Spain, since you did nothing to exact reparation for the ill treatment which the French experienced in those countries.

32. On 10 August you reviewed the Swiss Guards at five o'clock in the morning; and the Swiss Guards fired first on the citizens.

33. You caused the blood of Frenchmen to flow.

The Execution of Louis XVI (January 21, 1793)
HENRY EDGEWORTH DE FIRMONT

The carriage arrived . . . in the greatest silence, at the Place Louis XV, and came to a halt in the middle of a large empty space that had been left around the scaffold. This space was bordered with cannon; and beyond, as far as the eye could reach, was a multitude in arms. . . .

As soon as the king descended from the carriage, three executioners surrounded him and wished to take off his coat. He repulsed them with dignity and took it off himself. The executioners, whom the proud bearing of the king had momentarily disconcerted, seemed then to resume their audacity and, surrounding him again, attempted to tie his hands. "What are you trying to do?" asked the king, withdrawing his hands abruptly.

"Tie you," replied one of the executioners.

"Tie me!" returned the king in an indignant tone. "No, I will never consent; do what you are ordered to do, but I will not be tied; renounce that idea." The executioners insisted, they lifted their voices, and seemed about to call for help in order to use force. . . .

"Sire," I said to him with tears, "in this new outrage I see only a final resemblance between Your Majesty and the Saviour who is to reward you."

At these words he lifted his eyes to heaven with a sorrowing look that I cannot describe . . . and, turning to the executioners, said: "Do what you wish; I will drain the cup to the dregs."

The steps that led to the scaffold were extremely steep in ascent. The king was obliged to hold to my arm, and by the pains he seemed to take, feared that his courage had begun to weaken; but what was my astonishment when, upon arriving at the last step, I saw him escape, so to speak, from my hands, cross the length of the scaffold with firm step to impose silence, by a single glance, upon ten or fifteen drummers who were in front of him, and with a voice so strong that it could be heard at the Pont-Tournant, distinctly pronounce these words forever memorable: "I die innocent of all the crimes imputed to me. I pardon the authors of my death, and pray God that the blood you are about to shed will never fall upon France."

· · ·

The executioners seized him, the knife struck him, his head fell at fifteen minutes after ten. The executioners seized it by the hair, and showed it to the multitude, whose cries of "Long live the Republic!" resounded to the very bosom of the Convention, whose place of meeting was only a few steps from the place of execution.

Thus died, at the age of thirty-eight years, four months, and twenty-eight days, Louis, sixteenth of his name, whose ancestors had reigned in France for more than eight hundred years. . . .

Immediately after the execution, the body of Louis was transported to the cemetery of the ancient Church of the Madeleine. It was placed in a pit six feet square, close to the wall of the Rue d'Anjou, and dissolved instantly by a great quantity of quicklime with which they took the precaution to cover it.

Proclamation of the Convention to the French People (January 23, 1793)

Citizens, the tyrant is no more. For a long time the cries of the victims, whom war and domestic dissensions have spread over France and Europe, loudly protested his existence. He has paid his penalty, and only acclamations for the Republic and for liberty have been heard from the people.

We have had to combat inveterate prejudices, and the superstition of centuries concerning monarchy. Involuntary uncertainties and inevitable disturbances always accompany great changes and revolutions as profound as ours. This political crisis has suddenly surrounded us with contradictions and tumults.

But the cause has ceased, and the motives have disappeared; respect for liberty of opinion must cause these tumultuous scenes to be forgotten; only

"Proclamation of the Convention to the French People" is from E. L. Higgins, ed., *The French Revolution as Told by Contemporaries* (Boston: Houghton Mifflin, 1966), p. 392. Copyright © 1938, renewed 1966 by Houghton Mifflin Company. Used by permission of the publisher.

the good which they have produced through the death of the tyrant and of tyranny now remains, and this judgment belongs in its entirety to each of us, just as it belongs to the entire nation. The National Convention and the French people are now to have only one mind, only one sentiment, that of liberty and civic fraternity.

Now, above all, we need peace in the interior of the Republic, and the most active surveillance of the domestic enemies of liberty. Never did circumstances more urgently require of all citizens the sacrifice of their passions and their personal opinions concerning the act of national justice which has just been effected. Today the French people can have no other passion than that for liberty.

Reflections on Louis XVI

MME. ROLAND

Louis XVI was not exactly the man they were interested in painting in order to discredit him. He was neither the stupid imbecile that they presented for the disdain of the people, nor the fine, judicious, virtuous man that his friends described. Nature had made him an ordinary man, who would have done well in some obscure station. He was ruined in being educated for the throne, and lost through mediocrity in a difficult period when he could have been saved only through genius and strength. An ordinary mind, brought up near the throne and taught from infancy to dissemble, acquires many advantages for dealing with people; the art of letting each see only what is suitable for him to see is for it only a habit to which practice gives an appearance of cleverness: one would have to be an idiot to appear stupid in such a situation. Louis XVI had moreover, a good memory and much activity; he never remained idle, and read a great deal. He knew well the various treaties made by France with the neighboring powers, and he was the best geographer in his kingdom. The knowledge of names, the exact application to the faces of the court personages to whom they belonged, of anecdotes personal to them, had been extended by him to all the individuals who appeared in some manner in the Revolution. But Louis XVI, without elevation of soul without boldness of mind, without strength of character, still had his ideas narrowed and his sentiments perverted, so to say, by religious prejudices and jesuitical principles. . . . If he had been born two centuries earlier, and if he had had a reasonable wife, he would have made no more noise in the world than many other princes of his race who have passed across the stage without having done much good or much harm.

"Reflections on Louis XVI" is from E. L. Higgins, ed., *The French Revolution as Told by Contemporaries* (Boston: Houghton Mifflin, 1966), pp. 13–14. Copyright © 1938, renewed 1966 by Houghton Mifflin Company. Used by permission of the publisher.

Reality Check:
An Update on the Political Rights of Women (1793)

In the midst of the revolution, with the recent execution of the king and the various political groups scrambling to consolidate their power, the Convention was presented with a complaint regarding the impending dissolution of the Society of Revolutionary Republican Women. An investigation was ordered, and the Committee of General Security presented the following recommendations to the Convention. The Convention subsequently voted to outlaw "women's societies and popular clubs." Note carefully the committee's reasons for rejection of the organization.

The Committee thought it should carry its investigation further. It raised the following questions: . . . (1) Can women exercise political rights and take an active part in affairs of government? (2) Can they deliberate together in political associations or popular societies? With respect to these two questions, the Committee decided in the negative. . . .

We are going to put forward a few ideas which may shed light on [these questions]. In your wisdom you will know how to submit them to a thorough examination.

1. Should women exercise political rights and meddle in affairs of government? To govern is to rule the commonwealth by laws, the preparation of which demands extensive knowledge, unlimited attention and devotion, a strict immovability, and self-abnegation; again, to govern is to direct and ceaselessly to correct the action of constituted authorities. Are women capable of these cares and of the qualities they call for? In general, we can answer, no. Very few examples would contradict this evaluation.

The citizen's political rights are to debate and to have resolutions drawn up, by means of comparative deliberations, that relate to the interest of the state, and to resist oppression. Do women have the moral and physical strength which the exercise of one and the other of these rights calls for? Universal opinion rejects this idea.

2. Should women meet in political associations? The goal of popular associations is this: to unveil the maneuvers of the enemies of the commonwealth; to exercise surveillance both over citizens as individuals and over public functionaries—even over the legislative body; to excite the zeal of one and the other by the example of republican virtues; to shed light by public and in-depth discussion concerning the lack or reform of political laws. Can women devote themselves to these useful and difficult functions? No, because they would be obliged to sacrifice the more important cares to which nature calls them. The private functions for which women are

destined by their very nature are related to the general order of society; this social order results from the differences between man and woman. . . .

Man is strong, robust, born with great energy, audacity, and courage; he braves perils [and] the intemperance of seasons because of his constitution; he resists all the elements; he is fit for the arts, difficult labors; and as he is almost exclusively destined for agriculture, commerce, navigation, voyages, war—everything that calls for force, intelligence, capability, so in the same way, he alone seems to be equipped for profound and serious thinking which calls for great intellectual effort and long studies which it is not granted to women to pursue.

What character is suitable for woman? Morals and even nature have assigned her functions to her. To begin educating men, to prepare children's minds and hearts for public virtues, to direct them early in life towards the good, to elevate their souls, to educate them in the political cult of liberty; such are their functions, after household cares. . . . When they have fulfilled all these obligations, they will have deserved well of the Fatherland. . . .

We must say that this question is related essentially to morals, and without morals, no republic. Does the honesty of woman allow her to display herself in public and to struggle against men? to argue in full view of a public about questions on which the salvation of the republic depends? In general, women are ill suited for elevated thoughts and serious meditations, and if, among ancient peoples, their natural timidity and modesty did not allow them to appear outside their families, then in the French Republic do you want them to be seen coming into the gallery to political assemblies as men do? abandoning both reserve—source of all the virtues of their sex—and the care of their family? . . .

We believe, therefore, that a woman should not leave her family to meddle in affairs of government.

The Reign of Terror

One of the most dramatic personalities of the French Revolution was Maximilien Robespierre (1758–1794), who dominated the principal policy-making body in the state, the Committee of Public Safety. An ardent democrat, Robespierre believed in a republic of virtue that demanded selfless adherence to republican ideals. Those who supported the monarchy or were more moderate in their republican zeal became threats to the success of the revolution and had to be eliminated. Terror, according to Robespierre, was "swift, inflexible justice" and therefore virtuous. The Reign of Terror, which lasted from 1793 to 1794, saw the execution by the guillotine of more then 25,000 people, from both the political left and right, many without proper trials.

Perhaps the most amiable of the radical political leaders was Camille Desmoulins. Although he was one of the first to preach and write about republican ideals, he harbored none of the fanaticism or cruelty that so energized and blinded his friend Robespierre. In the first selection, Desmoulins pleads for clemency and an end to the Terror. Ultimately, his voice threatened the authority of Robespierre, who sent Desmoulins, Danton, and other former adherents to the guillotine three months later.

   The aims of the revolution are presented in the second selection by Robespierre. The next document is a law that transferred the administration of the Terror from the official government (called the Convention) to the Committee of Public Safety. This enactment provided a general definition of an "enemy of the Republic" and increased the number of victims sacrificed to the purity of the revolution. Historians generally agree that this law not only damaged the ideals of the French Revolution, but also was the ultimate cause of Robespierre's downfall. He fell victim to colleagues who feared his menacing power and was himself executed a month and a half after the law was ratified. With Robespierre's death, the Terror came to an end. The revolution continued, but without the bloodshed that had devoured its own children.

"You Would Exterminate All Your Enemies by the Guillotine!" (December 20, 1793)

CAMILLE DESMOULINS

Is this liberty that we desire a mere empty name? Is it only an opera actress carried about with a red cap on, or even that statue, forty-six feet high, which David proposes to make? If by liberty you do not understand, as I do, great principles, but only a bit of stone, there never was idolatry more stupid and expensive than ours. . . . No, heaven-born liberty is no nymph of the opera, nor a red liberty cap, nor a dirty shirt and rags. Liberty is happiness, reason, equality, justice, the Declaration of Rights, your sublime constitution.

   Would you have me recognize this liberty, have me fall at her feet, and shed all my blood for her? Then open the prison doors to the two hundred thousand citizens whom you call suspects, for in the Declaration of Rights no prisons for suspicion are provided for, only places of detention. Suspicion has no prison, but only the public accuser; there are no suspects, but only those accused of offenses established by law.

   Do not think that such a measure would be fatal to the republic. It would, on the contrary, be the most revolutionary that you have adopted. You would exterminate all your enemies by the guillotine! But was there ever greater madness? Can you possibly destroy one enemy on the scaffold without making ten others among his family and friends? Do you believe that those whom you have imprisoned—these women and old men, these

   " 'You Would Exterminate All Your Enemies by the Guillotine!' " is from James H. Robinson and Charles A. Beard, eds., *Readings in Modern European History*, vol. 1 (Boston: Ginn and Company, 1908), pp. 307–308.

stragglers of the Revolution—are really dangerous? Only those among your enemies have remained among you who are cowardly or sick. The strong and courageous have emigrated. They have perished at Lyons or in the Vendee. The remnant which still lingers does not deserve your anger. . . .

Moreover, it has not been love of the republic, but curiosity, which has every day attracted multitudes to the Place de la Revolution [site of the executions]; it was the new drama which was to be enacted but once. . . .

I am of a very different opinion from those who claim that it is necessary to leave Terror as the order of the day. I am confident . . . that liberty will be assured and Europe conquered as soon as you have a Committee of Clemency. This committee will complete the Revolution, for clemency is itself a Revolutionary measure, the most efficient of all when it is wisely dealt out.

"Virtue and Terror": Speech to the Convention (February 5, 1794)

MAXIMILIEN ROBESPIERRE

What is the aim we want to achieve? The peaceful enjoyment of liberty and equality, the reign of that eternal justice whose laws have been engraved, not in stone and marble, but in the hearts of all men, even in the heart of the slave who forgets them or of the tyrant who denies them.

We want a state of affairs where all despicable and cruel passions are unknown and all kind and generous passions are aroused by the laws; when ambition is the desire to deserve glory and to serve the fatherland; where distinctions arise only from equality itself; where the citizen submits to the magistrate, the magistrate to the people and the people to justice; where the fatherland guarantees the well-being of each individual, and where each individual enjoys with pride the prosperity and the glory of the fatherland; where all souls elevate themselves through constant communication of republican sentiments and through the need to deserve the esteem of a great people; where the arts are the decorations of liberty that ennobles them, where commerce is the source of public wealth and not only of the monstrous opulence of a few houses.

In our country we want to substitute morality for egoism, honesty for honor, principles for customs, duties for decorum, the rule of reason for the tyranny of custom, the contempt of vice for the contempt of misfortune, pride for insolence, magnanimity for vanity, love of glory for love of money, good people for well-bred people, merit for intrigue, genius for wit, truth for pompous action, warmth of happiness for boredom of sensuality, greatness of man for pettiness of the great; a magnanimous, power-

" 'Virtue and Terror' " is from Richard W. Lyman and Lewis W. Spitz, eds., *Major Crises in Western Civilization*, vol. 2 (New York: Harcourt, Brace & World, 1965), pp. 71–72.

ful, happy people for a polite, frivolous, despicable people—that is to say, all the virtues and all the miracles of the Republic for all the vices and all the absurdities of the monarchy.

In one word, we want to fulfill the wishes of nature, accomplish the destiny of humanity, keep the promises of philosophy, absolve Providence from the long reign of crime and tyranny.

What kind of government can realize these marvels? Only a democratic or republican government.

But what is the fundamental principle of the democratic or popular government, that is to say, the essential strength that sustains it and makes it move? It is virtue: I am speaking of the public virtue which brought about so many marvels in Greece and Rome and which must bring about much more astonishing ones yet in republican France; of that virtue which is nothing more than love of the fatherland and of its laws.

If the strength of popular government in peacetime is virtue, the strength of popular government in revolution is both virtue and terror; terror without virtue is disastrous, virtue without terror is powerless. Terror is nothing but prompt, severe, and inflexible justice; it is thus an emanation of virtue; it is less a particular principle than a consequence of the general principle of democracy applied to the most urgent needs of the fatherland. It is said that terror is the strength of despotic government. Does ours then resemble despotism? Yes, as the sword that shines in the hands of the heroes of liberty resemble the one with which the satellites of tyranny are armed. Let the despot govern his brutalized subjects through terror; he is right as a despot. Subdue the enemies of liberty through terror and you will be right as founders of the Republic. The government of revolution is the despotism of liberty against tyranny.

The Administration of Terror (June 10, 1794)

1. In the Revolutionary Tribunal there shall be a president and four vice-presidents, one public prosecutor, four substitutes for the public prosecutor, and twelve judges.

2. The jurors shall be fifty in number.

4. The Revolutionary Tribunal is instituted to punish the enemies of the people.

5. The enemies of the people are those who seek to destroy public liberty, either by force or by cunning.

6. The following are deemed enemies of the people: those who have instigated the re-establishment of monarchy, or have sought to disparage or dissolve the National Convention and the revolutionary and republican government of which it is the center;

Those who have betrayed the Republic in the command of places and armies, or in any other military function, carried on correspondence with the enemies of the Republic, labored to disrupt the provisioning or the service of the armies;

Those who have supported the designs of the enemies of France, either by countenancing the sheltering and the impunity of conspirators and aristocracy, by persecuting and calumniating patriotism, by corrupting the mandataries of the people, or by abusing the principles of the Revolution or the laws or measures of the government by false and perfidious applications;

Those who have deceived the people or the representatives of the people, in order to lead them into undertakings contrary to the interests of liberty;

Those who have sought to inspire discouragement, in order to favor the enterprises of the tyrants leagued against the Republic;

Those who have disseminated false news in order to divide or disturb the people;

Those who have sought to mislead opinion and to prevent the instruction of the people, to deprave morals and to corrupt the public conscience, to impair the energy and the purity of revolutionary and republican principles, or to impede the progress thereof, either by counter-revolutionary or insidious writings, or by any other machination; . . .

Finally, all who are designated in previous laws relative to the punishment of conspirators and counter-revolutionaries, and who, by whatever means or by whatever appearances they assume, have made an attempt against the liberty, unity, and security of the Republic, or labored to prevent the strengthening thereof.

7. The penalty provided for all offences under the jurisdiction of the Revolutionary Tribunal is death.

8. The proof necessary to convict enemies of the people comprises every kind of evidence, whether material or moral, oral or written, which can naturally secure the approval of every just and reasonable mind; the rule of judgments is the conscience of the jurors, enlightened by love of the *Patrie*; their aim, the triumph of the Republic and the ruin of its enemies; the procedure, the simple means which good sense dictates in order to arrive at a knowledge of the truth, in the forms determined by law.

9. Every citizen has the right to seize conspirators and counter-revolutionaries, and to arraign them before the magistrates. He is required to denounce them as soon as he knows of them.

The Execution of Robespierre (July 28, 1794)

DURAND DE MAILLANE

Robespierre's turn had come at last. By fawning upon the people he had become their idol, and this will happen to any man who declaims against the rich, causing the people to hope for a division of the spoils. Through the populace, he ruled the Jacobin Club; through the Jacobin Club, the Convention and through the Convention, France. He dictated decrees and directed the administration. Nothing was done except by his orders or with his approval. His caprices were flattered, and his very manias were praised. The tribunal beheaded those he designated without investigation. His power seemed too terrible to his accomplices as it did to his victims. A number had been sacrificed already and others feared the same fate. They banded together to pull down the idol they themselves had set up.

• • •

[The committee of general security] ordered that he [Robespierre] be taken to the prison of the Conciergerie. His trial was short. On the following day he was guillotined, together with Saint-Just, Couthon, and his other accomplices. It was quite a distance from the Palais de Justice to the scaffold, and the immensity of the long Rue Saint-Honore had to be traversed. Along the whole course, the people pursued Robespierre with hoots and maledictions. He had been given a conspicuous place in the tumbril, his face half covered by a dirty, bloodstained cloth which enveloped his jaw. It may be said that this man, who had brought so much anguish to others, suffered during these twenty-four hours all the pain and agony that a mortal can experience.

SECTION II: THE NAPOLEONIC ERA

The Rise of Napoleon

Napoleon Achieves Power (1799–1802)

After the Reign of Terror, the French Revolution entered a moderate period that retreated from the violent radicalism of Robespierre. A new government called the Directory was formed, and it governed the French Republic rather ineffectively until 1799. In this year, Napoleon Bonaparte, who had supported the Directory and had earned fame as the military protector of the Republic, returned to Paris from his Egyptian campaign and promptly overthrew the government. In its place he established the Consulate. Napoleon, as first consul, was given significant power over his other two colleagues. On December 15, 1799, the Consulate proclaimed the end of the French Revolution. The ideals that founded the Republic ostensibly had not changed, but the leadership certainly had. The first excerpt is from a conversation Napoleon had with one of his confidants in 1796, three years before coming into power. The second document is a proclamation to the French people that explains Napoleon's role in the overthrow of the Directory and the establishment of the Consulate. It is a fine example of effective propaganda. Both excerpts reveal much about Napoleon's ambition.

On the Realities of Power (1796)

NAPOLEON BONAPARTE

What I have done so far is nothing. I am but at the opening of the career I am to run. Do you suppose that I have gained my victories in Italy in order to advance the lawyers of the Directory? Do you think, either, that my object is to establish a Republic? What a notion! A republic of thirty million people, with our morals and vices! How could that ever be? It is a chimera with which the French are infatuated but which will pass away in time like all others. What they want is glory and the gratification of their vanity; as for liberty, of that they have no conception. Look at the army! The victories which we have just gained have given the French soldier his true character. I am everything to him. Let the Directory attempt to deprive me of my command and they will see who is master. The nation must have a head, a head rendered illustrious by glory and not by theories of government, fine phrases, or the talk of idealists, of which the French understand not a whit. Let them have their toys and they will be satisfied. They will amuse themselves and allow themselves to be led, provided the goal is cleverly disguised.

The First Consul: "A Citizen Devoted to the Republic" (November 10, 1799)

NAPOLEON BONAPARTE

On my return to Paris [from Egypt] I found division among all authorities, and agreement upon only one point, namely, that the Constitution was half destroyed and was unable to save liberty.

"On the Realities of Power" is from *Memoires of Miot de Melito*, in James H. Robinson, ed., *Translations and Reprints from the Original Sources of European History*, rev. ed., vol. 2, pt. 2 (Philadelphia: University of Pennsylvania Press, 1900), pp. 2–3.

"The First Consul" is reprinted with permission of Macmillan Publishing Company from *A Documentary Survey of the French Revolution*, edited by John Hall Stewart, pp. 763–765. Copyright 1951 by Macmillan Publishing Company, renewed 1979 by John Hall Stewart.

All parties came to me, confided to me their designs, disclosed their secrets, and requested my support; I refused to be the man of a party.

The Council of Elders summoned me; I answered its appeal. A plan of general restoration had been devised by men whom the nation has been accustomed to regard as the defenders of liberty, equality, and property; this plan required an examination, calm, free, exempt from all influence and all fear. Accordingly, the Council of Elders resolved upon the removal of the Legislative Body to Saint-Cloud; it gave me the responsibility of disposing the force necessary for its independence. I believe it my duty to my fellow citizens, to the soldiers perishing in our armies, to the national glory acquired at the cost of their blood, to accept the command.

The Councils assembled at Saint-Cloud; republican troops guaranteed their security from without, but assassins created terror within. Several deputies of the Council of Five Hundred, armed with stilettos and fire-arms, circulated threats of death around them.

The plans which ought to have been developed were withheld, the majority disorganized, the boldest orators disconcerted, and the futility of every wise proposition was evident.

I took my indignation and grief to the Council of Elders. I besought it to assure the execution of its generous designs; I directed its attention to the evils of the *Patrie* [Fatherland] . . . ; it concurred with me *by new* evidence of its steadfast will.

I presented myself at the Council of Five Hundred, alone, unarmed, my head uncovered, just as the Elders had received and applauded me; I came to remind the majority of its wishes, and to assure it of its power.

The stilettos which menaced the deputies were instantly raised against their liberator; twenty assassins threw themselves upon me and aimed at my breast. The grenadiers of the Legislative Body whom I had left at the door of the hall ran forward, placed themselves between the assassins and myself. One of these brave grenadiers had his clothes pierced by a stiletto. They bore me out.

At the same moment cries of "Outlaw" were raised against the defender of the law. It was the fierce cry of assassins against the power destined to repress them.

They crowded around the president, uttering threats, arms in their hands; they commanded him to outlaw me; I was informed of this: I ordered him to be rescued from their fury, and six grenadiers of the Legislative Body secured him. Immediately afterwards some grenadiers of the Legislative Body charged into the hall and cleared it.

The factions, intimidated, dispersed and fled. The majority, freed from their attacks, returned freely and peaceably into the meeting hall, listened to the proposals on behalf of public safety, deliberated, and prepared the salutary resolution which is to become the new and provisional law of the Republic.

Frenchmen, you will doubtless recognize in this conduct the zeal of a soldier of liberty, a citizen devoted to the Republic. Conservative, tutelary, and liberal ideas have been restored to their rights through the dispersal of the rebels who oppressed the Councils.

Napoleon's Consolidation of His Rule

In order to consolidate the new regime, Napoleon sought to control the flow of information in the state. In the first document, note the reasons given for suppression of the newspapers. Between July 1801 and April 1802 Napoleon sought to reorganize the religious institutions of France. The second document is the agreement between France and the papacy, which controlled the position of the Roman Catholic Church in France until 1905. The third selection is a legislative act of state that was promulgated without the pope's consent, but enforced nevertheless. There were other similar pronouncements for Protestants (1802) and Jews (1808).

Suppression of the Newspapers (1800)

The consuls of the Republic, considering that a part of the newspapers which are printed in the department of the Seine are instruments in the hands of the enemies of the Republic; that the government is particularly charged by the French people to look after their security, orders as follows:

1. The minister of police shall permit to be printed, published, and circulated during the whole course of the war only the following newspapers: . . . [Here follows the names of thirteen newspapers], and newspapers devoted exclusively to science, arts, literature, commerce, announcements and notices.

2. The minister of the general police shall immediately make a report upon all the newspapers that are printed in the other departments.

3. The minister of the general police shall see that no new newspaper be printed in the department of the Seine, as well as in all the other departments of the Republic.

4. The proprietors and editors of the newspapers preserved by the present order shall present themselves to the minister of the police in order to attest their character as French citizens, their residences and signatures, and they shall promise fidelity to the constitution.

5. All newspapers which shall insert articles opposed to the respect that is due to the social compact, to the sovereignty of the people and the glory of the armies, or which shall publish invectives against the governments and nations who are the friends or allies of the Republic, even when these

"Suppression of the Newspapers" is from Frank M. Anderson, ed., *The Constitutions and Other Illustrative Documents of the History of France*, 2nd ed., revised (New York: Russell and Russell, 1908), p. 282.

articles may be extracts from foreign periodicals, shall be immediately suppressed.

6. The minister of the general police is charged with the execution of the present order, which shall be inserted in the *Bulletin of the Laws.*

Reorganization of Religion: Convention between the French Government and His Holiness Pope Pius VII (1802)

The government of the French Republic recognizes that the Roman, catholic and apostolic religion is the religion of the great majority of French citizens.

His Holiness likewise recognizes that this same religion has derived and in this moment again expects the greatest benefit and grandeur from the establishment of catholic worship in France and from the personal profession of it which the consuls of the Republic make.

In consequence, after this mutual recognition, as well for the benefit of religion as for the maintenance of internal tranquility, they have agreed as follows:

1. The catholic, apostolic and Roman religion shall be freely exercised in France: its worship shall be public, and in conformity with the police regulations which the government shall deem necessary for the public tranquility.

4. The First Consul of the Republic shall make appointments, within the three months which shall follow the publication of the bull of His Holiness to the archbishoprics and bishoprics of the new circumscription. His Holiness shall confer the canonical institution, following the forms established in relation to France before the change of government.

6. Before entering upon their functions, the bishops shall take directly, at the hands of the First Consul, the oath of fidelity which was in use before the change of government, expressed in the following terms:

"I swear and promise to God, upon the holy scriptures, to remain in obedience and fidelity to the government established by the constitution of the French Republic. I also promise not to have any intercourse, nor to assist by any counsel, nor to support any league, either within or without, which is inimical to the public tranquility; and if, within my diocese or elsewhere, I learn that anything to the prejudice of the state is being contrived, I will make it known to the government."

"Reorganization of Religion" is from Frank M. Anderson, ed., *The Constitutions and Other Illustrative Documents of the History of France*, 2nd ed., revised (New York: Russell and Russell, 1908), pp. 296–297.

Articles for the Catholic Church (1802)

1. No bull, brief, rescript, decree, injunction, provision, signature serving as a provision, nor other documents from the court of Rome, even concerning individuals only, can be received, published, printed, or otherwise put into effect, without the authorization of the government.

4. No national or metropolitan council, no diocesan synod, no deliberative assembly, shall take place without the express permission of the government.

6. There shall be recourse to the Council of State in every case of abuse on the part of the Superiors and other ecclesiastical persons.

The cases of abuse are usurpation or excess of power, contravention of the laws and regulations of the Republic, infraction of the rules sanctioned by the canons received in France, attack upon the liberties, privileges and customs of the Gallican church, and every undertaking or any proceeding which in the exercise of worship can compromise the honor of the citizens, disturb arbitrarily their consciences, or degenerate into oppression or injury against them or into public scandal.

Consul for Life (1802)

On May 8, 1802, Napoleon's ten-year term as first consul of the Republic was extended by the senate for another ten years. Reasons for this vote of confidence are given in the first selection. Napoleon's reply to this action follows. His term of office was further extended for life just three months later. This accumulation of so much power in so short a time is extraordinary. The third selection is Napoleon's oath of office.

Reelection as Consul (May 8, 1802)

Considering that, under the circumstances in which the Republic finds itself, it is the duty of the Conservative Senate to employ all the means which the constitution has put in its power in order to give to the government the stability which alone multiplies resources, inspires confidence abroad, establishes credit within, reassures allies, discourages secret ene-

"Articles for the Catholic Church" is from Frank M. Anderson, ed., *The Constitutions and Other Illustrative Documents of the History of France*, 2nd ed., revised (New York: Russell and Russell, 1908), p. 299.

"Reelection as Consul" is from Frank M. Anderson, ed., *The Constitutions and Other Illustrative Documents of the History of France*, 2nd ed., revised (New York: Russell and Russell, 1908), p. 324.

mies, turns away the scourge of war, permits the enjoyment of the fruits of peace, and leaves to wisdom time to carry out whatever it can conceive for the welfare of a free people;

Considering, moreover, that the supreme magistrate who, after having so many times led the republican legions to victory, delivered Italy, triumphed in Europe, in Africa, in Asia, and filled the world with his renown, has preserved France from the horrors of anarchy which were menacing it, broken the revolutionary sickle, dispersed the factions, extinguished civil discords and religious disturbances, added to the benefits of liberty those of order and of security, hastened the progress of enlightenment, consoled humanity, and pacified the continent and the seas, has the greatest right to the recognition of his fellow citizens, as well as the admiration of posterity;

That the wish of the Tribunate, which has come to the Senate in the sitting of this day, under these circumstances, can be regarded as that of the French nation;

That the Senate cannot express more solemnly to the First Consul the recognition of the nation than in giving him a striking proof of the confidence which he has inspired in the French people;

Considering, finally, that the second and the third consuls have worthily seconded the glorious labors of the First Consul of the Republic;

In consequence of all these motives, and the votes having been collected by secret ballot;

The Senate decrees as follows:

1. The Conservative Senate, in the name of the French people, testifies to its recognition of the consuls of the Republic.
2. The Conservative Senate re-elects Citizen Napoleon Bonaparte, First Consul of the French Republic for the ten years which shall immediately follow the ten for which he has been appointed by article 39 of the constitution.

Reply to the Senate (May 11, 1802)

NAPOLEON BONAPARTE

Senators:

The honorable proof of esteem contained in your resolution of [May 8th] will ever be graven upon my heart.

The suffrage of the people has invested me with the supreme magistracy. I should not think myself assured of their confidence, if the act which retained me there was not again sanctioned by their suffrage.

In the three years which have just passed away fortune has smiled upon

"Reply to the Senate" is from Frank M. Anderson, ed., *The Constitutions and Other Illustrative Documents of the History of France*, 2nd ed., revised (New York: Russell and Russell, 1908), p. 325.

the Republic; but fortune is inconstant, and how many men whom it had crowned with its favors have lived on some years too many.

The interest of my glory and that of my happiness would seem to have marked the termination of my public life at the moment in which the peace of the world is proclaimed.

But the glory and happiness of the citizen must be silent, when the interest of the state and the public well-being summon him.

You deem that I owe to the people a new sacrifice: I will make it, if the wish of the people commands what your suffrage authorises.

Signed, Bonaparte

Oath as Consul for Life (August 4, 1802)
NAPOLEON BONAPARTE

"I swear to maintain the constitution, to respect liberty of conscience, to oppose a return to feudal institutions, never to make war except for the defence and glory of the Republic, and to employ the authority with which I shall be invested only for the good of the people, from whom and for whom I shall have received it."

Napoleon's Reforms and Institutions

Although Napoleon's rise was extraordinary and, some would say, not in keeping with the spirit of a free republic, it is true that the programs he advocated were progressive and contributed to the stability and morale of the French state. Of the many reforms and institutions created by Napoleon, the provisions for education and the Legion of Honor are among the most characteristic and enduring. Apart from these official decrees, note some of Napoleon's personal comments on the same topics, as excerpted from his diary.

General Provisions on Education (May 1, 1802)

143. The Imperial University and its grand master, charged exclusively by us with the care of education and public instruction in all the empire, shall aim without respite to improve the instruction of all sorts, and to favor the

"Oath as Consul for Life" is from Frank M. Anderson, ed., *The Constitutions and Other Illustrative Documents of the History of France*, 2nd ed., revised (New York: Russell and Russell, 1908), p. 331.

"General Provisions on Education" is from Frank M. Anderson, ed., *The Constitutions and Other Illustrative Documents of the History of France*, 2nd ed., revised (New York: Russell and Russell, 1908), p. 323.

composition of classical works; they shall particularly take care that the instruction of the sciences shall always be upon the level of acquired knowledge and that the spirit of system shall never arrest their progress.

The Legion of Honor (May 19, 1802)

Each person admitted to the legion shall swear upon his honor to devote himself to the service of the Republic, to the preservation of its territory in its integrity, to the defence of its government, its laws and the properties which they have consecrated; to combat with all the means that justice, reason and the laws authorise, every undertaking having a tendency to reestablish the feudal regime, or to reproduce the titles and qualities which were symbolical of it; lastly, to assist with all his power in the maintenance of liberty and equality.

All military men who have received arms of honor are members of the legion.

The military men who have rendered important services to the state in the war for liberty;

The citizens who by their knowledge, their talents or their virtues, have contributed to the establishment or defence of the principles of the Republic, or have made justice or the public administration loved and respected shall be eligible for appointment.

In times of peace one must have had twenty-five years of military service in order to be appointed a member of the legion; the years of service in time of war shall count double and each campaign of the last war shall count for four years.

Great services rendered to the state in legislative functions, diplomacy, administration, justice or the sciences, shall also be titles for admission, provided the person who shall have rendered them has made part of the national guard of the place his domicile.

Comments on Reform from Napoleon's Diary
NAPOLEON BONAPARTE

On Honors (May 14, 1802):

Where is the republic, ancient or modern, that has not granted honours? Call them trifles if you like, but it is by trifles that men are influenced. I would not utter such a sentiment as this in public, but here, among states-

"The Legion of Honor" is from Frank M. Anderson, ed., *The Constitutions and Other Illustrative Documents of the History of France*, 2nd ed., revised (New York: Russell and Russell, 1908), p. 337.

"Comments on Reform from Napoleon's Diary" is from R. M. Johnston, ed., *The Corsican: A Diary of Napoleon's Life in His Own Words* (Boston: Houghton Mifflin, 1910), pp. 160, 226, 469.

men and thinkers, things should be spoken of as they are. In my opinion the French do not care for liberty and equality; they have but one sentiment, that of honour. Therefore, that sentiment must be gratified; they must be given distinctions. Do you suppose you can persuade men to fight by a process of analysis? Never! That process is valid only for the man of science in his study. The soldier demands glory, distinction, rewards.

On the Education of Women (March 1, 1806):

I think it is unnecessary to take into consideration a system of education for girls, they can get no better teaching than that of their mothers. A public education does not suit them, for the reason that they are not called on to live in public; for them habit is everything, and marriage is the goal.

If we are to establish the nation, we must hasten to regulate by means of codes the principal fields of legislation. The Civil Code, though imperfect, has done much good. Everyone is familiar now with the first principles of conduct, and governs his property and business accordingly.

On Crime and Shakespeare (November 29, 1815):

My [Civil] Code alone, because of its simplicity, has done more good in France than the sum total of all the laws that preceded it. My schools are preparing unknown generations. And so during my reign, crime diminished rapidly, while on the contrary among our neighbours in England it increased with frightful rapidity. And that is enough, I think, to give a clear judgment on the two governments.

People take England on trust, and repeat that Shakespeare is the greatest of all authors. I have read him; there is nothing that compares with Racine or Corneille: his plays are unreadable, pitiful.

Napoleon Becomes Emperor (1804)

Five years after Napoleon became head of the French government as first consul, he moved to expand his power, and on May 18, 1804, the Senate decreed that he should be made emperor of the French. The people of France overwhelmingly approved of this measure through a plebiscite. Napoleon now had complete control of France's government and fate. In the following statement, before the legislative body of December 31, 1804, Napoleon recounts the reasons for establishing the government of the Empire in place of the Consulate. Note the importance of having the pope "officiate" at the coronation. In fact, Napoleon crowned himself emperor since he did not recognize the pope's authority as superior to his own. But why did the French people willingly submit to the despotism of Napoleon? In the second selection, the Comtesse de Rémusat (1780–1821), lady-in-waiting to Napoleon's wife Josephine and the author of some lively memoirs, gives her assessment. Appropriately, Napoleon

Napoleon as Emperor by Jacques Louis David. Having executed King Louis XVI in 1793 in support of republican government, the French overwhelmingly accepted Napoleon as emperor in 1804. Did France have more need of Napoleon than did he for France? *(Alinari/Art Resource, NY)*

found divine sanction for his power. The third offering recounts a catechism written during the reign of Louis XIV and modified to meet Napoleon's particular needs. Its questions and answers address the duties of French citizens toward their emperor.

Reasons for Establishing the Empire (December 1804)
NAPOLEON BONAPARTE

The internal situation of France is to-day as calm as it has ever been in the most peaceful periods. There is no agitation to disturb the public tranquility, no suggestion of those crimes which recall the Revolution. Everywhere useful enterprises are in progress, and the general improvements, both public and private, attest the universal confidence and sense of security. . . .

A plot conceived by an implacable government was about to replunge France into the abyss of civil war and anarchy. The discovery of this horrible crime stirred all France profoundly, and anxieties that had scarcely been calmed again awoke. Experience has taught that a divided power in the state is impotent and at odds with itself. It was generally felt that if power was delegated for short periods only, it was so uncertain as to discourage any prolonged undertakings or wide-reaching plans. If vested in an individual for life, it would lapse with him, and after him would prove a source of anarchy and discord. It was clearly seen that for a great nation the only salvation lies in hereditary power, which can alone assure a continuous political life which may endure for generations, even for centuries.

The Senate, as was proper, served as the organ through which this general apprehension found expression. The necessity of hereditary power in a state as vast as France had long been perceived by the First Consul. He had endeavored in vain to avoid this conclusion; but the public solicitude and the hopes of our enemies emphasized the importance of his task, and he realized that his death might ruin his whole work. Under such circumstances, and with such a pressure of public opinion, there was no alternative left to the First Consul. He resolved, therefore, to accept for himself, and two of his brothers after him, the burden imposed by the exigencies of the situation.

After prolonged consideration, repeated conferences with the members of the Senate, discussion in the councils, and the suggestions of the most prudent advisers, a series of provisions was drawn up which regulate the succession to the imperial throne. These provisions were decreed by a *senatus consultus* of the 28th Floreal last. The French people, by a free and independent expression, then manifested its desire that the imperial digni-

---

"Reasons for Establishing the Empire" is from James H. Robinson and Charles A. Beard, eds., *Readings in Modern European History*, vol. 1 (Boston: Ginn and Company, 1908), pp. 334–336.

ty should pass down in a direct line through the legitimate or adopted descendants of Napoleon Bonaparte, or through the legitimate descendants of Joseph Bonaparte, or of Louis Bonaparte.

From this moment Napoleon was, by the most unquestioned of titles, emperor of the French. No other act was necessary to sanction his right and consecrate his authority. But he wished to restore in France the ancient forms and recall those institutions which divinity itself seems to have inspired. He wished to impress the seal of religion itself upon the opening of his reign. The head of the Church, in order to give the French a striking proof of his paternal affection, consented to officiate at this august ceremony. What deep and enduring impressions did this leave on the mind of Napoleon and in the memory of the nation! What thoughts for future races! What a subject of wonder for all Europe!

In the midst of this pomp, and under the eye of the Eternal, Napoleon pronounced the inviolable oath which assures the integrity of the empire, the security of property, the perpetuity of institutions, the respect for Law, and the happiness of the nation. The oath of Napoleon shall be forever the terror of the enemies of France. If our borders are attacked, it will be repeated at the head of our armies, and our frontiers shall never more fear foreign invasion.

Why the French Submitted to Napoleon's Rule (1804)
COMTESSE DE RÉMUSAT

I can understand how it was that men worn out by the turmoil of the Revolution, and afraid of that liberty which had long been associated with death, looked for repose under the dominion of an able ruler on who Fortune was seemingly resolved to smile. I can conceive that they regarded his elevation as a decree of destiny and fondly believed that in the irrevocable they should find peace. I may confidently assert that those persons believed quite sincerely that Bonaparte, whether as Consul or Emperor, would exert his authority to oppose the intrigues of faction and would save us from the perils of anarchy.

None dared to utter the word "republic," so deeply had the Terror stained that name; and the government of the Directory had perished in the contempt with which its chiefs were regarded. The return of the Bourbons could only be brought about by the aid of a revolution; and the slightest disturbance terrified the French people, in whom enthusiasm of every kind seemed dead. Besides, the men in whom they had trusted had one after the other deceived them; and as, this time, they were yielding to force, they were at least certain they were not deceiving themselves.

"Why the French Submitted to Napoleon's Rule" is from James H. Robinson and Charles A. Beard, eds., *Readings in Modern European History*, vol. 1 (Boston: Ginn and Company, 1908), pp. 333–334.

The belief, or rather the error, that only despotism could at that epoch maintain order in France was very widespread. It became the mainstay of Bonaparte; and it is due to him to say that he also believed it. The factions played into his hands by imprudent attempts which he turned to his own advantage. He had some grounds for his belief that he was necessary; France believed it, too; and he even succeeded in persuading foreign sovereigns that he constituted a barrier against republican influences, which, but for him, might spread widely. At the moment when Bonaparte placed the imperial crown upon his head there was not a king in Europe who did not believe that he wore his own crown more securely because of that event. Had the new emperor granted a liberal constitution, the peace of nations and of kings might really have been forever secured.

The Imperial Catechism (April 1806)

Question: What are the duties of Christians toward those who govern them, and what in particular are our duties towards Napoleon I, our emperor?

Answer: Christians owe to the princes who govern them, and we in particular owe to Napoleon I, our emperor, love, respect, obedience, fidelity, military service, and the taxes levied for the preservation and defense of the empire and of his throne. We also owe him fervent prayers for his safety and for the spiritual and temporal prosperity of the state.

Question: Why are we subject to all these duties toward our emperor?

Answer: First, because God, who has created empires and distributes them according to his will, has, by loading our emperor with gifts both in peace and in war, established him as our sovereign and made him the agent of his power and his image on earth. To honor and serve our emperor is therefore to honor and serve God himself. Secondly, because our Lord Jesus Christ himself, both by his teaching and his example, has taught us what we owe to our sovereign. Even at his very birth he obeyed the edict of Caesar Augustus; he paid the established tax; and while he commanded us to render to God those things which belong to God, he also commanded us to render unto Caesar those things which are Caesar's.

Question: Are there not special motives which should attach us more closely to Napoleon I, our emperor?

Answer: Yes, for it is he whom God has raised up in trying times to reestablish the public worship of the holy religion of our fathers and to be its protector; he has reestablished and preserved public order by his profound and active wisdom; he defends the state by his mighty arm; he has

"The Imperial Catechism" is from James H. Robinson and Charles A. Beard, eds., *Readings in Modern European History*, vol. 1 (Boston: Ginn and Company, 1908), pp. 351–352.

become the anointed of the Lord by the consecration which he has received from the sovereign pontiff, head of the Church universal.

Question: What must we think of those who are neglecting their duties toward our emperor?

Answer: According to the apostle Paul, they are resisting the order established by God himself, and render themselves worthy of eternal damnation.

The Hero in History

Beginning in 1792 and continuing throughout much of the revolution, France was at war against various coalitions of European nations. Revolutionary ideology was exportable and threatened the very foundation of enlightened despotism. As the French revolutionaries attacked the Church, monarchy, and aristocracy, most of Europe, including Great Britain, reacted by repressing liberal reform movements. These wars at once threatened the revolution and also granted it purpose and unity. Napoleon, a military commander of genius and overreaching ambition, capitalized on this French "spirit of the times" and sought to dominate Europe both militarily and culturally from 1803 to his final defeat at Waterloo in 1815. In the process, he inspired France and certainly changed the course of history. Napoleon believed that his actions were directed toward a destiny that he was compelled to achieve by fate. The first selection is a good example of this belief. It is an address to Dutch representatives upon the annexation of Holland to the French empire in 1810. The second selection finds Napoleon in permanent exile on the South Atlantic island of St. Helena. His diary accounts give indication of his dominant personality and spirit. However, he remained on this isolated rock until his death in 1821.

Yet, what is the role of the "great man" or "hero" in history? Can the course of history be changed by a dynamic individual of ability and resolve? Or does history progress by uncontrollable economic and social "forces"? The third selection is by G. W. F. Hegel, a German philosopher who believed that "heroes" such as Caesar, Alexander, and Napoleon were unconscious instruments of a "world spirit" (Zeitgeist) that lay behind the development of human history. The chosen passage reveals Hegel's thoughts about how heroes could change the course of history. Hegel is representative of the romantic belief, current in the early nineteenth century, that human history was connected with much larger spiritual forces.

The last selection is an excerpt from the memoirs of Stanislaus Girardin (1762–1827), a French politician. As he and the then First Consul Napoleon stood by the grave of Jean Jacques Rousseau, Napoleon reflected on the influence of this great political philosopher.

"An End to the Woes of Anarchy" (1810)

NAPOLEON BONAPARTE

When Providence elevated me to the first throne in the world it became my duty, while establishing forever the destinies of France, to determine the fate of all those people who formed a part of the empire, to insure for all the benefits of stability and order, and to put an end everywhere to the woes of anarchy. I have done away with the uncertainty in Italy by placing upon my head the crown of iron. . . .

I gave you a prince of my own blood to govern you. . . . I have opened the continent to your industry, and the day will come when you shall bear my eagles upon the seas which your ancestors have rendered illustrious. You will then show yourself worthy of them and of me. . . .

"We Stand as Martyrs to an Immortal Cause!": Napoleon in Exile on St. Helena (1815)

NAPOLEON BONAPARTE

What infamous treatment they have held in store for us! This is the agony of death! To injustice, to violence, they add insult and slow torture! If I was so dangerous, why didn't they get rid of me? A few bullets in my heart or in my head would have settled it; there would have been some courage at least in such a crime! How can the Sovereigns of Europe permit the sacred nature of sovereignty to be attainted in me? Can't they see that they are killing themselves at St. Helena? I have entered their capitals as a conqueror; had I been moved by such motives, what would have become of them? They all called me their brother, and I had become so by the will of the people, the sanction of victory, the character of religion, the alliances of policy and of family. . . . Apart from that, who has there been in history with more partisans, more friends? Who has been more popular, more beloved? Who ever left behind more ardent regrets? Look at France: might not one say that from this rock of mine I still reign over her? . . .

Our situation may even have good points! The Universe watches us! We stand as martyrs to an immortal cause! Millions of men weep with us, our country sighs, and glory has put on mourning! We struggle here against the tyranny of the gods, and the hopes of humanity are with us! Misfortune itself knows heroism, and glory! Only adversity was wanting to complete my career! Had I died on the throne, in the clouds of my almightiness, I

" 'An End to the Woes of Anarchy' " is from James H. Robinson and Charles A. Beard, eds., *Readings in Modern European History*, vol. 1 (Boston: Ginn and Company, 1908), pp. 355–356.

" 'We Stand as Martyrs to an Immortal Cause!' " is from R. M. Johnston, ed., *The Corsican: A Diary of Napoleon's Life in His Own Words* (Boston: Houghton Mifflin, 1910), pp. 468–469.

would have remained a problem for many; as it is, thanks to my misfortunes, I can be judged naked.

The Role of Great Men in History
G. W. F. HEGEL

Such are all great historical men—whose own particular aims involve those large issues which are the will of the World-Spirit. They may be called Heroes, inasmuch as they have derived their purposes and their vocation, not from the clam, regular course of things, sanctioned by the existing order: but from a concealed fount—one which has not attained to phenomenal, present existence—from that inner Spirit, still hidden beneath the surface, which, impinging on the outer world as on a shell, bursts it in pieces, because it is another kernel than that which belonged to the shell in question. They are men, therefore, who appear to draw the impulse of their life from themselves; and whose deeds have produced a condition of things and a complex of historical relations which appear to be only their interest, and their work.

Such individuals had no consciousness of the general idea they were unfolding, while prosecuting those aims of theirs; on the contrary, they were practical, political men. But at the same time they were thinking men, who had an insight into the requirements of the time—what was ripe for development. This was the very Truth for their age, for their world: the species next in order, so to speak, and which was already formed in the womb of time. It was theirs to know this nascent principle; the necessary, directly sequent step in progress, which their world was to take; to make this their aim, and to expend their energy in promoting it. World-historical men—the Heroes of an epoch—must, therefore, be recognized as its clear-sighted ones: their deed, their words are the best of that time.

Napoleon on Rousseau
STANISLAUS GIRARDIN

When he reached the poplar island, Bonaparte stepped in front of Jean-Jacques' tomb and said, "It would have been better for the peace of France if this man had never lived."—"And why, Citizen Consul?"—"It was he who prepared the French Revolution."—"I should have thought, Citizen Con-

"The Role of Great Men in History" is from G. W. F. Hegel, *The Philosophy of History*, trans. J. Sibree (New York: Dover, 1956), pp. 30–31. Reprinted by permission of the publisher.

"Napoleon on Rousseau" is from J. Christopher Herold, ed., and trans., *The Mind of Napoleon* (New York: Columbia University Press, 1955), p. 67. Reprinted by permission of the publisher.

sul, that it was not for you to complain of the Revolution."—"Well," Napoleon replied, "the future will tell us whether it would not have been better if neither I nor Rousseau had ever lived." And he resumed his walk with a thoughtful air.

CHRONOLOGY: "Liberty, Equality, Fraternity!": The French Revolution and the Rise of Napoleon

May 1789–
June 1789
: *ESTATES GENERAL*: Monarchy still in control of the government. War is the expected foreign policy of the *ancien regime*.

1789–1791
: *NATIONAL ASSEMBLY*: Nominal absolute monarchy. State church exists with priests paid by the state.

June 20, 1789:	Tennis Court Oath
July 14, 1789:	Fall of Bastille
August 27, 1789:	Declaration of the Rights of Man
July 12, 1790:	Civil Constitution of the clergy adopted
June 24, 1791:	Louis XVI and family are caught trying to flee France

1791–1792
: *LEGISLATIVE ASSEMBLY*: Constitutional monarchy. War is promoted to solve domestic problems. State church.

October 1, 1791:	Legislative Assembly convenes
September 2, 1792:	The September Massacres

1792–1794
: *THE CONVENTION*: Committee of Public Safety administers government. Universal manhood suffrage. Cult of Reason promoted. Reign of Terror (1793–1794).

September 21, 1792:	The Convention meets and the monarchy is abolished
January 21, 1793:	Louis XVI is executed
July, 1793:	Robespierre enters the Committee of Public Safety
October 16, 1793:	Queen Marie Antoinette is executed
November 10, 1793:	The Cult of Reason is proclaimed
April 6, 1794:	Execution of Danton and Desmoulins
May 7, 1794:	Cult of the Supreme Being proclaimed
June 10, 1794:	Law of 22 Prairial is adopted (Administration of Terror)
July 28, 1794:	Execution of Robespierre

1795–1799	*THE DIRECTORY AND CONSULATE*: Thermidorian Reaction. Restricted franchise. Separation of church and state promoted.

August 22, 1795:	Directory established
November 10, 1799:	Consulate established with Napoleon as First Consul
December 15, 1799:	Consulate proclaims end of French Revolution

1801	Napoleon concludes a concordat with Pope Pius VII: clergy must swear loyalty oath to the state
1802	Napoleon proclaimed Consul for Life
1804	Napoleon crowned Emperor of the French; Civil Code issued
1805	Nelson defeats French fleet at Trafalgar; Napoleon's victory at Austerlitz
1806	Napoleon's victory at Jena
1812	Invasion of Russia and French defeat at Borodino
1813	French defeat at Leipzig (Battle of Nations)
1814	Congress of Vienna convenes in September
1815	Napoleon escapes from Elba and returns to Paris. The Duke of Wellington commands coalition forces in victory over Napoleon at Waterloo.
1821	Napoleon dies in exile on South Atlantic island of St. Helena.

STUDY QUESTIONS

Section I: The French Revolution

1. What are the arguments used by Locke, Montesquieu, and Rousseau to justify revolution? Who or what is the "sovereign power" Rousseau mentions? Comment in particular on Rousseau's belief that "whoever refuses to obey the general will shall be compelled to it by the whole body." Isn't this a form of tyranny?
2. Compare the views of Rousseau and Mary Wollstonecraft on the education and abilities of women. In what ways do Wollstonecraft's arguments mirror the ideals of the Enlightenment? In this regard, does Rousseau appear somewhat hypocritical? Or can one rationalize his arguments? Note in particular Napoleon's comment from his diary regarding the education of women. What does this say about Napoleon as an enlightened reformer?

3. Note the excerpts under the section "The Political Framework." In order to be enduring, must revolutions have precedents for action (like the Glorious Revolution or the American Revolution)? Must they have some philosophical justification?

4. What is a revolution? How do you distinguish it from a riot or a rebellion? What political, social, or economic conditions existed in eighteenth-century France that contributed to the French Revolution? In a general sense, do you think that difficult conditions precede any successful revolution?

5. What were the specific demands made by the Third Estate? Do they seem reasonable to you? Compare the demands made by the Abbé Sieyès with the requests made by the women of the Third Estate to the king. Assess the progress made by 1793 for women to achieve political equality as noted in the document "Update on the Political Rights of Women." Do you find it hypocritical that in a period where the "rights of man" are hotly contested, they don't apply to women?

6. Read the Tennis Court Oath carefully. Does it call for radical action? Why is it considered to be one of the most important documents of the French Revolution?

7. Why was the fall of the Bastille such an important event? After reading the pertinent selections, discuss how important violence is in a revolution. Do most successful revolutions promote violence to some degree?

8. What are the most important ideas contained in the Declaration of the Rights of Man? Why was it essential to the French Revolution? What does it tell you about the Old Regime of Louis XVI and his predecessors? Do you believe (as did most of the *philosophes*) that there are "natural rights" for all human beings and that a government should protect these rights? How is this "natural rights" argument reflected in the various documents of the revolution?

9. What were Edmund Burke's main criticisms of the revolution in France? Why did Burke anticipate plots, assassinations, and a "long roll of bloody maxims"? Was he right?

10. Compare Louis XVI's "Letter to Foreign Courts" with his "Declaration" of June 20, 1791. Do you find his arguments in the declaration to be legitimate and effective? Is the "Indictment of Louis XVI" a truthful or exaggerated account of the king's actions? To what extent, then, were the revolutionaries justified in executing Louis XVI as a tyrant and traitor to the revolution?

11. Analyze the speech of Robespierre. How did he justify the use of terror in the promotion of revolution? Note, in particular, the juxtaposition of virtue and terror. In an ethical sense, can virtue ever be promoted by terror?

Section II: The Napoleonic Era

12. How did Napoleon come to power in 1799? Carefully read the statement he made on becoming consul. Pay particular attention to the vocabulary. How did Napoleon justify his overthrow of the Directory? Balance this

public statement with the attitude found in the preceding excerpt "On the Realities of Power." What does this say about Napoleon's commitment to democratic ideals? At the time, though, to progress as a nation did France need less ideal and more practical inspiration and leadership? Was Napoleon a hypocrite who saved France from chaos? If so, do you condemn him for his hypocrisy?

13. On becoming first consul, Napoleon consolidated his position by suppressing the newspapers and reorganizing the state's religious institutions. Read these selections. Are these actions consistent with democratic government? From Napoleon's perspective, why were these actions essential to the stability of the state?

14. In 1802, Napoleon was voted consul for life. In practical terms, what does this title mean? How did the senate justify its decision to elect Napoleon to this position? Examine Napoleon's reply to the senate. Why did he decide to accept the position?

15. Look carefully at the statements concerning the reform of education and establishing the Legion of Honor. What special traits or characteristics of French citizens was Napoleon trying to reward or inspire in these measures? Were these reforms progressive and healthy for the French state? Why? Do Napoleon's revealing diary accounts on these topics detract from the reform ideals he set forth publicly?

16. In 1804, Napoleon became emperor of the French by decree of the senate. How does this position differ from that of first consul for life? Compare the reasons that Napoleon gives for assuming this position with those given when he became first consul and consul for life. Is there any pattern of justification? Note that the people of France approved of Napoleon's rise to power and his assumption of titles by supporting him with plebiscites. Were they in fact limiting their own freedom? Is freedom, most importantly, just a state of mind? Does progress often depend on a restriction of freedom in the interests of stability and security?

17. Compare the provisions for Napoleon's reorganization of the Church in 1802 with the imperial catechism of 1806. What comment can you make regarding Napoleon and religion? Was he a divine-right monarch? What role did religion play in the establishment of Napoleon's political power? In this sense, note also the "Clerical Oath of Loyalty" (1790). Why is it essential in time of revolution for the state to control religious organization?

18. Was Napoleon an absolute monarch in the tradition of Louis XIV? Was he a democrat, or the first of the "modern dictators" in the fascist mold of Mussolini and Hitler? Does the distinction between a democrat and a dictator blur when one is trying to achieve and consolidate power?

19. Note Napoleon's view of his destiny, entitled "An End to the Woes of Anarchy," and his comments in exile on St. Helena. Was he a progressive or destructive force in French history? Did he embody Hegel's conception of the term "hero"? How? Was the philosophy of Jean Jacques Rousseau every bit as much a force for the promotion of historical change as were the actions of Napoleon Bonaparte?

4

The Industrial Revolution

Two nations between whom there is no intercourse and no sympathy; who are as ignorant of each other's habits, thoughts and feelings as if they were . . . inhabitants of different planets; who are formed by a different breeding, are fed by a different food, are ordered by differ-ent manners, and are not governed by the same laws—the rich and the poor.

—Benjamin Disraeli

The inherent vice of capitalism is the unequal sharing of blessings; the inherent virtue of socialism is the equal sharing of miseries.

—Winston Churchill

The worth of a State, in the long run, is the worth of the individuals composing it.

—John Stuart Mill

Man is born free and everywhere he is in chains.

—Jean Jacques Rousseau

The word "revolution" implies drastic change, most often of a political nature, which results in a new form of government. There are other types of revolution as well. From the late eighteenth century to the late nineteenth century,

Europe underwent a social and economic revolution that was the result of technological process inspired by inventive minds. No longer would humans be harnessed to the land, completely dependent on the vicissitudes of nature for their livelihood; a new world was dawning, based in the city and filled with the prospect of employment and new lives. But this was not a move toward economic independence, for humans would soon be harnessed to an even more exacting master than the land—the machine.

Historically, the process of industrialization was a gradual one. The first stage of the Industrial Revolution began slowly, about 1760, and was made possible by several factors. First, Europe had reaped the benefits of an age of discovery during the sixteenth and seventeenth centuries. This fostered a commercial revolution that resulted in substantial economic growth. Indeed, the economic benefits of exploration were evident as nations sought to organize and compete on a grand scale. In addition, the English and French political revolutions of the seventeenth and eighteenth centuries began the ascendency of the middle class, which furnished the investment capital and expansive leadership necessary for the inception of the Industrial Revolution. At the same time, the population of Europe was growing dramatically, so much so that a rural-based economy simply could not support the growing tax requirements of governments and employ all who sought jobs.

These conditions were especially evident in England, where rural unemployment had been exacerbated by a conscious decision on the part of the wealthy landowners and the government itself to "enclose" farmland, release the tenantry from the security of farm labor, and use the land as pasture for sheep. Great profits were to be made in the textile trade, but the resulting displacement of the yeoman farmer added to the rural dilemma.

Yet England in the mid-eighteenth century was generally prosperous since it had developed a solid colonial foundation that provided ready markets for its goods. These markets were served by a maritime commercial and military fleet without peer and were supported by growing domestic production. This increase in the productive capacity of domestic industry resulted in large part from English ingenuity. The development of the flying shuttle, spinning jenny, power loom, and cotton gin in the mid-eighteenth century bespoke English technical superiority and advancement. The English had other natural advantages as well. Blessed with the existence of large quantities of coal and iron in close proximity, the English developed techniques for reducing the impurities in iron, thereby stimulating production; this eventually led to the development of the railroad in the mid-nineteenth century.

These new technologies were harnessed and organized in the factory. Men, women, and children were employed to keep the machines running, and the "factory system" was established to provide the greatest efficiency of material and labor, at the least expensive cost.

To many, industrialization became synonymous with progress. Increased production of goods meant greater potential for export, and this in turn created greater profit for the individual and government alike. The cultivation of new markets inspired competition among nations, exploration of new lands, and efficient management of time and labor. Yet industrialization, for all its glorification of the genius of the human mind, was never without its critics. It solved certain problems, but created others. What, for instance, was to be done with those people who moved to the city in search of factory employment and found themselves among the "technologically unemployed," looking for jobs that simply did not exist? And what of those who were fortunate enough to find work in the mills or the mines? The dull monotony and danger of their occupations, not to mention their subsistence living conditions, made life depressing. Factory workers dreaded unemployment, yet could do little to change their condition. As long as competition, efficiency, and profit were the primary catalysts of the Industrial Revolution, the laborer would have to be sacrificed.

The conflicts raised by industrialization were all the more bewildering because they were unprecedented. How, for example, was government to respond to the complex problems created by industrial progress? This question was of primary importance for Britain, the first industrial area and the subject of this chapter. British industrialization was stimulated in the nine-teenth century by the needs of national defense in view of the threat imposed by Napoleon. Criticism by reformers was not tolerated by the government, which viewed such acts as unpatriotic and incendiary. By the 1820s, however, tentative reforms were made that led to a rather prolonged debate resulting in the Reform Bill of 1832. This ensured that most middle-class British subjects would receive parliamentary representation and opened the franchise to some of the new industrial towns whose populations had never before been repre-sented. In the following years, further reforms were legislated, such as the Factory Act of 1833, that limited the working hours of women and children in the textile mills and provided government inspection of the workplace. Still, reform was not won without struggle. In the 1830s and 1840s, writers and literary figures such as Charles Dickens and historian Thomas Carlyle and political organizations such as the Chartists advocated constitutional and social change. Liberalism was born as a political philosophy, and intellectuals such as John Stuart Mill (1806–1873) advocated workers' cooperatives, unions, and even women's suffrage.

Change was advocated from other directions as well. It was during this time that Karl Marx and Friedrich Engels observed the conditions of the working class in England and composed one of the most influential documents of the modern world—the *Communist Manifesto* (1848). According to Marx, the true revolutionary force in society was the workers (proletarians) who were domi-nated and abused by capitalists interested in profit at the workers' expense. As Marx wrote: "Let the ruling classes tremble at a Communist revolution. The proletarians have nothing to lose but their chains. They have a world to win." Other socialists less radical than Marx preached the need and inevitability of change to a more balanced society, based less on privilege and more on equality of opportunity.

The Industrial Revolution can thus be viewed in two ways: as a force for progress, an example of human ability to mold the environment, and as a demonstration of man's abuse of man, for the Industrial Revolution intensified class animosities and provided the catalyst for social change. The questions that emerge from this chapter are thus philosophical in nature yet practical in application. In order for civilization to progress, to move forward technologically, must there always be a price to pay in human suffering or abuse? And if that is the case, is it worth it? What indeed constitutes "progress"? The twentieth century has experienced some of the greatest technological change, from the invention of the automobile to the exploration of space. Have we too paid a price?

The Factory System: Working Conditions

Sybil (1845)

BENJAMIN DISRAELI

One of the most ardent reformers who criticized working conditions was Benjamin Disraeli. A novelist and politician, he served as prime minister of Britain from 1867 to 1868 and from 1874 to 1880. His most famous novel, Sybil, or the Two Nations, *vividly describes working and living conditions in factory towns. Disraeli hoped to gain working-class support for a group of reforming aristocrats in his Tory party. The following selection from this novel demonstrates the power of his prose.*

They come forth: the mine delivers its gang and the pit its bondsmen, the forge is silent and the engine is still. The plain is covered with the swarming multitude: bands of stalwart men, broad-chested and muscular, wet with the toil, and black as the children of the tropics; troops of youth, alas! of both sexes, though neither their raiment nor their language indicates the difference; all are clad in male attire; and oaths that men might shudder at issue from lips born to breathe words of sweetness. Yet these are to be, some are, the mothers of England! But can we wonder at the hideous coarseness of their language, when we remember the savage rudeness of their lives? Naked to the waist, an iron chain fastened to a belt of leather runs between their legs clad in canvas trousers, while on hands and feet an English girl, for twelve, sometimes for sixteen hours a day, hauls and

"Sybil" is from Benjamin Disraeli, *Sybil, or the Two Nations* (New York: M. Walter Dunne, 1904), pp. 199–200.

hurries tubs of coals up subterranean roads, dark, precipitous, and plashy; circumstances that seem to have escaped the notice of the Society for the Abolition of Negro Slavery. Those worthy gentlemen, too, appear to have been singularly unconscious of the sufferings of the little trappers, which was remarkable, as many of them were in their own employ.

See, too, these emerge from the bowels of the earth! Infants of four and five years of age, many of them girls, pretty and still soft and timid; entrusted with the fulfillment of responsible duties, the very nature of which entails on them the necessity of being the earliest to enter the mine and the latest to leave it. Their labour indeed is not severe, for that would be impossible, but it is passed in darkness and in solitude. They endure that punishment which philosophical philanthropy has invented for the direst criminals, and which those criminals deem more terrible than the death for which it is substituted. Hour after hour elapses, and all that reminds the infant trappers of the world they have quitted, and that which they have joined, is the passage of the coal-wagons for which they open the air-doors of the galleries, and on keeping which doors constantly closed, except at this moment of passage, the safety of the mine and the lives of the persons employed in it entirely depend.

Testimony before the Sadler Committee (1832)

In 1831 and 1832, the British government was under popular pressure to regulate factories and protect men, women, and children from abusive working conditions. The Sadler Committee was established and heard testimony from both workers and factory owners. The following selection clearly describes working conditions in a flax mill.

What age are you?—Twenty-three.

Where do you live?—At Leeds.

What time did you begin to work at a factory?—When I was six years old.

At whose factory did you work?—At Mr. Busk's.

What kind of mill is it?—Flax-mill.

What was your business in that mill?—I was a little doffer.

What were your hours of labour in that mill?—From 5 in the morning till 9 at night, when they were thronged.

For how long a time together have you worked that excessive length of time?—For about half a year.

What were your usual hours of labour when you were not so thronged?—From 6 in the morning till 7 at night.

"Testimony before the Sadler Committee" is from *Parliamentary Papers*, Reports from Committees, XV, "Labour of Children in Factories 1831–1832" (London, 1832).

What time was allowed for your meals?—Forty minutes at noon.

Had you any time to get your breakfast or drinking?—No, we got it as we could.

And when your work was bad, you hardly had anytime to eat at all?—No; we were obliged to leave it or take it home, and when we did not take it, the overlooker took it, and gave it to his pigs.

Do you consider doffing a laborious employment?—Yes.

Explain what it is you had to do?—When the frames are full, they have to stop the frames, and take the flyers off, and take the full bobbins off, and carry them to the roller; and then put empty ones on, and set the frame going again.

Does that keep you constantly on your feet?—Yes, there are so many frames, and they run so quick.

Your labour is very excessive?—Yes; you have not time for anything.

Suppose you flagged a little, or were too late, what would they do?—Strap us.

Are they in the habit of strapping those who are last in doffing?—Yes.

Constantly?—Yes.

Have you ever been strapped?—Yes.

Severely?—Yes.

Is the strap used so as to hurt you excessively?—Yes, it is.

Were you strapped if you were too much fatigued to keep up with the machinery?—Yes; the overlooker I was under was a very severe man, and when we have been fatigued and worn out, and had not baskets to put the bobbins in, we used to put them in the window bottoms, and that broke the panes sometimes, and I broke one one time, and the overlooker strapped me on the arm, and it rose a blister, and I ran home to my mother.

How long did you work at Mr. Busk's?—Three or four years.

Where did you go to then?—Benyon's factory.

That was when you were about 10 years?—Yes.

What were you then?—A weigher in the card-room.

How long did you work there?—From half-past 5 till 8 at night.

Was that the ordinary time?—Till 9 when they were thronged.

What time was allowed for meals at that mill?—Forty minutes at noon.

Any time at breakfast or drinking?—Yes, for the card-rooms, but not for the spinning-rooms, a quarter of an hour to get their breakfast.

And the same for their drinking?—Yes.

So that the spinners in that room worked from half-past 5 till 9 at night?—Yes.

Having only forty minutes' rest?—Yes.

The carding-room is more oppressive than the spinning department?—Yes, it is so dusty they cannot see each other for dust.

It is on that account they are allowed a relaxation of those few minutes?—Yes; the cards get so soon filled up with waste and dirt, they are obliged to stop them, or they would take fire.

There is a convenience in that stoppage?—Yes, it is as much for their benefit as for the working people.

When it was not necessary no such indulgence was allowed?—No.

Never?—No.

Were the children beat up to their labour there?—Yes.

With what?—A strap; I have seen the overlooker go to the top end of the room, where the little girls hug the can to the backminders; he has taken a strap, and a whistle in his mouth, and sometimes he has got a chain and chained them, and strapped them all down the room.

All the children?—No, only those hugging the cans.

What was his reason for that?—He was angry.

Had the children committed any fault?—They were too slow.

Were the children excessively fatigued at that time?—Yes, it was in the afternoon.

Were the girls so struck as to leave marks upon their skin?—Yes, they have had black marks many times, and their parents dare not come to him about it, they were afraid of losing their work.

If the parents were to complain of this excessive ill-usage, the probable consequence would be the loss of the situation of the child?—Yes.

In what part of the mill did you work?—In the card-room.

It was exceedingly dusty?—Yes.

Did it affect your health?—Yes; it was so dusty, the dust got upon my lungs, and the work was so hard; I was middling strong when I went there, but the work was so bad; I got so bad in health, that when I pulled the baskets down, I pulled my bones out of their places.

You dragged the baskets?—Yes; down the rooms to where they are worked.

And as you had been weakened by excessive labour, you could not stand that labour?—No.

It has had the effect of pulling your shoulders out?—Yes; it was a great basket that stood higher than this table a good deal.

How heavy was it?—I cannot say; it was a very large one, that was full of weights up-heaped, and pulling the basket pulled my shoulders out of its place, and my ribs have grown over it.

You continued at that work?—Yes.

You think that work is too much for children?—Yes.

It is woman's work, not fit for children?—Yes.

Is that work generally done by women?—Yes.

How came you to do it?—There was no spinning for me.

Did they give you women's wages?—They gave me 5s. and the women had 6s. 6d.

What wages did you get as a spinner?—Six shillings.

Did you perceive that many other girls were made ill by that long labour?—Yes, a good many of them.

So that you were constantly receiving fresh hands to supply the places of those that could no longer bear their work?—Yes, there were fresh hands every week; they could not keep their hands.

Did they all go away on account of illness?—They were sick and ill with the dust.

Do you know whether any of them died in consequence of it?—No, I cannot speak to that.

You do not know what became of them?—No, we did not know that.

If a person was to take an account of a mill, and the hands in it that were ill, they would know very little of those who had suffered from their labour; they would be elsewhere?—Yes.

But you are sure of this, that they were constantly leaving on account of the excessive labour they had to endure?—Yes.

And the unhealthy nature of their employment?—Yes.

Did you take any means to obviate the bad effects of this dust?—No.

Did it make you very thirsty?—Yes, we drank a deal of water in the room.

Were you heated with your employment at the same time?—No, it was not so very hot as in the summer time; in the winter time they were obliged to have the windows open, it made no matter what the weather was, and sometimes we got very severe colds in frost and snow.

You were constantly exposed to colds, and were made ill by that cause also?—Yes.

You are considerably deformed in your person in consequence of this labour?—Yes, I am.

At what time did it come on?—I was about 13 years old when it began coming, and it has got worse since. . . .

Do you know of any body that has been similarly injured in their health?—Yes, in their health, but not many deformed as I am.

You are deformed in the shoulders?—Yes.

It is very common to have weak ankles and crooked knees?—Yes, very common indeed.

That is brought on by stopping the spindle?—Yes.

Do you know anything of wet-spinning?—Yes, it is very uncomfortable; I have stood before the frame till I have been wet through to my skin; and in winter time, when we have gone home, our clothes have been frozen, and we have nearly caught our death of cold.

Child Labor

Children were an integral part of the factory system. Mine owners depended on small boys to enter and work in restrictive areas that could not accommodate adults. The mills were common sources of employment for children who were

"Child Labor" is from John Saville, ed., *Working Conditions in the Victorian Age* (Westmead, England: Gregg International Publishers Limited, 1973), pp. 130–132, 378–380. Reprinted by permission of the publisher.

good with their hands. Many parents condoned this and often forced their children to work, since they depended on their children's wages to live at subsistence level. The following accounts were excerpted from various liberal journals such as the Edinburgh Review, *the* Westminster Review, *and* Fraser's Magazine; *they reveal the social conscience of Victorian England.*

With regard to the hours of work, the commissioners state, that when the work-people are in full employment, the regular hours of work for children and young persons are rarely less than eleven; more often they are twelve; in some districts they are thirteen; and in one district they are generally fourteen and upwards. Certainly, unless upon the ample testimony produced by the Commission, it would not be credible that there is one district in the centre of England in which children are regularly required to pursue the labours of the mine for fourteen and sixteen hours daily; but in Derbyshire, south of Chesterfield, from thirteen to sixteen hours are considered a day's work; from eleven to twelve hours are reckoned three quarters of a day's work; and eight hours make half a day's work.

"John Hawkins, eight years of age:—'Has worked in Sissons Pit, a year and a half; lives a mile from the pit; goes down from five to nine;' that is, this child, eight years old, is employed in the pit at work from five o'clock in the morning to nine at night, a period of 16 hours.—John Houghton, nine years old:—'Goes down from six to eight—it has been ten:' that is, this child is regularly employed at work in the pits 14 hours, and occasionally 16 hours.—Ephraim Riley, eleven years old:—'Had three miles to walk to the pit; left home at five o'clock, winter and summer, and did not get home again until nine o'clock at night (16 hours); his legs and thighs hurt him so with working so much that he remains in bed on Sunday mornings.'—John Chambers, thirteen years old:—'Has worked in pits since he was seven; works from six to nine or ten (from 15 to 16 hours). When first he worked in a pit he felt so tired, and his legs, arms, and back ached so much, that his brother has had to help him home many times. He could not go to school on a Sunday morning, he has been so stiff; he felt these pains until about a year since; he now feels tired, but his limbs do not ache as they did.'—James Creswell, fourteen years old:—'Has worked in pits four or five years; goes down at half-past six to nine, has this winter been after ten; half-days half-past six to three or four.'

"Of the fatigue of such labour, so protracted and carried on in such places of work, the following evidence exhibits a striking picture, and it will be observed that the witnesses of every class, children, young persons, colliers, underground stewards, agents, parents, teachers, and ministers of religion, all concur in making similar statements.

"John Bostock, aged seventeen, Babbington:—'Has often been made to work until he was so tired as to lie down on his road home until 12 o'clock, when his mother has come and led him home; he has done so many times when he first went to the pits; he has sometimes been so fatigued that he could not eat his dinner, but has been beaten and made to work until night; he never thought to play, was always too anxious to get to bed; is sure this is all true.'—John Leadbeater, aged eighteen, Babbington:—'Has two miles to go to the pit, and must be there before six, and works until eight; he has often worked all night, and been made by the butties to work as usual the next day; has often been so tired that he has lain in bed all Sunday. He knows no work so bad as that of a pit lad.'—Samuel Radford, aged nineteen, New Birchwood:—'Has been a week together and never seen daylight but on a Sunday, and not much then, he was so sleepy.'

An imperfect abstract from the registration of deaths for the year 1838, gives a total, in England alone, of 349 deaths by violence in coal mines, and shows the most common causes of them:—

Cause of death	Under 13 years of age	13 and not exceeding 18 years of age	Over 18 years of age
Fell down the shafts	13	12	31
Fell down the shaft from the rope breaking	1	—	2
Fell out when ascending	—	—	3
Drawn over the pulley	3	—	3
Fall of stone out of a skip down the shaft	1	—	3
Drowned in the mines	3	4	15
Fall of stones, coal, and rubbish in the mines	14	14	69
Injuries in coal-pits, the nature of which is not specified	6	3	32
Crushed in coal-pits	—	1	1
Explosion of gas	13	18	49
Suffocation of choke-damp	—	2	6
Explosion of gunpowder	—	1	3
By tram-wagons	4	5	12
Total	58	62	229

We proceed now to notice the great *Metal Manufactures* and their influence upon the health and well being of the children and youths employed in them. . . . In the blast-furnaces, mills, and forges, great numbers of children and youths are employed in night sets, between 6 P.M. and 6 A.M.; and in the miscellaneous trades overtime is very common, a great number of children working as long as the men, viz. from 6 A.M. to 11 P.M. Little girls are employed in bellows-blowing (very hard work for children) for fourteen hours a-day, standing on platforms to enable them to reach the handle of the bellows. Night work, overtime, and the very nature of the employment, cannot but have a very disastrous influence on their health.

The foundry-boys, it is admitted by the masters themselves, commence work at much too early an age, and are taxed far beyond their strength; and the children who work at home, in the various domestic manufactures, are so injured by premature labour, often commencing from the age of seven, that, as a rule, they are stunted, dwarfed, or deformed. An instance is given of a father having worked his three young boys from four in the morning until twelve at night for weeks together, until the other men 'cried shame upon him'. . . . Two girls, nine and ten years of age, were working as 'strikers' and a little girl of eight, occasionally relieved by a still younger one of six, was working the bellows. The gross earnings of this man amounted to two guineas per week. It may be doubted whether the world could not produce a more revolting instance of parental oppression than the spectacle of these two young girls, whose little hands would have been appropriately employed in hemming a kerchief or working a sampler, begrimed with the smoke, stifled with the heat and stunned with the din morning till night. A single instance of oppression has often had a greater effect in rousing indignation than the most powerful denunciation of a general wrong. The picture of these little Staffordshire girls thus unsexed by an imperious taskmaster, and that taskmaster their parent, is well adapted to expose for universal reprobation a system under which such an enormity could be possible, and to prove the necessity of immediate legislative interference.

Living Conditions

The living conditions of workers in urban industrial settings were a popular subject for reformers. One of the most important reformers, Friedrich Engels (1820–1895), was born to a family of German textile manufacturers. Engels was a keen observer of society and a talented, urbane writer. His close friendship and collaboration with Karl Marx was instrumental in the dissemination and success of communist ideology. In the first selection, Engels describes the condition of the working class in Manchester, the primary manufacturing town in England. In the second, he exposes the threat to women and the family engendered by the factory system.

The Condition of the Working Class in England (1844)
FRIEDRICH ENGELS

Above Ducie Bridge, the left bank grows more flat and the right bank steeper, but the condition of the dwellings on both banks grows worse

"The Condition of the Working Class in England" is from Friedrich Engels, *The Condition of the Working Class in England in 1844* (London: Sonenschein & Co., 1892), pp. 51–53.

rather than better. He who turns to the left here from the main street, Long Millgate, is lost; he wanders from one court to another, turns count-less corners, passes nothing but narrow, filthy nooks and alleys, until after a few minutes he has lost all clue, and knows not whither to turn. Everywhere half or wholly ruined buildings, some of them actually uninhabited, which means a great deal here; rarely a wooden or stone floor to be seen in the houses, almost uniformly broken, ill-fitting windows and doors, and a state of filth! Everywhere heaps of debris, refuse, and offal; standing pools for gutters, and a stench which alone would make it impossible for a human being in any degree civilised to live in such a district. The newly-built extension of the Leeds railway, which crosses the Irk here, has swept away some of these courts and lanes, laying others completely open to view. Immediately under the railway bridge there stands a court, the filth and horrors of which surpass all the others by far, just because it was hitherto so shut off, so secluded that the way to it could not be found without a good deal of trouble. I should never have discovered it myself, without the breaks made by the railway, though I thought I knew this whole region thoroughly. Passing along a rough bank, among stakes and washing-lines, one penetrates into this chaos of small one-storied, one-roomed huts, in most of which there is no artificial floor; kitchen, living and sleeping-room all in one. In such a hole, scarcely five feet long by six broad, I found two beds—and such bedsteads and beds!—which, with a staircase and chimney-place, exactly filled the room. In several others I found absolutely nothing, while the door stood open, and the inhabitants leaned against it. Every-where before the doors refuse and offal; that any sort of pavement lay underneath could not be seen but only felt, here and there with the feet. This whole collection of cattle-sheds for human beings was surrounded on two sides by houses and a factory, and on the third by the river, and besides the narrow stair up the bank, a narrow doorway alone led out into another almost equally ill-built, ill-kept labyrinth of dwellings. . . .

Such is the Old Town of Manchester, and on re-reading my description, I am forced to admit that instead of being exaggerated, it is far from black enough to convey a true impression of the filth, ruin, and uninhabitable-ness, the defiance of all considerations of cleanliness, ventilation, and health which characterise the construction of this single district, containing at least twenty to thirty thousand inhabitants. And such a district exists in the heart of the second city of England, the first manufacturing city of the world. If any one wishes to see in how little space a human being can move, how little air—and *such* air!—he can breathe, how little civilisation he may share and yet live, it is only necessary to travel hither. True, this is the *Old* Town, and the people of Manchester emphasise the fact whenever any one mentions to them the frightful condition of this Hell upon Earth; but what does that prove? Everything which here arouses horror and indignation is of recent origin, belongs to the *industrial epoch*.

The Impact of the Factory System on Women and the Family

FRIEDRICH ENGELS

The employment of women at once breaks up the family; for when the wife spends twelve or thirteen hours every day in the mill, and the husband works the same length of time there or elsewhere, what becomes of the children? They grow up like wild weeds; they are put out to nurse for a shilling or eighteenpence a week, and how they are treated may be imagined. . . . That the general mortality among young children must be increased by the employment of the mothers is self-evident, and is placed beyond all doubt by notorious facts.

Women often return to the mill three or four days after confinement [for childbirth], leaving the baby, of course; in the dinner hour they must hurry home to feed the child and eat something, and what sort of suckling that can be is also evident.

Lord Ashley repeats the testimony of several workwomen:

"M. H., twenty years old, has two children, the youngest a baby, that is tended by the other, a little older. The mother goes to the mill shortly after five o'clock in the morning, and comes home at eight at night; all day the milk pours from her breasts so that her clothing drips with it."

"H. W. has three children, goes away Monday morning at five o'clock, and comes back Saturday evening; has so much to do for the children then that she cannot get to bed before three o'clock in the morning; often wet through to the skin, and obliged to work in that state. She said: 'My breasts have given me the most frightful pain, and I have been dripping wet with milk.' "

The use of narcotics to keep the children still is fostered by this infamous system, and has reached a great extent in the factory districts. Dr. Johns, Registrar in Chief for Manchester, is of opinion that this custom is the chief source of the many deaths from convulsions. The employment of the wife dissolves the family utterly and of necessity, and this dissolution, in our present society, which is based upon the family, brings the most demoralizing consequences for parents, as well as children. . . .

Yet the working man cannot escape from the family, must live in the family, and the consequence is a perpetual succession of family troubles, domestic quarrels, most demoralizing for parents and children alike. Neglect of all domestic duties, neglect of the children, especially, is only too common among English working people, and only too vigorously fostered by the existing institutions of society. And children growing up in this savage way, amidst these demoralizing influences, are expected to turn out

"The Impact of the Factory System on Women and the Family" is from Friedrich Engels, *The Conditions of the Working Class in England in 1844* (London: Sonnenschein & Co., 1892).

goody-goody and moral in the end! Verily the requirements are naive which the self-satisfied bourgeois makes upon the working man!

Defense of the Factory System

The Philosophy of Manufactures (1835)

ANDREW URE

The factory system was not without its advocates. One of the most influential was Andrew Ure, a professor of applied science at the University of Glasgow. He was supportive of the efficiency and productive capabilities of mechanized manufacturing. Note how the major criticisms of the reformers (child labor, degrading and unhealthy work conditions, etc.) are methodically countered. Ure argued that the owners of the mills and mines were not devils, but were actually abused themselves by the demands of the workers.

Proud of the power of malefaction, many of the cotton-spinners, though better paid, as we have shown, than any similar set of artisans in the world, organized the machinery of strikes through all the gradations of their people, *terrifying* or *cajoling* the timid or the passive among them to join their vindictive union. They boasted of possessing a dark tribunal, by the mandates of which they could paralyze every mill whose master did not comply with their wishes, and so bring ruin on the man who had given them profitable employment for many a year. By flattery or intimidation, they levied contributions from their associates in the privileged mills, which they suffered to proceed, in order to furnish spare funds for the maintenance of the idle during the decreed suspension of labour. In this extraordinary state of things, when the inventive head and the sustaining heart of trade were held in bondage by the unruly lower members, a destructive spirit began to display itself among some partisans of the union. Acts of singular atrocity were committed, sometimes with weapons fit only for demons to wield, such as the corrosive oil of vitriol, dashed in the faces of most meritorious individuals, with the effect of disfiguring their persons, and burning their eyes out of the sockets with dreadful agony.

The true spirit of turn-outs [strikes] among the spinners is well described in the following statement made on oath to the Factory Commission, by Mr. George Royle Chappel, a manufacturer of Manchester, who employs 274 hands, and two steam-engines of sixty-four horse power.

"I have had several turn-outs, and have heard of many more, but never

"The Philosophy of Manufactures" is from Andrew Ure, *The Philosophy of Manufactures* (London: Charles Knight, 1835), pp. 282–284, 290, 300–301, 309–311, 398–399.

heard of a turn-out for short time. I will relate the circumstances of the last turn-out, which took place on the 16th October, 1830, and continued till the 17th January, 1831. The whole of our spinners, whose average (weekly) wages were 2£. 13s. 5d., turned out at the instigation, as they told us at the time, of the delegates of the union. They said they had no fault to find with their wages, their work, or their masters, but the union obliged them to turn out. The same week three delegates from the spinners' union waited upon us at our mill, and dictated certain advances in wages, and other regulations, to which, if we would not adhere, they said neither our own spinners not any other should work for us again! Of course we declined, believing our wages to be ample, and our regulations such as were necessary for the proper conducting of the establishment. The consequences were, they set watches on every avenue to the mill, night and day, to prevent any fresh hands coming into the mill, an object which they effec-

"[The children] seemed always to be cheerful and alert, taking pleasure in the light play of their muscles, enjoying the mobility natural to their age."–Andrew Ure, *The Philosophy of Manufactures* (1835). (*Library of Congress*)

tually attained, by intimidating some, and promising support to others (whom I got into the mill in a caravan), if they would leave their work. Under these circumstances, I could not work the mill, and advertised it for sale, without any applications, and I also tried in vain to let it. At the end of twenty-three weeks the hands requested to be taken to the mill again on the terms that they had left it, declaring, as they had done at first, that the union alone had forced them to turn out. . . .

Nothing shows in a clearer point of view the credulity of mankind in general, and of the people of these islands in particular, than the ready faith which was given to the tales of cruelty exercised by proprietors of cotton-mills towards young children. The systems of calumny somewhat resembles that brought by the Pagans against the primitive Christians, of enticing children into their meetings in order to murder and devour them. . . .

No master would wish to have any wayward children to work within the walls of his factory, who do not mind their business without beating, and he therefore usually fines or turns away any spinners who are known to maltreat their assistants. Hence, ill-usage of any kind is a very rare occurrence. I have visited many factories, both in Manchester and in the surrounding districts, during a period of several months, entering the spinning rooms, unexpectedly, and often alone, at different times of the day, and I never saw a single instance of corporal chastisement inflicted on a child, nor indeed did I ever see children in ill-humour. They seemed to be always cheerful and alert, taking pleasure in the light play of their muscles, enjoying the mobility natural to their age. The scene of industry, so far from exciting sad emotions in my mind, was always exhilarating. It was delightful to observe the nimbleness with which they pieced the broken ends, as the mule-carriage began to recede from the fixed roller-beam, and to see them at leisure, after a few seconds' exercise of their tiny fingers, to amuse themselves in any attitude they chose, till the stretch and winding-on were once more completed. The work of these lively elves seemed to resemble a sport, in which habit gave them a pleasing dexterity. Conscious of their skill, they were delighted to show it off to any stranger. As to exhaustion by the day's work, they evinced no trace of it on emerging from the mill in the evening; for they immediately began to skip about any neighbouring playground, and to commence their little amusements with the same alacrity as boys issuing from a school. It is moreover my firm conviction, that if children are not ill-used by bad parents or guardians, but receive in food and raiment the full benefit of what they earn, they would thrive better when employed in our modern factories, than if left at home in apartments too often ill-aired, damp, and cold. . . .

Of all the common prejudices that exist with regard to factory labour, there is none more unfounded than that which ascribes to it excessive tedium and irksomeness above other occupations, owing to its being carried on in conjunction with the "unceasing motion of the steam-engine." In an establishment for spinning or weaving cotton, all the hard work is performed by the steam-engine, which leaves for the attendant no hard labour at all, and literally nothing to do in general; but at intervals to perform some delicate operation, such as joining the threads that break, taking the cops off the spindle, &c. And it is so far from being true that the work in a factory is incessant, because the motion of the steam-engine is incessant, that the fact is, that the labour is not incessant on that very count, because it is performed in conjunction with the steam-engine. Of all manu-facturing employments, those are by far the most irksome and incessant in which steam-engines are not employed, as in lace-running and stocking-weaving; and the way to prevent an employment from being incessant, is to introduce a steam-engine into it. These remarks certainly apply more especially to the labour of children in factories. Three-fourths of the children so employed are engaged in piecing at the mules. "When the carriages of these have receded a foot and a half or two feet from the roll-ers," says Mr. Tufnell, "nothing is to be done, not even attention is required from either spinner or piecer." Both of them stand idle for a time, and in fine spinning particularly, for three-quarters of a minute, or more. Conse-quently, if a child remains at this business twelve hours daily, he has nine hours of inaction. And though he attends two mules, he has still six hours of non-exertion. Spinners sometimes dedicate these intervals to the perusal of books. The scavengers, who, in Mr. Sadler's report, have been described as being "constantly in a state of grief, always in terror, and every moment they have to spare stretched all their length upon the floor in a state of perspiration," may be observed in cotton factories idle for *four* minutes at a time, or moving about in a sportive mood, utterly unconscious of the tragical scenes in which they were dramatized. . . .

Mr. Hutton, who has been in practice as a surgeon at Stayley Bridge upwards of thirty-one years, and, of course, remembers the commence-ment, and has had occasion to trace the progress and effect, of the factory system, says that the health of the population has much improved since its introduction, and that they are much superior in point of comfort to what they were formerly. He also says that fever has become less common since the erection of factories, and that the persons employed in them were less attacked by the influenza in 1833, than other classes of work-people. Mr. Bott, a surgeon, who is employed by the operatives in Messrs. Lichfield's mills to attend them in all cases of sickness or accident, at the rate of one halfpenny a week (a sum which indicates pretty distinctly their small chances of ailment), says that the factory workmen are not so liable to epidemics as other persons; and that though he has had many cases of typhus fever in the surrounding district, nearly all the mill-hands have escaped, and not one was attacked by the cholera during its prevalence in the neighbourhood.

Reaction and Reform

The Iron Law of Wages (1817)

DAVID RICARDO

The Industrial Revolution began to develop in England while the economic practice of mercantilism was still widespread. Proponents of mercantilism argued that colonies existed for the benefit of the mother country, and indeed all economic activity should be regulated by the state for the good of the state. This concept was not in harmony with the rise of industrial capitalism. Adam Smith, in his important treatise The Wealth of Nations *(1776), advocated the economic doctrine of* laissez-faire. *He contended that every human being is motivated primarily by self-interest and that the marketplace is regulated by its own competitive laws of supply and demand, profit and loss. Therefore, the market must be left alone (hence the name* laissez-faire*) and free from government controls and monopolies. Adam Smith soon became the "Patron Saint of Free Enterprise" and capitalism as a theory was born.*

Two of the most important "classical economists" who subscribed to Smith's ideas were Thomas Malthus (1766–1834) and David Ricardo (1772–1823). Malthus employed statistics to develop the Malthusian doctrine: the world's population, unless checked by war, disease, famine, late marriage, or moral restraint, grows at a higher rate than the means of subsistence, resulting in a doubling of the population every twenty-five years. His prediction for world famine was pessimistic indeed. David Ricardo, who had made a fortune on the London Stock Exchange, developed a theory, based to some extent on Malthus' analysis, that later came to be called the Iron Law of Wages. Ricardo believed that the wages of laborers must necessarily remain at a subsistence level because of the working class's unchecked rate of reproduction that would continuously keep the supply of labor excessive. Ricardo advocated a restriction of "poor laws" that were enacted by Parliament in the early nineteenth century to relieve the poor through governmental assistance. Ricardo thus became a champion of the rising industrial capitalists. A selection from his treatise The Principles of Political Economy and Taxation *(1817) follows.*

The friends of humanity cannot but wish that in all countries the labouring classes should have a taste for comforts and enjoyments, and that they should be stimulated by all legal means in their exertions to procure them. There cannot be a better security against a superabundant population. In those countries where the labouring classes have the fewest wants, and are contented with the cheapest food, the people are exposed to the greatest vicissitudes and miseries. They have no place or refuge from calamity; they

"The Iron Law of Wages" is from David Ricardo, *The Principles of Political Economy and Taxation* (London: J. M. Dent & Sons, Ltd., 1911), pp. 57, 61–63.

cannot seek safety in a lower station; they are already so low that they can fall no lower. On any deficiency of the chief article of their subsistence there are few substitutes of which they can avail themselves and dearth to them is attended with almost all the evils of famine.

In the natural advance of society, the wages of labour will have a tendency to fall, as far as they are regulated by supply and demand; for the supply of labourers will continue to increase at the same rate, while the demand for them will increase at a slower rate. . . . I say that, under these circumstances, wages would fall if they were regulated only by the supply and demand of labourers; but we must not forget that wages are also regulated by the prices of the commodities on which they are expended.

As population increases, these necessaries will be constantly rising in price, because more labour will be necessary to produce them. If, then, the money wages of labour should fall, while every commodity on which the wages of labour were expended rose, the labourer would be doubly affected, and would be soon totally deprived of subsistence. . . . These, then, are the laws by which wages are regulated, and by which the happiness of far the greatest part of every community is governed. Like all other contracts, wages should be left to the fair and free competition of the market, and should never be controlled by the interference of the legislature.

The clear and direct tendency of the poor laws is in direct opposition to those obvious principles: it is not, as the legislature benevolently intended, to amend the condition of the poor, but to deteriorate the condition of both poor and rich; instead of making the poor rich, they are calculated to make the rich poor; and while the present laws are in force, it is quite in the natural order of things that the fund for the maintenance of the poor should progressively increase till it has absorbed all the net revenue of the country, or at least so much of it as the state shall leave to us, after satisfying its own never-failing demands for the public expenditure.

This pernicious tendency of these laws is no longer a mystery, since it has been fully developed by the able hand of Mr. Malthus; and every friend to the poor must ardently wish for their abolition. Unfortunately, however, they have been so long established, and the habits of the poor have been so formed upon their operation, that to eradicate them with safety from our political system requires the most cautious and skillful management. It is agreed by all who are most friendly to a repeal of these laws that, if it be desirable to prevent the most overwhelming distress to those for whose benefit they were erroneously enacted, their abolition should be effected by the most gradual steps.

It is a truth which admits not a doubt that the comforts and well-being of the poor cannot be permanently secured without some regard on their part, or some effort on the part of the legislature, to regulate the increase of their numbers, and to render less frequent among them early and improvident marriages. The operation of the system of poor laws has been directly contrary to this. They have rendered restraint superfluous, and have invited imprudence, by offering it a portion of the wages of prudence and industry.

The nature of the evil points out the remedy. By gradually contracting the sphere of the poor laws; by impressing on the poor the value of independence, by teaching them that they must look not to systematic or casual charity, but to their own exertions for support, that prudence and forethought are neither unnecessary nor unprofitable virtues, we shall by degrees approach a sounder and more healthful state.

No scheme for the amendment of the poor laws merits the least attention which has not their abolition for its ultimate object; and he is the best friend of the poor, and to the cause of humanity, who can point out how this end can be attained with the most security, and at the same time with the least violence. It is not by raising in any manner different from the present the fund from which the poor are supported that the evil can be mitigated. It would not only be no improvement, but it would be an aggravation of the distress which we wish to see removed, if the fund were increased in amount or were levied according to some late proposals, as a general fund from the country at large. . . . If by law every human being wanting support could be sure to obtain it, and obtain it in such a degree as to make life tolerably comfortable, theory would lead us to expect that all other taxes together would be light compared with the single one of poor rates. The principle of gravitation is not more certain than the tendency of such laws to change wealth and power into misery and weakness; . . . to confound all intellectual distinction; to busy the mind continually in supplying the body's wants; until at last all classes should be infected with the plague of universal poverty. Happily these laws have been in operation during a period of progressive prosperity, when the funds for the maintenance of labour have regularly increased, and when an increase of population would be naturally called for. But if our progress should become more slow; if we should attain the stationary state, from which I trust we are yet far distant, then will the pernicious nature of these laws become more manifest and alarming; and then, too, will their removal be obstructed by many additional difficulties.

On Liberty (1859)

JOHN STUART MILL

The classical economists such as Adam Smith and David Ricardo stressed the need for free enterprise in the marketplace and defied regulation by government. Other theoreticians accepted these principles of self-interest and self-determination and yet applied them more specifically to the social and political world. Jeremy Bentham (1748–1832) advocated a principle called "utilitari-

"On Liberty" is from John Stuart Mill, *On Liberty* (New York: John B. Alden, 1885), pp. 302–303, 305, 307.

anism," whereby all things could be judged on twin concepts of utility and happiness. The best government, for example, was one that ensured the greatest happiness for the greatest number of people. These utilitarians were also referred to as "philosophical radicals" because they lacked all reverence for tradition and believed that political, social, and economic problems could be addressed rationally, without reference to privilege or special interests. They were popularly characterized as unemotional intellectuals without a practical understanding of humanity. Yet their most distinguished spokesman went far in moderating this image. John Stuart Mill (1806–1878) was groomed by his father to carry on "the movement," but rebelled against the rigid educational system imposed on him. Mill believed, as did the classical economists, that human beings were motivated principally by self-interest and that individual freedom was a cherished necessity. Still, he had a true social conscience and believed in the dignity of the working class. Mill favored the education of workers as a means of social progress, the reform of working conditions, the establishment of unions, and women's suffrage. His distinguished presence and ideas gave legitimacy to the liberalization of English democracy. The following excerpt is from his work On Liberty (1859) and is representative of his concern for the rights of the individual in the state.

Of the Limits to the Authority of Society over the Individual

What, then, is the rightful limit to the sovereignty of the individual over himself? Where does the authority of society begin? How much of human life should be assigned to individuality, and how much to society?

Each will receive its proper share, if each has that which more particularly concerns it. To individuality should belong the part of life in which it is chiefly the individual that is interested; to society, the part which chiefly interests society.

Though society is not founded on a contract, and though no good purpose is answered by inventing a contract in order to deduce social obligations from it, every one who receives the protection of society owes a return for the benefit, and the fact of living in society renders it indispensable that each should be bound to observe a certain line of conduct towards the rest. This conduct consists, first, in not injuring the interests of one another; or rather certain interests, which, either by express legal provision or by tacit understanding, ought to be considered as rights; and secondly, in each person's bearing his share (to be fixed on some equitable principle) of the labours and sacrifices incurred for defending the society or its members from injury and molestation. These conditions society is justified in enforcing, at all costs to those who endeavour to withhold fulfilment. Nor is this all that society may do. The acts of an individual may be hurtful to others, or wanting in due consideration for their welfare, without going to the length of violating any of their constituted rights. The offender may then be justly punished by opinion, though not by law. As soon as any part of a person's conduct affects prejudicially the interests of others, society has jurisdiction over it, and the question whether the general welfare will or will not be promoted by interfering with it, becomes open to discussion. But there is no room for entertaining any such question when a person's conduct affects the interests of no persons besides himself, or needs not affect them unless they like (all the persons concerned being of full age, and the ordinary amount of understanding). In all such cases, there should be perfect freedom, legal and social, to do the action and stand the consequences.

It would be a great misunderstanding of this doctrine to suppose that it is one of selfish indifference, which pretends that human beings have no business with each other's conduct in life, and that they should not concern themselves about the well-doing or well-being of one another, unless their own interest is involved. Instead of any diminution, there is need of a great increase of disinterested exertion to promote the good of others. . . . Human beings owe to each other help to distinguish the better from the worse, and encouragement to choose the former and avoid the latter. They should be for ever stimulating each other to increased exercise of their higher faculties, and increased direction of their feelings and aims toward wise instead of foolish, elevating instead of degrading, objects and contemplations. But neither one person, nor any number of persons, is warranted in saying to another human creature of ripe years, that he shall not do with his life for his own benefit what he chooses to do with it. He is the person most interested in his own well-being: the interest which any other person, except in cases of strong personal attachment, can have in it, is trifling, compared with that which he himself has: the interest which society has in him individually (except as to his conduct to others) is fractional, and altogether indirect; while the respect to his own feelings and circumstances, the most ordinary man or woman has means of knowledge immeasurably surpassing those that can be possessed by any one else. The interference of society to overrule his judgment and purposes in what only regards himself must be grounded on general presumptions; which may be altogether wrong, and even if right, are as likely as not to be misapplied to individual cases, by persons no better acquainted with the circumstances of such cases than those are who look at them merely from without. In this department, therefore, of human affairs, Individuality has its proper field of action. In the conduct of human beings towards one another it is necessary that general rules should for the most part be observed, in order that people may know what they have to expect: but in each person's own concerns his individual spontaneity is entitled to free exercise. Considerations to aid his judgment, exhortations to strengthen his will, may be offered to him, even obtruded on him, by others: but he himself is the final judge. All errors which he is likely to commit against advice and warning are far outweighed by the evil of allowing others to constrain him to what they deem is good. . . .

The distinction here pointed out between the part of a person's life which concerns only himself, and that which concerns others, many persons will refuse to admit. How (it may be asked) can any part of the conduct of a member of society be a matter of indifference to the other members? No person is an entirely isolated being; it is impossible for a person to do anything seriously or permanently hurtful to himself, without mischief reaching at least to his near connections, and often far beyond them. If he injures his property, he does harm to those who directly or indirectly derived support from it, and usually diminishes, by a greater or less amount, the general resources of the community. If he deteriorates his bodily or mental faculties, he not only brings evil upon all who depended on him for any portion of their happiness, but disqualifies himself for rendering the services which he owes to his fellow creatures generally; perhaps becomes a burden on their affection or benevolence; and if such conduct were very frequent, hardly any offence that is committed would detract more from the general sum of good. Finally, if by his vices or follies a person does no direct harm to others, he is nevertheless (it may be said) injurious by his example; and ought to be compelled to control himself, for the sake of those whom the sight or knowledge of his conduct might corrupt or mislead.

And even (it will be added) if the consequences of misconduct could be confined to the vicious or thoughtless individual, ought society to abandon to their own guidance those who are manifestly unfit for it? If protection against themselves is confessedly due to children and persons under age, is not society equally bound to afford it to persons of mature years who are equally incapable of self-government? If gambling, or drunkenness, or incontinence, or idleness, or uncleanliness, are as injurious to happiness, and as great a hindrance to improvement, as many or most of the acts prohibited by law, why (it may be asked) should not law, so far as is consistent with practicability and social convenience, endeavour to repress these also? And as a supplement to the unavoidable imperfections of law, ought not opinion at least to organize a powerful police against these vices, and visit rigidly with social penalties those who are known to practise them? There is no question here (it may be said) about restricting individual experiments in living. The only things it is sought to prevent are things which have been tried and condemned from the beginning of the world until now; things which experience has shown not to be useful or suitable to any person's individuality. There must be some length of time and amount of experience after which a moral or prudential truth may be regarded as established: and it is merely desired to prevent generation after generation from falling over the same precipice which has been fatal to their predecessors. . . .

But the strongest of all the arguments against the interference of the public with purely personal conduct is that, when it does interfere, the odds are that it interferes wrongly, and in the wrong place. On questions of social morality, of duty to others, the opinion of the public, that is, of an overruling majority, though often wrong, is likely to be still oftener right; because on such questions they are only required to judge of their own interests; of the manner in which some mode of conduct, if allowed to be practised, would effect themselves. But the opinion of a similar majority, imposed as a law on the minority, on questions of selfregarding conduct, is quite as likely to be wrong as right; for in these cases public opinion means, at the best, some people's opinion of what is good or bad for other people; while very often it does not even mean that; the public, with the most perfect indifference, passing over the pleasure or convenience of those whose conduct they censure, and considering only their own preference. . . . It is easy for any one to imagine an ideal public which leaves the freedom and choice of individuals in all uncertain matters undisturbed, and only requires them to abstain from modes of conduct which universal experience has condemned. But where has there been seen a public which set any such limit to its censorship? or when does the public trouble itself about universal experience? In its interferences with personal conduct it is seldom thinking of anything but the enormity of acting or feeling differently from itself; and this standard of judgment, thinly disguised, is held up to mankind as dictate of religion and philosophy, by nine-tenths of all moralists and speculative writers. These teach that things are right because they are right; because we tell them to be so. They tell us to search in our own minds and hearts for laws of conduct binding on ourselves and on all others. What can the poor public do but apply these instructions, and make their own personal feelings of good and evil, if they are tolerably unanimous in them, obligatory on all the world?

A Middle-Class Perspective (1859)

SAMUEL SMILES

For many members of the middle class, the Victorian Age was not characterized by the slums of Glasgow or the dirt of industry. To their thinking, perseverance and hard work resulted in a better life and was always rewarded. In his book Self-Help *(1859), Samuel Smiles emphasized this principle through a series of biographies of men who had risen to fame and fortune. The guiding idea was that "the most important results in daily life are to be obtained, not through the exercise of extraordinary powers, such as genius and intellect, but through the energetic use of simple means and ordinary qualities with which nearly all human individuals have more or less been endowed." One was responsible for one's own fate; it was up to the individual to change a bad situation if so desired.*

The object of the book briefly is, to re-inculcate these old-fashioned but wholesome lessons—which perhaps cannot be too often urged,—that youth must work in order to enjoy,—that nothing creditable can be accomplished without application and diligence,—that the student must not be daunted by difficulties, but conquer them by patience and perseverance,—and that,

"A Middle-Class Perspective" is from Samuel Smiles, *Self-Help* (London: John Murray, 1882), pp. v, 1, 4.

above all, he must seek elevation of character, without which capacity is worthless and worldly success is naught. If the author has not succeeded in illustrating these lessons, he can only say that he has failed in his object.

"Heaven helps those who help themselves" is a well-tried maxim, embodying in a small compass the results of vast human experience. The spirit of self-help is the root of all genuine growth in the individual; and, exhibited in the lives of many, it constitutes the true source of national vigour and strength. Help from without is often enfeebling in its effects, but help from within invariably invigorates. Whatever is done *for* men or classes, to a certain extent takes away the stimulus and necessity of doing for themselves; and where men are subjected to over-guidance and over-government, the inevitable tendency is to render them comparatively helpless.

Even the best institutions can give a man no active help. Perhaps the most they can do is, to leave him free to develop himself and improve his individual condition. But in all times men have been prone to believe that their happiness and well-being were to be secured by means of institutions rather than by their own conduct. Hence the value of legislation as an agent in human advancement has usually been much over-estimated. To constitute the millionth part of a Legislature, by voting for one or two men once in three or five years, however conscientiously this duty may be performed, can exercise but little active influence upon any man's life and character. Moreover, it is every day becoming more clearly understood, that the function of Government is negative and restrictive, rather than positive and active; being resolvable principally into protection—protection of life, liberty, and property. Laws, wisely administered, will secure men in the enjoyment of the fruits of their labour, whether of mind or body, at a comparatively small personal sacrifice; but no laws, however, stringent, can make the idle industrious, the thriftless provident, or the drunken sober. Reforms can only be effected by means of individual action, economy, and self-denial; better habits, rather than by greater rights. . . .

Daily experience shows that it is energetic individualism which produces the most powerful effects upon the life and action of others, and really constitutes the best practical education. Schools, academies, and colleges, give but the merest beginnings of culture in comparison with it. Far more influential is the life-education daily given in our homes, in the streets, behind counters, in workshops, at the loom and the plough, in counting-houses and manufactories, and in the busy haunts of men. This is that finishing instruction as members of society, which Schiller designated "the education of the human race," consisting in action, conduct, self-culture, self-control,—all that tends to discipline a man truly, and fit him for the proper performance of the duties and business of life,—a kind of education not to be learnt from books, or acquired by any amount of mere literary training. With his usual weight of words Bacon observes, that "Studies teach not their own use; but that is a wisdom without them, and above them, won by observation;" a remark that holds true of actual life, as well as of the cultivation of the intellect itself. For all experience serves to illustrate and enforce the lesson, that a man perfects himself by work more than by reading,—that it is life rather than literature, action rather than study, and character rather than biography, which tend perpetually to renovate mankind.

The Communist Manifesto (1848)

KARL MARX AND FRIEDRICH ENGELS

The Communist Manifesto, written by Karl Marx (1818–1883) and Friedrich Engels in 1848, is the fundamental declaration of communist ideology. Marx was concerned with the process of change in history (dialectic). A keen observer of the industrial world around him, Marx saw the oppression of the worker (proletarian) by those who owned the means of production (bourgeoisie). Marx advocated a society that was devoid of capitalistic oppression, a society in which workers actually controlled the factories and regulated their own working conditions and environment. His call to revolution had little influence on the protests of 1848, but his ideas would serve as the foundation for the Russian Revolution in 1917 and are of great importance today.

Bourgeoisie and Proletariat

The history of all hitherto existing society is the history of class struggles.

Freeman and slave, patrician and plebian, lord and serf, guildmaster and journeyman, in a word, oppressor and oppressed, stood in constant opposition to one another, carried on an uninterrupted, now hidden, now open fight, a fight that each time ended, either in a revolutionary reconstitution of society at large, or in the common ruin of the contending classes.

In the earlier epochs of history, we find almost everywhere a complicated arrangement of society into various orders, a manifold graduation of social rank. In ancient Rome we have patricians, knights, plebians, slaves; in the Middle Ages, feudal lords, vassals, guildmasters, journeymen, apprentices, serfs; in almost all of these classes, again, subordinate gradations.

The modern bourgeois society that has sprouted from the ruins of feudal society, has not done away with class antagonisms. It has but established new classes, new conditions of oppression, new forms of struggle in place of the old ones.

Our epoch, the epoch of the bourgeoisie, possesses, however, this distinctive feature: it has simplified the class antagonisms. Society as a whole is more and more splitting up into two great hostile camps, into two great classes directly facing each other: Bourgeoisie and Proletariat. . . .

"The Communist Manifesto" is from Karl Marx and Friedrich Engels, *The Communist Manifesto*, trans. Samuel Moore (New York: Socialist Labor Party, 1888).

Each step in the development of the bourgeoisie was accompanied by a corresponding political advance of the class. An oppressed class under the sway of the feudal nobility, an armed and self-governing association in the medieval commune, here independent urban republic (as in Italy and Germany), there taxable "third estate" of the monarchy (as in France), afterwards, in the period of manufacture proper, serving either the semi-feudal or the absolute monarchy as a counterpoise against the nobility, and in fact, corner stone of the great monarchies in general, the bourgeoisie has at last, since the establishment of Modern Industry and of the world-market, conquered for itself, in the modern representative State, exclusive political sway. The executive of the modern State is but a committee for managing the common affairs of the whole bourgeoisie. . . .

The need of a constantly expanding market for its products chases the bourgeoisie over the whole surface of the globe. It must nestle everywhere, establish connections everywhere. . . .

The bourgeoisie, during its rule of scarce one hundred years, has created more massive and more colossal productive forces than have all preceding generations together. Subjection of Nature's forces to man, machinery, application of chemistry to industry and agriculture, steam-navigation, railways, electric telegraphs, clearing of whole continents for cultivation, canalization of rivers, whole populations conjured out of the ground—what earlier century had even a presentiment that such productive forces slumbered in the lap of social labor? . . .

In proportion as the bourgeoisie, i.e., capital, is developed, in the same proportion is the proletariat, the modern working-class, developed, a class of laborers, who live only so long as they find work, and who find work only so long as their labor increases capital. These laborers, who must sell themselves piecemeal, are a commodity, like every other article of commerce, and are consequently exposed to all the vicissitudes of competition, to all the fluctuations of the market.

Owing to the extensive use of machinery and to division of labor, the work of the proletarians has lost all individual character, and, consequently, all charm for the workman. He becomes an appendage of the machine, and it is only the most simple, most monotonous, and most easily acquired knack that is required of him. Hence, the cost of production of a workman is restricted, almost entirely, to the means of subsistence that he requires for his maintenance, and for the propagation of his race. But the price of commodity, and also of labor, is equal to its cost of production. In proportion, therefore, as the repulsiveness of the work increases, the wage decreases. Nay more, in proportion as the use of the machinery and division of labor increases, in the same proportion the burden of toil also increases, whether by prolongation of the working hours, by increase of the work enacted in a given time, or by increased speed of the machinery, etc.

Modern industry has converted the little workshop of the patriarchal master into the great factory of the industrial capitalist. Masses of laborers, crowded into the factory, are organized like soldiers. As privates of the

The grave memorial of Karl Marx at Highgate Cemetery in London: "The proletarians have nothing to lose but their chains. They have a world to win. Workers of the world, unite!"

industrial army they are placed under the command of a perfect hierarchy of officers and sergeants. Not only are they the slaves of the bourgeois class, and of the bourgeois State, they are daily and hourly enslaved by the machine, by the over-looker, and, above all, by the individual bourgeois manufacturer himself. The more openly despotism proclaims gain to be its end and aim, the more petty, the more hateful and the more embittering it is.

The less the skill and exertion or strength implied in manual labor, in other words, the more modern industry becomes developed, the more is the labor of men superseded by that of women. Differences of age and sex have no longer any distinctive social validity for the working class. All are instruments of labor, more or less expensive to use, according to their age and sex.

No sooner is the exploitation of the laborer by the manufacturer, so far at an end, that he receives his wages in cash, than he is set upon by the other portions of the bourgeoisie, the landlord, the shopkeeper, the pawnbroker, etc. . . .

But with the development of industry the proletariat not only increases in number, it becomes concentrated in greater masses, its strength grows, and it feels that strength more. The various interests and conditions of life within the ranks of the proletariat are more and more equalized, in proportion as machinery obliterates all distinctions of labor, and nearly everywhere reduces wages to the same low level. The growing competition among the bourgeois, and the resulting commercial crises, make the wages of the workers ever more fluctuating. The unceasing improvement of machinery, ever more rapidly developing, makes their livelihood more and more precarious; the collisions between individual workmen and individual bourgeois take more and more the character of collisions between two classes. Thereupon the workers begin to form combinations (Trades' Unions) against the bourgeois; they club together in order to keep up the rate of wages; they found permanent associations in order to make provision beforehand for these occasional revolts. Here and there the contest breaks out into riots.

Now and then the workers are victorious, but only for a time. The real fruit of their battle lies, not in the immediate result, but in the ever expanding union of the workers. This union is helped on by the improved means of communications that are created by modern industry, and that places the workers of different localities in contact with one another. It was just this contact that was needed to centralize the numerous local struggles, all of the same character, into one national struggle between classes. But every class struggle is a political struggle. . . .

This organization of the proletarians into a class, and consequently into a political party, is continually being upset again by the competition between the workers themselves. But it ever rises up again, stronger, firmer, mightier. It compels legislative recognition of particular interests of the workers, by taking advantage of the divisions among the bourgeoisie itself. Thus the ten-hour bill in England was carried. . . .

The essential condition for the existence, and for the sway of the bourgeois class, is the formation and augmentation of capital; the condition for capital is wage-labor. Wage-labor rests exclusively on competition between the laborers. The advance of industry, whose involuntary promoter is the bourgeoisie, replaces the isolation of the laborers, due to competition, by their revolutionary combination, due to association. The development of Modern Industry, therefore, cuts from under its feet the very foundation on which the bourgeoisie produces and appropriates products. What the bourgeoisie therefore produces, above all, are its own gravediggers. Its fall and the victory of the proletariat are equally inevitable.

Proletarians and Communists

In what relation do the Communists stand to the proletarians as a whole?

The Communists do not form a separate party opposed to other working class parties.

They have no interests separate and apart from those of the proletariat as a whole.

They do not set up any sectarian principles of their own, by which to shape and mould the proletarian movement.

The Communists are distinguished from the other working class parties by this only: 1. In the national struggles of the proletarians of the different countries, they point out and bring to the front the common interests of the entire proletariat independently of all nationality. 2. In the various stages of development which the struggle of the working class against the bourgeoisie has to pass through, they always and everywhere represent the interests of the movement as a whole.

The Communists, therefore, are on the one hand, practically, the most advanced and resolute section of the working class parties of every country, that section which pushes forward all other; on the other hand, theoretically, they have over the great mass of the proletariat the advantage of clearly understanding the line of march, the conditions, and the ultimate general results of the proletarian movement.

The immediate aim of the Communists is the same as that of all the other proletarian parties: formation of the proletariat into a class, overthrow of the bourgeois supremacy, conquest of political power by the proletariat.

The theoretical conclusions of the Communists are in no way based on ideas or principles that have been invented, or discovered, by this or that would-be universal reformer.

They merely express, in general terms, actual relations springing from an existing class struggle, from a historical movement going on under our very eyes. The abolition of existing property relations is not at all a distinctive feature of Communism.

All property relations in the past have continually been subject to historical change consequent upon the change in historical conditions.

The French Revolution, for example, abolished feudal property in favor of bourgeois property.

The distinguishing feature of Communism is not the abolition of property generally, but the abolition of bourgeois property. But modern bourgeois private property is the final and most complete expression of the system of producing and appropriating products, that is based on class antagonism, on the exploitation of the many by the few.

In this sense, the theory of the Communists may be summed up in the single sentence: Abolition of private property. . . .

The Communist revolution is the most radical rupture with traditional property-relations; no wonder that its development involves the most radical rupture with traditional ideas.

But let us have done with the bourgeois objections to Communism.

We have seen above, that the first step in the revolution by the working class, is to raise the proletariat to the position of ruling class, to win the battle of democracy.

The proletariat will use its political supremacy, to wrest, by degrees, all capital from the bourgeoisie, to centralize all instruments of production in the hands of the State, i.e., of the proletariat organized as the ruling class; and to increase the total of productive forces as rapidly as possible.

Of course, in the beginning, this cannot be effected except by means of despotic inroads on the rights of property, and on the conditions of bourgeois production; by means of measures, therefore, which appear economically insufficient and untenable, but which, in the course of the movement, outstrip themselves, necessitate further inroads upon the old social order, and are unavoidable as a means of entirely revolutionizing the mode of production.

These measures will of course be different in different countries.

Nevertheless in the most advanced countries the following will be pretty generally applicable:

1. Abolition of property in land and application of all rents of land to public purposes.
2. A heavy progressive or graduated income tax.
3. Abolition of all rights of inheritance.
4. Confiscation of the property of all emigrants and rebels.
5. Centralization of credit in the hands of the state, by means of a national bank with State capital and an exclusive monopoly.
6. Centralization of the means of communication and transport in the hands of the State.
7. Extension of factories and instruments of production owned by the State; the bringing into cultivation of waste lands, and the improvement of the soil generally in accordance with a common plan.
8. Equal liability of all to labor. Establishment of industrial armies, especially for agriculture.
9. Combination of agriculture with manufacturing industries; gradual abolition of the distinction between town and country, by a more equable distribution of population over the country.
10. Free education for all children in public schools. Abolition of children's factory labor in its present form. Combination of education with industrial production, etc., etc.

When, in the course of development, class distinctions have disappeared, and all production has been concentrated in the hands of a vast association of the whole nation, the public power will lose its political character. Political power, properly so called, is merely the organized power of one class for oppressing another. If the proletariat during its contest with the bourgeoisie is compelled, by the force of circumstances, to organize itself as a class, if, by means of a revolution, it makes itself the ruling class, and, as such, sweeps away by force the old conditions of production, then it will, along with these conditions, have swept away the conditions for the existence of class antagonisms, and of class generally, and will thereby have abolished its own supremacy as a class.

In place of the old bourgeois society, with its classes and class antagonisms, we shall have an association, in which the free development of each is the condition for the free development of all. . . .

In short, the Communists everywhere support every revolutionary movement against the existing social and political order of things.

In all these movements they bring to the front, as the leading question in each, the property question, no matter what its degree of development at the time.

Finally, they labor everywhere for the union and agreement of the democratic parties of all countries.

The Communists disdain to conceal their views and aims. They openly declare that their ends can be attained only by the forcible overthrow of all existing social conditions. Let the ruling classes tremble at a Communistic revolution. The proletarians have nothing to lose but their chains. They have a world to win.

Workers of the world, unite!

Rerum Novarum (1891)
POPE LEO XIII

One of the more influential associations against the abuses of industrialism was the Christian Socialist movement. It began in England about 1848 and stressed that one could overcome the evils of industrialism by following Christian principles: brotherly love was preferable to ruthless competition and exploitation. Quite apart from this movement, but adhering to the same basic principles, was the Catholic Church. Pope Leo XIII was an active commentator on political power and human liberty. In 1891, he issued the encyclical Rerum Novarum, *which addressed the continuing struggle between capitalists and workers. This official opinion of the pope demonstrates the Church's continuing interest in the affairs of the secular world.*

Rights and Duties of Capital Labor

That the spirit of revolutionary change, which has long been disturbing the nations of the world, should have passed beyond the sphere of politics and made its influence felt in the cognate sphere of practical economics is not surprising. The elements of the conflict now raging are unmistakable, in the vast expansion of industrial pursuits and the marvelous discoveries of science; in the changed relations between masters and workmen; in the

"Rerum Novarum" is from Claudia Carlen Ihm, ed., *The Papal Encyclicals, 1878–1903*, vol. 2 (New York: McGrath Publishing Company, 1981), pp. 241–242, 244–246, 248, 255–256.

enormous fortunes of some few individuals, and the utter poverty of the masses; in the increased self-reliance and closer mutual combination of the working classes; as also, finally, in the prevailing moral degeneracy. The momentous gravity of the state of things now obtaining fills every mind with painful apprehension; wise men are discussing it; practical men are proposing schemes; popular meetings, legislatures, and rulers of nations are all busied with it—actually there is no question which has taken a deeper hold on the public mind.

Therefore, . . . We thought it expedient now to speak on the condition of the working classes. It is a subject on which We have already touched more than once, incidentally. But in the present letter, the responsibility of the apostolic office urges Us to treat the question of set purpose and in detail, in order that no misapprehension may exist as to the principles which truth and justice dictate for its settlement. The discussion is not easy, nor is it void of danger. It is no easy matter to define the relative rights and mutual duties of the rich and of the poor, of capital and of labor. And the danger lies in this, that crafty agitators are intent on making use of these differences of opinion to pervert men's judgments and to stir up the people to revolt.

In any case we clearly see, and on this there is general agreement, that some opportune remedy must be found quickly for the misery and wretchedness pressing so unjustly on the majority of the working class: for the ancient working-men's guilds were abolished in the last century, and no other protective organization took their place. . . . Hence, by degrees it has come to pass that working men have been surrendered, isolated and helpless, to the hardheartedness of employers and the greed of unchecked competition. The mischief has been increased by rapacious usury, which, although more than once condemned by the Church, is nevertheless, under a different guise, but with like injustice, still practiced by covetous and grasping men. To this must be added that the hiring of labor and the conduct of trade are concentrated in the hands of comparatively few; so that a small number of very rich men have been able to lay upon the teeming masses of the laboring poor a yoke little better than that of slavery itself.

To remedy these wrongs the socialists, working on the poor man's envy of the rich, are striving to do away with private property, and contend that individual possessions should become the common property of all, to be administered by the State or by municipal bodies. They hold that by thus transferring property from private individuals to the community, the present mischievous state of things will be set to rights, inasmuch as each citizen will then get his fair share of whatever there is to enjoy. But their contentions are so clearly powerless to end the controversy that were they carried into effect the working man himself would be among the first to suffer. They are, moreover, emphatically unjust, for they would rob the lawful possessor, distort the functions of the State, and create utter confusion in the community. . . .

What is of far greater moment, however, is the fact that the remedy they propose is manifestly against justice. For, every man has by nature the right to possess property as his own. This is one of the chief points of distinction between man and the animal creation, for the brute has no power of self-direction, but is governed by two main instincts, which keep his powers on the alert, impel him to develop them in a fitting manner, and stimulate and determine him to action without any power of choice. One of these instincts is self-preservation, the other the propagation of the species. Both can attain their purpose by means of things which lie within range; beyond their verge the brute creation cannot go, for they are moved to action by their senses only, and in the special direction which these suggest. But with man it is wholly different. He possesses, on the one hand, the full perfection of the animal being, and hence enjoys at least as much as the rest of the animal kind, the fruition of things material. But animal nature, however perfect, is far from representing the human being in its completeness, and is in truth but humanity's humble handmaid, made to serve and to obey. It is the mind, or reason, which is the predominate element in us who are human creatures; it is this which renders a human being human, and distinguishes him essentially from the brute. And on this very account—that man alone among the animal creation is endowed with reason—it must be within his right to possess things not merely for temporary and momentary use, as other living things do, but to have and to hold them in stable and permanent possession. . . .

The contention, then, that the civil government should at its option intrude into and exercise intimate control over the family and the household is a great and pernicious error. True, if a family finds itself in exceeding distress, utterly deprived of the counsel of friends, and without any prospect of extricating itself, it is right that extreme necessity be met by public aid, since each family is a part of the commonwealth. In like manner, if within the precincts of the household there occur grave disturbance of mutual rights, public authority should intervene to force each party to yield to the other its proper due; for this is not to deprive citizens of their rights, but justly and properly to safeguard and strengthen them. But rulers of the commonwealth must go no further; here, nature bids them stop. Paternal authority can be neither abolished nor absorbed by the State; for it has the same source as human life itself. . . . The socialists, therefore, in setting aside the parent and setting up a State supervision, act against natural justice, and destroy the structure of the home. . . .

The great mistake in regard to the matter now under consideration is to take up with the notion that class is naturally hostile to class, and that the wealthy and the working men are intended by nature to live in mutual conflict. So irrational and so false is this view that the direct contrary is the truth. Just as the symmetry of the human frame is the result of the suitable arrangement of the different parts of the body, so in a State is it ordained by nature that these two classes should dwell in harmony and agreement, so as to maintain the balance of the body politic. Each needs the other: capital cannot do without labor, nor labor without capital. Mutual agreement results in the beauty of good order, while perpetual conflict necessarily produces confusion and savage barbarity. Now, in preventing such strife as this, and in uprooting it, the efficacy of Christian institutions is marvelous and manifold. First of all, there is no intermediary more powerful than religion (whereof the Church is the interpreter and guardian) in drawing the rich and the working class together, by reminding each of its duties to the other, and especially of the obligations of justice.

Of these duties, the following bind the proletarian and the worker: fully and faithfully to perform the work which has been freely and equitably agreed upon; never to injure the property, nor to outrage the person, of an employer; never to resort to violence in defending their own cause, nor to engage in riot or disorder; and to have nothing to do with men of evil principles, who work upon the people with artful promises of great results, and excite foolish hopes which usually end in useless regrets and grievous loss. The following duties bind the wealthy owner and the employer: not to look upon their work people as their bondsmen, but to respect in every man his dignity as a person ennobled by Christian character. They are reminded that, according to natural reason and Christian philosophy, working for gain is creditable, not shameful, to a man, since it enables him to earn an honorable livelihood; but to misuse men as though they were things in the pursuit of gain, or to value them solely for their physical powers—that is truly shameful and inhuman. Again justice demands that, in dealing with the working man, religion and the good of his soul must be kept in mind. Hence, the employer is bound to see that the worker has time for his religious duties; that he be not exposed to corrupting influences and dangerous occasions; and that he be not led away to neglect his home and family, or to squander his earnings. Furthermore, the employer must never tax his work people beyond their strength, or employ them in work unsuited to their sex and age. His great and principal duty is to give every one what is just. Doubtless, before deciding whether wages are fair, many things have to be considered; but wealthy owners and all masters of labor should be mindful of this—that to exercise pressure upon the indigent and the destitute for the sake of gain, and to gather one's profit out of the need of another, is condemned by all laws, human and divine. To defraud any one of wages that are his due is a great crime which cries to the avenging anger of Heaven. . . .

To sum up, then, We may lay it down as a general and lasting law that working men's associations should be so organized and governed as to furnish the best and most suitable means for attaining what is aimed at, that is to say, for helping each individual member to better his condition to the utmost in body, soul, and property. It is clear that they must pay special and chief attention to the duties of religion and morality, and that social betterment should have this chiefly in view; otherwise they would lose wholly their special character, and end by becoming little better than those societies which take no account whatever of religion. What advantage can it be to a working man to obtain by means of a society material well-being, if he endangers his soul for lack of spiritual food? "What doth it profit a man, if he gains the whole world and suffer the loss of his soul?" This, as our Lord teaches, is the mark of character that distinguishes the Christian from the heathen. . . . Let the working man be urged and led to the worship of God, to the earnest practice of religion. . . . Let him learn to reverence and love holy Church, the common Mother of us all; and hence to obey the precepts of the Church, . . . since they are the means ordained by God for obtaining forgiveness of sin and for leading a holy life. . . .

CHRONOLOGY: The Industrial Revolution

1733	James Kay invents flying shuttle, which increases productive capacity of weavers.
1769	James Watt patents steam engine, which provided for the first time in history a steady and unlimited source of inanimate power.
1769	Richard Arkwright patents waterframe, which permits the production of a purely cotton fabric thus allowing large-scale textile manufacturing in factories.
1770	James Hargreaves patents spinning jenny, which allows for faster production of thread.
1776	Adam Smith publishes *The Wealth of Nations*, which develops the theory of capitalism, an economic system based on individual self-interest.
1787	Edmund Cartwright invents the power loom for machine, rather than hand weaving.
1798	Thomas Malthus writes *Essay on the Principle of Population*, which contended that the plight of the working class could only become worse because the human population must eventually outstrip the food supply.
1817	David Ricardo's *Principles of Political Economy and Taxation* fashioned Malthus' theories into the "Iron Law of Wages."
1825	Death of Count Claude Henri de Saint-Simon, the earliest of socialist pioneers: private wealth, property, and enterprise should be subject to regulation.
1832	Great Reform Bill passed by British Parliament: eliminated "rotten boroughs" and extended franchise to a greater proportion of the middle class.

1833	Factory Act passed by British Parliament: limits the working hours of women and children in the textile mills and provides government inspection of the workplace.
1844	*The Condition of the Working Class in England* by Friedrich Engels appears.
1848	*The Communist Manifesto* by Karl Marx and Friedrich Engels is published. Revolutions throughout Europe in support of liberal agendas are unsuccessful.
1858	Death of Robert Owen, a "Utopian Socialist," who believed that a proper working environment would improve human character. Through enlightened management, his New Lanark textile mills were successful and humanely operated.
1891	Pope Leo XIII issues the encyclical, *Rerum Novarum*, which addresses the continuing struggle between capitalists and workers: brotherly love was preferable to ruthless competition and exploitation.

STUDY QUESTIONS

1. What was the "factory system"? How and why did it originate? What was it intended to do?
2. Do the descriptions of child labor and the testimony about degrading working conditions constitute a realistic and accurate portrayal of urban life during the Industrial Revolution? Or is this portrait an exaggeration? How does Engel's description of the impact of the factory system on women and the family seem to reflect some of the concerns of our contemporary society? How does Andrew Ure defend the factory system? What specific points does he address? Are his arguments persuasive? Why or why not?
3. Discuss David Ricardo's ideas on the wages of laborers. Why were the poor laws to be regarded as destructive to the basic economic health of the state? Do you find his argument logical and compelling? Can you apply it to our contemporary society?
4. Discuss John Stuart Mill's ideas on liberty. Is the state ever legitimate in restricting individual liberty? To what extent should a person be free in society?
5. What was the attitude of Samuel Smiles toward the plight of the working class? Why would this opinion be considered "middle class"? What do you think of the principle of "self-help"?
6. What do you consider to be the most important ideas or statements that can be found in the excerpt on the *Communist Manifesto*? Why is this considered to be one of the most influential documents in Western Civilization?

7. What is Pope Leo XIII's basic argument concerning the relationship between capital and labor? What specific measures does he advocate? How do his ideals compare with those of Karl Marx? Note especially his statement: "The great mistake . . . is to take up with the notion that class is naturally hostile to class, and that the wealthy and the working men are intended by nature to live in mutual conflict." Is this a naïve statement, or does the pope give a strong supporting argument?

8. How do you view the Industrial Revolution? Was it a progressive time that demonstrated human creativity, or was it born of human greed and exploitation of others who were less fortunate or less conscientious and determined to succeed? Is there always a price to pay in human suffering for a civilization to progress? How can you apply your ideas to our contemporary age?

5

Nationalism and Imperialism: The Motives and Methods of Expansion

No other factor in history, not even religion, has produced so many wars as has the clash of national egotisms sanctified by the name of patriotism.

—Preserved Smith

Lust for dominion inflames the heart more than any other passion.

—Tacitus

The Englishman does everything on principle. He fights you on patriotic principles; he robs you on business principles; he enslaves you on imperial principles. . . . His watchword is always Duty; and he never forgets that the nation which lets its duty get on the side opposite to its interest is lost.

—Napoleon Bonaparte

The right of conquest has no foundation other than the right of the strongest.

—Jean Jacques Rousseau

Nationalism and imperialism were two of the most important factors that shaped the nineteenth century. These terms, however, are difficult to define and have been used so loosely as nearly to be deprived of meaning. Nationalism involves devotion, a patriotism that implies unity and constructive action in the service of one's country. Imperialism is a policy of extending a nation's authority by establishing political or economic control over another area or people. It is important to note that nationalism need not cause imperialism, but it promotes domestic unity, which is a necessity for successful expansion. The term "expansion" is basically benign, connoting progress and dedication, but "imperialism" is often pejorative in connotation and recalls economic exploitation, racial prejudice, and even war. This chapter will seek to define more clearly the nature of nationalism and imperialism and to demonstrate how the two were inextricably linked during the nineteenth century.

Imperialism and nationalism were certainly not introduced in the nineteenth century. During the Renaissance and Reformation eras in the fifteenth and sixteenth centuries, countries such as Spain, France, and England, which had heretofore been decentralized feudal areas, were united under the leadership of strong monarchs. Although this unity was often achieved initially by the sword, the benefits of centralized rule soon became apparent. Unity fostered pride and cooperation among compatriots and soon provided the energy and direction that made possible an age of exploration and discovery.

In essence, the establishment of colonial empires was profitable and patriotic. But by the nineteenth century, the age of colonial empire building was at an end. Spain, Portugal, and France had lost much of their old empires, Great Britain had lost her American colonies, and Germany was too divided internally to attempt to acquire new territory. Of the continental powers, only France under Napoleon was somewhat successful in establishing overseas colonies but realized only small gains. From 1800 to 1870, Britain acquired New Zealand, central Canada, and western Australia; however, these territories generally were contiguous to areas Britain already held. There was a great deal of missionary activity from Christian organizations but little overt government support.

This period of relative disinterest did not last long. Suddenly, between 1870 and 1900, there was a general outburst of imperialistic activity among the nations of Europe. France, Belgium, Britain, and Portugal made extensive gains, especially in Africa. By 1871, both Italy and Germany were born as nations under the aggressive political and military leadership of Camillo Cavour (1810–1861) and Giuseppe Garibaldi (1807–1882) in the case of Italy, and Otto von Bismarck (1815–1898), the first chancellor of the German Empire. Appealing to abstractions such as "fate" and "duty," politicians immediately sought new territories that would keep them economically and politically competitive with the other nations of Europe. It has been estimated that in this thirty-year period from 1870 to 1900, Europeans expanded their colonial empires by over ten million square miles and nearly one hundred fifty million people. These intense economic rivalries were often expressed as well in political alliances. In 1882, the Triple Alliance was formed among Germany, Austria-Hungary, and Italy and, in 1907, the Triple Entente among Great Britain, France, and Russia. Such organized competition resulted in a polarization of European nations that contributed to the outbreak of World War I in 1914.

This drive for colonial acquisition was not limited to European powers, however. The United States had come of age in the mid-nineteenth century by expanding to its "natural boundaries" of Mexico and the Pacific. Impelled by the dictates of a policy called "manifest destiny," American settlers moved west in quest of new lives as farmers or in pursuit of the gold of California. They were supported militarily by the American government and ideologically by Christian missionaries who saw westward expansion as the fulfillment of the destiny of the United States, so ordained by God. Thus were Indians dehumanized and sent to reservations, and thus was Texas taken from Mexico in 1845. This expansion, however, was essentially "domestic." The United States did not become involved in foreign adventures until 1898 when the Spanish-American War resulted in the cession of the Philippines. The same arguments used by Europeans to legitimate their rule were now employed by the United States.

The imperialism of the late nineteenth century differed somewhat from the colonialism of the fifteenth to the eighteenth centuries. Earlier, nations had seized land with the intention of settling it with colonists or using it as a base from which to exploit the area economically. The "New Imperialism," as it was called, retained some of these goals, but also introduced new ones. European nations now invested capital in a "backward region" and set about building productive enterprises while also improving the area with hygienic and transportation facilities. In so doing, the colonial powers employed native labor and made cooperative arrangements with local rulers (through either enrichment or intimidation). Their main purpose was to control the region, and if such arrangements proved inadequate, the colonial power had other options, which frequently resulted in full annexation.

Our twentieth century has also seen its share of imperialism. Determined to secure Germany's "place in the sun," Kaiser Wilhelm II led Germany to war in 1914. Adolf Hitler resurrected a moribund German people, reminded them of their national heritage, gave them self-respect, and promised them more living space through expansion to "natural boundaries." Hitler's territorial demands could not be satisfied and became one of the primary causes of World War II. After Hitler's defeat in 1945, the Soviet Union and the United States moved from their role as allies to rivals in the scramble for territory and influence in the remains of war-ravaged Europe. In a more contemporary setting, the United States fought a war in Vietnam to maintain "principles of democracy" in a country 7500 miles from home. In 1979, the Soviet Union invaded Afghanistan and offered as justification the explanation that it was "asked in" by the Afghan people. In 1982, the Israelis invaded southern Lebanon in an attempt to eliminate dangerous Palestinian bases in the area; they ended up controlling Beirut itself. The United States in 1983 not only rescued American students from the perils of a coup d'état on the Caribbean island of Grenada, but also stayed to ensure the establishment of a democratic regime. Most recently, Panama was liberated from its dictator, Manuel Noriega, by U.S. forces in 1989, as was Kuwait from Saddam Hussein in 1991. The questions abound: What are the responsibilities of great powers? Impelled by their concept of rightness and geopolitical advantage, do "superpowers" constitute forces for civilization or obstructions to the principle of self-determination? Are they vanguards of freedom or proponents of narrowly defined self-interest? It is important to gain the perspective that history offers.

Nationalism

The Unification of Italy

The Duties of Man

GIUSEPPE MAZZINI

Before Italy finally became a single, independent state under the pragmatic leadership of Count Camillo Cavour, unification was an ideal kept alive through the liberal beliefs of advocates such as Giuseppe Mazzini. Active in the 1830s and 1840s, Mazzini, through his writings, helped define a basis for unification and proved influential in establishing a liberal constitutional monarchy in Italy by 1870. The following selection is from his address to Italian workers.

Your first duties—first as regards importance—are, as I have already told you, towards Humanity. You are *men* before you are either citizens or fathers. Embrace the whole human family in your affection. Bear witness to your belief in the Unity of that family, consequent upon the Unity of God, and in that fraternity among the peoples which is destined to reduce that unity of action. . . .

But what can each of you, singly, *do* for the moral improvement and progress of Humanity? You can from time to time give sterile utterance to your belief; you may, on some rare occasions, perform some act of charity towards a brother man not belonging to your own land;—no more. But charity is not the watchword of the Faith of the Future. The watchword of the faith of the future is *Association*, and fraternal co-operation of all towards a common aim; and this is as far superior to all *charity*, as the edifice which all of you should unite to raise would be superior to the humble hut each one of you might build alone, or with the mere assistance of lending, and borrowing stone, mortar, and tools.

But, you tell me, you cannot attempt united action, distinct and divided as you are in language, customs, tendencies, and capacity. The individual is too insignificant, and Humanity too vast. . . .

This means was provided for you by God when he gave you a country; when, even as a wise overseer of labour distributes the various branches of

---

"The Duties of Man" is from Emilie Ashurst Venturi, *Joseph Mazzini: A Memoir* (London: Alexander and Shepherd, 1875), pp. 312–315.

employment according to the different capacities of the workmen, he divided Humanity into distinct groups or nuclei upon the face of the earth, thus creating the germ of Nationalities. Evil governments have disfigured the divine design. Nevertheless you may still trace it, distinctly marked out. . . . They have disfigured it by their conquests, their greed, and their jealousy even of the righteous power of others; disfigured it so far that if we except England and France—there is not perhaps a single country whose present boundaries correspond to that design.

These governments did not, and do not, recognize any country save their own families or dynasty, the egotism of caste. But the Divine design will infallibly be realized. Natural divisions, and the spontaneous, innate tendencies of the peoples, will take the place of the arbitrary divisions sanctioned by evil governments. The map of Europe will be re-drawn. The countries of the Peoples, defined by the vote of free men, will arise upon the ruins of the countries of kings and privileged castes, and between these countries harmony and fraternity will exist. And the common work of Humanity, of general amelioration and the gradual discovery and application of its Law of life, being distributed according to local development and advance. Then may each one of you, fortified by the power and the affection of many millions, all speaking the same language, gifted with the same tendencies, and educated by the same historical tradition, hope, even by your own single effort, to be able to benefit all Humanity.

O my brothers, love your Country! Our country is our Home, the house that God has given us, placing therein a numerous family that loves us, and whom we love; a family with whom we sympathise more readily, and whom we understand more quickly than we do others; and which, from its being centered round a given spot, and from the homogeneous nature of its elements, is adapted to a special branch of activity. Our country is our common workshop, whence the products of our activity are sent forth for the benefit of the whole world; wherein the tools and implements of labour we can most usefully employ are gathered together: nor may we reject them without disobeying the plan of the Almighty, and diminishing our own strength.

Proclamation for the Liberation of Sicily (1860)

GIUSEPPE GARIBALDI

One of Mazzini's most devoted disciples was Giuseppe Garibaldi (1807–1882). A man of action, he was also an adventurer of military ability who succeeded in gaining military support for the king of Piedmont, Victor Emmanuel. In 1860, he organized a volunteer force to invade Sicily and offered the following appeal to the people. Note the emphasis on goals that transcend the individual boundaries and responsibilities of the small regions that heretofore composed Italy. Garibaldi was successful in gaining control of both Sicily and Naples.

"Proclamation for the Liberation of Sicily" is from Public Documents, *The Annual Register, 1860* (London: 1861), pp. 281–282.

Italians!—The Sicilians are fighting against the enemies of Italy, and for Italy. It is the duty of every Italian to succour them with words, money, and arms, and, above all, in person.

The misfortunes of Italy arise from the indifference of one province to the fate of the others.

The redemption of Italy began from the moment that men of the same land ran to help their distressed brothers.

Left to themselves, the brave Sicilians will have to fight, not only the mercenaries of the Bourbon, but also those of Austria and the Priest of Rome.

Let the inhabitants of the free provinces lift their voices in behalf of their struggling brethren, and impel their brave youth to the conflict.

Let the Marches, Umbria, Sabina, Rome, the Neapolitan, rise to divide the forces of our enemies.

Where the cities suffice not for the insurrection, let them send bands of their bravest into the country.

The brave man finds an arm everywhere. Listen not to the voice of cowards, but arm, and let us fight for our brethren, who will fight for us tomorrow.

A band of those who fought with me the country's battles marches with me to the fight. Good and generous, they will fight for their country to the last drop of their blood, nor ask for other reward than a clear conscience.

"Italy and Victor Emmanuel!" they cried, on passing the Ticino. "Italy and Victor Emmanuel!" shall re-echo in the blazing caves of Mongibello.

At this cry, thundering from the great rock of Italy to the Tarpeian, the rotton Throne of tyranny shall crumble, and, as one man, the brave descendants of Vespro shall rise.

To Arms! Let me put an end, once and for all, to the miseries of so many centuries. Prove to the world that it is no lie that Roman generations inhabited this land.

Address to Parliament (1871)

KING VICTOR EMMANUEL

Through years of idealistic and impassioned speeches by people like Giuseppe Mazzini, diplomatic maneuvering by Camillo Cavour, and the exercise of military might by Giuseppe Garibaldi, Italy became a unified, independent state in 1870 under the leadership of Victor Emmanuel (1820–1878), former king of Piedmont. This excerpt from his address to the Italian Parliament in 1871 discusses some of the challenges that a new nation must face.

Senators and Deputies, gentlemen!

The work to which we consecrated our life is accomplished. After long trials of expiation Italy is restored to herself and to Rome. Here, where our

"Address to Parliament" is from Christine Walsh, ed., *Prologue: A Documentary History of Europe: 1846–1960*. Originally published by Cassell Australia Ltd. (1968), pp. 103–104. Reprinted by permission of Macmillan Publishing Company.

people, after centuries of separation, find themselves for the first time solemnly reunited in the person of their representatives: here where we recognize the fatherland of our dreams, everything speaks to us of greatness; but at the same time it all reminds us of our duties. The joy that we experience must not let us forget them. . . .

We have proclaimed the separation of Church and State. Having recognized the absolute independence of the spiritual authority, we are convinced that Rome, the capital of Italy, will continue to be the peaceful and respected seat of the Pontificate. . . .

Economic and financial affairs, moreover, claim our most careful attention. Now that Italy is established, it is necessary to make it prosperous by putting in order its finances; we shall succeed in this only by persevering in the virtues which have been the source of our national regeneration. Good finances will be the means of re-enforcing our military organization. Our most ardent desire is for peace, and nothing can make us believe that it can be troubled. But the organization of the army and the navy, the supply of arms, the works for the defense of the national territory, demand long and profound study. . . .

Senators and deputies, a vast range of activity opens before you; the national unity which is today attained will have, I hope, the effect of rendering less bitter the struggles of parties, the rivalry of which will have henceforth no other end than the development of the productive forces of the nation.

I rejoice to see that our population already gives unequivocal proofs of its love of work. The economic awakening is closely associated with the political awakening. The banks multiply, as do the commercial institutions, the expositions of the products of art and industry, and the congresses of the learned. We ought, you and I, to favor this productive movement while giving to professional and scientific education more attention and efficiency, and opening to commerce new avenues of communication and new outlets. . . .

A brilliant future opens before us. It remains for us to respond to the blessings of Providence by showing ourselves worthy of bearing among the nations the glorious names of Italy and Rome.

The Unification of Germany

The People and the Fatherland (1807–1808)

JOHANN GOTTLIEB FICHTE

Like Italy, Germany did not achieve unification until 1871. But there were those who provided the philosophical and idealistic foundation for later policies that would prove more practical. Johann Gottlieb Fichte delivered a series of addresses in 1807–1808 that disclose the frustration of German disunity and

"The People and the Fatherland" is from Guy Carelton Lee, ed., *The World's Orators*, vol. 2 (New York: G. P. Putnam's Sons, 1900), pp. 190–193.

presage the intense nationalism that was to erupt in the latter part of the nineteenth century, propelling Germany toward what Kaiser Wilhelm II would later call her "place in the sun."

Our oldest common ancestors, the original people of the new culture, the Teutons, called Germans by the Romans, set themselves bravely in opposition to the overwhelming worldwide rule of the Romans. Did they not see with their own eyes the finest blossom of the Roman provinces beside them, the finer enjoyment in the same, together with laws, courts of justice, lictors' staves and axes in superabundance? Were not the Romans ready and generous enough to let them share in all these benefits? Did they not see proof of the famous Roman clemency in the case of several of their own princes, who allowed themselves to think that war against such benefactors of the human race was rebellion? For the compliant were decorated with the title of king and rewarded with posts of importance as leaders in the Roman army, with Roman sacrificial wreaths; and when they were expelled by their countrymen, the Romans furnished them with a refuge and support in their colonies. Had they no appreciation of the advantages of Roman culture, for better organization of their armies, for example, in which even Arminius himself did not refuse to learn the art of war? It cannot be charged against them that in any one of these respects they were ignorant. Their descendants have appropriated that culture, as soon as they could do so without loss of their own freedom, and as far as it was possible without loss of their distinctive character. Wherefore, then, have they fought for so many generations in bloody wars which have been repeatedly renewed with undiminished fury? A Roman writer represents their leaders as asking if anything else remained for them but to maintain their freedom or to die before they became slaves. Freedom was their possession, that they might remain Germans, that they might continue to settle their own affairs independently and originally and in their own way, and at the same time to advance their culture and to plant the same independence in the hearts of their posterity. Slavery was what they called all the benefits which the Romans offered them, because through them they would become other than Germans, they would have to become semi-Romans. It was perfectly clear, they assumed, that every man, rather than become this, would die, and that a true German could wish to live only to be and to remain a German, and to have his sons the same.

They have not all died; they have not seen slavery; they have bequeathed freedom to their children. To their constant resistance the whole new world owes that it is as it is. Had the Romans succeeded in subjugating them also, and, as the Romans everywhere did, destroying them as a nation, the entire development of the human race would have taken a different direction, and it cannot be thought a better one. We who are the nearest heirs of their land, their language, and their sentiments, owe to them that we are still Germans, that the stream of original and independent life still bears us on; to them we owe that we have since then become a nation; to them, if now perhaps it is not at an end with us and the last drops of blood inherited from them are not dried in our veins, we owe all that which we have become. To them, even the other tribes, who have become to us aliens but through them our brethren, owe their existence; when they conquered eternal Rome, there were no others of all those peoples present; at that time was won for them the possibility of their future origin. . . .

These orations have attempted, by the only means remaining after others have been tried in vain, to prevent this annihilation of every noble action that may in the future arise among us, and this degradation of our entire nation. They have attempted to implant in your minds the deep and immovable foundations of the true and almighty love of the fatherland, in the conception of our nation as eternal and the people as citizens of our own eternity through the education of all hearts and minds.

Speech to the Reichstag (1888)

OTTO VON BISMARCK

In 1862, Otto von Bismarck was appointed prime minister of Prussia. At that time he declared that German unity would be realized "not by speeches and majorities . . . but by blood and iron." By 1871, after several wars, Bismarck had formed the unified fatherland of which Fichte had dreamed: the nation of Germany existed under the leadership of Kaiser Wilhelm I. The following excerpt is from Bismarck's speech to the Reichstag (parliament) in 1888. Unity demands great goals.

Great complications and all kinds of coalitions, which no one can foresee, are constantly possible, and we must be prepared for them. We must be so strong, irrespective of momentary conditions, that we can face any coalition with the assurance of a great nation which is strong enough under circumstances to take her fate into her own hands. We must be able to face our fate placidly with that self reliance and confidence in God which are ours when we are strong and our cause is just. And the government will see to it that the German cause will be just always.

We must, to put it briefly, be as strong in these times as we possibly can be, and we can be stronger than any other nation of equal numbers in the world. I shall revert to this later—but it would be criminal if we were not to make use of our opportunity. If we do not need our full armed strength, we need not summon it. The only problem is the not very weighty one of money—not very weighty I say in passing, because I have no wish to enter upon a discussion of the financial and military figures, and of the fact that France has spent three milliards for the improvement of her armaments these last years, while we have spent scarcely one and one half milliards, including what we are asking of you at this time. But I leave the elucidation of this to the minister of war and the representatives of the treasury department.

When I say that it is our duty to endeavor to be ready at all times and for all emergencies, I imply that we must make greater exertions than other people for the same purpose, because of our geographical position. We are situated in the heart of Europe, and have at least three fronts open to an attack. France has only her eastern, and Russia only her western frontier where they may be attacked. We are also more exposed to the dangers of a coalition than any other nation, as is proved by the whole development of history, by our geographical position, and the lesser degree of cohesiveness, which until now has characterized the German nation in comparison with others. God has placed us where we are prevented, thanks to our neighbors, from growing lazy and dull. He has placed by our side the most warlike and restless of all nations, the French, and He has permitted warlike inclinations to grow strong in Russia, where formerly they existed to a lesser degree. Thus we are given the spur, so to speak, from both sides, and are compelled to exertions which we should perhaps not be making otherwise. The pikes in the European carp-pond are keeping us from being carps by making us feel their teeth on both sides. They also are forcing us to an exertion which without them we might not make, and to a union among us Germans, which is abhorrent to us at heart. By nature we are rather tending away, the one from the other. But the Franco-Russian press within which we are squeezed compels us to hold together, and by pressure our cohesive force is greatly increased. This will bring us to that state of being inseparable which all other nations possess, while we do not yet enjoy it. But we must respond to the intentions of Providence by making ourselves so strong that the pikes can do nothing but encourage us. . . .

If we Germans wish to wage a war with the full effect of our national strength, it must be a war which satisfies all who take part in it, all who sacrifice anything for it, in short the whole nation. It must be a national war, a war carried on with the enthusiasm of 1870, when we were foully attacked. I still remember the earsplitting, joyful shouts in the station at Köln. It was the same all the way from Berlin to Köln, in Berlin itself. The waves of popular approval bore us into the war, whether or not we wished it. That is the way it must be, if a popular force like ours is to show what it can do. . . . A war into which we are not borne by the will of the people will be waged, to be sure, if it has been declared by the constituted authorities who deemed it necessary; it will even be waged pluckily, and possibly victoriously, after we have once smelled fire and tasted blood, but it will lack from the beginning the nerve and enthusiasm of a war in which we are attacked. In such a one the whole of Germany from Memel to the Alpine Lakes will flare up like a powder mine; it will be bristling with guns, and no enemy will dare to engage this *furor teutonicus* which develops when we are attacked. We cannot afford to lose this factor of preeminence even if many military men—not only ours but others as well—believe that today we are superior to our future opponents. Our own officers believe this to a man, naturally. Every soldier believes this. He would almost cease to be a useful soldier if he did not wish for war, and did not believe that we would be victorious in it. If our opponents by any chance are thinking that we are pacific because we are afraid of how the war may end, they are mightily mistaken. We believe as firmly in our victory in a just cause as any foreign lieutenant in his garrison, after his third glass of champagne, can believe in his, and we probably do so with greater certainty. It is not fear, therefore, which makes us pacific, but the consciousness of our strength. We are strong enough to protect ourselves, even if we should be attacked at a less favorable moment, and we are in a position to let divine providence determine whether a war in the meanwhile may not become unnecessary after all.

I am, therefore, not in favor of any kind of an aggressive war, and if war could result only from our attack—somebody must kindle a fire, we shall not kindle it. Neither the consciousness of our strength, which I have described, nor our confidence in our treaties, will prevent us from continuing our former endeavors to preserve peace. In this we do not permit ourselves to be influenced by annoyances or dislikes. The threats and insults, and the challenges, which have been made have, no doubt, excited also with us a feeling of irritation, which does not easily happen with Germans, for they are less prone to national hatred than any other nation. We are, however, trying to calm our countrymen, and we shall work for peace with our neighbors, especially with Russia, in the future as in the past. . . .

We are easily influenced—perhaps too easily—by love and kindness, but quite surely never by threats! We Germans fear God, and naught else in the world! It is this fear of God which makes us love and cherish peace. If in spite of this anybody breaks the peace, he will discover that ardent patriotism . . . has today become the common property of the whole German nation. Attack the German nation anywhere, and you will find it armed to a man, and every man with the firm belief in his heart: God will be with us.

Motives for Imperialism

Racism and Social Darwinism

In general, imperialistic nations have felt compelled to justify their actions by explaining why they have taken control of territory or populations. One of the most popular justifications has been the policy of Social Darwinism, a vulgarization of the scientific theory of Charles Darwin contained in The Origin of Species *(1859). Social Darwinists held that only the fittest peoples would survive and that "lesser breeds" would of necessity perish or be taken over. Indeed, some argued that an empire was a living organism that must either grow or die. Racism, therefore, provided a potent thrust to imperial expansion. The first selection, by American clergyman Josiah Strong (1847–1916), is typical of the racist argument. The second excerpt is from a lecture delivered in 1900 by the German scientist Karl Pearson; in it he presents racism as being consistent with the directives of nature. The last account is by Sir Henry Johnston, British explorer and administrator in Central and East Africa at the turn of the century.*

Our Country (1885)

JOSIAH STRONG

God, with infinite wisdom and skill, is training the Anglo-Saxon race for an hour sure to come in the world's future. Heretofore there has always been in the history of the world a comparatively unoccupied land westward, into which the crowded countries of the East have poured their surplus populations. But the widening waves of migration, which millenniums ago rolled east and west from the valley of the Euphrates meet to-day on our Pacific coast. There are no more new worlds. . . . The time is coming when the pressure of population on the means of subsistence will be felt here as it is now felt in Europe and Asia. Then will the world enter upon a new stage of its history—*the final competition of races, for which the Anglo-Saxon is being schooled.* Long before the thousand millions are here, the mighty *centrifugal* tendency, inherent in this stock and strengthened in the United States, will assert itself. Then this race of unequaled energy, with all the majesty of numbers and the might of wealth behind it—the representative, let us hope, of the largest liberty, the purest Christianity, the highest civilization—having developed peculiarly aggressive traits calculated to impress its institutions upon mankind, will spread itself over the earth. If I read not amiss, this powerful race will move down upon Mexico, down upon Central and South America, out upon the islands of the sea, over upon Africa and beyond. And can any one doubt that the result of this competition of races will be the "survival of the fittest"? . . . Nothing can save the inferior race but a ready and pliant assimilation. Whether the feebler and more abject races are going to be regenerated and raised up, is already very much of a question. What if it should be God's plan to people the world with better and finer material? Certain it is, whatever expectations we may indulge, that there is a tremendous overbearing surge of power in the Christian nations, which, if the others are not speedily raised to some vastly higher capacity, will inevitably submerge and bury them forever. . . . To this result no war of extermination is needful; the contest is not one of arms, but of

"Our Country" is from Josiah Strong, *Our Country* (New York: The Baker and Taylor Publishing Company, 1885), pp. 174–178.

vitality and of civilization. "At the present day," says Mr. Darwin, "civilized nations are everywhere supplanting barbarous nations. . . ."

Some of the stronger races, doubtless, may be able to preserve their integrity; but, in order to compete with the Anglo-Saxon, they will probably be forced to adopt his methods and instruments, his civilization and his religion. . . . The contact of Christian with heathen nations is awakening the latter to new life. Old superstitions are loosening their grasp. The dead crust of fossil faiths is being shattered by the movements of life underneath. In Catholic countries, Catholicism is losing its influence over educated minds, and in some cases the masses have already lost all faith in it. Thus, while on this continent God is training the Anglo-Saxon race for its mission, a complemental work has been in progress in the great world beyond. God has two hands. Not only is He preparing in our civilization the die with which to stamp the nations, but . . . he is preparing mankind to receive our impress.

Is there room for reasonable doubt that this race, unless devitalized by alcohol and tobacco, is destined to dispossess many weaker races, assimilate others, and mold the remainder, until, in a very true and important sense, it has Anglo-Saxonized mankind?

The Standpoint of Science (1900)

KARL PEARSON

How many centuries, how many thousand of years, have the Kaffir or the Negro held large districts in Africa undisturbed by the white man? Yet their intertribal struggles have not yet produced a civilization in the least comparable with the Aryan. Educate and nurture them as you will, I do not believe that you will succeed in modifying the stock. History shows me one way, and one way only, in which a high state of civilization has been produced, namely, the struggle of race with race, and the survival of the physically and mentally fitter race. If you want to know whether the lower races of man can evolve a higher type, I fear the only course is to leave them to fight it out among themselves, and even then the struggle for existence between individual and individual, between tribe and tribe, may not be supported by that physical selection due to a particular climate on which probably so much of the Aryan's success depended.

If you bring the white man into contact with the black, you too often suspend the very process of natural selection on which the evolution of a higher type depends. You get superior and inferior races living on the same soil, and that coexistence is demoralizing for both. They naturally sink into the position of master and servant, if not admittedly or covertly into that of slave-owner and slave. Frequently they inter-cross, and if the

"The Standpoint of Science" is from Karl Pearson, *National Life from the Standpoint of Science*, 2nd ed. (Cambridge: Cambridge University Press, 1907), pp. 21–25.

bad stock be raised the good is lowered. Even in the case of Eurasians, of whom I have met mentally and physically fine specimens, I have felt how much better they would have been had they been pure Asiatics or pure Europeans. Thus it comes about that when the struggle for existence between races is suspended, the solution of great problems may be unnaturally postponed; instead of the slow, stern processes of evolution, cataclysmal solutions are prepared for the future. Such problems in suspense, it appears to me, are to be found in the Negro population of the Southern States of America, in the large admixture of Indian blood in some of the South American races, but, above all, in the Kaffir factor in South Africa.

You may possibly think that I am straying from my subject, but I want to justify natural selection to you. I want you to see selection as something which renders the inexorable law of heredity a source of progress which produces the good through suffering, an infinitely greater good which far outbalances the very obvious pain and evil. Let us suppose the alternative were possible. Let us suppose we could prevent the white man, if we liked, from going to lands of which the agricultural and mineral resources are not worked to the full; then I should say a thousand times better for him that he should not go than that he should settle down and live alongside the inferior race. The only healthy alternative is that he should go and completely drive out the inferior race. That is practically what the white man has done in North America. . . . The civilization of the white man is a civilization dependent upon free white labour, and when that element of stability is removed it will collapse like those of Greece and Rome. I venture to assert, then, that the struggle for existence between white and red man, painful and even terrible as it was in its details, has given us a good for outbalancing its immediate evil. In place of the red man, contributing practically nothing to the work and thought of the world, we have a great nation, mistress of many arts, and able, with its youthful imagination and fresh, untrammelled impulses, to contribute much to the common stock of civilized man. Against that we have only to put the romantic sympathy for the Red Indian generated by the novels of Cooper and the poems of Longfellow, and then—see how little it weighs in the balance! . . .

You will see that my view—and I think it may be called the scientific view of a nation—is that of an organized whole, kept up to a high pitch of internal efficiency by insuring that its numbers are substantially recruited from the better stocks, and kept up to a high pitch of external efficiency by contest, chiefly by way of war with inferior races, and with equal races by the struggle for trade-routes and for the sources of raw material and of food supply. This is the natural history view of mankind, and I do not think you can in its main features subvert it. Some of you may refuse to acknowledge it, but you cannot really study history and refuse to see its force. Some of you may realize it, and then despair of life; you may decline to admit any glory in a world where the superior race must either eject the inferior, or, mixing with it, or even living alongside it, degenerate itself. What beauty can there be when the battle is to the stronger, and the weaker must suffer in the struggle of nations and in the struggle of individual men? You may say: Let us cease to struggle; let us leave the lands of the world to the races that cannot profit by them to the full; let us cease to compete in the markets of the world. Well, we could do it, if we were a small nation living off the produce of our own soil, and a soil so worthless that no other race envied it and sought to appropriate it. We should cease to advance; but then we should naturally give up progress as a good which comes through suffering. I say it is impossible for a small rural community to stand apart from the world-contest and to stagnate, if no more powerful nation wants its possessions.

The Backward Peoples (1920)

SIR HARRY JOHNSTON

[L]et us proceed to define who and what these backward or unprogressive peoples are and to what extent they may be considered to be retrograde and ineffective as compared with the dominating white race. The chief and obvious distinction between the backward and forward peoples is that the former, with the exception of about 20,000,000 in the Mediterranean basin and the Near East, are of coloured skin; while the latter are white-skinned, or, as in the case of the Japanese and the inhabitants of Northern China, nearly white.

I think if we took all the factors into consideration—religion, education (especially knowledge concerning the relations between this planet and the universe of which it is a minute speck, the history and geography of the planet, the sciences that are a part of earth-study), standard of living, respect for sanitation, infant death rate, bodily strength, manner of government, regard for law and order, position in agriculture and manufactures,—we might appraise mathematically, according to the following ratio, the principal nations and peoples into which humanity is divided:

100 percent.

1. Great Britain and Ireland, Canada and Newfoundland, White Australia, New Zealand, White South Africa (south of the Zambezi), Malta and Mauritius, United States, France, Corsica, much of Algeria and Tunis, Belgium and Luxembourg, Holland, Germany, Austria, Chekho-Slovakia, Italy, Switzerland, Hungary, Norway, Sweden, Denmark and Iceland, Finland, Estonia, Spain, Chile, Argentina, Japan

"The Backward Peoples" is from Sir Harry Johnston, *The Backward Peoples and Our Relations with Them* (London: Oxford University Press, 1920), pp. 7–9.

98 per cent.

2. Poland and Lithuania, Serbia and Croatia, Bulgaria, Rumania, Portugal, Greece, Cyprus, Brazil, Peru, Columbia, British Guiana, French and Dutch Guiana, British and French West Indies, Cuba and Puerto Rico, Hawaii, Uruguay

97 per cent.

3. Russia, Russian Siberia, Russian Central Asia, the Caucasus, Egypt, British India, French Indo-China, Siam, British Malaysia, Mexico, Central America, Bolivia, Venezuela, Ecuador, Paraguay, Java, . . . Armenia

95 per cent.

4. Albania, Asia Minor, Morocco, Southern Algeria, Tripoli, Palestine, Syria, Persia, China, Tibet, Afghanistan, Zanzibar

90 per cent.

5. Madagascar, Black South Africa, French West Africa, British West Africa, Uganda, British Central and East Africa, Sumatra, Borneo, the Philippines, the Anglo-Egyptian Sudan, Angola, Santo Domingo

80 per cent.

6. Abyssinia, Arabia, Portuguese East Africa, the Belgian Congo, Portuguese Congo, Liberia, Haiti, Celebes, Timor, New Caledonia, British Papas

75 per cent.

7. Dutch New Guinea and New Hebrides, Portuguese Guinea, French Central Africa

This rough estimate of civilization and culture does not imply that the nations or peoples which are classed together resemble one another in all their stages of culture. Some will excel in one direction, some in another. In certain directions a people may be very forward, coupled with retrograde features which reduce their average value.

Obviously, the foremost nations in the world at the present day are Britain and the regions of the British Empire in which the white race predominates; the United States; France; and Germany,—not only by the numbers of their peoples and the degree of their national wealth, but by their industry, commerce and the proportion of educated to uneducated people in the population. In all elements of greatness, but not in potency of numbers, Denmark, Sweden, Norway, Finland, Holland, Luxembourg and Belgium, are on an equal footing. From their magnificent parts in history one would like to class Spain, Portugal and Italy with these powers of the first rank. . . .

It is the peoples of 95 per cent. to 90 per cent. that may be put in the unprogressive or retrograde class, unable at present to govern themselves in a manner conducive to progress; while those that are graded 80 to 75 per cent. still contain in their midst elements of sheer savagery. Such regions, if left alone by the controlling white men, might easily relapse into the unprofitable barbarism out of which they have been lifted with the white man's efforts during the past fifty years.

For God and Country

The Mandate System: Britain's Duty in Egypt (1890)

JOSEPH CHAMBERLAIN

The British in the late nineteenth century often justified their imperialism on the premise of duty. As a civilized power, it was imperative that they spread God's word and the fruits of civilization to those peoples who were not sufficiently advanced to develop them on their own. In essence, Britain held a nation "in trust" until the backward peoples could be educated and made ready to assume the responsibilities of self-government. The "mandate system," as it came to be called, is described in the following excerpt by the liberal statesman Joseph Chamberlain (1836–1914). The motive for British expansion in Egypt was not completely altruistic, however. Britain also wanted to protect the strategic Suez Canal, which controlled access to the riches of Britain's empire in India and the Far East. In 1882, Britain occupied Cairo and set about reorganizing the country. Chamberlain's address to Parliament must also be viewed in this light.

I want to say a word or two to you about the future. I am going to make a confession. I admit I was one of those—I think my views were shared by the whole Cabinet of Mr. Gladstone—who regretted the necessity for the occupation of Egypt. I thought that England had so much to do, such enormous obligations and responsibilities, that we might well escape, if we could, this addition to them; and, when the occupation was forced upon us, I looked forward with anxiety to an early, it might be even, to an immediate evacuation. The confession I have to make is that having seen what are the results of this occupation, having seen what is the nature of the task we have undertaken, and what progress we have already made towards its accomplishment, I have changed my mind. (Cheers.) I say it would be unworthy of this great nation if we did not rise to the full height of our duty, and complete our work before we left the country. (Cheers.) We have no right to abandon the duty which has been cast upon us, and the work

"The Mandate System: Britain's Duty in Egypt" is from Joseph Chamberlain, *Foreign and Colonial Speeches* (London: George Routledge and Sons, 1897), pp. 41–44.

which already shows so much promise for the advantage of the people with whose destinies we have become involved.

This great alteration is due to the influence of a mere handful of your fellow-countrymen. . . . They, by their persevering devotion, and their single-minded honesty, have wrought out this great work, and have brought Egypt from a condition which may fairly be described as one of ruin, to the promise of once more being restored to its ancient prosperity. I hear sometimes of pessimists who think the work of England is accomplished, who will tell you that we have lost the force and the capacity to govern. No; that is not true; and as long as we can spare from our abundance men like these, who, after all, are only ordinary Englishmen— men like these, who are able and willing to carry their zeal and their intelligence wherever it may conduce to the service of humanity, and to the honour of their native land—so long as we can do that we need not despair of the future of the United Kingdom. (Cheers.) But we owe it to them, we owe it to ourselves, that their work shall not be in vain. You cannot revolutionise a country like Egypt—you cannot reform all that is wrong in her system, all that is poor and weak in the character of the people—in a few minutes, or a few years. Egypt has been submitted for centuries to arbitrary despotism. I believe there is hardly any time in her history, even if you go back to almost prehistoric ages, when she has not been in the grasp of some foreign ruler; and, under these circumstances, you cannot expect to find ready to your hands a self-governing people. They are not able— they cannot be able—to stand alone; and they do not wish to stand alone. They ask for your support and assistance, and without it, it is absolutely impossible that their welfare can be secured. If you were to abandon your responsibility, your retirement would be followed by an attempt once more to restore the old arbitrary methods and the old abuses, which in turn would no doubt be followed by anarchy and disorder; and then in time there would be again a foreign intervention, this time the intervention of some other European country. I have too much confidence in the public spirit of the country to believe that it will ever neglect a national duty. (Hear, hear.) A nation is like an individual; it has duties which it must fulfill, or else it cannot live honoured and respected as a nation. (Loud cheers.)

American Imperialism in the Philippines (1900)

ALBERT J. BEVERIDGE

Through much of the nineteenth century, the United States was involved with establishing its own borders "from sea to shining sea," but did not try to expand internationally. In 1898, however, because of the Spanish-American War, the

"American Imperialism in the Philippines" is from *Congressional Record*, vol. 33 (1900), pp. 704–705, 708, 710–712.

United States inaugurated a policy of foreign imperialism. One of the Spanish colonies ceded to the United States was the Philippine Islands. There was a strong independence movement in the islands, however, and actual warfare broke out in 1899 between Filipinos and American forces. Congress was divided about setting up a government for the newly acquired territory. One of the champions of imperialism was Albert J. Beveridge, senator from Indiana. In January 1900, he addressed Congress in support of a resolution that decreed that the United States "establish and maintain such government control throughout the archipelago as the situation may demand."

Mr. President, the times call for candor. The Philippines are ours forever, "territory belonging to the United States," as the Constitution calls them. And just beyond the Philippines are China's illimitable markets. We will not retreat from either. We will not repudiate our duty in the archipelago. We will not abandon our opportunity in the Orient. We will not renounce our part in the mission of our race, trustee under God, of the civilization of the world. And we will move forward to our work, not howling our regrets like slaves whipped to their burdens, but with gratitude for a task worthy of our strength, and thanksgiving to Almighty God that He has marked us as His chosen people, henceforth to lead in the regeneration of the world. . . .

Senators, it would be better to abandon this combined garden and Gibraltar of the Pacific, and count our blood and treasure already spent a profitable loss, than to apply any academic arrangement of self-government to these children. They are not capable of self-government. How could they be? They are not of a self-governing race. They are Orientals, Malays, instructed by Spaniards in the latter's worst estate.

They know nothing of practical government except as they have witnessed the weak, corrupt, cruel, and capricious rule of Spain. What magic will anyone employ to dissolve in their minds and characters those impressions of governors and governed which three centuries of misrule have created? What alchemy will change the Oriental quality of their blood and set the self-governing currents of the American pouring through their Malay veins? How shall they, in the twinkling of an eye, be exalted to the heights of self-governing peoples which required a thousand years for us to reach, Anglo-Saxon though we are? . . .

Mr. President, self-government and internal development have been the dominant notes of our first century; administration and the development of other lands will be the dominant notes of our second century. And administration is as high and holy a function as self-government, just as the care of a trust estate is as sacred an obligation as the management of our own concerns. . . .

The Declaration of Independence does not forbid us to do our part in the regeneration of the world. If it did, the Declaration would be wrong, just as the Articles of Confederation, drafted by the very same men who signed the Declaration, were found to be wrong. The Declaration has no application to the present situation. It was written by self-governing men for self-governing men. . . .

Mr. President, this question is deeper than any question of party politics; deeper than any question of the isolated policy of our country even; deeper even than any question of constitutional power. It is elemental. It is racial. God has not been preparing the English-speaking and Teutonic peoples for a thousand years for nothing but vain and idle self-contemplation and self-admiration. No! He has made us the master organizers of the world to establish system where chaos reigns. He has given the spirit of progress to overwhelm the forces of reaction throughout the earth. He has made us adept in government that we may administer government among savage and senile peoples. Were it not for such a force as this the world would relapse into barbarism and night. And of all our race He has marked the American people as His chosen nation to finally lead in the regeneration of the world. This is the divine mission of America, and it holds for us all the profit, all the glory, all the happiness possible to man. We are trustees of the world's progress, guardians of its righteous peace. The judgment of the Master is upon us: "Ye have been faithful over a few things; I will make you ruler over many things."

What shall history say of us? Shall it say that we renounced that holy trust, left the savage to his base condition, the wilderness to the reign of waste, deserted duty, abandoned glory, forgot our sordid profit even, because we feared our strength and read the charter of our powers with the doubter's eye and the quibbler's mind? Shall it say that, called by events to captain and command the proudest, ablest, purest race of history in history's noblest work, we declined that great commission? Our fathers would not have had it so. No! They founded no paralytic government, incapable of the simplest acts of administration. They planted no sluggard people, passive while the world's work calls them. They established no reactionary nation. They unfurled no retreating flag. . . .

Blind indeed is he who sees not the hand of God in events so vast, so harmonious, so benign. Reactionary indeed is the mind that perceives not that this vital people is the strongest of the saving forces of the world; that our place, therefore, is at the head of the constructing and redeeming nations of the earth; and that to stand aside while events march on is a surrender of our interests, a betrayal of our duty as blind as it is base. Craven indeed is the heart that fears to perform a work so golden and so noble; that dares not win a glory of immortal. . . .

Mr. President and Senators, adopt the resolution offered, that peace may quickly come and that we may begin our saving, regenerating, and uplifting work. . . . Reject it, and the world, history, and the American people will know where to forever fix the awful responsibility for the consequences that will surely follow such failure to do our manifest duty. How dare we delay when our soldiers' blood is flowing?

The White Man's Burden (1899)

RUDYARD KIPLING

In commemoration of successful U.S. imperialism in the Philippines, the great British poet Rudyard Kipling wrote "The White Man's Burden" in 1899. It reflects a devotion to the demands of empire and the duty of civilized nations. In Kipling's eyes, imperialism was a nationalistic venture—a heroic necessity.

Take up the White Man's burden—
Send forth the best ye breed—
Go bind your sons to exile
To serve your captive's need;
To wait in heavy harness,
On fluttered folk and wild—
Your new-caught, sullen peoples,
Half-devil and half-child.

Take up the White Man's burden—
In patience to abide,
To veil the threat of terror
And check the show of pride;
By open speech and simple,
An hundred times made plain
To seek another's profit,
And work another's gain.

Take up the White Man's burden—
The savage wars of peace—
Fill full the mouth of Famine
And bid the sickness cease;
And when you goal is nearest
The end for others sought,
Watch sloth and heathen Folly
Bring all your hopes to nought.

Take up the White Man's burden—
No tawdry rule of kings,
But toil of serf and sweeper—
The tale of common things.
The ports ye shall not enter,
The roads ye shall not tread,
Go mark them with your living,
And mark them with your dead.

"The White Man's Burden" is from Rudyard Kipling, *Collected Verse* (New York: Doubleday and Page, 1911), pp. 215–217.

Take up the White Man's burden—
And reap his old reward:
The blame of those ye better,
The hate of those ye guard—
The cry of hosts ye humour
(Ah, slowly!) toward the light:—
'Why brought he us from bondage,
Our loved Egyptian night?

Take up the White Man's burden—
Ye dare not stoop to less—
Nor call too loud on Freedom
To cloke your weariness;
By all ye cry or whisper,
By all ye leave or do,
The silent, sullen peoples
Shall weigh your gods and you.

Take up the White Man's burden—
Have done with childish days—
The lightly proferred laurel,
The easy, ungrudged praise.
Comes now, to search your manhood
Through all the thankless years,
Cold, edged with dear-bought wisdom,
The judgment of your peers!

The Economic Argument

Probably the most obvious motive for imperialism is in the economic profit to be made from the colonization of territory and the subjugation of people. Sir Frederick Lugard, British soldier and administrator of some of Britain's colonial possessions in the late nineteenth century, analyzes the "scramble for Africa."

"A Natural Inclination to Submit to a Higher Authority" (1893)

SIR FREDERICK DEALTRY LUGARD

The Chambers of Commerce of the United Kingdom have unanimously urged the retention of East Africa on the grounds of commercial advantage. The Presidents of the London and Liverpool chambers attended a

" 'A Natural Inclination to Submit to a Higher Authority' " is from Sir Frederick Dealtry Lugard, *The Rise of Our East African Empire*, vol. 1 (London: William Blackwood and Sons, 1893), pp. 379–382.

deputation to her Majesty's Minister for Foreign Affairs to urge "the absolute necessity, for the prosperity of this country, that new avenues for commerce such as that in East Equatorial Africa should be opened up, in view of the hostile tariffs with which British manufacturers are being everywhere confronted." Manchester followed with a similar declaration; Glasgow, Birmingham, Edinburgh, and other commercial centres gave it as their opinion that "there is practically no middle course for this country, between a reversal of the freetrade policy to which it is pledged, on the one hand, and a prudent but continuous territorial extension for the creation of new markets, on the other hand. . . .

The "Scramble for Africa" by the nations of Europe—an incident without parallel in the history of the world—was due to the growing commercial rivalry, which brought home to civilised nations the vital necessity of securing the only remaining fields for industrial enterprise and expansion. It is well, then, to realise that it is for our *advantage*—and not alone at the dictates of duty—that we have undertaken responsibilities in East Africa. It is in order to foster the growth of the trade of this country, and to find an outlet for our manufactures and our surplus energy, that our far-seeing statesmen and our commercial men advocate colonial expansion. . . .

There are some who say we have no *right* in Africa at all, that "it belongs to the natives". I hold that our right is the necessity that is upon us to provide for our ever-growing population—either by opening new fields for emigration, or by providing work and employment which the development of over-sea extension entails—and to stimulate trade by finding new markets, since we know what misery trade depression brings at home.

While thus serving our own interests as a nation, we may, by selecting men of the right stamp for the control of new territories, bring at the same time many advantages to Africa. Nor do we deprive the natives of their birthright of freedom, to place them under a foreign yoke. It has ever been the key-note of British colonial method to rule through and by the natives, and it is this method, in contrast to the arbitrary and uncompromising rule of Germany, France, Portugal, and Spain, which has been the secret of our success as a colonising nation, and has made us welcomed by tribes and peoples in Africa, who ever rose in revolt against the other nations named. In Africa, moreover, there is among the people a natural inclination to submit to a higher authority. That intense detestation of control which animates our Teutonic races does not exist among the tribes of Africa, and if there is any authority that we replace, it is the authority of the Slavers and Arabs, or the intolerable tyranny of the "dominant tribe."

Power and Pride

The next three selections provide another motive for imperialism. The desire for power can be justified through the pride that one has in one's nation. Nationalism and imperialism seem to be intimately connected. The first excerpt is from a

*speech made by the German Kaiser Wilhelm II in 1901. The second selection,
by John Louis O'Sullivan, promotes the concept of "manifest destiny," which
legitimized the American annexation of land as settlers moved west. The
fulfillment of the "destiny" of the nation necessarily involved the sacrifice of
Mexican and Indian populations in Texas and throughout the plains.*

Germany's Place in the Sun (1901)

KAISER WILHELM II

In spite of the fact that we have no such fleet as we should have, we have
conquered for ourselves a place in the sun. It will now be my task to see to it
that this place in the sun shall remain our undisputed possession, in order
that the sun's rays may fall fruitfully upon our activity and trade in foreign
parts, that our industry and agriculture may develop within the state and
our sailing sports upon the water, for our future lies upon the water. The
more Germans go out upon the waters . . . whether it be in journeys across
the ocean, or in the service of the battleflag, so much the better will it be for
us. For when the German has once learned to direct his glance upon what is
distant and great, the pettiness which surrounds him in daily life on all
sides will disappear. . . .

As head of the empire I therefore rejoice over every citizen, whether
from Hamburg, Bremen, or Lubeck, who goes forth with this large outlook
and seeks new points where we can drive in the nail on which to hang our
armour.

Manifest Destiny: The Annexation of Texas (1845)

JOHN LOUIS O'SULLIVAN

Texas is now ours. . . . It is wholly untrue, and unjust to ourselves, the
pretence that the Annexation has been a measure of spoliation, unrightful
and unrighteous—of military conquest under forms of peace and law—of
territorial aggrandizement at the expense of justice, and justice due by a
double sanctity to the weak. This view of the question is wholly unfounded,
and has been before so amply refuted in these pages, as well as in a
thousand other modes, that we shall not again dwell upon it. The independence of Texas was complete and absolute. It was an independence, not
only in fact but of right. . . .

Texas has been absorbed into the Union in the inevitable fulfillment of
the general law which is rolling our population westward; the connection of
which with that ratio of growth in population which is destined within a
hundred years to swell our numbers to the enormous population of two

"Germany's Place in the Sun" is from Christian Gauss, excerpted from *The German Emperor*,
pp. 181–183. Copyright 1915 Charles Scribner's Sons. Reprinted with the permission of
Charles Scribner's Sons.

"Manifest Destiny: The Annexation of Texas" is from *The United States Magazine and
Democratic Review*, vol. 17, no. 85 (1845).

hundred and fifty millions (if not more), is too evident to leave us in doubt of the manifest design of Providence in regard to the occupation of this continent. It was disintegrated from Mexico in the natural course of events, by a process perfectly legitimate on its own part, blameless on ours; and in which all the censures due to wrong, perfidy and folly, rest on Mexico alone. And possessed as it was by a population which was in truth but a colonial detachment from our own, and which was still bound by myriad ties of the very heartstrings to its old relations, domestic and political, their incorporation into the Union was not only inevitable, but the most natural, right and proper thing in the world—and it is only astonishing that there should be any among ourselves to say it nay. . . .

California will, probably, next fall away from the loose adhesion which, in such a country as Mexico, holds a remote province in a slight equivocal kind of dependence on the metropolis. Imbecile and distracted, Mexico never can exert any real governmental authority over such a country. A population will soon be in actual occupation of California, over which it will be idle for Mexico to dream of dominion. They will necessarily become independent. Whether they will then attach themselves to our Union or not, is not to be predicted with any certainty. Unless the projected railroad across the continent to the Pacific be carried into effect, perhaps they may not; though even in that case, the day is not distant when the Empires of the Atlantic and Pacific would again flow together into one, as soon as their inland border should approach each other. . . .

Away then with all idle French talk of balances of power on the American Continent. There is no growth in Spanish America! Whatever progress of population there may be in the British Canada, is only for their own early severance of their present colonial relation to the little island three thousand miles across the Atlantic; soon to be followed by Annexation, and destined to swell the still accumulating momentum of our progress. And whosoever may hold the balance, though they should cast into the opposite scale all the bayonets and cannon, not only of France and England, but of Europe entire, how would it kick the beam against the simple solid weight of the two hundred millions—destined to gather beneath the flutter of the stripes and stars, in the fast hastening year of the Lord 1945!

A Criticism of British Imperialism (1900)

WILFRID SCAWEN BLUNT

The next selection includes entries in the diary of Wilfrid Scawen Blunt (1840–1922), a diplomat and poet who ardently opposed British imperialism in Egypt, India, and Ireland. He was one of several who resisted the attractions of power and glory and advocated the right of national self-determination.

"A Criticism of British Imperialism" is from Wilfrid Scawen Blunt, *My Diaries: Being a Personal Narrative of Events 1888–1914*, vol. 1 (New York: Alfred A. Knopf, 1921), pp. 375–377. Reprinted by permission of the publisher.

22nd Dec., 1900—The old century is very nearly out, and leaves the world in a pretty pass, and the British Empire is playing the devil in it as never an empire before on so large a scale. We may live to see its fall. All the nations of Europe are making the same heel upon earth in China, massacring and pillaging and raping in the captured cities as outrageously as in the Middle Ages. The Emperor of Germany gives the word for slaughter and the Pope looks on and approves. In South Africa our troops are burning farms under Kitchener's command, and the Queen and the two houses of Parliament, and the bench of bishops thank God publicly and vote money for the work. The Americans are spending fifty millions a year on slaughtering Filipinos; the King of the Belgians has invested his whole fortune on the Congo, where he is brutalizing the Negroes to fill his pockets. The French and Italians for the moment are playing a less prominent part in the slaughter, but their inactivity grieves them. The whole white race is reveling openly in violence, as though it had never pretended to be Christian. God's equal curse be on them all! So ends the famous nineteenth century into which we were so proud to have been born. . . .

31st Dec., 1900—I bid good-bye to the old century, may it rest in peace as it has lived in war. Of the new century I prophesy nothing except that it will see the decline of the British Empire. Other worse empires will rise perhaps in its place, but I shall not live to see the day. It all seems a very little matter here in Egypt, with the pyramids watching us as they watched Joseph, when, as a young man four thousand years ago, perhaps in this very garden, he walked and gazed at the sunset behind them, wondering about the future just as I did this evening. And so, poor wicked nineteenth century, farewell!

Interpretations of Imperialism

This section is composed of classic interpretations of imperialism and seeks to investigate why human beings, in an abstract sense, are seemingly determined to take over territory at the expense of others. Is it a part of human nature to possess what is not yours? Or is nationalism, which promotes unity and energy, the root of imperialism? Or is the primary motive the desire for economic gain? More specifically, does capitalism, by its very nature, cause imperialism? To what extent is war a concomitant of imperialism, a factor in the progress of civilization? The following opinions span a wide chasm of interpretation from Marxist thought to that of the Social Darwinists. The first two selections are by the English economist John Hobson (1858–1940), whose analysis of imperialism became the standard of comparison. V. I. Lenin (1870–1924), a disciple of Karl Marx and leader of the Russian Revolution of 1917, attacked imperialism as "a special stage of capitalism" in his much debated analysis. Finally, Charles Morris, a popularizer of Social Darwinist theories, discusses war as a progressive force in civilization.

Nationalism and Imperialism (1902)

JOHN HOBSON

Nationalism is a plain highway to internationalism, and if it manifests divergence we may well suspect a perversion of its nature and its purpose. Such a perversion is imperialism, in which nations trespassing beyond the limits of facile assimilation transform the wholesome stimulative rivalry of varied national types into the cutthroat struggle of competing empires.

Not only does aggressive imperialism defeat the movement toward internationalism by fostering animosities among competing empires: its attacks upon the liberties and the existence of weaker or lower races stimulate in them a corresponding excess of national self-consciousness. A nationalism that bristles with resentment and is all astrain with the passion of self-defense is only less perverted from its natural genius than the nationalism which glows with the animus of greed and self-aggrandisement at the expense of others. From this aspect aggressive imperialism is an artificial stimulation of nationalism in peoples too foreign to be absorbed and too compact to be permanently crushed. We have welded Africanderdom into just such a strong dangerous nationalism, and we have joined with other nations in creating a resentful nationalism hitherto unknown in China. The injury to nationalism in both cases consists in converting a cohesive, pacific, internal force into an exclusive, hostile force, a perversion of the true power and use of nationality. The worst and most certain result is the retardation of internationalism. The older nationalism was primarily an inclusive sentiment; its natural relation to the same sentiment in another people was lack of sympathy, not open hostility; there was no inherent antagonism to prevent nationalities from growing and thriving side by side. Such in the main was the nationalism of the earlier nineteenth century, and the politicians of free trade had some foundation for their dream of a quick growth of effective, profitable, intercommunication of goods and ideas among nations recognizing a just harmony of interests in free peoples. . . .

Economics and Imperialism (1902)

JOHN HOBSON

What is the direct economic outcome of imperialism? A great expenditure of public money upon ships, guns, military and naval equipment and stores, growing and productive of enormous profits when a war, or an alarm of war, occurs; new public loans and important fluctuations in the

"Nationalism and Imperialism" is from John Hobson, *Imperialism: A Study*, 3rd ed. (London: George Allen and Unwin, 1938), pp. 9–10. Reprinted by permission of Routledge.

"Economics and Imperialism" is from John Hobson, *Imperialism: A Study*, 3rd ed. (London: George Allen and Unwin, 1938), pp. 48, 51, 85–86, 88–89, 93, 109. Reprinted by permission of Routledge.

home and foreign bourses; more posts for soldiers and sailors and in the diplomatic and consular services; improvement of foreign investments by the substitution of the British flag for a foreign flag; acquisition of markets for certain classes of exports, and some protection and assistance for trades representing British houses in these manufactures; employment for engineers, missionaries, speculative miners, ranchers, and other emigrants. . . .

In all the professions, military and civil, the army, diplomacy, the church, the bar, teaching and engineering, Greater Britain serves for an overflow, relieving the congestion of the home market and offering chances to more reckless or adventurous members, while it furnishes a convenient limbo for damaged characters and careers. The actual amount of profitable employment thus furnished by our recent acquisitions is inconsiderable, but it arouses that disproportionate interest which always attaches to the margin of employment. To extend this margin is a powerful motive in imperialism.

These influences, primarily economic, though not unmixed with other sentimental motives, are particularly operative in military, clerical, academic, and civil service circles, and furnish an interested bias toward imperialism throughout the educated classes. . . .

Thus we reach the conclusion that imperialism is the endeavor of the great controllers of industry to broaden the channel for the flow of their surplus wealth by seeking foreign markets and foreign investments to take off the goods and capital they cannot sell or use at home.

The fallacy of the supposed inevitability of imperial expansion as a necessary outlet for progressive industry is now manifest. It is not industrial progress that demands the opening up of new markets and areas of investment, but maldistribution of consuming power which prevents the absorption of commodities and capital within the country. The oversaving which is the economic root of imperialism is found by analysis to consist of rents, monopoly profits, and other unearned or excessive elements of income, which, not being earned by labor of head or hand, have no legitimate *raison d'être*. Having no natural relation to effort of production, they impel their recipients to no corresponding satisfaction of consumption: they form a surplus wealth, which, having no proper place in the normal economy of production and consumption, tends to accumulate as excessive savings. Let any turn in the tide of politico-economic forces divert from these owners their excess of income and make it flow, either to the workers in higher wages, or to the community in taxes, so that it will be spent instead of being saved, serving in either of these ways to swell the tide of consumption—there will be no need to fight for foreign markets or foreign areas of investment. . . .

There is no necessity to open up new foreign markets; the home markets are capable of indefinite expansion. Whatever is produced in England can be consumed in England, provided that the "income," or power to demand commodities, is properly distributed. This only appears untrue because of the unnatural and unwholesome specialization to which this country has been subjected, based upon a bad distribution of economic resources, which had induced an overgrowth of certain manufacturing trades for the express purpose of effecting foreign sales. . . . An economy that assigns to the "possessing" classes an excess of consuming power which they cannot use, and cannot convert into really serviceable capital, is a dog-in-the-manger policy. The social reforms which deprive the possession classes of their surplus will not, therefore, inflict upon them the real injury they dread; they can only use this surplus by forcing on their country a wrecking policy of imperialism. The only safety of nations lies in removing the unearned increments of income from the possessing classes, and adding them to the wage income of the working classes or to the public income, in order that they may be spent in raising the standard of consumption. . . . It is idle to attack imperialism or militarism as political expedients or policies unless the axe is laid at the economic root of the tree, and the classes for whose interest imperialism works are shorn of the surplus revenues which seek this outlet.

Imperialism with its wars and its armaments is undeniably responsible for the growing debts of the Continental nations, and while the unparalleled industrial prosperity of Great Britain and the isolation of the United States have enabled these great nations to escape this ruinous competition during the recent decades, the period of their immunity is over; both, committed as they seem to an imperialism without limit, will succumb more and more to the money-lending classes dressed as imperialists and patriots.

Imperialism: The Highest Stage of Capitalism (1916)

V. I. LENIN

The enormous dimensions of finance capital concentrated in a few hands and creating an extremely extensive and close network of ties and relationships which subordinate not only the small and medium, but also even the very small capitalists and small masters, on the one hand, and the intense struggle waged against other national state groups of financiers for the division of the world and domination over other countries, on the other hand, cause wholesale transition of the possessing classes to the side of imperialism. The signs of the times are a "general" enthusiasm regarding its prospects, a passionate defence of imperialist ideology also penetrates the working class. There is no Chinese Wall between it and the other classes. The leaders of the so-called "Social-Democratic" Party of Germany are today justly called "'social-imperialists," that is, socialists in words and imperialists in deeds; but as early as 1902, Hobson noted the existence of "Fabian Imperialists" who belonged to the opportunist Fabian Society in England.

"Imperialism: The Highest Stage of Capitalism" is from V. I. Lenin, *Imperialism: The Highest Stage of Capitalism* (New York: International Publishers Co., 1939), pp. 109–111, 123–124. Reprinted by permission of the publisher.

Bourgeois scholars and publicists usually come out in defence of imperialism in a somewhat veiled form, and obscure its complete domination and its profound roots; they strive to concentrate attention on partial and secondary details and do their very best to distract attention from the main issue by means of ridiculous schemes for "reform," such as police supervision of the trusts and banks, etc. Less frequently, cynical and frank imperialists speak out and are bold enough to admit the absurdity of the idea of reforming the fundamental features of imperialism. . . .

The question as to whether it is possible to reform the basis of imperialism, whether to go forward to the accentuation and deepening of the antagonisms, which it engenders, or backwards, towards allaying these antagonisms, is a fundamental question in the critique of imperialism. As a consequence of the fact that the political features of imperialism are reaction all along the line, and increased national oppression, resulting from the oppression of the financial oligarchy and the elimination of free competition, a petty-bourgeois–democratic opposition has been rising against imperialism in almost all imperialist countries since the beginning of the twentieth century. . . .

In the United States, the imperialist war waged against Spain in 1898 stirred up the opposition of the "anti-imperialists," the last of the Mohicans of bourgeois democracy. They declared this war to be "criminal"; they denounced the annexation of foreign territories as being a violation of the Constitution, and denounced the "Jingo treachery" by means of which Aguinaldo, leader of the native Filipinos, was deceived (the Americans promised him the independence of his country, but later they landed troops and annexed it). They quoted the words of Lincoln: "When the white man governs himself, that is self-government, but when he governs himself and also governs another man, that is more than self-government—that is despotism."

But while all this criticism shrank from recognising the indissoluble bond between imperialism and the trusts, and, therefore, between imperialism and the very foundations of capitalism; while it shrank from joining up with the forces engendered by large-scale capitalism and its development—it remained a "pious wish." . . .

We have seen that the economic quintessence of imperialism is monopoly capitalism. This very fact determines its place in history, for monopoly that grew up on the basis of free competition, and precisely out of free competition, is the transition from the capitalist system to a higher social-economic order. We must take special note of the four principal forms of monopoly, or the four principal manifestations of monopoly capitalism, which are characteristic of the epoch under review.

Firstly, monopoly arose out of the concentration of production at a very advanced stage of development. This refers to the monopolist capitalist combines, cartels, syndicates and trusts. We have seen the important part that these play in modern economic life. At the beginning of the twentieth century, monopolies acquired complete supremacy in the advanced countries. And although the first steps toward the formation of the cartels were first taken by countries enjoying the protection of high tariffs (Germany, America), Great Britain, with her system of free trade, was not far behind in revealing the same basic phenomenon, namely, the birth of monopoly out of the concentration of production.

Secondly, monopolies have accelerated the capture of the most important sources of raw materials, especially for the coal and iron industries, which are the basic and most highly cartelised industries in capitalist society. The monopoly of the most important sources of raw materials has enormously increased the power of big capital, and has sharpened the antagonism between cartelised and non-cartelised industry.

Thirdly, monopoly has sprung from the banks. The banks have developed from modest intermediary enterprises into the monopolists of finance capital. Some three to five of the biggest banks in each of the foremost capitalist countries have achieved the "personal union" of industrial and bank capital, and have concentrated in their hands the disposal of thousands upon thousands of millions which form the greater part of the capital and income of entire countries. A financial oligarchy, which throws a close net of relations of dependence over all the economic and political institutions of contemporary bourgeois society without exception—such is the most striking manifestation of this monopoly.

Fourthly, the monopoly has grown out of colonial policy. To the numerous "old" motives of colonial policy, finance capital has added the struggle for the sources of raw materials, for the export capital, for "spheres of influence," i.e., for spheres for profitable deals, concessions, monopolist profits and so on; in fine, for economic territory in general. When the colonies of the European powers in Africa, for instance, comprised only one-tenth of that territory (as was the case in 1876,), colonial policy was able to develop by methods other than those of monopoly—by the "free grabbing" of territories, so to speak. But when nine-tenths of Africa had been seized (approximately by 1900), when the whole world had been divided up, there was inevitably ushered in a period of colonial monopoly and, consequently, a period of particularly intense struggle for the division and the redivision of the world.

The extent to which monopolist capital has intensified all the contradictions of capitalism is generally known. It is sufficient to mention the high cost of living and the oppression of the cartels. This intensification of contradictions constitutes the most powerful driving force of the transitional period of history, which began from the time of the definite victory of world finance capital.

Monopolies, oligarchy, the striving for domination instead of the striving for liberty, the exploitation of an increasing number of small or weak nations by an extremely small group of the richest or most powerful nations—all these have given birth to those distinctive characteristics of imperialism which compel us to define it as parasitic or decaying capitalism. . . .

The receipt of high monopoly profits by the capitalists in one of the numerous branches of industry, in one of numerous countries, etc., makes it economically possible for them to corrupt certain sections of the working class, and for a time a fairly considerable minority, and win them to the side of the bourgeoisie of a given industry or nation against all other. The intensification of antagonisms between imperialist nations for the division of the world increases this striving. And so there is created that bond between imperialism and opportunism, which revealed itself first and most clearly in England, owing to the fact that certain features of imperialist development were observable there much earlier than in other countries. . . .

From all that has been said . . . on the economic nature of imperialism, it follows that we must define it as capitalism in transition, or, more precisely, as moribund capitalism.

War and Civilization (1895)

CHARLES MORRIS

It may seem to many readers absurd to speak of war as a helpful agency in civilization. It is the general impression that a state of profound peace, with its consequent agricultural and mechanical industries, is most conducive to human advancement. Warfare is usually looked upon as simply destructive, and as destitute of any redeeming feature; and yet I venture to claim that all the civilizations to-day existing were in their origin largely the results of ancient wars; and that peace, in the long past of the human race, was almost a synonym for social and intellectual stagnation. . . .

If we ask what is the philosophy of this, the answer may not be difficult to reach. Unlike the fixed conservatism of peace, war introduces new conditions, new foundations for human thought, on which the edifice of future civilization may be erected; and, breaking up the isolation of peace, it spreads these conditions throughout the world, making distant nations participants in their influences. The progress of mankind means simply the development of the human mind. Ideas are the seeds of civilization, and under whatever form it appears the idea must be born first, the embodiment must come afterward. In seeking for the causes of advancement, then, we must seek for the sources of new ideas; but, as experience lies at the root of ideas, new ideas can only arise from new experiences. Whence, then, do we derive our experiences? No isolated individual can learn much of himself. His own powers of observation and thought are limited. Our minds can only rapidly develop when we avail ourselves of the experience of others. In this way only can they become storehouses of new thoughts. There is a common stock of such thought abroad in the world, from which

"War and Civilization" is from Charles Morris, "War As a Factor in Civilization," *Popular Science Monthly* 47 (1895), pp. 823, 826.

we derive the great mass of the ideas which we call our own. And, obviously, that mind will be most developed which comes into contact with and assimilates the greatest number of these thoughts.

The same holds good with nations. An isolated nation is in the same position as an isolated individual. Its experiences are limited, its ideas few and narrow in range. Its thoughts move in one fixed channel, and the other powers of its mind are apt to become virtually aborted. An isolated nation, then, is not likely rapidly to gain new ideas. Yet peace, in all barbarian and semi-civilized nations, seems to tend strongly toward this condition of isolation; and such isolation in its conservative influence is a fatal bar to any wide or continuous progress. The long persistence of one form of government, of one condition of social customs, of one line of thought, tends to produce that uniformity of character which is so fatally opposed to any width of development of breadth of mental grasp. From uniformity arises stagnation. Its final result is a dead pause in mental advancement. Variety of influences and conditions alone can yield a healthy and vigorous growth of thought. The movement of the national mind in any one line must soon cease. Its limit is quickly reached, unless it be aided by development in other directions.

CHRONOLOGY: Nationalism and Imperialism: The Motives and Methods of Expansion

1854–1856	Crimean War: Britain, France, and the Ottoman Empire vs. Russia. Opposition to Russian expansion in Balkans leads to an ineptly managed war that shatters the invincible image of Russia and the Concert of Europe.
1859	War of Piedmont and France against Austria.
1859	*The Origin of Species* by Charles Darwin is published and promotes the theory of "natural selection."
1860	Garibaldi lands his forces in Sicily and invades southern Italy. These southern states join the northern union forged by Piedmont under the direction of Camillo Cavour.
1861	Victor Emmanuel II proclaimed King of Italy. Cavour dies three months later.
1861	Serfdom abolished in Russia by Tsar Alexander II.
1862	Otto von Bismarck becomes prime minister of Prussia.
1864	Danish-Prussian War results in quick Prussian victory. Prussia and Austria respectively rule Schleswig and Holstein.
1866	Austro-Prussian war breaks out over the Austrian administration of Holstein. Prussian victory in seven weeks: Austria is permanently excluded from German affairs.

1867	Dual Monarchy established in a compromise solution between Austria and Hungary.
1868–1874	Liberal ministry of William Gladstone in Great Britain.
1869	Suez Canal completed.
1870	France declares war on Prussia over Ems dispatch. France defeated at Sedan and Emperor Napoleon III captured. Third French republic proclaimed.
1870	Italian state annexes Rome. Italian unification completed under King Victor Emmanuel II.
1871	Proclamation of the German Empire at Versailles. Paris Commune in existence from March to May with goal to administer Paris separately from the rest of the country. The Commune is suppressed with heavy loss of life.
1874–1880	Ministry of Benjamin Disraeli in Great Britain highlighted by social legislation such as The Public Health Act and Artisans Dwelling Act, both in 1875.
1875	Britain gains control of Suez. Britain begins to establish Protectorate over Egypt.
1882	France controls Algeria.
1884–1885	Germany establishes Protectorate over Southwest Africa, Togoland, Cameroons, and East Africa.
1894	Captain Dreyfus accused of passing secret information to the Germany army and convicted on forged evidence by a military court. Dreyfus conviction set aside in 1906, but military discredited and France divided politically.
1898	Spanish-American War: United States acquires Puerto Rico, Philippines, Guam; annexes Hawaiian Islands and establishes Protectorate over Cuba.
1899	"Open Door Policy" in the Far East is proposed by the United States.
1899–1902	Britain crushes a rebellion by Dutch farmers in South Africa called the Boer War.

STUDY QUESTIONS

1. What are the main ideas contained in Giuseppe Mazzini's address "The Duties of Man"? This piece was directed toward Italian workers. How does it appeal to them specifically? How does Garibaldi's speech to the Italians differ from that of Mazzini? How is Garibaldi *using* nationalism?

2. Why does Johann Gottlieb Fichte refer to Rome and the Germanic tribes to such an extent? What specifically does he demonstrate by these examples? How does he define the German "people"?

3. According to Bismarck, why must Germany be armed? Does Bismarck advocate imperialism? How does he use God in his arguments? How does this relate to nationalism? How is religion (specifically Christianity) used in other sources as justification for imperial expansion?

4. Explain Social Darwinism and give several specific examples from the reading selections that demonstrate its practice and use as justification for imperial expansion. What phrases and ideas are consistently used? What are some of Karl Pearson's arguments? Are they compelling?

5. Discuss the "mandate system." What was it and how is it evident in the speech by Joseph Chamberlain regarding Britain's duty in Egypt? Cite specific phrases in this regard.

6. Analyze Senator Beveridge's speech on American control of the Philippines. What does he advocate and what are the specific arguments he uses to justify his beliefs? Note especially how he uses the abstraction of "history." Is this a *logical*, if not satisfying, argument? Why would it be appealing to many? How does Kipling's poem "The White Man's Burden" complement Beveridge's statements? How do this source and other sources in this chapter define imperialism as an agent of "progress and civilization"?

7. How does Sir Frederick Lugard connect nationalism with the economic argument for imperialism? How does he respond to the arguments presented by critics of imperialism? How does he justify his support of imperial expansion?

8. Explain the concept of "manifest destiny." What is "Providence" and how is it used to justify expansion into Indian lands and the annexation of Texas? What other arguments does O'Sullivan use for justification?

9. What does Wilfrid Blunt have to say about the civility of British imperialism, or American or European imperialism, for that matter? What specific justifications for imperialism, presented in earlier accounts, do his comments attack?

10. Discuss the various interpretations of imperialism. In your opinion, based on the evidence provided, does nationalism necessarily cause imperialism, or is economic profit a more important factor? What are Hobson's and Lenin's thoughts on the subject? Which are more firmly grounded in the evidence and therefore more persuasive? Do you agree or disagree with the arguments of Charles Morris on war as a factor of civilization? Why?

6

The Great War
(1914–1918)

The next dreadful thing to a battle lost is a battle won.

—Arthur Wellesley, Duke of Wellington

There never was a good war or a bad peace.

—Benjamin Franklin

Only a general who was a barbarian would send his men to certain death against the concentrated power of my new gun.

—Hiram Maxim (inventor of the machine gun)

Diplomats are just as essential to starting a war as soldiers are for finishing it. . . . You take diplomacy out of war and the whole thing would fall flat in a week.

—Will Rogers

After the defeat of Napoleon at the Battle of Waterloo in 1815, it was decided by the victors at the Congress of Vienna that Europe had to be governed by a policy of deterrence that resisted dominance by any one country. Nations required comparable strength in order to maintain the balance of power and thus preserve the peace. Great Britain led the way and applied this policy successfully throughout the nineteenth century. During this time, however, Europe was changing. The Industrial Revolution had increased the demand for trade, and various countries sought markets in Africa and the East, establishing hegemony over a region by military force. Imperialism and competition abroad affected the sense of security and the balance of power that were crucial to the preservation of peace at home. In addition, new factors were being introduced that further threatened to disrupt the balance.

The first serious threat to the *Pax Britannica* of the nineteenth century came from the expansion of industry and the accompanying scientific progress. In the first decade of the twentieth century, new weapons were being developed, as were more rapid forms of communication and transportation, including the telegraph, the automobile, the railway, and the steamship. These technological advancements presented new possibilities for highly mobilized warfare that could be better coordinated and managed.

The second serious threat to the balance of European power in the late nineteenth century was Germany. By 1870, the Prussians had unified north and west Germany through a policy of "blood and iron." The various regions of Germany had always been disunited, defying such masters as the Romans, Charlemagne, the Holy Roman Emperors, and Napoleon. But Kaiser Wilhelm I of Prussia (1797–1888), together with his master statesman Otto von Bismarck (1815–1898) and his general Count Helmut von Moltke, made highly effective use of the military capabilities of a thoroughly disciplined and well-supported army. To achieve unification, Prussia had beaten and humiliated the French in 1870 and succeeded in forging a unified German Reich. The balance of power had been upset and the lesson was clear: No nation in Europe could feel secure without training all of its young men for war, establishing a system of reserves, and creating a general staff that would prepare plans for potential wars and oversee a scheme for mobilization.

The concept of mobilization is very important in understanding why Europe and the world went to war. By 1914, every continental power had a complex plan and timetable for mobilizing against the most likely opponent or combination of enemies. When a country mobilized for war, its reserve troops were called to active duty, placed in the field, and supported with necessary rations, equipment, and armament. Timing was essential. Full mobilization took weeks, and it was important to get the process started before your enemy was ready to commit to such a policy. Hence the beginning of hostilities came when the various chiefs of state were convinced that military "necessity" required a mobilization order and that further delay would spell defeat by allowing the opponent to gain a military advantage that could not be overcome. Since mobilization involved a radical shift of the economy to maximum production and since troop movements could be detected by other nations within hours, the mobilization order could not be rescinded without the prospect of diplomatic and economic disaster. William H. McNeill, in *The Rise of the West*, notes that "the first weeks of World War I presented the amazing spectacle of vast human machines operating in a truly inhuman fashion and moving at least approximately according to predetermined and irreversible plans. The millions of persons composing the rival machines behaved almost as though they had lost individual will and intelligence." The "predetermined and irreversible" plans were centered on a military theory by Karl von Clausewitz that was accepted by all the general staffs of Europe: A swift and decisive battle that led to the initial destruction of the enemy's forces would achieve ultimate success. None planned for a long war—three or four months at most.

Thus, the nations of Europe were powderkegs waiting to go off when in June 1914 the heir to the Austro-Hungarian Empire, the Archduke Franz Ferdinand, was assassinated at Sarajevo. The diplomats talked and then the armies mobilized one by one. The "guns of August" soon enveloped Europe in a war that was to last not four months but four years. Over 8.5 million people were killed, with a total casualty count of over 37.5 million.

This chapter seeks to give an overall picture of World War I, or what has been more accurately called the Great War. This was war on a world scale, involving hostilities in Africa and the Balkans, as well as an American presence. And it was war on some of the cruelest terms. Rules were changing. There were no longer strict orders to exempt the civilian population from harm. Nor were there moral constraints on the use of submarines, machine guns, and poisonous gas; all became permanent fixtures. The Great War stands unequaled in terms of blood sacrificed for miserable accomplishment. To die for a "victory" of a hundred yards of land needed justification, which was rarely forthcoming. The questions are disturbing and perhaps unanswerable: Why did commanders send their men repeatedly "over the top" of the trenches, across "no man's land," and into the bloody rain of machine gun fire? Why was this slaughter of human life condoned by the diplomats and even the soldiers themselves? Why did Europe lose an entire generation of men?

When the war ended in 1918, the world of the nineteenth century had been forever altered. The thin veneer of civilization had been shattered and the nations of Europe had difficulty defining what had happened and why. Europe would be led out of this abyss of disillusionment and despair by those promising order and respect: Benito Mussolini and Adolf Hitler.

The Road to War

Assassination at Sarajevo

For decades the Balkan areas of Bosnia and Serbia had been in turmoil, causing the neighboring Austro-Hungarian empire great anxiety. The Serbs had their own language and customs and had always been wary of Austrian attempts to unify the region politically and culturally. Several extremist organizations, inspired by patriotic idealism, sought to eliminate the Austro-Hungarian presence through terror and violence. Among these organizations was the pan-Serbian nationalist group Union or Death, also known as The

Black Hand. Statutes of this representative group are included in the first selection.

The second selection recounts the famous assassination of the heir to the Austro-Hungarian throne, Archduke Franz Ferdinand. The murderer, a nineteen-year-old Serb student named Gavrilo Princip, was a member of a patriotic society similar to The Black Hand, called Narodna Odbrana. *One of the leaders of this organization who was arrested along with Princip gave this first-hand account of the assassination, an event that propelled the world to war.*

Statutes of The Black Hand

Article 1. This organization has been created with the object of realising the national ideal: The union of all the Serbs. All Serbs without distinction of sex, religion, place of birth, and all who are sincerely devoted to this cause, may become members.

Article 2. This organization prefers terrorist action to intellectual propaganda and for this reason must be kept absolutely secret from persons who do not belong to it.

Article 3. This organization bears the name "Union or Death."

Article 4. To accomplish its task, the organization:

1. Brings influence to bear on Government circles, on the various social classes and on the whole social life of the Kingdom of Serbia, regarded as Piedmont.

2. Organizes revolutionary action in all territories inhabited by Serbs.

3. Outside the frontiers of Serbia uses every means available to fight the adversaries of this idea.

4. Maintains amicable relations with all states, peoples, organizations, and individuals who entertain feelings of friendship towards Serbia and the Serbian element.

5. Lends help and support in every way possible to all people and all organizations struggling for their national liberation and for their union.

Article 5. A central Committee having its headquarters at Belgrade is at the head of this organization and exercises executive authority. . . .

Article 25. Members of the organization are not known to each other personally. It is only the members of the Central Committee who are known to one another.

"Statutes of The Black Hand" is from p. 309 of *Readings in European International Relations* by W. Henry Cooke and Edith P. Stickney. Copyright, 1931, by Harper & Row, Publishers, Inc.; renewed 1959 by W. Henry Cooke. Reprinted by permission of Harper & Row, Publishers, Inc.

Article 26. In the organization itself the members are known by numbers. Only the Central Committee at Belgrade is to know their names. . . .

Article 31. Anyone who once enters the organization may never withdraw from it. . . .

Article 33. When the Central Committee at Belgrade has pronounced penalty of death [on one of the members] the only matter of importance is that the execution take place without fail. . . .

The Plot and Murder (June 28, 1914)

A tiny clipping from a newspaper, mailed without comment from a secret band of terrorists in Zagreb, capital of Croatia, to their comrades in Belgrade, was the torch which set the world afire with war in 1914. That bit of paper wrecked old, proud empires. It gave birth to new, free nations.

I was one of the members of the terrorist band in Belgrade which received it.

The little clipping declared that the Austrian Archduke Francis Ferdinand would visit Sarajevo, the capital of Bosnia, June 28, to direct army maneuvers in the neighboring mountains.

It reached our meeting place, the cafe called Zeatna Moruna, one night the latter part of April, 1914. To understand how great a sensation that little piece of paper caused among us when it was passed from hand to hand almost in silence, and how greatly it inflamed our hearts, it is necessary to explain just why the *Narodna Odbrana* existed, the kind of men that were in it, and the significance of that date, June 28, on which the Archduke dared to enter Sarajevo.

As every one knows, the old Austrio-Hungarian Empire was built by conquest and intrigues, by sales and treacheries, which held in subjugation many peoples who were neither Austrian nor Hungarian. It taxed them heavily; it diverted the products of their toil to serve the wealth of the master state. It interfered in their old freedom by a multiplicity of laws administered with arrogance.

Several years before the war, a little group of us, thirty-five in all, living in several Bosnian and Herzegovinian cities and villages, formed the *Narodna Odbrana*, the secret society, the aim of which was to work for freedom from Austria and a union with Serbia. So strict was the police vigilance in Bosnia and Herzegovina that we set up our headquarters in Belgrade, the capital of our mother country.

The men who were terrorists in 1914 embraced all classes. Most of them were students. Youth is the time for the philosophy of action. There were also teachers, tradesmen and peasants, artisans and even men of the upper

"The Plot and Murder" is from *New York World,* June 28, 1924, the North American Newspaper Alliance.

classes were ardent patriots. They were dissimilar in everything except hatred of the oppressor.

Such were the men into whose hands the tiny bit of newsprint was sent by friends in Bosnia that April night in Belgrade. At a small table in a very humble cafe, beneath a flickering gas jet we sat and read it. There was no advice nor admonition sent with it. Only four letters and two numerals were sufficient to make us unanimous, without discussion, as to what we should do about it. They were contained in the fateful date, June 28.

How dared Francis Ferdinand, not only the representative of the oppressor but in his own person an arrogant tyrant, enter Sarajevo on that day? Such an entry was a studied insult.

June 28 is a date engraved deep in the heart of every Serb, so that the day has a name of its own. It is called the *vidovnan* [St. Vitus Day]. It is the day on which the old Serbian kingdom was conquered by the Turks at the battle of Amselfelde in 1389. It is also the day on which in the second Balkan War the Serbian armies took glorious revenge on the Turk for his old victory and for the years of enslavement. . . .

As we read that clipping in Belgrade we knew what we would do to Francis Ferdinand. We would kill him to show Austria there yet lived within its borders defiance of its rule. We would kill him to bring once more to the boiling point the fighting spirit of the revolutionaries and pave the way for revolt.

Our decision was taken almost immediately. Death to the tyrant!

Then came the matter of arranging it. To make his death certain twenty-two members of the organization were selected to carry out the sentence. At first we thought we would choose the men by lot. But here Gavrilo Princip intervened. . . . From the moment Ferdinand's death was decided upon, he took an active leadership in its planning. Upon his advice we left the deed to members of our band, who were in and around Sarajevo, under his direction and that of Gabrinovic, a linotype operator on a Serbian newspaper. Both were regarded as capable of anything in the cause. . . .

The fateful morning dawned. Two hours before Francis Ferdinand arrived in Sarajevo all the twenty-two conspirators were in their allotted positions, armed and ready. They were distributed five hundred yards apart over the whole route along which the Archduke must travel from the railroad station to the town hall.

When Francis Ferdinand and his retinue drove from the station they were allowed to pass the first two conspirators. The motor cars were driving too fast to make an attempt feasible and in the crowd were many Serbians; throwing a grenade would have killed many innocent people.

When the car passed Chabrinovic, the compositor, he threw his grenade. It hit the side of the car, but Francis Ferdinand with presence of mind threw himself back and was uninjured. Several officers riding in his attendance were injured.

The cars sped to the Town Hall and the rest of the conspirators did not interfere with them. After the reception in the Town Hall General Potiorek, the Austrian Commander, pleaded with Francis Ferdinand to leave the city, as it was seething with rebellion. The Archduke was persuaded to drive the shortest way out of the city and to go quickly.

The road to the maneuvers was shaped like the letter V, making a sharp turn at the bridge over the River Nilgacka. Francis Ferdinand's car could go fast enough until it reached this spot but here it was forced to slow down for the turn. Here Princip had taken his stand.

As the car came abreast he stepped forward from the curb, drew his automatic pistol from his coat and fired two shots. The first struck the wife of the Archduke, the Archduchess Sofia, in the abdomen. She was an expectant mother. She died instantly.

The second bullet struck the Archduke close to the heart.

He uttered only one word, "Sofia"—a call to his stricken wife. Then his head fell back and he collapsed. He died almost instantly.

The officers seized Princip. They beat him over the head with the flat of their swords. They knocked him down, they kicked him, scraped the skin from his neck with the edges of their swords, tortured him, all but killed him.

The next day they put chains on Princip's feet, which he wore till his death. . . .

I was placed in the cell next to Princip's, and when Princip was taken out to walk in the prison yard I was taken along as his companion.

By Oct. 12, the date of Princip's trial, his prison sufferings had worn him to a skeleton.

His sentence was twenty years imprisonment at hard labor, the death sentence being inapplicable because he was a minor.

Awakened in the middle of the night and told that he was to be carried off to another prison, Princip made an appeal to the prison governor:

"There is no need to carry me to another prison. My life here is already ebbing away. I suggest that you nail me to a cross and burn me alive. My flaming body will be a torch to light my people on their path to freedom."

Diplomatic Maneuvers

For several years Europe had been diplomatically divided into two rival camps. The Triple Alliance was formed in 1882 among Germany, Italy, and Austria-Hungary. In 1907, the Triple Entente was established among Great Britain, France, and Russia. Both organizations were pledged by treaty to support their respective allies militarily should their mutual interests or existence be threatened. Thus, the European world was shocked by the assassination of Archduke Franz Ferdinand. Poised on the brink of crisis, each nation took stock of its diplomatic commitments, its military arsenal, and its long-range goals. Such a slap in the face of the powerful Austro-Hungarian empire by Serbian terrorists had wide-ranging implications. Response had to be quick in order to preserve the honor and integrity of the throne and to assure that such action would not invite further insolence, which could lead to outright revolt. There were other factors to consider as well. How would Russia react to a severe stand against the Serbs? Russia, after all, was a Slavic nation and was promoting a policy that advocated the independence and cultural integrity of Balkan Slavs.

Count Leopold von Berchtold, the Austro-Hungarian foreign minister, sought German support in his plans to punish Serbia for the assassination of the Austrian heir. Germany would be an important ally in countering the potential hostility of Russia. On July 6, 1914, the German kaiser, Wilhelm II, and his chancellor, Theobold von Bethmann-Hollweg, sent the following dispatch to Vienna. Berchtold regarded this telegram as a "blank check" that guaranteed German support for whatever punishment he decided to inflict upon Serbia.

The Austrians, thus secure in their relationship with Germany, sent an ultimatum to Serbia demanding the dissolution of nationalist societies, the suppression of anti-Austrian propaganda, and permission to allow Austrian officials to aid in suppressing disorders in Serbia. The Serbian government agreed to all conditions except the last, noting that this violated Serbia's sovereignty as a nation. Austria thereupon rejected Serbia's reply, declared war, and started mobilizing her military forces.

The "Blank Check" Telegram (July 6, 1914)

CHANCELLOR THEOBOLD VON BETHMANN-HOLLWEG

His Majesty sends his thanks to the Emperor Francis Joseph for his letter and would soon answer it personally. In the meantime His Majesty desires to say that he is not blind to the danger which threatens Austria-Hungary and thus the Triple Alliance as a result of the Russian and Serbian Pan-Slavic agitation. . . . As far as concerns Serbia, His Majesty, of course, cannot interfere in the dispute now going on between Austria-Hungary and that country, as it is a matter not within his competence. The Emperor Francis Joseph may, however, rest assured that His Majesty will faithfully stand by Austria-Hungary, as is required by the obligations of his alliance and of his ancient friendship.

"The 'Blank Check' Telegram" is from Max Montgelas and Walter Schucking, eds., *Outbreak of the European War: Documents Collected by Karl Kautsky* (New York: Oxford University Press, 1924), p. 79. Reprinted by permission of the Carnegie Endowment for International Peace.

Austro-Hungarian Declaration of War on Serbia (July 28, 1914)
COUNT LEOPOLD VON BERCHTOLD

[Telegraphic]

Vienna, July 28, 1914

The Royal Serbian Government not having answered in a satisfactory manner the note of July 23, 1914, presented by the Austro-Hungarian Minister at Belgrade, the Imperial and Royal Government are themselves compelled to see to the safeguarding of their rights and interests, and, with this object, to have recourse to force of arms. Austria-Hungary consequently considers herself henceforward in state of war with Serbia.

Telegram: Kaiser to Tsar (July 29, 1:45 A.M.)
KAISER WILHELM II

The Great War was, in some ways, an intensely personal war. The monarchs of Great Britain, Germany, and Russia were all cousins and had been on rather good terms for years. Personal relationships, however, were being strained as Europe drifted closer to war. The following telegrams reflect a confidence that personal communication between cousin "Willy" and cousin "Nicky" might salvage the deteriorating relationship between Germany and Russia. However, the secret telegram from the Russian minister of foreign affairs, Sergei Sazonoff, to Paris suggests that war was fast becoming inevitable despite the private and perhaps naïve attempts of the monarchs to control the situation.

It is with the gravest concern that I hear of the impression which the action of Austria against Serbia is creating in your country. The unscrupulous agitation that has been going on in Serbia for years has resulted in the outrageous crime, to which Archduke Francis Ferdinand fell a victim. The spirit that led Serbians to murder their own king and his wife still dominates the country. You will doubtless agree with me that we both, you and I, have a common interest as well as all Sovereigns to insist that all the persons morally responsible for the dastardly murder should receive their deserved punishment. In this case politics plays no part at all.

On the other hand, I fully understand how difficult it is for you and your Government to face the drift of your public opinion. Therefore, with regard to the hearty and tender friendship which binds us both from long

"Austro-Hungarian Declaration of War" is from Great Britain Foreign Office, *Collected Documents Relating to the Outbreak of the European War*, 1915; Serbian Blue Book, no. 45, p. 392.

"Telegram: Kaiser to Tsar" and "Telegram: Tsar to Kaiser" are from Max Montgelas and Walter Schucking, eds., *Outbreak of the European War: Documents Collected by Karl Kautsky* (New York: Oxford University Press, 1924), pp. 295–297. Reprinted by permission of the Carnegie Endowment for International Peace.

ago with firm ties, I am exerting my utmost influence to induce the Austrians to deal straightly to arrive to a satisfactory understanding with you. I confidently hope that you will help me in my efforts to smooth over difficulties that may still arise.

Your very sincere and devoted friend and cousin,

WILLY

Telegram: Tsar to Kaiser (July 29, 8:20 P.M.)

TSAR NICHOLAS II

Am glad you are back. In this serious moment, I appeal to you to help me. An ignoble war has been declared to a weak country. The indignation in Russia shared fully by me is enormous. I foresee that very soon I shall be overwhelmed by the pressure forced upon me and be forced to take extreme measures which will lead to war. To try and avoid such a calamity as a European war I beg you in the name of our old friendship to do what you can to stop your allies from going too far.

NICKY

Secret Telegram of the Russian Minister of Foreign Affairs to the Russian Ambassador at Paris (July 29, 1914)

SERGEI SAZONOFF

No. 1551 Urgent

Saint Petersburg, July 29, 1914

Communicate to London

The German Ambassador informed me today of the decision of his Government to mobilize its forces if Russia did not stop its military preparations. Now, these preparations have been begun by us only as a consequence of the mobilization of eight corps which the Austrians have already effected and of the evident unwillingness on the part of the Austrians to accept any means of arriving at a peaceful settlement of their differences with Serbia. As we cannot comply with the wishes of Germany, we have no alternative but to hasten on our own military preparations and to envisage the inevitable eventuality of war. Please inform the French Government and at the same time express to it our sincere gratitude for the declaration which the French Ambassador made to me on its behalf, to the effect that we could count fully upon the support of France. In the present circumstances this declaration is particularly valuable to us. It will be extremely desirable that England join France without loss of time, for only in this way can she succeed in anticipating a dangerous rupture of the European equilibrium.

Russia Enters the War

Kaiser Wilhelm II was known for his bellicose personality. He dearly loved his military forces and felt a personal responsibility as a self-styled divine-right monarch. The following excerpt from a speech delivered two days after his telegram to Nicholas reveals his intentions. On August 1, Germany declared war on Russia.

Speech from the Balcony of the Royal Palace (July 31, 1914)
KAISER WILHELM II

A momentous hour has struck for Germany. Envious rivals everywhere force us to legitimate defense. The sword has been forced into our hands. I hope that in the event that my efforts to the very last moment do not succeed in bringing our opponents to reason and in preserving peace, we may use the sword, with the help of God, so that we may sheathe it again with honor. War will demand enormous sacrifices by the German people, but we shall show the enemy what it means to attack Germany. And so I commend you to God. Go forth into the churches, kneel down before God, and implore his help for our brave army.

The German Declaration of War on Russia (August 1, 1914)

The Imperial German Government have used every effort since the beginning of the crisis to bring about a peaceful settlement. In compliance with a wish expressed to him by His Majesty the Emperor of Russia, the German Emperor had undertaken, in concert with Great Britain, the part of mediator between the Cabinets of Vienna and St. Petersburg; but Russia, without waiting for any result, proceeded to a general mobilisation of her forces

"Speech from the Balcony" is from Louis L. Snyder, ed., *Historic Documents of World War I* (Princeton: Van Nostrand, 1958), p. 80. Reprinted by permission of Louis Snyder.

"The German Declaration" is from Great Britain Foreign Office, *Collected Diplomatic Documents Relating to the Outbreak of the European War*, 1915: Russian Orange Book, no. 76, pp. 294–295.

both on land and sea. In consequence of this threatening step, which was not justified by any military proceedings on the part of Germany, the German Empire was faced by a grave and imminent danger. If the German Government had failed to guard against this peril, they would have compromised the safety and the very existence of Germany. The German Government were, therefore, obliged to make representations to the Government of His Majesty the Emperor of All the Russians and to insist upon a cessation of the aforesaid military acts. Russia having refused to comply with this demand, and having shown by this refusal that her action was directed against Germany, I have the honor, on the instruction of my Government, to inform your Excellency as follows:

His Majesty the Emperor, by august Sovereign, in the name of the German Empire, accepts the challenge, and considers itself at war with Russia.

The Question of Belgian Neutrality

On August 1, Germany declared war on Russia. At the same time, France began to mobilize her forces, and Germany declared war on August 3. The British, removed from the fray by the English Channel, could not long remain out of the conflict. On August 2, Germany issued an ultimatum that Belgium allow German troops to pass through her territory in order to invade France. Belgium refused and appealed to Britain to intervene diplomatically in order "to safeguard the integrity of Belgium." The British Parliament responded favorably and demanded that Germany withdraw its ultimatum. She refused and Britain declared war on August 4, 1914.

The following speech was by the German chancellor, Bethmann-Hollweg, who admitted that the violation of Belgian neutrality was unjust but necessary to ensure German security. The second selection is another of Kaiser Wilhelm's militaristic speeches. The European world was now at war.

German Defense for Invading Belgium (August 4, 1914)
CHANCELLOR THEOBOLD VON BETHMANN-HOLLWEG

A stupendous fate is breaking over Europe. For forty-four years, since the time we fought for and won the German Empire and our position in the world, we have lived in peace and have protected the peace of Europe. In

"German Defense for Invading Belgium" is from Great Britain Foreign Office, *Collected Diplomatic Documents Relating to the Outbreak of the European War*, 1915: German White Book, pp. 436–439.

the works of peace we have become strong and powerful, and have thus aroused the envy of others. With patience we have faced the fact that, under the pretense that Germany was desirous of war, enmity has been awakened against us in the East and the West, and chains have been fashioned for us. The wind then sown has brought forth the whirlwind which has now broken loose. We wished to continue our work of peace, and, like a silent vow, the feeling that animated everyone from the Emperor down to the youngest soldier was this: Only in defense of a just cause shall our sword fly from its scabbard.

The day has now come when we must draw it, against our wish, and in spite of our sincere endeavors. Russia has set fire to the building. We are at war with Russia and France—a war that has been forced upon us.

From the first moment of the Austro-Serbian conflict we declared that this question must be limited to Austria-Hungary and Serbia, and we worked with this end in view. All governments, especially that of Great Britain, took the same attitude. Russia alone asserted that she had to be heard in the settlement of this matter.

Thus the danger of a European crisis raised its threatening head.

As soon as the first definite information regarding the military preparations in Russia reached us, we declared at St. Petersburg in a friendly but emphatic manner that military measures against Austria would find us on the side of our ally, and that military preparations against ourselves would oblige us to take countermeasures; but that mobilization would come very near to actual war.

Russia assured us in the most solemn manner of her desire for peace, and declared that she was making no military preparations against us.

In the meantime, Great Britain, warmly supported by us, tried to mediate between Vienna and St. Petersburg.

On July 28th the Emperor telegraphed to the Tsar asking him to take into consideration the fact that it was both the duty and the right of Austria-Hungary to defend herself against the Pan-Serb agitation, which threatened to undermine her existence. . . . About the same time, and before receipt of this telegram, the Tsar asked the Emperor to come to his aid and to induce Vienna to moderate her demands. The emperor accepted the role of mediator.

But scarcely had active steps on these lines begun, when Russia mobilized all her forces directed against Austria, while Austria-Hungary had mobilized only those of her corps which were directed against Serbia. To the north she has mobilized only two of her corps, far from the Russian frontier. The Emperor immediately informed the Tsar that this mobilization of Russian forces against Austria rendered the role of mediator, which he accepted at the Tsar's request, difficult, if not impossible.

The Emperor ordered that the French frontier was to be unconditionally respected. This order, with one single exception, was strictly obeyed. France, who mobilized at the same time as we did, assured us that she would respect a zone of ten kilometers on the frontier. What really happened? Aviators dropped bombs, and cavalry patrols and French infantry detachments appeared on the territory of the Empire! Though war had not been declared, France thus broke the peace and actually attacked us. . . .

Gentlemen, we are now in a state of necessity (*Notwehr*), and necessity (*Not*) knows no law. Our troops have occupied Luxembourg and perhaps have already entered Belgian territory.

Gentlemen, that is a breach of international law. It is true that the French government declared at Brussels that France would respect Belgian neutrality as long as her adversary respected it. We knew, however, that France stood ready for an invasion. France could wait, we could not. A French attack on our flank on the lower Rhine might have been disastrous. Thus we were forced to ignore the rightful protests of the governments of Luxembourg and Belgium. The wrong—I speak openly—the wrong we thereby commit we will try to make good as soon as our military aims have been attained.

Gentlemen, we stand shoulder to shoulder with Austria-Hungary.

Gentlemen, so much for the facts. I repeat the words of the Emperor: "With a clear conscience we enter the lists." We are fighting for the fruits of our works of peace, for the inheritance of a great past and for our future. The fifty years are not yet past during which Count Moltke said we should have to remain armed to defend the inheritance that we won in 1870. Now the great hour of trial has struck for our people. But with clear confidence we go forward to meet it. Our army is in the field, our navy is ready for battle—behind them stands the entire German nation—the entire German nation united to the last man.

"The Sword Is Drawn!" (August 18, 1914)
KAISER WILHELM II

Former generations as well as those who stand here today have often seen the soldiers of the First Guard Regiment and My Guards at this place. We were brought together then by an oath of allegiance which we swore before God. Today all have gathered to pray for the triumph of our weapons, for now that oath must be proved to the last drop of blood. The sword, which I have left in its scabbard for decades, shall decide.

I expect My First Guard Regiment on Foot and My Guards to add a new page of fame to their glorious history. The celebration today finds us confident in God in the Highest and remembering the glorious days of

" 'The Sword Is Drawn!' " is from Louis L. Snyder, ed., *Historic Documents of World War I* (Princeton: Van Nostrand, 1958), pp. 80–81. Reprinted by permission of Louis Snyder.

Leuthen, Chlum, and St. Privat. Our ancient fame is an appeal to the German people and their sword. And the entire German nation to the last man has grasped the sword. And so I draw the sword which with the help of God I have kept in its scabbard for decades. [*At this point the Kaiser drew his sword from its scabbard and held it high above his head.*]

The sword is drawn, and I cannot sheathe it again without victory and honor. All of you shall and will see to it that only in honor is it returned to the scabbard. You are my guarantee that I can dictate peace to my enemies. Up and at the enemy! Down with the enemies of Brandenburg!

Three cheers for our army!

"They Shall Not Pass": The War

The Horror of Battle

The German strategy in August 1914 had been planned long in advance by Count Alfred von Schlieffen, German chief of staff until 1905. The essence of the strategy was to sweep through Belgium and overwhelm French defenses in one swift onslaught; about 90 percent of the German army would be used for that purpose, while the remaining fraction, together with the Austrians, would hold off Russia. Once France was defeated, Germany and Austria-Hungary could concentrate their forces against the Russian army. Quite unexpectedly, however, the Belgians put up a gallant resistance, and the German attack was stalled long enough to upset the timetable. The British were able to land troops in Europe, and the war degenerated into a struggle for position that was characterized by trench warfare. New weapons such as the machine gun, the tank, and barbed wire eliminated thousands of men as attacks failed and comrades were left to die in the region between the trenches called "No Man's Land."

The following accounts of soldiers testify to the horrors of ceaseless shelling and destruction. The Battle of Verdun in 1916 raged for ten months, resulting in a combined total of about one million casualties. The Battle of the Somme lasted five months, with well over one million killed or wounded. Very little ground or tactical advantage was gained. Battle cries such as the French "They Shall Not Pass" were indicative of the stalemated defensive war. In such a situation, propaganda leaflets dropped into enemy trenches by balloons attempted to gain advantage in what was as much psychological as physical combat.

The section begins, however, with "laws of war" established at the Hague Convention of 1907. These laws were designed to control hostilities and promote peaceful coexistence; the convention was to meet next in 1915 but ironically was canceled because of the Great War.

Establishing "Laws of War":
The Hague Convention (1907)

SECTION II.—HOSTILITIES

Chapter I.—*Means of Injuring the Enemy, Sieges, and Bombardments*

ARTICLE 22

The right of belligerents to adopt means of injuring the enemy is not unlimited.

ARTICLE 23

In addition to the prohibitions provided by special Conventions, it is especially forbidden—

(a) To employ poison or poisoned weapons;
(b) To kill or wound treacherously individuals belonging to the hostile nation or army;
(c) To kill or wound an enemy who, having laid down his arms, or having no longer the means of defence, has surrendered at discretion;

ARTICLE 25

The attack or bombardment, *by whatever means*, of towns, villages, dwellings, or buildings which are undefended is prohibited.

ARTICLE 26

The officer in command of an attacking force must, before commencing a bombardment, except in cases of assault, do all in his power to warn the authorities.

ARTICLE 27

In sieges and bombardments all necessary steps must be taken to spare, as far as possible, buildings dedicated to religion, art, science, or charitable purposes, *historic monuments*, hospitals, and places where the sick and wounded are collected, provided they are not being used at the time for military purposes.

"Establishing 'Laws of War' " is from Carnegie Endowment for International Peace, *The Hague Conventions and Declarations of 1899 and 1907* (New York: Oxford University Press, 1915), pp. 116–118.

It is the duty of the besieged to indicate the presence of such buildings or places by distinctive and visible signs, which shall be notified to the enemy beforehand.

ARTICLE 28

The pillage of a town or place, even when taken by assault, is prohibited.

The Battle of Verdun (February–December 1916)

During three days (February 26–29th) after their initial advance over devastated and useless ground, they assaulted with the greatest dash and determination the main French positions. But the defenders were now in strength; and the French guns at length took matters in hand. The German assaulting waves dashed themselves in vain against the Talou heights, the Pepper ridge, and the Vaux position. They were ripped open with cannon, broken by the French bayonets, and driven back with fearful slaughter, time and again. Finally the mauled and battered German columns collapsed, and they were withdrawn from the fray; the casualties of the assailants for the first full week of uninterrupted fighting being estimated, on the lowest computation, at 60,000.

For such heavy sacrifice the enemy technically had won nothing, although, as usual, he indulged in much boasting and he magnified tremendously the barren results he had obtained from the action—an insignificant and useless gain of ground, a few prisoners, and some disabled guns; this was really all he could show as the outcome of his plan which was meant to open to him the gates of Verdun and to place him in possession of the Heights of the Meuse. The French, who had lost 20,000 men, continued to hold Verdun and the main positions surrounding it. . . .

Thousands of projectiles are flying in all directions, some whistling, others howling, others moaning low, and all uniting in one infernal roar. From time to time an aerial torpedo passes, making a noise like a gigantic motor car. With a tremendous thud a giant shell bursts quite close to our observation post, breaking the telephone wire and interrupting all communication with our batteries.

A man gets out at once for repairs, crawling along on his stomach through all this place of busting mines and shells. It seems quite impossible that he should escape in the rain of shell, which exceeds anything imaginable; there has never been such a bombardment in war. Our man seems to be enveloped in explosions, and shelters himself from time to time in the

"The Battle of Verdun" is from Charles F. Horne, ed., *Source Records of the Great War*, vol. 4 (Indianapolis: The American Legion, 1931), pp. 45, 54–57. Reprinted by permission of The American Legion.

shell craters which honeycomb the ground; finally he reaches a less stormy spot, mends his wires, and then, as it would be madness to try to return, settles down in a big crater and waits for the storm to pass.

Beyond, in the valley, dark-masses are moving over the snow-covered ground. It is German infantry advancing in packed formation along the valley to the attack. They look like a big gray carpet being unrolled over the country. We telephone through to the batteries and the ball begins. The sight is hellish. In the distance, in the valley and upon the slopes, regiments spread out, and as they deploy fresh troops come pouring in.

There is a whistle over our heads. It is our first shell. It falls right in the middle of the enemy infantry. We telephone through, telling our batteries of their hit, and a deluge of heavy shells is poured on the enemy. Their position becomes critical. Through glasses we can see men maddened, men covered with earth and blood, falling one upon the other. When the first wave of the assault is decimated, the ground is dotted with heaps of corpses, but the second wave is already pressing on. Once more our shells carve awful gaps in their ranks. Nevertheless, like an army of rats the Boches [Germans] continue to advance in spite of our "marmites." Then our heavy artillery bursts forth in fury. The whole valley is turned into a volcano, and its exit is stopped by the barrier of the slain.

Despite the horror of it, despite the ceaseless flow of blood, one wants to see. One's soul wants to feed on the sight of the brute Boches falling. I stopped on the ground for hours, and when I closed my eyes I saw the whole picture again. The guns are firing at 200 and 300 yards, and shrapnel is exploding with a crash, scything them down. Our men hold their ground; our machine guns keep to their work, and yet they advance.

The Boches are returning again massed to the assault, and they are being killed in bulk. It makes one think that in declaring war the Kaiser had sworn the destruction of his race, and he would have shown good taste in doing so. Their gunfire is slackening now, and ours redoubles. The fort has gone, and if under its ruins there are left a few guns and gunners the bulk of the guns are firing from outside. The machine guns are coming up and getting in position, and our men are moving on in numerous waves.

I find a rifle belonging to a comrade who has fallen and join the Chasseurs with the fifty cartridges that I have left. What a fight it is, and what troops! From time to time a man falls, rises, shoots, runs, shoots again, keeps on firing, fights with his bayonet, and then, worn out, falls, to be trampled on without raising a cry. The storm of fire continues. Everything is on fire—the wood nearby, the village of Douaumont, Verdun, the front of Bezonvaux, and the back of Thiaumont. There is fire everywhere. The acid smell of carbonic acid and blood catches at our throats, but the battle goes on.

They are brave, but one of our men is worth two of theirs, especially in hand-to-hand fighting. . . . Our reenforcements continue to arrive. We are the masters.

The Battle of the Somme (July–November 1916)

The German Command was not thinking much about the human suffering of its troops. It was thinking, necessarily, of the next defensive line upon which they would have to fall back if the pressure of the British offensive could be maintained. . . . It was getting nervous. Owing to the enormous efforts made in the Verdun offensive the supplies of ammunition were not adequate to the enormous demand.

The German gunners were trying to compete with the British in continuity of bombardments and the shells were running short. Guns were wearing out under this incessant strain, and it was difficult to replace them. General von Gallwitz received reports of "an alarmingly large number of bursts in the bore, particularly in the field guns."

In all the letters written during those weeks of fighting and captured by us from dead or living men there is one great cry of agony and horror.

"I stood on the brink of the most terrible days of my life," wrote one of them. "They were those of the battle of the Somme. It began with a night attack on August 13th–14th. The attack lasted till the evening of the 18th, when the English wrote on our bodies in letters of blood: 'It is all over with you.' A handful of the half-mad, wretched creatures, worn out in body and mind, were all that was left of a whole battalion. We were that handful."

In many letters this phrase was used. The Somme was called the "Bath of Blood" by the German troops who waded across its shell-craters, and in the ditches which were heaped with their dead. But what I have described is only the beginning of the battle, and the bath was to be filled deeper in the months that followed.

It was in no cheerful mood that men went away to the Somme battle-fields. Those battalions of gray-clad men entrained without any of the old enthusiasm with which they had gone to earlier battles. Their gloom was noticed by the officers.

"Sing, you sheep's heads, sing!" they shouted.

They were compelled to sing, by order.

"In the afternoon," wrote a man of the 18th Reserve Division, "we had to go out again: we were to learn to sing. The greater part did not join in, and the song went feebly. Then we had to march round in a circle, and sing, and that went no better."

"After that we had an hour off, and on the way back to billets we were to sing 'Deutschland über Alles,' but this broke down completely. One never hears songs of the Fatherland any more."

They were silent, grave-eyed men who marched through the streets of French and Belgian towns to be entrained for the Somme front, for they had forebodings of the fate before them. Yet none of their forebodings

"The Battle of the Somme" is from Charles F. Horne, ed., Source Records of the Great War, vol. 4 (Indianapolis: The American Legion, 1931), pp. 248–251. Reprinted by permission of The American Legion.

were equal in intensity of fear to the frightful reality into which they were flung.

No Man's Land

J. KNIGHT-ADKIN

No Man's Land is an eerie sight
At early dawn in the pale gray light.
Never a house and never a hedge
In No Man's Land from edge to edge,
And never a living soul walks there
To taste the fresh of the morning air.
Only some lumps of rotting clay,
That were friends or foemen yesterday.

What are the bounds of No Man's Land?
You can see them clearly on either hand,
A mound of rag-bags gray in the sun,
Or a furrow of brown where the earth works run
From the eastern hills to the western sea,
Through field or forest o'er river and lea;
No man may pass them, but aim you well
And Death rides across on the bullet or shell.

But No Man's Land is a goblin sight
When patrols crawl over at dead o' night;
Boche or British, Belgian or French,
You dice with death when you cross the trench.
When the "rapid," like fireflies in the dark,
Flits down the parapet spark by spark,
And you drop for cover to keep your head
With your face on the breast of the four months' dead.

The man who ranges in No Man's Land
Is dogged by the shadows on either hand
When the star-shell's flares, as it bursts o'erhead,
Scares the great gray rats that feed on the dead,
And the bursting bomb or the bayonet-snatch
May answer the click of your safety-catch.
For the lone patrol, with his life in his hand,
Is hunting for blood in No Man's Land.

"No Man's Land" is from W. Reginald Wheeler, ed., *A Book of Verse of the Great War* (New Haven: Yale University Press, 1917), pp. 90–91. Reprinted by permission of *The Spectator*.

Life in the Trenches

ROBERT GRAVES

Those were early days of trench warfare, the days of the jamtin bomb and the gas-pipe trench mortar: still innocent of Lewis or Stokes guns, steel helmets, telescopic rifle-sights, gas-shells, pillboxes, tanks, well-organized trench-raids, or any of the later refinements of trench warfare.

After a meal of bread, bacon, rum, and bitter stewed tea sickly with sugar, we went through the broken trees to the east of the village and up a long trench to battalion headquarters. The wet and slippery trench ran through dull red clay. I had a torch with me, and saw that hundreds of field mice and frogs had fallen into the trench but found no way out. The light dazzled them, and because I could not help treading on them, I put the torch back in my pocket. We had no mental picture of what the trenches would be like, and were almost as ignorant as a young soldier who joined us a week or two later. He called out excitedly to old Burford, who was cooking up a bit of stew in a dixie, apart from the others: 'Hi, mate, where's the battle? I want to do my bit.'

We now came under rifle-fire, which I found more trying than shell-fire. The gunner, I knew, fired not at people but at map-references—cross-roads, likely artillery positions, houses that suggested billets for troops, and so on. Even when an observation officer in an aeroplane or captive balloon or on a church spire directed the guns, it seemed random, somehow. But a rifle-bullet, even when fired blindly, always seemed purposely aimed. And whereas we could usually hear a shell approaching, and take some sort of cover, the rifle-bullet gave no warning. So, though we learned not to duck a rifle-bullet because, once heard, it must have missed, it gave us a worse feeling of danger. Rifle-bullets in the open went hissing into the grass without much noise, but when we were in a trench, the bullets made a tremendous crack as they went over the hollow. Bullets often struck the barbed wire in front of the trenches, which sent them spinning with a head-over-heels motion—ping! rockety-ockety-ockety into the woods behind.

I went on patrol fairly often, finding that the only thing respected in young officers was personal courage. Besides, I had cannily worked it out like this. My best way of lasting through to the end of the war would be to get wounded. The best time to get wounded would be at night and in the open, with the rifle fire more or less unaimed and my whole body exposed. Best, also, to get wounded when there was no rush on the dressing-station services, and while the back areas were not being heavily shelled. Best to get

"Life in the Trenches" is from Robert Graves, *Goodbye to All That*, 3rd ed. (London: Cassell & Co., 1961), pp. 84–85, 115–116. Reprinted by permission of A. P. Watt Ltd. on behalf of The Executors of the Estate of Robert Graves.

"A rifle bullet, even when fired blindly always seemed purposefully aimed. . . . When we were in a trench, the bullets made a tremendous crack as they went over the hollow." *(Wide World Photos)*

wounded, therefore, on a night patrol in a quiet sector. One could usually manage to crawl into a shell hole until help arrived.

Still, patrolling had its peculiar risks. If a German patrol found a wounded man, they were as likely as not to cut his throat. The bowie-knife was a favourite German patrol weapon because of its silence. . . . The most important information that a patrol could bring back was to what regiment and division the troops opposite belonged. So if it were impossible to get a wounded enemy back without danger to oneself, he had to be stripped of his badges. To do that quickly and silently, it might be necessary to cut his throat or beat in his skull.

Like everyone else, I had a carefully worked out formula for taking risks. In principle, we would all take any risk, even the certainty of death, to save life or to maintain an important position. To take life we would run, say, a one-in-five risk, particularly if there was some wider object than merely reducing the enemy's manpower; for instance, picking off a well-known sniper, or getting fire ascendancy in trenches where the lines came dangerously close.

French Propaganda Leaflet

Pass this along!
  German War Comrades!
Think about this:

1. Only greedy rulers want war. The people want peace, and work, and bread.
2. Only the German Kaiser with his militarists, Junkers, and arms manufacturers wanted war, prepared for it, and brought it on. No one wanted to fight Germany, no one opposed her desires for a "place in the sun."
3. If a murderer shoots a revolver on the street, it is the duty of every peace-loving, dutiful citizen to hurry to the aid of the fallen. For that reason Italy, Rumania, and the United States went to war against Germany; to free Belgium, Serbia, and France from the clutches of the murderer. . . .
10. Stop *[fighting]*! Turn your cannons around! Come over to us. Shoot anyone who wants to hinder you from coming.

YOUR DEMOCRATIC GERMAN COMRADES IN FRENCH PRISONS

What Are You Fighting For, Michel?

They tell you that you are fighting to secure victory for your Fatherland. But have you ever thought about what you are fighting for?

You are fighting for the glory of, and for the enrichment of the Krupps. You are fighting to save the Kaiser, the Junkers and the War Lords who caused the war from the anger of the people.

The Junkers [German nobility] are sitting at home with their bejewelled wives and mistresses. Their bank accounts are constantly growing, accounts to which you and your comrades pay with your lives. For your wives and brides there are no growing bank accounts. They are at home working and starving, sacrifices like yourselves to the greed of the ruling class to whose pipes you have to dance.

What a dance! The dance of death. But yesterday you marched over the

"French Propaganda Leaflet" is from George G. Bruntz, *Allied Propaganda and the Collapse of the German Empire in 1918,* Hoover War Library Publication No. 13 (Stanford: Stanford University Press, 1938), pp. 98. Reprinted by permission of the publisher.

"What Are You Fighting For, Michel?" is from George G. Bruntz, *Allied Propaganda and the Collapse of the German Empire in 1918,* Hoover War Library Publication No. 13 (Stanford: Stanford University Press, 1938), pp. 99. Reprinted by permission of the publisher.

corpses of your comrades against the English cannon. Tomorrow another German soldier will march over your corpse.

You have been promised victory and peace. You poor fool! Your comrades were also promised these things more than three years ago. Peace indeed they have found—deep in the grave. But victory did not come.

Your Kaiser has adorned the glorious Hindenburg with the Iron Cross with golden beams. What has the Kaiser awarded to you? Ruin, suffering, poverty, hunger for your wives and children, misery, disease, and tomorrow the grave.

It is for the Fatherland, you say, that you go out as a brave patriot to death for the Fatherland.

But of what does your Fatherland consists? Is it the Kaiser with his fine speeches? Is it the Crown Prince with his jolly companions, who sacrificed 600,000 men at Verdun? Is it [Field Marshall] Hindenburg, who sits with [General] Ludendorf, both covered with medals many kilometers behind you and who plans how he can furnish the English with still more cannon fodder. Is it Frau Bertha Krupp for whom through year after year of war you pile up millions upon millions of marks? Is it the Prussian Junkers who cry out over your dead bodies for annexation?

No, the Fatherland is not any of these. You are the Fatherland, Michel! You and your sisters and your wives and your parents and your children. You, the common people are the Fatherland. And yet it is you and your comrades who are driven like slaves into the hell of English cannon-fire, driven by the command of the feelingless slave-drivers.

When your comrades at home were striking, they were shot at with machine guns. If you, after the war, strike a blow for your rights, the machine guns will be turned upon you, for you are fighting only to increase the power of your lords.

Do you perhaps believe your rulers who love war as you hate it? Of course not. They love war for it brings them advancement, honor, power, profit. The longer the war lasts, the longer they will postpone the revolution.

They promise you that you can compel the English to beg for peace. Do you really believe that? You have advanced a few kilometers but for every Englishman whom you have shot down, six Germans have fallen. And all America is still to come.

Your commanders report to you wonderful stories of English losses. But did they tell you that Germany in the first five days of battle lost 315,000 men?

Arrayed against Germany in battle today stands the entire world because it knows that German rulers caused the war to serve their own greedy ambition. The entire power of the Western World stands behind England and France and America. Soon it will go forth to battle. Have you thought of that, Michel?

The Red Baron: Glory in the Skies?

BARON MANFRED VON RICHTHOFEN

While the infantryman was exposed to the frustration and chaos of land combat, there was another war that existed with less restriction. By 1916, airplanes had been developed for combat, and the sky became the haven for men who relished the opportunity to test individual skill in "dog-fights" high above the earth. The romantic notion of the solitary warrior, with scarf flying high in the wind, was established by men who played by their own rules of honor and death in the air. Baron Manfred von Richthofen, a member of the Prussian aristocracy, became the ace of the war, shooting down eighty planes within two years before he himself was felled. In spite of his romantic aura, Richthofen was a methodical killer, a hunter with a morbid curiosity for death, who flew with his brains and not with the innocent courage of other pilots. The Red Baron discriminated between a sportsman and a butcher: "The latter shoots for fun. When I have shot down an Englishman, my hunting passion is satisfied for a quarter of an hour. If one of them comes down, I have a feeling of complete satisfaction. Only much much later I have overcome my instinct and have become a butcher." The first excerpt is from his autobiography, The Red Battle Flyer; *the second selection is an assessment of the Red Baron by one of his fellow pilots.*

My First English Victim (September 17, 1915)

We were all at the butts trying our machine guns. On the previous day we had received our new aeroplanes and the next morning Boelcke was to fly with us. We were all beginners. None of us had had a success so far. Consequently everything that Boelcke told us was to us gospel truth. Every day, during the last few days, he had, as he said, shot one or two Englishmen for breakfast.

Slowly we approached the hostile squadron. It could not escape us. We had intercepted it, for we were between the Front and our opponents. If they wished to go back they had to pass us. We counted the hostile machines. They were seven in number. We were only five. All the Englishmen flew large bomb-carrying two-seaters. In a few seconds the dance would begin.

Boelcke had come very near the first English machine but he did not yet shoot. I followed. Close to me were my comrades. The Englishman nearest to me was traveling in a large boat painted with dark colors. I did not reflect very long but took my aim and shot.

Apparently he was no beginner, for he knew exactly that his last hour

"The Red Baron" is from Manfred von Richthofen, *The Red Battle Flyer* (New York: McBride Co., 1918), pp. 131–133.

had arrived at the moment when I got at the back of him. At that time I had not yet the conviction "He must fall!" which I have now on such occasions, but on the contrary, I was curious to see whether he would fall. There is a great difference between the two feelings. When one has shot down one's first, second or third opponent, then one begins to find out how the trick is done.

In a fraction of a second I was at his back with my excellent machine. I give a short series of shots with my machine gun. I had gone so close that I was afraid I might dash into the Englishman. Suddenly, I nearly yelled with joy for the propeller of the enemy machine had stopped turning. I had shot his engine to pieces; the enemy was compelled to land, for it was impossible for him to reach his own lines.

The Englishman landed close to the flying ground of one of our squadrons. I was so excited that I landed also and my eagerness was so great that I nearly smashed up my machine. The English flying machine and my own stood close together. I rushed to the English machine and saw that a lot of soldiers were running towards my enemy. When I arrived I discovered that my assumption had been correct. I had shot the engine to pieces and both the pilot and observer were severely wounded. The observer died at once and the pilot while being transported to the nearest dressing station. I honored the fallen enemy by placing a stone on his beautiful grave.

English and French Flying (February 1917)

The great thing in air fighting is that the decisive factor does not lie in trick flying but solely in the personal ability and energy of the aviator. A flying man may be able to loop and do all the stunts imaginable and yet he may not succeed in shooting down a single enemy. In my opinion the aggressive spirit is everything and that spirit is very strong in us Germans. Hence we shall always retain the domination of the air.

The French have a different character. They like to put traps and to attack their opponents unawares. That cannot easily be done in the air. Only a beginner can be caught and one cannot set traps because an aeroplane cannot hide itself. The invisible aeroplane has not yet been discovered. Sometimes, however, the Gaelic blood asserts itself. The Frenchmen will then attack. But the French attacking spirit is like bottled lemonade. It lacks tenacity.

The Englishmen, on the other hand, one notices that they are of Germanic blood. Sportsmen easily take to flying, and Englishmen see in flying nothing but a sport. They take a perfect delight in looping the loop, flying on their back, and indulging in other stunts for the benefit of our soldiers in the trenches. All these tricks may impress people who attend a Sports Meeting, but the public at the battle-front is not as appreciative of these things. It demands higher qualifications than trick flying. Therefore, the blood of English pilots will have to flow in streams.

An Assessment of the Red Baron

ERNST UDET

What a man he was! The others, admittedly, were doing their share, but they had wives at home, children, a mother or a profession. And only on rare occasions could they forget it. But Richthofen always lived on the other side of the boundary which we crossed only in our great moments. When he fought, his private life was thrust ruthlessly behind him. Eating, drinking and sleeping were all he granted life, and then only the minimum that was necessary to keep flesh and blood in working order. He was the simplest man I ever met. He was a Prussian through and through. A great soldier.

It Is Sweet and Proper to Die for One's Country

Wilfred Owen, a poet and soldier who was killed a week before the war ended, wrote that the "Lie" of the conflict lay in the belief that it was honorable and proper to give your life for the benefit of your country (Dulce et decorum est pro patria mori). *Indeed, the war seemed to people an absurd and tragic event. Why were they fighting? Why did old men send young men off to die "for their country"? How could poisonous gas, which burned out the lungs and led to a painfully slow death, be justified—or submarines, which destroyed under cover, thus eliminating a "fair fight"? The rules of war had changed. Disillusionment was evident in mutinies and in the poetry written in the trenches and in the letters sent home. It was not enough to be complimented by your general for victory in battle.*

Order of the Day
(Battle of the Marne, September 1914)

GENERAL JOSEPH JOFFRE

September 11th

The battle which we have been fighting for the last five days has ended in an undoubted victory. The retreat of the 1st, 2nd, and 3rd German Armies before our left and center becomes more and more marked. The enemy's 4th Army in its turn has begun to withdraw to the north of Vitry and Sermaise.

"An Assessment of the Red Baron" is from Ernst Udet, *Ace of the Black Cross*, trans. Kenneth Kirkness (London: Newnes, 1937), p. 72.

"Order of the Day" is from Charles F. Horne, ed., *Source Records of the Great War*, vol. 2 (Indianapolis: The American Legion, 1931), p. 281. Reprinted by permission of the American Legion.

Everywhere the enemy has left on the field numerous wounded and a quantity of munitions. Everywhere we have made prisoners while gaining ground. Our troops bear witness to the intensity of the fight, and the means employed by the Germans in their endeavors to resist our *elan*. The vigorous resumption of the offensive has determined our success.

Officers, non-commissioned officers, and men! You have all responded to my appeal; you have all deserved well of your country.

Five Souls

W. N. EWER

FIRST SOUL—
> I was a peasant of the Polish plain;
> I left my plow because the message ran:
> Russia, in danger, needed every man
> To save her from the Teuton; and was slain.
> *I gave my life for freedom—this I know;*
> *For those who bade me fight had told me so.*

SECOND SOUL—
> I was a Tyrolese, a mountaineer;
> I gladly left my mountain home to fight
> Against the brutal, treacherous Muscovite;
> And died in Poland on a Cossack spear.
> *I gave my life for freedom—this I know;*
> *For those who bade me fight had told me so.*

THIRD SOUL—
> I worked in Lyons at my weaver's loom,
> When suddenly the Prussian despot hurled
> His felon blow at France and at the world;
> Then I went forth to Belgium and my doom.
> *I gave my life for freedom—this I know;*
> *For those who bade me fight had told me so.*

FOURTH SOUL—
> I owned a vineyard by the wooded Main,
> Until the Fatherland, begirt by foes
> Lusting her downfall, called me, and I rose
> Swift to the call—and died in fair Lorraine.
> *I gave my life for freedom—this I know;*
> *For those who bade me fight had told me so.*

"Five Souls" is from W. Reginald Wheeler, ed., *A Book of Verse of the Great War* (New Haven: Yale University Press, 1917), pp. 46–47. Reprinted by permission.

FIFTH SOUL—
    I worked in a great shipyard by the Clyde,
      There came a sudden word of wars declared,
      Of Belgium, peaceful, helpless, unprepared,
    Asking our aid; I joined the ranks, and died.
      I gave my life for freedom—this I know;
      For those who bade me fight had told me so.

German Student's War Letter

RICHARD SCHMIEDER, Student of Philosophy, Leipzig
Born January 24th, 1888.
Killed July 14th, 1916, near Bethenville.

In the Trenches near Vaudesincourt, March 13th, 1915.

Anybody who, like myself, has been through the awful days near Penthy since the 6th of February, will agree with me that a more appalling struggle could not be imagined. It has been a case of soldier against soldier, equally matched and both mad with hate and anger, fighting for days on end over a single square of ground, till the whole tract of country is one blood-soaked, corpse-strewn field. . . .

On February 27th, tired out and utterly exhausted in body and mind, we were suddenly called up to reinforce the VIIIth Reserve Corps, had to reoccupy our old position at Ripont, and were immediately attacked by the French with extraordinary strength and violence. It was a gigantic murder, by means of bullets, shells, axes, and bombs, and there was such a thundering, crashing, bellowing and screaming as might have heralded the Day of Judgment.

In three days, on a front of about 200 yards, we lost 909 men, and the enemy casualties must have amounted to thousands. The blue French cloth mingled with the German grey upon the ground, and in some places the bodies were piled so high that one could take cover from shell-fire behind them. The noise was so terrific that orders had to be shouted by each man into the ear of the next. And whenever there was a momentary lull in the tumult of battle and the groans of the wounded, one heard, high up in the blue sky, the joyful song of birds! Birds singing just as they do at home in spring-time! It was enough to tear the heart out of one's body!

Don't ask about the fate of the wounded! Anybody who was incapable of walking to the doctor had to die a miserable death; some lingered in agony for hours, some for days, and even for a week. And the combatants stormed regardlessly to and fro over them: 'I can't give you a hand,—

"German Student's War Letter" is from *German Students' War Letters*, translated and arranged from the original edition of Dr. Philipp Witkop by A. F. Wedd (New York: E. P. Dutton, 1929), pp. 208–209. Reprinted by permission of Methuen and Company.

"This is the way the world ends/Not with a bang but a whimper."—T. S. Eliot. (*Library of Congress*)

You're for the Promised Land,—My Comrade good and true.' A dog, dying in the poorest hovel at home, is enviable in comparison.

There are moments when even the bravest soldier is so utterly sick of the whole thing that he could cry like a child. When I heard the birds singing at Ripont, I could have crushed the whole world to death in my wrath and fury. If only those gentlemen—Grey, Asquith, and Poincaré—could be transported to this spot, instead of the war lasting ten years, there would be peace tomorrow!

Dulce et Decorum Est

WILFRED OWEN

Bent double, like old beggars under sacks,
Knocked-kneed, coughing like hags, we cursed through sludge,
Till on the haunting flares we turned our backs
And towards our distant rest began to trudge.
Men marched asleep. Many had lost their boots
But limped on, blood-shod. All went lame; all blind;
Drunk with fatigue; deaf even to the hoots
Of tired, outstripped Five-Nines that dropped behind.

Gas! Gas! Quick Boys!—An ecstasy of fumbling,
Fitting the clumsy helmets just in time;
But someone still was yelling out and stumbling
And flound'ring like a man in fire or lime. . . .
Dim, through the misty panes and thick green light,
As under a green sea, I saw him drowning.
In all my dreams, before my helpless sight,
He plunges at me, guttering, choking, drowning.

If in some smothering dreams you too could pace
Behind the wagon that we flung him in,
And watch the white eyes writhing in his face,
His hanging face, like a devil's sick of sin;
If you could hear, at every jolt, the blood
Come gargling from the froth-corrupted lungs,
Obscene as cancer, bitter as the cud

Of vile, incurable sores on innocent tongues,—
My friend, you would not tell with such high zest
To children ardent for some desperate glory,
The old Lie: Dulce et decorum est
Pro patria mori.

The Framework of Peace

In January 1917, Germany informed the United States that it intended to resume unrestricted submarine warfare. Consequently, three American merchant ships were sunk, and at President Woodrow Wilson's request Congress declared war with Germany on April 6. As fresh American troops arrived in Europe, German resistance became increasingly tenuous. It was left to President Wilson to provide the framework for a peace treaty. In his address to Congress, he proposed a fourteen-point plan.

The Fourteen Points (January 8, 1918)
WOODROW WILSON

Gentlemen of the Congress:

It will be our wish and purpose that the processes of peace, when they are begun, shall be absolutely open and that they shall involve and permit henceforth no secret understandings of any kind. The day of conquest and aggrandizement is gone by; so is also the day of secret covenants entered

"The Fourteen Points" is from *Congressional Record* (January 8, 1918), vol. 56, pt. 1, p. 691.

into in the interest of particular governments and likely at some unlooked-for moment to upset the peace of the world. It is this happy fact, now clear to the view of every public man whose thoughts do not still linger in an age that is dead and gone, which makes it possible for every nation whose purposes are consistent with justice and the peace of the world to avow now or at any other time the objects it has in view.

We entered this war because violations of right had occurred which touched us to the quick and made the life of our own people impossible unless they were corrected and the world secured once for all against their recurrence. What we demand in this war, therefore, is nothing peculiar to ourselves. It is that the world be made fit and safe to live in; and particularly that it be made safe for every peace-loving nation which, like our own, wishes to live its own life, determine its own institutions, be assured of justice and fair dealing by the other peoples of the world as against force and selfish aggression. All the peoples of the world are in effect partners in this interest, and for our own part we see very clearly that unless justice be done to others it will not be done to us. The program of the world's peace, therefore, is our program; and that program, the only possible program, as we see it, is this:

1. Open covenants of peace, openly arrived at, after which there shall be no private international understandings of any kind but diplomacy shall proceed always frankly and in the public view.

2. Absolute freedom of navigation upon the seas. . . .

4. Adequate guarantees given and taken that national armaments will be reduced to the lowest point consistent with domestic safety.

5. A free, open-minded, and absolutely impartial adjustment of all colonial claims, based upon a strict observance of the principle that in determining all such questions of sovereignty the interests of the populations concerned must have equal weight with the equitable claims of the government whose title is to be determined.

6. The evacuation of all Russian territory and such a settlement of all questions affecting Russia as will secure . . . the independent determination of her own political development and national policy and assure her of a sincere welcome into the society of free nations under institutions of her own choosing. . . .

7. Belgium, the whole world will agree, must be evacuated and restored, without any attempt to limit the sovereignty which she enjoys in common with all other free nations. No other single act will serve as this will serve to restore confidence among the nations in the laws which they have themselves set and determined for the government of their relations with one another. Without this healing act the whole structure and validity of international law is forever impaired.

8. All French territory should be freed and the invaded portions restored, and the wrong done to France by Prussia in 1871 in the matter of Alsace-Lorraine, which has unsettled the peace of the world for nearly fifty

years, should be righted, in order that peace may once more be made secure in the interest of all.

10. The peoples of Austria-Hungary, whose place among the nations we wish to see safeguarded and assured, should be accorded the freest opportunity of autonomous development.

11. Rumania, Serbia, and Montenegro should be evacuated; occupied territories restored; Serbia accorded free and secure access to the sea. . . .

13. An independent Polish state should be erected which should include the territories inhabited by indisputably Polish populations. . . .

14. A general association of nations must be formed under specific covenants for the purpose of affording mutual guarantees of political independence and territorial integrity to great and small states alike.

In regard to these essential rectifications of wrong and assertions of right we feel ourselves to be intimate partners of all the governments and peoples associated together against the Imperialists. We cannot be separated in interest or divided in purpose. We stand together until the end.

For such arrangements and covenants we are willing to fight and to continue to fight until they are achieved; but only because we wish the right to prevail and desire a just and stable peace such as can be secured only by removing the chief provocations to war, which this program does not remove. We have no jealously of German greatness, and there is nothing in this program that impairs it. We grudge her no achievement or distinction of learning or of pacific enterprise such as have made her record very bright and very enviable. We do not wish to injure her or to block in any way her legitimate influence or power. We do not wish to fight her either with arms or with hostile arrangements of trade if she is willing to associate herself with us and the other peace-loving nations of the world in covenants of justice and law and fair dealing. We wish her only to accept a place of equality among the peoples of the world,—the new world in which we now live,—instead of a place of mastery.

Neither do we presume to suggest to her any alteration or modification of her institutions. But it is necessary, we must frankly say, and necessary as a preliminary to any intelligent dealings with her on our part, that we should know whom her spokesmen speak for when they speak to us, whether for the Reichstag majority or for the military party and the men whose creed is imperial domination.

We have spoken now, surely, in terms too concrete to admit to any further doubt or question. An evident principle runs through the whole program of justice to all peoples and nationalities, and their right to live on equal terms of liberty and safety with one another, whether they be strong or weak. Unless this principle be made its foundation no part of the structure of international justice can stand. The people of the United States could act upon no other principle; and to the vindication of this principle they are ready to devote their lives, their honor, and everything that they possess. The moral climax of this, the culminating and final war for human liberty has come, and they are ready to put their own strength, their own highest purpose, their own integrity and devotion to the test.

The Aftermath of War

On November 9, 1918, the German kaiser abdicated his throne and fled the country. The armistice, which ended the war, was signed on November 11. The European world of 1914 had been shattered, people were changed, and the foremost question was, how to begin again?

The first selection is from the diary of Anna Eisenmenger, an Austrian whose son returned home after the armistice a changed man. The treaty of 1922 was an attempt to civilize war and to protect the lives of noncombatants by regulating submarine warfare and by banning the use of poisonous gas. Both weapons were considered to have been immorally used during the war and remained a subject of controversy. The next two selections argue similar viewpoints, but The Great Illusion *was written in 1910, four years before the war, and* The International Anarchy *was written in 1926. The authors were struggling with the relationship between war and civilization. The final piece is an excerpt from a poem by T. S. Eliot. Where is the bluster and confidence that gave rise to the Great War?*

A German Soldier Returns Home: "A Complete Stranger"

ANNA EISENMENGER

Karl looked very ill. He had no underlinen or socks. His uniform was dirty and in rags. "Mother, I am famished!" he said, and walking straight into the kitchen without waiting for me to bring him something he began to devour our rations of bread and jam. "Forgive me, Mother, but we have got into the habit of taking what we can find." He only greeted us very casually and did not notice until much later that Erni, who had come in to welcome him on Liesbeth's arm, was wounded. "Hullo! So it's caught you too!" and then, still hurriedly chewing and swallowing: "Well, just wait! We'll pay them out yet, the war profiteers and parasites. We've grown wiser out there in the trenches, far wiser than we were. Everything must be changed, utterly changed."

I got ready the bath and clean underlinen. After his bath Karl went straight to bed, but he was too excited to sleep, although it was almost 11

"A German Soldier Returns Home" is from Anna Eisenmenger, *Blockade: The Diary of an Austrian Middle-Class Woman, 1914–1924* (London: Constable Publishers, 1932), pp. 39–42. Reprinted by permission of the publisher.

o'clock at night. He telephoned to Edith, and then he made us all come to his bedside, for he wanted to tell us about himself. He told us that . . . the Italians had gone on attacking in spite of the Armistice. For another whole day they had fired on our retreating columns in the Fellathal and had captured several divisions. That, however, was the only victory they had won. It was contemptible, but war made every one base and contemptible. He had become so too. . . . After the proclamation of the Armistice all military discipline went to pieces. Everyone was intent only on getting home and made for home by the way that seemed to him quickest and surest. The men trampled down whatever stood in their way, even if the obstacle were their own officers. Woe to the officers who were unpopular with their men. . . . In the next war there would be no one foolish enough to risk his life, they would see to that. . . . Karl was evidently in a nervous, over-excited state, but he went on talking, and only after I had entreated him several times did he consent to try to get to sleep.

"We are all tired, Karl, and it is already past midnight. . . ."

"Do you know, Mother, how I feel here? In a clean bed, washed and fed? As if I were in heaven. . . . Oh no, there is no heaven so beautiful. . . . As if I were in a beautiful dream . . . and in that dream I shall try to find sleep."

We left Karl's room in order to go to bed ourselves. As I was helping Erni undress, he said: "Mother, Karl seems to me like a complete stranger."

Although I was nervously and physically exhausted, sleep refused to close my eyelids. For a long, long time I lay awake, agitated by the horrors of the War. I found myself marvelling that civilised human beings could live through all the brutalities which war entailed for themselves and others without going utterly to pieces. . . .

Treaty Concerning Submarines and Poisonous Gases in Warfare (1922)

The United States of America, the British Empire, France, Italy and Japan, hereinafter referred to as the Signatory Powers, desiring to make more effective the rules adopted by civilized nations for the protection of the lives of neutrals and noncombatants at sea in time of war, and to prevent the use in war of noxious gases and chemicals, have determined to conclude a Treaty to this effect:

ARTICLE 1

The Signatory Powers declare that among the rules adopted by civilized nations for the protection of the lives of neutrals and noncombatants at sea in time of war, the following are to be deemed an established part of international law:

"Treaty Concerning Submarines and Poisonous Gases" is from *Department of State Bulletin* (February 6, 1922).

(1) A merchant vessel must be ordered to submit to visit and search to determine its character before it can be seized.

A merchant vessel must not be attacked unless it refuse to submit to visit and search after warning, or to proceed as directed after seizure.

A merchant must not be destroyed unless the crew and passengers have been first placed in safety.

(2) Belligerent submarines are not under any circumstances exempt from universal rules above stated; and if a submarine can not capture a merchant vessel in conformity with these rules the existing law of nations requires it to desist from attack and from seizure and to permit the merchant vessel to proceed unmolested.

ARTICLE IV

The Signatory Powers recognize the practical impossibility of using submarines as commerce destroyers without violating, as they were violated in the recent war of 1914–1918, the requirements universally accepted by civilized nations for the protection of the lives of neutrals and noncombatants, and to the end that the prohibition of the use of submarines as commerce destroyers shall be universally accepted as a part of the law of nations, they now accept that prohibition as henceforth binding as between themselves and they invite all other nations to adhere thereto.

ARTICLE V

The use in war of asphyxiating, poisonous or other gases, and all analogous liquids, materials or devices, having been justly condemned by the general opinion of the civilized world and a prohibition of such use having been declared in treaties to which a majority of the civilized Powers are parties.

The Signatory Powers, to the end that this prohibition shall be universally accepted as a part of international law binding alike the prohibitions, agree to be bound thereby as between themselves and invite all other civilized nations to adhere thereto.

The Great Illusion (1910)

NORMAN ANGELL

What are the fundamental motives that explain the present rivalry of armaments in Europe, notably the Anglo-German? Each nation pleads the need for defence; but this implies that someone is likely to attack, and has therefore a presumed interest in so doing. What are the motives which each State thus fears its neighbors may obey?

"The Great Illusion" is from Norman Angell, *The Great Illusion* (New York: G. P. Putnam's Sons, 1913), pp. ix–xiiiff, 381–382.

They are based on the universal assumption that a nation, in order to find outlets for expanding population and increasing industry, or simply to ensure the best conditions possible for its people, is necessarily pushed to territorial expansion and the exercise of political force against others. . . . It is assumed that a nation's relative prosperity is broadly determined by its political power; that nations being competing units, advantage in the last resort goes to the possessor of preponderant military force, the weaker goes to the wall, as in the other forms of the struggle for life. The author challenges this whole doctrine. . . .

War has no longer the justification that it makes for the survival of the fittest; it involves the survival of the less fit. The idea that the struggle between nations is a part of the evolutionary law of man's advance involves a profound misreading of the biological analogy.

The warlike nations do not inherit the earth; they represent the decaying human element. . . .

Are we, in blind obedience to primitive instincts and old prejudices, enslaved by the old catchwords and that curious indolence which makes the revision of old ideas unpleasant, to duplicate indefinitely on the political and economic side a condition from which we have liberated ourselves on the religious side? Are we to continue to struggle, as so many good men struggled in the first dozen centuries of Christendom—spilling oceans of blood, wasting mountains of treasure—to achieve what is at bottom a logical absurdity, to accomplish something which, when accomplished, can avail us nothing, and which, if it could avail us anything, would condemn the nations of the world to never-ending bloodshed and the constant defeat of all those aims which men, in their sober hours, know to be alone worthy of sustained endeavor?

The International Anarchy (1926)

G. LOWES DICKINSON

I have written, consciously and deliberately, to point a moral. I believe, with most instructed people, that modern war, with all the resources of science at its disposal, has become incompatible with the continuance of civilization. If this be true, it is a mistake to look back upon the course of history and say: There has always been war, and yet civilization has survived. At the best, what has survived is a poor thing compared to what might have been, had there been no war. But even such poor survival cannot be counted upon in the future. . . .

My thesis is, that whenever and wherever the anarchy of armed states exists, war becomes inevitable. That was the condition in ancient Greece, in republican Rome, in medieval Italy, and in Europe for several centuries

"The International Anarchy" is from G. Lowes Dickinson, *The International Anarchy, 1904–1914* (London: Allen & Unwin, 1926). pp. v, 47–48.

after its emergence from the feudal chaos. That chaos also involved war. But such war is not properly to be called civil or international; and with that particular condition we are not now concerned. International war, in our own age as in the others referred to, is a clash between sovereign armed States. It arises in consequence of the international anarchy. . . .

States armed, and therefore a menace to one another; policies ostensibly defensive, but really just as much offensive; these policies pursued in the dark by a very few men who, because they act secretly, cannot act honestly; and this whole complex playing upon primitive passions, arousable at any moment by appropriate appeals from a Press which has no object except to make money out of the weaknesses of men—that is the real situation of the world under the conditions of the international anarchy.

These conditions are commonly regarded as unalterable. Hence the view that war is a fate from which we cannot escape. I will cite in illustration the words of a typical militarist which express, I believe, the real opinion of most soldiers, sailors, politicians, journalists, and plain men: "Possibly in the future great coalitions of Powers will be able to keep the peace for long epochs and to avoid conflict with arms; but this will not be possible in permanence. The life of man is unbroken combat in every form; eternal peace, unfortunately, a Utopia in which only philanthropists ignorant of the world believe. A nation which lays down its arms thereby seals its fate."

Those who hold this philosophy also devoted their lives to making sure that it shall come true; for it is impossible to hold any view about life without thereby contributing to its realization. The confusion, in the passage quoted, between military conflict and other forms of struggle is patent to any one who can think. The same philosophy should conclude that civil war also is an eternal fact, a conclusion to which militarists are usually much averse. But this much is certainly true, that until men lay down their arms, and accept the method of peaceable decision of their disputes, war can never cease.

The Hollow Men (1925)

T. S. ELIOT

A penny for the Old Guy

We are the hollow men
We are the stuffed men
Leaning together

Headpiece filled with straw. Alas!
Our dried voices, when
We whisper together
Are quiet and meaningless
As wind in dry grass
Or rats' feet over broken glass
In our dry cellar

Shape without form, shade without colour,
Paralysed force, gesture without motion;

Those who have crossed
With direct eyes, to death's other Kingdom
Remember us—if at all—not as lost
Violent souls, but only
As the hollow men
The stuffed men.

•   •   •

For Thine is
Life is
For Thine is the

This is the way the world ends
This is the way the world ends
This is the way the world ends
Not with a bang but a whimper.

CHRONOLOGY: The Great War (1914–1918)

June 14, 1914 Assassination of Archduke Franz Ferdinand, heir to the Austro-Hungarian Empire.

July 28, 1914 Austria-Hungary declares war on Serbia after receiving "blank check" of support from Germany.

August 1914 Germany declares war on Russia (Aug. 1) and France (Aug. 3); Germany invades Belgium followed immediately by Britain's declaration of war on Germany (Aug. 4).

September 5–9, 1914 Battle of the Marne: French and British are able to stop the German advance in the west. Thereafter, the nature of the war in the west changed completely and became one of position instead of movement.

April 22, 1915 Germans employ poisonous gas for the first time at the Second Battle of Ypres.

April 25, 1915	British land at Gallipoli, start of Dardanelles Campaign.
May 7, 1915	German submarine sinks the American ship, *Lusitania.* Among 1200 drowned were 118 Americans.
February–December 1916	Battle of Verdun results in 550,000 French and 450,000 German casualties.
July–November 1916	Battle of the Somme fails to achieve major breakthrough for Allied forces; British use tanks for the first time.
March 1917	Revolution in Russia leads to abdication of Tsar Nicholas II.
April 6, 1917	United States declares war on Germany.
November 8, 1917	Bolsheviks seize power in Petrograd. Russia pulls out of the war.
January 8, 1918	President Woodrow Wilson issues the "Fourteen Points" framework for peace.
March 3, 1918	Bolsheviks accept German peace terms at Brest-Litovsk.
November 11, 1918	Kaiser Wilhelm II abdicates German throne and flees to Holland. Armistice concluded on Western Front.

STUDY QUESTIONS

1. In any conflict there are underlying tensions within countries or between countries that depend on a precipitating action to upset the status quo. What was the "spark" that ignited the Great War, and what were the underlying causes for the conflict? Do you regard the German dispatch to the Austro-Hungarian government as a "blank check" supporting any Austrian action against Serbia?
2. Note the speech of German Chancellor Bethmann-Hollweg in which he defends the German violation of Belgian neutrality. What are his arguments and is his defense a convincing one?
3. Did the diplomats and other personalities of the time do enough to try to prevent war? On the basis of the evidence at your disposal, do you think war could have been avoided? If so, how? Or was it inevitable? What is your reaction to the quotation by Will Rogers at the beginning of this chapter?
4. What are your most vivid impressions from the personal accounts of combat under the section "The Horrors of War"? Granted that all wars are horrible, what made this war unique? What makes the propaganda leaflet an effective weapon?
5. Apart from the physical differences, how was war in the air different from war on land? Is killing more palatable when it is romanticized? Do you find the Red Baron an exciting or intriguing personality?
6. Evaluate the statement, "It is sweet and proper to die for one's country." Is it an "Old Lie" as Wilfred Owen said? Was this war a game started by the

old, fought by the young, and suffered by the innocent? What about patriotism and honor? Were they hollow concepts in this war? How about in World War II or in Vietnam, or more recently in the Persian Gulf War?

7. In his Fourteen Points and at the Paris Peace Conference (1919), President Woodrow Wilson advocated idealistic principles: self-determination for nationalities, open diplomacy, disarmament, and the establishment of an international organization to discuss the concerns of the world community. Would these measures have helped stop the war? What do Norman Angell and G. Lowes Dickinson advocate? Does the fact that their books were written before and after the war say anything about political leadership in the early decades of the twentieth century?

8. In 1864, the English prelate John Henry Cardinal Newman said, "There is such a thing as legitimate warfare: war has its laws; there are things which may fairly be done, and things which may not be done." Do you agree or disagree? Analyze the articles of the Hague Convention of 1907. Are "laws of war" so unrealistic? Which of the articles do you respect the most? Note the treaty of 1922 concerning submarines and poisonous gas. Why were these weapons considered immoral at the time? By mutual consent poisonous gas was not used in World War II—yet this was a "total war." Does total war preclude "laws of humanity"? In the same sense, consider the Persian Gulf War of 1990–1991. Since modern technology now provides laser-controlled missiles to destroy specific targets, do such "surgical strikes" allow us to fight antiseptic campaigns where civilian casualties are considerably reduced and war is thus made more palatable and civilized?

9. The Great War has sometimes been viewed as the logical outcome of the intense nationalism and imperialism of the late nineteenth century. Do you agree with this view? What evidence exists in this chapter that indicates that nationalism and imperialism played a role in the Great War?

10. Although terrible in its ferocity, can the Great War be viewed as an agent of change and progress in civilization? Can you find evidence of this in the sources?

7

The Russian Revolution

The essence of Bolshevism, the essence of Soviet power, lies in exposing the fraud and hypocrisy of bourgeois democracy, in abolishing the private ownership of the land, the factories, and in concentrating all political power in the hands of the toilers and the exploited masses.

—V. I. Lenin

Even if for every hundred correct things we did, we committed ten thousand mistakes, our revolution would still be—and it will be in the judgment of history—great and invincible; for this is the first time that the working people are themselves building a new life.

—V. I. Lenin

The Russian dictatorship of the proletariat has made a farce of the whole Marxist vision: developing a powerful, privileged ruling class to prepare for a classless society, setting up the most despotic state in history so that the state may *wither away*, establishing by force a colonial empire to combat imperialism and unite the workers of the world.

—Herbert J. Muller

A proletarian revolution is never proletarian.

—Will Durant

The events of the year 1917 remain among the most significant in the history of the twentieth century. The world was in the midst of a war that could no longer be viewed as glorious and patriotic, but had degenerated in people's minds to what war really is—suffering, destruction, and death. In such a crisis, it is important for governments to justify their actions, inspire soldiers, and assuage the populace. Statesmen require domestic stability in order to focus attention on the war effort. However, Russia was not afforded this tranquility, and the monarchy of Tsar Nicholas II fell in March 1917, a prelude to a power struggle that by November of that year would see the imposition of a new regime, born of Marxist revolutionary philosophy and led by Vladimir Ulyanov, better known as Lenin (1870–1924). This was a complex revolution, and any simplification distorts the intricacy of events and political philosophies. Yet, for our purposes, it can be divided into three separate but related phases: the revolution of 1905, the March revolution of 1917, and the Bolshevik revolution of November 1917. This chapter seeks to unravel the conditions and pressures that led to the overthrow of the Romanov dynasty and the eventual Bolshevik seizure of power.

As in the French and American revolutions, social and economic conditions, as well as ideology, played an important role in providing the underlying causes and inspiration for revolution. Tsar Nicholas II was heir to a long tradition of autocracy that regarded change as dangerous to the stability of the dynasty. In the nineteenth century alone, Tsar Alexander I (1801–1825) continued the long-standing policy of absolutism, and his successor, Nicholas I (1825–1855), became Europe's most reactionary monarch with the slogan "Autocracy, Orthodoxy and National Unity." Under Nicholas' leadership, Russia became a closed society. Nicholas employed a secret police and a network of paid informers that successfully exiled over 150,000 persons to the frigid wastes of Siberia. And yet there existed reform movements. Alexander Herzen (1812–1870), called the "father of Russian liberalism," advocated moderate socialist policies. But other dissidents were not so polite. Michail Bakunin (1814–1876) founded the anarchist movement and advocated the use of terror to effect change. Tsar Alexander II (1855–1881) instituted a series of liberal measures, including the emancipation of Russian serfs (1861), and reforms of the judiciary, army, and local and municipal governments. Yet his actions, though revolutionary for the absolutist government of Russia, were incomplete, and his failure to provide a constitution led to growing opposition and a populist movement (Narodnik), which preached revolution to the peasant masses and was suppressed by the tsar. On March 13, 1881, Alexander II was assassinated by the terrorist group "People's Will"—ironically on the very day he had signed a decree that was to lead to constitutional reform. His son, Alexander III (1881–1894), refused to conform to the decree and set about reimplementing a policy of reactionary oppression. Thus when Nicholas II came to the throne in 1894, a long tradition of violent repression and terrorist response already existed.

One of the most influential philosophies that gave inspiration to the Russian Revolution was Marxism. Karl Marx and Friedrich Engels published the *Com-*

munist Manifesto in 1848. In it they advocated a classless society that would come about through struggle between the exploiting *bourgeoisie* or middle-class capitalists and the working class, or proletariat. Marx intoned, "Workers of the world unite! You have nothing to lose but your chains!" Marx's ideas became popular among the Russian revolutionary intelligentsia, and converts met in secret societies throughout Europe and Russia to discuss and plan action. One of his most dedicated disciples was Lenin. By 1905, Tsar Nicholas II's political opposition was more firmly organized. The Social Democratic party had been formed among industrial workers and was truly Marxist in philosophy. Yet party members differed among themselves; the Menshevik faction was more moderate and wanted to concentrate on improving the lot of the industrial worker, instead of concentrating on the world revolution that Marx predicted would become a reality. The other faction of the Social Democrats, the Bolsheviks, were led by Lenin and were more extreme in their insistence on a core of "professional revolutionaries," dedicated to the immediate overthrow of capitalist society. Other political groups existed in 1905 as well, including the Constitutional Democratic party (Cadets) and the Social Revolutionary party, which sought agricultural land reform.

Although Russian tsars had long resisted demands for basic civil rights, equality before the law and representative government, Nicholas II especially seemed to live in a vacuum—his own world of yachts and tennis, crystal and caviar. He remained unaware of the plight of the Russian peasantry, half-starved and oppressed by landlords who often confiscated their land, or of the urban worker who was burdened by low wages and long hours. Following the massacre of Russian workers during a peaceful demonstration in January 1905 (called "Bloody Sunday"), the popular outcry forced the tsar to establish an Imperial Duma, or representative assembly, and to provide a new constitution, guaranteeing civil rights for the people. The first phase of the Russian Revolution had taken place. Still, the Duma had no real authority over the tsar and its liberal recommendations were stifled. From 1906 to 1907, Nicholas merely dismissed Dumas that sought to encroach upon his power. From 1907 to 1916, the Dumas were controlled by the tsar through voting restrictions and altered election laws.

In the summer of 1914, Europe gravitated toward disaster. When Germany declared war on Russia (August 1, 1914), France supported her Russian ally. On August 4, Great Britain also joined in the struggle against Germany and Austria. The Great War had begun. Conditions among the Russian people deteriorated as thousands died in battle or as victims of disease or famine. The refugee problem was acute and people wandered homeless throughout Russia. The government was simply not able to cope with the economic and logistic demands of military mobilization and war. In March of 1917, the tsar was persuaded to abdicate, hoping that such action would assure Russia's continued participation in the war. This action came as a surprise to almost everyone. Even the most vitriolic detractors of the tsarist regime, notably Lenin in Switzerland, were caught off-guard. The second phase of the revolution had just begun.

With the fall of the tsar, a power vacuum existed and the competition to fill it was intense. A Provisional Government was chosen from members of the sitting Imperial Duma. The Provisional Government generally was made up of liberals and moderate socialists who promised an elected Constituent Assembly that was representative of the Russian people; they also pledged to draw up a new constitution that guaranteed civil liberties. However, the Provisional Government also supported Russia's continuation of the war. The other competitor for power was the Petrograd Soviet of Workers and Soldiers' Deputies. A soviet was simply a council of elected representatives that advocated reforms for the working classes. The soviets were generally composed of Social Revolutionaries, Mensheviks, and initially only a minority of Bolsheviks. They regarded the war as a struggle between capitalists at the expense of the working classes (proletariat) and therefore wanted Russia to cease hostilities immediately. However, the Petrograd Soviet did not advocate armed rebellion against the Provisional Government. On the contrary, some members of the Soviet even believed that they held a kind of dual power with it. No one proposed a government of national unity, and this lack of cooperation was to prove fatal to political stability.

Perhaps too much was expected of the Provisional Government. Soldiers wanted an end to the war, peasants needed more land, the workers in the cities demanded better living conditions, the national and religious minorities of Russia wanted official recognition, as well as political and cultural autonomy, and the Allies wanted Russia's continued support in the war. For a temporary government composed of people who lacked experience and an organized plan of action, the burden was too great.

Lenin arrived in Petrograd in April and started organizing the opposition. As leader of the more radical Bolshevik faction of the Social Democratic party, he denounced the Provisional Government and worked independently of the other socialist groups in an effort to seize control. Lenin proclaimed "all power to the soviets" and in July led a premature uprising that failed. Several Bolsheviks were arrested (including Lenin's brilliant associate Leon Trotsky), but Lenin escaped to Finland. Bolshevik fortunes changed when the leader of the Provisional Government, Alexander Kerensky (1881–1970), was confronted with a military rebellion—a right-wing revolt led by General Lavr Kornilov that was quelled only with the assistance of the Petrograd Soviet. In November 1917, Lenin, against the judgment of some of his colleagues, made another attempt to topple the Provisional Government. This time he was successful and his Bolshevik faction of radical socialists was able to maintain its power. This third phase of the Russian Revolution established a regime of a very different order.

The Provisional Government failed for many reasons. The members had little experience in government and administration and could not counter the effective propaganda of Lenin, which offered "Peace, Bread, and Land." Kerensky believed that he had an obligation to act in a legal, democratic fashion, to demonstrate that his leadership was progressive and superior to that of the tsar. Lenin played by his own rules and would not share power. His organization and insistence in the rightness of his ideas, coupled with a measure of luck, produced a revolution that indeed shook the world.

Lenin's Bolshevik government survived a counterrevolutionary threat from supporters of the tsar as the Civil War came to an end in 1921. Lenin had started the transition toward Marx's concept of a Communist society, but fell ill in 1922 and died two years later. His position as leader of the revolution would eventually be assumed by Joseph Stalin (1879–1953). Under Stalin's brutal direction, and the leadership of his successors, the Soviet Union emerged as a formidable political, military, and ideological adversary to the United States in the late twentieth century.

From 1945 to 1989, we lived under a cloud of mutual suspicion, fostered by intense propaganda, massive nuclear arsenals, and geopolitical competition. It is only in the 1990s with the Soviet preoccupation with domestic affairs that the rhetoric has cooled, the Cold War ended, and the future seemed less threatening. Viewed from this perspective, the Russian Revolution of 1917 remains one of the most significant political events of the modern world.

The Fall of the Monarchy

Bloody Sunday (January 1905)

Successful revolutions often depend on an incident or immediate crisis that serves as a rallying point for mass protest and outrage. It is at this moment that underlying problems between rulers and governed are brought into focus and the revolution given justification and incentive. Just such an incident occurred on January 22, 1905, when elite Russian troops called Cossacks attacked unarmed workers who were protesting in a peaceful demonstration. The workers wanted to address the tsar regarding civil rights, popular representation, and the needs of the Russian laborer. A correspondent of the London Times *dispatched the first account below of the massacre. The second account was telegraphed to the Paris newspaper* Le Matin *by its correspondent.*

Report of the *London Times*

A more perfect and lovely day never dawned. The air was crisp and the sky almost cloudless. The gilded domes of the cathedrals and churches, brilliantly illuminated by the sun, formed a superb panorama. I noticed a significant change in the bearing of the passers-by. They were all wending their way, singly or in small groups, in the direction of the Winter Palace.

"Report of the *London Times*" is from James H. Robinson and Charles A. Beard, eds., *Readings in Modern European History*, vol. 2 (Boston: Ginn & Company, 1909), pp. 373–374.

Bloody Sunday (January 1905). Russian Cossacks fire on a group of protesting workers. This incident became a rallying point for governmental reform. (*Sovfoto*)

Joining in the stream of workingmen, I proceeded in the direction of the Winter Palace. No observer could help being struck by the look of sullen determination on every face. Already a crowd of many thousands had collected, but was prevented from entering the square by mounted troops drawn up across the thoroughfare. The cavalry advanced at a walking pace, scattering the people right and left.

Event has succeeded event with such bewildering rapidity that the public is staggered and shocked beyond measure. The first trouble began at 11 o'clock, when the military tried to turn back some thousands of strikers at one of the bridges. The same thing happened almost simultaneously at other bridges, where the constant flow of workmen pressing forward refused to be denied access to the common rendezvous in the Palace Square. The Cossacks at first used their knouts, then the flat of their sabers, and finally they fired. The strikers in the front ranks fell on the knees and implored the Cossacks to let them pass, protesting that they had no hostile intentions. They refused, however, to be intimidated by blank cartridges, and orders were given to load with ball.

The passions of the mob broke loose like a bursting dam. The people, seeing the dead and dying carried away in all directions, the snow on the streets and pavements soaked with blood, cried aloud for vengeance. Meanwhile the situation at the Palace was becoming momentarily worse. The troops were reported to be unable to control the vast masses which were constantly surging forward. Reenforcements were sent, and at 2 o'clock here also the order was given to fire. Men, women, and children fell at each volley, and were carried away in ambulances, sledges, and carts. The indignation and fury of every class were aroused. Students, merchants, all classes of the population alike were inflamed. At the moment of writing, firing is going on in every quarter of the city.

Father Gapon, marching at the head of a large body of workmen, carrying a cross and other religious emblems, was wounded in the arm and shoulder. The two forces of workmen are now separated. Those on the other side of the river were arming with swords, knives, and smiths' and carpenters' tools, and are busy erecting barricades. The troops are apparently reckless, firing right and left, with or without reason. The rioters continue to appeal to them, saying, "You are Russians! Why play the part of bloodthirsty butchers?"

Dreadful anxiety prevails in every household where any members are absent. Distracted husbands, fathers, wives, and children are searching for those missing. The surgeons and Red Cross ambulances are busy. A night of terror is in prospect.

Report of *Le Matin*

The soldiers of the Preobrazhensky regiment, without any summons to disperse, shoot down the unfortunate people as if they were playing at bloodshed. Several hundred fall; more than a hundred and fifty are killed. They are almost all children, women, and young people. It is terrible. Blood flows on all sides. At 5 o'clock the crowd is driven back, cut down and repelled on all sides. The people, terror-stricken, fly in every direction. Scared women and children slip, fall, rise to their feet, only to fall again farther on. At this moment a sharp word of command is heard and the victims fall *en masse*. There had been no disturbances to speak of. The whole crowd is unarmed and has not uttered a single threat.

As I proceeded, there were everywhere troops and Cossacks. Successive discharges of musketry shoot down on all sides the terrorized mob. The soldiers aim at the people's heads and the victims are frightfully disfigured. A woman falls almost at my side. A little farther I slip on a piece of brain. Before me is a child of eight years whose face is no longer human. Its mother is kneeling in tears over its corpse. The wounded, as they drag themselves along, leave streams of blood on the snow.

"Report of *Le Matin*" is from James H. Robinson & Charles A. Beard, eds., *Readings in Modern European History*, vol 2 (Boston: Ginn and Company, 1909) pp. 374–375.

Duma and Constitution

The public outcry following the massacre on Bloody Sunday contributed to a more responsive attitude on the part of the tsar. Nicholas decided to institute a duma, or representative assembly, which was to exist as a testament to reform, but with no real power to change conditions. The Duma convened in May 1906; it tried to direct the tsar's attention to liberal reforms but was dismissed as a consequence (1906). In all, there were four Dumas from 1905 to 1917. The first two selections recall the institution and dismissal of the first Duma. Note the tsar's reasons for his actions. The last document excerpts articles from the Russian Imperial Constitution of April 1906. Has Nicholas compromised on his autocracy?

Manifesto for the First Duma (August 1905)

TSAR NICHOLAS II

The empire of Russia is formed and strengthened by the indestructible union of the Tsar with the people and the people with the Tsar. This concord and the union of the Tsar and the people is the great moral force which has created Russia in the course of centuries by protecting her from all misfortunes and all attacks, and has constituted up to the present time a pledge of unity, independence, integrity, material well-being, and intellectual development in the present and in the future.

In our manifesto of February 26, 1903, we summoned all faithful sons of the fatherland in order to perfect, through mutual understanding, the organization of the State, founding it securely on public order and private welfare. We devoted ourselves to the task of coordinating local elective bodies [zemstvos] with the central authorities, and removing the disagreements existing between them, which so disturbed the normal course of the national life. Autocratic Tsars, our ancestors, have had this aim constantly in view, and the time has now come to follow out their good intentions and to summon elected representatives from the whole of Russia to take a constant and active part in the elaboration of laws, adding for this purpose to the higher State institutions a special consultative body entrusted with the preliminary elaboration and discussion of measures and with the examination of the State Budget. It is for this reason that, while preserving the fundamental law regarding autocratic power, we have deemed it well to form a *Gosundarstvennaia* Duma (i.e. State Council) and to approve regulations for elections to this Duma, extending these laws to the whole territory of the empire, with such exceptions only as may be considered necessary in the case of some regions in which special conditions obtain. . . .

"Manifesto for the First Duma" is from James H. Robinson and Charles A. Beard, eds., *Readings in Modern European History*, vol. 2 (Boston: Ginn & Company, 1909), pp. 375–377.

We are convinced that those who are elected by the confidence of the whole people, and who are called upon to take part in the legislative work of the government, will show themselves in the eyes of all Russia worthy of the imperial trust in virtue of which they have been invited to cooperate in this great work; and that in perfect harmony with the other institutions and authorities of the State, established by us, they will contribute profitably and zealously to our labors for the well-being of our common mother, Russia, and for the strengthening of the unity, security, and greatness of the empire, as well as for the tranquillity and prosperity of the people.

In invoking the blessing of the Lord on the labors of the new assembly which we are establishing, and with unshakable confidence in the grace of God and in the assurance of the great historical destinies reserved by Divine Providence for our beloved fatherland, we firmly hope that Russia with the help of God Almighty, and with the combined efforts of all her sons, will emerge triumphant from the trying ordeals through which she is now passing, and will renew her strength in the greatness and glory of her history extending over a thousand years.

Given at Peterhof on the nineteenth day of August, in the year of grace 1905, and the eleventh year of our reign.

Dissolution of the Duma (July 1906)

TSAR NICHOLAS II

We summoned the representatives of the nation by our will to the work of productive legislation. Confiding firmly in divine clemency and believing in the great and brilliant future of our people, we confidantly anticipated benefits for the country from their labors. We proposed great reforms in all departments of the national life. We have always devoted our greatest care to the removal of the ignorance of the people by the light of instruction, and to the removal of their burdens by improving the conditions of agricultural work.

A cruel disappointment has befallen our expectations. The representatives of the nation, instead of applying themselves to the work of productive legislation, have strayed into spheres beyond their competence, and have been making inquiries into the acts of local authorities established by ourselves, and have been making comments upon the imperfections of the fundamental laws, which can only be modified by our imperial will. In short, the representatives of the nation have undertaken really illegal acts, such as the appeal by the Duma to the nation.

The peasants, disturbed by such anomalies, and seeing no hope of the amelioration of their lot, have resorted in a number of districts to open

"Dissolution of the Duma" is from James H. Robinson and Charles A. Beard, eds., *Readings in Modern European History*, vol. 2 (Boston: Ginn & Company, 1909), pp. 377–378.

pillage and the destruction of other people's property, and to disobedience of the law and of the legal authorities. But our subjects ought to remember that an improvement in the lot of the people is only possible under conditions of perfect order and tranquillity. We shall not permit arbitrary or illegal acts, and we shall impose our imperial will on the disobedient by all the power of the State.

In dissolving the Duma we confirm our immutable intention of maintaining this institution, and in conformity with this intention we fix March 5, 1907 as the date of the convocation of a new Duma. With unshakable faith in divine clemency and in the good sense of the Russian people, we shall expect from the new Duma the realization of our efforts and their promotion of legislation in accordance with the requirements of a regenerated Russia.

Faithful sons of Russia, your Tsar calls upon you as a father upon his children to unite with him for the regeneration of our holy fatherland. We believe that giants in thought and action will appear, and that, thanks to their assiduous efforts, the glory of Russia will continue to shine.

Russian Imperial Constitution (April 1906)

Art. 4. The supreme autocratic power is vested in the Tsar of all the Russians. It is God's command that his authority should be obeyed not only through fear but for conscience' sake.

Art. 5. The person of the Tsar is sacred and inviolable.

Art. 7. The Tsar exercises the legislative power in conjunction with the Council of the Empire and the imperial Duma.

Art. 8. The initiative in all branches of legislation belongs to the Tsar. Solely on his initiative may the fundamental laws of the empire be subjected to a revision in the Council of the Empire and the imperial Duma.

Art. 9. The Tsar approves the laws, and without his approval no law can come into existence.

Art. 10. All governmental powers in their widest extent throughout the whole Russian empire are vested in the Tsar. . . .

Art. 62. The established and ruling faith of the Russian Empire is the Christian, Orthodox Catholic, Eastern faith.

Art. 64. The Tsar as Christian ruler is the supreme defender and upholder of the doctrines of the ruling faith, the protector of the true belief, and of every ordinance in the holy Church.

Art. 66. All those subjects of the Russian State who do not belong to the ruling Church, natives as well as the inhabitants of annexed districts, foreigners in the Russian service, or temporary sojourners in Russia, enjoy the free exercise of their respective faiths and religious services according to their particular usages.

"Russian Imperial Constitution" is from James H. Robinson and Charles A. Beard, eds., *Readings in Modern European History*, vol. 2 (Boston: Ginn & Company, 1909), pp. 379–381.

Art. 73. No one shall be arrested except in the cases determined by law.

Art. 74. No one shall be brought into court or punished for an offense which was not a crime according to the law when committed.

Art. 75. The dwelling of every one is inviolable.

Art. 76. Every Russian subject is entitled freely to choose his residence and occupation.

Art. 77. Property is inviolable. Property shall be taken only for public use and after just compensation.

Art. 78. Russian subjects are entitled to meet peaceably and without arms for such purposes as are not contrary to law.

Art. 79. Within the limits fixed by law every one may express his thoughts by word or writing and circulate them by means of the press or otherwise.

What Is to Be Done? (1902)

The above question was asked time and again by revolutionaries who fought against the autocracy of the Russian monarchy during the nineteenth century. The famous solution written in 1902 came from Vladimir Ulyanov (Lenin), who was a disciple of Karl Marx but was rather impatient with the disorganization and amateurism of his fellow revolutionaries. Lenin saw the communist revolution as an all-consuming goal, to be obtained only by hard work and commitment to the cause of revolution itself. Lenin advocated the strict organization of a party composed of "professional revolutionaries." In this he went far beyond Marx's conception of revolution as "eventual." Lenin's answer to the question "What is to be done?" marks the beginning of Leninism as a distinct political philosophy.

"We Shall Overturn Russia!"

V. I. LENIN

Without a revolutionary theory there can be no revolutionary movement. This thought cannot be insisted upon too strongly at a time when the fashionable preaching of opportunism goes hand in hand with an infatuation for the narrowest forms of practical activity. . . . Our Party is only in process of formation, its features are only just becoming outlined, and it is yet far from having settled accounts with other trends of revolutionary thought, which threaten to divert the movement from the correct path. . . . The national tasks of Russian Social-Democracy are such as have never

" 'We Shall Overturn Russia!' " is from Robert V. Daniels, *A Documentary History of Communism*. vol 1 (Hanover, N.H.: University Press of New England, 1984), pp. 8, 12–13. Reprinted by permission of the publisher.

confronted any other socialist party in the world. . . . *The role of vanguard fighter can be fulfilled only by a party that is guided by the most advanced theory.* . . .

The strikes of the nineties represented the class struggle in embryo, but only in embryo. Taken by themselves, these strikes were simply trade union struggles, but not yet Social-Democratic struggles. They testified to the awakening antagonisms between workers and employers, but the workers were not, and could not be, conscious of the irreconcilable antagonism of their interests to the whole of the modern political and social system, i.e., theirs was not yet Social-Democratic consciousness. In this sense, the strikes of the nineties in spite of the enormous progress they represented as compared with the "riots," remained a purely spontaneous movement.

I assert: 1) that no revolutionary movement can endure without a stable organization of leaders that maintains continuity; 2) that the wider the masses spontaneously drawn into the struggle, forming the basis of the movement and participating in it, the more urgent the need of such an organization, and the more solid this organization must be (for it is much easier for demagogues to sidetrack the more backward sections of the masses); 3) that such an organization must consist chiefly of people professionally engaged in revolutionary activity; 4) that in an autocratic state, the more we *confine* the membership of such an organization to people who are professionally engaged in revolutionary activity and to have been professionally trained in the art of combatting the political police, the more difficult will it be to wipe out such an organization, and 5) the *greater* will be the number of people of the working class of the other classes of society who will be able to join the movement and perform active work in it. . . .

Our chief sin with regard to organization is that *by our amateurishness we have lowered the prestige of revolutionaries in Russia.* A person who is flabby and shaky in questions of theory, who has a narrow outlook, who pleads the spontaneity of the masses as an excuse for his own sluggishness, who resembles a trade union secretary more than a people's tribune, who is unable to conceive of a broad and bold plan that would command the respect even of opponents, and who is inexperienced and clumsy in his own professional art—the art of combatting the political police—why, such a man is not a revolutionary but a wretched amateur!

Let no active worker take offense at these frank remarks, for as far as insufficient training is concerned, I apply them first and foremost to myself. I used to work in a circle that set itself very wide, all-embracing tasks; and all of us, members of that circle, suffered painfully, acutely from the realization that we were proving ourselves to be amateurs at a moment in history when we might have been able to say, paraphrasing a well-known epigram: "Give us an organization of revolutionaries, and we shall overturn Russia!" And the more I recall the burning sense of shame I then experienced, the more bitter are my feelings towards those pseudo Social-Democrats whose teachings "bring disgrace on the calling of a revolutionary," who fail to understand that our task is not to champion the degrading of the revolutionary to the level of an amateur, but to *raise* the amateurs to the level of revolutionaries. . . .

War and the Abdication of the Tsar

The following selections range in time from August 1914, when Russia entered the Great War, to March 1917, when Nicholas abdicated the throne. They recount the reasons given for Russia's entrance into the war, the problems associated with the abdication of the tsar, and the debate over the continued existence of the Romanov dynasty.

Imperial Manifesto for Entrance (August 2, 1914)

TSAR NICHOLAS II

Compelled, by the force of circumstances thus created, to adopt the necessary measures of precaution, We commanded that the army and the navy be put on a war footing, but, at the same time, holding the blood and the treasure of Our subjects dear, We made very effort to obtain a peaceable issue of the negotiations that had been started.

In the midst of friendly communications, Austria's Ally, Germany, contrary to our trust in century-old relations of neighborliness, and paying no heed to Our assurances that the measures We had adopted implied no hostile aims whatever, insisted upon their immediate abandonment, and, meeting with a rejection of this demand, suddenly declared war on Russia.

We have now to intercede not only for a related country, unjustly attacked, but also to safeguard the honor, dignity, and integrity of Russia, and her position among the Great Powers. We firmly believe that all Our loyal subjects will rally self-sacrificingly and with one accord to the defense of the Russian soil.

At this hour of threatening danger, let domestic strife be forgotten. Let the union between the Tsar and His people be stronger than ever, and let Russia, rising like one man, repel the insolent assault of the enemy.

With a profound faith in the justice of Our cause, and trusting humbly in Almighty Providence, We invoke prayerfully the Divine blessing for Holy Russia and our valiant troops.

Given at Saint Petersburg, on the second day of August, in the year of Our Lord one thousand nine hundred and fourteen, and the twentieth year of Our reign.

"Imperial Manifesto for Entrance" is from Frank A Golder, ed., *Documents of Russian History (1914–1917)*, trans. Emanuel Aronsberg (New York: The Century Company, 1927), pp. 29–30.

The Refugee Problem (August 17, 1915)

[Discussion in a meeting of the Council of Ministers]

Of all the grave consequences of the war this one [refugee] is the most unexpected, the most serious and the most difficult to remedy. . . . It has been worked out by the wise strategists to frighten the enemy. . . . Misery, sickness, sorrow and poverty go with them [refugees] all over Russia. They create panics wherever they go and put out whatever still remains of the ardor of the first days of the war. They move like a wall, knocking down the grain, trampling down the plowed fields and destroying the forests. . . . Their trail is like that of the flight of locusts or the band of Tamerlane on the warpath. The railways are choked, and pretty soon it will be impossible to move war freight and food supplies. . . . I have an idea that the Germans watch with pleasure the result of this attempt to repeat the tactics of 1812. If on the one hand they [Germans] are deprived of certain local provisions, they are, on the other hand, freed from the care of the population and have full freedom of action in the depopulated areas. . . . In my capacity as member of the Council of Ministers I should like to say that this undertaking of Headquarters to bring about a second migration of peoples will lead Russia into darkness, revolution and ruin.

Abdication of the Russian Throne (March 15, 1917)

TSAR NICHOLAS II

In the midst of the great struggle against a foreign foe, who has been striving for three years to enslave our country, it has pleased God to lay on Russia a new and painful trial. Newly arisen popular disturbances in the interior imperil the successful continuation of the stubborn fight. The fate of Russia, the honor of our heroic army, the welfare of our people, the entire future of our dear land, call for the prosecution of the conflict, regardless of the sacrifices, to a triumphant end. The cruel foe is making his last effort and the hour is near when our brave army, together with our glorious Allies, will crush him.

In these decisive days in the life of Russia, we deem it our duty to do what we can to help our people to draw together and unite all their forces with the State Duma. We therefore think it best to abdicate the throne of the Russian State and to lay down the Supreme Power.

Not wishing to be separated from our beloved son, we hand down our

"The Refugee Problem" is from Frank A. Golder, ed., *Documents of Russian History (1914–1917)*, trans. Emanuel Aronsberg (New York: The Century Company, 1927), p. 182.

"Abdication of the Russian Throne" is from Frank A. Golder, ed., *Documents of Russian History (1914–1917)*, trans. Emanuel Aronsberg (New York: The Century Company, 1927), pp. 297–298.

inheritance to our brother, Grand Duke Michael Alexandrovich, and give him our blessing on mounting the throne of the Russian Empire.

We enjoin our brother to govern in union and harmony with the representatives of the people on such principles as they shall see fit to establish. He should bind himself to do so by an oath in the name of our beloved country.

We call on all faithful sons of the Fatherland to fulfil their sacred obligations to their country by obeying the Tsar at this hour of national distress, and to help him and the representatives of the people to take the path of victory, well-being, and glory.

May the Lord God help Russia!

March 15, 1917, 3 P.M.
City of Pskov

Shall the Romanov Dynasty Remain? (March 15, 1917)

[Newspaper editorial from *Izvestiia*]

The revolutionary people should carry through to the end the revolution and the democratization of its political and social organization. To return to the old is unthinkable. The revolutionary people should organize the State in the way that will best satisfy its interests, strength and great zeal, and will make impossible a new attempt on its rights and liberty. This can be done by handing the power over to the people, that is to say, by forming a democratic republic, in which the officers of government are elected by universal equal, secret, and direct suffrage. All the revolutionary elements in Russia, who have made tremendous sacrifices in the fight and the forging of freedom, should strive for such a government.

If the power were entrusted to a monarch, one, with his responsible ministry, the latter might make an attempt on the liberty of the people and bind it with chains of slavery. Then again, in a constitutional monarchy there is the right of succession which again creates the possibility of rulers of the type of Nicholas, the Last.

In a constitutional monarchy, the army serves not the people, but the monarch, giving him great power, which he could use to harm the people.

The Romanov dynasty is now overthrown. . . . There must be no going back to it. The revolutionary people will find enough strength to form a new republican government, which will guarantee its rights and freedom.

"Shall the Romanov Dynasty Remain?" is from Frank A. Golder, ed., *Documents of Russian History (1914–1917)*, trans. Emanuel Aronsberg (New York: The Century Company, 1927), pp. 296–297.

Last Address to the Army (March 21, 1917)

TSAR NICHOLAS II

I appeal to you for the last time, my beloved troops. After the abdication of myself and my son, all the authority has passed into the hands of the Provisional Government, formed by the State Duma. So may God help them lead Russia on the way to prosperity and glory!

And you, my valiant troops, God help you to defend our country against the cruel foe! For two and a half years you have daily and hourly borne on your shoulders the heavy burden of war. Much blood has been shed; many efforts have been made; and the day is near when Russia, closely united to her gallant allies in their common aspiration to victory, will break the resistance of the enemy. This war, unprecedented in history, must be continued and brought to a victorious end. Any one who dreams of peace at the present moment is a traitor to his country. I know that every honest soldier thinks so. Go on fulfilling your duty; stand to guard your glorious fatherland; obey the Provisional Government and your chiefs. Do not forget that all disorder, all weakening of discipline, are so many assets for the foe.

I firmly believe that the love for your great country is, and ever will be, alive in your hearts. God will give you his blessing, and St. George, the Victorious, will help you to triumph over the foe!

The Provisional Government

After the abdication of the tsar in March 1917, a temporary body called the Provisional Government was installed to maintain stability in the country until a representative constituent assembly could be elected by the Russian people. The Petrograd Soviet, an elected council of workers and soldiers, immediately threatened the authority of the Provisional Government. Lenin, who had just arrived in Petrograd from Switzerland, reasserted leadership of the Bolshevik party and set forth his demands in the last selection, the famous "April Theses."

First Declaration of the Provisional Government (March 19, 1917)

Citizens of Russia:

A great event has taken place. By the mighty assault of the Russian people, the old order has been overthrown. A new, free Russia is born. The great

"Last Address to the Army" is from Frank A Golder, ed. *Documents of Russian History (1914–1917)*, trans. Emanuel Aronsberg (New York: The Century Company, 1927), pp. 53–54.

"First Declaration of the Provisional Government" is from Frank A. Golder, ed., *Documents of Russian History (1914–1917)*, trans. Emanuel Aronsberg (New York: The Century Company, 1927), pp. 311–313.

revolution crowns long years of struggle. By the act of October 17, [30] 1905, under the pressure of the awakened popular forces, Russia was promised constitutional liberties. Those promises, however, were not kept. The First State Duma, interpreter of the nation's hopes, was dissolved. The Second Duma suffered the same fate, and the Government, powerless to crush the national will, decided, by the act of June 3, [16] 1907, to deprive the people of a part of those rights of participation in legislative work which had been granted.

In the course of nine long years, there were taken from the people, step by step, all the rights that they had won. Once more the country was plunged into an abyss of arbitrariness and despotism. All attempts to bring the Government to its senses proved futile, and the titanic world struggle, into which the country was dragged by the enemy, found the Government in a state of moral decay, alienated from the people, indifferent to the fate of our native land, and steeped in the infamy of corruption. Neither the heroic efforts of the army, staggering under the crushing burdens of internal chaos, nor the appeals of the popular representatives who had united in the face of the national peril, were able to lead the former Emperor and his Government into the path of unity with the people. And when Russia, owing to the illegal and fatal actions of her rulers, was confronted with gravest disasters, the nation was obliged to take the power into its own hands.

The unanimous revolutionary enthusiasm of the people, fully conscious of the gravity of the moment, and the determination of the State Duma, have created the Provisional Government, which considers it to be its sacred and responsible duty to fulfill the hopes of the nation, and lead the country out onto the bright path of free civic organization.

The Government trusts that the spirit of lofty patriotism, manifested during the struggle of the people against the old regime, will also inspire our valiant soldiers on the field of battle. For its own part, the Government will make every effort to provide our army with everything necessary to bring the war to a victorious end.

The Government will sacredly observe the alliances which bind us to other powers, and will unswervingly carry out the agreements entered into by the Allies. While taking measures to defend the country against the foreign enemy, the Government will, at the same time, consider it to be its primary duty to make possible the expression of the popular will as regards the form of government, and will convoke the Constituent Assembly within the shortest time possible, on the basis of universal, direct, equal, and secret suffrage, also guaranteeing participation in the elections to the gallant defenders of our native land, who are now shedding their blood on the fields of battle.

The Constituent Assembly will issue the fundamental laws, guaranteeing to the country the inalienable rights of justice, equality, and liberty. Conscious of the heavy burden which the country suffers because of the lack of civic rights, which lack stands in the way of its free, creative power at this time of violent national commotion, the Provisional Government deems it necessary, at once, before the convocation of the Constituent Assembly, to provide the country with laws for the safeguard of civic liberty and equality, in order to enable all citizens freely to apply their spiritual forces to creative work for the benefit of the country. The Government will also undertake the enactment of legal provisions to assure to all citizens, on the basis of universal suffrage, an equal share in the election of local governments.

At this moment of national liberation, the whole country remembers with reverent gratitude those who, in the struggle for their political and religious convictions, fell victims to the vindictive old regime, and the Provisional Government will regard it as its joyful duty to bring back from their exile, with full honors, all those who have suffered for the good of the country.

In fulfilling these tasks, the Provisional Government is animated by the belief that it will thus execute the will of the people, and that the whole nation will support it in its honest efforts to insure the happiness of Russia. This belief inspires it with courage. Only in the common effort of the entire nation and the Provisional Government can it see a pledge of triumph of the new order.

March 19, 1917

Policy of the Petrograd Soviet (March 27, 1917)

Comrade-proletarians, and toilers of all countries:

We, Russian workers and soldiers, united in the Petrograd Soviet of Workers' and Soldiers' Deputies, send you warmest greetings and announce the great event. The Russian democracy has shattered in the dust the age-long despotism of the Tsar and enters your family [of nations] as an equal, and as a mighty force in the struggle for our common liberation. Our victory is a great victory for the freedom and democracy of the world. The chief pillar of reaction in the world, the "Gendarme of Europe" is no more. May the earth turn to heavy granite on his grave! Long live freedom! Long live the international solidarity of the proletariat, and its struggle for final victory!

Our work is not yet finished: the shades of the old order have not yet been dispersed, and not a few enemies are gathering their forces against the Russian revolution. Nevertheless our achievement so far is tremendous. The people of Russia will express their will in the Constituent Assembly, which will be called as soon as possible on the basis of universal, equal, direct, and secret suffrage. And it may already be said without a doubt that a democratic republic will triumph in Russia. The Russian

"Policy of the Petrograd Soviet" is from Frank A. Golder, ed., *Documents of Russian History (1914–1917)*, trans. Emanuel Aronsberg (New York: The Century Company, 1927), pp. 325–326.

people now possess full political liberty. They can now assert their mighty power in the internal government of the country and in its foreign policy. And, appealing to all people who are being destroyed and ruined in the monstrous war, we announce that the time has come to start a decisive struggle against the grasping ambitions of the governments of all countries; the time has come for the people to take into their own hands the decision of the question of war and peace.

Conscious of its revolutionary power, the Russian democracy announces that it will, by every means, resist the policy of conquest of its ruling classes, and it calls upon the peoples of Europe for concerted, decisive action in favor of peace.

We are appealing to our brother-proletarians of the Austro-German coalition, and, first of all, to the German proletariat. From the first days of the war, you were assured that by raising arms against autocratic Russia, you were defending the culture of Europe from Asiatic despotism. Many of you saw in this a justification of that support which you were giving to the war. Now even this justification is gone: democratic Russia cannot be a threat to liberty and civilization.

We will firmly defend our own liberty from all reactionary attempts from within, as well as from without. The Russian revolution will not retreat before the bayonets of conquerors, and will not allow itself to be crushed by foreign military force. But we are calling to you: Throw off the yoke of your semi-autocratic rule, as the Russian people have shaken off the Tsar's autocracy; refuse to serve as an instrument of conquest and violence in the hands of kings, landowners, and bankers—and then by our united efforts, we will stop the horrible butchery, which is disgracing humanity and is beclouding the great days of the birth of Russian freedom.

Toilers of all countries: We hold out to you the hand of brotherhood across the mountains of our brothers' corpses, across rivers of innocent blood and tears, over the smoking ruins of cities and villages, over the wreckage of the treasures of civilization;—we appeal to you for the reestablishment and strengthening of international unity. In it is the pledge of future victories and the complete liberation of humanity.

Proletarians of all countries, Unite!

PETROGRAD SOVIET OF WORKERS'
AND SOLDIERS' DEPUTIES

The April Theses (April 20, 1917)

V. I. LENIN

The class conscious proletariat can consent to a revolutionary war, which would really justify revolutionary defencism, only on condition: (a) that the

"The April Theses" is from Martin McCauley, *The Russian Revolution and the Soviet State* (New York: Barnes & Noble, 1975), pp. 52–54. Permission granted by Barnes & Noble Books, Totowa, New Jersey.

power of government pass to the proletariat and the poor sections of the peasantry bordering on the proletariat; (b) that all annexations be renounced in deed as well as in words; (c) that a complete and real break be made with all capitalist interests.

In view of the undoubted honesty of the mass of the rank-and-file believers in revolutionary defencism, who accept the war as a necessity only and not as a means of conquest; in view of the fact that they are being deceived by the bourgeoisie, it is necessary thoroughly, persistently and patiently to explain their error to them, to explain the indissoluble connection between capital and the imperialist war, and to prove that *it is impossible* to end the war by a truly democratic, non-coercive peace without overthrow of capital.

The widespread propaganda of this view among the army on active service must be organised.

Fraternisation

(2) The specific feature of the present situation in Russia is that it represents a *transition* from the first stage of the revolution—which owing to the insufficient class consciousness and organisation of the proletariat, led to the assumption of power by the bourgeoisie—*to the second stage*, which must place power in the hands of the proletariat and the poor strata of the peasantry.

This transition is characterised, on the one hand, by a maximum of freedom (Russia is *now* the freest of all the belligerent countries in the world); on the other, by the absence of violence in relation to the masses, and, finally, by the naive confidence of the masses in the government of capitalists, the worst enemies of peace and socialism.

This specific situation demands on our part an ability to adapt ourselves to the specific requirements of Party work among unprecedently large masses of proletarians who have just awakened to political life.

(3) No support must be given to the Provisional Government, the utter falsity of all its promises must be exposed, particularly of those relating to the renunciation of annexations. Exposure, and not the unpardonable illusion-breeding 'demand' that this government, a government of capitalists, should *cease* to be an imperialist government.

(4) The fact must be recognised that in most of the Soviets of Workers' Deputies our Party is in a minority, and so far in a small minority, as against *a bloc of all* the petty-bourgeois opportunist elements, who have yielded to the influence of the bourgeoisie and are the conveyors of its influence to the proletariat. . . .

It must be explained to the masses that the Soviet of Workers' Deputies is the *only possible* form of revolutionary government and that therefore our task is, as long as *this* government submits to the influence of the bourgeoisie, to present a patient, systematic, and persistent *explanation* of its errors and tactics, an explanation especially adapted to the practical needs of the masses.

As long as we are in the minority we carry on the work of criticising and exposing errors and at the same time advocate the necessity of transferring the entire power of state to the Soviets of Workers' Deputies, so that the masses may by experience overcome their mistakes.

(5) Not a parliamentary republic—to return to a parliamentary republic from the Soviets of Workers' Deputies would be a retrograde step—but a republic of Soviets of Workers', Agricultural Labourers' and Peasants' Deputies throughout the country, from top to bottom.

Abolition of the police, the army and the bureaucracy.

(6) The agrarian programme must be centered around the Soviets of Agricultural Labourers' Deputies.

Confiscation of All Landed Estates

Nationalisation of *all* lands in the country, the disposal of such *lands* to be in the charge of the local Soviets of Agricultural Labourers' and Peasants' Deputies. The organisation of separate soviets of Deputies of the Poor Peasants. The creation of model farms on each of the large estates. . . .

(7) The immediate amalgamation of all banks in the country into a single national bank, control over which shall be exercised by the Soviet of Workers' Deputies.

(8) Our *immediate* task shall be not the 'introduction of socialism,' but to bring social production and distribution of products at once under the *control* of the Soviet of Workers' Deputies.

(9) Party tasks:

   (a) Immediate summoning of a Party congress.
   (b) Alteration of the Party programme, mainly:
      1. On the question of imperialism and the imperialist war;
      2. On the question of our attitude towards the state and our demand for a 'commune state.'
      3. Amendment of our antiquated minimum programme;
   (c) A new name for the Party.

(10) A new International.

The November Revolution (November 8, 1917)

The Bolshevik faction, led by Lenin and his very competent colleague Leon Trotsky, had suffered reversals during an abortive uprising in July 1917. Trotsky was imprisoned and Lenin fled to Finland. Finally in November 1917, Lenin persuaded his faction that the time was ripe for a coup. The first selection is Lenin's speech after his successful storming of the Winter Palace in Petrograd. Note the critical editorial from the newspaper Izvestiia *on November 8. It was the last before the Bolsheviks censored the press. Lenin's seizure of power also included the establishment of a secret police (Cheka), an institution that had been used (in another form) by the autocratic tsar to eliminate opposition.*

Speech after the Overthrow of the Provisional Government

V. I. LENIN

Comrades, the workmen's and peasant's revolution, the need of which the Bolsheviks have emphasized many times, has come to pass.

What is the significance of this revolution? Its significance is, in the first place, that we shall have a soviet government, without the participation of bourgeoisie of any kind. The oppressed masses will of themselves form a government. The old state machinery will be smashed into bits and in its place will be created a new machinery of government by the soviet organizations. From now on there is a new page in the history of Russia, and the present, third Russian revolution shall in its final result lead to the victory of Socialism.

One of our immediate tasks is to put an end to the war at once. But in order to end the war, which is closely bound up with the present capitalistic system, it is necessary to overthrow capitalism itself. In this work we shall have the aid of the world labor movement, which has already begun to develop in Italy, England, and Germany.

A just and immediate offer of peace by us to the international democracy will find everywhere a warm response among the international proletariat masses. In order to secure the confidence of the proletariat, it is necessary to publish at once all secret treaties.

In the interior of Russia a very large part of the peasantry has said: Enough playing with the capitalists; we will go with the workers. We shall secure the confidence of the peasants by one decree, which will wipe out the private property of the landowners. The peasants will understand that their only salvation is in union with the workers.

We will establish a real labor control on production.

We have now learned to work together in a friendly manner, as is evident from this revolution. We have the force of mass organization which has conquered all and which will lead the proletariat to world revolution.

We should now occupy ourselves in Russia in building up a proletarian socialist state.

Long live the world-wide socialistic revolution!

"Speech after the Overthrow of the Provisional Government" is from Frank A. Golder, ed., *Documents of Russian History (1914–1917)*, trans. Emanuel Aronsberg (New York: The Century Company, 1927), pp. 618–619.

"Little Good Is to Be Expected" (November 8, 1917)

[*Izvestiia* newspaper editorial]

Yesterday we said that the Bolshevik uprising is a mad adventure and today, when their attempt is crowned with success, we are of the same mind. We repeat: that which is before us is not a transfer of power to the Soviets, but a seizure of power by one party—the Bolsheviks. Yesterday we said that a successful attempt meant the breaking up of the greatest of the revolution—the Constituent Assembly. Today we add that it means, also, the breaking up of the Congress of Soviets, and perhaps the whole soviet organization. They can call themselves what they please; the fact remains that the Bolsheviks alone took part in the uprising. All the other socialistic and democratic parties protest against it.

How the situation may develop we do not know, but little good is to be expected. We are quite confident that the Bolsheviks cannot organize a state government. As yesterday, so today, we repeat that what is happening will react worst of all on the question of peace.

Censorship of the Press (November 9, 1917)

V. I. LENIN

In the trying critical period of the revolution and the days that immediately followed it the Provisional Revolutionary Committee was compelled to take a number of measures against the counter-revolutionary press of different shades.

Immediately outcries were heard from all sides that the new, socialist power had violated a fundamental principle of its programme by encroaching upon the freedom of the press.

The Workers' and Peasants' Government calls the attention of the population to the fact that what this liberal facade actually conceals is freedom for the propertied classes, having taken hold of the lion's share of the entire press, to poison, unhindered, the minds and obscure the consciousness of the masses.

Every one knows that the bourgeois press is one of the most powerful weapons of the bourgeoisie. Especially at the crucial moment when the new power, the power of workers and peasants, is only affirming itself, it was impossible to leave this weapon wholly in the hands of the enemy, for in such moments it is no less dangerous than bombs and machine-guns. That is why temporary extraordinary measures were taken to stem the torrent of

" 'Little Good Is to Be Expected' " is from Frank A. Golder, ed., *Documents of Russian History (1914–1917)* trans. Emanuel Aronsberg (New York: The Century Company, 1927), p. 619.

"Censorship of the Press" is from Martin McCauley, *The Russian Revolution and the Soviet State* (New York: Barnes & Noble, 1975), pp. 190–191. Permission granted by Barnes & Noble Books, Totowa, New Jersey.

filth and slander in which the yellow and green press would be only too glad to drown the recent victory of the people.

As soon as the new order becomes consolidated, all administrative pressure on the press will be terminated and it will be granted complete freedom within the bounds of legal responsibility, in keeping with a law that will be broadest and most progressive in this respect.

However, being aware that a restriction of the press, even at critical moments, is permissible only within the limits of what is absolutely necessary, the Council of People's Commissars resolves:

General Provisions on the Press

1. Only those publications can be suppressed which (1) call for open resistance or insubordination to the Workers' and Peasants' Government; (2) sow sedition through demonstrably slanderous distortion of facts; (3) instigate actions of an obviously criminal, i.e. criminally punishable, nature.
2. Publications can be proscribed, temporarily or permanently, only by decision of the Council of People's Commissars.
3. The present ordinance is of a temporary nature and will be repealed by a special decree as soon as normal conditions of social life set in.

Chairman of the Council of People's Commissars,
VLADIMIR ULYANOV (LENIN)

Establishment of the Secret Police (December 20, 1917)

V. I. LENIN

The Commission is to be called the All-Russian Extraordinary Commission for the Struggle with Counter-Revolution and Sabotage and is to be attached to the Council of People's Commissars.

The duties of the Commission are to be as follows:

1. To investigate and nullify all acts of counter-revolution and sabotage throughout Russia, irrespective of origin.
2. To bring before the Revolutionary Tribunal all counter-revolutionaries and saboteurs and to work out measures to combat them.
3. The Commission is to conduct the preliminary investigation only, sufficient to suppress (the counter-revolutionary act). The Commission to be divided into sections: (1) the information (section) (2) the orga-

"Establishment of the Secret Police" is from Martin McCauley, *The Russian Revolution and the Soviet State* (New York: Barnes & Noble, 1975), pp. 181–182. Permission granted by Barnes & Noble Books, Totowa, New Jersey.

nization section (in charge of organizing the struggle with counter-revolution section (in charge of organizing the struggle with counter-revolution throughout Russia) with branches, and (3) the fighting section.

The Commission shall be set up finally tomorrow. Then the fighting section of the All-Russian Commission shall start its activities. The Commission shall keep an eye on the press, saboteurs, right Socialist Revolutionaries and strikers. Measures to be taken are confiscation, imprisonment, confiscation of cards, publication of the names of the enemies of the people, etc.

Chairman of the Council of People's Commissars
V. ULYANOV (LENIN)

Dissolution of the Constituent Assembly (December 1917)

V. I. LENIN

A major responsibility of the Provisional Government had been to organize an election and establish a Constituent Assembly that was truly representative of the Russian people. Lenin, after achieving power through political manipulation and force of arms, decided to hold the election anyway. The results were not encouraging since the Bolsheviks were soundly defeated. Lenin, however, would not concede defeat and chose to dissolve the Constituent Assembly instead. Note Lenin's reasons for his actions. The second document is a questionnaire that all delegates to the Tenth All Russian Congress of the Russian Communist Party had to fill out. This was Lenin's view of himself in 1921.

At its very inception, the Russian revolution produced the Soviets of Workers', Soldiers' and Peasants' Deputies as the only mass organization of all the working and exploited classes capable of giving leadership to the struggle of these classes for their complete political and economic emancipation.

Throughout the initial period of the Russian revolution the Soviets grew in number, size and strength, their own experience disabusing them of the illusions regarding compromise with the bourgeoisie, opening their eyes to the fraudulence of the forms of bourgeois-democratic parliamentarism, and leading them to the conclusion that the emancipation of the oppressed classes was unthinkable unless they broke with these forms and with every kind of compromise. Such a break came with the October [November] Revolution, with the transfer of power to the Soviets.

"Dissolution of the Constituent Assembly" is from Martin McCauley, *The Russian Revolution and the Soviet State* (New York: Barnes & Noble, 1975), pp. 184–186. Permission granted by Barnes & Noble Books, Totowa, New Jersey.

The Constituent Assembly, elected on the basis of lists drawn up before October Revolution, was expressive of the old correlation of political forces, when the conciliators and Constitutional-Democrats were in power.

The working classes learned through experience that old bourgeois parliamentarism had outlived its day, that it was utterly incompatible with the tasks of Socialism, and that only class institutions (such as the Soviets) and not national ones were capable of overcoming the resistance of the propertied classes and laying the foundations of socialist society.

Any renunciation of the sovereign power of the Soviets, of the Soviet Republic won by the people, in favour of bourgeois parliamentarism and the Constituent Assembly would now be a step backwards and would cause a collapse of the entire October Workers' and Peasants' Revolution.

By virtue of generally known circumstances the Constituent Assembly, opening on January 18, gave the majority to the party of Right-Wing Socialist-Revolutionaries, the party of Kerensky, Avksentev and Chernov. Naturally, this party refused to recognize the programme of Soviet power, to recognize the Declaration of Rights of the Working and Exploited People, to recognize the October Revolution and Soviet power. . . .

Obviously, under such circumstances the Constituent Assembly can only serve as a cover for the struggle of the bourgeois counter-revolution to overthrow the power of the Soviets.

In view of this, the Central Executive Committee resolves:

The Constituent Assembly is hereby dissolved.

A Self-Portrait (March 7, 1921)
V. I. LENIN

Name: Ulyanov (Lenin), Vladimir Ilyich

Party organization: Central Committee, Russian Communist Party

Number of delegate mandate (voting/advisory):   No. 21 advisory

By whom elected: Central Committee

No. of Party members represented at meeting at which elected: Central Committee—19 members

Which All-Russian party Congresses have you attended: All except July (August?) 1917

Date of birth—age: 1870—51 years

State of health: Good

Family—no. of members of dependents: Wife and sister

"A Self-Portrait" is from Warren B. Walsh, ed., *Readings in Russian History,* 3rd ed. (Syracuse, N.Y.: Syracuse University Press, 1959), pp. 622–623. Reprinted by permission of the publisher.

Portrait of V. I. Lenin (October 1918). Could the Russian Revolution have succeeded without Lenin's firm direction? (*Sovfoto*)

Nationality: Russian

Native tongue: Russian

Knowledge of other languages: English, German, French—poor, Italian—very poor

What parts of Russia do you know well, and how long have you lived there: Know Volga country where I was born best; lived there until age 17

Have you been abroad (when, where, how long): In a number of West European countries—1895, 1900–1905, 1908–1917

Military training: None

Education: Graduate (passed examination as externe) Petrograd University Law Faculty, 1891

Basic occupation before 1917: Writer

Special training: None

Occupation since 1917 besides Party, Soviet, trade union, and similar work: Besides those enumerated, only writing

What trade union do you belong to: Union of Journalists

Positions held since 1917: October 1917 to March 1921; Moscow; Council People's Commissars and Council of Labor and Defense; Chairman

Present position: Since October 1917; Moscow; Chairman, Council of People's Commissars and Council of Labor and Defense

How long have you been a member of the R.C.P. (Bolsheviks):   Since 1894

Have you ever belonged to any other parties: No

Participation in the revolutionary movement before 1917:   Illegal Social-Democratic circles; member of the Russian Social-Democrats Workers' Party since its foundation. 1892–3, Samara; 1894–5, St. Petersburg; 1895–7, prison; 1898–1900, Siberia; 1900–05, abroad; 1905–07, St. Petersburg; 1908–1917, abroad

Penalties incurred for revolutionary activities: 1887 prison; 1895—7 prison; 1898–1900 Siberia; 1900 prison

How long in prison: Several days and 14 months

How long at hard labor: None

How long in exile: Three years

How long a political refugee: 9–10 years

Party functions since 1917:   October 1917 to March 1921, Moscow, Member of the Central Committee

Present Party function: as above

Have you ever been tried by the courts of the RSFSR or of the Party: No

Date: March, 1921

Signature of delegate: V. Ulyanov (Lenin)

The Aftermath

The Bolsheviks were thrust into a difficult situation on achieving power. Lenin was true to his slogan "Peace, Bread, and Land," and took Russia out of the war, negotiating a peace with Germany (Brest-Litovsk) that conceded much Russian territory. Lenin then applied his energies to quelling a civil war that pitted his Red Army (led by Trotsky) against the "White" forces, which consisted of supporters of the tsar or of other anti-Bolshevik elements. The tsar's execution in 1918 removed a possible impediment to the progress of the revolution. The Civil War ended in 1921, and Lenin spent the next three years until his death consolidating his gains and preparing for Russia's transition from a capitalist to a communist state. In this, Lenin endeavored to apply Marxist theory to the realities of the situation. The first selection is from a pamphlet entitled State and Revolution *written in August 1917, two months before the Bolshevik seizure of power. In it Lenin discusses this crucial period of transition. Events were to move in logical progression: from bourgeois capitalism to the dictatorship of the proletariat, to the "withering away" of the state, and finally to the justice and equality of the purely communist society. But things did not quite go as planned. The chaos of the Civil War and a great drought rendered the socialization of the economic system an unrealistic proposition. Lenin thus allowed a "partial return to capitalism" by permitting the revival of private industry and authorizing the peasantry to produce and trade for profit as part of his New Economic Plan (NEP). Although Russia would sitll move toward Marx's dream of a truly communist existence, the journey would take longer than Lenin expected. In any event, Lenin envisioned an egalitarian future, one that included women as integral members of society, valued for their talents and abilities. His thoughts on the role of women in the new state are included in the second selection.*

When Lenin died, apparently of a stroke, in 1924, Bolshevik leadership was assumed by Trotsky and Stalin. Their shaky relationship resulted in a power struggle that was eventually won by Stalin. Trotsky was exiled and finally executed abroad in 1940. Stalin led the Soviet state toward rapid industrialization, state collectivization of privately owned land, and repression. His execution of over 10 million Soviet dissidents in the collectivization struggle and purges of the 1930s established his reputation as one of the great scourges of history. His imposing figure and totalitarian regime became the model for the repressive world of "Big Brother" in George Orwell's 1984. Lenin himself doubted Stalin's character, as he revealed in a note written about a year before his death.

State and Revolution: The Transition from Capitalism to Communism (August 1917)

V. I. LENIN

Earlier the question was put thus: to attain its emancipation, the proletariat must overthrow the Bourgeoisie, conquer political power and establish its own revolutionary dictatorship.

Now the question is put somewhat differently: the transition from capitalist society, developing towards Communism, towards a Communist society, is impossible without a "political transition period", and the state in this period can only be the revolutionary dictatorship of the proletariat.

What, then, is the relation of this dictatorship to democracy?

We have seen that the *Communist Manifesto* simply places side by side the two ideas: the "transformation of the proletariat into the ruling class" and the "establishment of democracy". On the basis of all that has been said above, one can define more exactly how democracy changes in the transition from capitalism to Communism.

In capitalist society, under the conditions most favourable to its development, we have more or less complete democracy in the democratic republic. But this democracy is always bound by the narrow framework of capitalist exploitation, and consequently always remains, in reality, a democracy for the minority, only for the possessing classes, only for the rich. . . .

Democracy for an insignificant minority, democracy for the rich—that is the democracy of capitalist society. If we look more closely into the mechanism of capitalist democracy, everywhere, both in the . . . details of suffrage (residential qualification, exclusion of women, etc.), and in the technique of the representative institutions . . . on all sides we see restriction after restriction upon democracy. These restrictions, exceptions, exclusions, obstacles for the poor, seem slight, especially in the eyes of one who has himself never known want and has never been in close contact with the oppressed classes in their mass life (and nine-tenths, if not ninety-nine hundredths, of the bourgeois publicists and politicians are of this class), but in their sum total these restrictions exclude and squeeze out the poor from politics and from an active share in democracy.

Marx splendidly grasped this *essence* of capitalist democracy, when . . . he said that the oppressed were allowed once every few years, to decide which particular representatives of the oppressing class should be in parliament to represent and repress them!

But from this capitalist democracy—inevitably narrow, subtly rejecting the poor, and therefore hypocritical and false to the core—progress does not march onward, simply, smoothly and directly, to "greater and greater democracy", as the liberal professors and petty-bourgeois opportunists would have us believe. No, progress marches onward, i.e., towards Communism, through the dictatorship of the proletariat; it cannot do otherwise, for there is no one else and no other way to *break the resistance* of the capitalist exploiters.

But the dictatorship of the proletariat—i.e., the organisation of the vanguard of the oppressed as the ruling class for the purpose of crushing the oppressors—cannot produce merely an expansion of democracy. *Together* with an immense expansion of democracy which *for the first time* becomes democracy for the poor, democracy for the people, and not democracy for the rich folk, the dictatorship of the proletariat produces a series of restrictions of liberty [by itself oppressing] the exploiters, the capitalists. We must crush them in order to free humanity from wage-slavery; their resistance must be broken by force; it is clear that where there is suppression there is also violence, there is no liberty, no democracy.

Engels expressed this splendidly . . . when he said . . . that "as long as the proletariat still *needs* the state, it needs it not in the interests of freedom, but for the purpose of crushing its antagonists; and as soon as it becomes possible to speak of freedom, then the state, as such, ceases to exist."

Democracy for the vast majority of the people, and suppression by force, i.e., exclusion from democracy, of the exploiters and oppressors of the people—this is the modification of democracy during the *transition* from capitalism to Communism.

Only in Communist society, when the resistance of the capitalists has been completely broken, when the capitalists have disappeared, when there are no classes (i.e., there is no difference between the members of society in their relation to the social means of production), *only then* "the state ceases to exist", and "*it becomes possible to speak of freedom.*" Only then a really full democracy, a democracy without any exceptions, will be possible and will be realised. And only then will democracy itself begin to *wither away* due to the simple fact that, free from capitalist slavery, from the untold horrors, savagery, absurdities and infamies of capitalist exploitation, people will gradually *become accustomed* to the observance of the elementary rules of social life that have been known for centuries and repeated for thousands of years in all school books; they will become accustomed to observing them without force, without compulsion, without subordination, without the *special apparatus* for compulsion which is called the state.

The expression "the state *withers away*", is very well chosen, for it indicates both the gradual and the elemental nature of the process. Only habit can, and undoubtedly will, have such an effect; for we see around us millions of times how readily people get accustomed to observe the necessary rules of life in common, if there is no exploitation, if there is nothing that causes indignation, that calls forth protest and revolt and has to be *suppressed.*

Thus, in capitalist society, we have a democracy that is curtailed, poor, false; a democracy only for the rich, for the minority. The dictatorship of the proletariat, the period of transition to Communism, will, for the first time, produce democracy for the people, for the majority, side by side with the necessary suppression of the minority—the exploiters. Communism alone is capable of giving a really complete democracy, and the more complete it is the more quickly will it become unnecessary and wither away of itself. . . .

Again, during the *transition* from capitalism to Communism, suppression is *still* necessary; but it is the suppression of the minority of exploiters by the majority of exploited. . . . Finally, only Communism renders the state absolutely unnecessary, for there is *no one* to be suppressed—"no one" in the sense of a *class*, in the sense of a systematic struggle with a definite section of the population.

The Communist Emancipation of Women (1920)

V. I. LENIN

The thesis must clearly point out that real freedom for women is possible only through communism. The inseparable connection between the social and human position of the woman, and private property in the means of production, must be strongly brought out . . . And it will also supply the basis for regarding the woman question as a part of the social question, of the workers' problem, and so bind it firmly to the proletarian class struggle and the revolution. The Communist women's movement must itself be a mass movement, a part of the general mass movement. Not only of the proletariat, but of all the exploited and oppressed, all the victims of capitalism or any other mastery . . . We must win over to our side the millions of toiling women in the towns and villages. Win them for our struggles and in particular for the communist transformation of society. There can be no real mass movement without women. . .

Could there be more damning proof of [female exploitation] than the callous acquiescence of men who see how women grow worn out in the petty, monotonous household work, their strength and time dissipated and wasted, their minds growing narrow and stale, their hearts beating slowly, their will weakened? Of course, I am not speaking of the ladies of the bourgeoisie who shove onto servants the responsibility of all household work, including the care of children. What I am saying applies to the overwhelming majority of women, to the wives of workers and to those who stand all day in a factory.

So few men—even among the proletariat—realize how much effort and trouble they could save women, even quite do away with, if they were to lend a hand in "woman's work." But no, that is contrary to the "right and dignity of a man." They want their peace and comfort. The home life of the woman is a daily sacrifice to a thousand unimportant trivialities. The old master right of the man still lives in secret. His slave takes her revenge, almost secretly. The backwardness of women, their lack of understanding for the revolutionary ideals of the man decrease his joy and determination in fighting. They are like little worms which, unseen slowly but surely rot and corrode. I know the life of the worker, and not only from books. Our Communist work among the women, our political work, embraces a great deal of educational work among men. We must root out the old "master" idea to its last and smallest root, in the party and among the masses. That is one of our political tasks, just as is the urgently necessary task of forming a staff of men and women comrades, well trained in theory and practice, to carry on party activity among working women.

The government of the proletarian dictatorship, together with the Communist Party and trade unions, is of course leaving no stone unturned in the effort to overcome the backward ideas of men and women, to destroy the old Communist psychology. In law there is naturally complete equality of rights for men and women. And everywhere there is evidence of a sincere wish to put this equality into practice. We are bringing the women into the social economy, into legislation and government. All educational institutions are open to them, so that they can increase their professional and social capacities. We are establishing communal kitchens and public eating-houses, laundries and repair shops, infant asylums, kindergartens, children's homes, educational institutes of all kinds. In short, we are seriously carrying out the demand in our program for the transference of the economic and educational functions of the separate household to society. That will mean freedom for the women from the old household drudgery and dependence on man. That enables her to exercise to the full her talents and her inclinations . . . We have the most advanced protective laws for women workers in the world, and the officials of the organized workers carry them out. We are establishing maternity hospitals, homes for mothers and children, mothercraft clinics, organizing lecture courses on child care, exhibitions teaching mothers how to look after themselves and their children, and similar things. We are making the most serious efforts to maintain women who are unemployed and unprovided for.

We realize clearly that that is not very much, in comparison with the needs of the working women, that it is far from being all that is required for their real freedom. But still, it is tremendous progress, as against conditions in tsarist-capitalist Russia. It is even a great deal compared with conditions in countries where capitalism still has a free hand. It is a good beginning in the right direction, and we shall develop it further. With all our energy, you may believe that. For every day of the existence of the Soviet state proves more clearly that we cannot go forward without the women.

"Stalin Is Too Rude" (January 4, 1923)

V. I. LENIN

Stalin is too rude and this defect, which can be freely tolerated in our midst and in contacts among us Communists, can become an intolerable defect in one holding the position of the Secretary General. Because of this, I proposed that the comrades consider ways and means by which Stalin can be removed from this position and another man selected, a man who, above all, would differ from Com. Stalin in only one quality, namely, attitude toward his comrades, less capricious temper, etc. This circumstance could appear to be a meaningless trifle. I think, however, that from the viewpoint of preventing a split and from the viewpoint of what I have written above concerning the relationship between Stalin and Trotsky, this is not a trifle, or if it is one, then it is a trifle which can acquire a decisive significance.

CHRONOLOGY: The Russian Revolution

1894   Nicholas II becomes Tsar.

1895   Vladimir I. Ulyanov (Lenin) is arrested and sent to Siberia. Released in 1900 and leaves for the West, spending most of the next seventeen years in Switzerland.

" 'Stalin Is Too Rude' " is from Warren B. Walsh, ed., *Readings in Russian History*, 3rd ed. (Syracuse, N.Y.: Syracuse University Press, 1959), p. 626. Reprinted by permission of the publisher.

1902   Lenin writes *What Is to Be Done?* in which he criticized accommodations and short-term gains rather than true revolutionary change for the working class. He advocates a small elite party of professional revolutionaries. In *Two Tactics of Social Democracy* (1905), Lenin urges that the socialist revolution unite the proletariat and the peasants.

1904   Russo-Japanese war breaks out.

1905   Revolution breaks out in St. Petersburg after Bloody Sunday massacre (January 22). Japan defeats Russia (January). Manifesto establishes constitutional government and institution of the Duma, or representative assembly.

1906   Meeting of the First Duma (April). It is dissolved in July. Three subsequent Dumas elected and dismissed.

1914   Outbreak of the Great War.

March 15, 1917 Tsar Nicholas II abdicates the Russian throne.

March 19, 1917 Provisional Government established until a representative constituent assembly could be elected by the Russian people. Leadership assumed by Alexander Kerensky.

April 20, 1917 Lenin arrives in Petrograd, reasserts his leadership of the Bolshevik party, and issues the *April Theses*, which declares war on the Provisional Government and advocates the confiscation of all landed estates for redistribution to the people at a later time.

July 1917   Bolsheviks attempt a *coup* that is premature and fails. Lenin flees to Finland and his collaborator, Leon Trotsky, is arrested.

November 8, 1917 Lenin returns to Petrograd, convinces his skeptical colleagues to act. Trotsky organizes a successful *coup* on the Provisional Government. Bolsheviks seize power.

December 1917   Lenin, after achieving power through political manipulation and force of arms, decides to hold elections to legitimize the popular mandate of the people. Bolsheviks soundly defeated. Lenin does not concede defeat and dissolves Constituent Assembly. Freedom of the press curtailed and secret police (*Cheka*) organized.

March 3, 1918   Treaty of Brest-Litovsk formally ends Russian involvement in World War I. Poland, the Baltic States, and the Ukraine are ceded to Germany. The Bolsheviks agree to pay a heavy war indemnity.

1918–1921 Civil war between supporters of the Tsar (White Army) and the communists with the Red Army organized by Trotsky. Tsar Nicholas II is executed in the summer of 1918. In spite of aid to the Tsarist faction from the West, the Red Army eventually overcomes the domestic opposition. Under the economic policy of "War Communism," the revolutionary government confiscated and then operated the banks, transport facilities and heavy industry.

March 1921 Following the Kronstadt mutiny and in the face of peasant resistance to the requisition of grain necessary to feed the urban population, Lenin issues the New Economic Policy (NEP). Peasants allowed to farm for a profit and could sell surplus grain on the open market. Russia becomes a country of family farmers and small, private shops and businesses.

1924 Lenin dies after suffering a series of strokes starting in 1922. Two factions emerge: Trotsky and Stalin. Stalin uses the party apparatus to edge out Trotsky who is exiled in 1929 and murdered in 1940, presumably by Stalin's agents.

1929 Start of forced collectivization of land among kulaks. Resistance harshly dealt with by force and deportation.

1935–1939 Purge trials of Communist Party members in opposition to Stalin.

STUDY QUESTIONS

1. Why did Tsar Nicholas institute the first Imperial Duma? Analyze the Imperial Constitution. Would you consider this a liberal constitution presented by a progressive ruler? Why or why not? Consider the "First Declaration of the Provisional Government" in this regard.
2. Even before the events of 1905 and 1906, Lenin opposed the Russian monarchy. He asked the question "What is to be done?" What was his answer?
3. What reasons does Nicholas give for entering the war? What problems did the Russian people encounter? Compare the manifesto for entrance into the war with the tsar's abdication manifesto and the last address to the troops? Did his perspective change at all?
4. Analyze the demands of the Provisional Government and the Petrograd Soviet just after the abdication of the tsar. How are they similar and what are their differences? Note Lenin's ideas in his "April Theses." What action does he advocate? Is this consistent with his earlier ideas in "What Is to Be Done?"

5. What measures did Lenin take to protect the position of the Bolsheviks once they had achieved power? How does Lenin justify censorship of the press? Do fallacies or inconsistencies exist in his argument? Note especially the vocabulary. For example, how is the phrase "workmen's and peasants' revolution" used? How was the *Izvestiia* newspaper editorial dangerous to the Bolshevik revolution?

6. What are the duties of the secret police? What elements of society was this organization directed against? The tsar also had an active secret police that protected against "enemies of the monarchy." What is the difference between "enemies of the monarchy" and "enemies of the people"? Is a secret police therefore a necessary instrument for maintaining power, regardless of political philosophy?

7. What arguments do the Bolsheviks give to justify the dissolution of the Constituent Assembly? What gave them the authority to invalidate an assembly that was chosen by vote of the Russian people? Why did the Bolsheviks allow the election to occur in the first place?

8. What social or economic conditions contributed to the outbreak of the Russian Revolution? Although the Russian Revolution involved such strong personalities as Kerensky, Trotsky, and Stalin, it was Lenin who was the guiding spirit. What do his comments on the emancipation of women tell you about the man? Analyze his self-portrait. What kind of a man emerges? In Marxist theory, the individual is of little or no importance in contributing to the social and economic forces that result in the eventual destruction of capitalism and capitalist society. If so, how then does one explain Lenin? What was his role in the revolution? Without his presence, would the Russian Revolution have succeeded? To what extent can the individual change the course of history?

8

Adolf Hitler and the Nazi Rise to Power

Power is given only to him who dares to stoop and seize it. There is only one thing that matters, just one thing: you have to dare!

—Fyodor Dostoyevsky

Tyranny consists in the desire of universal power beyond its scope; it is the wish to have in one way what can only be had in another.

—Blaise Pascal

Order is the mother of civilization and liberty; chaos is the midwife of dictatorship.

—Will Durant

It is too difficult to think nobly when one only thinks to get a living.

—Jean Jacques Rousseau

There is nothing more terrible than ignorance in action.

—Johann von Goethe

With the end of the war in 1918, Europe entered a new age of change and development. Democratic governments had won the "war to make the world safe for democracy" and the aggressive German monarchy had been abolished.

Indeed, most other European nations adopted or maintained democratic institutions. The dominant theme, however, in the political history of Europe from 1919 to 1939 is the decline of these democratic governments. By the beginning of World War II in 1939, authoritarian regimes had been established in Italy, Germany, Spain, and throughout most of central and eastern Europe. The world was introduced to two of the most intriguing and destructive individuals of the twentieth century: Benito Mussolini and Adolf Hitler.

In order to understand the success of Hitler and the Nazis in particular, we must first look at the doctrine of fascism to which Hitler and many other twentieth-century dictators have subscribed. Fascism varies in its particular details of application, but in the simplest of terms, it is a doctrine that sanctifies the interests of the state and minimizes the rights of the individual. Fascism promotes as its great benefit the stability and security of the state.

Nearly all fascist governments have certain features in common. For example, fascism was born in direct opposition to liberal democracy, and as such regards personal freedom as dangerous to the stability of the state. Democracy, according to fascist doctrine, promotes individual expression and self-aggrandizement, which in turn results in disagreement and class conflict. Fascists also oppose socialism and communism since they promote the welfare of the masses over the good of the state. Communism, in fact, with its Leninist emphasis on the immediacy of world revolution, has dangerous potential for destabilization by its very insistence on class warfare. Fascism also depends on extreme nationalism. This goes far beyond the patriotic love of one's nation, but is based on pride in the allegedly unique characteristics and achievements of a "special" people. Therefore, fascist national pride is exclusive and implies a hostility toward other countries that are considered inferior in their outlook, governmental organization, or national heritage. This hostility is a unifying factor and is often vented against particular minority groups within the state itself. Thus, Hitler promoted hatred of the Jews as a rallying point for his support. This fascist national pride often expresses itself through imperialism, since military and economic expansion actually strengthens the state. Because stability and security of the state are the watchwords of fascism, it is important to implement a strong, highly centralized, and efficient government that only dictatorial rule can provide. One man with total control over the affairs of state ensures coordination and consistency of rule. Such a dictatorship is achieved and maintained through control of the national army, but most practically through paramilitary organizations like secret police, private armies, and bodyguards, which do not hesitate to use violence.

Fascism traditionally derives its support from the "right-wing" or conservative forces of society. The military represents, by its very nature, order and discipline. Big industrialists want to enjoy the lucrative profits that state stability affords; in a fascist society, general workers' strikes, which can often cripple an economy and interrupt production, are forbidden. Socially, fascism derives its mass support from the lower middle class. In general, these are people who have worked hard within the confines of society to attain some measure of self-respect. Sociologically, they are individuals of commitment and pride who harbor dreams of social mobility, have faith in traditional values, and love their country; they have much to lose from instability and chaos. The fascist, total-itarian regime is intended to eliminate class conflict by concentrating the energy of all its members in the service of the state.

Fascism is often born of the frustration and discontent of people who have been in some way humiliated or robbed of their dignity either as individuals or collectively as a nation. According to the philosopher Eric Hoffer, in his book *The True Believer* (New York: Harper & Row, 1951), people who are most susceptible to mass movements are filled with the burden of their present existence and seek inspiration from those who have a vision of a proud and stable future.

Fascism first took hold in Italy during the 1920s, when unemployment greeted returning war veterans and disruptive strikes crippled the economy. Liberal middle-class politicians lost control of the state and four Socialist governments fell in three years. In addition, Italy felt deprived of the "fruits of victory" from her involvement in World War I. She failed to obtain any of the German colonies in Africa and was frustrated in her attempt to acquire Albania as well. Amidst this frustration and dislocation, Benito Mussolini rose to power with his Italian National Fascist party ("Black Shirts"). Mussolini (1883-1945) promised stability and the vision of a "corporate state" in which each individual worked for the welfare of the entire nation. Mussolini guaran-teed employment and satisfactory wages for labor but did not permit strikes. He favored industrialists by allowing lucrative profits and gave respect to Italy by closely identifying his regime with the glorious heritage of the ancient Roman Empire. Mussolini succeeded in giving Italy direction and dignity, but he accomplished this through suppression of civil rights and individual liber-ties. He was, indeed, the quintessential fascist.

But perhaps the most important and influential of the authoritarian re-gimes in the subsequent history of Europe was established legally in Germany by Adolf Hitler and the National Socialist party.

After the abolition of the aggressive German monarchy in 1918, the Weimar Republic was established amid lofty ideals. Yet it labored under the burden of antirepublican pressures from the army, judiciary, bureaucracy, and even mon-archists who wanted to reinstate the kaiser. Germany had never had a strong democratic tradition and had been united under a central monarch for only about fifty years. The German republic was also weakened because it had been created during a time of national defeat and humiliation. Critics used the Republic as a scapegoat for Germany's ills and accused its democratic leaders of betraying the German armies by making an unacceptable peace. Faced with the threat of communist revolution in Germany and economic dislocation, which was prompted by incredible price inflation and devaluation of currency, the Weimar Republic struggled through the early 1920s. Even during a period of relative economic stability after 1924, the leaders of the Republic were unable to foster a coherent program because of the conflicting demands of coalition government.

In the summer of 1929, Germany felt the first effects of the worldwide depression. By the winter of 1929-1930, three million Germans were unemployed, a figure that increased to six million by 1933. The deepening depression made it increasingly difficult for the various parties in the coalition government to work together. In the elections of 1930, the moderate and prorepublican parties suffered a significant defeat; the greatest gains were made by the National Socialist party, headed by Adolf Hitler. The Nazis, as its members were called, had been a small, violent group on the fringes of antirepublican politics during the early 1920s. But by 1930, their membership had increased greatly and they were the most dynamic of the antidemocratic parties. Their success and popularity lay in providing, or at least promising, something for everyone. The Nazis promised a renegotiation of peace treaties and reestablishment of German honor and power to those who saw Germany's greatness shattered by the defeat in 1918 and the Treaty of Versailles in 1919. They promised efficient authoritarianism to those who were frustrated by the inadequacy of republican politics. The Nazis promised a strong economy to those (especially in the middle class) whose savings were threatened by the depression. Hitler also promised protection to the industrialists whose profits and very existence were jeopardized by the communist movement.

The central doctrine, however, of the National Socialist party was anti-Semitism. In his autobiography, *Mein Kampf* (My Struggle), and in speeches and party announcements, Hitler blamed the Jews for the economic crises of the 1920s. The inflation and depression, he argued, had been caused by Jewish international financiers. The Nazis also believed that the Jews controlled the international communist movement. Jews had to be excluded from German life, they concluded. In the unstable and violent years after 1929, more and more Germans seemed willing to accept this explanation for their difficult times.

As Hitler's influence grew, his followers advocated a violent seizure of power. Although he sanctioned violent political disruption and intimidation, Hitler insisted on attaining power legally. On January 30, 1933, after much political maneuvering, Hitler was appointed chancellor of the Weimar Republic. By July 1934, Hitler had legally altered the Weimar constitution, changed the nature of the Republic, removed all Jews and "politically unreliable" people from the bureaucracy, dissolved all opposition political parties, and purged the army. On August 2, 1934, President von Hindenburg died, and Hitler combined the offices of president and chancellor. The army formally supported these developments by swearing "unconditional obedience to the Fuehrer of the German Reich and People, Adolf Hitler." Hitler than began fashioning his own dictatorship.

In this chapter, we will look carefully at the political, social, and economic conditions that existed in Germany during the 1920s and early 1930s in an effort to understand why the Nazis were able to gain power. Themes that will emerge from the material include the use of racism and propaganda in the pursuit of power, as well as the role of the individual in history. Could Hitler have risen to lead Germany had he not been presented with the devastating social and economic conditions of the time? To what extent did Hitler change the course of history? In essence, why did Germany follow the leadership of Adolf Hitler? The complicated political maneuverings are not at issue here. Rather, it is important to try to understand people in crisis.

The Doctrine of Fascism

Before discussing the Nazi rise to power, one must understand the doctrine of fascism to which most of the right-wing dictatorships in the decades between the wars adhered. Benito Mussolini (1883–1945) was perhaps its most articulate spokesman. Mussolini was born the son of a blacksmith and worked as a school teacher and day laborer before becoming editor of a Socialist newspaper prior to World War I. He supported Italy's entry into the war and was wounded in the conflict. In 1919, he was one of many small-time candidates trying to make a mark in Italian politics. An amazing orator and opportunist, Mussolini's message of order and action won him the support of working and middle-class Italians who had been hit hard by the inflation that plagued Europe after the war. Mussolini even organized terrorist squads to contribute to the very instability that drew him adherents.

By 1922, the fascists controlled local governments in many cities in northern Italy. Mussolini initiated a march on Rome that met with no resistance from King Victor Emmanuel III. Concerned with violence and his personal safety, the king asked Mussolini to become prime minister and form a government. Although Mussolini had achieved power legally, he did not enjoy even a near majority in the Chamber of Deputies. He immediately disrupted the parliamentary government with threats and physical acts of violence against its elected members. Mussolini was then given temporary dictatorial powers by the king to stabilize the political situation; he soon turned these into a permanent and personal dominance.

The following selection is perhaps the quintessential defining statement of fascism. Mussolini believed that the twentieth century was a new historical epoch that required a different political premise based on popular loyalty to the State and supported by violent force.

"This Will Be the Century of the State"
BENITO MUSSOLINI

Fascism was not the nursling of a doctrine worked out beforehand with detailed elaboration; it was born of the need for action and it was itself from the beginning practical rather than theoretical; it was not merely another political party but, even in the first two years, in opposition to all

" 'This Will Be the Century of the State' " is from Benito Mussolini, "The Political and Social Doctrine of Fascism," in *International Conciliation*, no. 306 (January 1935), pp. 5–17. Reprinted by permission of the Carnegie Endowment for International Peace.

political parties as such. . . . If one were to re-read . . . the report of the meeting in which the *Fasci Italiani di Combattimento* [Italian Bands of Combat] were constituted, one would there find no ordered expression of doctrine, but a series of aphorisms, anticipations, and aspirations which, when refined by time from the original ore, were destined after some years to develop into an ordered series of doctrinal concepts, forming the Fascists' political doctrine—different from all others either of the past or the present day. . . .

We want to accustom the working-class to real and effectual leadership, and also to convince them that it is no easy thing to direct an industry or a commercial enterprise successfully. . . . We shall combat every retrograde idea, technical or spiritual. . . . When the succession to the seat of government is open, we must not be unwilling to fight for it. We must make haste; when the present regime breaks down, we must be ready at once to take its place. It is we who have the right to the succession, because it was we who forced the country into the War, and led her to victory. . . .

The years which preceded the March to Rome were years of great difficulty, during which the necessity for action did not permit research of any complete elaboration of doctrine. The battle had to be fought in the towns and villages. There was much discussion, but—what was more important and more sacred—men died. They knew how to die. Doctrine, beautifully defined and carefully elucidated, with headlines and paragraphs, might be lacking; but there was to take its place something more decisive—Faith. . . . But, since there was inevitably some lack of system, the adversaries of Fascism have disingenuously denied that it had any capacity to produce a doctrine of its own, though that doctrine was growing and taking shape under their very eyes . . . in the laws and institutions of the regime as enacted successively in the years 1926, 1927 and 1928. . . .

Above all, Fascism, the more it considers and observes the future and the development of humanity quite apart from political considerations of the moment, believes neither in the possibility nor the utility of perpetual peace. It thus repudiates the doctrine of Pacifism—born of a renunciation of the struggle and an act of cowardice in the face of sacrifice. War alone brings up to its highest tension all human energy and puts the stamp of nobility upon the peoples who have the courage to meet it. All other trials are substitutes, which never really put men into the position where they have to make the great decision—the alternative of life or death. Thus a doctrine which is founded upon this harmful postulate of peace is hostile to Fascism. . . . This anti-pacifist spirit is carried by Fascism even in the life of the individual. . . . The Fascist accepts life and loves it, knowing nothing of and despising suicide; he rather conceives of life as duty and struggle and conquest, life which would be high and full, lived for oneself, but above all for others—those who are at hand and those who are far distant contemporaries, and those who will come after. . . .

Such a conception of life makes Fascism the complete opposite of that doctrine, the base of the so-called scientific and Marxian Socialism, the materialist conception of history; according to which the history of human civilization can be explained simply through the conflict of interests among the various social groups and by the change and development in the means and instruments of production. That the changes in the economic field . . . have their importance no one can deny; but that these factors are sufficient to explain the history of humanity excluding all others is an absurd delusion. Fascism now and always, believes in holiness and in heroism; that is to say, in actions influenced by no economic motive, direct or indirect. . . . And above all Fascism denies that class war can be the preponderant force in the transformation of society. . . .

After Socialism, Fascism combats the whole complex system of democratic ideology; and repudiates it, whether in its theoretical premises or in its practical application. Fascism denies that the majority, by the simple fact that it is a majority, can direct human society; it denies that numbers alone can govern by means of a periodical consultation, and it affirms the immutable, beneficial, and fruitful inequality of mankind, which can never be permanently leveled through the mere operation of a mechanical process such as universal suffrage. The democratic regime may be defined as from time to time giving the people the illusion of sovereignty, while the real effective sovereignty lies in the hands of other concealed and irresponsible forces. Democracy is a regime nominally without a king, but it is ruled by many kings—more absolute, tyrannical, and ruinous than one sole king, even though a tyrant. . . .

Political doctrines pass, but humanity remains; and it may rather be expected that this will be a century of Fascism. For if the nineteenth century was the century of individualism (Liberalism always signifying individualism) it may be expected that this will be the century of collectivism, and hence the century of the State. . . .

The foundation of Fascism is the conception of the State. Fascism conceives of the State as an absolute, in comparison with which all individuals or groups are relative, only to be conceived of in their relation to the State. . . .

The Fascist State has drawn into itself even the economic activities of the nation, and through the corporative social and educational institutions created by it, its influence reaches every aspect of the national life and includes, framed in their respective organizations, all the political, economic and spiritual forces of the nation. A State which reposes upon the support of millions of individuals who recognize its authority, are continually conscious of its power and are ready at once to serve it, is not the old tyrannical State of the medieval lord nor has it anything in common with the absolute governments either before or after 1789. The individual in the Fascist State is not annulled but rather multiplied, just in the same way that a soldier in a regiment is not diminished but rather increased by the number of his comrades. The Fascist State organizes the nation, but leaves a sufficient margin of liberty to the individual; the latter is deprived of all useless and possibly harmful freedom, but retains what is essential. . . .

The Fascist State is an embodied will to power and government; the Roman tradition is here an ideal of force in action. According to Fascism, government is not so much a thing to be expressed in territorial or military terms as in terms of morality and the spirit. It must be thought of as an empire—that is to say, a nation which directly or indirectly rules other nations, without the need for conquering a single square yard of territory. For Fascism, the growth of empire, that is to say the expansion of the nation, is an essential manifestation of vitality, and its opposite a sign of decadence. Peoples which are rising, or rising again after a period of decadence, are always imperialist: any renunciation is a sign of decay and of death.

Fascism is the doctrine best adapted to represent the tendencies and the aspirations of a people, like the people of Italy, who are rising again after many centuries of abasement and foreign servitude. But empire demands discipline, the coordination of all forces and a deeply felt sense of duty and sacrifice; . . . for never before has the nation [Italy] stood more in need of authority, of direction, and of order. If every age has its own characteristic doctrine, there are a thousand signs which point to Fascism as the characteristic doctrine of our time. For if a doctrine must be a living thing, this is proved by the fact that Fascism has created a living faith; and that this faith is very powerful in the minds of men, is demonstrated by those who have suffered and died for it.

The Legacy of World War I

"I Resolved Now to Become a Politician"

ADOLF HITLER

On November 11, 1918, German representatives signed terms of surrender and the Great War came to an end. Although they were clearly beaten militarily, defeat came as a shock to the majority of Germans because they had been told, as late as September, that victory was certain. Adolf Hitler, a corporal at the time, was gassed during the night of October 13, 1918. While recuperating in a military hospital, he heard rumors of German surrender.

But then as the old gentleman tried to continue and began to tell us that now we had to end the long war, that even our fatherland would now be submitted to severe oppressions in the future, that now the War was lost and that we had to surrender to the mercy of the victors . . . that the armistice should be accepted with confidence in the generosity of our previous enemies . . . there I could stand it no more. It was impossible for

" 'I Resolved Now to Become a Politician' " is from *Mein Kampf* by Adolf Hitler, translated by Ralph Manheim, pp. 266–269. Copyright 1943 and copyright © renewed 1971 by Houghton Mifflin Company. Reprinted by permission of Houghton Mifflin Company.

me to stay any longer. While everything began to go black again before my eyes, stumbling, I groped my way back to the dormitory, threw myself on my cot and buried by burning head in the covers and pillows. . . .

Now all had been in vain. In vain all the sacrifices and deprivations, in vain the hunger and thirst of endless months, in vain the hours during which, gripped by the fear of death, we nevertheless did our duty, and in vain the death of two millions who died thereby. Would not the graves of all the hundred of thousands open up, the graves of those who once had marched out with faith in the fatherland, never to return? Would they not open up and send the silent heroes, covered with mud and blood, home as spirits of revenge, to the country that had so mockingly cheated them of the highest sacrifice which in this world man is able to bring to his people? Was it for this that they had died, the soldiers of August and September, 1914, was it for this that the regiments of volunteers followed the old comrades in the fall of the same year? Was it for this that boys of seventeen sank into Flanders Fields? Was that the meaning of the sacrifice which the German mother brought to the fatherland when in those days, with an aching heart, she let her most beloved boys go away, never to see them again? Was it all for this that now a handfull of miserable criminals was allowed to lay hands on the fatherland? . . .

I . . . resolved now to become a politician.

"Stabbed in the Back" (1919)

PAUL VON HINDENBURG

The following is a statement by the German field marshal Paul von Hindenburg (1847–1934) to the Committee of Enquiry in November 1919. The committee was established to investigate charges that Germany had provoked the war and committed war crimes. Hindenburg was one of the most influential German commanders during World War I and later became president of the German Weimar Republic (1925–1934). His statement reveals the dissatisfaction and betrayal that many Germans felt upon surrender.

In spite of the superiority of the enemy in men and materials, we could have brought the struggle to a favourable conclusion if determined and unanimous cooperation had existed between the army and those at home. But while the enemy showed an ever greater will for victory, divergent party interests began to show themselves with us. These circumstances soon led to a breaking up of our will to conquer. . . . Our operations therefore failed, as they were bound to, and the collapse became inevitable; the Revolution was merely that last straw. As an English General has truly said,

" 'Stabbed in the Back' " is from John W. Wheeler-Bennet, *Wooden Titan: Hindenburg in Twenty Years of German History, 1914–34*, pp. 235–236. Copyright © 1950. Reprinted by permission of Macmillan and Co., Ltd., London and Basingstoke.

"The German Army was stabbed in the back." It is plain enough on whom the blame lies.

The Treaty of Versailles (1919)

The Treaty of Versailles, which was signed by Germany on June 28, 1919, was a dictated peace designed to affix blame and to punish. The reduction of the army to 100,000 men and the territorial clauses, which eliminated areas abundant in natural resources, were viewed with outrage. The Germans were particularly incensed by the reparation clauses and the statement of German responsibility for the war contained in Article 231.

Article 227. The Allied and Associated Powers publicly arraign William II of Hohenzollern, formerly German Emperor, for a supreme offence against international morality and the sanctity of treaties.

A special tribunal will be constituted to try the accused, thereby assuring him the guarantees essential to the right of defence. It will be composed of five judges, one appointed by each of the following Powers: namely, the United States of America, Great Britain, France, Italy and Japan.

In its decision the tribunal will be guided by the highest motives of international policy, with a view to vindicating the solemn obligations of international undertakings and the validity of international morality. It will be its duty to fix the punishment which it considers should be imposed.

Article 228. The German Government recognises the right of the Allied and Associated Powers to bring before military tribunals persons accused of having committed acts of violation of the laws and customs of war. Such persons shall, if found guilty, be sentenced to punishments laid down by law.

Article 231. The Allied and Associated Governments affirm and Germany accepts the responsibility of Germany and her allies for causing all the loss and damage to which the Allied and Associated Governments and their nationals have been subjected as a consequence of the war imposed upon them by the aggression of Germany and her allies.

Article 232. The Allied and Associated Governments recognise that the resources of Germany are not adequate . . . to make complete reparation for all such loss and damage.

The Allied and Associated Governments, however, require, and Germany undertakes, that she will make compensation for all damage done to the civilian population of the Allied and Associated Powers . . . by such aggression by land, by sea, and from the air. . . .

Article 428. As a guarantee for the execution of the present Treaty by Germany, the German territory situated to the west of the Rhine together with the bridgeheads,will be occupied by Allied and Associated troops for a period of fifteen years from the coming into force of the present Treaty.

"The Treaty of Versailles" is from Great Britain, *State Papers*, vol. 112 (1919), pp. 104 ff.

Article 430. In case either during the occupation or after the expiration of the fifteen years referred to above the Reparation Commission finds that Germany refuses to observe the whole or part of her obligations under the present Treaty with regard to reparation, the whole or part of the areas specified will be re-occupied immediately by the Allied and Associated forces.

Article 431. If before the expiration of the period of fifteen years Germany complies with all the undertakings resulting from the present Treaty, the occupying forces will be withdrawn immediately.

The Weimar Republic

The Weimar Republic, burdened by the specter of defeat and shame, was impotent to meet the economic and political problems of the 1920s. The portion of the constitution that follows reflects the liberal idealism of the Social Democratic, Catholic Center, and Democratic parties that shaped it. Although there was much opposition to these beliefs from the National Socialist (Nazi) party among others, many Germans were still loyal to the Republic, as the second selection reveals.

The Weimar Constitution: Fundamental Rights and Duties of the Germans (1919)

Section I: The Individual

Article 109. All Germans are equal before the law. Men and women have the same fundamental civil rights and duties. Public legal privileges or disadvantages of birth or of rank are abolished. Titles of nobility . . . may be bestowed no longer . . . Orders and decorations shall not be conferred by the state. No German shall accept titles or orders from a foreign government.

Article 110. Citizenship of the Reich and the states is acquired in accordance with the provisions of a Reich law. . . .

Article 111. All Germans shall enjoy liberty of travel and residence throughout the whole Reich. . . .

Article 112. Every German is permitted to emigrate to a foreign country. . . .

Article 114. Personal liberty is inviolable. Curtailment or deprivation of personal liberty by a public authority is permissible only by authority of law.

Persons who have been deprived of their liberty must be informed at the latest on the following day by whose authority and for what reasons they have been held. They shall receive the opportunity without delay of submitting objections to their deprivation of liberty.

Article 115. The house of every German is his sanctuary and is inviolable. Exceptions are permitted only by authority of law. . . .

Article 117. The secrecy of letters and all postal, telegraph, and telephone communications is inviolable. Exceptions are inadmissable by national law.

Article 118. Every German has the right, within the limits of the general laws, to express his opinion freely by word, in writing, in print, in picture form, or in any other way. . . . Censorship is forbidden. . . .

Section II. The General Welfare

Article 123. All Germans have the right to assemble peacefully and unarmed without giving notice and without special permission. . . .

Article 124. All Germans have the right to form associations and societies for purposes not contrary to the criminal law. . . .

Article 126. Every German has the right to petition. . . .

Section III. Religion and Religious Societies

Article 135. All inhabitants of the Reich enjoy full religious freedom and freedom of conscience. The free exercise of religion is guaranteed by the Constitution and is under public protection. . . .

Article 137. There is no state church. . . .

Section IV. Education and the Schools

Article 144. The entire school system is under the supervision of the state. . . .

Article 145. Attendance at school is compulsory. . . .

Section V: Economic Life

Article 151. The regulation of economic life must be compatible with the principles of justice, with the aim of attaining humane conditions of existence for all. Within these limits the economic liberty of the individual is assured. . . .

Article 152. Freedom of contract prevails . . . in accordance with the laws. . . .

Article 153. The right of private property is guaranteed by the Constitution. . . . Expropriation of property may take place . . . by due process of law. . . .

Article 159. Freedom of association for the preservation and promotion of labor and economic conditions is guaranteed to everyone and to all vocations. All agreements and measures attempting to restrict or restrain this freedom are unlawful. . . .

Article 161. the Reich shall organize a comprehensive system of [social] insurance. . . .

Article 165. Workers and employees are called upon to cooperate, on an equal footing, with employers in the regulation of wages and of the conditions of labor, as well as in the general development of the productive forces. . . .

Loyalty to the Weimar Republic

LILO LINKE

A procession was formed, headed by the military band with triangles and drums and clarinets and followed by the members of the movement, two abreast, holding their torches in their upraised hands. We marched through the town, our ghostly magnified shadows moving restlessly over the fronts of the houses.

Never before had I followed the flag of the Republic, which was now waving thirty yards in front of me, spreading its colours overhead, the black melting in one with the night, the red glowing in the light of the torches, and the gold overshining them like a dancing sun. It was not just a torchlight march for me, it was a political confession. I had decided to take part in the struggle for German democracy. I wanted to fight for it although I knew that this meant a challenge to my parents and my whole family, who all lived with their eyes turned towards the past and thought it disloyal and shameful to help the Socialists.

We marched out of the town to the cemetery, where the first President of the Republic, Fritz Ebert, has been buried. Silently we assembled round the grave. Wilhelm Wismar, national leader of the Young Democrats and youngest member of the Reichstag, stepped forward and spoke slowly the oath.

"We vow to stand for the Republic with all our abilities and strength."

"We vow to work for the fulfillment of the promises given to the German people in the Weimar Constitution."

"We vow to shield and defend democracy against all its enemies and attackers whoever they might be."

And out of the night in a rolling echo two thousand citizens of tomorrow answered, repeating solemnly word for word:

"We vow to stand for the Republic with all our abilities and strength."

"We vow to work for the fulfillment of the promises given to the German people in the Weimar Constitution."

"We vow to shield and defend democracy against all its enemies and attackers whoever they might be."

Inflation: "The Boiling Kettle of a Wicked Witch"

LILO LINKE

Inflation, or the decline in the value of currency with the attendant rise in prices, engulfed Germany in the early 1920s, reaching a peak in 1923. The following accounts reflect some of the difficulties and frustrations felt by people of the time. The middle classes were especially affected and their hard-earned savings became worthless. Both Lilo Linke and Konrad Heiden witnessed the hardship of these days. Heiden was particularly active against the Nazis in street confrontations as a student at the University of Munich in 1923.

The time for my first excursions into life was badly chosen. Rapidly Germany was precipitated into the inflation, thousands, millions, milliards of marks whirled about, making heads swim in confusion. War, revolution, and the wild years after had deprived everyone of old standards and the possibility of planning a normal life. Again and again fate hurled the helpless individual into the boiling kettle of a wicked witch. Now the inflation came and destroyed the last vestige of steadiness. Hurriedly one had to make use of the moment and could not consider the following day.

The whole population had suddenly turned into maniacs. Everyone was buying, selling, speculating, bargaining, and dollar, dollar, dollar was the magic word which dominated every conversation, every newspaper, every poster in Germany. Nobody understood what was happening. There seemed to be no sense, no rules in the mad game, but one had to take part in it if one did not want to be trampled underfoot at once. Only a few people were able to carry through to the end and gain by the inflation. The majority lost everything and broke down, impoverished and bewildered.

The middle class was hurt more than any other, the savings of a lifetime and their small fortunes melted into a few coppers. They had to sell their most precious belongings for ten milliard inflated marks to buy a bit of food or an absolutely necessary coat, and their pride and dignity were bleeding out of many wounds. Bitterness remained for ever in their hearts. Full of hatred, they accused the international financiers, the Jews and Socialists—their old enemies—of having exploited their distress. They never forgot and never forgave and were the first to lend a willing ear to Hitler's fervent preaching.

In the shop, notices announced that we should receive our salaries in weekly parts; after a while we queued up at the cashier's desk every evening, and before long we were paid twice daily and ran out during the lunch hour to buy a few things, because as soon as the new rate of exchange became known in the early afternoon our money had again lost half its value.

In the beginning I did not concern myself much with these happenings.

They merely added to the excitement of my new life, which was all that mattered to me. Living in the east of Berlin and in hard times, I was long accustomed to seeing people around me in hunger, distress, and poverty. My mother was always lamenting that it was impossible for her to make both ends meet, my father—whenever he was at home—always asking what the deuce she had done with all the money he had given her yesterday. A few tears, a few outbreaks more did not make a difference great enough to impress me deeply.

Yet, in the long run, the evil influence of the inflation, financially as well as morally, penetrated even to me. Berlin had become the centre of international profiteers and noisy new rich. For a few dollars they could buy the whole town, drinks and women, horses and houses, virtue and vice, and they made free use of these possibilities.

The Devaluation of Currency
KONRAD HEIDEN

They all stood in lines outside the pay-windows, staring impatiently at the electric wall clock, slowly advancing until at last they reached the window and received a bag full of paper notes. According to the figures inscribed on them, the paper notes amounted to seven hundred thousand or five hundred million, or three hundred and eighty billion, or eighteen trillion marks—the figures rose from month to month, then from week to week, finally from day to day. With their bags the people moved quickly to the doors, all in haste, the younger ones running. They dashed to the nearest food store, where a line had already formed. Again they moved slowly, oh how slowly, forward. When you reached the store, a pound of sugar might have been obtainable for two millions; but, by the time you came to the counter, all you could get for two millions was half a pound, and the saleswoman said the dollar had just gone up again. With the millions and billions you bought sardines, sausages, sugar, perhaps even a little butter, but as a rule the cheaper margarine—always things that would keep for a week, until next pay-day, until the next stage in the fall of the mark.

Hitler's Response to Germany's Problems

The National Socialist party produced a program in 1920 that formed the basis of Hitler's campaign against the Weimar Republic. The succeeding selections of speeches and rally announcements not only reveal Nazi ideology but also testify to the dynamism of Nazi propaganda.

"The Devaluation of Currency" is from *Der Fuehrer* by Konrad Heiden, translated by Ralph Manheim, p. 126. Copyright 1944 by Konrad Heiden. Copyright © renewed 1971 by Bernhard E. Bartels, Executor of the Estate. Reprinted by permission of the Houghton Mifflin Company.

The Nazi Program (1920)

The program is the political foundation of the NSDAP [Nazi Party] and accordingly the primary political law of the State. It has been made brief and clear intentionally.

All legal precepts must be applied in the spirit of the party program.

Since the taking over of control, the Fuehrer has succeeded in the realization of essential portions of the Party program from the fundamentals to the detail.

The Party Program of the NSDAP was proclaimed on the 24 February 1920 by Adolf Hitler at the first large Party gathering in Munich and since that day has remained unaltered. Within the national socialist philosophy is summarized in 25 points:

1. We demand the unification of all Germans in the Greater Germany on the basis of the right of self-determination of peoples.

2. We demand equality of rights for the German people in respect to the other nations; abrogation of the peace treaties of Versailles and St. Germain.

3. We demand land and territory [colonies] for the sustenance of our people, and colonization for our surplus population.

4. Only a member of the race can be a citizen. A member of the race can only be one who is of German blood, without consideration of creed. Consequently no Jew can be a member of the race.

5. Whoever has no citizenship is to be able to live in Germany only as a guest, and must be under the authority of legislation for foreigners.

6. The right to determine matters concerning administration and law belongs only to the citizen. Therefore we demand that every public office, of any sort whatsoever, whether in the Reich, the county or municipality, be filled only by citizens. . . .

7. We demand that the state be charged first with providing the opportunity for a livelihood and way of life for citizens. If it is impossible to sustain the total population of the State, then the members of foreign nations (non-citizens) are to be expelled from the Reich.

8. Any further immigration of non-citizens is to be prevented. We demand that all non-Germans, who have immigrated to Germany since the 2 August 1914, be forced immediately to leave the Reich.

9. All citizens must have equal rights and obligations.

10. The first obligation of every citizen must be to work both spiritually and physically. . . .

13. We demand the nationalization of all [previous] associated industries [trusts].

"The Nazi Program" is from "National Socialist Yearbook, 1941," Office of the U.S. Chief Counsel for Prosecution of Axis Criminality, *Nazi Conspiracy and Aggression* (Washington, D.C.: Government Printing Office, 1946), vol.4, pp. 208–211.

14. We demand a division of profits of all heavy industries.

15. We demand an expansion on a large scale of old age welfare.

16. We demand the creation of a healthy middle class and its conservation. . . .

18. We demand struggle without consideration against those whose activity is injurious to the general interest. Common national criminals, usurers . . . and so forth are to be punished with death, without consideration of confession or race.

20. The state is to be responsible for a fundamental reconstruction of our whole national education program, to enable every capable and industrious German to obtain higher education and subsequently introduction into leading positions. . . .

21. The State is to care for the elevating of national health by protecting the mother and child, by outlawing child-labor, by the encouragement of physical fitness, by means of the legal establishment of a gymnastic and sport obligation, by the utmost support of all organizations concerned with the physical instruction of the young.

23. We demand legal opposition to known lies and their promulgation through the press. In order to enable the provision of a German press, we demand, that: (a) All writers and employees of the newspapers appearing in the German language be members of the race: (b) Non-German newspapers be required to have the express permission of the State to be published. They may not be printed in the German language: (c) Non-Germans are forbidden by law any financial interest in German publications, or any influence on them, and as punishment for violations the closing of such a publication as well as the immediate expulsion from the Reich of the non-German concerned. Publications which are counter to the general good are to be forbidden. We demand legal prosecution of artistic and literary forms which exert a destructive influence on our national life, and the closure of organizations opposing the above made demands.

24. We demand freedom of religion for all religious denominations within the state so long as they do not endanger its existence or oppose the moral senses of the Germanic race. The Party as such advocates the standpoint of a positive Christianity without binding itself confessionally to any one denomination. It combats the Jewish-materialistic spirit within and around us, and is convinced that a lasting recovery of our nation can only succeed from within on the framework: common utility precedes individual utility.

25. For the execution of all of this we demand the formation of a strong central power in the Reich. Unlimited authority of the central parliament over the whole Reich and its organizations in general. The forming of state and profession chambers for the execution of the laws made by the Reich within the various states of the confederation. The leaders of the Party promise, if necessary by sacrificing their own lives, to support the execution of the points set forth above without consideration.

Speech on the Treaty of Versailles (April 17, 1923)

ADOLF HITLER

With the armistice begins the humiliation of Germany. If the Republic on the day of its foundation had appealed to the country: "Germans, stand together! Up and resist the foe! The Fatherland, the Republic expects of you that you fight to your last breath," then millions who are now enemies of the Republic would be fanatical Republicans. Today they are the foes of the Republic not because it is a Republic but because this Republic was founded at the moment when Germany was humiliated, because it so discredited the new flag that men's eyes must turn regretfully towards the old flag.

So long as this Treaty stands there can be no resurrection of the German people; no social reform of any kind is possible! The Treaty was made in order to bring 20 million Germans to their deaths and to ruin the German nation. But those who made the Treaty cannot set it aside. As its foundation our Movement formulated three demands:

1. Setting aside of the Peace Treaty.
2. Unification of all Germans.
3. Land and soil [*Grund und Boden*] to feed our nation.

Our movement could formulate these demands, since it was not our Movement which caused the War, it has not made the Republic, it did not sign the Peace Treaty.

There is thus one thing which is the first task of this Movement: it desires to make the German once more National, that his Fatherland shall stand for him above everything else. It desires to teach our people to understand afresh the truth of the old saying: He who will not be a hammer must be an anvil. An anvil are we today, and that anvil will be beaten until out of the anvil we fashion once more a hammer, a German sword!

Nazi Political Rally Announcement (February 1921)

NATIONAL SOCIALIST GERMAN WORKERS' PARTY

Fellow Citizens!

A year ago we called you to the Zirkus Krone. For the first time we invited you to a giant protest against making Germany defenseless by disarmament. We declared that this making her defenseless would be the prelude for the loss of Upper Silesia.

"Speech on the Treaty of Versailles" is from Norman H. Baynes, trans. and ed., *The Speeches of Adolf Hitler, April 1922–1939*, vol. 1 (London: Oxford University Press, 1942), pp. 56–57. Reprinted by permission of the publisher.

"Nazi Political Rally Announcement" is from *Mein Kampf* by Adolf Hitler, translated by Ralph Manheim, pp. 546–547. Copyright 1943 and copyright © renewed 1971 by Houghton Mifflin Company. Reprinted by permission of Houghton Mifflin Company.

For the second time we invite you to resist against the Paris Dictate. We called it the permanent enslavement of Germany. . . .

Poverty no longer begins to appear, it is here. And though one does not feel it in the armchairs of the parliaments and in the soft cushions of our people's leaders it is felt all the more by the millions who have been cheated, by the masses of the people who do not live by cheating, profiteering and usury, but by the sweat of their honest work. But we are not only a poor people, we are also a miserable people.

We have forgotten the millions of our fellow citizens who once, during a long four and a half years, bled for Germany's existence on innumerable battlefields, and of whom our fatherland has been robbed by a cruel fate.

We have forgotten the millions of those Germans who longingly await the day which brings them home to a country that even as the poorest would still present the happiness of being their fatherland. We have forgotten the Rhineland and Upper Silesia, forgotten German-Austria and the millions of our brothers in Czechoslovakia, forgotten Alsace-Lorraine and the Palatinate, and while our beloved Germany thus lies dismembered, powerless and torn, disgracefully robbed, a colony of the international world criminals, there—we dance.

We invite you to come Thursday, February 2, 1921, to a GIANT DEMONSTRATION for a coming GREATER GERMANY to the Zirkus Krone, Engineer Rudolf JUNG, Deputy of the Prague Parliament, and Party Member Adolf HITLER will speak about:

'GERMANY IN HER DEEPEST HUMILIATION'

Beginning 8 p.m., end 10 p.m.   Jews not admitted

To cover expenses of the hall and posters, admission M.I. War invalids free.

Fellow citizens, white collar and manual workers, Germans from all countries of our fatherland, come in masses!

[The meeting was attended by more than seven thousand persons.]

Nazi Appeal and Victory

Nazi Propaganda

In order to rise to power, an organization or individual must promote ideas, gain converts, and feed on mistakes of the opposition. Where no problems exist, they must be created, and where they are real, they must be exposed and used to advantage. Such is the nature and purpose of propaganda. The first selection is a pamphlet composed in 1930 by Dr. Joseph Goebbels, the future minister of propaganda for the Third Reich. It was important to focus on enemies, whether they were cowards, communists, or Jews, since fear and hatred can often unify a people more readily than positive ideas.

Unity must also be achieved through leadership. Above anything else, the Nazis promoted faith over rational thought. The National Socialist program

could be reduced to two words: Adolf Hitler. His mythic presence is seen in the second selection, which appeared in the newspaper Völkischer Beobachter *just before an election on March 13, 1932. As Hitler noted, "The most brilliant propaganda technique must concentrate on a few points and repeat them over and over." He understood that in troubled times, people want a simple explanation for their pain and insecurity—and then they want the pain to go away.*

Nationalists, Socialists, and Jews (1930)

JOSEPH GOEBBELS

WHY ARE WE NATIONALISTS?

We are NATIONALISTS because we see in the NATION the only possibility for the protection and the furtherance of our existence.

The NATION is the organic bond of a people for the protection and defense of their lives. He is nationally minded who understands this IN WORD AND IN DEED.

Today, in GERMANY, NATIONALISM has degenerated into BOURGEOIS PATRIOTISM, and its power exhausts itself in tilting at windmills. . . .

Young nationalism has its unconditional demands. BELIEF IN THE NATION is a matter of all the people, not for individuals of rank, a class, or an industrial clique. The eternal must be separated from the contemporary. The maintenance of a rotten industrial system has nothing to do with nationalism. I can love Germany and hate capitalism; not only CAN I do it, I also MUST do it. The germ of the rebirth of our people LIES ONLY IN THE DESTRUCTION OF THE SYSTEM OF PLUNDERING THE HEALTHY POWER OF THE PEOPLE.

WE ARE NATIONALISTS BECAUSE WE, AS GERMANS, LOVE GERMANY. And because we love Germany, we demand the protection of its national spirit and we battle against its destroyers.

WHY ARE WE SOCIALISTS?

We are SOCIALISTS because we see in SOCIALISM the only possibility for maintaining our racial existence and through it the reconquest of our political freedom and the rebirth of the German state. SOCIALISM has its peculiar form first of all through its comradeship in arms with the forward-driving energy of a newly awakened nationalism. Without nationalism it is nothing, a phantom, a theory, a vision of air, a book. With it, it is everything, THE FUTURE, FREEDOM, FATHERLAND!

It was a sin of the liberal bourgeoisie to overlook THE STATEBUILDING POWER OF SOCIALISM. It was the sin of MARXISM to degrade SOCIALISM to a system of MONEY AND STOMACH.

We are SOCIALISTS because for us THE SOCIAL QUESTION IS A MATTER OF NECESSITY AND JUSTICE, and even beyond that A MATTER FOR THE VERY EXISTENCE OF OUR PEOPLE.

DOWN WITH POLITICAL BOURGEOIS SENTIMENT: FOR REAL NATIONALISM!

DOWN WITH MARXISM: FOR TRUE SOCIALISM!

UP WITH THE STAMP OF THE FIRST GERMAN NATIONAL SOCIALIST STATE!

AT THE FRONT THE NATIONAL SOCIALIST GERMAN WORKERS PARTY! . . .

WHY DO WE OPPOSE THE JEWS?

We are ENEMIES OF THE JEWS, because we are fighters for the freedom of the German people. THE JEW IS THE CAUSE AND THE BENEFICIARY OF OUR MISERY. He has used the social difficulties of the broad masses of our people to deepen the unholy split between Right and Left among our people. He has made two halves of Germany. He is the real cause for our loss of the Great War.

The Jew has no interest in the solution of Germany's fateful problems. He CANNOT have any. FOR HE LIVES ON THE FACT THAT THERE HAS BEEN NO SOLUTION. If we could make the German people a unified community and give them freedom before the world, then the Jew can have no place among us. He has the best trumps in his hands when a people lives in inner and outer slavery. THE JEW IS RESPONSIBLE FOR OUR MISERY AND HE LIVES ON IT.

That is the reason why we, AS NATIONALISTS and AS SOCIALISTS, oppose the Jew. HE HAS CORRUPTED OUR RACE, FOULED OUR MORALS, UNDERMINED OUR CUSTOMS, AND BROKEN OUR POWER.

THE JEW IS THE PLASTIC DEMON OF THE DECLINE OF MANKIND.

THE JEW IS UNCREATIVE. He produces nothing. HE ONLY HANDLES PRODUCTS. As long as he struggles against the state, HE IS A REVOLUTIONARY; as soon as he has power, he preaches QUIET AND ORDER, so that he can consume his plunder at his convenience.

ANTI-SEMITISM IS UN-CHRISTIAN. That means, then, that he is a Christian who looks on while the Jew sews straps around our necks. TO BE A CHRISTIAN MEANS: LOVE THY NEIGHBOR AS THYSELF! MY NEIGHBOR IS ONE WHO IS TIED TO ME BY HIS BLOOD. IF I LOVE HIM, THEN I MUST HATE HIS ENEMIES. HE WHO THINKS GERMAN MUST DESPISE THE JEWS. The one thing makes the other necessary.

WE ARE ENEMIES OF THE JEWS BECAUSE WE BELONG TO THE GERMAN PEOPLE. THE JEW IS OUR GREATEST MISFORTUNE.

It is not true that we eat a Jew every morning at breakfast.

It is true, however, that he SLOWLY BUT SURELY ROBS US OF EVERYTHING WE OWN.

THAT WILL STOP, AS SURELY AS WE ARE GERMANS.

Free Germany! (1932)

The National Socialist movement, assembled, at this hour, as a fighting squad around its leader, today calls on the entire German people to join its ranks, and to pave a path that will bring Adolf Hitler to the head of the nation, and thus

HITLER is the password of all who believe in Germany's resurrection.

HITLER is the last hope of those who were deprived of everything: of farm and home, of savings, employment, survival; and who have but one possession left: their faith in a just Germany which will once again grant to its citizens honor, freedom, and bread.

HITLER is the word of deliverance for millions, for they are in despair, and see only in this name a path to new life and creativity.

HITLER was bequeathed the legacy of the two million dead comrades of the World War, who died not for the present system of the gradual destruction of our nation, but for Germany's future.

HITLER is the man of the people hated by the enemy because he understands the people and fights for the people.

HITLER is the furious will of Germany's youth, which, in the midst of a tired generation, is fighting for new forms, and neither can nor will abandon its faith in a better German future. Hence Hitler is the password and the flaming signal of all who wish for a German future.

All of them, on March 13, will call out to the men of the old system who promised them freedom, and dignity, and delivered stones and words instead: We have known enough of you. Now you are to know us!

Statistical Evidence

The statistical table on the following page reveals the increasing popularity of the National Socialist party from 1924, when the Nazis first appeared on a ballot, to 1932, the last free election before Hitler's accession to power. Note the direct relationship of Nazi popularity to the unemployment figures.

"Free Germany!" is from *The Nazi Years: A Documentary History,* edited by Joachim Remak, p. 45. © 1969. Used by permission of Prentice-Hall, Inc., Englewood Cliffs, N.J.

Elections to the German Reichstag (1924–1932)

	May 4, 1924	December 7, 1924	May 20, 1928	September 14, 1930	July 31, 1932	November 6, 1932
Number of eligible voters (in millions)	38.4	39.0	41.2	43.0	44.2	44.2
Votes cast (in millions)	29.7	30.7	31.2	35.2	37.2	35.7
National Socialist German Workers party (Nazi)	1,918,000 6.6%	908,000 3%	810,000 2.6%	6,407,000 18.3%	13,779,000 37.3%	11,737,000 33.1%
German Nationalist People's party (Conservative)	5,696,000 19.5%	6,209,000 20.5%	4,382,000 14.2%	2,458,000 7%	2,187,000 5.9%	3,131,000 8.8%
Center party (Catholic)	3,914,000 13.4%	4,121,000 13.6%	3,712,000 12.1%	4,127,000 11.8%	4,589,000 12.4%	4,230,000 11.9%
Democratic party (The German State Party)	1,655,000 5.7%	1,921,000 6.3%	1,506,000 4.9%	1,322,000 3.8%	373,000 1%	339,000 1%
Social Democratic party	6,009,000 20.5%	7,886,000 26%	9,153,000 29.8%	8,575,000 24.5%	7,960,000 21.6%	7,251,000 20.4%
Communist party	3,693,000 12.6%	2,712,000 9%	3,265,000 10.6%	4,590,000 13.1%	5,370,000 14.3%	5,980,000 16.9%

Unemployment in Germany (1924–1932)*

1924	1928	1930	July 31, 1932	October 31, 1932
978,000	1,368,000	3,076,000	5,392,000	5,109,000

*The figures are those of annual average unemployment, except for 1932, where some precise end-of-the-month figures are available, and the two dates that coincide with the Reichstag elections are given.

"Elections to the German Reichstag" is from *The Nazi Years: A Documentary History*, edited by Joachim Remak, p. 44. © 1969. Used by permission of Prentice-Hall, Inc., Englewood Cliffs, N.J.

Parade through Brandenburg Gate (January 30, 1933). The Nazi celebrated the appointment of Adolf Hitler as chancellor of the Weimar Republic with a night rally. The dismantling of the Weimar Constitution began almost immediately. (*Bundesarchiva*)

Chancellor to Dictator

By 1932, the Nazis had emerged as Germany's strongest single party. Hitler demanded the chancellorship of the Weimar Republic. The president, Paul von Hindenburg, disliked Hitler and resisted entrusting all governmental authority to a single party which "held to such a one-sided attitude toward people with convictions different from theirs." But on January 30, 1933, Hindenburg gave in to political pressure and popular demand and appointed Hitler chancellor. The Nazis were confirmed in power and immediately began to dismantle the Weimar Constitution. On the night of February 27, 1933, the Reichstag building burned. The Nazis blamed the communists and issued the "Decree for the Protection of the People and State," an article of which is presented in the first selection.

The second selection is the famous Enabling Act, which allowed Hitler and his Reich Cabinet to issue laws that could deviate from the established constitution, yet could not practically be challenged by representatives of the Reichstag. Its overwhelming passage (444 to 94) gave the destruction of parliamentary democracy an appearance of legality; from then on, the Reichstag became a rubber stamp of approval for Hitler's decrees. The succeeding documents show the conversion of Hitler's chancellorship to a dictatorship.

Decree for the Protection of the People and State (February 28, 1933)

In virtue of Section 48 (2) of the German Constitution, the following is decreed as a defensive measure against Communist acts of violence endangering the state:

Article 1

Sections 114, 115, 117, 118, 123, 124, and 153 of the Constitution of the German Reich are suspended until further notice. Thus, restrictions on personal liberty, on the right of free expression of opinion, including freedom of the press, on the right of assembly and the right of association, and violations of the privacy of postal, telegraphic, and telephone communications, and warrants for house-searches, orders for confiscations as well as restrictions on property, are also permissible beyond the legal limits otherwise prescribed.

"Decree for the Protection of the People and State" is from Office of the U.S. Chief Counsel for Prosecution of Axis Criminality, *Nazi Conspiracy and Aggression* (Washington, D.C.: Government Printing Office, 1946), vol. 1, p. 126 (PS-1390).

The Enabling Act (March 24, 1933)

The Reichstag has passed the following law, which is, with the approval of the Reichsrat [upper house], herewith promulgated, after it has been established that it satisfies the requirements for legislation altering the Constitution.

Article 1: In addition to the procedure for the passage of legislation outlined in the Constitution, the Reich Cabinet is also authorized to enact Laws.

Article 2: The national laws enacted by the Reich Cabinet may deviate from the Constitution provided they do not affect the position of the Reichstag and the Reichsrat. The powers of the President remain unaffected.

Article 3: The national laws enacted by the Reich Cabinet shall be prepared by the Chancellor and published in the official gazette. They come into effect, unless otherwise specified, upon the day following their publication. Articles 68–77 of the Constitution [concerning the enactment of new legislation] do not apply to the laws enacted by the Reich Cabinet.

Article 4: Treaties of the Reich with foreign states which concern matters of domestic legislation do not require the consent of the bodies participating in legislation. The Reich Cabinet is empowered to issue the necessary provisions for the implementing of these treaties.

Article 5: This law comes into effect on the day of its publication.

Law against the New Formation of Parties (July 14, 1933)

The government has passed the following law, which is being proclaimed herewith:

ARTICLE 1

The sole political party existing in Germany is the National Socialist German Workers' Party.

ARTICLE 2

Whoever shall undertake to maintain the organization of another party, or to found a new party, shall be punished with a sentence of hard labor of up

"The Enabling Act" is from Jeremy Noakes and Geoffrey Pridham, eds., *Documents on Nazism, 1919–1945*, p. 195. Reprinted by permission of A. D. Peters & Co., Ltd.

"Law against the New Formation of Parties" and "Law Concerning the Head of the German State" are from *The Nazi Years: A Documentary History*, edited by Joachim Remak, p. 54. © 1969. Used by permission of Prentice-Hall, Inc., Englewood Cliffs, N.J.

to three years, or of prison between six months and three years, unless other regulations provide for heavier punishment.

> The Chancellor
> s. ADOLF HITLER
> The Minister of the Interior
> s. FRICK
> The Minister of Justice
> s. GURTNER

Law Concerning the Head of the German State (August 1, 1934)

The government has passed the following law, which is being proclaimed herewith:

ARTICLE 1

The office of President shall be combined with that of Chancellor. Thus all the functions heretofore exercised by the President are transferred to the Fuhrer and Chancellor Adolf Hitler. He has the right to appoint his deputy.

The Role of Women in the Nazi State

> *Once Hitler and his National Socialist party were firmly seated in power, he began to enact legislation designed to restrict Jews and other racial groups whose presence threatened his plans for a racially pure society. Women became the cornerstone of the new social policy. Their role in the state as wives and mothers was crucial to Hitler's sense of future and the establishment of his "thousand-year" Reich. Two weeks after Hitler received 88 percent of the votes in a plebiscite and assumed the title "Reichführer," he delivered this speech at Nuremberg and articulated his vision of the role of women in the Nazi state.*

"Our Fanatical Fellow-Combatants" (September 8, 1934)

ADOLF HITLER

If one says that man's world is the State, his struggle, his readiness to devote his powers to the service of the community, one might be tempted to say that the world of woman is a smaller world. For her world is her

" 'Our Fanatical Fellow-Combatants' " is from Raoul de Roussy de Sales, ed., *My New Order* (New York: Reynal & Hitchcock, Inc., 1941), pp. 286–289. Reprinted by permission of Harcourt Brace Jovanovich.

husband, her family, her children, and her house. But where would the greater world be if there were no one to care for the small world? How could the greater world survive if there were none to make the cares of the smaller world the content of their lives? . . . Providence has entrusted to woman the cares of that world which is peculiarly her own, and only on the basis of this smaller world can the man's world be formed and built up. These two worlds are never in conflict. They are complementary to each other, they belong together as man and woman belong together. . . .

Every child that a woman brings into the world is a battle, a battle waged for the existence of her people. Man and woman must therefore mutually value and respect each other when they see that each performs the task which Nature and Providence have ordained. And from this separation of the functions of each there will necessarily result this mutual respect. It is not true, as Jewish intellectuals assert, that respect depends upon the overlapping of the spheres of activity of the sexes: this respect demands that neither sex should try to do that which belongs to the other's sphere. Respect lies in the last resort in this: that each knows that the other is doing everything which is necessary to maintain the whole community. . . .

We National Socialists have for many years protested against bringing woman into political life; that life in our eyes was unworthy of her. A woman said to me once: You must see to it that women go into Parliament; that is the only way to raise the standard of Parliamentary life. I do not believe, I answered, that man should try to raise the level of that which is bad in itself. And the woman who enters into this business of Parliament will not raise it, it will dishonor her. I would not leave to woman what I intend to take away from men. My opponents thought that in that case we would never gain women for our Movement, but in fact we gained more women than all the other parties together, and I know we should have won over the last German woman if she had only had the opportunity to study Parliament and the dishonoring role which women have played there. . . .

So our Women's Movement is for us not something which inscribes on its banner as its program the fight *against* man, but something which sets on its program the common fight of woman *together with man:* For the new National Socialist community of the people was set on a firm basis precisely because we gained in millions of women our truest, our fanatical fellow-combatants, women who fought for the common life in the service of the common task of maintaining life, who in that combat did not set their gaze on rights which a Jewish intellectualism mirrored before their eyes, but rather on duties which nature imposes on all of us in common. . . .

The program of our National Socialist Women's Movement has in truth but one single point, and that point is The Child—that tiny creature which must be born and should grow strong, for in the child alone the whole life-struggle gains its meaning. . . . It is a glorious sight, this golden youth of ours: we know that it is the Germany of the future when we shall be no more. What we create and construct, that youth will maintain. For youth we work; it is that fact which gives its significance to all this effort of ours.

Conversion and Resistance

The people of Germany were generally enthusiastic about Hitler, his image of a strong, successful fatherland, and his promises of prosperity. Membership in the National Socialist party rose steadily. Some people found that joining the Nazis was even more than a political experience; for them it was almost a religious conversion. The following section presents the experience of two such converts. But it must be remembered that there were still many who were alarmed at Hitler's actions. Among those who refused to support the "Fuehrer" was S. Ricarda Huch, a distinguished novelist and popular historian. In protest to the recent expulsion of writers who were politically or racially undesirable from the Prussian Academy of Arts and Sciences, Huch decided to resign. Her letter to the president of the academy, Max von Schillings, explains her decision.

"Now I Know Which Road to Take"

JOSEPH GOEBBELS

Someone was standing up and had begun to talk, hesitatingly and shyly at first. . . . Then suddenly the speech gathered momentum. I was caught, I was listening. . . . The crowd began to stir. The haggard grey faces were reflecting hope. . . . Two seats to my left, an old officer was crying like a child. I felt alternately hot and cold. . . . It was as though guns were thundering. . . . I was beside myself. I was shouting hurrah. Nobody seemed surprised. The man up there looked at me for a moment. His blue eyes met my glance like a flame. This was a command. At that moment I was reborn. . . . Now I know which road to take.

[Goebbels became member No. 8,762.]

"I Had Given Him My Heart"

KURT LUDECKE

Hitler's words were like a scourge. When he spoke of the disgrace of Germany, I felt ready to spring on any enemy . . . glancing around, I saw that his magnetism was holding these thousands as one. . . . I was a man of 32, weary of disgust and disillusionment, a wanderer seeking a cause . . . a yearner after the heroic without a hero. The intense will of the man, the passion of his sincerity, seemed to flow from him into me. I experienced a feeling that could be likened only to a religious conversion. . . . I felt sure that no-one who heard Hitler that night could doubt he was the man of destiny. . . . I had given him my heart.

Nazi propaganda poster: "Youth Serve the Führer. All ten-year-olds in Hitler Youth."
(*Bundesarchiva*)

A Matter of Principle

S. RICARDA HUCH

Heidelberg, April 9, 1933

Dear President von Schillings:

Let me first thank you for the warm interest you have taken in having me remain in the Academy. I would very much like you to understand why I cannot follow your wish. That a German's feelings are German I would consider to be just about self-evident, but the definition of what is German, and what acting in a German manner means—those are things where opinions differ. What the present government prescribes by way of the use of compulsion, the brutal methods, the defamation of those who hold different convictions, the boastful self-praise—these are matters which I consider un-German and disastrous. As I consider the divergence between this opinion of mine and that being ordered by the state, I find it impossible to remain in an Academy that is a part of the state. You say that the

"A Matter of Principle" is from *The Nazi Years: A Documentary History,* edited by Joachim Remak, p. 162. © 1969. Used by permission of Prentice-Hall, Inc., Englewood Cliffs, N.J.

declaration submitted to me by the Academy would not prevent me from the free expression of my opinions. But "loyal cooperation, in the spirit of the changed historical situation, on matters affecting national and cultural tasks that fall within the jurisdiction of the Academy" requires an agreement with the government's program which in my case does not exist. Besides, I would find no newspaper or magazine that would print an opposition opinion. Thus the right to the free expression of opinion would remain quite theoretical. . . .

I hereby resign from the Academy.

CHRONOLOGY: Adolf Hitler and the Nazi Rise to Power

November 11, 1918	Kaiser Wilhelm II abdicates German throne and flees to Holland. Armistice concluded on Western Front.
June 28, 1919	Treaty of Versailles signed between Germany and the Allies. Germany ceded territory and all her colonies to the Allies, returned Alsace-Lorraine to France, promised to pay large reparations and had its armed forces restricted. The Rhineland was demilitarized and occupied, and the League of Nations was created. Germany admitted "war guilt."
August, 1919	Constitution of the Weimar Republic promulgated.
October– November 1922	After Fascist takeovers in Bologna and Milan, Mussolini marches on Rome where an intimidated King Victor Emmanuel asks him to form a government. Mussolini is granted temporary dictatorial powers to institute reforms.
January 11, 1923	German nonpayment of reparations leads to French and Belgian troops occupying the industrial Ruhr; Germany adopts passive resistance to the occupation. France leaves in 1925.
September– November 1923	Massive inflation in Germany. Interest rates raised to 90 percent, but by October German mark trading at 10,000 million to the English pound.
November 8–9, 1923	Unsuccessful "Beer Hall" putsch in Munich led by Hitler and Ludendorff. Hitler spends eight months in jail where he writes *Mein Kampf*.
April 9, 1924	Dawes Plan provides a modified settlement of the reparations issue.
December 1, 1924	Locarno Pact signed which guarantees Franco-German and Belgian-German frontiers and demilitarization of the Rhineland.

December 24, 1925	Mussolini's dictatorial powers increased in Italy. Press censorship tightened, secret non-fascist organizations banned, and widespread arrests.
February 6, 1929	Germany accepts Kellogg-Briand Pact, outlawing war and providing for the pacific settlements of disputes.
October 29, 1929	Wall Street Crash and cessation of American loans to Europe.
September 14, 1930	In Reichstag elections, Hitler and the National Socialists (Nazis) emerge as a major party with 107 seats, second only to the Social Democrats with 143 seats.
July, 1931	Worsening economic crisis in Germany. Unemployment reaches over 4 million.
July 31, 1932	In Reichstag elections, Nazis win 230 seats and become largest party.
January 30, 1933	President von Hindenburg accepts a cabinet with Hitler as chancellor.
February 27, 1933	Reichstag fire blamed on Communists and made pretext for suspension of civil liberties and freedom of the press.
March 23, 1933	Hitler obtains Enabling Law, granting him dictatorial powers for four years.
July 14, 1933	All parties, other than the Nazis, suppressed. The National Socialist Party is formally declared the only political party in Germany.
August 2, 1934	Death of President von Hindenburg. Hitler assumes Presidency, but retains title *Der Führer*. Army swears oath of allegiance.

STUDY QUESTIONS

1. According to Benito Mussolini, what are the primary tenets of fascist doctrine? Why was he especially critical of socialism (Marxism) and democracy? Do you find his arguments compelling or flawed? Why is war such an important requirement for the fascist state? What did Mussolini mean by "[the individual] is deprived of all useless and possibly harmful freedom, but retains what is essential." What is "harmful freedom" as opposed to "essential freedom"? In what ways was Hitler's concept of fascism (as expressed in the various documents) consistent or inconsistent with Mussolini's concept?

2. Why was the National Socialist party able to rise to power? What were the main political, social, and economic problems of the 1920s and early 1930s, and what were the solutions offered by the Nazis? Why was the

Weimar Republic unable to cope with the major problems facing Germany? Was its destruction inevitable?

3. Compare the constitution of the Weimar Republic with the Nazi program of 1920. How are they similar in outlook and what are the main differences? Pay particular attention to the presentation of specific points and the vocabulary.

4. Analyze the propaganda documents included in this chapter. In particular, what messages does Goebbels promote in "Nationalists, Socialists, and Jews"? Is he logical in the presentation of his arguments, or can you find inconsistencies? What emotions does the propaganda exploit? What is the message in "Free Germany!"? Would you call it effective propaganda?

5. Statistics often reveal much after close analysis. What statements about the comparative strength of political parties can you make based on these data? Which party lost the most support from 1924 to 1932? How successful was the Communist party? What relationships do you see between political election and unemployment?

6. Many have viewed the Nazi rise to power as a legitimate act, fully sanctioned by law. Others have called it a revolution in which Hitler seized power. What do you think? To what extent was Hitler justified in stressing the legality of the Nazi assumption of power?

7. According to Hitler's speech of September 8, 1934, what was the intended role of women in the Nazi state? What does this document say about Nazi society and the future? Compare this statement with that of V. I. Lenin in the preceding chapter on the Russian Revolution entitled "The Communist Emancipation of Women" (1920). Why are the concepts for the position of women in these two states so different?

8. Carefully read the conversion accounts of Joseph Goebbels and Kurt Ludecke. Why did they join the Nazi party? The philosopher Eric Hoffer, in his book *The True Believer* (New York: Harper & Row, 1951, p. 50), described such converts as "permanent misfits." He noted that no achievement can give them a sense of fulfillment; they pursue goals passionately, but never arrive: "The permanent misfits can find salvation only in a complete separation from the self; and they usually find it by losing themselves in the compact collectivity of a mass movement. By renouncing individual will, judgment, and ambition, and dedicating all their powers to the service of an eternal cause, they are at last listed off the endless treadmill which can never lead them to fulfillment. A rising mass movement attracts and holds a following not by its doctrine or promises, but by the refuge it offers from the anxieties [and] barrenness of an individual existence." Do you agree? Why do people give their fanatical devotion to a cause?

9. Was the victory of National Socialism in Germany dependent on Adolf Hitler? How important was he to the Nazi movement? To what extent can the individual mold the events of history? What conditions in a state present the greatest opportunity for individual assertion of will and power?

10. Konrad Heiden. in his book *Der Fuehrer* (New York: Houghton Mifflin,

1944, p. v), stated that "Hitler was able to enslave his own people because he gave them something that even the traditional religions could no longer provide; the belief in a meaning to existence beyond the narrowest self-interest." How do you see this statement reflected in the various sources?

11. During the 1930s and 1940s, Hitler and Germany could lead the world to war, with all its attendant suffering and destruction. Some historians argue that the victory of Adolf Hitler and the National Socialist party was consistent with the racism, militarism, and blind obedience to authority that marks the German national character. Can you describe French, Italian, British, Russian, or American character? Is there even such a thing as "national character," and is it legitimate to explain historical events on the basis of such a characterization?

9

The Jewish Holocaust

I mean the clearing out of the Jews, the extermination of the Jewish race. . . . Most of you must know what it means when 100 corpses are lying side by side, or 500, or 1,000. To have stuck it out and at the same time . . . to have remained decent fellows, that is what has made us hard. This is a page of glory in our history which has never been written and is never to be written. . . .

—Heinrich Himmler to his SS Officers

In spite of everything, I still believe that people are really good at heart.

—Anne Frank

Whoever fights monsters should see to it that in the process he does not become a monster; and when you look long into an abyss, the abyss also looks into you.

—Friedrich Nietzsche

Man does not deny that terrible things have happened and still go on happening, but it is always the others who do them. And when such deeds belong to the recent or remote past, they quickly and conveniently sink into the sea of forgetfulness. . . . [but] Man has done these things; I am a man, who has his share of human nature; therefore, I am guilty with the rest and bear . . . within me the inclination to do them again at any time. Even if . . . we were not accessories to the crime, we are always, thanks to our human nature, potential criminals. In reality, we merely lacked a suitable opportunity to be drawn into the infernal melee. None of us stands outside humanity's black collective shadow.

—Carl Jung

In 1933, Adolf Hitler was appointed chancellor of the German Weimar Republic, a post of prestige and authority. His National Socialist party was swept into power on the promises made to end the rampant inflation and unemployment that plagued the German economy, and to restore the dignity of the German people, who had been humiliated by the onorous Treaty of Versailles. Germany had to accept the harsh terms of this peace that resolved World War I and was especially dissatisfied with the stipulation that Germany alone had been responsible for the war. Hitler's program presented a vision of the future, and his speeches inspired a defeated nation. His constant demands for more "living space" (*Lebensraum*) extended the boundaries of Germany, as Austria and the Sudetenland of Czechoslovakia were incorporated. By 1939, Hitler had revived the German economy and set the people back to work building the armaments that were to maintain a strong, united Germany. The other nations of Europe, particularly Great Britain, had generally appeased Hitler and allowed him to incorporate more territory, thinking that each demand would be his last. When Hitler invaded Poland in 1939, he went too far and the world once again went to war.

The road to World War II is, of course, a twisted one, and there are many different aspects to Hitler's rise and ultimate destruction. The name Adolf Hitler has become synonymous with evil. Much of this reputation has been derived from his attempt to commit genocide, to exterminate an entire race of people. One of the more distinctive differences between Italian fascism under Benito Mussolini (1883–1945) and the Nazi movement was Hitler's use of anti-Semitism. Hitler demanded that Germany be composed of racially pure Aryan stock. The blond, blue-eyed German, untainted by inferior blood, became Hitler's ideal and the image he tried to cultivate in his propaganda. Hitler saw the Jews as the source of all of Germany's trouble. According to Hitler, Jews were cowards who did not support the fatherland in the Great War. They had deep communist sympathies, controlled international finance, and dominated the most important offices in government. Jews also controlled the purse strings of the nation and thus prevented worthier and more talented individuals from holding jobs and contributing to German culture. Indeed, Hitler had once been a frustrated artist in Vienna who blamed his failure on such Jewish influence. Hitler understood that hatred often unifies a nation more readily than does love. In troubled times, people want a simple explanation for their pain and insecurity. For Hitler, and consequently for Germany, that explanation was the Jew.

Anti-Semitism certainly did not originate with Hitler. Jews had been persecuted since the Middle Ages and even blamed for such things as outbreaks of bubonic plague. Still, never before was there such a systematic, methodical attempt to exterminate an entire race.

Although Hitler had exhibited his racism from the early 1920s in speeches and writings, and had incorporated it into the philosophy of National Socialism, nothing could be implemented until the Nazis came into power. By 1935, Jews were excluded from citizenship by law in order to preserve German blood and honor. Germany was saturated with propaganda that presented the Jew as an immoral pervert whose presence was a threat to the health and morality of the German community. Nazi policy slowly evolved toward deportation and then toward isolation of the Jews in city ghettos. The "Final Solution" to the Jewish problem actually began in June 1941. As Hitler's armies drove into Russia, special mobile killing units (*Einsatzgruppen*) were set up and followed just behind the front lines. For eighteen months, the *Einsatzgruppen* operated and killed over 1.3 million Jews. The Nazis also built several concentration camps generally designed to house workers and remove Jews from society. The treatment of prisoners was cruel, and hundreds of thousands died of exhaustion, starvation, and disease. The Nazi commitment to Jewish extermination even exceeded the bounds of practicality. Although there was a widespread shortage of labor throughout German-controlled Europe during the war, the Nazis continued to wipe out valuable workers. The camps, run by Hitler's private army called the "SS" (*Schutzstaffel*), often served as holding pens until the inmates were sent by train to six death camps located in Poland. Created solely for the task of killing, the camps at Auschwitz and Treblinka have become infamous—over 2.7 million Jews were eliminated, 1 million in Auschwitz alone. Thousands of other undesirable people such as gypsies, Slavs, and even dissident Germans were also killed.

Many questions arise out of the Holocaust that make this a particularly important and relevant historical problem. How could such a violation against humanity have happened? Could it happen again? Can one view the Jewish Holocaust as a precedent that legitimized the dropping of the atomic bomb on Hiroshima and Nagasaki? Can one say, "War is Hell," and let it go at that? How deep and penetrating is the racial argument? Do we all have prejudices, which, if exploited properly, can lead to such results? The urgency of these questions is intensified when we consider other issues such as the policy of apartheid in South Africa or the influence of the Ku Klux Klan; the millions who were murdered by Stalin during Soviet collectivization, industrialization, and the Great Purges of the 1930s; the ruthlessness of the Cambodian dictator Pol Pot; or the maniacal ranting of Muammar Gaddafi or Saddam Hussein.

Not forgetting is the responsibility of the living.

The Evolution of Nazi Jewish Policy

Anti-Semitism was one of the cornerstones of Nazi dogma. When Hitler became chancellor in 1933, he began the process of excluding Jews from life in the German Reich. Note the charges that are leveled against the Jews in one of Hitler's early speeches. Indeed, Jews felt compelled to defend themselves against

accusations that they were in control of international finance and the German
government, or that they were cowards who forsook Germany in World War I.
With the adoption of the Nuremberg Laws in 1935, Hitler excluded Jews from
German citizenship and made provisions to restrict their social relations.

Jewish Responsibility

The Jewish Peril (April 1923)

ADOLF HITLER

The German people was once clear thinking and simple: why has it lost these characteristics? Any inner renewal is possible only if one realizes that this is a question of race: America forbids the yellow peoples to settle there, but this is a lesser peril than that which stretches out its hand over the entire world—the Jewish peril. Many hold that the Jews are not a race, but is there a second people anywhere in the wide world which is so determined to maintain its race?

As a matter of fact the Jew can never become a German however often he may affirm that he can. If he wished to become a German, he must surrender the Jew in him. And that is not possible: he cannot, however much he tries, become a German at heart, and that for several reasons: first because of his blood, second because of his character, thirdly because of his will, and fourthly because of his actions. His actions remain Jewish: he works for the "greater idea" of the Jewish people. Because that is so, because it cannot be otherwise, therefore the bare existence of the Jew as part of another State rests upon a monstrous lie. It is a lie when he pretends to the peoples to be a German, a Frenchman, etc.

What then are the specifically Jewish aims?

To spread their invisible State as a supreme tyranny over all other States in the whole world. The Jew is therefore a disintegrator of peoples. To realize his rule over the peoples he must work in two directions: in economics he dominates peoples when he subjugates them politically and morally: in politics he dominates them through the propagation of the principles of democracy and the doctrines of Marxism—the creed which makes a Proletarian a Terrorist in the domestic sphere and a Pacifist in foreign policy. Ethically the Jew destroys the peoples both in religion and in morals. He who wishes to see that can see it, and him who refuses to see it no one can help.

The Jew, whether consciously or unconsciously, whether he wishes it or not, undermines the platform on which alone a nation can stand.

We are now met by the questions: Do we wish to restore Germany to

"The Jewish Peril" is from Norman H. Baynes, translator and editor, *The Speeches of Adolf Hitler, April, 1922–1939*, vol. 1, pp. 59–60 (London, RIIA/Oxford University Press, 1942). Reprinted by kind permission of the Royal Institute of International Affairs, London.

freedom and power? If "yes": then the first thing to do is to rescue it from him who is ruining our country. Admittedly it is a hard fight that must be fought here. We National Socialists on this point occupy an extreme position: but we know only one people: it is for that people we fight and that is our own people. . . . We want to stir up a storm. Men must not sleep: they ought to know that a thunder-storm is coming up. We want to prevent our Germany from suffering, as Another did, the death upon the Cross.

We may be inhumane, but if we rescue Germany we have achieved the greatest deed in the world! We may work injustice, but if we rescue Germany then we have removed the greatest injustice in the world. We may be immoral, but if our people is rescued we have once more opened up the way for morality!

Jewish Defense
"Not a Single Jew" (1932)

Jewish World Finance

Today, capital formation takes place in large industry. Its largest enterprises are almost entirely dominated by non-Jewish interests: Krupp, Vereinigte Stahlwerke, Klockner, Stinnes, Siemeins, Stumm, I. G. Farben, Hugenberg, Hapag, Nordlloyd.

International connections are concentrated most heavily in those industries in which Jews are without influence or altogether unrepresented: the German-French iron cartel, wooden matches trust, oil trust, potash industry, and shipping conventions are all "clean of Jews," and so are the international chemical cartel, nylon production and all the other raw material and key industries in which Jews have no influence either as owners or directors. . . .

Jewish Government

The anti-Semites assert that the German government is full of Jews. The 19 post-war cabinets consisted of 237 ministers of whom three (Preuss and twice Rathenau) were Jews and four (Landsberg, Gradnauer, and twice Hilferding) of Jewish descent. The last few governments have had no Jewish ministers.

In the German provinces, the situation is not different: none of the provincial cabinets contain a Jew. The administration is not full of Jews, either. For example, in Prussia, among the twelve chief presidents, thirty-five government presidents and four hundred provincial counsellors, there is not a single Jew. . . .

" 'Not a Single Jew' " is from Raul Hilberg, ed., *Documents of Destruction* (Chicago: Quadrangle Books, 1971), pp. 8–11. Reprinted by permission of the author.

The Jews in World War I

Of 538,000 Jews in Germany, more than 96,000 were under arms, including 10,000 volunteers; about 80,000 were on the front lines, 35,000 received decorations, 23,000 were promoted, including more than 2000 to officer rank (without medical corps). One hundred sixty-eight Jews who volunteered as flyers are known by name. At the top of the list is Lieutenant D. R. Frankl who received the *Pour le merite* [combat medal] and *who like 29 other Jewish flyers was killed in battle.*

Twelve thousand Jewish soldiers did not see their homeland again; they *died a hero's death for their German fatherland.* More than 10,000 of their names have now been recorded with personal information, unit, and number. The dead of Hamburg, Alsace-Lorraine and ceded Posen (with its relatively large Jewish population) have not yet been registered.

It is heartless to demand today that the widows and orphans, parents and brothers, brides and relatives of 12,000 fallen Jews be deprived of equality in Germany.

Legal Restriction of the Jews: The Nuremberg Laws

Law for the Protection of German Blood and German Honor (September 1935)

Entirely convinced that the purity of German blood is essential to the further existence of the German people, and inspired by the uncompromising determination to safeguard the future of the German nation, the Reichstag has unanimously resolved upon the following law, which is promulgated herewith:

Section 1

Marriages between Jews and citizens of German or kindred blood are forbidden. Marriages concluded in defiance of this law are void, even if, for the purpose of evading this law, they were concluded abroad.

Proceedings for annulment may be initiated only by the Public Prosecutor.

Section 2

Sexual relations outside marriage between Jews and nationals of German or kindred blood are forbidden.

"Law for the Protection of German Blood and German Honor" is from Jeremy Noakes and Geoffrey Pridham, eds., *Documents on Nazism, 1919–1945*, pp. 463–464. Reprinted by permission of A. D. Peters & Co., Ltd.

Section 3

Jews will not be permitted to employ female citizens of German or kindred blood as domestic servants.

Section 4

Jews are forbidden to display the Reich and national flag or the national colours.

On the other hand they are permitted to display the Jewish colours. The exercise of this right is protected by the State.

Section 5

A person who acts contrary to the prohibition of Section 1 will be punished with hard labour.

A person who acts contrary to the prohibition of Section 2 will be punished with imprisonment or with hard labour.

A person who acts contrary to the provisions of Sections 3 or 4 will be punished with imprisonment up to a year and with a fine, or with one of these penalties.

The Reich Citizenship Law (September 1935)

Article 1

1. A subject of the State is a person who belongs to the protective union of the German Reich, and who therefore has particular obligations towards the Reich.

2. The status of subject is acquired in accordance with the provisions of the Reich and State Law of Citizenship.

Article 2

1. A citizen of the Reich is that subject only who is of German or kindred blood and who, through his conduct, shows that he is both desirous and fit to serve the German people and Reich faithfully.

2. The right to citizenship is acquired by the granting of Reich citizenship papers.

3. Only the citizen of the Reich enjoys full political rights in accordance with the provision of the laws.

"The Reich Citizenship Law" is from Jeremy Noakes and Geoffrey Pridham, eds., *Documents on Nazism, 1919–1945*, pp. 464–465. Reprinted by permission of A. D. Peters & Co., Ltd.

Anti-Jewish Propaganda

In 1936, Germany hosted the Olympic Games, and Hitler ordered the tempo-
rary removal of anti-Jewish placards in order to appease foreign opinion. Still,
the propaganda continued to flow, especially from Der Stürmer, *a sensa-*
tionalistic journal published by Julius Streicher. In the first selection, note the
accusation of cannibalism and the misrepresentation of the two Jewish festivals
of Purim and Passover, which commemorate not murder but deliverance from
oppression. The second excerpt is from a book for older children called Der
Giftpilz *(The Poisonous Mushroom), which presented the Jew as an evil*
deviate who preyed on the innocence of children.

Ritual Murder: *Der Stürmer* (1937)

The murder of the 10 year old Gertrud Lenhoff in Quirschied (Saarpfalz)

* * *   The Jews are our MISFORTUNE!   * * *

Also the numerous confessions made by the Jews show that the execution of ritual murders is a law to the Talmud Jew. The former Chief Rabbi
(and later monk) Teofiti declares . . . that the ritual murders take place
especially on the Jewish Purim (in memory of the Persian murders) and
Passover (in memory of the murder of Christ).

The instructions are as follows:

The blood of the victims is to be tapped by force. On Passover, it is to be
used in wine and matzos; thus, a small part of the blood is to be poured into
the dough of the matzos and into the wine. The mixing is done by the
Jewish head of the family.

The procedure is as follows: the family head empties a few drops of the
fresh and powdered blood into the glass, wets the fingers of the left hand
with it and sprays (blesses) with it everything on the table. The head of the
family then says: "Dam Izzardia chynim heroff dever Isyn porech harbe
hossen maschus pohorus" (Exod. 7.12) ("Thus we ask God to send the ten
plagues to all enemies of the Jewish faith.") Then they eat, and at the end
the head of the family exclaims: "Sfach, chaba, moscho kol hagoym!" ("May
all Gentiles perish—as the child whose blood is contained in the bread and
wine!")

The fresh (or dried and powdered) blood of the slaughtered is further
used by young married Jewish couples, by pregnant Jewesses, for circumci-
sions, and so on. Ritual murder is recognized by all Talmud Jews. The Jew
believes he absolves himself thus of his sins.

"Ritual Murder: *Der Stürmer*" is from the Office of the U.S. Chief of Counsel for the
Prosecution of Axis Criminality, *Nazi Conspiracy and Aggression* (Washington, D.C.: Government Printing Office, 1947), vol. 5, pp. 372–373 (PS-2699).

The Poisonous Mushroom (1938)

ERNST HIEMER

"It is almost noon," he said, "now we want to summarize what we have learned in this lesson. What did we discuss?"

All the children raise their hands. The teacher calls on Karl Scholz, a little boy on the first bench. "We talked about how to recognize a Jew."

"Good! Now tell us about it!"

Little Karl takes the pointer, goes to the blackboard and points to the sketches.

"One usually recognizes a Jew by his nose. The Jewish nose is crooked at the end. It looks like the figure 6. Therefore it is called the "Jewish Six." Many non-Jews have crooked noses, too. But their noses are bent, not at the end but further up. Such a nose is called a hook nose or eagle's beak. It has nothing to do with a Jewish nose."

"Right!" says the teacher. "But the Jew is recognized not only by his nose. . . ." The boy continues. The Jew is also recognized by his lips. His lips are usually thick. Often the lower lip hangs down. This is called "sloppy." And the Jew is also recognized by his eyes. His eyelids are usually thicker and more fleshy than ours. The look of the Jew is lurking and sharp.

Then the teacher goes to the desk and turns over the blackboard, on its back is a verse. The children recite it in chorus:

> From a Jew's countenance—the evil devil talks to us,
> The devil, who in every land—is known as evil plague.
> If we shall be free of the Jew—and again will be happy and glad,
> Then the youth must struggle with us—to subdue the Jew devil.

Inge sits in the reception room of the Jew doctor. She has to wait a long time. She looks through the journals which are on the table. But she is almost too nervous to read even a few sentences. Again and again she remembers the talk with her mother. And again and again her mind reflects on the warnings of her leader of the BDM [League of German Girls]: "A German must not consult a Jew doctor! And particularly not a German girl! Many a girl that went to a Jew doctor to be cured, found disease and disgrace!"

When Inge had entered the waiting room, she experienced an extraordinary incident. From the doctor's consulting room she could hear the sound of crying. She heard the voice of a young girl: "Doctor, doctor leave me alone!"

Then she heard the scornful laughing of a man. And then all of a sudden it became absolutely silent. Inge had listened breathlessly.

"The Poisonous Mushroom" is from the Office of the U.S. Chief of Counsel for the Prosecution of Axis Criminality, *Nazi Conspiracy and Aggression* (Washington, D.C.: Government Printing Office, 1947), vol. 4, pp. 358–359 (PS-1778).

"What may be the meaning of all this?" she asked herself and her heart was pounding. And again she thought of the warning of her leader in the BDM.

Inge was already waiting for an hour. Again she takes the journals in an endeavor to read. Then the door opens. Inge looks up. The Jew appears. She screams. In terror she drops the paper. Frightened she jumps up. Her eyes stare into the face of the Jewish doctor. And this face is the face of the devil. In the middle of this devil's face is a huge crooked nose. Behind the spectacles two criminal eyes. And the thick lips are grinning. A grinning that expresses: "Now I got you at last, you little German girl!"

And then the Jew approaches her. His fleshy fingers stretch out after her. But now Inge has her wits. Before the Jew can grab hold of her, she hits the fat face of the Jew doctor with her hand. Then one jump to the door. Breathlessly she escapes the Jew house.

The Radicalization of Anti-Semitism (1938–1941)

On November 9–10, 1938, the Nazis, in retaliation for the assassination of a German diplomat, set fire to Jewish synagogues and systematically destroyed 7,500 Jewish stores. The incident became known as Kristallnacht (Crystal Night) *because of the broken glass that covered the street. A few days later, Reich Marshal Hermann Goering called a meeting of some of the Nazi hierarchy (Reinhard Heydrich and Joseph Goebbels) to place ultimate responsibility for the destruction on the Jews. It was decided that the Jews would have to pay for the damage they "provoked." In the first selection, note the mention of ideas (separate schools, badges, and ghettos) that achieved fruition later as indicated in the second selection. Hitler gave little doubt as to his intentions regarding the Jews in a speech given before the Reichstag in 1939. Joseph Goebbels, the minister of propaganda, capitalized on this official anti-Semitic stance of the German government in his tract, which blamed the war on the Jews.*

Conference on the Jewish Question
(November 12, 1938)

Goering: I should not want to leave any doubt, gentlemen, as to the aim of today's meeting. We have not come together merely to talk again, but to make decisions, and I implore the competent agencies to take all measures for the elimination of the Jew from German economy and to submit them to me, as far as it is necessary. . . .

Furthermore, I advocate that the Jews be eliminated from all positions in public life in which they may prove to be provocative. . . . Jews should not

"Conference on the Jewish Question" is from Office of the U.S. Chief of Counsel for the Prosecution of Axis Criminality, *Nazi Conspiracy and Aggression* (Washington, D.C.: Government Printing Office, 1947), vol. 4, pp. 426, 432–434 (PS-1816).

be allowed to sit around in German parks. I am thinking of the whispering campaign on the part of Jewish women in the public gardens at Fehrbelliner Platz. They go and sit with German mothers and their children and begin to gossip and incite. I see in this a particularly grave danger. I think it is imperative to give the Jews certain public parks, not the best ones—and tell them: "You may sit on these benches," these benches shall be marked, "For Jews only." Besides that they have no business in German parks. Furthermore, Jewish children are still allowed in German schools. That's impossible. It is out of the question that any boy should sit beside a Jewish boy in a German gymnasium and receive lessons in German history. Jews ought to be eliminated completely from German schools; they may take care of their own education in their own communities. . . .

Heydrich: As another means of getting the Jews out, measures for Emigration are to be taken in the rest of the Reich for the next 8 to 10 years. The highest number of Jews we can possibly get out during one year is 8,000 to 10,000. Therefore, a great number of Jews will remain. Because of aryanizing and other restrictions, Jewry will become unemployed. The remaining Jews gradually become proletarians. Therefore, I shall have to take steps; to isolate the Jew so he won't enter into the German normal routine of life. On the other hand, I shall have to restrict the Jew to a small circle of consumers, but I shall have to permit certain activities within professions; lawyers, doctors, barbers, etc. This question shall also have to be examined.

As for the isolation, I'd like to make a few proposals regarding police measures which are important also because of their psychological effect on public opinion. For example, who is Jewish according to the Nuremberg laws shall have to wear a certain insignia. That is a possibility which shall facilitate many other things. I don't see any danger of excuses, and it shall make our relationship with the foreign Jew easier.

Goering: A uniform?

Heydrich: An insignia. This way we could also put an end to it that the foreign Jews who don't look different from ours, are being molested.

Goering: But, my dear Heydrich, you won't be able to avoid the creation of ghettos on a very large scale, in all the cities. They shall have to be created.

Police Decree Concerning the Marking of Jews (September 1941)

Paragraph 1

1. Jews over the age of six are forbidden to show themselves in public without a Jew's star.

"Police Decree Concerning the Marking of Jews" is from *The Nazi Years: A Documentary History*, edited by Joachim Remak, p. 151. © 1969. Used by permission of Prentice-Hall, Inc., Englewood Cliffs, N.J.

2. The Jew's star consists of a six-pointed star of yellow cloth with black borders, equivalent in size to the palm of the hand. The inscription is to read "JEW" in black letters. It is to be sewn to the left breast of the garment, and to be worn visibly.

Paragraph 2

Jews are Forbidden

a) to leave their area of residence without carrying, on their person, written permission from the local police.
b) to wear medals, decorations, or other insignia. . . .

Speech to the Reichstag (January 30, 1939)
ADOLF HITLER

One thing I should like to say on this day which may be memorable for others as well as for us Germans. In the course of my life I have very often been a prophet, and have usually been ridiculed for it. During the time of my struggle for power it was in the first instance only the Jewish race that received my prophecies with laughter when I said that I would one day take over the leadership of the State, and with it that of the whole nation, and that I would then among other things settle the Jewish problem. Their laughter was uproarious, but I think that for some time now they have been laughing on the other side of their face. Today I will once more be a prophet: if the international Jewish financiers in and outside Europe should succeed in plunging the nations once more into a world war, then the result will not be the Bolshevizing of the earth, and thus the victory of Jewry, but the annihilation of the Jewish race in Europe!

The Jews Are to Blame! (1941)
JOSEPH GOEBBELS

World Jewry's historic guilt for the outbreak and extension of this war has been so abundantly proven that no additional words need to be lost over the matter. The Jews wanted their war. Now they have it. But what is also

"Speech to the Reichstag" is from Norman H. Baynes, translator and editor, *The Speeches of Adolf Hitler, April, 1922–1939*, vol. 1, pp. 740–741 (London, RIIA/Oxford University Press, 1942). Reprinted by kind permission of the Royal Institute of International Affairs, London.
"The Jews Are to Blame" is from *The Nazi Years: A Documentary History*, edited by Joachim Remak, pp. 155–156. © 1969. Used by permission of Prentice-Hall, Inc., Englewood Cliffs, N.J.

coming true for them is the Führer's prophecy which he voiced in his Reichstag speech of January 30, 1939. It was that if international financial Jewry succeeded in plunging the nations into another world war, the result would not be the Bolshevization of the world and thus the victory of Jewry, but the destruction of the Jewish race in Europe.

We are now witnessing the acid test of this prophecy, and thus Jewry is experiencing a fate which is hard but more than deserved. Pity or even regrets are entirely out of place here. World Jewry, in starting this war, made an entirely wrong estimate of the forces at its disposal, and is now suffering the same gradual process of destruction which it had planned for us, and which it would apply without hesitation were it to possess the power to do so. It is in line with their own law, "An eye for an eye, a tooth for a tooth," that the ruin of the Jews is now taking place. . . .

So, superfluous though it might be, let me say once more:

1. The Jews are our destruction. They provoked and brought about this war. What they mean to achieve by it is to destroy the German state and nation. This plan must be frustrated.

2. There is no difference between Jew and Jew. Every Jew is a sworn enemy of the German people. If he fails to display his hostility against us, it is merely out of cowardice and slyness, but not because his heart is free of it.

3. Every German soldier's death in this war is the Jew's responsibility. They have it on their conscience; hence they must pay for it.

4. Anyone wearing the Jew's star has been marked as an enemy of the nation. Any person who still maintains social relations with him is one of them, and must be considered a Jew himself and treated as such. He deserves the contempt of the entire nation, which he has deserted in its gravest hour to join the side of those who hate it.

5. The Jews enjoy the protection of the enemy nations. No further proof is needed of their destructive role among our people.

6. The Jews are the messengers of the enemy in our midst. Anyone joining them is going over to the enemy in time of war.

7. The Jews have no claim to pretend to have rights equal to ours. Wherever they want to open their mouths, in the street, in the lines in front of the stores, or on public transportation, they are to be silenced. They are to be silenced not only because they are wrong on principle, but because they are Jews and have no voice in the community.

8. If Jews pull a sentimental act for you, bear in mind that they are speculating on your forgetfullness. Show them immediately that you see right through them and punish them with contempt.

9. A decent enemy, after his defeat, deserves our generosity. But the Jew is no decent enemy. He only pretends to be one.

10. The Jews are to blame for this war. The treatment we give them does them no wrong; they have more than deserved it. . . .

The Final Solution (1941–1945)

By 1940, the Nazis had embarked on a policy that was designed to "cleanse" the German homeland of Jews by confining them to ghettos in cities, especially in Poland. There the Nazis could control them and, upon demand, export them to concentration camps where they would be put to work or die. But in July 1941, preparations were made for a secretive "Final Solution" to the Jewish problem. It was discussed in more detail at the Wansee Conference in January 1942, as the following excerpts indicate.

Official Policy

Decree of the Reich Marshal (July 31, 1941)

HERMANN GOERING

To: The Chief of the Security Police and the Security Service; SS-Gruppenfuehrer Heydrich

Complementing the task that was assigned to you on 24 January 1939, which dealt with the carrying out of emigration and evacuation, a solution of the Jewish problem, as advantageous as possible, I hereby charge you with making all necessary preparations in regard to organizational and financial matters for bringing out a complete solution of the Jewish question in the German sphere of influence in Europe.

Wherever other governmental agencies are involved, these are to cooperate with you.

I charge you furthermore to send me, before long, an overall plan concerning the organizational, factual and material measures necessary for the accomplishment of the desired solution of the Jewish question.

Wansee Conference (January 20, 1942)

II. At the beginning of the meeting the Chief of the Security Police and the SD, SS Lieutenant General Heydrich, reported his appointment by the Reich Marshal to service as Commissioner for the Preparation of the Final

"Decree of the Reich Marshal" is from the Office of the U.S. Chief Counsel for Prosecution of Axis Criminality, *Nazi Conspiracy and Aggression* (Washington, D.C.: Government Printing Office, 1947), vol. 3, pp. 525–526 (PS-710).

"Wansee Conference" is from the Nuremberg Military Tribunals, *Trials of War Criminals* (Washington, D.C.: Government Printing Office, 1947–1949), vol. 13, pp. 211–213.

Solution of the European Jewish Problem, and pointed out that the officials had been invited to this conference in order to clear up the fundamental problems. The Reich Marshal's request to have a draft submitted to him on the organizational, factual, and material requirements with respect to the Final Solution of the European Jewish Problem, necessitated this previous general consultation by all the central offices directly concerned, in order that there should be coordination in the policy.

The primary responsibility for the administrative handling of the Final Solution of the Jewish Problem will rest centrally with the Reich Leader SS and the Chief of the German Police (Chief of the Security Police and the SD)—regardless of geographic boundaries.

The Chief of the Security Police and the SD thereafter gave a brief review of the battle conducted up to now against these enemies. The most important are—

a. Forcing the Jews out of the various fields of the community life of the German people.
b. Forcing the Jews out of the living space [*Lebensraum*] of the German people.

•   •   •

Meanwhile, in view of the dangers of emigration during the war and in view of the possibilities in the East, the Reich Leader SS and Chief of the German Police had forbidden the emigrating of the Jews.

III. The emigration program has now been replaced by the evacuation of the Jews to the East as a further solution possibility, in accordance with previous authorization by the Fuehrer.

These actions are of course to be regarded only as a temporary substitute; nonetheless, here already, the coming Final Solution of the Jewish Question is of great importance. In the course of this Final Solution of the European Jewish Problem, approximately 11 million Jews are involved.

Under proper direction the Jews should now in the course of the Final Solution be brought to the East in a suitable way for use as labor. In big labor gangs, with separation of the sexes, the Jews capable of work are brought to these areas and employed in road building, in which task undoubtedly a great part will fall out through natural diminution.

The remnant that finally is able to survive all this—since this is undoubtedly the part with the strongest resistance—must be treated accordingly since these people, representing a natural selection, are to be regarded as the germ cell of a new Jewish development. (See the experience of history.)

In the program of the practical execution of the Final Solution, Europe is combed through from the West to the East.

The evacuated Jews are brought first group by group into the so-called transit ghettos, in order to be transported from these farther to the East.

The Death Camps

The "Final Solution" ordered the implementation of a policy of genocide. Hitler wanted to rid the world of a people whom he found responsible for most of humanity's ills. The following selections present the system of extermination from the trip to the death camp by train through the selection process and the gas chambers. Much of the testimony in this section comes from the Nuremberg trial proceedings in 1946. Hermann Gräbe ("The Pit") was a German construction engineer working in the Ukraine in 1942. Kurt Gerstein ("Gas") was the SS Head of Disinfection Services in early 1942. The gassing of Jews did not take place at concentration or death camps alone, as is noted by the selection entitled "Mobile Killing." This is a top secret dispatch concerning the Einsatzgruppen *that often followed advancing troops. Excerpts from the autobiography and Nuremberg testimony of Rudolf Hoess are also included. He was commandant of the notorious Auschwitz death camp and was himself executed there in 1947 after being judged guilty of crimes against humanity.*

Sites of Nazi Concentration Camps

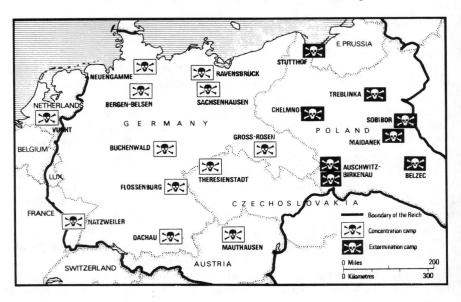

"Sites of Nazi Concentration Camps" is from Louis L. Snyder, *Encyclopedia of the Third Reich* (New York: McGraw-Hill Book Company, 1976), p. 57. Reprinted by permission of the publisher.

Arrival: The Death Train

ELIE WIESEL

Indescribable confusion reigned.

Parents searched for their children, children for their parents, and lonely captives for their friends. The people were beset by loneliness. Everyone feared that the outcome of the journey would be tragic and would claim its toll of lives. And so one yearned to have the companionship of someone who would stand by with a word, with a loving glance.

Afterward, an ominous silence fell upon us. We squatted on the soft snow that covered the floor of the railroad car like a carpet, and tried to keep warm by drawing closer to our neighbors.

When the train started to move, no one paid any attention to it. Careworn and burdened with conflicting thoughts, each of us wondered if he was wise to continue on the journey. But in our weariness, whether one died today, tomorrow, a week or a generation later, hardly seemed to matter.

The night dragged on interminably, as though it were to go on to the end of time. When the gray dawn appeared in the east, I felt as though I had spent a night in a tomb haunted by evil spirits. Human beings, defeated and broken, sat like dusty tombstones in the dim light of early dawn. I looked about the subdued throng and tried to distinguish one from another. And, indeed, perhaps there was no distinction.

My gaze fell on one who stared blankly ahead. A wry smile seemed to play on his ice-encrusted face. Those glazed eyes, whether living or dead, seemed to ensnare my gaze. A hundred and twenty captives, shadows of human lives, extinguished flames of burned-out candles lit on the anniversaries of the deaths of their loved ones.

Wrapped in a drenched blanket, his black cap pulled down over his ears, a layer of snow on his shoulders, my father sat beside me. Could it be that he, too, was dead? The thought flashed across my mind. I tried to talk to him. I wanted to shout, but all I could do was mutter. He did not reply, he did not utter a sound. I was certain that from then on I was to be all alone, all alone. Then I was filled with a numbing sense of indifference to everyone and to myself. Well, the Lord giveth and the Lord taketh away. The struggle was over. There was nothing and no one for whom to fight now.

The train ground to an abrupt halt in a snow-covered field. Awakened by the jolt, a few curious captives struggled to their feet to look out. The scene was reminiscent of cattle staring stupidly from a livestock car.

"Arrival: The Death Train" is from E. Wiesel, *The World Was Silent*, trans. Moshe Spiegel (Buenos Aires, 1956), in *An Anthology of Holocaust Literature*, ed. J. Glatstein, I. Knox, and S. Margoshes (Philadelphia: The Jewish Publication Society, 1969), pp. 3–5, 10. Reprinted by permission of the publisher.

Halt during railway journey near Jassy: "German S.S. guards surrounded the human cargo, shouting, 'All the dead are to be thrown out! All the dead are to be thrown out!' "—Elie Wiesel. (*Yad Vashem, Jerusalem*)

German S.S. guards surrounded the human cargo, shouting, "All the dead are to be thrown out! All the dead are to be thrown out!"

The living were pleased; there would be more space. It would not be as crowded now.

Strong men appeared and examined each one who could not stand up, and rapped out, "Here's one! Get hold of him!"

Whereupon two men would pick the corpse by the shoulders and feet and fling it out of the car like a sack of flour.

From various parts of the car came such cries as, "Here's another—my neighbor! He doesn't move. Help me get rid of him!"

There were some twenty-odd dead in our one car, and after they were stripped of their clothes, which the living snatched up, they were flung out of the car.

This task took several hours. Then the train chugged along, and as icy gusts shrieked about it, it seemed that through the accursed world about us could be heard the far-away, muffled wail of the naked bodies that had been abandoned on Polish snow-covered fields.

The journey was insufferable; and every one who lived through it later questioned the natural laws that their survival seemed to disprove.

We were deprived of even bread and water, and snow was our only source of water. Cramped for space and thoroughly chilled, we were very weak by the third day of the journey. Days were turned into nights, and the nights cast a shadow of doom over our very souls.

The train plodded along for what seemed countless days, and the snow fell, fell, fell incessantly. And the exhausted, travel-weary unfortunates lay huddled for days on end, without uttering a word, eyes closed, waiting for one thing only—the next station, where the new yield of corpses would be got rid of. That was what we looked forward to.

The journey lasted ten interminable days and nights. Each day claimed its toll of victims and each night paid its homage to the Angel of Death.

We passed through German settlements, generally in the early morning hours, only in a few instances. Sometimes men on their way to work would halt in their tracks to glare at us as though we were animals in a kind of demonic circus. Once a German churled a chunk of bread into our car and caused pandemonium to break out as scores of famished men fought each other in an effort to pounce upon it. And the German workers eyed the spectacle with sneering amusement.

We arrived at the Buchenwald concentration camp late at night. "Security police" of the camp came forward to unload the human cargo. The dead were left in the cars. Only those who were able to drag their feet got out. Meir Katz was left in the car; like so many others, he had frozen to death a short time before we reached our destination. The journey itself was the worst part of the ordeal. About forty of the deportees were claimed by death on that one day alone. Our car had originally started out with a hundred and twenty souls; twelve—among them my father and I—had survived the ordeal.

Genocide

RUDOLF HOESS

I, Rudolf Franz Ferdinand Hoess, being first duly sworn, depose and say as follows:

1. I am forty-six years old, and have been a member of the NSDAP since 1922; a member of the SS since 1934; a member of the Waffen-SS since 1939. I was a member from 1 December 1934 of the SS Guard Unit, the so-called Deathshead Formation [*Totenkopf Verband*].

2. I have been constantly associated with the administration of concentration camps since 1934, serving at Dachau until 1938; then as Adjutant in Sachenhausen from 1938 to May 1, 1940, when I was appointed Commandant of Auschwitz. I commanded Auschwitz until 1 December 1943, and estimate that at least 2,500,000 victims were executed and exterminated

"Genocide" is from the Office of the U.S. Chief of Counsel for the Prosecution of Axis Criminality, *Nazi Conspiracy and Aggression* (Washington, D.C.: Government Printing Office, 1947), vol. 6, pp. 787–790 (PS-3868).

there by gassing and burning, and at least another half million succumbed to starvation and disease making a total dead of about 3,000,000. This figure represents about 70% or 80% of all persons sent to Auschwitz as prisoners, the remainder having been selected and used for slave labor in the concentration camp industries. Included among the executed and burnt were approximately 20,000 Russian prisoners of war (previously screened out of Prisoner of War cages by the Gestapo) who were delivered at Auschwitz in Wehrmacht transports operated by regular Wehrmacht officers, 100,000 German Jews, and great numbers of citizens, mostly Jewish from Holland, France, Belgium, Poland, Hungary, Czechoslovakia, Greece, or other countries. We executed about 400,000 Hungarian Jews alone at Auschwitz in the summer of 1944. . . .

4. Mass executions by gassing commenced during the summer 1941 and continued until fall 1944. I personally supervised executions at Auschwitz until the first of December 1943 and know by reason of my continued duties . . . that these mass executions continued as stated above. All mass executions by gassing took place under the direct orders, supervisions, and responsibility of RSHA [Reich Security Main Office]. I received all orders for carrying out these mass executions directly from RSHA. . . .

6. The "final solution" of the Jewish question meant the complete extermination of all Jews in Europe. I was ordered to establish extermination facilities at Auschwitz in June 1941. At that time, there were already in the general government three other extermination camps; Belzek, Treblinka, and Wolzek. These camps were under the *Einsatzkommando* of the Security Police and SD. I visited Treblinka to find out how they carried out their extermination. The Camp Commandant at Treblinka told me that he had liquidated 80,000 in the course of one-half year. He was principally concerned with liquidating all the Jews from the Warsaw ghetto. He used monoxide gas and I did not think that his methods were very efficient. So when I set up the extermination building at Auschwitz, I used Cyclon B, which was a crystallized prussic acid which we dropped into the death chamber from a small opening. It took from 3 to 15 minutes to kill the people in the death chamber depending upon climatic conditions. We knew when the people were dead because their screaming stopped. We usually waited about one-half hour before we opened the doors and removed the bodies. After the bodies were removed our special commandos took off the rings and extracted the gold from the teeth of the corpses.

7. Another improvement we made over Treblinka was that we built our gas chambers to accommodate 2,000 people at one time, whereas at Treblinka their 10 gas chambers only accommodated 200 people each. The way we selected our victims was as follows: we had two SS doctors on duty at Auschwitz to examine the incoming transports of prisoners. The prisoners would be marched by one of the doctors who would make spot decisions as they walked by. Those who were fit for work were sent into the Camp. Others were sent immediately to the extermination plants. Children of tender years were invariably exterminated since by reason of their youth they were unable to work. Still another improvement we made over Treb-

linka was that at Treblinka the victims almost always knew that they were to be exterminated and at Auschwitz we endeavored to fool the victims into thinking that they were to go through a delousing process. Of course, frequently they realized our true intentions and we sometimes had riots and difficulties due to that fact. Very frequently women would hide their children under their clothes but of course when we found them we would send the children in to be exterminated. We were required to carry out these exterminations in secrecy but of course the foul and nauseating stench from the continuous burning of bodies permeated the entire area and all of the people living in the surrounding communities knew that exterminations were going on at Auschwitz.

8. We received from time to time special prisoners from the local Gestapo office. The SS doctors killed such prisoners by injections of benzine. Doctors had orders to write ordinary death certificates and could put down any reason at all for the cause of death.

9. From time to time we conducted medical experiments on women inmates, including sterilization and experiments relating to cancer. Most of the people who died under these experiments had been already condemned to death by the Gestapo. . . .

I understand English as it is written above. The above statements are true; this declaration is made by me voluntarily and without compulsion; after reading over the statements, I have signed and executed the same at Nuremberg, Germany, on the fifth day of April 1946.

Rudolf Franz Ferdinand Hoess

Subscribed and sworn to before me this 5th day of April 1946, at Nuremberg, Germany
Smith W. Brookhart Jr., Lt. Colonel, IGD

The Pit

HERMANN GRÄBE

On October 5, 1942, when I visited the building office at Dubno, my foreman told me that in the vicinity of the site, Jews from Dubno had been shot in three large pits, each about 30 metres long and 3 metres deep. About 1,500 persons had been killed daily. All the 5,000 Jews who had still been living in Dubno before the pogrom were to be liquidated. As the shooting had taken place in his presence, he was still much upset.

Thereupon, I drove to the site accompanied by my foreman and saw near it great mounds of earth, about 30 metres long and 2 metres high. Several trucks stood in front of the mounds. Armed Ukrainian militia

"The Pit" is from Louis L. Snyder, ed., *Documents of German History*, pp. 462–463. Copyright 1958 by Rutgers, The State University. Reprinted by permission of Rutgers University Press.

"I remember and I am afraid."—Elie Wiesel. (*Yad Vashem, Jerusalem*)

drove the people off the trucks under the supervision of an S.S. man. The militiamen acted as guards on the trucks and drove them to and from the pit. All these people had the regulation yellow patches on the front and back of their clothes, and thus could be recognized as Jews.

My foreman and I went directly to the pits. Nobody bothered us. Now I heard rifle shots in quick succession from behind one of the earth mounds. The people who had got off the trucks—men, women and children of all ages—had to undress upon the orders of an S.S. man, who carried a riding or dog whip. They had to put down their clothes in fixed places, sorted according to shoes, top clothing and underclothing. I saw a heap of shoes of about 800 to 1,000 pairs, great piles of underlinen and clothing.

Without screaming or weeping, these people undressed, stood around in family groups, kissed each other, said farewells, and waited for a sign from another S.S. man, who stood near the pit, also with a whip in his hand. During the fifteen minutes that I stood near I heard no complaint or plea for mercy. I watched a family of about eight persons, a man and a woman both about fifty with their children of about one, eight and ten, and two grown-up daughters of about twenty to twenty-nine. An old woman with snow-white hair was holding the one-year old child in her arms and singing to it and tickling it. The child was cooing with delight. The couple were looking on with tears in their eyes. The father was holding the hand of a boy about ten years old and speaking to him softly; the boy was fighting his tears. The father pointed to the sky, stroked his head, and seemed to explain something to him.

At that moment the S.S. man at the pit shouted something to his comrade. The latter counted off about twenty persons and instructed them to go behind the earth mound. Among them was the family which I have mentioned. I well remember a girl, slim and with black hair, who, as she passed close to me pointed to herself and said "23." I walked around the mound and found myself confronted by a tremendous grave. People were closely wedged together and lying on top of each other so that only their heads were visible. Nearly all had blood running over their shoulders from their heads. Some of the people shot were still moving. Some were lifting their arms and turning their heads to show that they were still alive. The pit was already two-thirds full. I estimated that it already contained about 1,000 people.

Gas

KURT GERSTEIN

In January, 1942, I was named chief of the Waffen SS technical disinfection services, including a section for extremely toxic gases. . . . SS Gruppenfuhrer Globocnik was waiting for us at Lublin. He told us, "This is one of the most secret matters there are, even the most secret. Anybody who talks about it will be shot immediately." He explained to us that there were three installations:

1) Belzec, on the Lublin-Lwow road. A maximum of 15,000 people per day.
2) Sobibor (I don't know exactly where it is), 20,000 people a day.
3) Treblinka, 120 kilometers NNE of Warsaw.
4) Maidanek, near Lublin (under construction).

Globocnik said: "You will have to disinfect large piles of clothing coming from Jews, Poles, Czechs, etc. Your other duty will be to improve the workings of our gas chambers, which operate on the exhaust from a Diesel engine. We need a more toxic and faster working gas, something like prussic acid. . . .

The following morning, a little before seven there was an announcement: "The first train will arrive in ten minutes!" A few minutes later a train arrived from Lemberg: 45 cars with more than 6,000 people. Two hundred Ukrainians assigned to this work flung open the doors and drove the Jews out of the cars with leather whips. A loud speaker gave instructions: Strip, even artificial limbs and glasses. Hand all money and valuables in at the 'valuables window.' Women and young girls are to have their hair cut in the 'barber's hut.' "

Then the march began. Barbed wire on both sides, in the rear two dozen Ukrainians with rifles. They drew near. Wirth and I found ourselves in front of the death chambers. Stark naked men, women, children, and cripples passed by. A tall SS man in the corner called to the unfortunates in a loud minister's voice: "Nothing is going to hurt you! Just breathe deep

---

"Gas" is from Leon Poliakov, *Harvest of Hate*, pp. 193–196. Copyright © 1954, The American Jewish Committee. Reprinted by permission.

and it will strengthen your lungs. It's a way to prevent contagious diseases. It's a good disinfectant!" They asked him what was going to happen and he answered: "The men will have to work, build houses and streets. The women won't have to do that, they will be busy with the housework and the kitchen." This was the last hope for some of these poor people, enough to make them march toward the death chambers without resistance. The majority knew everything; the smell betrayed it! They climbed a little wooden stairs and entered the death chambers, most of them silently, pushed by those behind them. A Jewess of about forty with eyes like fire cursed the murderers; she disappeared into the gas chambers after being struck several times by Captain Wirth's whip. . . . All were dead after thirty-two minutes! Jewish workers on the other side opened the wooden doors. They had been promised their lives in return for doing this horrible work, plus a small percentage of the money and valuables collected. The men still standing, like columns of stone, with no room to fall or lean. Even in death you could tell the families, all holding hands. It was difficult to separate them while emptying the rooms for the next batch. The bodies were tossed out, blue, wet with sweat and urine, the legs smeared with excrement and menstrual blood. Two dozen workers were busy checking mouths which they opened with iron hooks. "Gold to the left, no gold to the right." Others checked anus and genitals, looking for money, diamonds, gold, etc. Dentists knocked out gold teeth, bridges and crowns, with hammers. . . .

Then the bodies were thrown into big ditches near the gas chambers, about 100 by 20 by 12 meters. After a few days the bodies swelled and the whole mass rose up 2–3 yards because of the gas in the bodies. When the swelling went down several days later, the bodies matted down again. They told me later they poured Diesel oil over the bodies and burned them on railroad ties to make them disappear.

Mobile Killing

Kiev, 16 May 1942

Field Post Office
No 32704
B Nr 40/42

TOP SECRET

To: SS-Obersturmbannfuehrer Rauff
    Berlin, Prinz-Albrecht-Str. 8

pers.

R/29/5   Pradel n.R

b/R

Sinkkel [?] b.R., p 16/6
    The overhauling of vans by groups D and C is finished. . . .
    I ordered the vans of group D to be camouflaged as housetrailers by

putting one set of window shutters on each side of the small van and two on each side of the larger vans, such as one often sees on farm-houses in the country. The vans became so well-known, that not only the authorities, but also the civilian population called the van "death van", as soon as one of these vehicles appeared. It is my opinion, the van cannot be kept secret for any length of time, not even camouflaged. . . .

I ordered that during application of gas all the men were to be kept as far away from the vans as possible, so they should not suffer damage to their health by the gas which eventually would escape. I should like to take this opportunity to bring the following to your attention: several commands have had the unloading after the application of gas done by their own men. I brought to the attention of the commanders of the *Sonder-Kommando* [special unit] concerning the immense psychological injuries and damages to their health which that work can have for those men, even if not immediately, at least later on. The men complained to me about headaches which appeared after each unloading. Nevertheless prisoners called for that work, could use an opportune moment to flee. To protect the men from these damages, I request orders be issued accordingly.

The application of gas usually is not undertaken correctly. In order to come to an end as fast as possible, the driver presses the accelerator to the fullest extent. By doing that the persons to be executed suffer death from suffocation and not death by dozing off as was planned. My directions now have proved that by correct adjustment of the levers death comes faster and the prisoners fall asleep peacefully. Distorted faces and excretions, such as could be seen before, are no longer noticed.

Today I shall continue my journey to group B, where I can be reached with further news.

Signed: D. Becker
SS Untersturmfuehrer

Commandant of Auschwitz

RUDOLF HOESS

I must emphasise here that I have never personally hated the Jews. It is true that I looked upon them as the enemies of our people. But just because of this I saw no difference between them and the other prisoners, and I treated them all in the same way. I never drew any distinctions. In

"Mobile Killing" is from the Office of the U.S. Chief Counsel for Prosecution of Axis Criminality, *Nazi Conspiracy and Aggression* (Washington, D.C.: Government Printing Office, 1946), vol. 3, pp. 418–419 (PS-501).

"Commandant of Auschwitz" is from Rudolf Hoess, *Commandant of Auschwitz: The Autobiography of Rudolf Hoess,* trans. Constantine Fitzgibbon, pp. 147–149, 202–203. Copyright © 1959 by George Weidenfeld & Nicholson, Ltd. Copyright © 1961 by Pan Books, Ltd. Reprinted by permission.

any event the emotion of hatred is foreign to my nature. But I know what hate is, and what it looks like. I have seen it and I have suffered it myself.

When the Reichsfuhrer SS modified his original Extermination Order of 1941, by which all Jews without exception were to be destroyed, and ordered instead that those capable of work were to be separated from the rest and employed in the armaments industry, Auschwitz became a Jewish camp. It was a collecting place for Jews, exceeding in scale anything previously known.

Whereas the Jews who had been imprisoned in former years were able to count on being released one day and were thus far less affected psychologically by the hardships of captivity, the Jews in Auschwitz no longer had any such hope. They knew, without exception, that they were condemned to death, that they would live only so long as they could work.

Nor did the majority have any hope of a change in their sad lot. They were fatalists. Patiently and apathetically, they submitted to all the misery and distress and terror. The hopelessness with which they accepted their impending fate made them psychologically quite indifferent to their surroundings. This mental collapse accelerated its physical equivalent. They no longer had the will to live, everything had become a matter of indifference to them, and they would succumb to the slightest physical shock. Sooner or later, death was inevitable. I firmly maintain from what I have seen that the high mortality among the Jews was due not only to the hard work, to which most of them were unaccustomed, and to the insufficient food, the overcrowded quarters and all the severities and abuses of camp life, but principally and decisively to their psychological state. . . .

What I have just written applies to the bulk, the mass of the Jewish prisoners. The more intelligent ones, psychologically stronger and with a keener desire for life, that is to say in most cases those from the western countries, reacted differently.

These people, especially if they were doctors, had no illusions concerning their fate. But they continued to hope, reckoning on a change of fortune that somehow or other would save their lives. They also reckoned on the collapse of Germany, for it was not difficult for them to listen to enemy propaganda.

For them the most important thing was to obtain a position which would lift them out of the mass and give them special privileges, a job that would protect them to a certain extent from accidental and mortal hazards, and improve the physical conditions in which they lived.

They employed all their ability and all their will to obtain what can truly be described as a 'living' of this sort. The safer the position the more eagerly and fiercely it was fought for. No quarter was shown, for this was a struggle in which everything was at stake. They flinched from nothing, no matter how desperate, in their efforts to make such safe jobs fall vacant and then to acquire them for themselves. Victory usually went to the most unscrupulous man or woman. Time and again I heard of these struggles to oust a rival and win his job. . . .

So it can be seen that even in a small prison the governor is unable to prevent such behavior; how much more difficult was it in a concentration camp the size of Auschwitz!

I was certainly severe and strict. Often perhaps, when I look at it now, too severe and too strict.

In my disgust at the errors and abuses that I discovered, I may have spoken many hard words that I should have kept to myself. But I was never cruel, and I have never maltreated anyone, even in a fit of temper. A great deal happened in Auschwitz which was done ostensibly in my name, under my authority and on my orders, which I neither knew about nor sanctioned. But all these things happened in Auschwitz and so I am responsible. For the camp regulations say: the camp commandant is *fully* responsible for *everything* that happens in his sphere.

Jewish Resistance

As Hoess noted in his autobiography, many Jews went to their deaths as lambs to slaughter without struggling against their apparent fate. Still, it is misleading to characterize the acts of the condemned under duress as devoid of courage. In fact, there was constant Jewish resistance to the Nazis in the camps and ghettos. A Jewish Fighting Organization was active in the Warsaw ghetto, and resistance continued from January to mid-May 1943, when the Jews were finally defeated. Joseph Goebbels was rather surprised at their tenacity, as the excerpt from his diary indicates. An account by the Nazi SS chief in Warsaw of the destruction of the ghetto follows. The Treblinka death camp was often the final stop for Jews from the Warsaw ghetto. In August 1943, the inmates rebelled. Although the rebellion was ultimately unsuccessful, the camp was shut down shortly afterward. The last selection is a manifesto of a Jewish resistance organization in the Vilna ghetto dated a month after the revolt at Treblinka.

Nazi Problems in the Warsaw Ghetto (May 1, 1943)
JOSEPH GOEBBELS

Reports from the occupied areas contain no sensational news. The only noteworthy item is the exceedingly serious fights in Warsaw between the police and even a part of our Wehrmacht on the one hand and the rebellious Jews on the other. The Jews have actually succeeded in making a defensive position of the Ghetto. Heavy engagements are being fought there which led even to the Jewish Supreme Command's issuing daily communiques. Of course this fun won't last very long. But it shows what is to be expected of the Jews when they are in possession of arms. Unfortunately, some of their weapons are good German ones, especially machine guns. Heaven only knows how they got them. . . .

The Destruction of the Warsaw Ghetto (May 1943)
JÜRGEN STROOP

On 23 April 1943 the Reichsführer SS issued through the higher SS and Police Führer East at Cracow his order to complete the combing out of the Warsaw Ghetto with the greatest severity and relentless tenacity. I therefore decided to destroy the entire Jewish residential area by setting every block on fire, including the blocks of residential buildings near the armament works. One concern after the other was systematically evacuated and later destroyed by fire. In almost every case, the Jews then emerged from their hiding places and dug-outs. Not infrequently, the Jews stayed in the burning buildings until, because of the heat and the fear of being burned alive, they preferred to jump down from the upper storeys after having thrown mattresses and other upholstered articles into the street from the burning buildings. With their bones broken, they still tried to crawl across the streets into blocks of buildings which had not yet been set on fire or were only partly in flames. Often Jews changed their hiding places during the night, by moving into the ruins of burnt-out buildings, taking refuge there until they were found by our patrols. Their stay in the sewers also ceased to be pleasant after the first week. From the street we could frequently hear loud voices coming through the sewer shafts. Then the men of the Waffen SS, the police or the Wehrmacht engineers courageously climbed down the shafts to bring out the Jews and not infrequently they then stumbled over Jews already dead, or were shot at. It was always necessary to use smoke candles to drive out the Jews. Thus, one day we opened 183 sewer entrance holes and at a fixed time lowered smoke candles into them, so that the bandits fled from what they believed to be gas to the centre of the former Ghetto, where they could then be pulled out of the sewer holes. A great number of Jews, beyond counting, were exterminated by the blowing up of the sewers and dug-outs. . . .

Only through the continuous and untiring work of all involved did we succeed in catching a total of 56,065 Jews, whose extermination can be proved. To this should be added the number of Jews who lost their lives in explosions or fires, whose numbers could not be ascertained.

During the large-scale operation the Aryan population was informed by posters that it was strictly forbidden to enter the former Jewish Ghetto and

"The Destruction of the Warsaw Ghetto" is from Jeremy Noakes and Geoffrey Pridham, eds., *Documents on Nazism, 1919–1945*, pp. 491–492. Reprinted by permission of A. D. Peters & Co. Ltd.

Warsaw Jews on the way to the Treblinka death camp. (*Yad Vashem, Jerusalem*)

that anybody caught within the former Ghetto without a valid pass would be shot. At the same time these posters informed the Aryan population again that the death penalty would be imposed on anyone who intentionally gave refuge to a Jew, especially on anyone who lodged, supported or concealed a Jew outside the Jewish residential area. . . .

The large-scale action was terminated on 16 May 1943 with the blowing up of the Warsaw synagogue at 20.15 hours.

The Treblinka Revolt (August 1943)

STANISLAW KOHN

Before I arrived at Treblinka, in other words before October 1, 1942, cases of rebellion on the part of Jews had been reported. Thus, for example, a Jewish youth from Warsaw who worked in one of the death companies, having seen his wife and child escorted to the gas chamber, attacked the S.S. man, Max Bill, with a knife and killed him on the spot. From that day the S.S. barracks bore the name of this Hitlerite "martyr." Neither the plate on the wall of the barracks nor the massacre of Jews after this attack deterred us. This episode encouraged us to fight and take our revenge. The Warsaw youth became our ideal.

"The Treblinka Revolt" is from *An Anthology of Holocaust Literature*, ed. J. Glatstein, I. Knox, and S. Margoshes (Philadelphia: The Jewish Publication Society, 1969), pp. 319, 321–324. Reprinted by permission of the publisher.

A desire for revenge burned within us as we witnessed Hitler's extermination methods, and ripened each day and began to concretize into something precise, particularly from the moment when the fifty-year-old doctor, Choronzicki, of Warsaw, began to be active. The doctor worked in the camps as sanitation adviser, a task invented by the Germans to mock the humiliated victims even more vilely before despatching them to the gas chamber. He was a calm, cautious man who, on the surface, appeared very cold. He wandered around in his white apron with the sign of the Red Cross on his arm as in the olden days in his Warsaw consulting room, and seemed completely disinterested. But beneath his apron beat a warm Jewish heart, burning with desire for revenge. . . .

The date of the revolt was postponed several times for various reasons. And then the last transports of the Warsaw Jews were brought to Treblinka. From them we learned about the ghetto revolt. The Germans treated them with particular savagery; most of the trucks were full of corpses of ghetto combatants who had refused to leave the ghetto alive. Those who now arrived were no longer resigned and indifferent creatures like their predecessors. . . .

The desire for revenge increased continuously. The terror-stricken eyes of the Jews being led to their death, and throngs into the gas chamber, called for revenge.

At last the leader, Galewski, gave the signal for the revolt. The date fixed was for Monday, August 2, 1943, at five o'clock in the afternoon. This was the plan of action: to lay an ambush for the chief murderers, to liquidate them, to disarm the warders, cut the telephone wires and then burn and destroy all the extermination plants so that they could never function again; to free the Poles from the detention camp of Treblinka, to flee into the forest to organize a partisan band. . . .

At two o'clock in the afternoon the distribution of weapons began. It was very difficult to purloin the hand grenades from the armory. . . . Marcus and Salzberg took up the carpets and beat them in front of the armory. The guards were obliged to move away for a while. At that moment the door of the armory was opened with our key [which had been stolen] and Jacek, the Hungarian boy, slipped inside, climbed onto the window sill at the end of the room, cut out a small square in the glass with a diamond and handed out the bombs and other weapons to Jacob Miller who put them on his refuse cart. The arms were carried to the garage. This time the hand grenades acted as a spur.

Spirits grew agitated and no one could keep the secret. The leaders therefore decided to start the revolt an hour before the agreed time.

Punctually at four o'clock in the afternoon messages were sent to all groups with orders to assemble immediately in the garage to fetch their weapons.

Anyone coming to fetch weapons had to give the password, "Death," to which the reply was "life." "Death-Life," "Death-Life!" Cries of enthusiasm arose as the long-hoped-for guns, revolvers and hand grenades were distributed. At the same time the chief murderers of the camp were attacked. Telephonic communication was cut and the watchtowers were set on fire with petrol. The armory was taken by assault and the weapons distributed. We already had two hundred armed men. The others attacked the Germans with axes and spades.

We set fire to the gas chambers, burned the railway station with all the notices. . . . We burned the barracks. . . .

The flames and the reports of the firing roused the Germans who began to arrive from all sides. S.S. and police arrived from Kosow, soldiers from the nearby airfield and finally a special section of the Warsaw S.S. Orders had been given to make for the neighboring forest. Most of our fighters fell but there were many German casualties. Very few of us survived.

Manifesto of the Jewish Resistance in Vilna (September 1943)

Offer armed resistance! Jews, defend yourselves with arms!

The German and Lithuanian executioners are at the gates of the ghetto. They have come to murder us! Soon they will lead you forth in groups through the ghetto door.

Tens of thousands of us were despatched. But we shall not go! We will not offer our heads to the butcher like sheep.

Jews, defend yourselves with arms!

Do not believe the false promises of the assassins or believe the words of the traitors.

Anyone who passes through the ghetto gate will go to Ponar! [Death Camp]

And Ponar means death!

Jews, we have nothing to lose. Death will overtake us in any event. And who can still believe in survival when the murderer exterminates us with so much determination? The hand of the executioner will reach each man and woman. Flight and acts of cowardice will not save our lives.

Active resistance alone can save our lives and our honor.

Brothers! It is better to die in battle in the ghetto than to be carried away to Ponar like sheep. And know this: within the walls of the ghetto there are organized Jewish forces who will resist with weapons.

Support the revolt!

Do not take refuge or hide in the bunkers, for then you will fall into the hands of the murderers like rats.

Jewish people, go out into the squares. Anyone who has no weapons should take an ax, and he who has no ax should take a crowbar or a bludgeon!

"Manifesto of the Jewish Resistance in Vilna" is from *An Anthology of Holocaust Literature*, ed. J. Glatstein, I. Knox, and S. Margoshes (Philadelphia: The Jewish Publication Society, 1969), pp. 332–333. Reprinted by permission of the publisher.

For our ancestors!
For our murdered children!
Avenge Ponar!
Attack the murderers!

In every street, in every courtyard, in every house within and without the ghetto, attack these dogs!

Jews, we have nothing to lose! We shall save our lives only if we exterminate our assassins.

Long live liberty! Long live armed resistance! Death to the assassins!

The Commander of the F.P.A.

Vilna, the Ghetto, September 1, 1943.

Judgment and Reflection

The Nuremberg Trials
(November 1945–October 1946)

In the spring of 1945, Allied troops fought their way into the heart of Nazi Germany. Infamous concentration camps such as Dachau and Buchenwald were liberated by soldiers; the German inhabitants of the area were forced to view the horrors perpetrated by their "neighbors." Judgment was demanded and an international court was established in Nuremberg. Its responsibility was to pass sentence on the various Nazi leaders after first examining documentary evidence and transcripts of oral testimony. No court has ever attained such universal recognition. Transcripts and documents of the proceedings fill forty-two large volumes. The following selection is from the summation of Justice Robert H. Jackson, the chief American prosecutor.

The Crimes of the Nazi Regime
JUSTICE ROBERT H. JACKSON

The Nazi movement will be an evil memory in history because of its persecution of the Jews, the most far-flung and terrible racial persecution of all time. Although the Nazi party neither invented nor monopolized anti-Semitism, its leaders from the very beginning embraced it, and exploited it. They used it as "the psychological spark that ignites the mob."

"The Crimes of the Nazi Regime" is from Office of the U.S. Chief of Counsel for the Prosecution of Axis Criminality, *Nazi Conspiracy and Aggression* (Washington, D.C.: Government Printing Office, 1947), Supplement A, pp. 15–16, 44.

After the seizure of power, it became an official state policy. The persecution began in a series of discriminatory laws eliminating the Jews from the civil service, the professions, and economic life. As it became more intense it included segregation of Jews in ghettos, and exile. Riots were organized by party leaders to loot Jewish business places and to burn synagogues. Jewish property was confiscated and a collective fine of a billion marks was imposed upon German Jewry. The program progressed in fury and irresponsibility to the "final solution." This consisted of sending all Jews who were fit to work to concentration camps as slave laborers, and all who were not fit, which included children under 12 and people over 50, as well as any others judged unfit by an SS doctor, to concentration camps for extermination. . . .

The chief instrumentality for persecution and extermination was the concentration camp, sired by defendant Goering and nurtured under the overall authority of defendants Frick and Kaltenbrunner.

The horrors of these iniquitous places have been vividly disclosed by documents and testified to by witnesses. The Tribunal must be satiated with ghastly verbal and pictorial portrayals. From your records it is clear that the concentration camps were the first and worst weapons of oppression used by the National Socialist State, and that they were the primary means utilized for the persecution of the Christian Church and the extermination of the Jewish race. This has been admitted to you by some of the defendants from the witness stand. In the words of defendant Frank: "A thousand years will pass and this guilt of Germany will still not be erased.". . .

It is against such a background that these defendants now ask this Tribunal to say that they are not guilty of planning, executing, or conspiring to commit this long list of crimes and wrongs. They stand before the record of this trial. . . . If you were to say of these men that they are not guilty, it would be as true to say there has been no war, there are no slain, there has been no crime.

Judgment and Sentence

At Nuremberg, the accused Nazis were indicted on one or more charges: (1) Crimes against Peace (conspiracy), (2) War Crimes, (3) Crimes against Humanity, (4) Membership in a Criminal Organization. The verdict on some of the major Nazi figures of the Holocaust are presented next, followed by an account of the execution of Julius Streicher as described by Kingsbury Smith, European general manager of International News Service. Streicher, a former elementary school teacher and fanatical Nazi, published Der Stürmer, *the most violently anti-Semitic journal in the Reich.*

"Judgment and Sentence" is from International Military Tribunal, *Nuremberg Trials of the Major War Criminals* (Nuremberg: Allied Central Commission, 1948), vol. 22, pp. 524, 527, 544–549.

Hermann Goering

Goering is indicted on all four Counts. The evidence shows that after Hitler he was the most prominent man in the Nazi regime. He was Commander-in-Chief of the *Luftwaffe*. Plenipotentiary for the Four Year Plan, he had tremendous influence with Hitler, at least until 1943, when their relationship deteriorated, ending in his arrest in 1945. He testified that Hitler kept him informed of all important military and political problems. . . .

Goering persecuted the Jews, particularly after the November 1938 riots, and not only in Germany . . . but in the conquered territories as well. . . . As these countries fell before the German Army, he extended the Reich anti-Jewish laws to them. . . . Although their extermination was in Himmler's hands, Goering was far from disinterested or inactive, despite his protestations in the witness box. By decree of 31 July 1941 he directed Himmler and Heydrich to "bring about a complete solution of the Jewish question in the German sphere of influence in Europe."

There is nothing to be said in mitigation. For Goering was often, indeed almost always, the moving force, second only to his leader. He was the leading war aggressor, both as political and as military leader; he was the director of the slave labor program and the creator of the oppressive program against the Jews and other races, at home and abroad. All of these crimes he frankly admitted. On some specific cases there may be conflict of testimony, but in terms of the broad outline his own admissions are more than sufficiently wide to be conclusive of his guilt. His guilt is unique in its enormity. The record discloses no excuses for this man.

The Tribunal finds the Defendant Goering guilty of all four Counts of the Indictment.

Wilhelm Frick

Frick is indicted on all four Counts. Recognized as the chief Nazi administrative specialist and bureaucrat, he was appointed Reich Minister of the Interior in Hitler's first cabinet.

Always rabidly anti-Semitic, Frick drafted, signed, and administered many laws designed to eliminate Jews from German life and economy. His work formed the basis of the Nuremberg Decrees, and he was active in enforcing them. Responsible for prohibiting Jews from following various professions and for confiscating their property, he signed a final decree in 1943, after the mass destruction of Jews in the East, which placed them "outside the law" and handed them over to the *Gestapo*. These laws paved the way for the "final solution," and were extended by Frick to the incorporated territories and to certain of the occupied territories. While he was Reich Protector of Bohemia and Moravia, thousands of Jews were transferred from the Terezin ghetto in Czechoslovakia to Auschwitz, where they were killed. He issued a decree providing for special penal laws against Jews and Poles in the Governmental General. . . .

During the war nursing homes, hospitals, and asylums in which euthanasia was practised as described elsewhere in this Judgment, came under Frick's jurisdiction. He had knowledge that insane, sick, and aged people, "useless eaters," were being systematically put to death. Complaints of these murders reached him, but he did nothing to stop them. A report of the Czechoslovak War Crimes Commission estimated that 275,000 mentally deficient and aged people, for whose welfare he was responsible, fell victim to it.

The Tribunal finds that Frick is not guilty on Count One. He is guilty on Counts Two, Three and Four.

Julius Streicher

Streicher is indicted on Counts One and Four. One of the earliest members of the Nazi Party, joining in 1921, he took part in the Munich Putsch. From 1925 to 1940 he was Gauleiter of Franconia. Elected to the Reichstag in 1933, he was an honorary general in the SA. His persecution of the Jews was notorious. He was the publisher of *Der Stürmer*, an anti-Semitic weekly newspaper, from 1923 to 1945 and was its editor until 1933. . . .

For his 25 years of speaking, writing, and preaching hatred of the Jews, Streicher was widely known as "Jew-Baiter Number One." In his speeches and articles, week after week, month after month, he infected the German mind with the virus of anti-Semitism and incited the German people to active persecution. Each issue of *Der Stürmer*, which reached a circulation of 600,000 in 1935, was filled with such articles, often lewd and disgusting. . . .

As the war in the early stages proved successful in acquiring more and more territory for the Reich, Streicher even intensified his efforts to incite the Germans against the Jews. In the record are 26 articles from *Der Stürmer*, published between August 1941 and September 1944, 12 by Streicher's own hand, which demanded annihilation and extermination in unequivocal terms. He wrote and published on 25 December 1941:

"If the danger of the reproduction of that curse of God in the Jewish blood is finally to come to an end, then there is only one way—the extermination of that people whose father is the devil." And in February 1944 his own article stated: "Whoever does what a Jew does is a scoundrel, a criminal. And he who repeats and wishes to copy him deserves the same fate: annihilation, death."

With knowledge of the extermination of the Jews in the Occupied Eastern Territories, this defendant continued to write and publish his propaganda of death. Testifying in this Trial, he vehemently denied any knowledge of mass executions of Jews. But the evidence makes it clear that he continually received current information on the progress of the "final solution."

Streicher's incitement to murder and extermination at the time when Jews in the East were being killed under the most horrible conditions clearly constitutes persecution on political and racial grounds in connection with War Crimes, as defined by the Charter, and constitutes a Crime against Humanity.

The Tribunal finds that Streicher is not guilty on Count One, but that he is guilty on Count Four.

The Execution of Julius Streicher (1946)
KINGSBURY SMITH

The only one, however, to make any reference to Nazi ideology was Julius Streicher, that arch Jew-baiter. Displaying the most bitter and enraged defiance of any of the condemned, he screamed "Heil Hitler" at the top of his voice as he was about to mount the steps leading to the gallows.

Streicher appeared in the execution hall, which had been used only last Saturday night for a basketball game by American security guards, at twelve and a half minutes after two o'clock.

As in the case of all the condemned, a warning knock by a guard outside preceded Streicher's entry through a door in the middle of the hall.

An American lieutenant colonel sent to fetch the condemned from the death row of the cell block to the near-by prison wing entered first. He was followed by Streicher, who was stopped immediately inside the door by two American sergeants. They closed in on each side of him and held his arms while another sergeant removed the manacles from his hands and replaced them with a leather cord.

The first person whom Streicher and the others saw upon entering the gruesome hall was an American lieutenant colonel who stood directly in front of him while his hands were being tied behind his back as they had been manacled upon his entrance.

This ugly, dwarfish little man, wearing a threadbare suit and a well-worn bluish shirt buttoned to the neck but without a tie, glanced at the three wooden scaffolds rising up menacingly in front of him.

Two of these were used alternately to execute the condemned men while the third was kept in reserve.

After a quick glance at the gallows, Streicher glared around the room, his eyes resting momentarily upon the small group of American, British, French, and Russian officers on hand to witness the executions.

By this time Streicher's hands were tied securely behind his back. Two

"The Execution of Julius Streicher" is from *New York Journal-American* (October 16, 1946). Reprinted by permission of United Press International, Copyright 1946.

guards, one to each arm, directed him to No. 1 gallows on the left entrance. He walked steadily the six feet to the first wooden step, but his face was twitching nervously. As the guards stopped him at the bottom of the steps for official identification requests, he uttered his piercing scream:

"Heil Hitler!"

His shriek sent a shiver down the back of this International News Service correspondent, who is witnessing the executions as sole representative of the American press.

As its echo died away, another American colonel standing by the steps said sharply:

"Ask the man his name."

In response to the interpreter's query Streicher shouted:

"You know my name well."

The interpreter repeated his request, and the condemned man yelled:

"Julius Streicher."

As he mounted the platform Streicher cried out:

"Now it goes to God!"

After getting up the thirteen steps to the eight-foot-high and eight-foot-square black-painted wooden platform, Streicher was pushed two steps to the mortal spot beneath the hangman's rope.

This was suspended from an iron ring attached to a crossbeam which rested on two posts. The rope was being held back against a wooden rail by the American Army sergeant hangman.

Streicher was swung around to face the front.

He glanced again at the Allied officers and the eight Allied correspondents representing the world's press who were lined up against a wall behind small tables directly facing the gallows.

The American officer standing at the scaffold said:

"Ask the man if he has any last words."

When the interpreter had translated, Streicher shouted:

"The Bolsheviks will hang you one day."

As the black hood was being adjusted about his head, Streicher was heard saying:

"Adele, my dear wife."

At that moment the trap was sprung with a loud bang. With the rope snapped taut and the body swinging wildly, a groan could be heard distinctly within the dark interior of the scaffold.

Why?

The most difficult question to answer regarding a genocidal policy is why people participate in such action. In the first selection, Rudolf Hoess, the commandant of Auschwitz, speaks of the formation of his character. The next sections are from two influential authors who have written books about fanaticism.

"Whatever They Said Was Always Right"

RUDOLF HOESS

I had been brought up by my parents to be respectful and obedient towards all grown-up people, and especially the elderly, regardless of their social status. I was taught that my highest duty was to help those in need. It was constantly impressed upon me in forceful terms that I must obey promptly the wishes and commands of my parents, teachers and priests, and indeed of all grown-up people, including servants, and that nothing must distract me from this duty. Whatever they said was always right.

These basic principles on which I was brought up became part of my flesh and blood. I can still clearly remember how my father, who on account of his fervent Catholicism was a determined opponent of the Reich government and its policy, never ceased to remind his friends that, however strong one's opposition might be, the laws and decrees of the State had to be obeyed unconditionally.

From my earliest youth I was brought up with a strong awareness of duty. In my parents' house it was insisted that every task be exactly and conscientiously carried out. Each member of the family had his own special duties to perform. My father took particular care to see that I obeyed all his instructions and wishes with the greatest meticulousness. I remember to this day how he hauled me out of bed one night, because I had left the saddle-cloth lying in the garden instead of hanging it up in the barn to dry, as he had told me to do. I had simply forgotten all about it. Again and again he impressed on me how great evils almost always spring from small, apparently insignificant misdeeds. At that time I did not fully understand the meaning of this dictum, but in later years I was to learn, through bitter experience, the truth of his words.

I remain, as I have always been, a convinced National-Socialist in my attitude to life. When a man has adhered to a belief and an attitude for nigh on twenty-five years, has grown up with it and become bound to it body and soul, he cannot simply throw it aside because the embodiments of this ideal, the National-Socialist State and its leaders have used their powers wrongly and even criminally, and because as a result of this failure and misdirection his world has collapsed and the entire German people been plunged for decades into untold misery. I, at least, cannot.

From the documents published and from the Nuremberg trials I can see that the leaders of the Third Reich, because of their policy of force, were guilty of causing this vast war and all its consequences. I see that these leaders, by means of exceptionally effective propaganda and of limitless terrorism, were able to make the whole German people so docile and submissive that they were ready, with very few exceptions, to go wherever they were led, without voicing a word of criticism. . . .

In order to disguise a policy of force it is necessary to use propaganda so that a clever distortion of all the facts, the policies and measures of the rulers of the State can be made palatable. Terrorism must be used from the outset, to stifle all doubt and opposition.

The True Believer

ERIC HOFFER

The impulse to fight springs less from self-interest than from intangibles such as tradition, honor (a word), and, above all, hope. Where there is no hope, people either run, or allow themselves to be killed without a fight. They will hang on to life as in a daze. How else explain the fact that millions of Europeans allowed themselves to be led into annihilation camps and gas chambers, knowing beyond doubt that they were being led to death? It was not the least of Hitler's formidable powers that he knew how to drain his opponents (at least in continental Europe) of all hope. His fanatical conviction that he was building a new order that would last a thousand years communicated itself both to followers and antagonists. To the former it gave the feeling that in fighting for the Third Reich they were in league with eternity, while the latter felt that to struggle against Hitler's new order was to defy inexorable fate. . . .

To rely on the evidence of the senses and of reason is heresy and treason. It is startling to realize how much unbelief is necessary to make belief possible. What we know as blind faith is sustained by innumerable unbeliefs. The fanatical Japanese in Brazil refused to believe for years the evidence of Japan's defeat. The fanatical Communist refuses to believe any unfavorable report or evidence about Russia, nor will he be disillusioned by seeing with his own eyes the cruel misery inside the Soviet promised land.

It is the true believer's ability to "shut his eyes and stop his ears" to facts that do not deserve to be either seen or heard which is the source of his unequaled fortitude and constancy. He cannot be frightened by danger nor disheartened by obstacle nor baffled by contradictions because he denies their existence. Strength of faith . . . manifests itself not in moving mountains but in not seeing mountains move. And it is the certitude of his infallible doctrine that renders the true believer impervious to the uncertainties, surprises and the unpleasant realities of the world around him.

Thus the effectiveness of a doctrine should not be judged by its profundity, sublimity or the validity of the truths it embodies, but by how thoroughly it insulates the individual from his self and the world as it is. What Pascal said of an effective religion is true of any effective doctrine: It must be "contrary to nature, to common sense and to pleasure."

Darkness at Noon

ARTHUR KOESTLER

There are only two conceptions of human ethics, and they are at opposite poles. One of them is Christian and humane, declares the individual to be sacrosanct, and asserts that the rules of arithmetic are not to be applied to human units. The other starts from the basic principle that a collective aim justifies all means, and not only allows, but demands, that the individual should in every way be subordinated and sacrificed to the community— which may dispose of it as an experimentation rabbit or a sacrificial lamb. The first conception could be called anti-vivisection morality, the second, vivisection morality. Humbugs and dilettantes have always tried to mix the two conceptions; in practice, it is impossible. Whoever is burdened with power and responsibility finds out on the first occasion that he has to choose; and he is fatally driven to the second alternative. Do you know, since the establishment of Christianity as a state religion, a single example of a state which really followed a Christian policy? You can't point out one. In times of need—and politics are chronically in a time of need—the rulers were always able to evoke 'exceptional circumstances,' which demanded exceptional measures of defence. Since the existence of nations and classes, they live in a permanent state of mutual self-defence, which forces them to defer to another time the putting into practice of humanism. . . .

Could the Holocaust Happen Again?

> *One of the foremost authorities on the Holocaust is Raul Hilberg. In his book* The Destruction of the European Jews, *he offers some perspective on the possibilities of reoccurrence. The second selection is by Elie Wiesel, himself a survivor of the death camps and now a professor of philosophy and winner of the 1986 Nobel Peace Prize. He wrote this newspaper article in 1974.*

The Destruction of the European Jews

RAUL HILBERG

The destruction of the European Jews between 1933 and 1945 appears to us now as an unprecedented event in history. Indeed, in its dimensions and total configuration, nothing like it had ever happened before. Five million people were killed as a result of an organized undertaking in the short space of a few years. The operation was over before anyone could grasp its enormity, let alone its implications for the future.

Yet if we analyze that singularly massive upheaval, we discover that most of what happened in those twelve years had already happened before. The Nazi destruction process did not come out of a void; it was the culmination of a cyclical trend. We have observed the trend in the three successive goals of anti-Jewish administrators. The missionaries of Christianity had said in effect: You have no right to live among us as Jews. The secular rulers who followed had proclaimed: You have no right to live among us. The German Nazis at last decreed: You have no right to live. . . .

As time passes, the destruction of the European Jews will recede into the background. Its most immediate consequences are almost over, and whatever developments may henceforth be traced to the catastrophe will be consequences of consequences, more and more remote. Already the Nazi outburst has become historical. But this is a strange page in history. Few events of modern times were so filled with unpredicted action and suspected death. A primordial impulse had suddenly surfaced among the Western nations; it had been unfettered through their machines. From this moment, fundamental assumptions about our civilization have no longer stood unchallenged, for while the occurrence is past, the phenomenon remains.

Before the emergence of the 20th century and its technology, a destructive mind could not play in fantasy with the thoughts that the Nazis were to translate into action. The administrator of earlier centuries did not have the tools. He did not possess the network of communications; he did not dispose over rapid small arms fire and quick-working poison gasses. The bureaucrat of tomorrow would not have these problems; already, he is better equipped than the German Nazis were. Killing is not as difficult as it used to be. The modern administrative apparatus has facilities for rapid, concerted movements and for efficient massive killings. These devices not only trap a larger number of victims; they also require a greater degree of specialization, and with that division of labor the moral burden too is fragmented among the participants. The perpetrator can now kill his victims without touching them. He may feel sure of his success and safe from its repercussions. This ever-growing capacity for destruction cannot be arrested anywhere. . . .

Since the end of the Jewish catastrophe, basic decisions have been made about the future. In the Christian world the remaining alternatives are gradually moving toward polar ends. After two thousand years there is no defensible middle ground. The ancient compromise, with all its contradictions, is weakening day by day. To the Jewish community that growing dichotomy conveys unique opportunities and unprecedented vulnerabilities. Jewry is faced with ultimate weapons. It has no deterrent. The Jews can live more freely now. They can also die more quickly. The summit is within sight. An abyss has opened below.

Ominous Signs and Unspeakable Thoughts (1974)

ELIE WIESEL

I admit it sadly: I feel threatened. For the first time in many years I feel that I am in danger. For the first time in my adult life I am afraid that the nightmare may start all over again, or that it has never ended, that since 1945 we have lived in parentheses. Now they are closed.

Could the Holocaust happen again? Over the years I have often put the question to my young students. And they, consistently, have answered yes, while I said no. I saw it as a unique event that would remain unique. I believed that if mankind had learned anything from it, it was that hate and murder reach beyond the direct participants; he who begins by killing others, in the end will kill his own. Without Auschwitz, Hiroshima would not have been possible. The murder of one people inevitably leads to that of mankind.

In my naivete I thought, especially in the immediate postwar period, Jews would never again be singled out, handed over to the executioner. That anti-Semitism had received its death-blow long ago, under the fiery skies of Poland. I was somehow convinced that—paradoxically—man would be shielded, protected by the awesome mystery of the Event.

I was wrong. What happened once, could happen again. Perhaps I am exaggerating. Perhaps I am oversensitive. But then I belong to a traumatized generation. We have learned to take threats more seriously than promises.

There are signs and they are unmistakable. The sickening spectacle of a diplomatic gathering wildly applauding a spokesman for killers. The scandalous exclusion of Israel from UNESCO. The arrogant self-righteousness of certain leaders, the cynicism of others. The dramatic solitude of Israel. The anti-Semitic statements made by America's top general. Anti-Semitism has become fashionable once more both in the East and in the West.

No wonder then that suddenly one hears discussions on a subject that many of us had thought buried long ago: Jewish survival. Can Israel—the country, the people—survive another onslaught? How many times must it sacrifice the best of its children? How long can one go on living in a hostile world? Is it conceivable that Hitler could be victorious posthumously?

For those of us who have lived and endured the human and Jewish condition in its ultimate depth know: at this turning point in history, the Jewish people and the Jewish State are irrevocably linked; one cannot survive without the other. As a community, we have rarely been so united. And never so alone.

And so, the idea of another catastrophe is no longer unthinkable. I say it reluctantly. In fact, it is the first time I say it. I have chosen until now to place the Holocaust on a mystical or ontological level, one that defies language and transcends imagination. I have quarreled with friends who built entire theories and doctrines on an event which, in my view, is not to be used or approached casually. If I speak of it now, it is only because of my realization that Jewish survival is being recalled into question.

Hence the fear in me. All of a sudden, I am too much reminded of past experiences. The enemy growing more and more popular. The aggressiveness of the blackmailers, the permissiveness of some leaders and the total submissiveness of others. The overt threats. The complacency and diffidence of the bystanders. I feel as my father must have felt when he was my age.

Not that I foresee the possibility of Jews being massacred in the cities of America or in the forests of Europe. Death-factories will not be built again. But there is a certain climate, a certain mood in the making. As far as the Jewish people are concerned, the world has remained unchanged: as indifferent to our fate as to its own.

And so I look at my young students and tremble for their future; I see myself at their age surrounded by ruins. What am I to tell them?

I would like to be able to tell them that in spite of endless disillusionments one must maintain faith in man and in mankind; that one must never lose heart. I would like to tell them that, notwithstanding the official discourses and policies, our people do have friends and allies and reasons to advocate hope. But I have never lied to them, I am not going to begin now. And yet. . . .

Despair is no solution. I know that. What is the solution? Hitler had one. And he tried it while a civilized world kept silent.

I remember. And I am afraid.

CHRONOLOGY: THE JEWISH HOLOCAUST

March 23, 1933	Hitler obtains the Enabling Law granting him dictatorial powers for four years.
April 1, 1933	National boycott of all Jewish businesses and professions.
April 7, 1933	Civil Service law permits removal of Jews and other opponents.
August 2, 1934	Death of President Hindenburg. Hitler assumes Presidency but retains title *Der Führer*. Army swears allegiance.
September 15, 1935	Nuremberg laws prohibit marriage and sexual intercourse between Jews and German nationals.
November 9–10, 1938	Anti-Jewish pogrom, the *Kristallnacht* (Crystal Night).
September 1, 1939	Germany invades Poland forcing declarations of war from Britain and France two days later.

September 21, 1939	Polish Jews ordered into ghettos.
October 12, 1939	Austrian Jews deported to east.
May 10, 1940	Germany invades Holland, France, and Belgium.
June 22, 1941	German forces launch invasion of Russia.
July 31, 1941	Reich Marshall Hermann Goering gives SS Lt. Colonel Reinhard Heydrich a written order to achieve a "general solution to the Jewish problem in areas of Jewish influence in Europe."
January 20, 1942	Heydrich proposes Final Solution to the "Jewish problem" at Wansee Conference.
July 1942	Liquidation of Jewish ghetto in Warsaw begins.
August–September 1942	German advance in North Africa halted at El Alamein.
February 2, 1943	German army at Stalingrad surrenders.
June 6, 1944	D-Day invasion of allied forces on Normandy coast. Liberation of concentration camps begins as allies gradually secure territory from German control.
May 2, 1945	Fall of Berlin to Soviet forces.
May 7, 1945	German surrender. Resettlement of Jews becomes a political and moral issue in post-war Europe.

STUDY QUESTIONS

1. What were the main accusations leveled against the Jews by Hitler and the Nazis? Does the Jewish defense seem convincing? Why were the Jews legally restricted?
2. In the conference on the Jewish question (November 12, 1938), the topic concerned the isolation of the Jews. What measures does Heydrich advocate? Why is Goering's solution inevitable?
3. What solutions to the Jewish problem were presented at the Wansee Conference? On the basis of this evidence and on the directive of Hermann Goering, how would you define the "Final Solution"? What did it entail? Why was there no specific talk of extermination in these documents?
4. After reading through the accounts concerning the death camps, what are your feelings? What statements by Rudolf Hoess in his testimony at Nuremberg and in his autobiography stand out in your mind? Why? How does he free himself from guilt while still accepting it?

5. Granted that Jews were both submissive and resistant to Nazi atrocities during the Holocaust, how do you think you would react under the same stress and abuse?

6. In your opinion, was justice served and the dead avenged by the Nuremberg trials and execution of Nazi leaders?

7. In the opinion of Eric Hoffer, why were the Jews killed and why are people able to commit such acts? Do you agree with him?

8. Comment on another statement of Eric Hoffer's: "It is obvious . . . that in order to be effective, a doctrine must not be understood, but has to be believed in. We can be absolutely certain only about things we do not understand; a doctrine that is understood is shorn of its strength." Do you agree? How can you relate this to the Holocaust?

9. What meaning does Arthur Koestler's message in *Darkness at Noon* have for the Holocaust?

10. After reading the selections by Raul Hilberg, "The Destruction of the European Jews," and Elie Wiesel, "Ominous Signs and Unspeakable Thoughts," do you think such a thing as the Holocaust could happen again? In a way, was the Holocaust the inevitable outcome of the racist and Social Darwinist ideas that were discussed in the chapter on "Nationalism and Imperialism"? Was the Holocaust "conditioned" by the expendability of life that was so characteristic of battles during World War I? Was the Holocaust itself a precedent for the American bombing of Hiroshima? As you look at the world today, give some examples of attitudes, specific organizations, or individuals that might threaten reoccurrence of genocide. What can be done?

10

Our Contemporary World: The Progress of Civilization

The reasonable man adapts himself to the world: the unreasonable one persists in trying to adapt the world to himself. Therefore all progress depends upon the unreasonable man.

—George Bernard Shaw

I have always considered that the substitution of the internal combustion engine for the horse marked a very gloomy milestone in the progress of mankind.

—Sir Winston Churchill

In their worship of the machine, many Americans have . . . confused progress with mechanization.

—Lewis Mumford

Progress, far from consisting of change, depends on retentiveness. Those who cannot remember the past are condemned to repeat it.

—George Santayana

All progress is based upon a universal innate desire, on the part of every organism to live beyond its income.

—Samuel Butler

The necessary has never been man's top priority. The passionate pursuit of the nonessential and the extravagant is one of the chief traits of human uniqueness. Unlike other forms of life, man's greatest exertions are made in the pursuit not of necessities, but of superfluities. Man is the only creature who strives to surpass himself, and yearns for the impossible.

—Eric Hoffer

And the end of all our exploring, will be to arrive where we started, and know the place for the first time.

—T. S. Eliot

————————

The twentieth century has been a most extraordinary time in which to live—extraordinary because the changes that have taken place in science, technology, governmental systems, and especially daily life have occurred in such a short span of time. We live today with computers that can calculate, store, and retrieve information far more quickly and efficiently than is humanly possible. We were amazed in 1969 when a human finally walked on the moon, and we still anticipate news from interplanetary probes, which hold out the possibility of discovering other forms of life. Medical research has developed vaccines for dreaded diseases, extended life by transplanting organs, and even unlocked the possibilities of changing the human condition itself through discovery of DNA and genetic engineering. All these accomplishments bespeak progress. But this progress entails risks that threaten to destroy all that has been created.

There is a curious paradox that technological progress contributes to the ultimate insecurity of humankind. We marvel at the computer revolution, yet fear the specter of "Big Brother," which looms large and threatens personal freedom by controlling information. We in the twentieth century are faced with the ultimate concern: the survival of civilization itself. The obliteration of the human species has never before been within its own power. Those who were born after 1945 have inherited the responsibility of maintaining peace and therefore existence.

So how does one define the word "progress"? Far too often we forget that progress is not necessarily a technological or scientific preserve. Indeed, one must also measure progress on a human scale in terms of moral and ethical considerations. Have we learned anything from history, from the attitudes and mistakes of our ancestors? In 1912, the great ocean liner *Titanic* set sail from Britain to America. It was described as the quintessential expression of human technology—"unsinkable" said its creators. In 1985, the *Titanic* was finally discovered on the bottom of the Atlantic, the victim of a natural disaster on its maiden voyage, when the impact from a collision with an iceberg split the ship in two. More than this, its sinking was symbolic of an ordered world on the path to destruction. Two years after the *Titanic* vanished, the world went to war, a war unparalleled for its ferocity and barbarism. The new technology played its role as machine guns, tanks, airplanes, submarines, and poisonous gas were introduced. This new style of "total war," in which innocents died and thousands of men walked into barbed wire and machine gun fire, must be seen as a retreat from progress on a human scale. The succeeding events of the century—World War II, Hitler's destruction of the Jews, the nuclear devastation of Hiroshima, and the Cold War—have led many to view this less as a century of progress and more as a century of holocaust. And yet, have we in the late twentieth century advanced on an ideal plane of existence toward a more just and equal international community? How much further must we go to secure the political and social equality of women? Is racism generally on the decline? Have we gone beyond totalitarian government and the dictates of imperialism? Can new holocausts be prevented through the force of world opinion? One needs to question human nature and the value of history in this regard. And what influence does the individual have in all this? Personal roles in revolution (V. I. Lenin) and destruction (Adolf Hitler and Joseph Stalin) have been confirmed. But how successful has the individual been in promoting peaceful change and coexistence? Mahatma Gandhi, Martin Luther King, Jr., Desmond Tutu, Albert Schweitzer, Elie Wiesel, Albert Einstein, Mother Theresa—have they too made a difference?

Humanity seems to wage a perpetual duel between progress and holocaust, between inclusion and exclusion. Reasons for this are difficult to discern. The explanation of human action is necessarily fraught with frustration, for humans are ruled more often by their passions than by their intellect. But it is precisely this unpredictability that contributes to the progress of civilization; the new idea, the desire to compete and achieve, the will to give life or take it away—all enter into the equation of success or failure, of progress or destruction. We do not have the benefit of "20/20 hindsight." In fact, we often suffer from the stress of myopia, of not being able to "see the forest for the trees." So the need to understand where we are going in life and what things are of greatest value ceases to be a concern of the historian and becomes more a responsibility of each individual.

This chapter seeks to develop the dichotomy between the desire of humans for progress and coexistence, and our established record of destruction. It is broken into three separate thematic sections, which can be studied individually or compared for analytic purposes. The role of science and the responsibilities of scientists and politicians are especially at question in this historical problem. But ultimately, responsibility for our own civilization rests in each individual. It is important to understand the problems and struggle toward the solutions.

SECTION I: POLITICAL AND TECHNOLOGICAL DEVELOPMENTS
The Cold War (1945–1990)

The Nuclear Age

On August 6, 1945, the world entered the nuclear age with the detonation of the atomic bomb over the city of Hiroshima, Japan. Persuaded by the argument that such use would ultimately save Allied lives, President Truman ordered another bomb dropped on Nagasaki two days later. The Japanese surrendered, and the race was on to match America's technological achievement. The selections below relate the events, from Albert Einstein's famous letter to President Roosevelt proposing the possibility of such a weapon, to U.S. attempts at responsibly controlling the destructive power it had unleashed.

The Theory: Letter to President Roosevelt (1939)
ALBERT EINSTEIN

Albert Einstein
Old Grove Rd.
Nassau Point
Peconic, Long Island

August 2nd, 1939

F. D. Roosevelt,
President of the United States,
White House
Washington, D.C.

Sir:

Some recent work by E. Fermi and L. Szilard, which has been communicated to me in manuscript, leads me to expect that the element uranium may be turned into a new and important source of energy in the immediate future. Certain aspects of the situation which has arisen seem to call for watchfulness and, if necessary, quick action on the part of the Administration. I believe therefore that it is my duty to bring to your attention the following facts and recommendations:

"The Theory: Letter to President Roosevelt" is from Albert Einstein's Letter to President Roosevelt, August 2, 1939. Reprinted by permission of The Hebrew University of Jerusalem, Israel.

In the course of the last four months it has been made probable—through the work of Joliot in France as well as Fermi and Szilard in America—that it may become possible to set up a nuclear chain reaction in a large mass of uranium, by which vast amounts of power and large quantities of new radium-like elements would be generated. Now it appears almost certain that this could be achieved in the immediate future.

This new phenomenon would also lead to the construction of bombs, and it is conceivable—though much less certain—that extremely powerful bombs of a new type may thus be constructed. A single bomb of this type, carried by boat and exploded in a port, might very well destroy the whole port together with some of the surrounding territory. However, such bombs might very well prove to be too heavy for transportation by air.

The United States has only very poor ores of uranium in moderate quantities. There is some good ore in Canada and the former Czechoslovakia, while the most important source of uranium is the Belgian Congo. . . .

I understand that Germany has actually stopped the sale of uranium from the Czechoslovakian mines which she has taken over. That she should have taken such early action might perhaps be understood on the ground that the son of the German Under-Secretary of State, von Weizsacker, is attached to the Kaiser-Wilhelm-Institut in Berlin where some of the American work on uranium is now being repeated.

Yours very truly,
(Albert Einstein)

The Reality: Announcement of the Destruction of Hiroshima (August 6, 1945)

HARRY S. TRUMAN

Sixteen hours ago an American airplane dropped one bomb on Hiroshima, an important Japanese Army base. That bomb had more power than 20,000 tons of T.N.T. It had more than two thousand times the blast power of the British "Grand Slam" which is the largest bomb ever yet used in the history of warfare.

The Japanese began the war from the air at Pearl Harbor. They have been repaid many fold. And the end is not yet in sight. With this bomb we have now added a new and revolutionary increase in destruction to supplement the growing power of our armed forces. In their present form these bombs are now in production and even more powerful forms are in development.

"The Reality: Announcement of the Destruction of Hiroshima" is from *Public Papers of the President, Harry S Truman, 1947* (Washington, D.C.: Government Printing Office, 1963), pp. 197–200.

Explosion of the atomic bomb over Nagasaki, Japan (August 9, 1945). (*U.S. Air Force Photo*)

It is an atomic bomb. It is a harnessing of the basic power of the universe. The force from which the sun draws its power has been loosed against those who brought war to the Far East.

Before 1939, it was the accepted belief of scientists that it was theoretically possible to release atomic energy. But no one knew any practical method of doing it. By 1942, however, we knew that the Germans were working feverishly to find a way to add atomic energy to the other engines of war with which they hoped to enslave the world. But they failed. We may be grateful to Providence that the Germans got the V-1's and V-2's late and in limited quantities and even more grateful that they did not get the atomic bomb at all. . . .

We are now prepared to obliterate more rapidly and completely every productive enterprise the Japanese have above ground in any city. We shall destroy their docks, their factories, and their communications. Let there be no mistake; we shall completely destroy Japan's power to make war. . . .

I shall recommend that the Congress of the United States consider promptly the establishment of an appropriate commission to control the production and use of atomic power within the United States. I shall give further consideration and make further recommendations to the Congress as to how atomic power can become a powerful and forceful influence towards the maintenance of world peace.

In Defense of the Use of the Atomic Bomb (August 16, 1946)

SIR WINSTON CHURCHILL

There are voices which assert that the bomb should never have been used at all. I cannot associate myself with such ideas. Six years of total war have convinced most people that, had the Germans or Japanese discovered this new weapon, they would have used it upon us to our complete destruction with utmost alacrity. I am surprised that very worthy people, but people who in most cases had no intention of proceeding to the Japanese front themselves, should adopt the position that, rather than throw this bomb, we should have sacrificed a million American and a quarter million British lives in the desperate battles and massacres of an invasion of Japan. Future generations will judge these dire decisions, and I believe if they find themselves dwelling in a happier world from which war has been banished, and where freedom reigns, they will not condemn those who struggled for their benefit amid the horrors and the miseries of this gruesome and ferocious epoch.

The Control of Atomic Energy (1946)

BERNARD BARUCH

We are here to make a choice between the quick and the dead.

This is our business.

Behind the black portent of the new atomic age lies a hope which, seized upon with faith, can work our salvation. If we fail, then we have damned

"In Defense of the Use of the Atomic Bomb" is from Sir Winston S. Churchill, in an address to the House of Commons, *Parliamentary Papers*, August 16, 1946.

"The Control of Atomic Energy" is from *Department of State Bulletin* (June 23, 1946), pp. 1057–1062.

every man to be the slave of Fear. Let us not deceive ourselves: We must elect World Peace or World Destruction.

Science has torn from nature a secret so vast in its potentialities that our minds cower from the terror it creates. Yet terror is not enough to inhibit the use of the atomic bombs. The terror created by weapons has never stopped man from employing them. For each new weapon a defense has been produced, in time. But now we face a condition in which adequate defense does not exist. . . .

The United States proposes the creation of an International Atomic Development Authority, to which should be entrusted all phases of the development and use of atomic energy, starting with the raw material and including—

1. Managerial control or ownership of all atomic-energy activities potentially dangerous to world security.
2. Power to control, inspect, and license all other atomic activities.
3. The duty of fostering the beneficial uses of atomic energy.
4. Research and development responsibilities of an affirmative character intended to put the Authority in the forefront of atomic knowledge and thus to enable it to comprehend, and therefore to detect, misuse of atomic energy. To be effective, the Authority must itself be the world's leader in the field of atomic knowledge and development and thus supplement its legal authority with the great power inherent in possession of leadership in knowledge.

I offer this as a basis for beginning our discussion. . . .

We of this nation, desirous of helping to bring peace to the world and realizing the heavy obligations upon us arising from our possession of the means of producing the bomb and from the fact that it is part of our armament, are prepared to make our full contribution toward effective control of atomic energy.

When an adequate system for control of atomic energy, including the renunciation of the bomb as a weapon, has been agreed upon and put into effective operation and condign punishments set up for violations of the rules of control which are to be stigmatized as international crimes, we propose that—

1. Manufacture of atomic bombs shall stop;
2. Existing bombs shall be disposed of pursuant to the terms of the treaty; and
3. The Authority shall be in possession of full information as to the know-how for production of atomic energy. . . .

Let me repeat, so as to avoid misunderstanding: My country is ready to make its full contribution toward the end we seek, subject of course to our constitutional processes and to an adequate system of control becoming fully effective, as we finally work it out.

The bomb does not wait upon debate. To delay may be to die. The time between violation and preventive action or punishment would be all too short for extended discussion as to the course to be followed.

"Pacem in Terris" (1963)
POPE JOHN XXIII

The papacy, which played such an important role in the Middle Ages, declined in international authority after the Protestant Reformation. However, with the emergence of twentieth-century leaders such as John XXIII, Paul VI, and John Paul II, the papacy has played an important role in international affairs apart from the 800 million Catholics it represents. For example, John Paul II (1978–   ) was a formidable figure in defying Soviet threats to invade his native Poland in 1980; his knowledge of languages and frequent travel have made him a vital force, especially in Third World countries. The encyclical presented below, translated as "Peace on Earth," was issued by Pope John XXIII in 1963. It speaks to the issue of nuclear arms escalation and is indicative of the active papacy of the late twentieth century.

It is with deep sorrow that We note the enormous stocks of armaments that have been and still are being made in more economically developed countries, with a vast outlay of intellectual and economic resources. And so it happens that, while the people of these countries are loaded with heavy burdens, other countries as a result are deprived of the collaboration they need in order to make economic and social progress.

The production of arms is allegedly justified on the grounds that in present-day conditions peace cannot be preserved without an equal balance of armaments. And so, if one country increases its armaments, others feel the need to do the same; and if one country is equipped with nuclear weapons, other countries must produce their own, equally destructive.

Consequently, people live in constant fear lest the storm that every moment threatens should break upon them with dreadful violence. And with good reason, for the arms of war are ready at hand. Even though it is difficult to believe that anyone would deliberately take the responsibility for the appalling destruction and sorrow that war would bring in its train, it cannot be denied that the conflagration may be set off by some unexpected and obscure event. And one must bear in mind that, even though the monstrous power of modern weapons acts as a deterrent, it is to be feared that the mere continuance of nuclear tests, undertaken with war in mind, will prove a serious hazard for life on earth.

Justice, then, right reason and humanity urgently demand that the arms race should cease; that the stockpiles which exist in various countries should be reduced equally and simultaneously by the parties concerned;

" 'Pacem in Terris' " is from Pope John XXIII, *Pacem in Terris* (New York: Paulist Press, 1963), pp. 38–40.

that nuclear weapons should be banned; and that a general agreement should eventually be reached about progressive disarmament and an effective method of control. In the words of Pius XII, Our Predecessor of happy memory: *The calamity of a world war, with the economic and social ruin and the moral excesses and dissolution that accompany it, must not be permitted to envelop the human race for a third time.*

All must realize that there is no hope of putting an end to the building up of armaments, nor of reducing the present stocks, nor, still less, of abolishing them altogether, unless the process is complete and thorough and unless it proceeds from inner convictions: unless, that is, everyone sincerely cooperates to banish the fear and anxious expectation of war with which men are oppressed. If this is to come about, the fundamental principle on which our present peace depends must be replaced by another, which declares that the true and solid peace of nations consists not in equality of arms but in mutual trust alone. We believe that this can be brought to pass, and We consider that it is something which reason requires, that it is eminently desirable in itself and that it will prove to be the source of many benefits.

In the first place, it is an objective demanded by reason. There can be, or at least there should be, no doubt that relations between States, as between individuals, should be regulated not by the force of arms but by the light of reason, by the rule, that is, of truth, of justice and of active and sincere cooperation.

Secondly, We say that it is an objective earnestly to be desired in itself. Is there anyone who does not ardently yearn to see war banished, to see peace preserved and daily more firmly established?

And finally, it is an objective which will be a fruitful source of many benefits, for its advantages will be felt everywhere, by individuals, by families, by nations, by the whole human family. The warning of Pius XII still rings in our ears: *Nothing is lost by peace; everything may be lost by war.*

The "Super-Power" Rivalry and the Rejection of Stalin

The Charter of the United Nations (June 1945)

In June 1945, the Charter of the United Nations was signed. This organization was dedicated to the proposition that international cooperation was not only preferable to war but also possible to attain. The organization has been criticized and applauded throughout the years. Some have seen it as effective in

"The Charter of the United Nations" is from Department of State, *The United Nations Conference on International Organization* (Washington, D.C.: Government Printing Office, 1946), pp. 943–944.

settling disputes and maintaining peace; others have viewed it as impotent and devoid of any authority to enforce its verdicts.

We the peoples of the United Nations determined to save succeeding generations from the scourge of war, which twice in our lifetime has brought untold sorrow to mankind, and

To reaffirm faith in fundamental human rights, in the dignity and worth of the human person, in the equal rights of men and women and of nations large and small, and

To establish conditions under which justice and respect for the obligations arising from treaties and other sources of international law can be maintained, and

To promote social progress and better standards of life in larger freedom,

and for these ends to practice tolerance and live together in peace with one another as good neighbors, and

To unite our strength to maintain international peace and security, and

To ensure, by the acceptance of principles and the institution of methods, that armed force shall not be used, save in the common interest, and

To employ international machinery for the promotion of the economic and social advancement of all peoples,

have resolved to combine our efforts to accomplish these aims; accordingly; our respective Governments, through representatives assembled in the city of San Francisco, who have exhibited their full powers found to be in good and due form, have agreed to the present Charter of the United Nations and do hereby establish an international organization to be known as the United Nations.

PURPOSES AND PRINCIPLES

Article 1

The Organization and its Members . . . shall act in accordance with the following Principles.

1. The Organization is based on the principle of the sovereign equality of all its Members.

2. All Members, in order to ensure to all of them the rights and benefits resulting from membership, shall fulfill in good faith the obligations assumed by them in accordance with the present Charter.

3. All Members shall settle their international disputes by peaceful means in such a manner that international peace and security, and justice, are not endangered.

4. All Members shall refrain in their international relations from the threat or use of force against the territorial integrity or political independence of any state, or in any other manner, inconsistent with the Purposes of the United Nations.

5. All Members shall give the United Nations every assistance in any action it takes in accordance with the present Charter, and shall refrain

from giving assistance to any state against which the United Nations is taking preventive or enforcement action.

6. The Organization shall ensure that states which are not Members of the United Nations act in accordance with these Principles so far as may be necessary for the maintenance of international peace and security.

7. Nothing contained in the present Charter shall authorize the United Nations to intervene in matters which are essentially within the domestic jurisdiction of any state or shall require the Members to submit such matters to settlement under the present Charter. . . .

The Soviet Victory: Capitalism versus Communism (February 1946)

JOSEPH STALIN

The term "Cold War" describes the era of uneasy relations between the western Allies and the Soviet Union after World War II. Each was competing for influence in Europe through propaganda and troop placement. In the first excerpt, the Soviet leader Joseph Stalin offered a glimpse of the ideological combat that was to be waged in the future. A month later, Winston Churchill, who had largely directed the British war effort, warned the West of the deceptive Soviet Union in his famous "Iron Curtain" speech.

It would be wrong to believe that the Second World War broke out accidentally or as a result of the mistakes of some or other statesmen, though mistakes certainly were made. In reality, the war broke out as an inevitable result of the development of world economic and political forces on the basis of modern monopoly capitalism.

Marxists have stated more than once that the capitalist system of world economy conceals in itself the elements of general crisis and military clashes, that in view of this in our time the development of world capitalism takes place not as a smooth and even advance but through crises and war catastrophes.

The reason is that the unevenness of the development of capitalist countries usually results, as time passes, in an abrupt disruption of the equilibrium within the world system of capitalism, and that a group of capitalist countries which believes itself to be less supplied with raw materials and markets usually attempts to alter the situation and re-divide the "spheres of influence" in its own favour by means of armed force. . . .

This results in the splitting of the capitalist world into two hostile camps and in war between them.

Perhaps the catastrophes of war could be avoided if there existed the possibility of re-distributing periodically raw materials and markets among the countries in accordance with their economic weight—by means of

"The Soviet Victory" is from *Embassy of the U.S.S.R., Speech Delivered by J. V. Stalin at a Meeting of Voters of the Stalin Electoral Area of Moscow* (Washington, D.C.: Government Printing Office, 1946).

adopting coordinated and peaceful decisions. This, however, cannot be accomplished under present capitalist conditions of the development of world economy. . . .

As to our country, for her the war was the severest and hardest of all the wars our Motherland has ever experienced in her history.

But the war was not only a curse. It was at the same time a great school in which all the forces of the people were tried and tested. The war laid bare all the facts and events in the rear and at the front, it mercilessly tore off all the veils and covers which had concealed the true faces of States, governments, and parties, and placed them on the stage without masks, without embellishments, with all their shortcomings and virtues.

• • •

And so, what are the results of the war? . . .

Our victory means, in the first place, that our Soviet social system has won, that the Soviet social system successfully withstood the trial in the flames of war and proved its perfect viability.

It is well known that the foreign press more than once asserted that the Soviet social system is a "risky experiment" doomed to failure, that the Soviet system is a "house of cards," without any roots in life, imposed upon the people by the organs of the "Cheka," [secret police] that a slight push from outside would be enough to blow this "house of cards" to smithereens.

Now we can say that the war swept away all these assertions of the foreign press as groundless. The war has shown that the Soviet social system is a truly popular system, which has grown from the people and enjoys its powerful support, that the Soviet social system is a perfectly viable and stable form of organisation of society.

More than that, the point is now not whether the Soviet social system is viable or not, since after the objective lessons of the war no single skeptic now ventures to come out with doubts concerning the viability of the Soviet social system. The point now is that the Soviet social system has proved more viable and stable than a non-Soviet social system, that the Soviet social system is a better form of organisation of society than any non-Soviet social system.

"An Iron Curtain Has Descended across the Continent" (March 1946)

SIR WINSTON CHURCHILL

I now come to the . . . danger which threatens the cottage home and ordinary people, namely tyranny. We cannot be blind to the fact that the liberties enjoyed by individual citizens throughout the United States and

"'An Iron Curtain Has Descended across the Continent'" is from *Congressional Record*, 79th Congress, 2nd session, pp. A1145–A1147.

British Empire are not valid in a considerable number of countries, some of which are very powerful. In these states control is forced upon the common people by various kinds of all-embracing police governments, to a degree which is overwhelming and contrary to every principle of democracy. The power of the state is exercised without restraint, either by dictators or by compact oligarchies operating through a privileged party and a political police. It is not our duty at this time, when difficulties are so numerous, to interfere forcibly in the internal affairs of countries whom we have not conquered in war, but we must never cease to proclaim in fearless tones the great principles of freedom and the rights of man, which are the joint inheritance of the English-speaking world and which, through Magna Carta, the Bill of Rights, the habeas corpus, trial by jury, and the English common law find their famous expression in the Declaration of Independence. . . .

A shadow has fallen upon the scenes so lately lighted by the Allied victory. Nobody knows what Soviet Russia and its Communist international organization intends to do in the immediate future, or what are the limits, if any, to their expansive and proselytizing tendencies . . . From Stettin in the Baltic to Trieste in the Adriatic, an iron curtain has descended across the continent. Behind that line lie all the capitals of the ancient states of central and eastern Europe. Warsaw, Berlin, Prague, Vienna, Budapest, Belgrade, Bucharest, and Sofia, all these famous cities and the populations around them lie in the Soviet sphere and all are subject, in one form or another, not only to Soviet influence but to a very high and increasing measure of control from Moscow. Athens alone, with its immortal glories, is free to decide its future at an election under British, American, and French observation.

In a great number of countries, far from the Russian frontiers and throughout the world, Communist fifth columns are established and work in complete unity and absolute obedience to the directions they receive from the Communist center. Except in the British Commonwealth, and in the United States, where communism is in its infancy, the Communist parties and fifth columns constitute a growing challenge and peril to Christian civilization. These are somber facts for anyone to have to recite on the morrow of a victory gained by so much splendid comradeship in arms and in the cause of freedom and democracy, and we should be most unwise not to face them squarely while time remains. . . .

On the other hand, I repulse the idea that a new war is inevitable, still more that it is imminent. It is because I am so sure that our fortunes are in our own hands and that we hold the power to save the future, that I feel the duty to speak out now that I have occasion to do so. I do not believe that Soviet Russia desires war. What they desire is the fruits of war and the indefinite expansion of their power and doctrines. But what we have to consider here today while time remains, is the permanent prevention of war and the establishment of conditions of freedom and democracy as rapidly as possible in all countries.

Our difficulties and dangers will not be removed by closing our eyes to them; they will not be removed by mere waiting to see what happens; nor will they be relieved by a policy of appeasement. What is needed is a settlement, and the longer this is delayed, the more difficult it will be and the greater our dangers will become. From what I have seen of our Russian friends and allies during the war, I am convinced that there is nothing they admire so much as strength, and there is nothing for which they have less respect than for military weakness. For that reason the old doctrine of a balance of power is unsound. We cannot afford, if we can help it, to work on narrow margins, offering temptations to a trial of strength. If the western democracies stand together in strict adherence to the principles of the United Nations Charter, their influence for furthering these principles will be immense and no one is likely to molest them. If, however, they become divided or falter in their duty, and if these all-important years are allowed to slip away, then indeed catastrophe may overwhelm us all.

The Truman Doctrine (March 1947)

HARRY S. TRUMAN

In the first months of 1946, President Truman received urgent requests from the Greek government for economic assistance, which, it was hoped, would put an end to the chaos and strife hindering its recovery from the war. Hoping to forestall Communist dissidents who were threatening the stability of the government, Truman appealed to Congress to appropriate such financial assistance. He also asked for military as well as economic aid to Turkey. The controversial Truman Doctrine, as it came to be called, committed the United States to an active policy of promoting ideological divisions between it and the Soviet Union, and further escalated Cold War tensions. The Marshall Plan of 1947, which advocated the rebuilding of West Germany after the war, is an example of this policy of Soviet containment.

One of the primary objectives of the foreign policy of the United States is the creation of conditions in which we and other nations will be able to work out a way of life free from coercion. This was a fundamental issue in the war with Germany and Japan. Our victory was won over countries which sought to impose their will, and their way of life, upon other nations.

To ensure the peaceful development of nations, free from coercion, the United States has taken a leading part in establishing the United Nations. The United Nations is designed to make possible lasting freedom and independence for all its members. We shall not realize our objectives, however, unless we are willing to help free peoples to maintain their free institutions and their national integrity against aggressive movements that

"The Truman Doctrine" is from *Public Papers of the President, Harry S. Truman, 1947* (Washington, D.C.: Government Printing Office, 1963), pp. 177–180.

seek to impose upon them totalitarian regimes. This is no more than a frank recognition that totalitarian regimes imposed upon free peoples, by direct or indirect aggression, undermine the foundations of international peace and hence the security of the United States.

The peoples of a number of countries of the world have recently had totalitarian regimes forced upon them against their will. The Government of the United States has made frequent protests against coercion and intimidation, in violation of the Yalta agreement, in Poland, Rumania, and Bulgaria. I must also state that in a number of other countries there have been similar developments.

At the present moment in world history nearly every nation must choose between alternative ways of life. The choice is too often not a free one.

One way of life is based upon the will of the majority, and is distinguished by free institutions, representative government, free elections, guarantees of individual liberty, freedom of speech and religion, and freedom from political oppression.

The second way of life is based upon the will of a minority forcibly imposed upon the majority. It relies upon terror and oppression, a controlled press and radio, fixed elections, and the suppression of personal freedoms.

I believe that it must be the policy of the United States to support free peoples who are resisting attempted subjugation by armed minorities or by outside pressures.

I believe that we must assist free peoples to work out their own destinies in their own way.

I believe that our help should be primarily through economic and financial aid which is essential to economic stability and orderly political processes.

The world is not static, and the *status quo* is not sacred. But we cannot allow changes in the *status quo* in violation of the Charter of United Nations by such methods as coercion, or by such subterfuges as political infiltration. In helping free and independent nations to maintain their freedom, the United States will be giving effect to the principles of the Charter of the United Nations. . . .

The seeds of totalitarian regimes are nurtured by misery and want. They spread and grow in the evil soil of poverty and strife. They reach their full growth when the hope of a people for a better life has died.

We must keep that hope alive.

The free peoples of the world look to us for support in maintaining their freedoms.

If we falter in our leadership, we may endanger the peace of the world— and we shall surely endanger the welfare of this Nation.

Great responsibilities have been placed upon us by the swift movement of events.

I am confident that the Congress will face these responsibilities squarely.

The Marshall Plan (June 1947)

GEORGE C. MARSHALL

The truth of the matter is that Europe's requirements for the next three or four years of foreign food and other essential products—principally from America—are so much greater than her present ability to pay that she must have substantial additional help or face economic, social, and political deterioration of a very grave character.

The remedy lies in breaking the vicious circle and restoring the confidence of the European people in the economic future of their own countries and of Europe as a whole. The manufacturer and the farmer throughout wide areas must be able and willing to exchange their products for currencies the continuing value of which is not open to question.

Aside from the demoralizing effect on the world at large and the possibilities of disturbances arising as a result of the desperation of the people concerned, the consequences to the economy of the United States should be apparent to all. It is logical that the United States should do whatever it is able to do to assist in the return of normal economic health in the world, without which there can be no political stability and no assured peace. Our policy is directed not against any country or doctrine but against hunger, poverty, desperation, and chaos. Its purpose should be the revival of a working economy in the world so as to permit the emergence of political and social conditions in which free institutions can exist. Such assistance, I am convinced, must not be on a piecemeal basis as various crises develop. Any assistance that this Government may render in the future should provide a cure rather than a mere palliative. Any government that is willing to assist in the task of recovery will find full cooperation, I am sure, on the part of the United States Government. Any government which maneuvers to block the recovery of other countries cannot expect help from us. Furthermore, governments, political parties, or groups which seek to perpetuate human misery in order to profit therefrom politically or otherwise will encounter the opposition of the United States.

It is already evident that, before the United States Government can proceed much further in its efforts to alleviate the situation and help start the European world on its way to recovery, there must be some agreement among the countries of Europe as to the requirements of the situation and the part those countries themselves will take in order to give proper effect to whatever action might be undertaken by this Government. It would be neither fitting nor efficacious for this Government to undertake to draw up unilaterally a program designed to place Europe on its feet economically. This is the business of the Europeans. The initiative, I think, must come from Europe. The role of this country should consist of friendly aid in the drafting of a European program and of later support of such a program so far as it may be practical for us to do so. The program should be a joint one, agreed to by a number, if not all, European nations.

"The Marshall Plan" is from *Department of State Bulletin* (June 15, 1947), pp. 1159–1160.

An essential part of any successful action on the part of the United States is an understanding on the part of the people of America of the character of the problem and the remedies to be applied. Political passion and prejudice should have no part. With foresight, and a willingness on the part of our people to face up to the vast responsibility which history has clearly placed upon our country, the difficulties I have outlined can and will be overcome.

The Sources of Soviet Conduct (July 1947)

"X"

Distrust and tension between the United States and the Soviet Union continued to mount in 1948 as the Russians stopped all traffic, including food transports, into their zone of German occupation. From June 1948 to May 1949, the United States airlifted supplies to the people of Berlin and defied Soviet heavy-handedness. This tenacious policy in the face of Soviet aggression was greatly influenced by the containment ideas of George Kennan, director of the State Department's policy-planning staff. The following is an excerpt from his seminal paper published in 1947 under the pseudonym "X."

In actuality the possibilities for American policy are by no means limited to holding the line and hoping for the best. It is entirely possible for the United States to influence by its actions the internal developments, both within Russia and throughout the international Communist movement, by which Russian policy is largely determined. This is not only a question of the modest measure of informational activity which this government can conduct in the Soviet Union and elsewhere, although that, too, is important. It is rather a question of the degree to which the United States can create among the peoples of the world generally the impression of a country which knows what it wants, which is coping successfully with the problems of its internal life and with the responsibilities of a world power, and which has a spiritual vitality capable of holding its own among the major ideological currents of the time. To the extent that such an impression can be created and maintained, the aims of Russian Communism must appear sterile and quixotic, the hopes and enthusiasm of Moscow's supporters must wane, and added strain must be imposed on the Kremlin's foreign policies. For the palsied decrepitude of the capitalist world is the keystone of Communist philosophy. Even the failure of the United States to experience the early economic depression which the ravens of the Red Square have been predicting with such complacent confidence since hostilities ceased would have deep and important repercussions throughout the Communist world.

By the same token, exhibitions of indecision, disunity and internal disintegration within this country have an exhilarating effect on the whole Communist movement. At each evidence of these tendencies, a thrill of hope and excitement goes through the Communist world; a new jauntiness can be noted in the Moscow tread; new groups of foreign supporters climb on to what they can only view as the bandwagon of international politics; and Russian pressure increases all along the line in international affairs.

It would be an exaggeration to say that American behavior unassisted and alone could exercise a power of life and death over the Communist movement and bring about the early fall of Soviet power in Russia. But the United States has it in its power to increase enormously the strains under which Soviet policy must operate, to force upon the Kremlin a far greater degree of moderation and circumspection than it has had to observe in recent years, and in this way to promote tendencies which must eventually find their outlet in either the breakup or the gradual mellowing of Soviet power. For no mystical, messianic movement—and particularly not that of the Kremlin—can face frustration indefinitely without eventually adjusting itself in one way or another to the logic of that state of affairs.

Thus the decision will really fall in large measure on this country itself. The issue of Soviet-American relations is in essence a test of the overall worth of the United States as a nation among nations. To avoid destruction the United States need only measure up to its own best traditions and prove itself worthy of preservation as a great nation.

An Assessment of Communism (1953)
THEODORE WHITE

By 1950, it was natural to begin assessing the events that had transpired during the first half of the century and to speculate on developments for the future. In 1953, the Soviet leader Joseph Stalin died, and many wondered how this might change the face of communism and subsequently the nature of the Cold War. Theodore White, a journalist who had spent much of his early career in China and became famous for his political analysis of the presidency, offered this view of communism in 1953.

Americans are so frightened by the evil in communism that they fail to see that the greatest danger is not the evil but the attraction in it. Only Americans live in a society in which communism can seduce no healthy mind. Most of our senior Allies and the myriad-man countries who live outside our Alliance are made of people who stand transfixed by fear of communism and its sinister charm at the same time.

The magic appeal in the Communist faith is simple. It is the belief that

"As Assessment of Communism" is from Theodore H. White, *Fire in the Ashes* (New York: William Sloane Associates Publishers, 1953), pp. 318–320.

pure logic applied to human affairs is enough to change the world and cure it of all its human miseries. It is buttressed by the belief that the processes of history are governed by certain "scientific" laws, which automatically guarantee the triumph of communism when the situation is ripe, if only its protestants have the courage to strike and act.

This simple credo carries an almost irresistible attraction to two kinds of people everywhere in the world: first, to small coteries of able and ambitious young men hungry for the ecstasy of leadership, and, secondly, to larger masses of ignorant people who have just begun to hope.

To both these schools of converts, the fatal flaw in the Communist faith is neither apparent nor important. This fatal flaw is embedded in the nature of human beings whenever they gather politically. Human beings tend to be illogical. The logic of which communism boasts is never certain, therefore, of success in any political operation unless simultaneously it imposes so rigid a discipline as to make ordinary people mere bodies in the sequence of their masters' planning. Logic cannot succeed if its premises are to be shaken over and over again by vagrant human emotions allowed freely to express themselves in all their passion and frailty. Any political organization which sets out to be totally logical thus calls for total discipline; total discipline inevitably requires police, and police bring terror.

But the weakness of communism lies less in the calculated immorality of terror than in the inevitable internal appetite of the discipline. The discipline feeds on itself; it shrinks the area of discussion and decision into ever narrower, ever tighter, even more cramped circles. Fewer and fewer men have less and less access to the raw facts which are necessary for wise judgment. The discipline they control and impose inevitably sneaks back to weaken them, to blind or deafen them into stupidity and error.

To those who come to communism out of ambition or out of misguided intelligence, this flaw is not immediately apparent. Each of this type of convert cherishes the illusion until too late that the ever-shrinking circle of discipline will leave him safe at its center of creative leadership, rather than crushed and tortured as discipline contracts about his own soft human body. To the second category of converts, those who come to it out of hunger and ignorance, this flaw in communism (even if it could be explained to them) seems unimportant. They have always been excluded from decision and control over their own lives. Communism promises them simply "more"; they are ready to believe. The hungrier and more ignorant they are, the more difficult it is to explain to them that their own hopes and welfare are directly dependent on the freedom of creative minds, with which they are unfamiliar, to think independently of all discipline.

To the Western world, so challenged by communism, this flaw in the adversary presents a grotesque problem. Communism's prison-logical system of human organization grows in strength decade by decade even as its leadership becomes less and less capable of wise and sensible decision. For all its dynamism and strength, the Communist world falls into blunders with increasing frequency, blunders which are only rectified by great wrenchings of policy that shake the world with disaster. To deal with communism, one must recognize both its strength and its blunders clearly. . . .

Such an event as the death of Stalin, by shaking the superstructure of discipline, by admitting for a brief moment the clash of several opinions and the consequent opportunity for a slightly larger area of discussion at the summit, has given the Communist machinery of politics a momentary opportunity to review some of its errors. But, unless communism ceases to be communism, the process of discipline calls for a new tightening of control, a new struggle to apply the logic of a single man to a world of dark and uncertain phenomena.

How to Spot a Communist (1955)

The following article was issued by the U.S. First Army Headquarters for public dissemination and reveals the Cold War paranoia that was so much a part of the decade of the 1950s.

Events of recent years have made it obvious that there is no fool-proof way of detecting a Communist. The Communist individual is no longer a "type" exemplified by the bearded and coarse revolutionary with time bomb in briefcase. U.S. Communists come from all walks in life, profess all faiths, and exercise all trades and professions. In addition, the Communist Party, USA, has made concerted efforts to go underground for the purpose of infiltration.

If there is no fool-proof system in spotting a Communist, there are, fortunately, indications that may give him away. These indications are often subtle but always present, for the Communist, by reason of his "faith" must act and talk along certain lines.

While a certain heaviness of style and preference for long sentences is common to most Communist writing, a distinct vocabulary provides the . . . more easily recognized feature of the "Communist Language."

Even a superficial reading of an article written by a Communist or a conversation with one will probably reveal the use of some of the following expressions: integrative thinking, vanguard, comrade, hootenanny, chauvinism, book-burning, syncretistic faith, bourgeois-nationalism, jingoism, colonialism, hooliganism, ruling class, progressive, demagogy, dialectical, witch-hunt, reactionary, exploitation, oppressive, materialist.

This list, selected at random, could be extended almost indefinitely. While all of the above expressions are part of the English language, their use by Communists is infinitely more frequent than by the general public. . . .

The tell-tale signs of the "Communist Religion" are not easy to detect. There is, above all, a rigidity in views insofar as they pertain to the Communist doctrine. This is not to say that the Communist lacks persuasiveness or variety of expression. It does mean, however, that he will stubbornly cling to the "line" even when proven wrong in debate. The Communist has implicit faith in Marxist philosophy and in the truth of the "line" as transmitted from Moscow. Because of this faith, he cannot and will not give ground when challenged on basic Marxist issues or political pronouncements made by his leaders. The possibility of compromising on these issues is utterly beyond his comprehension. . . .

His "religion," then, can give away the Communist. His naive and unquestioning acceptance of the "line," his refusal to accept criticism are excellent indications. Last but not least, the Communist feels a strong compulsion to speak his "faith" and can frequently be spotted by his never-ceasing attempts at conversion of others.

The "Communist Logic" . . . is diametrically opposed to our own. Thus, the Communist refers to the iron curtain police states as "democracies," and any defensive move on the part of the Western powers is condemned as "aggression." The Communist thus builds for himself a topsy-turvy world with a completely distorted set of values. For this reason, it is practically impossible to win an argument with a hard-core Communist. . . . The Communist mind cannot and will not engage in a detached examination of ideas. Talking to a Communist about his own ideas, then, is like listening to a phonograph record. His answers will invariably follow a definite pattern because he can never admit, even hypothetically, that the basis for his ideas may not be sound. This attitude is typical not only for the individual but also on a national scale. . . . The answer is final and no arguments are permitted so far as the Communists are concerned. The Communist, then, is not really "logical." The finality of his arguments and the completeness of his condemnation marks him clearly, whether as a speaker, a writer or a conversation partner.

In addition to these very general principles common to Communist tactics, a number of specific issues have been part of the Communist arsenal for a long period of time. These issues are raised not only by Communist appeals to the public, but also by the individual Party member or sympathizer who is a product of his Communist environment. They include: "McCarthyism," violation of civil rights, racial or religious discrimination, immigration laws, anti-subversive legislation, any legislation concerning labor unions, the military budget, "peace."

While showing standard opposition to certain standard issues, the U.S. Communist has traditionally identified himself with certain activities in the hope of furthering his ultimate purposes. Such hobbies as "folk dancing" and "folk music" have been traditionally allied with the Communist movement in the United States. . . . The reason for their choice [of hobbies] is not altogether an attempt to hide political activities. The Communist's fondness for everything that comes from "the people" is not an entirely theoretical preference and has found expression in his everyday life. Most Communists are likely to show preference for group activities rather than such bourgeois forms of recreation as ballroom dancing. . . .

A study such as this can lead to only one certain conclusion: There is no sure-fire way of spotting a Communist. . . . The principle difficulty involved is the distinction between the person who merely dissents in the good old American tradition and the one who condemns for the purpose of abolishing that tradition.

In attempting to find the answer to the question: "Is this man a Communist?" a checklist such as this can prove helpful, although in itself it cannot provide the answer:

Does the individual use unusual language? ("Communist Language")
Does he stubbornly cling to Marxist ideals without being willing to question them?
Does he condemn our American institutions and praise those of Communist countries?
Does he pick on any event, even the most insignificant occurrences in this country for his criticism?
Is he secretive about certain of his contacts?
Does he belong to groups exploiting controversial subjects?

Above all, the approach to the problem of discovering Communists must be detached and completely free from prejudice. Using some of the clues mentioned in this study in connection with a factual approach provides the best system at present of spotting a Communist.

Self-Renewal: The Attack on Stalin (June 1956)
NIKITA KHRUSHCHEV

After Stalin's death in 1953, the power vacuum was eventually filled by Sergeyevich (Nikita) Khrushchev. At the 20th Communist Party Congress, Khrushchev quite unexpectedly attacked Stalin and his legacy of fear. The Soviets were looking for a new beginning.

Comrades, in the report of the Central Committee of the Party at the 20th Congress, in a number of speeches by delegates to the Congress . . . quite a lot has been said about the cult of the individual and about its harmful consequences.

After Stalin's death the Central Committee of the Party began to implement a policy of explaining concisely and consistently that it is impermissi-

"Self-Renewal" is from *Congressional Record*, 84th Congress, 2nd session, pp. 9390–9402 (June 4, 1956).

ble and foreign to the spirit of Marxism-Leninism to elevate one person, to transform him into a superman possessing supernatural characteristics akin to those of a god. Such a man supposedly knows everything, sees everything, thinks for everyone, can do anything, is infallible in his behavior.

Such a belief about a man, and specifically about Stalin, was cultivated among us for many years. . . .

Stalin originated the concept "enemy of the people." This term automatically rendered it unnecessary that the ideological errors of a man or men engaged in a controversy be proven; this term made possible the usage of the most cruel repression, violating all norms of revolutionary legality, against anyone who in any way disagreed with Stalin, against those who were only suspected of hostile intent, against those who had bad reputations. This concept, "enemy of the people," actually eliminated the possibility of any kind of ideological fight or the making of one's views known on this or that issue, even those of a practical character. In the main, and in actuality, the only proof of guilt used, against all norms of current legal science, was the "confession" of the accused himself; and, as subsequent probing proved, "confessions" were acquired through physical pressures against the accused.

This led to glaring violations of revolutionary legality, and to the fact that many entirely innocent persons, who in the past had defended the Party line, became victims.

We must assert that in regard to those persons who in their time had opposed the Party line, there were often no sufficient serious reasons for their physical annihilation. The formula, "enemy of the people" was specifically introduced for the purpose of physically annihilating such individuals. . . .

Thus, Stalin had sanctioned in the name of the Central Committee of the All-Union Communist Party (Bolsheviks) the most brutal violation of Socialist legality, torture and oppression, which led as we have seen to the slandering and self-accusation of innocent people.

Speech to the 22nd Communist Party Congress (1962)

NIKITA KHRUSHCHEV

Although there may have been hope that the fears of the Cold War would be reduced, the decade from 1955 to 1966 was especially intense in its rhetoric and ideological conflict. As Khrushchev menacingly said of capitalist states in 1956, "Whether you like it or not, history is on our side. We will bury you!" This was the era of Senator Joseph McCarthy, who played on the fears of Americans with his deceitful rantings that communists had infiltrated the highest echelons of government. It was during this time (1961) that the Berlin

"Speech to the 22nd Communist Party Congress" is from *Current Soviet Policies*, IV (New York, 1962), pp. 44–45, 50, 77. Reprinted by permission of *The Current Digest of The Soviet Press.*

Wall was built, sealing off the city into communist and democratic sectors—a symbolic as well as practical measure. And finally, in 1962, the two super-powers nearly went to nuclear war as President Kennedy demanded the removal of Soviet missiles from Cuba. The following excerpt is from Khrushchev's speech to the 22nd Congress of the Communist party. Note the argument carefully.

The most rabid imperialists, acting on the principle of "after us the del-uge," openly voice their desire to undertake a new war venture. The ideologists of imperialism, intimidating the peoples, try to instill a kind of philosophy of hopelessness and desperation. Hysterically they cry: "Better death under capitalism than life under communism." They do not like free peoples to flourish, you see. They fear that the peoples in their countries too will take the path of socialism. Blinded by class hatred, our enemies are ready to doom all mankind to the catastrophe of war. The imperialists' opportunities to carry out their aggressive designs, however, are becoming smaller and smaller. They behave like a feeble and greedy old man whose powers have been exhausted, whose physical capacity has weakened, but whose avid desires remain. . . .

As long as the imperialist aggressors exist, we must be on guard, keep our powder dry, improve the defense of the socialist countries, their armed forces and the state security agencies. If, in the face of common sense, the imperialists dare attack the socialist countries and plunge mankind into the abyss of a world war of annihilation, this mad act of theirs would be their last, it would be the end of the whole system of capitalism. (*Applause.*)

Our party clearly understands its tasks, its responsibility, and will do everything in its power to see to it that the world socialist system continues to grow stronger, gathers fresh strength and develops. We believe that in the competition with capitalism socialism will win. (*Prolonged applause.*) We believe that this victory will be won in peaceful competition and not by way of unleashing a war. We have stood, we stand and we will stand by the positions of peaceful competition of states with different social systems; we will do everything to strengthen world peace. (*Prolonged applause.*)

The most important component of our party's foreign policy activities is *the struggle for general and complete disarmament.* The Soviet Union has been waging this struggle for many years now, and doing so firmly and perse-veringly. We have always been resolutely opposed to the arms race, since rivalry in this sphere in the past not only saddled the peoples with a terrible burden but inevitably led to world wars. We are even more resolutely opposed to the arms race now that there has been a colossal technical revolution in the art of war and the use of today's weapons would inevitably entail the deaths of hundreds of millions of people.

The stockpiling of these weapons, proceeding as it is in a setting of cold war and war hysteria, is fraught with disastrous consequences. All that has to happen is for the nerves of some fellow in uniform to crack while he is on duty at a "push-button" somewhere in the West, and things may happen that will bring more than a little misfortune upon the peoples of the whole world.

Naturally, when we put forward a program of general and complete disarmament, we are talking not about the unilateral disarmament of socialism in the face of imperialism or vice versa, but about universal renunciation of arms as a means of solving problems at issue among states. . . .

The example of the Soviet Union inspires all progressive mankind. Never has the great vital forces of Marxist-Leninist teaching been so clearly evident as in our days, now that socialism has triumphed fully and finally in the Soviet Union, the cause of socialism is winning new victories in the countries of the world socialist commonwealth, and the international Communist and workers' movement and the national liberation struggle of peoples are growing and expanding tempestuously.

The revolution awakened the great energy of peoples, which is transforming the world on the principles of socialism and communism. Colossal changes are taking place and will take place throughout the world under the influence of the successes of communism.

The victory of communism is inevitable! (*Stormy applause.*)

The great army of Communists and of Marxist-Leninists acts as the vanguard of the peoples in the struggle for peace, for social progress and for communism, the bright future of mankind. New and ever newer millions of people will assemble and rally under the great banner of communism. The cause of progress, the cause of communism will triumph! (*Stormy applause.*)

Long live the great and heroic Soviet people, the builders of communism! (*Stormy applause.*)

Long live the indestructible unity and fraternal friendship of the peoples of the world socialist camp! (*Stormy applause.*)

Long live the heroic party of the Communists of the Soviet Union, created and tempered in struggle by the great Lenin! (*Stormy applause.*)

Long live the indestructible unity of the international Communist and workers' movement and the fraternal solidarity of the proletarians of all countries! (*Stormy applause.*)

Long live peace the world over! (*Stormy applause.*)

Under the all-conquering banner of Marxism-Leninism, under the leadership of the Communist Party, forward to the victory of communism! (*Stormy, prolonged applause, turning into an ovation. All rise.*)

Currents of Dissent and the "Evil Empire" (1974–1984)

During the early 1970s, the Soviet Union and United States, under the leadership, respectively, of Leonid Brezhnev and Richard Nixon, demonstrated cooperation through cultural exchanges and even negotiated a Strategic Arms

Limitation Treaty (SALT) in 1972. This policy of détente, *as it was called, was a hopeful sign that the world was becoming a safer place. But internally, the Soviet Union continued to stifle dissent in an effort to preserve the integrity of its image as a united and stable state, proof of the success and superiority of the communist philosophy.*

Two of the most outspoken dissenters became international spokesmen against arbitrary political and social repression. The first selection is by Andrei Sakharov (1921–1989), who was a brilliant physicist and helped develop the Soviet Union's first hydrogen bomb. Like Albert Einstein, Sakharov was outspoken in his fear of nuclear proliferation and called on all nuclear powers for arms reduction. He also criticized Soviet leadership and predicted the eventual integration of communist and capitalist systems in a form of democratic socialism. He won the Nobel Peace Prize in 1975 but was censured by the Soviet government and exiled to Gorky in 1980. Released six years later by Mikhail Gorbachev, Sakharov and his wife, human rights activist Yelena Bonner, continued to advocate political and intellectual liberty, and international coexistence.

The next selection is from the dissident writer Alexander Solzhenitsyn. A winner of the Nobel Prize for Literature in 1970, his fame was secured by his book The Gulag Archipelago *(1973), which examined the brutal Soviet prison system in Siberia. Exiled in 1974, Solzhenitsyn commanded international recognition and focused concern on the inadequacies and repression of Soviet society. His comments seem prescient in light of some of the current changes in the Soviet Union under Mikhail Gorbachev.*

"Freedom of Thought Is the Only Guarantee" (1974)
ANDREI SAKHAROV

The division of mankind threatens it with destruction. Civilization is imperiled by: a universal thermonuclear war, catastrophic hunger for most of mankind, stupefaction from the narcotic of "mass culture," and bureaucratized dogmatism, a spreading of mass myths that put entire peoples and continents under the power of cruel and treacherous demagogues, and destruction or degeneration from the unforeseeable consequences of swift changes in the conditions of life on our planet.

In the face of these perils, any action increasing the division of mankind, any preaching of the incompatibility of world ideologies and nations is madness and a crime. Only universal cooperation under conditions of intellectual freedom and the lofty moral ideals of socialism and labor, accompanied by the elimination of dogmatism and pressures of the concealed interests of ruling classes, will preserve civilization. . . .

Millions of people throughout the world are striving to put an end to poverty. They despise oppression, dogmatism, and demagogy (and their more extreme manifestations—racism, fascism, Stalinism, and Maoism). They believe in progress based on the use, under conditions of social justice and intellectual freedom, of all the positive experience accumulated by mankind. . . .

Intellectual freedom is essential to human society—freedom to obtain and distribute information, freedom for open-minded and unfearing debate, and freedom from pressure by officialdom and prejudices. Such a trinity of freedom of thought is the only guarantee against an infection of people by mass myths, which, in the hands of treacherous hypocrites and demagogues, can be transformed into bloody dictatorship. Freedom of thought is the only guarantee of the feasibility of a scientific democratic approach to politics, economy, and culture.

But freedom of thought is under a triple threat in modern society—from the deliberate opium of mass culture, from cowardly, egotistic, and philistine ideologies, and from the ossified dogmatism of a bureaucratic oligarchy and its favorite weapon, ideological censorship. Therefore, freedom of thought requires the defense of all thinking and honest people. This is a mission not only for the intelligentsia, but for all strata of society, particularly its most active and organized stratum, the working class. The world-wide dangers of war, famine, cults of personality, and bureaucracy—these are perils for all of mankind.

"What Have You to Fear?" (1974)
ALEXANDER I. SOLZHENITSYN

But what about *us*? Us, with our unwieldiness and our inertia, with our flinching and inability to change even a single letter, a single syllable, of what Marx said in 1848 about industrial development? Economically and physically we are perfectly capable of saving ourselves. But there is a road block on the path to our salvation—the sole Progressive World View. If we renounce industrial development, what about the working class, socialism, Communism, unlimited increase in productivity and all the rest? Marx is not to be corrected, that's revisionism. . . .

But you are already being called "revisionists" anyway, whatever you may do in the future. So wouldn't it be better to do your duty soberly, responsibly and firmly, and give up the dead letter for the sake of a living people who are utterly dependent on your power and your decisions? And you must do it without delay. Why dawdle if we shall have to snap out of it sometime anyway? Why repeat what others have done and loop the agoniz-

" 'What Have You to Fear?' " is an excerpt from Alexander I. Solzhenitsyn, *Letter to the Soviet Leaders* (New York, 1974), pp. 25–26, 41–43, 56–58. Copyright © 1974 by Aleksandr I. Solzhenitsyn. English translation by Hilary Sternberg. Copyright © 1974 by Writers and Scholars International Ltd. Reprinted by permission of HarperCollins Publishers, Inc.

ing loop right to the end, when we are not too far into it to turn back? If the man at the head of the column cries, "I have lost my way," do we absolutely have to plow right on to the spot where he realized his mistake and only there turn back? Why not turn and start on the right course from wherever we happen to be? . . .

This Ideology [Marxism] that fell to us by inheritance is not only decrepit and hopelessly antiquated now; even during its best decades it was totally mistaken in its predictions and was never a science.

A primitive, superficial economic theory, it declared that only the worker creates value and failed to take into account the contribution of either organizers, engineers, transportation or marketing systems. It was mistaken when it forecast that the proletariat would be endlessly oppressed and would never achieve anything in a bourgeois democracy—if only we could shower people with as much food, clothing and leisure as they have gained under capitalism! It missed the point when it asserted that the prosperity of the European countries depended on their colonies—it was only after they had shaken the colonies off that they began to accomplish their "economic miracles." It was mistaken through and through in its prediction that socialists could never come to power except through an armed uprising. It miscalculated in thinking that the first uprisings would take place in the advanced industrial countries—quite the reverse. And the picture of how the whole world would rapidly be overtaken by revolutions and how states would soon wither away was sheer delusion, sheer ignorance of human nature. And as for wars being characteristic of capitalism alone and coming to an end when capitalism did—we have already witnessed the longest war of the twentieth century so far, and it was not capitalism that rejected negotiations and a truce for fifteen to twenty years; and God forbid that we should witness the bloodiest and most brutal of all mankind's wars—a war between two Communist superpowers. Then there was nationalism, which this theory also buried in 1848 as a "survival"—but find a stronger force in the world today! And its the same with many other things too boring to list.

Marxism is not only not accurate, is not only not a science, has not only failed to predict a *single event* in terms of figures, quantities, time-scales or locations . . . —it absolutely astounds one by the economic and mechanistic crudity of its attempts to explain that most subtle of creatures, the human being, and that even more complex synthesis of millions of people, society. Only the cupidity of some, the blindness of others and a craving for *faith* on the part of others can serve to explain this grim jest of the twentieth century: how can such a discredited and bankrupt doctrine still have so many followers in the West! In *our* country are left the fewest of all! *We* who have had a taste of it are only pretending willy-nilly. . . .

So that the country and people do not suffocate, and so that they all have the chance to develop and enrich us with ideas, allow competition on an equal and honorable basis—not for power, but for truth—between all ideological and moral currents, in particular between *all religions*. . . . Allow us a free art and literature, the free publication not just of political books—God preserve us!—and exhortations and election leaflets; allow us philosophical, ethical, economic and social studies, and you will see what a rich harvest it brings and how it bears fruit—for the good of Russia. . . .

What have you to fear? Is the idea really so terrible? Are you really so unsure of yourselves? You will still have absolute and impregnable power, a separate, strong and exclusive Party, the army, the police force, industry, transportation, communications, mineral wealth, a monopoly of foreign trade, an artificial rate of exchange for the ruble—but let the people breathe, let them think and develop! If you belong to the people heart and soul, there can be nothing to hold you back!

After all, does the human heart not still feel the need to atone for the past?

Your dearest wish is for our state structure and our ideological system never to change, to remain as they are for centuries. But history is not like that. Every system either finds a way to develop or else collapses.

The Merger of Nationalities (1982)

R. I. KOSOLAPOV

After the 1979 census showed that population growth among Soviet minorities would soon place them in a majority over Russians, pressure was increased for them to learn the Russian language and in other ways to assimilate to the Russian culture. R. I. Kosolapov, editor of the Communist party's main theoretical journal, stressed the need to merge nationalities. He was optimistic in his 1982 assessment of a united Soviet state. The problems of ethnic violence that occurred at the beginning of the 1990s in the Soviet Union were never supposed to have taken place.

The Soviet people constitute an unprecedented phenomenon in history. Internationalist in terms of its very essence, this new community of people has united in a single family over one hundred nations and ethnic groups belonging to various races but has not submerged them within itself; on the contrary, it has secured the flourishing of each one of them while at the same time evolving numerous common psychological and moral features conditioned by the unity of their political, economic and ideological life. . . .

It is no exaggeration to say that the Russian people have become the backbone of our new internationalist community of people. The rulers of czarist Russia made great endeavors to instill in Russians a sense of "superiority" over a contemptuously hostile attitude toward "outsiders." But nothing could eliminate sensitivity to other people's troubles from the soul of

"The Merger of Nationalities" is from *Kommunist*, no. 12, 1982 editorial, "We Are the Soviet People" (English translation: Washington, Joint Publications Research Service, no. 82130, November 1, 1982, pp. 1, 4–10). Reprinted by permission.

the Russian people, who became a good friend to all the country's peoples, large and small. The misanthropic ideas of chauvinism and racism never took root in practice on Russian soil, and superpatriotic intoxication never turned the heads of indigenous Russians. . . . The [Communist] Party relied primarily on the Russian people in implementing the nationalities policy. . . . The Russian language became the means of communication between nationalities, which made a supreme contribution to the consolidation of the entire complex of internationalist ties. . . .

Under our country's specific conditions following the republics' voluntary unification in the Soviet Union it would have been a crime against the socialist revolution and the future of socialism and an irresponsible attitude to the people's destiny to have made centralized leadership of the union state formalistic, telling the republics "govern yourselves as you wish." This would have been a conscious deviation from the principles of proletarian internationalism to the benefit of national sovereignty interpreted in an egotistical, narrow and formalistic manner. Under such conditions it would have been extremely difficult if not impossible for many of our peoples to have extricated themselves from poverty and backwardness. But today it is common knowledge what national flourishing they have achieved under the conditions of comprehensive fraternal mutual aid attentively and skillfully administered by the central union authorities.

But maybe it is not a question of the past? Maybe now, when all the nations and ethnic groups comprising the Soviet people have achieved economic and cultural equality—they have had political equality from the start—when every union Soviet republic constitutes an economically strong and highly cultured state formation, maybe, proceeding from all this, we should weaken the bonds of democratic centralism for the sake of that notorious self-government? . . .

The social structure of Soviet society is developing intensively in the direction of the intensification of its homogeneity: The working class peasantry and people's intelligentsia are drawing closer together in terms of their qualitative indicators, mutual relations between them are improving, and their alliance is strengthening. . . . Time will tell what this projected new fusion of peoples of different ethnic groups and races will be like, but it seems perfectly clear that it will be a human community of an unprecedentedly high level since it will be effected on the threshold of the full implementation of the great humanist ideals of communism.

America's Foreign Policy (1983)

GEORGE SHULTZ

During the presidency of Jimmy Carter, the Soviet Union invaded the sovereign state of Afghanistan (December 1979), an act that drew international criticism and contributed to the Carter Doctrine of January 1980: Any threat

"America's Foreign Policy" is from George Shultz, speech delivered before the United Nations, September 30, 1983.

upon American oil interests in the Persian Gulf would be considered provoca-
tive and tantamount to war. In 1981, Ronald Reagan was inaugurated as
president, having won the election in part on a "get-tough" stance toward the
U.S.S.R. His verbal attacks characterized the Soviet Union as "the evil
Empire" and "the focus of evil in the world." Such rhetoric did little to
encourage cooperation between the two nations. It was only late in 1985,
during Reagan's second term, that a summit conference was held. George
Shultz, secretary of state, offered this assessment of American foreign policy in
1983.

Americans are, by history and by inclination, a practical and pragmatic
people—yet a people with a vision. It is the vision—usually simple and
sometimes naive—that has so often led us to dare and to achieve. President
Reagan's approach to foreign policy is grounded squarely on standards
drawn from the pragmatic American experience. As de Tocqueville pointed out, "To achieve its objective, America relies on personal interest, and
gives full reign to the strength and reason of the individual." That is as true
now as when it was said 150 years ago. Our principal instrument, now as
then, is freedom. Our adversaries are the oppressors, the totalitarians, the
tacticians of fear and pressure.

On this foundation, President Reagan's ideas and the structure of his
foreign policy are so straight forward that those of us enmeshed in day-to-
day details may easily lose sight of them. The President never does; he
consistently brings us back to fundamentals. Today, I will talk about those
fundamentals. They consist of four ideas that guide our actions.

- We will start from realism.
- We will act from strength, both in power and purpose.
- We will stress the indispensable need to generate consent, build agree-
  ments, and negotiate on key issues.
- We will conduct ourselves in the belief that progress is possible, even
  though the road to achievement is long and hard.

Reality

If we are to change the world we must first understand it. We must face
reality—with all its anguish and all its opportunities. Our era needs those
who, as Pericles said, have the clearest vision of what is before them, glory
and danger alike, and, notwithstanding, go out to meet it.

Reality is not an illusion nor a sleight of hand, though many would have
us believe otherwise. The enormous, grinding machinery of Soviet propaganda daily seeks to distort reality, to bend truth for its own purposes. Our
world is occupied by far too many governments which seek to conceal truth
from their own people. They wish to imprison reality by controlling what
can be read or spoken or heard. They would have us believe that black is
white and up is down.

Unpleasant Reality

Much of present day reality is unpleasant. To describe conditions as we see them, as I do today and as President Reagan has over the course of his presidency, is not to seek confrontation. Far from it. Our purpose is to avoid misunderstanding and to create the necessary preconditions for change. And so, when we see aggression, we will call it aggression. When we see subversion, we will call it subversion. When we see repression, we will call it repression.

- Events in Poland, for example, cannot be ignored or explained away. The Polish people want to be their own master. Years of systematic tyranny cannot repress this desire, and neither will martial law. But in Poland today, truth must hide in corners.
- Nor can we simply turn our heads and look the other way as Soviet divisions brutalize an entire population in Afghanistan. The resistance of the Afghan people is a valiant saga of our times. We demean that valor if we do not recognize its source.
- And Soviet surrogates intervene in many countries, creating a new era of colonialism at the moment in history when peoples around the globe had lifted that burden from their backs. . . .

Strength

America's yearning for peace does not lead us to be hesitant in developing our strength or in using it when necessary. Indeed, clarity about the magnitude of the problems we face leads inevitably to a realistic appreciation of the importance of American strength. The strength of the free world imposes restraint, invites accommodation, and reassures those who would share in the creative work that is the wonderful consequence of liberty.

Strength means military forces to insure that no other nation can threaten us, our interests, or our friends. But when I speak of strength, I do not mean military power alone. To Americans, strength derives as well from a solid economic base and social vitality at home and with our partners. And, most fundamentally, the true wellspring of strength lies in America's moral commitment.

Military Strength

The bulwark of America's strength is military power for peace. The American people have never accepted weakness, nor hesitancy, nor abdication. We will not put our destiny into the hands of the ruthless. Americans today are emphatically united on the necessity of a strong defense. This year's defense budget will insure that the United States will help its friends and allies defend themselves—to make sure that peace is seen clearly by all to be the only feasible course in world affairs. . . .

Economic Strength

The engine of America's strength is a sound economy. . . . The United States, with its vast resources, can survive an era of economic strife and decay. But our moral commitment and our self-interest require us to use our technological and productive abilities to build lasting prosperity at home and to contribute to a sound economic situation abroad. . . .

Moral Strength

The bedrock of our strength is our moral and spiritual character. The sources of true strength lie deeper than economic or military power—in the dedication of a free people which knows its responsibility. America's institutions are those of freedom accessible to every person and of government as the accountable servant of the people. Equal opportunity; due process of law; open trial by jury; freedom of belief, speech, and assembly—our Bill of Rights, our guarantees of liberty and limited government—were hammered out in centuries of ordeal. Because we care about these human values for ourselves, so must we then be concerned, and legitimately so, with abuses of freedom, justice, and humanitarian principles beyond our borders. This is why we will speak and act for prisoners of conscience, against terrorism. . . . This is why we are anxious to participate in periodic reviews of the human rights performance of ourselves as well as others. We welcome scrutiny of our own system. We are not perfect, and we know it, but we have nothing to hide.

Our belief in liberty guides our policies here in the United Nations as elsewhere. Therefore, in this forum the United States will continue to insist upon fairness, balance, and truth. We take the debate on human rights seriously. We insist upon honesty in the use of language; we will point out inconsistencies, double standards, and lies. We will not compromise our commitment to truth. . . .

Progress

Perhaps the most common phrase spoken by the American people in our more than two centuries of national life has been: "You can't stop progress." Our people have always been imbued with the conviction that the future of a free people would be good.

America continues to offer that vision to the world. With that vision and with the freedom to act creatively, there is nothing that people of goodwill need fear.

I am not here to assert, however, that the way is easy, quick, or that the future is bound to be bright. There is a poem by Carl Sandburg in which a traveler asks the sphinx to speak and reveal the distilled wisdom of all the ages. The sphinx does speak. Its words are: "Don't expect too much."

That is good counsel for all of us here. It does not mean that great accomplishments are beyond our reach. We can help shape more constructive international relations and give our children a better chance at life. It does mean, however, that risk, pain, expense, and above all endurance are needed to bring those achievements into our grasp.

We must recognize the complex and vexing character of this world. We should not indulge ourselves in fantasies of perfection or unfulfillable plans or solutions gained by pressure. It is the responsibility of leaders not to feed the growing appetite for easy promises and grand assurances. The plain truth is this: We face the prospect of all too few decisive or dramatic breakthroughs; we face the necessity of dedicating our energies and creativity to a protracted struggle toward eventual success.

That is the approach of my country—because we see not only the necessity, but the possibility, of making important progress on a broad front.

"A World Turned Upside Down!": The Gorbachev Era and Beyond

There is nothing more difficult to take in hand, more perilous to conduct, or more uncertain in its success than to take the lead in a new order of things.

—Niccolò Machiavelli

It is in no way a question of destroying the values of the October Revolution. Rather, we must restore and purify them; they must be reinforced and built upon. Only if there is a systematic and consistent democratization of the whole of our political and social life on a socialist basis will our country be able to retain its role and influence among the progressive forces of the world.

—Roy Medvedev

Much of what accumulated in the stifling and repressive atmosphere of Stalinism and stagnation, and is now surfacing, is far from pleasant and constructive. But this has to be tolerated. This is what a revolution is all about. Its primary function is always to give people freedom. And perestroika with its democratization and glasnost has already fulfilled its primary task.

—Mikhail Gorbachev

A new era in international relations dawned on the death of the old-guard Soviet leader Constantine Chernenko in 1985. His government had been transitional, a geriatric accommodation to the demands of a new-style Soviet leadership waiting in the wings. Mikhail Gorbachev was forty-eight years old when he secured entry to the Politburo in 1979 and only fifty-four when he assumed the position of general secretary of the Communist party in 1985. A career bureaucrat with primary assignments in agricultural administration, Gorbachev was nevertheless ready to embark on a radical departure from established Soviet policies. He sought to define and implement the new concepts of perestroika ("restructuring") *and* glasnost *("openness") through which he hoped to liberalize the political, economic, and cultural bases of Soviet society. Change was imminent, but no one could predict its full impact on travel restrictions and emigration, censorship, state control of artistic expression, and ultimately political organization itself through democratization and self-determination of ethnic nationalities.*

Gorbachev's initial declarations in 1985 were met with international and domestic astonishment. Gorbachev was hailed in the West as the "man of the century," personally responsible for overcoming the legacy of Stalinism, for eliminating an authoritarian mindset, for offering flexible positions on arms reduction in pursuit of a safer world. The "Evil Empire" was fast losing its threatening aura as each of the eastern European "satellite" nations broke away from Soviet control in popular revolutions throughout 1989. This time there was no military attempt to maintain Soviet control as in Hungary (1954) and in Czechoslovakia (1968). The symbolic culmination of this process occurred on November 10, 1989, with the destruction of the Berlin Wall by the people of East and West Germany.

But Mikhail Gorbachev also faced severe opposition at home, both from the political right, which feared chaos and a loss of influence, and from the political left, led by Boris Yeltsin, who argued that perestroika *was not being instituted fast enough, nor with a deep democratic conviction. Also in the late 1980s, the various ethnic minorities in the Soviet republics of Armenia, Azerbaijan, and Georgia began testing the limits of Gorbachev's commitment to democracy and self-determination of peoples. So too did the Baltic states of Estonia, Latvia, and Lithuania seek to break away from the Soviet "Union" and once again run their own affairs independent of Moscow.*

Add to this turmoil a tense domestic background of deprivation as evidenced by food shortages and a heritage of consumer neglect, and Gorbachev was pressed at every turn. However, he was a maneuverer, a political tactician, an orchestrator of change. In an effort to maintain the union of the Soviet republics, Gorbachev tried to run a center position against the divergent agendas of the reformists and conservatives. He promised the former continued democratization and progress toward a market economy, and he reassured the latter that he was a loyal Communist party man, who would respect them and protect their traditional interests. In late 1990, Gorbachev felt the need to conciliate the right wing of the party, which was increasingly concerned about demonstrations of independence in the republics. Gorbachev regarded this placation as necessary for the maintenance of his authority; however, it drove away some of the most talented and avid reformers in the Gorbachev orbit. Eduard Shevardnadze resigned as Foreign Minister and warned of dictator-

ship. On August 19, 1991, Shevardnadze's fears threatened to become reality as hard-line members of Gorbachev's advisory cabinet tried to institute a coup d'etat. Gorbachev was confined in the Crimea for three days while an "emergency committee" of eight coup leaders explained that he was "ill" and needed a long rest. The incompetency of the conspirators, the refusal of the army and KGB security forces to fire on the Russian people, and most importantly the defiance of the Soviet citizenry and their commitment to the tenets of popular sovereignty resulted in the swift collapse of the coup. But the Soviet state emerged from this drama a changed entity. Boris Yeltsin, the popularly elected president of the republic of Russia, now seemed to hold the keys to the future. By August 24, Gorbachev's cabinet had been reappointed with reformers scrutinized by Yeltsin; the Communist party newspaper, Pravda, *had been shut down; and Gorbachev had resigned from his position as General Secretary of the Communist party. Indeed, the Communist party was in complete disarray after having ruled the country for nearly seventy-five years. Each of the Baltic states as well as the Ukraine and other Soviet republics had declared independence, a foreshadowing of the dissolution of the Soviet empire. Some scholars have already hailed this as the "Second Russian Revolution." That revolution may in fact have left Gorbachev behind. He had styled himself a reforming communist and a convinced socialist, an image essential to the initial phases of reform. Paradoxically, this close identification with the Communist party afforded him the path to success, but it also sowed the seeds of failure. Gorbachev faced the great challenge of transition, of* creating *revolution and* controlling *it at the same time. As Lenin, Napoleon, Robespierre, and the Roman emperor, Augustus, understood in earlier ages, it is difficult to hold onto a world turned upside down. The future of the Soviet Republics continues to be a tentative brew of economic dislocation and political uncertainty.*

The following selections are excerpted from the speeches of Mikhail Gorbachev. They address the transitional dilemmas facing the Communist party and the Soviet government and people during the most important years of Gorbachev's leadership.

Perestroika and the Socialist Renewal of Society (September 11, 1989)

MIKHAIL GORBACHEV

Good evening, comrades, I am here to talk to you about our current affairs. The situation in the country is not simple. We all know and feel this. Everything has become entangled in a tight knot: scarcity on the consumer goods market, conflicts in ethnic relations, and difficult and sometimes painful processes in the public consciousness, resulting from the overcom-

"*Perestroika* and the Socialist Renewal of Society" is from Mikhail Gorbachev, speech delivered to the people of the U.S.S.R., September 11, 1989. Contained in *Vital Speeches of the Day*, October 15, 1989, pp. 5–7.

ing of distortions and from the renewal of socialism. People are trying to understand where we have found ourselves at the moment, evaluating the pluses and minuses of the path we have covered during the last four-plus years, the development of democracy and the pace of the economic and political reforms.

It is only natural that people want to know the real causes of our weaknesses and failures in carrying out specific programs for perestroika and in tackling urgent problems and to find out why the situation in some areas has deteriorated rather than improved.

In short, political life today is characterized by intense debate. But the main thing I want to emphasize is that the mass of people have become involved in this movement and they play an ever growing role in discussing and accomplishing social, economic, and political tasks.

Comrades, this is a fact of fundamental importance because it gives perestroika the elements of constructive and businesslike effort and helps overcome people's alienation from power. Yet one cannot fail to see a different tend. Against the background of heated debate and a rapid succession of events, things are happening that must not be ignored or left unaccounted for. Efforts are being made to discredit perestroika from conservative, leftist and sometimes unmistakably anti-socialist positions. One can hear in this discordant choir voices predicting an imminent chaos and speculation about the threat of a coup and even civil war. It is a fact that some people would like to create an atmosphere of anxiety, despair and uncertainty in society. . . .

In effect, the conservative forces are trying to impose on us such evaluations of the situation that would provoke resistance to perestroika and mold in people's mind the view that the process of change begun in society should be halted or at least slowed down; these forces demand that the old command methods of government should be restored. Otherwise, they say, chaos will set in. Meanwhile, the leftist elements suggest tackling extremely difficult problems in one go, without taking into account our actual possibilities or the interests of society. Such demands are presented as concern for the people and its well-being.

Recommendations have also been made lately from which one can assume that our only "salvation" is renouncing the values of socialism and conducting perestroika in the capitalist manner. Such views do exist. Needless to say, such ideas go against the grain of perestroika, which implies socialist renewal of society. . . .

True, perestroika is meeting with many difficulties. But it is radical change, a revolution in the economy and in policy, in the ways of thinking and in people's consciousness, in the entire pattern of our life. Besides, we have not been able to avoid mistakes in our practical actions in the course of perestroika.

But perestroika has opened up realistic opportunities for society's renewal, for giving society a new quality and for creating truly humane and democratic socialism. It has returned to the great nation a sense of dignity and given the Soviet people a sense of freedom. It is a powerful source of social, spiritual, and, I should say, patriotic energy for decades to come.

That is why we must do everything to continue perestroika on the basis of the ideas and principles proclaimed by the party. And we must not stop. We must continue along the way of changes we have embarked upon. . . . The community is casting off its illusions. It no longer believes that there are simple solutions to be brought ready-made from above for all our problems. . . .

I think it very important that the community is coming to better understand the primary link between perestroika and labor—dedicated, creative, efficient work fully implementing every worker's knowledge and abilities. This is essential because until recently, we concentrated not so much on labor as on the distribution of benefits. One could think that redistribution of fictitious wealth was all perestroika was about. We have at last begun to shed this delusion. . . .

The Government of the U.S.S.R. is elaborating a program of extraordinary measures to improve the economy and, above all, to normalize the consumer market. The program is to be submitted to the Congress of People's Deputies. We believe that this program will give clear answers to the questions of how and when the most urgent social and economic problems will be solved. I think society will not accept it if the program does not determine clear and concrete measures, stages, and time limits as well as the responsibility of the republic and local bodies and labor collectives. I presume that this package may include unpopular, probably tough and even painful measures. This will be justified, however, only if they are prompted by the need to get out of the present situation.

Shortages, which arouse the sharpest criticisms and discontent of the people, are a special issue. The government is to give an explanation on this urgent social problem and come up with practical measures shortly. . . .

Of major political importance will be the laws on republic and regional cost-accounting and self-government. They are an important step toward realistically strengthening the sovereignty of the republics and expanding the rights of the local Soviets [councils].

The party, which is society's consolidating and vanguard force, has a unique role to play in this process. Those who strive to use the difficulties of the transition period for certain unseemly purposes and try to undermine the influence of the party should know that they will not succeed. We are sure that with all the critical sentiments concerning that activities of some or other party committee or communists, the working people realize perfectly well the importance of the party of Lenin for the fate of socialism, which today is inseparable from the success of perestroika. On the other hand, it is clear that the new tasks call for a deep renewal of the party.

By restructuring itself, getting rid of all that hinders its activities, overcoming dogmatism and conservatism, mastering a new style and new methods of work, renewing its personnel, and working side by side with the working people, the Communist Party of the Soviet Union will be able to fulfill its role of the political vanguard of society. The party will firmly pursue the policy of perestroika, heading the revolutionary transformation of society. We should realistically assess all processes and phenomena of the present-day situation, show restraint, see clearly where we are and not become confused. On this basis we should draw conclusions for our action at the given moment and in the future. We must act responsibly and prudently, without deviating from the course of perestroika in society.

Dear comrades, I wish you success in work, determination and firm spirit.

Political Pluralism: The Changing Role of the Communist Party (February 5, 1990)

MIKHAIL GORBACHEV

We should abandon everything that led to the isolation of socialist [Communist] countries from the mainstream of world civilisation. We should abandon the understanding of progress as a permanent confrontation with a socially different world.

We are giving up the notion of building socialism on an earlier construed pattern which serves as a rigid framework for the ingenious creativity of the masses. . . . The [Communist] Party's renewal presupposes a fundamental change in its relations with state and economic bodies and the abandonment of the practice of commanding them and fulfilling for their functions.

The Party in a renewing society can exist and play its role as the vanguard only as a democratically recognised force. This means that its status should not be imposed through constitutional endorsement.

The Soviet Communist Party, it goes without saying, intends to struggle for the status of the ruling party. But it will do so strictly within the framework of the democratic process by giving up any legal and political advantages, offering its program and defending it in discussions, cooperating with other social and political forces, always working amidst the masses, living according to their interests and their needs.

The extensive democratisation currently under way in our society is being accompanied by mounting political pluralism. Various social and political organisations and movements are emerging. This process may lead at a certain stage to the establishment of [other] parties. The Soviet Communist Party is prepared to act with due account for these new circumstances, cooperate and conduct a dialogue with all organisations committed to the Soviet Constitution and the social system endorsed in this Constitu-

"Political Pluralism" is from Mikhail Gorbachev, speech delivered at the Soviet Communist Party Central Committee's Plenary Meeting, Moscow, U.S.S.R., February 5, 1990. Contained in *Vital Speeches of the Day*, March 15, 1990, p. 323.

tion. At the same time, we openly state that at this crucial period the Soviet Communist Party is able to play the consolidating, integrating role and ensure progress of perestroika for the benefit of the entire nation.

The Party's renewal presupposes its thorough, comprehensive democratisation and a rethinking of the principle of democratic centralism with emphasis on democratism and power of the Party masses.

The Soviet Federation and the Ethnic Issue (1990)
MIKHAIL GORBACHEV

Comrades, our society is concerned, no less than with the situation in the economy, with a number of complex problems that have arisen in inter-ethnic relations, which affect the future of the Soviet federation. . . . The 1989 pre-congress platform points to the possibility of and the need for the further development of the treaty principle of the Soviet Federation. This would involve the creation of legal conditions that would open up the possibility for the existence of diverse forms of federative ties.

We stand for the diversity of modes of ethnic life in an integral and united Soviet state. We all have lately had the opportunity to think seriously about the state of affairs and developments in the sphere of ethnic relations. . . .

I think the Party and society are coming to understand . . . that one must act in a well-balanced and responsible way in this sphere. People are coming to see where separatist nationalist, especially extremist, slogans may lead and what they can entail for people, nationalities and the whole country. We must display principled approaches in opposing nationalism, chauvinism and separatism and, at the same time, understand that ethnic problems are no fantasy, they are real and are waiting to be solved by perestroika.

• • •

I believe there is every reason to say that the country and the people are becoming increasingly convinced that it is vitally important to preserve the Union, of course, in a revamped form and on democratic principles, combining the U.S.S.R.'s sovereignty with that of the republics.

At the same time, I wish to stress that our republics' sovereignty is a historically irreversible stage in the development of our multinational state. But in our effort to do away with excessive centralism and unitarism, we

"The Soviet Federation and the Ethnic Issue" is from Mikhail Gorbachev, speeches delivered respectively to the Soviet Communist Party Central Committee's Plenary meeting, Moscow, U.S.S.R., February 5, 1990, and to the Congress of the U.S.S.R., Moscow, U.S.S.R., December 12, 1990. Contained in *Vital Speeches of the Day*, March 15, 1990, p. 325, and January 15, 1991, pp. 196, 200.

must not allow the Union to be turned into something amorphous or to disintegrate. This would hit hard at the destinies of millions of people and the world situation as a whole.

Today we have embarked upon the stage of radical reforms in our multinational state. Its future is being decided, and this means our own future, the future of every nation making it up. We proceed from the inviolability of the principle: every nation has the right to self-determination. But only the whole nation. Its will can best be expressed by referendum. And I submit the proposal to hold a nation-wide referendum, which will allow every citizen to say "yes" or "no" to the union of sovereign states built on federal lines. Results of referenda in every republic will provide the final verdict. As to secession from the U.S.S.R., it can be effected only in accordance with the existing law and with due account for all the aspects of this complicated political and socio-economic process.

And there is one more question of principle. We have been recently confronted by a situation when republics and other national-territorial formations announce all kinds of changes in their legal status, ignoring the existing constitution of the U.S.S.R. Roughly speaking, this "guerrilla-like" behaviour is fraught with grave disturbances and even chaos. It leads nowhere. And we have already felt this.

This is why I believe that Congress of People's Deputies must firmly declare: the Constitution of the U.S.S.R. remains the supreme legislative act and must be observed without fail until the Union Treaty is concluded, which will decide the legal status of each signatory. . . .

Our urgent tasks and our immediate prospects and goals are now clear. All of us should get down to practical work. We should decisively do away with politicking, sloganeering, passion-fomenting and confrontation.

We need discipline, including self-discipline, civil accord and hard self-less work now like never before. We also need confidence in ourselves. We should neither give up ourselves nor scare other people with talk of impending catastrophe.

"This Is What Our Time Is About": The Rebirth of the United Nations (September 25, 1990)

EDUARD SHEVARDNADZE

The Soviet Union has enjoyed great success in the international arena since 1985. At nearly each step, the Soviets provided the impetus, flexibility, and commitment to arms reduction that earned Gorbachev the Nobel Peace Prize. After removing Soviet military forces from Afghanistan and announcing

" 'This Is What Our Time Is About' " is from Eduard Shevardnadze, speech delivered to the United Nations General Assembly, New York, New York, on September 25, 1990. Contained in *Vital Speeches of the Day*, October 15, 1990, p. 8–9, 12.

*significant reductions in standing forces stationed in eastern Europe in 1989,
the Soviet Union garnered new accolades in world affairs. Nowhere are these
changes in international relations more in evidence than in the United Nations.*

*Built on idealistic foundations in 1945, the United Nations was seen by
Franklin Roosevelt, Winston Churchill, and others as the supreme acknowl-
edgment of a cooperative spirit among human beings that transcended ideological and territorial boundaries. The United Nations, however, has often been
regarded as a weak compendium of nations, without the authority or means of
enforcing the collective will of its members. However, on August 2, 1990,
Iraq, under the leadership of Saddam Hussein, invaded and occupied the
sovereign nation of Kuwait. This event provided President George Bush the
opportunity to promote and defend a concept that he has termed the "New
World Order" of nations. The first selection is a revealing speech on the
progress of international relations since 1945 delivered by Soviet Foreign
Minister Eduard Shevardnadze shortly after the Iraqi invasion of Kuwait. His
speech signaled a new cooperative Soviet presence in the world.*

*But this attempt at international leadership was tempered just three months
later upon the resignation of Shevardnadze as foreign minister, as noted in the
second selection. His action was prompted by Gorbachev's increasing preoc-
cupation with the domestic scene and his placation of the right wing. Shevardnadze warned: "No one knows what this dictatorship will be like, what kind
of dictator will come to power and what order will be established." Given the
tremendous changes after the abortive coup attempt of August 1991, and the
unknown potential of Boris Yeltsin's leadership, perhaps Shevardnadze's confidence in a democratic future may take years of experimentation, restraint, and
cooperation to prove secure. This kind of political interplay will have an impact
on the effectiveness of the Soviet Republics to contribute to a future perhaps
characterized more by internal consolidation and international cooperation
than by ideological polarization and confrontation.*

From the exceptional vantage point of this forty-fifth session of the United
Nations General Assembly, one might look back in amazement at how
strikingly different is the terrain we have covered in just one year from the
familiar landscape of the more than four decades which had preceded it.

Politically, this was not just a calendar year, but a light year in the history
of the world. The Cold War, which is—with its accompanying stress,
psychoses and anticipation of disaster—no longer a part of our life. Gone is
the strain of daily confrontation, propaganda, bickering and reciprocal
threats.

This has been a year during which pieces of the Berlin Wall were a
popular souvenir. And now an end has been put to the division of Europe,
and a final line has been drawn unto the Second World War. The unification of the two German states has been completed. The German
question, this great and classical problem of world politics, which only

yesterday seemed intractable, has been resolved calmly and to mutual satisfaction. . . .

Almost unnoticed, the military alliances have lost their enemies. They are beginning to build their relations on a new basis, moving away from confrontation, which is being eroded by disarmament, by lower defense spending, more wide-ranging confidence-building measures, and the emergence of collective and cooperative security structures.

Unprecedented progress has been made in the peaceful resolution of regional conflicts by political means. . . . All of this has been done with the most active participation of the United Nations.

These positive changes in the world, we can safely say, have been propelled by a new relationship between the Soviet Union and the United States, which is evolving from cooperation to partnership. . . . The political environment is clearly being defined by the global recognition of the supremacy of universal human values. . . .

The central concepts of today's politics are cooperation, interaction, and partnership in facing the global challenges of combating severe problems, such as economic backwardness, poverty, and social inequality, and protecting the environment.

Had this session taken place before last August, we would have had every reason to say that mankind had cleared a narrow and dangerous passage. . . . But now, our field of vision has been obscured by the dark cloud of aggression against Kuwait.

On that black Thursday [August 2, 1990], Iraq flagrantly violated the United Nations charter, the principles of international law, the universally recognized norms of morality, and the standards of civilized behavior. Iraq committed an unprovoked aggression, and next the neighboring sovereign states seized thousands of hostages and resorted to unprecedented blackmail, threatening to use weapons of mass destruction.

There is also another dimension to Iraq's action. It has dealt a blow to all that mankind has recently achieved, all that we have been able to accomplish together by adopting the new political thinking, as our guide to the future. . . . In a way the Gulf crisis is not just a tragedy and an extremely dangerous threat to peace; it is also a serious challenge for all of us to review the ways and means of maintaining security in our world; methods of protecting law and order on our planet; the mechanisms for controlling the processes which affect the state of human civilization in the broadest meaning of this term. . . .

As we meet for the organization's 45th General Assembly, we are speaking not so much of the organization's maturity, but of the beginning of its rebirth, its restoration according to the blueprints of 1945, and wiping off the grime left by Cold War, we see a work of collective wisdom. The United Nations devised it—the organization as an instrument of action, and we must see to it that from now on all of us gear our words, to joint actions. This is what our time is about.

The Onset of Dictatorship (December 20, 1990)

EDUARD SHEVARDNADZE

Comrade deputies! I have perhaps the shortest and the most difficult speech in my life. I did not ask for the floor, but since certain deputies have insisted, . . . I have drawn up the text of such a speech. . . .

Democrats, I'll put it bluntly: Comrade democrats! In the widest meaning of this work: You have scattered. The reformers have gone into hiding. A dictatorship is approaching—I tell you that with full responsibility. No one knows what this dictatorship will be like, what kind of dictator will come to power and what order will be established.

I want to make the following statement. I am resigning. Let this be—and do not react and do not curse me—let this be my contribution, if you like, my protest against the onset of dictatorship.

I would like to express sincere gratitude to Mikhail Sergeyevich Gorbachev. I am his friend. I am a fellow thinker of his. I have always supported, and will support to the end of my day, the ideas of perestroika, the ideas of renewal, the ideas of democracy, of democratization.

We did great work in international affairs. But I think that it is my duty. As a man, as a citizen, as a Communist, I cannot reconcile myself with what is happening in my country and to the trials which await our people. I nevertheless believe that the dictatorship will not succeed, that the future belongs to democracy and freedom.

Thank you very much.

The Future of Europe

The Reunification of Germany

> History teaches us that enmities between nations . . . do not last forever. However fixed our likes and dislikes, the tide of time and events will often bring surprising changes in the relations between nations and neighbors.
>
> —John F. Kennedy

Few years have seen such fundamental political, social, and economic changes as occurred throughout eastern Europe in 1989. Poland, Hungary, Czechoslovakia, and East Germany all peacefully established new governments

"The Onset of Dictatorship" is from Eduard Shevardnadze, speech delivered before the Fourth Congress of the People's Deputies, Moscow, U.S.S.R. on December 20, 1990. Contained in *Vital Speeches of the Day*, January 15, 1991, pp. 201 and 202.

with democratic overtones after more than four decades of Marxist rule. The Soviet Union, continuing to pursue its own liberalization, gave most of its former satellites wide latitude in carrying out reforms in contrast to its earlier suppression of popular movements in Hungary (1956) and Czechoslovakia (1968). Only in Romania was the transition violent as a swift, but bloody revolution toppled the regime of hard-line Communist dictator Nicolae Ceausescu in December 1989. He and his wife were charged with genocide and were executed.

Perhaps the most symbolic act of freedom occurred on November 9, 1989, as East Germany opened all its borders and allowed its citizens to travel and emigrate freely. The notorious Berlin Wall, constructed in 1961 at the height of the Cold War, was subsequently torn down, and thousands made their way to the West in search of new lives. This act would have serious consequences for the future of Germany.

Germany has occupied a central position in the history of the late nineteenth and twentieth centuries. After nearly forty-five years of division, the events of 1989 presented opportunities for reunification. But the new realities posed new problems for Europe: Would Germany once again threaten its neighbors militarily? Would the financial costs of reunification stall the process? Who would bear the economic burden? Would the new Germany be politically neutral or maintain its central position in the NATO alliance? German Chancellor Helmut Kohl addressed several of these questions in his speech to the American Council on Germany in New York City.

A United Germany in a United Europe (June 5, 1990)

HELMUT KOHL

We Germans are not oblivious of the fact that here and in other countries we are being asked questions as we head for unity:

—What kind of Germany will emerge?

—What will German unity mean for peace and security in the heart of Europe?

—Will this Germany revert to old patterns of behaviour, or has it learned the lessons of history?

I shall attempt to provide answers here for the future, bearing in mind that we Germans can build on proven foundations as we move towards unity. Moreover, we Germans are determined, as we prove by our actions, to heed the lessons of our and of European history.

"A United Germany in a United Europe" is from Helmut Kohl, speech delivered to the American Council on Germany, New York City, New York on June 5, 1990. Contained in *Vital Speeches of the Day*, July 1, 1990, pp. 546–548.

My first answer is this: A future united Germany will remain linked to the United States in close friendship and responsible partnership. . . . We shall remain together! This responsible partnership entails a future united Germany being a full member of the North Atlantic defence alliance.

We are thus drawing the first and most important conclusion from history: Peace, stability and security in Europe were ensured whenever Germany, the country in the heart of Europe, maintained firm ties, a fair balance of interests and mutually beneficial interchange with all its neighbours. On the other hand, when the Germans chose to go it alone or follow a separate nationalistic path, whether out of blind arrogance or criminal hubris, or when they were forced into isolation after a lost war, this resulted in discord, instability and insecurity for the whole of Europe.

A future Germany cannot and will not, therefore, drift back and forth between two camps. We do not seek neutrality or demilitarization, and we reject a non-aligned status. We Germans want to exercise our sovereign right, as enshrined in the Charter of the United Nations. . . . We want to be a member of . . . the North Atlantic defense alliance. Our immediate neighbours in the East—the Poles, Czechs and Hungarians support this position.

Our commitment to the Western Alliance—and this is my second answer—implies above all our commitment to the Western community of shared values. A future Germany will be a free and democratic state based on social justice and the rule of law, on respect for human dignity and human rights. Right or left-wing extremism does not, as more than forty years of domestic stability prove, stand a chance in our country in the future either.

A future Germany will also remain a federal state. . . . There is no better a means of preventing tyranny and totalitarianism than a constitution which not only provides for checks and balances, but also envisages a federal system. We in the Federal Republic of Germany have such a constitution: Our Basic Law has in more than forty years proved to be the most liberal constitution in German history. . . .

My third answer is this: A united Germany will be an economically sound and socially stable country. The unanimous opinion of international economic organizations is that German unification will significantly boost world economic growth. The pent-up demand in the GDR [formerly East Germany] and in the reformist countries of Central, Eastern and South-Eastern Europe affords substantial market opportunities for everyone. . . .

The Federal Republic of Germany will strongly support this new economic and social start in the GDR. We are well prepared for this. For eight years our economy has been expanding. Business earnings, investments and employment are at a high level. We want to pave the way for private enterprise and the influx of private capital into the GDR. . . . I would like to repeat my invitation to American business: Become actively involved in the GDR to the mutual benefit. We Germans do not seek a monopoly; on the contrary, we seek competition and the common advantages of the international division of labour.

A future Germany—and this is my fourth answer—will from the very beginning be a member of the European Community. A united Germany will take part in 1992 when the large single market with 336 million people is completed. A united Germany will, together with France, be a driving force behind European unification. Before the end of this year two parallel intergovernmental conferences will be started to lay the contractual foundation not only for economic and monetary union, but also for political union.

Finally, our commitment to federalism does not end at our borders. Federalism is our real goal for Europe as a whole. A united Germany will therefore also espouse the ambitious goal of laying the groundwork for a United States of Europe before the end of this century. We are thus drawing a further conclusion from our history: German unity has a future only if it is achieved in harmony with our neighbours, and not through confrontation with them. . . .

A future Germany, firmly anchored in the West, will—and this is my fifth answer—in the future, too, live up to its share of responsibility for ensuring peaceful and stable reforms in the neighbouring Eastern and South-Eastern countries. In following our path to national unity, we Germans do not call borders into question. On the contrary, we want to make them more permeable. We are willing to achieve lasting understanding and comprehensive, forward-looking cooperation. Our goal is international reconciliation. In particular we are willing to take account of the legitimate security interests of all our neighbours, not the least the Soviet Union.

We are convinced that this recognition will soon prevail in the whole of Europe: A future united Germany as a member of the Western defence alliance will increase the security of everyone concerned and thus become a cornerstone of a stable, peaceful order in Europe.

European Economic Unity

The future of Europe is closely tied to its ability to transcend the physical boundaries and political divisions that have existed for centuries. In response to the success of Japan in establishing new markets throughout the world, there has been a greater impetus for the nations of Europe to open their borders and permit free trade among the partners of the European Economic Community in 1992. Rainer Gut, chairman of the Board of Directors, Credit Suisse, discussed some of the trade implications for the United States in a speech delivered in Los Angeles in October 1988. There is now talk of future global trading blocs with a united Europe competing against a North and South American or Asian block. The complexities of international competition and cooperation should be a dominant theme as we head into the next century.

The Impact of the European Community's 1992 Project

RAINER E. GUT

The European Community plans to achieve a completely integrated internal market by the end of 1992, with full liberalization of movements of goods, persons, services and capital. Is it by coincidence or design that this landmark is timed to come exactly five hundred years after the discovery of the New World?

The immediate objective of the single EC [European Community] internal market is to make Europe more competitive. Its relative decline is to be halted. For some years, Europe's growth has been slower than that of the other major economic regions, North America and the Far East. . . . In order to cure this "Eurosclerosis," the Community plans to tear down the physical, technical and fiscal barriers between its member states. . . . The removal of all barriers is a Herculean task. . . . The Community is adopting a new strategic approach in an effort to tackle this problem. The old approach consisted of trying to bring into line the regulations already in force in individual member states. However, this attempt at gradual harmonization proved extremely drawn-out, because each EC member's approval was required for every single detail.

So what form does the *new* strategy take? First, the EC will issue only minimum statutory requirements which have to be observed by all member states. The next step is to build on these minimum requirements and achieve mutual recognition of national regulations. In practice, this means that goods and services legitimately produced in *one* member state can be marketed without hindrance anywhere in the EC.

I believe non-EC countries would be wise not to underestimate the momentum that the EC's 1992 project has acquired. Certainly, the path to the single market is likely to become increasingly bumpy, and it will take more time than envisaged to sort out many of the details. It will probably be much later than 1992 before all borders within the Community are removed. Nevertheless, the project will almost definitely go through.

The single integrated market will have a major impact on the corporate landscape and national economies of the twelve members. Stiffer competition will weed out inefficient firms and strengthen efficient ones. At the macroeconomic level, the effects of the barrier-free market are likely to be higher growth rates, slower inflation, an easing of the pressure on govern-

"The Impact of the European Community's 1992 Project" is from Rainer E. Gut, speech delivered at the Town Hall of California, Los Angeles, California, on October 5, 1988. Contained in *Vital Speeches of the Day*, November 1, 1988, pp. 34–35, 36. Reprinted by permission.

ment budgets and, at least in the long run, more jobs. However, in the medium term there might well be job losses as fiercer competition pushes marginally profitable producers out of business and forces others to rationalize their operations. We are also likely to see the gap between the North and South of Europe gradually becoming narrower.

Against this background it is understandable that the establishment of the single EC market is sometimes compared with the creation of the U.S. . . . But this comparison . . . is anything but watertight. Cultural and linguistic barriers still exist between individual parts of the Community. Also, the various EC countries are in very different situations from an economic point of view. This means that optimal use of resources will take a few decades to establish—if ever. . . .

As it stands, the EC program is not designed to erect new walls to keep other countries out. . . . In any event, the nightmare that haunts Americans when times are hard, that of a trade pact between the EC and Japan, will probably never come true. Europeans are too aware of the economic and political strength of the U.S. to make the mistake of pushing the U.S. eagle too far.

A more serious matter for America will be the effects of a stronger European economy. EC companies are providing ever fiercer competition on all world markets. How will this newfound vigor influence the U.S. balance of trade in the next few decades? To what extent will production facilities be shifted away from the U.S. towards the increasingly attractive EC? What add-on effects will this have on employment in non-member states? . . .

Companies from non-EC countries need to undertake an exhaustive study of the implication of EC-92. There are no set recipes for success. Each firm must try to establish the most promising strategy for itself. In coming to terms with the future of the EC, it is important that corporate policy is not determined by fear but by courage and a willingness to adapt and take risks. Thanks to their global presence, the big American companies can look to the future with confidence.

What the Community is planning is not some sort of gigantic protection system. The EC's project should be seen in the context of today's worldwide efforts to liberalize trade and capital movements. . . .

The [nightmare vision] of a Europe united under Soviet hegemony, in which Western Europe turns its back on the United States . . . is not what any single Western European nation strives for or even discusses in any seriousness. Western Europe remains oriented towards the United States, and pro-Americanism is a growing force among the younger generation in Europe. Many Americans are still very conscious of their European roots, while we in Europe are deeply aware of America's crucial role as a bastion of liberty, free enterprise and Western values in today's complex and challenging world.

A New Europe

As Europe moves away from the wasteland of World War II and the intellectual confines of the Cold War, toward a new era of intranational economic cooperation, many variables exist that may radically alter the face of Europe. A tunnel under the English Channel has just been completed (dubbed "the Chunnel"), which not only physically links Great Britain and France but "threatens" to meld the cultures as well. Britain will lose the island status that has protected it and offered a unique identity for centuries, in exchange for a more intimate link with the economic destiny of continental Europe. So too will the great enemies of the first half of the twentieth century, France and Germany, lie down together and reconcile past offenses for future gains. With the reunification of Germany and the reintroduction of eastern countries such as Czechoslovakia and Poland into the heart of Europe, there are great financial opportunities and the very real potential for domestic chaos. Certainly, the Soviet Union in its struggle to revamp an ossified economy would like to promote its own vast markets, and it increasingly sees Europe as a "common home." The following speeches by contemporary European leaders testify to the changing nature of Europe and the progress of Western Civilization.

A Common European Home (1989)

MIKHAIL GORBACHEV

Now that the twentieth century is drawing to a close and the postwar period and the Cold War are becoming things of the past, the Europeans are beginning to face the unique opportunity of playing their role in building a new world, a role that is worthy of their history and their economic and intellectual potential.

The international community is now more subject to profound change than at any time in its history. Many of its integral elements are at the crossroads of destinies. The material basis of life and its spiritual parameters are sharply changing. New, ever more powerful factors of progress are emerging. At the same time, threats connected with this very progress continue to exist and even to grow alongside and following these factors. . . .

The concept of the "decline of Europe" circulated widely in the 1920's. This subject is still in fashion in some quarters. We do not share the pessimism about the future of Europe. . . .

"A Common European Home" is from Mikhail Gorbachev, speech delivered to the Council of Europe in Strasbourg, July 6, 1989. Contained in *Vital Speeches of the Day*, September 15, 1989, pp. 706–708, 710–711.

Is it realistic to raise [the question of European unity]? I know that many people in the West regard the existence of two social systems as the major difficulty. But the difficulty is rather in the very common conviction—or even a political directive—that overcoming the split of Europe implies the "overcoming of socialism." This is a course toward confrontation, if not worse. There will be no European unity along these lines.

European states belong to different social systems. That is a reality. Recognition of this historical fact and respect for the sovereign right of every nation freely to choose a social system constitute the major prerequisites for a normal European process.

Social and political orders in one or another country have changed in the past and may change in the future. But this change is the exclusive affair of the people of that country and is their choice. Any interference in domestic affairs and any attempts to restrict the sovereignty of states—friends, allies, or any others—are inadmissible. . . .

As a result of its restructuring [*perestroika*], the U.S.S.R. will be able fully to take part in this honest, equitable, and constructive competition. Given all the existing shortcomings and lagging, we well know the intrinsic strengths of our social system. And we are sure that we will be able to put them to use for the benefit of ourselves and for the benefit of Europe.

It is time to deposit in the archives the postulates of the Cold War period, when Europe was regarded as an arena of confrontation, divided into "spheres of influence," somebody's "outpost," and as an object of military rivalry, a battlefield. In today's interdependent world, the geopolitical notions born of another era are just as useless in real politics as are the laws of classical mechanics in quantum theory.

Meanwhile, on the basis of outdated stereotypes, the Soviet Union is suspected of planning domination and intending to tear the United States away from Europe. There are some who would like to place the U.S.S.R. outside Europe from the Atlantic to the Urals, by limiting its expanse. . . . The U.S.S.R., it is alleged, is too large for co-existence: Others would feel ill at ease with it. The present-day realities and prospects for the foreseeable future are obvious: The U.S.S.R. and the United States constitute a natural part of the European international-political structure. And their participation in its evolution is not only justified, but also historically determined. No other approach is acceptable, nor will it bring forth any results. . . .

Our idea of the common European home was born of the comprehension of new realities and the understanding of the fact that the linear continuation of the movement along which intra-European relations developed up to the last quarter of the twentieth century no longer matches these realities.

The idea is connected with our domestic economic and political restructuring, which was in need of new relationships primarily in that part of the world to which we, the Soviet Union, belong and with which we had been connected most of all for centuries. . . . I do not claim today that I have a ready-made blueprint for such a "home." Instead, I shall speak of what, in my view, is the main point—namely the need for a restructuring of the international order in Europe to bring to the fore all European values and make it possible to replace the traditional balance of forces by a balance of interests. . . .

In the face of . . . the whole of Europe, I would like to speak once again of our simple and clear-cut positions on disarmament issues . . . :

—we are for a nuclear-weapon-free world and for the elimination of all nuclear weapons by the turn of the century;

—we are for the full elimination of chemical weapons at the earliest date and for the elimination forever of the production basis for the development of such weapons;

—we are for a radical cut in conventional arms and armed forces down to the level of reasonable defense sufficiency. . . .

—we are for complete withdrawal of all foreign troops from the territories of other countries;

—we are categorically against the development of any space weapons whatsoever;

—we are for the elimination of military blocs and the development of a political dialogue [toward] the establishment of an atmosphere of trust. . . .

—we are for profound, consistent, and effective verification of compliance with all treaties and agreements that may be concluded on disarmament issues.

I am convinced: It is high time that the Europeans brought their policy and conduct into line with new logic, [and] to learn to lay jointly for foundations for peace. If security is the foundation of the common European home, multifarious cooperation is its superstructure. . . .

Europeans can meet the challenges of the next century only by pooling their efforts. We are convinced that they need one Europe—peaceful and democratic—a Europe that preserves all of its diversity and abides by common humane ideals, a prospering Europe that extends a hand to the rest of the world. A Europe that confidently marches into the future. We see our own future in this Europe.

The Reconciliation of France and Germany (September 24, 1990)

FRANÇOIS MITTERRAND

Think of the events that have shaken up Europe and the World in 1939, the popular movements that have emerged from the depths which, like the French revolution of two hundred years ago, have triumphed over struc-

"The Reconciliation of France and Germany" is from François Mitterrand, speech delivered to the 45th Session of the United Nations General Assembly, New York, New York, on September 24, 1990. Contained in *Vital Speeches of the Day*, October 15, 1990, pp. 5, 7–8.

tures and systems, set ways of thinking and acting, powers and fears, because of the simple, irresistible need to live differently, in accordance with the requirements of the mind. When the walls separating peoples came down, walls built on the foolish assumption that the order they were protecting would never be untouched by the great winds of space, dreams and ideas, I remember saying to my compatriots in France . . . that the end of one order did not necessarily mean that another order would be born immediately thereafter, and that it would be a very difficult process. And I would ask you this: what are we to do with this era we are entering, so promising, so perilous? What shall we make of it? . . .

I think that an era of hope is opening up for mankind, if the peoples of the world accept to overcome what they take to be the fatality of history, and of their own interest. Believe me, such a goal is within our reach. After destroying each other in three wars in less than a century, France and Germany have sealed their reconciliation, a rare occurrence indeed: They belong to the same community, they meet together, they are forging a genuine friendship. While I speak, on the eve of German unity, instead of harping on the tragic events they experienced in the past because of each other, our two peoples are turned toward the same future. And so it is that here in New York, I can send the best wishes of France to the Germans, who are preparing to celebrate a great moment of their history. The deep understanding between France and Germany is a reality. As you know, it makes itself felt in the twelve nation European Community. Can you imagine the trouble and strife, the conflicts of age-old ambitions that were overcome forty years ago by a bold, almost unbelievable undertaking engaged in first by six, nine, then ten, now twelve countries of Europe? . . .

We Europeans are looking beyond the Community, to the horizon of the continent of Europe, the Europe of geography and history. . . . Where would our old continent be now if audacity had not managed to overthrow well established patterns of thought? And if peoples and their leaders had not accepted to build a future different from the past? In this Europe these are countries which yesterday were known as Eastern bloc countries and which belonged to a rival system. Now they control their own destiny, but with what means at their disposal? . . . We must think of them, they are our brethren and we will be by their side, until as I said in France, a more fixed relationship will bring together all the countries of Europe, those of the East, those of the Community, those of the Free Trade Area, these who are part of no system, in what I have called a Confederation. . . . Europe has been the first field of application thereof and a very real one. . . .

At the beginning of this century and at the end of the previous one, our forebears expressed their dreams of peace with these three words: disarmament, arbitration, collective security. Theirs came to be an era of unrest, dictatorship and war. Let us act in such a way, I beseech you, that through the United Nations, law, solidarity and peace may finally rule over a new era.

"Czechoslovakia Is Returning to Europe" (February 21, 1990)

VACLAV HAVEL

Czechoslovakia is returning to Europe. In the general interest and in its own interest as well, it wants to coordinate this return—both politically and economically—with the other returnees, which means, above all, with its neighbors the Poles and the Hungarians. We are doing what we can to coordinate these returns. And at the same time, we are doing what we can so that Europe will be capable of really accepting us, its wayward children. Which means that it may open itself to us, and may begin to transform its structures—which are formally European but de facto Western European—in that direction, but in such a way that it will not be to its detriment, but rather to its advantage. . . .

The Communist type of totalitarian system has left . . . all the nations of the Soviet Union and the other countries the Soviet Union subjugated in its time, a legacy of countless dead, an infinite spectrum of human suffering, profound economic decline, and above all enormous human humiliation. It has brought us horrors that fortunately you have not known.

At the same time, however—unintentionally, of course—it has given us something positive: a special capacity to look, from time to time, somewhat further than someone who has not undergone this bitter experience. A person who cannot move and live a somewhat normal life because he is pinned under a boulder has more time to think about his hopes than someone who is not trapped that way. . . . We too can offer something to you: our experience and the knowledge that has come from it. . . . Consciousness precedes Being, and not the other way around, as the Marxists claim.

For this reason, the salvation of the human world lies nowhere else than in the human heart, in the human power to reflect, in human meekness and in human responsibility. . . . If we are no longer threatened by world war, or by the danger that the absurd mountains of accumulated nuclear weapons might blow up the world, this does not mean that we have definitively won. We are in fact far from the final victory. . . .

In other words, we still don't know how to put morality ahead of politics, science and economics. We are still incapable of understanding that the only genuine backbone of all our actions—if they are to be moral—is responsibility. Responsibility to something higher than my family, my country, my company, my success. Responsibility to the order of Being, where all our actions are indelibly recorded and where, and only where, they will be properly judged. . . .

" 'Czechoslovakia Is Returning to Europe' " is from Vaclav Havel, speech delivered to the Joint Session of Congress, Washington, D.C., on February 21, 1990. Contained in *Vital Speeches of the Day*, March 15, 1990, pp. 329–330.

I end where I began: history has accelerated. I believe that once again it will be the human mind that will notice this acceleration, give it a name, and transform those words into deeds.

Technological Advance

Medical Research and Ethical Dilemmas

One of the areas in which progress in the twentieth century is most evident is in the field of health care. People tend to regard mumps, measles, and whooping cough as childhood diseases of little importance. Yet in the nineteenth century these, as well as tetanus and typhoid, were dangerous and sometimes devastating diseases. Even the bubonic plague (Black Death), which destroyed one-third of the population of Europe in 1348, can be treated today with antibiotics. The development of polio vaccine in 1955 freed humanity from the physical ravages of a disease that afflicted even the rich and powerful: Franklin Roosevelt, who was later to become president of the United States, was struck in 1921. Medical research also led to great advances in heart surgery and organ transplants by the late 1960s, and even to the potential for changing our very "humanness" through genetic engineering. Therein lies the great ethical question of this age of high technology. To what extent do we "play God" if we have the technology to create or alter life forms? Does euthanasia become an ethical option, a defense of individuality in an impersonal, technological world? And what progress is being made in the war against cancer or AIDS, the two most threatening diseases of our contemporary world? The following selections lend perspective to the challenges facing medical science and the underlying human concerns in a world where technological progress outstrips the legal and ethical limits of society.

Genetic Engineering (1977)

TED HOWARD AND JEREMY RIFKIN

Throughout this unfolding process, which we call civilization, scientific and technological progress has never been equally distributed. New discoveries have always been applied selectively, with some group, class, or race using knowledge of the external world to control not only it but their fellow humans as well. As the late C. S. Lewis observed, "Man's power over nature

"Genetic Engineering" is excerpted from the book *Who Should Play God? The Artificial Creation of Life and What It Means for the Future of the Human Race* by Ted Howard and Jeremy Rifkin, pp. 8–10. Copyright © 1977 by Center for Urban Education. Reprinted by permission of Delacorte Press.

is really the power of some men over others with nature as their instrument."

Now a dramatic new scientific discovery has given some people the power, for the first time, to shift attention from shaping and controlling the external world of matter and energy to shaping and controlling the internal world of life itself. With the discovery of DNA and its workings, scientists have unlocked the very secrets of life. It is now only a matter of a handful of years before biologists will be able to irreversibly change the evolutionary wisdom of billions of years with the creation of new plants, new animals, and new forms of human and post-human beings.

Today, only a tiny handful of people are privy to the secret of life and how to manipulate and change it. Most people are totally unaware of this newfound power. The concept of designing and engineering life, especially human life, is so utterly fantastic that it is difficult even to comprehend its meaning and implications. yet, even as the public is kept virtually ignorant of this unparalleled new scientific discovery, microbiologists are busy at work in hundreds of laboratories across the country, spending tens of millions of dollars in pursuit of the "mastery of life." . . .

For many years social commentators have looked on nuclear weaponry as the most powerful and dangerous tool at the disposal of humanity. With the development of human genetic engineering, a tool even more awesome is now available. It is true that nuclear weaponry poses the ever-present threat of annihilation of human life on this planet. But with genetic engineering there is a threat of a very different kind: that by calculation and planning, not accident or the precipitous passion of the moment, some people will make conscious and deliberate decisions to irreversibly alter the biological structure of millions of other men and women and their descendants for all time. This is a form of annihilation every bit as deadly as nuclear holocaust, and even more profound—whatever forms of future beings are developed will be forced to live the consequences of the biological designs that were molded for them.

"Some Diseases Are Less Equal than Others": The War against AIDS (1990)

ROBERT K. GRAY

AIDS is both a communicable disease and a disease of communications. Today, the maladies of aging or heredity are given full public discussion, championed by celebrities, generously funded by private giving and public funds. But some diseases are less equal than others. For decades mental

" 'Some Diseases Are Less Equal than Others' " is from Robert K. Gray, speech delivered to the International Conference on AIDS, Vatican City, on November 15, 1989. Contained in *Vital Speeches of the Day*, March 1, 1990, pp. 297–300. Reprinted by permission.

illness was a forbidden topic. And today there are strong inhibitions to a smooth flow of information in discussing sexually-transmitted diseases.

The even stronger barriers to communications on AIDS are many and include prejudices, taboos, superstitions and fears. Yes, fear; for in a period in history when we profess to have all the answers, those moments when it is obvious we do not, are all the more frightening. In the case of AIDS, there are added communications barriers in the powerful stigma attached by both society and religion to the behaviors most prominently associated with HIV infection.

Yet nearly half the babies born to HIV-infected mothers have the virus. And Central Africa, where millions have the disease although homosexuality and IV drug use are rare, shows what can happen when AIDS is unleashed on the general population. This virus once was restricted to monkeys in Africa. Now all it needs for a delayed-action global explosion is for each infected person to infect one other.

In forty-five days we will enter the decade of the 90's, a decade when, unless one of you is guided to a cure, the number of AIDS cases— according to the World Health Organization—could reach six million and the number infected with the virus could reach twenty-four million! And World Health Organization experts believe *that* number may prove far too conservative if transmission of the infection increases drastically in Asia where the virus has just begun to gain a foothold. Every indication is that it will do exactly that. The HIV infection rate among drug addicts in Bangkok has risen from one percent in 1987 to forty percent this year. In Southeastern India seven percent of prostitutes have tested HIV positive. . . .

[Among] those mighty voices which should be brought to full decibel is the voice of world governments. AIDS knows no boundaries. It touches all humanity. If the disease is not halted more lives could be lost than in all of mankind's past wars. Also at very serious risk are the fragile economies of the developing world and centuries of painful progress around the globe. So much is at stake, yet when the seven industrial nations met in Paris last July, the topic of AIDS was not even on the agenda. . . . The actions of governments can establish national priorities and communicate seriousness and urgency. . . . The leadership of nations have mighty megaphones to carry their messages. And when they are used to educate and lead the people they serve, those messages seldom fail.

With AIDS, where there are ethical and spiritual questions abounding, there also is a great need for the voice of moral persuasion and authority to guide, to convince and to calm. It is for these reasons I believe [another] voice can be the Church which at this moment may make the most important of all communications contributions to combat AIDS. For without focused, coherent and mature public support for those who have AIDS; without beneficial and wise programs for those at risk; and without realistic information campaigns to help stop the contamination, the public debate can decay into a cacophony of sexual politics and false mythologies perpetuated by mean-spirited groups with a macabre view of the human condition.

Without an underlying message of hope and redemption, without a loud, realistic and unequivocal message of forgiveness and understanding—and without Church programs for AIDS patients which offer clear evidence of the Church's commitment to the sick and dying, public opinion could continue to be a confused mass. . . . The Church is controlled by no government. It has no political body to which it is answerable. It has no tourist revenues to protect. It has a global following of nearly one billion citizens. No other single institution, political entity or organization so cuts across national boundaries, socioeconomic strata and political systems. For these reasons, the Church, which has been the epicenter for modern man's struggles, is the logical leader, the logical entity to embark upon a realistic, mature and modern communications program designed to stop the spread of AIDS, comfort and protect those with the disease, and educate those who have been so bewildered and confounded since its outbreak.

The Church has the moral authority to combat the mythology that AIDS is a direct punishment from God. As the disease spreads, so spreads fear and bigotry and the pulpit of the Catholic Church is the mightiest of weapons against these dark forces. . . .

A Washington friend is waging war on the disease with a lapel button which reads, "Heal AIDS with Love." My first reaction was, "How naive, how very desperate." But now I think, "How wise, how very wise." For we *will* win this war against this devastating disease of the body and the destructive diseases of fear, prejudice and ignorance which add to the suffering.

The Computer Revolution

Big Brother has arrived, and he is your computer!

—Norman Lear

Among the many technological advancements that have taken place since 1945, the development of the microchip has produced some of the most profound changes in our modern world. It has become the essential component of our modern communication systems and has made possible the computer revolution by storing vast amounts of information in a minute space. Whether on a network system at the office or in the privacy of one's home, the computer has opened new dimensions in communication, architectural design, engineering, medical analysis, and even artistic expression. The 1980s in particular saw the widespread integration of computers into Western culture. The processing and control of information will remain a key to political and social influence in the future.

But with all the advantages that the computer revolution can offer, it also raises new questions about the progress of civilization, especially regarding the protection of individual rights to privacy. Thomas Jefferson warned that "the natural process of things is for liberty to yield and government to gain ground." In a message to Congress in 1979, President Jimmy Carter lamented, "We confront threats to privacy undreamed of two hundred years ago. . . . Personal information on millions of Americans is being flashed across the nation from computer to computer." Indeed, data gained by businesses, credit bureaus, banks, medical agencies, the FBI, and the IRS place the individual more at risk in a technologically advanced society than ever before. The dilemma is acute: Must we always assume a risk to our personal liberties and even to our humanity itself in order to progress technologically?

The first selection is a speech by David Linowes, professor of political economy and public policy at the University of Illinois, delivered at the White House Conference on Libraries and Information Services in 1990. His analysis of the impact of information technology on learning, democracy, and the interdependence of nations is thoughtful and provocative. It is followed by a more philosophical discussion of computers and their impact on the human spirit by MIT sociologist and psychologist Sherry Turkle.

The Information Age (1990)

DAVID F. LINOWES

In this Information Age, information is inextricably linked to electronic technology. Computers in particular. That combination is causing a profound revolution in every aspect of our lives.

Just as the machine had become the extension of a person's limbs and muscles during the Industrial Revolution, so is the computer becoming the extension of one's mind and memory during the Computer Revolution, spawning the Information Age. Technology we currently have in place is one hundred years behind what has already been developed. Pushing these developments is the fact observed by Walter Wriston that eighty-five percent of all the scientists who have ever lived are alive today. The time between the realization of an idea and its arrival in the marketplace is now the shortest it has ever been in history—usually just a few months. In contrast it took gunpowder almost two hundred years to move from laboratory to use in artillery.

"The Information Age" is from David F. Linowes, speech delivered to the White House Conference on Libraries and Information Services, Krannert Center for the Performing Arts, Urbana, Illinois, October 27, 1990. Contained in *Vital Speeches of the Day*, January 1, 1991, pp. 168–171. Reprinted by permission.

During the past twenty years—during our lifetime—we have learned more about the human brain than in the rest of history. With that new knowledge, the brain is being recreated in computers.

This ultra-sophisticated software or "artificial intelligence" is being used to solve complex mathematical problems and to make medical diagnoses. Researchers at IBM and Texas Instruments are using artificial intelligence to analyze geographical formations, design new biological genes and to read, digest and answer correspondence.

Computers are being programmed to duplicate the decision-making process of leading experts in given fields. These "expert" programs are designed by programming all known information of a given subject into the computer. Programmers then interview recognized experts in the field to determine how they process information to form judgments. That process is then also programmed into the same computer. . . .

In the coming decade people will talk to computers the same as they do with one another. A number of computers already allow communication in written English. . . . During the next decade the Japanese Ministry for International Trade and Industry expects to have a thinking computer. It will understand natural speech, read written language, and translate documents. The machine will draw inferences and make its own judgments. It will learn by studying its errors.

The computer is being educated! It is acquiring unorganized and unrelated facts, what we commonly recognize as "information." It is being taught knowledge, i.e., extensive facts in a particular field just as any specialized professional. And through "Artificial Intelligence" it is acquiring wisdom, i.e., knowledge of people and human life so as to produce sound judgments. . . . Computers even are acquiring the ability of psychological reasoning, making decisions based on emotional understanding. All of this adds to the mountains of information that is being amassed, processed, classified, and stored for retrieval.

It took from the time of Christ to the mid-eighteenth century for knowledge to double. It doubled again one hundred fifty years later, and then again in only fifty years. Today it doubles every four or five years. More new information has been produced in the last thirty years than in the previous five thousand.

Some look askance at this avalanche of information. . . . They argue we have reached the point of "negative information" where we are being bombarded with so much data that useful information is actually reduced instead of increased. In the United States, . . . one thousand new book titles are printed each day. The entire contents of a 250,000-page encyclopedia can now be stored on a single compact disk. Our laws and institutional mores have not been adequate to deal with these challenges. Information has always been essential to a democracy. It is an observed fact that the economic, political, and social strength of the United States depends on people's ability to acquire and use information.

Information and Learning

Nowhere is the clash between technological development and societal impact more acute than in the field of education, for education involves information and communication. . . . In the long term, the school building or campus and even the concept of "going to school" may increasingly become obsolete. . . . Instead of confining formal learning to the classroom, students would be taught wherever they might be, at home, the work place, or at the playground by giving them access to centralized information networks. People of any age who wanted to learn something would go to a reference library counselor.

Just as the inventions of writing and the printing press necessitated a reformulation of pedagogic philosophy and technique, so the current advances will require the same careful re-examination of means, purpose, and policy in education. . . .

Privacy

As sophisticated computer and communications equipment has been introduced into public agencies, so information has become far easier to collect, store, manipulate, and disseminate. On the one hand, this has enhanced the management, decision-making, and analytical capabilities of governmental organizations. However, the advantages that contemporary data-processing techniques have brought are offset by certain dangers. . . . Data on almost any given subject is instantly available. Information companies which serve as libraries of giant computer warehouses can analyze a topic or person in seconds, running searches for newspaper and magazine stories or anything else. . . . The subject of an electronic inquiry, for instance, can be victimized by the increased ability to manipulate video images as well as the factual elements of the public record. . . . This personal information is used not only as a tool for those who make organizational decisions, but it is marketable for a variety of commercial and political purposes, and even as an instrument of surveillance and possible abuse. . . . We [in the United States] do not have adequate national public policy privacy protection legislation . . . designed to minimize intrusiveness in the collection of personal information. . . .

Information and Democracy

It is widely believed that the balance of power in our society is becoming more and more dangerously weighted in favor of large institutions—government and business alike. A chief reason is that they are the ones with the information about people, and the people don't know it. . . .

In the political arena, computerized information has given pressure groups the power to influence candidate selection and important legislative issues as never before. By pressing a key, a clerk obtains your profile that includes voting history, address, family composition, model of car, neighborhood characteristics, ethnic group, and even indication of sexual orientation. The candidate then targets you with either a telephone call or a direct mail message. GOP headquarters in Washington maintains voter lists with millions of names and relevant personal information in its computers. . . .

Impact On Institutions and Nations

The problems of information combined with technology are not problems confined to the United States; but, in fact impact on relations between countries. For instance, some nations want to create electronic barriers to halt the flow of information. They consider information within a country a national resource, much like copper or oil. If information does cross their borders electronically, they want to charge a tariff on it.

The lack of controls over information transmission for processing or use in another country leaves developed nations concerned and developing nations alarmed. . . . Technology in the United States has advanced so far that many developed countries, and especially Third World countries, lag hopelessly behind. . . . Once computer and telecommunications facilities are established by multinational corporation or by government agencies there is no technological means presently in existence to prevent its use for other purposes. All information has become inextricably intertwined. . . .

Have-not nations are of the conviction that divisions are widening between nations possessing sophisticated information and those that do not, creating greater disparities than have the differences in material wealth. It is this recognition that gives rise to many of the problems we are having with developing nations today and it will continue, even intensify. In time, economic exploitation, they argue, can be overcome but disparities between information-rich and information-poor societies based on continually advancing sophisticated technology and knowledge, can never be balanced. The flood of new knowledge, coupled with the negative tide of information flow, make it impossible for them to catch up and become self-sufficient, resulting in a new and more sinister form of colonialism. . . .

Disintegration of the Nation-State

Some studies of history point to the possible disintegration of the nation-state as we know it. The rise of the nation-state occurred shortly after the invention of the printing press making it possible to transmit information to large groups of people over broad geographic areas. The printing press was invented about 1455 and was widely used throughout Europe by 1487. The nation-state, using the printed word as the basic communication medium for its laws and edicts followed immediately, coming into being in Europe around 1500.

Communication today no longer depends on the physical distribution of the printed word. Satellites send information to all people of all nations instantaneously in their own languages. The impact of evolving technology transmitting all kinds of information is now creating what centuries of war and statesmanship could not establish, namely, One World. The question is "Whose world will it be?"

The Human Spirit in a Computer Culture (1984)

SHERRY TURKLE

The images of the computer offering a new expressive medium and of the computer offering a "schizoid compromise" between loneliness and fear of intimacy are emblematic of the encounter between the machine and our emotional lives. Along with this encounter comes another: between computers and our philosophical lives, in particular our thinking about human nature. Because they stand on the line between mind and not-mind, between life and not-life, computers excite reflection about the nature of mind and the nature of life. They provoke us to think about who we are. They challenge our ideas about what it is to be human, to think and feel. They present us with more than a challenge. They present us with an affront, because they hold up a new mirror in which mind is reflected as machine.

The effect is subversive. It calls into question our ways of thinking about ourselves: most dramatically, if mind is machine, who is the actor? Where is responsibility, spirit, soul? There is a new disorder. . . .

When Copernicus ousted earth and its travelers from their illusion of a central place in the universe, his assertion went beyond physics: it called into question our privileged relationship to God. It was as if the status of humankind had been reduced—from the center of creation to an inhabitant of a speck of dust in the vastness of space. It was unthinkable, and yet, with time, the unthinkable becomes taken for granted. This is not just because people get used to the new idea, or get tired of fighting against it. Something else happens as well. What happens is that ways are found to reassert a centered view of the human within the new context. . . .

This pattern of challenge and reassertion has been repeated time and time again. A first reaction to the Darwinian idea that humans are descended from animals was moral repulsion. Again, we were taken from a privileged position and turned into something that this time, seemed not so much insignificant as ignoble. But here too, after the shock comes a fresh reassertion of the uniqueness of humanity: we may be animals, kin to the others, but we are the crown of the evolutionary process.

The computational model of mind is yet another blow to our sense of centrality. Copernicus and Darwin took away our special role as the centerpiece of creation, but we could still think of ourselves as the center of ourselves. Now the computer culture, like the psychoanalytic culture before it, threatens the very idea of "self". . . . In response, a quest has already begun for ways to hold on to an understanding of human mind as other than machine. . . .

Arguments about human uniqueness based on what computers can't do leave us vulnerable to technical progress and what clever engineers might come up with. . . . No matter what a computer can do, human thought is something else, . . . the product of our specific biology, the product of a human brain. . . .

What makes us biological is our life cycle: we are born, we are nurtured by parents, we grow, we develop sexually, we become parents in our turn, we die. This cycle is what gives meaning to our lives. It brings us the knowledge that comes from understanding loss—from knowing that those we love will die and so will we. A being that is not born of a mother, that does not feel the vulnerability of childhood, a being that does not know sexuality or anticipate death, this being is alien. We may be machines, but it is our mortality that impels us to search for transcendence—in religion, history, art, the relationships in which we hope to live on. . . .

Before the computer, the animals, mortal though not sentient, seemed our nearest neighbors in the known universe. Computers, with their inter-activity, their psychology, with whatever fragments of intelligence they have, now bid for this place. . . . Where we once were rational animals, now we are feeling computers, emotional machines. But we have no way to really put these terms together. The hard-to-live-with, self-contradictory notion of the emotional machine captures the fact that what we live now is a new and deeply felt tension. . . .

One thing is certain: the riddle of mind, long a topic for philosophers, has taken on new urgency. Under pressure from the computer, the question of mind in relation to machine is becoming a central cultural preoc-cupation. It is becoming for us what sex was to the Victorians—threat and obsession, taboo and fascination.

SECTION II: SOCIAL AND SPIRITUAL DIMENSIONS

Social and Humanitarian Movements

The Women's Movement

> Humanity has begun to outgrow nature: we can no longer justify the maintenance of a discriminatory sex class system on grounds of its origins in Nature. Indeed, for pragmatic reasons alone, it is beginning to look as if we *must* get rid of it.
>
> —Shulamith Firestone

("Doonesbury." Copyright © 1987 by G. B. Trudeau. Reprinted by permission of Universal Press Syndicate.)

I thought that women were going to come along and save us with new humane values. And what do they do? They adopt the worst values of the young male and go off to law school.

—Charles A. Peters

Certainly one of the most dramatic and singular roads to progress in Western society was traveled by courageous and determined women who strove for equal political and social rights in the face of established male opposition. The origin of this movement is difficult to pinpoint and might be said to have existed throughout history, at random moments, in the inner recesses of the personal heart, in occasional diary accounts, in the political tracts of Mary Wollstonecraft, the street demonstrations of Emmeline Pankhurst, the jail cells of Elizabeth Cady Stanton and Susan B. Anthony, the munitions factories during World Wars I and II, in the forceful prose of Betty Friedan and Gloria Steinem. The following selections attest to some of the major attitudes of a movement that has been more directly defined in the twentieth century, with great impact on Western society. The issues of equal pay and discrimination in the workplace and the continuing controversy over abortion and reproductive freedom continue to provide a focus for the ideal of complete equality between the sexes.

At the heart of the women's movement during the nineteenth and early twentieth centuries was the demand for equal voting rights, or women's suffrage. The goal in America had been clearly detailed in a declaration of equal rights established at the Seneca Falls Convention in 1848. By 1852, the movement to secure the vote had picked up momentum. The reaction to such agitation was intense and polarizing. Advocates of the complete equality of women included the English philosopher John Stuart Mill, who together with his wife, Harriet, became a crusader for the cause. His fundamental tracts On Liberty *(1859) and* On the Subjection of Women *(1869) were especially persuasive in advocating voting rights for women. Opposition forces, however, could also claim their intellectual champions.*

The first selection comes from the pen of the great American historian Francis Parkman. A writer of unusual depth and narrative skill, Parkman was universally acknowledged for his ability to characterize the figures of colonial American history. His account of the westward movement, The Oregon Trail, *became one of the most popular personal narratives of the nineteenth century. He wrote this pamphlet against women's suffrage "at the request of an association of women." It reveals the attitudes and fears of conservatives in the face of an established threat to the status quo.*

Some of the Reasons against Woman Suffrage (1884)

FRANCIS PARKMAN

It has been said that the question of the rights and employment of women should be treated without regard to sex. It should rather be said that those who consider it regardless of sex do not consider it at all. . . . Whatever liberty the best civilization may accord to women, they must always be subject to restrictions unknown to the other sex, and they can never dispense with the protecting influences which society throws about them. A man, in lonely places, has nothing to lose but life and property; and he has nerve and muscles to defend them. He is free to go whither he pleases, and run what risks he pleases. Without a radical change in human nature, of which the world has never given the faintest sign, women cannot be equally emancipated. . . . Everybody knows that the physical and mental constitution of woman is more delicate than in the other sex; and, we may add, the relations between mind and body are more intimate and subtle. . . . It is these and other inherent conditions, joined to the engrossing nature of a woman's special functions, that have determined through all time her relative position. . . . Men did not make [these limitations], and they cannot unmake them. Through them, God and Nature have ordained that those subject to them shall not be forced to join in the harsh conflicts of the world militant. It is folly to ignore them, or try to counteract them by political and social quackery. . . .

The frequent low state of health among American women is a fact as undeniable as it is deplorable. In this condition of things, what do certain women demand for the good of their sex? To add to the excitements that are wasting them, other and greater excitements, and to cares too much for their strength, other and greater cares. Because they cannot do their own work, to require them to add to it the work of men, and launch them into the turmoil where the most robust sometimes fail. It is much as if a man in a state of nervous exhaustion were told by his physician to enter at once a foot-race or a boxing match.

Woman suffrage must have one of two effects. If, as many of its advocates complain, women are subservient to men, and do nothing but what

"Against Woman Suffrage" is from Francis Parkman, *Some of the Reasons against Woman Suffrage* (Printed at the Request of an Association of Women, 1884), pp. 1–7, 10–16.

they desire, then woman suffrage will have no other result than to increase the power of the other sex; if, on the other hand, women vote as they see fit, without regarding their husbands, then unhappy marriages will be multiplied and divorces redoubled. We cannot afford to add to the elements of domestic unhappiness.

One of the chief dangers of popular government is that of inconsiderate and rash legislation. . . . This danger would be increased immeasurably if the most impulsive and excitable half of humanity had an equal voice in the making of laws, and in the administration of them. . . . If the better class of women flatter themselves that they can control the others, they are doomed to disappointment. The female vote . . . is often more numerous, always more impulsive and less subject to reason, and almost devoid of the sense of responsibility. Here the bad politician would find his richest resources. He could not reach the better class of female voters, but the rest would be ready to his hand. Three fourths of them, when not urged by some pressing need or contagious passion, would be moved, not by principles, but by personal predilections.

Again, one of the chief arguments of the agitators is that government without the consent of the governed is opposed to inalienable right. But most women, including those of the best capacity and worth, fully consent that their fathers, husbands, brothers, or friends shall be their political representatives. . . . We venture to remind those who demand woman suffrage as a right that, even if it were so, the great majority of intelligent women could judge for themselves whether to exercise it better than the few who assume to teach them their duty. The agitators know well that, in spite of their persistent importunity, the majority of their sex are averse to the suffrage. . . .

On women of the intelligent and instructed classes depends the future of the nation. If they are sound in body and mind, impart this soundness to a numerous offspring, and rear them to a sense of responsibility and duty, there are no national evils that we cannot overcome. If they fail to do this their part, then the masses of the coarse and unintelligent, always of rapid increase, will overwhelm us and our institutions. When these indispensable duties are fully discharged, then the suffrage agitators may ask with better grace, if not with more reason, that they may share the political functions of men. . . .

Many women of sense and intelligence are influenced by the fact that the woman-suffrage movement boasts itself a movement of progress, and by a wish to be on the liberal or progressive side. But the boast is unfounded. Progress, to be genuine, must be in accord with natural law. If it is not, it ends in failure and in retrogression. To give women a thorough and wholesome training both of body and mind . . . [is] in the way of normal and healthy development: but to plunge them into politics, where they are not needed and for which they are unfit, would be scarcely more a movement of progress than to force them to bear arms and fight. . . .

Suppose, again, a foreign war in which the sympathies of our women were enlisted on one side or the other. Suppose them to vote against the judgment of the men that we should take part in it; or, in other words, that their male fellow citizens should fight whether they like it or not. Would the men be likely to obey?

There is another reason why the giving of the suffrage to women would tend to civil discord. . . . Most of us have had occasion to observe how strong the social rivalries and animosities of women are. They far exceed those of men. . . . The wives and daughters of the poor would bring into the contest a wrathful jealousy and hate against the wives and daughters of the rich, far more vehement than the corresponding passions in their husbands and brothers. . . .

The suffragists' idea of government is not practical, but utterly unpractical. It is not American, but French. It is that government of abstractions and generalities which found its realization in the French Revolution, and its apostle in the depraved and half-crazy man of genius, Jean Jacques Rousseau. The French had an excuse for their frenzy in the crushing oppression they had just flung off and in their inexperience of freedom. We have no excuse. Since the nation began we have been free and our liberty is in danger from nothing but its own excesses. . . .

Neither Congress, nor the States, nor the united voice of the whole people could permanently change the essential relations of the sexes. Universal female suffrage, even if decreed, would undo itself in time; but the attempt to establish it would work deplorable mischief. The question is, whether the persistency of a few agitators shall plunge us blindfold into the most reckless of all experiments; whether we shall adopt this supreme device for developing the defects of women, and demolish their real power to build an ugly mockery instead. For the sake of womanhood, let us hope not.

"The Brain Weight of Women Is Five Ounces Less than That of Men" (1887)

GEORGE ROMANES

Parkman's arguments against suffrage included the inability of women to participate effectively in the political arena, a world ill-suited to their excitable and passionate nature. Women's physical anatomy and psychological composition underwent even closer scientific scrutiny during the late nineteenth century. This study flowed from the resounding confidence of the age in the discipline of science to solve the dilemmas and mysteries of past decades. Human relationships were left open to scientific inquiry, often with misleading and damaging results. Thus were Charles Darwin's theories on natural selection applied quite loosely to the human realm with the excesses of Social

" 'The Brain Weight of Women' " is from George J. Romanes, "Mental Differences between Men and Women," *Nineteenth Century* 26 (1887), pp. 654–672.

Darwinism the result. It is therefore not surprising that several fallacious scientific treatises like the following often confirmed in people's minds the inherent genetic inferiority of women. Such attitudes retarded progress toward social equality and proved influential even late into the twentieth century in justifying negative perceptions of women's ability to compete with men on an equal footing.

I will now briefly enumerate what appear to me the leading features of this distinction in the case of mankind, adopting the ordinary classification of mental faculties as those of intellect, emotion, and will.

Seeing that the average brain-weight of women is about five ounces less than that of men, on merely anatomical grounds we should be prepared to expect a marked inferiority of intellectual power in the former. Moreover, as the general physique of women is less robust than that of men—and therefore less able to sustain the fatigue of serious or prolonged brain action—we should also on physiological grounds be prepared to entertain a similar anticipation. In actual fact, we find that the inferiority displays itself most conspicuously in a comparative absence of originality, and this more especially in the higher levels of intellectual work. In her powers of acquisition [of knowledge] the woman certainly stands nearer to the man than she does in her powers of creative thought, although even as regards the former there is a marked difference. The difference, however, is one which does not assert itself till the period of adolescence. . . . But as soon as the brain, and with it the organism as a whole, reaches the stage of full development, it becomes apparent that there is a greater power of amassing knowledge on the part of the male. Whether we look to the general average or to the intellectual giants of both sexes, we are similarly met with the general fact that a woman's information is less wide and deep and thorough than that of a man. What we regard as a highly cultured woman is usually one who has read largely but superficially; and even in the few instances that can be quoted of extraordinary female industry—which on account of their rarity stand out as exceptions to prove the rule—we find a long distance between them and the much more numerous instances of profound erudition among men. . . .

But it is in original work . . . that the disparity is most conspicuous. . . . In no one department of creative thought can women be said to have at all approached men, save in fiction. Yet in poetry, music, and painting, if not also in history, philosophy, and science, the field has always been open to both. For . . . the disabilities under which women have laboured with regard to education, social opinion, and so forth, have certainly not been sufficient to explain this general dearth among them of the products of creative genius.

Lastly, with regard to judgment, I think there can be no real question that the female mind stands considerably below the male. It is much more apt to take superficial views of circumstances calling for decision, and also to be guided by less impartiality. Undue influence is more frequently exercised from the side of the emotions. . . . As a general rule, that the judgment of women is inferior to that of men has been a matter of universal recognition from the earliest times. The man has always been regarded as the rightful lord of the woman, to whom she is by nature subject, as both mentally and physically the weaker vessel.

But if woman has been a loser in the intellectual race as regards acquisition, origination, and judgment, she has gained, even on the intellectual side, certain very conspicuous advantages. First among these we must place refinement of the senses, or higher evolution of sense-organs. Next we must place rapidity of perception, which no doubt in part arises from this higher evolution of the sense-organs. . . .

Turning now to the emotions, we find that in woman, as contrasted with man, these are almost always less under control of the will—more apt to break away, as it were, from the restraint of reason, and to overwhelm the mental chariot in disaster. Whether this tendency displays itself in the overmastering form of hysteria, or in the more ordinary form of comparative childishness, ready annoyance, and a generally unreasonable temper, . . . we recognize it as more of a feminine than a masculine characteristic. . . .

Of course the greatest type of manhood, or the type wherein our ideal of manliness reaches its highest expression, is where the virtues of strength are purged from its vices. To be strong and yet tender, brave and yet kind, to combine in the same breast the temper of a hero with the sympathy of a maiden—this is to transform the ape and the tiger into what we know ought to constitute the man. And if in actual life we find that such an ideal is but seldom realised, this should make us more lenient in judging the frailties of the opposite sex. . . . This truth is, that the highest type of manhood can only then be reached when the heart and mind have been so far purified from the refuse of a brutal ancestry as genuinely to appreciate, to admire, and to reverence the greatness, the beauty, and the strength which have been made perfect in the weakness of womanhood.

A Room of One's Own (1929)

VIRGINIA WOOLF

The suffrage movement gained great impetus from the participation of women in the factories and hospitals during World War I (1914–1918). By 1920, women won full or partial political rights in Soviet Russia, Canada, Germany, Austria, Poland, Czechoslovakia, Hungary, Great Britain, and the United States. Still, there was to be a long road toward achieving a recognition among men and even among women of their potential for complete social equality.

Postwar societies conceded initial change and then demanded stability and a reestablishment of "normalcy."

One of the most personal and articulate commentators on women in Western society was Virginia Woolf (1882–1941). A distinguished critic of her time, she stressed in her novels and essays the continuous flow of human experience. In her famous essay A Room on One's Own *(1929), she described the difficulties encountered by women writers in a man's world and offered her insight regarding the role of women in influencing history.*

Women have served all these centuries as looking-glasses possessing the magic and delicious power of reflecting the figure of man at twice its natural size. Without that power probably the earth would still be swamp and jungle. The glories of all our wars would be unknown. We should still be scratching the outlines of deer on the remains of mutton bones and bartering flints for sheepskins or whatever simple ornament took our unsophisticated taste. Supermen and Figures of Destiny would never have existed. The Czar and the Kaiser would never have worn their crowns or lost them. Whatever may be their use in civilised societies, mirrors are essential to all violent and heroic action. That is why Napoleon and Mussolini both insist so emphatically upon the inferiority of women, for if they were not inferior, they would cease to enlarge. That serves to explain in part the necessity that women so often are to men. And it serves to explain how restless they are under her criticism; how impossible it is for her to say to them this book is bad, this picture is feeble, or whatever it may be, without giving far more pain and rousing far more anger than a man would do who gave the same criticism. For if she begins to tell the truth, the figure in the looking-glass shrinks; his fitness for life is diminished. How is he to go on giving judgement, civilising natives, making laws, writing books, dressing up and speechifying at banquets, unless he can see himself at breakfast and at dinner at least twice the size he really is? So I reflected, crumbling my bread and stirring my coffee and now and again looking at the people in the street. The looking-glass vision is of supreme importance because it charges the vitality; it stimulates the nervous system. Take it away and man may die, like the drug fiend deprived of his cocaine. Under the spell of that illusion, I thought, looking out of the window, half the people on the pavement are striding to work. They put on their hats and coats in the morning under its agreeable rays. They start the day confident, braced, believing themselves desired at Miss Smith's tea party; they say to themselves as they go into the room, I am the superior of half the people here, and it is thus that they speak with that self-confidence, that self-assurance, which have had such profound consequences in public life and lead to such curious notes in the margin of the private mind. . . .

I need not hate any man; he cannot hurt me. I need not flatter any man; he has nothing to give me. So imperceptibly I found myself adopting a new attitude towards the other half of the human race. It was absurd to blame any class or any sex, as a whole. Great bodies of people are never responsible for what they do. They are driven by instincts which are not within their control. They too, the patriarchs, the professors, had endless difficulties, terrible drawbacks to contend with. Their education had been in some ways as faulty as my own. It had bred in them defects as great. True, they had money and power, but only at the cost of harbouring in their breasts an eagle, a vulture, forever tearing the liver out and plucking at the lungs— the instinct for possession, the rage for acquisition which drives them to desire other people's fields and goods perpetually; to make frontiers and flags; battleships and poison gas; to offer up their own lives and their children's lives. . . .

I thought how much harder it is now than it must have been even a century ago to say which . . . employments [are] the higher, the more necessary. Is it better to be a coal-heaver or a nursemaid; is the charwoman who has brought up eight children of less value to the world than the barrister who has made a hundred thousand pounds? It is useless to ask such questions; for nobody can answer them. Not only do the comparative values of charwomen and lawyers rise and fall from decade to decade, but we have no rods with which to measure them even as they are at the moment. . . . Even if one could state the value of any one gift at the moment, those values will change; in a century's time very possibly they will have changed completely. Moreover, in a hundred years, I thought, reaching my own doorstep, women will have ceased to be the protected sex. Logically they will take part in all the activities and exertions that were once denied them. The nursemaid will heave coal. The shop-woman will drive an engine. All assumptions founded on the facts observed when women were the protected sex will have disappeared. . . . Anything may happen when womanhood has ceased to be a protected occupation, I thought, opening the door.

The Feminine Mystique (1963)

BETTY FRIEDAN

Following significant gains made during the 1920s and 1930s, women retreated to their traditional roles after World War II. The image of 1950s life in America as stolid, conservative, and suburban, was cemented by a desire to find stability after the chaos of war, to start over with clearly defined sex roles. The emphasis was on traditional family values, supported by Norman Rockwell's paintings and Betty Crocker's recipes. Communism and Rock n' Roll were the enemies, but God was an American and our salvation lay in patriotism. In a sense, it was simpler when women knew the expectations of society and could commit total energy to the primary domestic goal of childrearing. There was purpose, even zeal in the retreat to domesticity.

"The Feminine Mystique" is from Betty Friedan, *The Feminine Mystique* (New York: W. W. Norton & Co., 1983), pp. 18–20, 32, 67–68. Copyright © 1983, 1974, 1973, 1963 by Betty Friedan. Reprinted by permission of W. W. Norton & Co.

Betty Friedan's publication of The Feminine Mystique *in 1963 provided impetus for a new women's movement. Friedan found an underlying frustration in women who had been mesmerized by an abstract ideal, a feminine mystique, and were now measured by society and their husbands for contentment and evaluated by the advertising industry for profit.*

In the fifteen years after World War II, this mystique of feminine fulfillment became the cherished and self-perpetuating core of contemporary American culture. Millions of women lived their lives in the image of those pretty pictures of the American suburban housewife, kissing their husbands goodbye in front of the picture window, depositing their stationwagonsful of children at school, and smiling as they ran the new electric waxer over the spotless kitchen floor. They baked their own bread, sewed their own and their children's clothes, kept their new washing machines and dryers running all day. They changed the sheets on the beds twice a week instead of once, took the rug-hooking class in adult education, and pitied their poor frustrated mothers, who had dreamed of having a career. Their only dream was to be perfect wives and mothers; their highest ambition to have five children and a beautiful house, their only fight to get and keep their husbands. They had no thought for the unfeminine problems of the world outside the home; they wanted the men to make the major decisions. They gloried in their role as women, and wrote proudly on the census blank: "Occupation: housewife."

For over fifteen years, the words written for women, and the words women used when they talked to each other, while their husbands sat on the other side of the room and talked shop or politics or septic tanks, were about problems with their children, or how to keep their husbands happy, or improve their children's school, or cook chicken or make slipcovers. Nobody argued whether women were inferior or superior to men; they were simply different. Words like "emancipation" and "career" sounded strange and embarrassing; no one had used them for years. When a Frenchwoman named Simone de Beauvoir wrote a book called *The Second Sex*, an American critic commented that she obviously "didn't know what life was all about," and besides, she was talking about French women. The "woman problem" in America no longer existed.

If a woman had a problem in the 1950's and 1960's, she knew that something must be wrong with her marriage, or with herself. Other women were satisfied with their lives, she thought. What kind of a woman was she if she did not feel this mysterious fulfillment waxing the kitchen floor? She was so ashamed to admit her dissatisfaction that she never knew how many other woman shared it. If she tried to tell her husband, he didn't understand what she was talking about. She did not really understand it herself. For over fifteen years women in America found it harder to talk about this problem than about sex. Even the psychoanalysts had no name for it. When a woman went to a psychiatrist for help, as many women did, she would say, "I'm so ashamed," or "I must be hopelessly neurotic." "I don't know what's wrong with women today," a suburban psychiatrist said uneasily. "I only know something is wrong because most of my patients happen to be women. And their problem isn't sexual." Most women with this problem did not go to see a psychoanalyst, however. "There's nothing wrong really," they kept telling themselves. "There isn't any problem."

But on an April morning in 1959, I heard a mother of four, having coffee with four other mothers in a suburban development fifteen miles from New York, say in a tone of quiet desperation, "the problem." And the others knew, without words, that she was not talking about a problem with her husband, or her children, or her home. Suddenly they realized they all shared the same problem, the problem that has no name. They began, hesitantly, to talk about it. Later, after they had picked up their children at a nursery school and taken them home to nap, two of the women cried, in sheer relief, just to know they were not alone. Gradually I came to realize that the problem that has no name was shared by countless women in America. . . .

If I am right, the problem that has no name stirring in the minds of so many American women today is not a matter of loss of femininity or too much education, or the demands of domesticity. It is far more important than anyone recognizes. It is the key to these other new and old problems which have been torturing women and their husbands and children, and puzzling their doctors and educators for years. It may well be the key to our future as a nation and a culture. "I want something more than my husband and my children and my home." . . .

This is the real mystery: why did so many American women, with the ability and education to discover and create, go back home again, to look for "something more" in housework and rearing children? For, paradoxically, in the same fifteen years in which that spirited New Women was replaced by the Happy Housewife, the boundaries of the human world have widened, the pace of world change has quickened, and the very nature of human reality has become increasingly free from biological and material necessity. Does the mystique keep American woman from growing with the world? Does it force her to deny reality to believe she is a queen? Does it doom women to be displaced persons, if not virtual schizophrenics, in our complex, changing world?

It is more than a strange paradox that as all professions are finally open to women in America, "career women" has become a dirty word; that as higher education becomes available to any woman with the capacity for it, education for women has become so suspect that more and more drop out of high school and college to marry and have babies; that as so many roles in modern society become theirs for the taking, women so insistently confine themselves to one role. Why, with the removal of all the legal, political, economic, and education barriers that once kept woman from being man's equal, a person in her own right, an individual free to develop her own potential, should she accept this new image which insists she is not a person but a "woman," by definition barred from the freedom of human existence and a voice in human destiny?

The feminine mystique is so powerful that women grow up no longer knowing that they have the desires and capacities the mystique forbids. But such a mystique does not fasten itself on a whole nation in a few short years, reversing the trends of a century, without cause. What gives the mystique its power? Why did women go home again?

United Nations Declaration of Women's Rights (1967)

The women's movement of the 1960s was not confined to the United States. Some of the most radical change took place in western Europe as socialist governments in West Germany, France, Great Britain, the Netherlands, Belgium, and the Scandinavian countries adopted health care and job tenure legislation that offered several benefits to women and mothers in particular. In 1967, the United Nations passed a declaration that addressed the issue of women's equality across legal and educational lines. It equated equal rights for women with basic human rights and challenged the male-dominated political structures to attend even to the question of attitudes and customs that encouraged the subordination of women. Although this declaration was not legally binding upon the membership (and more still needs to be done in passing binding covenants), it serves as a universal recognition of intent.

The General Assembly,

Considering that the peoples of the United Nations have, in the Charter, reaffirmed their faith in fundamental human rights, in the dignity and worth of the human person and in the equal rights of men and women,

Considering that the Universal Declaration of Human Rights asserts the principle of nondiscrimination and proclaims that all human beings are born free and equal in dignity and rights and that everyone is entitled to all the rights and freedoms set forth therein, without distinction of any kind, including any distinction as to sex,

Concerned that, despite the Charter, the Universal Declaration of Human Rights, International Covenants on Human Rights and other instruments of the United Nations, . . . there continues to exist considerable discrimination against women,

Considering that discrimination against women is incompatible with human dignity, and with the welfare of the family and of society, prevents their participation on equal terms with men, in the political, social, economic and cultural life of their countries, and is an obstacle to the full development of the potentialities of women in the service of their countries and humanity,

Bearing in mind the great contribution made by women to social, politi-

"United Nations Declaration of Women's Rights" is from Declaration on the Elimination of Discrimination Against Women, adopted by the General Assembly of the United Nations, Resolution 2263 (XXII), November 7, 1967.

cal, economic and cultural life and the part they play in the family and particularly in the rearing of children,

Convinced that the full and complete development of a country, the welfare of the world and the cause of peace require the maximum participation of women as well as men in all fields,

Considering that it is necessary to ensure the universal recognition in law and in fact of the principle of equality of men and women,

Solemnly proclaims this Declaration:

ARTICLE 1

Discrimination against women, denying or limiting as it does their equality of rights with men, is fundamentally unjust and constitutes an offense against human dignity.

ARTICLE 2

All appropriate measures shall be taken to abolish existing laws, customs, regulations and practices which are discriminatory against women, and to establish adequate legal protection for equal rights of men and women. . . .

ARTICLE 3

All appropriate measures shall be taken to educate public opinion and direct national aspirations toward the eradication of prejudice and the abolition of customary and all other practices which are based on the ideas of the inferiority of women.

ARTICLE 4

All appropriate measures shall be taken to ensure to women on equal terms with men without any discrimination:

a) The right to vote in all elections and be eligible for election to all publicly elected bodies;
b) The right to vote in all public referenda;
c) The right to hold public office and to exercise all public functions.

Such rights shall be guaranteed by legislation.

ARTICLE 6

All appropriate measures shall be taken to ensure the principle of equality of status of the husband and wife, and in particular:

a) Women shall have the same right as men to free choice of a spouse and to enter into marriage only with their free and full consent;
b) Women shall have equal rights with men during marriage and at its dissolution. . . .

Child marriage and the betrothal of young girls before puberty shall be prohibited, and effective action, including legislation, shall be taken to specify a minimum age for marriage and to make the registration of marriages in an official registry compulsory.

ARTICLE 8
All appropriate measures, including legislation, shall be taken to combat all forms of traffic in women and exploitation of prostitution of women.

ARTICLE 9
All appropriate measures shall be taken to ensure to girls and women, married or unmarried, equal rights with men in education at all levels. . . .

ARTICLE 10
1. All appropriate measures shall be taken to ensure to women, married or unmarried, equal rights with men in the field of economic and social life, and in particular:

a) The right to equal remuneration with men and to equality of treatment in respect of work of equal value;
b) The right to leave with pay, retirement privileges and provision for social security in respect of unemployment, sickness, old age or other incapacity to work. . . .

2. In order to prevent discrimination against women on account of marriage or maternity and to ensure their effective right to work, measures shall be taken to prevent their dismissal in the event of marriage or maternity and to provide maternity leave, and the guarantee of returning to former employment, and to provide the necessary social services, including childcare facilities. . . .

ARTICLE 11
Governments, nongovernmental organizations and individuals are urged, therefore, to do all in their power to promote the implementation of the principles in this Declaration.

"If Men Could Menstruate" (1978)

GLORIA STEINEM

Betty Friedan opened up the search for the "modern woman" who could find worth in the cultivation of her potential, who was intimately in tune with the heritage of the women's movement and could tap the future through vision and energy. Perhaps the quintessential example of this "modern woman" who staked a claim to high profile leadership of the feminist movement in the 1970s and 1980s was Gloria Steinem. The commentator, Bill Moyers, called her "a lightning rod for the cause of other women who would sing but have no voice." She began her career as a journalist and landed a job as a Playboy Club bunny in order to investigate the operations. She was a founding editor of Ms. magazine in 1972 and through this vehicle became a persuasive spokesperson for what has been called the "Feminist Movement." Her voice in her writings has taken on a wide range, from pathos to satire. In the following excerpt from a compilation of her work entitled Outrageous Acts and Everyday Rebellions *(1983), what appears to be a humorous and irreverent parody also contains some rather profound commentary on male and female power relationships in our contemporary society.*

. . . . Whatever a "superior" group has will be used to justify its superiority, and whatever an "inferior" group has will be used to justify its plight. Black men were given poorly paid jobs because they were said to be "stronger" than white men, while all women were relegated to poorly paid job because they were said to be "weaker." As the little boy said when asked if he wanted to be a lawyer like his mother, "Oh no, that's women's work." Logic has nothing to do with oppression.

So what would happen if suddenly, magically, men could menstruate and women could not?

Clearly, menstruation would become an enviable, boast-worthy masculine event:

Men would brag about how long and how much.

Young boys would talk about it as the envied beginning of manhood. Gifts, religious ceremonies, family dinners, and stag parties would mark the day.

To prevent monthly work loss among the powerful, Congress would fund a National Institute of Dysmenorrhea. Doctors would research little about heart attacks, from which men were hormonally protected, but everything about cramps.

Sanitary supplies would be federally funded and free. Of course, some men would still pay for the prestige of such commercial brands as Paul Newman Tampons, Muhammad Ali's Rope-a-Dope Pads, John Wayne

Maxi Pads, and Joe Namath Jock Shields—"For Those Light Bachelor Days."

Statistical surveys would show that men did better in sports and won more Olympic medals during their periods.

Generals, right-wing politicians, and religious fundamentalists would cite menstruation ("*men*-struation") as proof that only men could serve God and country in combat ("You have to give blood to take blood"), occupy high political office ("Can women be properly fierce without a monthly cycle governed by the planet Mars?"), be priests, ministers, God Himself ("He gave His blood for our sins"), or rabbis ("Without a monthly purge of impurities, women are unclean").

Male liberals or radicals, however, would insist that women are equal, just different; and that any woman could join their ranks if only she were willing to recognize the primacy of menstrual rights. . . .

Street guys would invent slang ("He's a three-pad-man") and "give fives" on the corner with some exchange like, "Man, you lookin' *good*!"

"Yeah, man, I'm on the rag!"

TV shows would treat the subject openly. (*Happy Days*: Richie and Potsie try to convince Fonzie that he is still "The Fonz," though he has missed two periods in a row. *Hill Street Blues*: The whole precinct hits the same cycle.) So would newspapers. (SUMMER SHARK SCARE THREATENS MEN-STRUATING MEN. JUDGE CITES MONTHLIES IN PARDONING RAPIST.) And so would movies. (Newman and Redford in *Blood Brothers*!)

Men would convince women that sex was *more* pleasurable at "that time of the month." Lesbians would be said to fear blood and therefore life itself, though all they needed was a good menstruating man.

Medical schools would limit women's entry ("they might faint at the sight of blood").

Of course, intellectuals would offer the most moral and logical arguments. Without that biological gift for measuring the cycles of the moon and planets, how could a woman master any discipline that demanded a sense of time, space, mathematics—or the ability to measure anything at all? . . .

Menopause would be celebrated as a positive event, the symbol that men had accumulated enough years of cyclical wisdom to need no more. . . .

And how would women be trained to react? One can imagine right-wing women agreeing to all these arguments with a staunch and smiling masochism. . . . Radical feminists would add that the oppression of the non-menstrual was the pattern for all other oppressions. ("Vampires were our first freedom fighters!") . . . Socialist feminists would insist that, once capitalism and imperialism were overthrown, women would menstruate, too. . . .

In short, we would discover, as we should already guess, that logic is in the eye of the logician. . . .

The truth is that, if men could menstruate, the power justifications would go on and on.

If we let them.

("Doonesbury." Copyright © 1987 by G. B. Trudeau. Reprinted by permission of Universal Press Syndicate.)

Women in the Marketplace (1990)

JOAN KONNER

Throughout the 1980s, both men and women refined a competitive, often uncooperative, relationship in the workplace that had been established in the 1970s. As more women applied and were admitted to professional schools, the face of corporate industry began to change. The workplace was in transition, and women faced new challenges in juggling traditional responsibilities in the home with the demands of the office. A new image of the "modern woman" was created by advertising agencies that placed emphasis on "having it all." The "two-income" family became a standard in society, and women were faced with the demands of both "brining home the bacon and frying it in a pan." Men, too, were faced with changing realities in personal relationships and found themselves judged by a new standard of the modern, sensitive male, who was comfortable with himself and understood the necessity of intimate communication. "Macho" was out and became acceptable only as a part of a males' guilty fantasyland of Rambo and Dirty Harry.

The 1990s have seen a reaction against the Yuppie "boomers" of the previous decade. Both men and women are more seriously considering the worth of "free time" and family stability. Women still exist in a world where their market value has not yet been fully realized. But they are bringing new perspectives and attitudes to that marketplace that may well again change the face of contemporary society.

Joan Konner, Dean of Columbia University's School of Journalism, reflected on these developments in a speech delivered to the New Jersey Press Women's Association in May 1990.

I always tried to follow a piece of advice I picked up when I was a student at the Columbia Graduate School of Journalism. The school had a ritual for

"Women in the Marketplace" is from Joan Konner, speech delivered to the New Jersey Press Women's Association on May 5, 1990. Contained in *Vital Speeches of the Day*, September 15, 1990, pp. 726–728.

the women students in the class at the end of the school year. A panel of women journalists was invited to discuss how to manage home and career.

One of the panelists, if I recall correctly, was Betsy Wade of the New York *Times*, who advised:

"When you're sick, go to work, because when your children are sick, you're going to have to say home and you can't be absent for both."

Such was the balancing act of women who worked in the newsroom at the time, and I'm not sure that it's much changed today. . . .

The guest on the program ("Not for Women Only" with Barbara Walters) that day was Clare Booth Luce, and they were talking about the time Mrs. Luce served in Congress.

Mrs. Luce said it was the worst experience of her professional life, and further, she thought that women would never become a strong presence in Congress.

"Why?" Barbara Walters asked.

Mrs. Luce replied, "because women do not have the instinct for the jugular, and men do."

Barbara Walters replied: "We'll learn."

I remember thinking that wasn't the point at all. We weren't supposed to be trying to become like men. We were supposed to be trying to get into the decision-making roles so that we could change the way business is done to the advantage of both sexes. What's the point of women getting into the positions of power if, in the process, we have to turn ourselves into killers, psychologically, at least, with an instinct for the jugular? Aren't those killer values the ones we are trying to change?

That's still the question today when we ask: Are women in journalism, especially now that there are more of us, some of us in positions of leadership, making a difference? Given the impact of the media in shaping our social, political, and economic life, are we seeing changes not only in numbers in the newsrooms, but in the agenda and priorities of society?

I suggest the answer is "yes," but it is only a beginning. . . .

We shouldn't mistake quantity for quality, and the quieter history includes the accomplishments of many women off-camera in television news-

("Doonesbury." Copyright © 1987 by G. B. Trudeau. Reprinted by permission of Universal Press Syndicate.)

rooms as well as many more in newspapers and magazines throughout the country. For one, the remarkable *Ms.* magazine, which legitimized women's issues by producing a serious magazine about them. It no doubt can take the credit for the greater seriousness of women's magazines in general, and for leading the way to the changing definition of news generally—the inclusion of domestic and workplace issues like battered wives, child abuse, and maternity leave, in so-called hard-news; values and quality of life stories; stories about children, health, education, social trends, community, and the environment—not only on the front page, but on every page and on television news as well. . . .

Are women better equipped to cover this "new" news? It is possible we are. The psychologist Carol Gilligan, in her book, *In A Different Voice*, described a difference between the moral development of men and women.

Women, she says, develop an ethic of care, an empathy based on their identification with the primary parent, usually the mother. Women define themselves in terms of relationship and responsibility.

Men develop an ethic of justice as they separate from the mother. They define themselves in terms of difference, position and hierarchy. If we accept this, then I think we can assume the responsibility that comes with our capacity to adopt a broader perspective and show the human, caring side of the news.

The feminine sensibility is growing everywhere in our culture today—in literature, in art, in history, politics, and the media. It coincides with concerns about the environment, a growing awareness of Mother Earth, as our life support system. There is talk of the Gaia principle, a world view that says we are all part of one living body. We find the principle expressed in the mythology of the Goddess, in which there is also a revival of interest today. The Goddess was worshipped for thousands of years in agrarian, egalitarian societies in which there was a love of life, of nature and beauty.

There seems at this time to be a great hunger in the American culture for the values of the goddess—the values of life, generation, and creation. There seems to be a growing reverence for nature, for a collective spirit, and relationship based on the awareness of the interconnectedness of life. We are becoming more concerned that our competitive Western culture that developed along the lines of the Darwinian principle of the survival of the fittest may have been a life-supporting pattern for one period of human evolution but it may no longer be a life-supporting pattern for another—this one. Human intelligence creates systems to protect human life. Today those very systems are threatening it—industrial development which threatens the environment, nuclear weapons that threaten all of life. In such a world, those with a wider perspective and greater awareness are turning out to be the fittest.

We are coming around a bend, and we realize there is a need for other values, values of collaboration, community, care. These are the values that used to belong to the private sphere of home and family. But we are beginning to see these values in the workplace and in public life as well. One hypothesis is that women, as they succeed in the marketplace, retain what is valuable from what used to be considered the domestic sphere and bring that wider perspective into view. It does seem some of us—women and men—have had enough of the instinct for the jugular. I think that women in positions of power—in politics, public service, and the media— are helping to make that difference.

The International Challenge of Human Rights

> Human dignity is best preserved not by developing the capacity to deal destruction, but by refusing to retaliate. If it is possible to train millions in the black art of violence, which is the art of the beast, it is more possible to train them in the white art of non-violence, which is the law of regenerate man.
>
> —Mahatma Gandhi

The topic of human rights has been a focal point of the decades following 1945. Enlightened thinkers of the eighteenth century sought to define and advocate the natural rights of human beings. They produced some of the seminal documents of Western Civilization, including the American Declaration of Independence and the French Declaration of the Rights of Man. After the destruction perpetrated during World War II, with its concomitant horrors of nuclear holocaust and genocide, the topic of human rights remained an issue of paramount importance.

Following the concerns of Presidents Abraham Lincoln, Woodrow Wilson, and Franklin Roosevelt, Jimmy Carter echoed this theme once again at his inauguration in 1977 as the foundation of his future international policy: "Our commitment to human rights must be absolute. . . . Because we are free, we can never be indifferent to the fate of freedom elsewhere." His foreign policy based on this commitment was not altogether successful in a political world more Machiavellian than moral. The succeeding Reagan administration was quick to disavow such principles on the argument of national self-interest. Perhaps the most eloquent expression of Carter's vision was contained in a 1978 White House speech on the thirtieth anniversary of the passage of the United Nations Universal Declaration of Human Rights.

The second selection describes the goals and philosophical foundations of the British-based organization Amnesty International. Its yearly compilation of human rights violations draws attention to prisoners of conscience throughout the world and serves as a barometer of the progress of human freedom.

("Doonesbury." Copyright © 1987 by G. B. Trudeau. Reprinted by permission of Universal Press Syndicate.)

"Human Rights Is the Soul of Our Foreign Policy" (1978)

JIMMY CARTER

What I have to say today is fundamentally very simple. It's something I've said many times, including my acceptance speech when I was nominated as President and my inaugural speech when I became President. But it cannot be said too often or too firmly nor too strongly.

As long as I am President, the government of the United States will continue throughout the world to enhance human rights. No force on earth can separate us from that commitment.

This week we commemorate the thirtieth anniversary of the Universal Declaration of Human Rights. We rededicate ourselves—in the words of Eleanor Roosevelt, who was the chairperson of the Human Rights Commission—to the Universal Declaration as, and I quote from her, "a common standard of achievement of all peoples of all nations."

The Universal Declaration and the human rights conventions that derive from it do not describe the world as it is. But these documents are very important, nonetheless. They are a beacon, a guide to a future of personal security, political freedom, and social justice. . . .

Political killings, tortures, arbitrary and prolonged detention without trial or without a charge, these are the cruelest and the ugliest of human rights violations. Of all human rights, the most basic is to be free of arbitrary violence, whether that violence comes from government, from terrorists, from criminals, or from self-appointed messiahs operating under the cover of politics or religion.

But governments—because of their power, which is so much greater than that of an individual—have a special responsibility. The first duty of a

" 'Human Rights Is the Soul of Our Foreign Policy' " is from President Jimmy Carter, speech delivered on December 6, 1978, in the East Room of the White House, Washington D.C.

government is to protect its own citizens, and when government itself becomes the perpetrator of arbitrary violence against its citizens, it undermines its own legitimacy.

There are other violations of the body and the spirit which are especially destructive of human life. Hunger, disease, poverty, are enemies of human potential which are as relentless as any repressive government.

The American people want the actions of their government, our government, both to reduce human suffering and to increase human freedom. . . . We will speak out when individual rights are violated in other lands. The Universal Declaration means that no nation can draw the cloak of sovereignty over torture, disappearances, officially sanctioned bigotry, or the destruction of freedom within its own borders. . . .

In distributing the scarce resources of our foreign assistance programs, we will demonstrate that our deepest affinities are with nations which commit themselves to a democratic path to development. Toward regimes which persist in wholesale violation of human rights, we will not hesitate to convey our outrage, nor will we pretend that our relations are unaffected.

In the coming year, I hope that Congress will take a step that has been long overdue for a generation, the ratification of the Convention on the Prevention and Punishment of the Crime of Genocide. As you know, the genocide convention was also adopted by the United Nations General Assembly thirty years ago this week, one day before the adoption of the Universal Declaration. It was the world's affirmation that the lesson of the Holocaust would never be forgotten, but unhappily, genocide is not peculiar to any one historical era. . . .

This action must be the first step toward the ratification of other human rights instruments, including those I signed a year ago. Many of the religious and human rights groups represented here have undertaken a campaign of public education on behalf of these covenants. I commend and appreciate your efforts.

Refugees are the living, homeless casualties of one very important failure on the part of the world to live by the principles of peace and human rights. To help these refugees is a simple human duty. As Americans, as a people made up largely of the descendants of refugees, we feel that duty with special keenness. . . .

The effectiveness of our human rights policy is now an established fact. It has contributed to an atmosphere of change—sometimes disturbing— but which has encouraged progress in many ways and in many places. In some countries, political prisoners have been released by the hundreds, even thousands. In others, the brutality of repression has been lessened. In still others, there's a movement toward democratic institutions or the rule of law when these movements were not previously detectable. To those who doubt the wisdom of our dedication, I say this: Ask the victims. Ask the exiles. Ask the governments which continue to practice repression. . . .

But I want to stress again that human rights are not peripheral to the foreign policy of the United States. Our human rights policy is not a decoration. It is not something we've adopted to polish up our image abroad or to put a fresh coat of moral paint on the discredited policies of the past. Our pursuit of human rights is a part of a broad effort to use our great power and our tremendous influence in the service of creating a better world, a world in which human beings can live in peace, in freedom, and with their basic needs adequately met.

Human rights is the soul of our foreign policy. And I say this with assurance, because human rights is the soul of our sense of nationhood. . . .

What unites us—what makes us Americans—is a common belief in peace, in a free society, and a common devotion to the liberties enshrined in our Constitution. That belief and that devotion are the sources of our sense of national community. Uniquely, ours is a nation founded on an idea of human rights. From our own history we know how powerful that idea can be. . . .

For most of the first half of our history, black Americans were denied even the most basic human rights. For most of the first two-thirds of our history, women were excluded from the political process. Their rights and those of native Americans are still not constitutionally guaranteed and enforced. Even freedom of speech has been threatened periodically throughout our history. . . . And the struggle for full human rights for all Americans—black, brown, and white; male and female; rich and poor—is far from over. . . .

For millions of people around the world today the Universal Declaration of Human Rights is still only a declaration of hope. Like all of you, I want that hope to be fulfilled. The struggle to fulfill it will last longer than the lifetimes of any of us. Indeed, it will last as long as the lifetime of humanity itself. But we must persevere.

And we must persevere by ensuring that this country of ours, leader in the world, which we love so much, is always in the forefront of those who are struggling for that great hope, the great dream of universal human rights.

Amnesty International (1982)

Amnesty International plays a specific role in the international protection of human rights. It seeks the immediate and unconditional release of men and women detained anywhere because of their beliefs, colour, sex, ethnic origin, language or religious creed, provided they have not used or advocated violence. These are termed prisoners of conscience. It works for fair and prompt trials for all political prisoners, and works on behalf of such people detained without charge or trial. It opposes the death penalty and torture or other cruel, inhuman or degrading treatment or punishment of all prisoners without reservation. . . . The record shows how much remains to be done.

As the year ended, thousands of men and women were in prison because of their beliefs, many were still held after years without charge or trial. Prisoners were subject to torture, and people had been executed or were under sentence of death in a number of countries, often for politically related offences. Still others were put to death without any pretence of judicial or legal process, selected and killed by governments or their agents.

In many countries men, women and children remained unaccounted for after being taken into custody, often violently, by security forces, or abducted by agents acting with the complicity of governments; they had "disappeared". Their families and friends could gain no information about their fate or whereabouts.

The International Council of Amnesty International, the movement's supreme governing body, stated this year that governments and state security forces who attempt to cover up the abduction and "disappearance" of their political opponents should be made publicly accountable for the fate of the victims. It called for a global publicity campaign to counter this contemporary technique of official repression. This campaign was launched on Human Rights Day, 10 December 1981.

Unlawful and deliberate killings carried out by order of a government or with its complicity have claimed the lives of countless victims. During the year Amnesty International determined the campaign against such killings worldwide. . . .

These two practices which are often related—the "disappearance" of people abducted by the authorities and deliberate killings by governments—represent an outright attack on values and rights which the world community has struggled to establish. These are not new abuses, but the international community must now take effective measures to end them. Governments must not be allowed to evade responsibility when they choose to obliterate suspected opponents. They must accept real accountability by permitting independent investigations, pressing for investigations of complaints in other countries and taking the other actions necessary to expose these abuses.

Human rights transcend the boundaries of nation, race and belief; so does the international responsibility for protecting those rights. The pressure of world public opinion, expressed in the concerted actions of ordinary people from all around the world, must be brought to bear if this principle is to be universally respected. This is the vision which launched Amnesty International. Today, it has more than 325,000 members, subscribers and supporters in over 150 countries and territories committed to that ambition.

The protection of the individual citizen goes beyond the boundaries of the individual state—it is a matter of international responsibility and concern. This is the principle on which Amnesty International is founded, and the concept that lies behind the creation of international human rights standards and mechanisms to monitor and enforce those standards. To promote international standards, to strengthen them and to try to ensure effective means of enforcing them are important aspects of Amnesty International's work, particularly through the United Nations (UN), but also through other international and regional bodies. . . . The purpose of this report is to record the efforts Amnesty International made to protect individuals in the diverse situations where their inalienable rights were transgressed. This is a report about people, not statistics.

South African Apartheid

One of the most influential factors in Western Civilization has been racism. It has been used to justify imperialism and to inspire genocide. The twentieth century has indeed seen its share of racism at the hands of Adolf Hitler, the Ku Klux Klan, and other white supremacist groups. Still, there have been significant strides to correct the injustices of the past. The civil rights movement in the United States during the mid-1960s, as well as affirmative action programs and Supreme Court decisions, give evidence to a continuing effort to achieve racial equality. South Africa, once a bastion of racial segregation in its advocacy of apartheid—or enforced, legal segregation—has since 1989, moved toward a more equitable arrangement. Yet the problem still persists and will take a continuing commitment to racial equality and a deft political hand in order to accommodate the many factions on the road to an integrated, yet stable society.

One of the most outspoken critics of apartheid is South African Archbishop Desmond Tutu. In the first excerpt from 1983, he discusses the South African policy of "population removal." At that time, the black majority were barred from living in the affluent cities and were forced into "homelands" or townships where they provided an inexpensive labor force to be exploited by the white minority. His commitment to the inevitability of political and racial accommodation sustained the movement in the face of the abuses of Anglo-Boer rule.

On August 14, 1989, South African President P. W. Botha resigned and was succeeded by Frederik de Klerk. De Klerk's commitment to liberalization and an integrated nation is noted in his speech to the South African Parliament. Note its visionary, yet cautious tone. De Klerk must walk a political tightrope in order to keep the process of racial accommodation truly viable. One of the most important acts in this process was the release of Nelson Mandela, leader of the African National Congress, after nearly thirty years in jail. Mandela's speech to his followers was given just nine days after de Klerk's address. The move away from apartheid and toward an integrated South African society will remain one of the great challenges of the century.

"Blacks Will Be Free Whatever You Do or Don't Do" (1983)

ARCHBISHOP DESMOND TUTU

1948 and After

When the [South African] Nationalists came to power in 1948 they resurrected their ideal of the Boer republics of the late nineteenth century and early twentieth century. They developed discriminatory legislation that was to hand, and initiated their own amazing creativity—the Race Classification, the Job Reservation, Mixed Marriages, Immorality and other racist laws . . . Basically, the South African crisis is one that hinges on political power, for it is this, if you have it, which commands access to other kinds of power—economic well-being, social amenities and facilities. That is why it is such a charade to talk about improving the quality of life of Blacks in their own areas, in talking about the so-called changes which have been wrought in the matter of sport, the creation of international hotels and restaurants, in the removal of discriminatory signs. It is a charade because no matter how wonderful the improvements in the Black person's lot may be (and I don't doubt that there will be very significant improvements) these will always be mere concessions that are always at risk, and vulnerable because they depend on the whim of those who have political power. When they deem it convenient for themselves they will withhold these privileges and when they think otherwise they will dole them out lavishly, or not, from their bounty.

Basically it is a question of how you an maintain political power in the hands of a White Oligarchy. Perhaps there is a preliminary stage—how do you, as a White minority outnumbered five to one, survive in a continent that has on the whole shown itself hostile to White presence? And the answer which the imperialistic Europeans decided upon with almost uncanny unanimity was to subjugate the native peoples and to retain most power in White hands. And so Africa in particular, but much of the so-called Third World in general, found itself ruled by these White foreigners. In time most of this colonial empire came to throw off the yoke of oppression. Southern Africa has been tardy in joining the liberation movement, but the waves of freedom have now washed away most White minority rule even in this sub-continent, the latest to fall being that in Zimbabwe, where we had famous last words from Mr. Ian Smith [former Prime Minister of Rhodesia (Zimbabwe)], such as that it would not happen during his lifetime or only over his dead body and not in a thousand years.

During our period it has been quite clear that the Whites were determined to keep political power in their hands exclusively. It did not strike them as at all odd (at least, the majority of them) that the way they were going about things was totally at variance with the accepted meaning of that democracy whose virtues they extolled so much, as they vilified Communism and Marxism.

On accession to power the Nationalist Party made no bones about their determination to maintain White domination with policies that were nakedly racist. They had stepped into the corridors of political power on the waves of White apprehension of the so-called Black period . . . and they did not conceal this from anybody. . . .

And the Total Strategy is a developing one. Some very specially blessed Blacks (urban Blacks) will also be part of this "gravy train." Their quality of life will be significantly enhanced, their children are likely to go to good White schools, they will get very good salaries, etc. etc., and they will be coopted into the system as a Black middle class to be a buffer between the *have*-Whites and the *have-not*-Blacks, and being so greatly privileged they will be supporters of the status quo such as you cannot ever hope to find anywhere. That is the new strategy of the Nationalist Government. The bitter pill is very significantly coated with sugar. Those who will belong to this core economy and society will be numerically insignificant, and will pose hardly any threat to the power-wielding White group. But what of the rest—the hapless *hoi polloi*? They will be, and are being, relegated to the outer darkness, the limbo of the forgotten. They must get out . . . Nobody repudiated Mr. Mulder when he pointed out in Parliament that the logical conclusion of apartheid was that there would be no Black South Africans.

And to get to that conclusion, they have with very little compunction moved nearly two million Blacks. They have moved them often from places where they had reasonably adequate housing, where they were able to work—some in the informal sector, as casual labourers, within walking or reasonable distance of their places of work. They have moved them, dumped them as if they were potatoes, in largely inhospitable areas, often with no alternative accommodation. . . .

People are starving in most of these resettlement camps. I know, for I have seen it. They are starving not because of an accident or a misfortune. No, they are starving because of deliberate Government policy made in the name of White Christian civilization. They are starving; a little girl can tell you that when they can't borrow food, they drink water to fill their stomachs. This is the solution the Nationalists have decided upon. Many can't work, not because they won't work but because there is no work available. So they sit listlessly while we reap the benefits of a soaring gold price and our boom, which makes us want to import skilled labour from overseas. They are there as a reservoir, deliberately created, of cheap labour. When Black labour is needed, the laws forced Blacks into town when they were often well-to-do farmers. They had to become wage earners in order to pay the taxes levied on them. Now they are not really wanted, so they are endorsed out. There are probably two million Blacks unemployed and another million likely to lose their jobs, but they are out of sight and so are out of mind. . . .

The Cost

The cost in terms of human suffering is incalculable. Undernourishment, starvation and malnutrition have serious consequences in growing children. They may suffer irreversible brain damage . . . But how do we compute the cost in the legacy of bitterness, anger, frustration and indeed hatred which we are leaving behind for our children? In the body of this paper I have described many things that have happened to us Blacks in this country during the several decades of our oppression and exploitation and deprivation. It is, I believe, a miracle of God's grace that Blacks still talk to Whites, to any Whites. It is a miracle of God's grace that Blacks still say that we want a non-racial South Africa for all of us, Black and White together. It is a miracle of God's grace that Blacks can still say they are committed to a ministry of justice and reconciliation and that they want to avert the bloodbath which seems more and more inevitable as we see little bending and give on the crucial issue of power-sharing. We are told that the Afrikaners [White, South African minority of Dutch extraction] have found it very difficult to forgive, certainly difficult to forget what the British did to them in the concentration camps. I want to say that Blacks are going to find it difficult, very difficult, to forgive, certainly difficult to forget what Whites have done and are doing to us in this matter of population removals.

All Blacks live in a constant state of uncertainty. Even I, a bishop in the Church of God and General Secretary of the South African Council of Churches, have no security. The township manager could in his wisdom decide that my continued presence in Soweto [impoverished black suburb of Johannesburg] was detrimental to its good ordering and peace, and by the stroke of his pen would withdraw my permission to reside there, just like that. We each have such a sword of Damocles hanging over our heads. I don't suppose many Whites know this or, if they do, care too much about it. . . .

What the Church Can Do

The solutions are both long-term and short-term. The short-term strategy is to oppose all removals. We suggest that representations are made to the authorities to persuade them to desist forthwith. If we know about any removals likely to happen then let us do all we can to oppose them. If all our efforts to dissuade the authorities fail, then we should be there, physically present as the witnessing and caring Church. We must use all non-violent methods to hinder the act of demolition.

We should support those in resettlement camps, providing them with as much relief that they will need as possible—food, blankets, etc. And the

Church should help to rehabilitate these shocked persons by being a serving Church, helping to develop a community spirit and helping the people help themselves. . . .

In the long term, the solution must be political. There are not two ways about it. Either there is going to be power-sharing or there is not. If not, then we must give up hope of a peaceful settlement in South Africa. If the Government is determined to go ahead with its Balkanization of South Africa on ethnic lines, and depriving Blacks of their South African citizenship, then we have had it, the ghastly alternative will be upon us. Population removals must stop immediately if we are to be able to work for a new kind of South Africa, and the Church should be in the forefront to prepare all of us for this new South Africa.

There is still a chance, but if we let it slip then it will be gone for ever. Neither the most sophisticated arsenal nor the best army or police force will give White South Africa true security, for that will come and come automatically when all of us, Black and White, know we count as of equal worth in the land of our birth, which we love with a passionate love. Please God, we pray you, let them hear us, let them hear us before it is too late.

White South Africa, please know that you are deluding yourselves, or you are allowing yourselves to be deluded, if you think that the present ordering of our society can continue. Blacks will be free whatever you do or don't do. That is not in question. Don't let the *when* and the *how* be in doubt. Don't delay our freedom, which is your freedom as well, for freedom is indivisible. Let it be now, and let it be reasonably peaceful. . . .

"Walk Through the Open Door": Normalizing the Political Process in South Africa (February 2, 1990)

F. W. DE KLERK

Mr. Speaker, Members of Parliament. The general election on September the 6th, 1989, placed our country irrevocably on the road of drastic change. Underlying this is the growing realisation by an increasing number of South Africans that only a negotiated understanding among the representative leaders of the entire population is able to ensure lasting peace.

The alternative is growing violence, tension and conflict. That is unacceptable and in nobody's interest. The well-being of all in this country is linked inextricably to the ability of the leaders to come to terms with one another on a new dispensation. No one can escape this simple truth.

On its part, the Government will accord the process of negotiation the highest priority. The aim is a totally new and just constitutional dispensa-

" 'Walk through the Open Door' " is from F. W. de Klerk, speech delivered to the Second Session of the Ninth Parliament of the Republic of South Africa, Capetown, February 2, 1990. *Vital Speeches of the Day*, March 1, 1990, pp. 290–295.

tion in which every inhabitant will enjoy equal rights, treatment and opportunity in every sphere of endeavour—constitutional, social and economic.

I hope that this new Parliament will play a constructive part in both the prelude to negotiations and the negotiating process itself. I wish to ask all of you who identify yourselves with the broad aim of a new South Africa, and that is the overwhelming majority:

—Let us put petty politics aside when we discuss the future during this Session.

—Help us build a broad consensus about the fundamentals of a new, realistic and democratic dispensation.

—Let us work together on a plan that will rid our country of suspicion and steer it away from domination and radicalism of any kind. . . .

The government accepts the principle of the recognition and protection of the fundamental individual rights which form the constitutional basis of most Western democracies. We acknowledge, too, that the most practical way of protecting those rights is vested in a declaration of rights justifiable by an independent judiciary. However, it is clear that a system for the protection of the rights of individuals, minorities and national entities has to form a well-rounded and balanced whole. South Africa has its own national composition and our constitutional dispensation has to take this into account. The formal recognition of individual rights does not mean that the problems of a heterogeneous population will simply disappear. Any new constitution which disregards this reality will be inappropriate and even harmful.

Naturally, the protection of collective, minority and national rights may not bring about an imbalance in respect of individual rights. It is neither the Government's policy nor its intention that any group—in whichever way it may be defined—shall be favoured above or in relation to any of the others.

The Government is requesting the Law Commission to undertake further task and report on it. This task is directed at the balanced protection in a future constitution of the human rights of all our citizens, as well as of collective units, associations, minorities, and nations. This investigation will also serve the purpose of supporting negotiations towards a new constitution.

The terms of reference also include:

—the identification of the main types and models of democratic constitutions which deserve consideration in the aforementioned context;

—an analysis of the ways in which the relevant rights are protected in every model; and

—possible methods by means of which such constitutions may be made to succeed and be safeguarded in a legitimate manner. . . .

Practically every leader agrees that negotiation is the key to reconciliation, peace and a new and just dispensation. However, numerous excuses for refusing to take part, are advanced. Some of the reasons being advanced are valid. Others are merely part of a political chess game. And while the game of chess proceeds, valuable time is being lost.

Against this background, I committed the Government during my inauguration to giving active attention to the most important obstacles in the way of negotiation. Today I am able to announce far-reaching decisions in this connection.

I believe that these decisions will shape a new phase in which there will be a movement away from measures which have been seized upon as a justification for confrontation and violence. The emphasis has to move, and will move now, to a debate and discussion of political and economic points of view as part of the process of negotiation.

I wish to urge every political and community leader, in and outside Parliament, to approach the new opportunities which are being created, constructively. There is no time left for advancing all manner of new conditions that will delay the negotiating process.

The steps that have been decided, are the following:

—The prohibition of the African National Congress, the Pan Africanist Congress, the South African Communist Party and a number of subsidiary organisations is being rescinded.

—People serving prison sentences merely because they were members of one of these organisations or because they committed another offence which was merely an offence because a prohibition on one of the organisations was in force, will be identified and released. Prisoners who have been sentenced for other offenses such as murder, terrorism or arson are not affected by this.

—The media emergency regulations as well as the education emergency regulations are being abolished in their entirety.

—The security emergency regulations will be amended to still make provision for effective control over visual material pertaining to scenes of unrest.

—The conditions imposed in terms of the security emergency regulations on 374 people on their release, are being rescinded and the regulations which provide for such conditions are being abolished. . . .

These decisions by the Cabinet are in accordance with the Government's declared intention to normalise the political process in South Africa without jeopardising the maintenance of the good order. They were preceded by thorough and unanimous advice by a group of officials which included members of the security community. Implementation will be immediate. . . .

At the same time I wish to emphasize that the maintenance of law and order dare not be jeopardised. The Government will not forsake its duty in this connection. Violence from whichever source, will be fought with all available might. Peaceful protest may not become the springboard for lawlessness, violence and intimidation. No democratic country can tolerate that. . . .

Therefore, I repeat my invitation with greater conviction than ever: Walk through the open door, take your place at the negotiating table together with the Government and other leaders who have important power bases inside and outside of Parliament.

Henceforth everybody's political points of view will be tested against their realism, their workability and their fairness. The time of negotiation has arrived.

"Apartheid Has No Future" (February 11, 1990)
NELSON MANDELA

My friends, comrades and fellow South Africans, I greet you all in the name of peace, democracy and freedom for all. . . . Your tireless and heroic sacrifices have made it possible for me to be here today. I therefore place the remaining years of my life in your hands. On this day of my release, I extend my sincere and warmest gratitude to the millions of my compatriots and those in every corner of the globe who have campaigned tirelessly for my release. . . .

Today the majority of South Africans, black and white, recognize that apartheid has no future. It has to be ended by our own decisive mass actions in order to build peace and security. The mass campaigns of defiance and other actions of our organizations and people can only culminate in the establishment of democracy.

The apartheid destruction on our subcontinent is incalculable. The fabric of family life of millions of my people has been shattered. Millions are homeless and unemployed. . . . The factors which necessitated the armed struggle still exist today. We have no option but to continue. We express the hope that a climate conducive to a negotiated settlement would be created soon so that there may no longer be the need for the armed struggle. . . .

Today, I wish to report to you that my talks with the Government have been aimed at normalizing the political situation in the country. We have not as yet begun discussing the basic demands of the struggle. I wish to stress that I myself had at no time entered into negotiations about the future of our country, except to insist on a meeting between the A.N.C. [African National Congress] and the government. Mr. de Klerk has gone further than any other Nationalist president in taking real steps to normalize the situation. . . .

I reiterate our call for *inter alia* the immediate ending of the state of emergency and the freeing of all, and not only some, political prisoners. . . . Negotiations cannot take place . . . above the heads or behind the backs of our people. It is our belief that the future of our country can only be determined by a body which is democratically elected on a nonracial basis.

Negotiations on the dismantling of apartheid will have to address the overwhelming demand of our people for a democratic nonracial and unitary South Africa. There must be an end to while monopoly on political

" 'Apartheid Has No Future' " is from Nelson Mandela, speech delivered to the public, Cape Town, South Africa, February 11, 1990. *Vital Speeches of the Day*, March 1, 1990, pp. 295–297.

power. And a fundamental restructuring of our political and economic systems to insure that the inequalities of apartheid are addressed and our society thoroughly democratized.

It must be added that Mr. de Klerk himself is a man of integrity who is acutely aware of the dangers of a public figure not honoring his undertakings. But as an organization, we base our policy and strategy on the harsh reality we are faced with, and this reality is that we are still suffering under the policies of the Nationalist Government.

Our struggle has reached a decisive moment. We call on our people to seize this moment so that the process toward democracy is rapid and uninterrupted. We have waited too long for our freedom. We can no longer wait. Now is the time to intensify the struggle on all fronts. To relax our efforts now would be a mistake which generations to come will not be able to forgive. The sight of freedom looming on the horizon should encourage us to redouble our efforts. It is only through disciplined mass action that our victory can be assured. . . .

In conclusion, I wish to go to my own words during my trial in 1964. They are as true today as they were then. I wrote: "I have fought against white domination, and I have fought against black domination. I have cherished the idea of a democratic and free society in which all persons live together in harmony and with equal opportunities. It is an ideal which I hope to live for and to achieve. But if needs be, it is an ideal for which I am prepared to die." My friends, I have no words of eloquence to offer today except to say that the remaining days of my life are in your hands.

I hope you will disperse with discipline. And not a single one of you should do anything which will make other people say that we can't control our own people.

Reflections on the Twentieth Century

Human Nature and Human Relationships

A Portrait of Albert Einstein: "As Long as There Will Be Man, There Will Be Wars" (1947)

PHILLIPPE HALSMAN

One of the most fertile and influential scientific minds in history belonged to Albert Einstein. Besides his contributions to the field of physics, Einstein was also a great humanist who believed in mankind's ability to change society and

---

"A Portrait of Albert Einstein" is from Phillippe Halsman, *Halsman Sight and Insight* (Garden City, N.Y.: Doubleday, 1972), p. 8.

progress toward international cooperation. It is ironic that is was Einstein who brought the destructive potential of nuclear energy to the attention of President Roosevelt in 1939. In this excerpt, Phillippe Halsman, one of the most famous photographers of distinguished people, describes his meeting with Einstein in 1947.

I admired Albert Einstein more than anyone I ever photographed, not only as the genius who singlehandedly had changed the foundation of modern physics, but even more as a rare and idealistic human being.

Personally, I owed him an immense debt of gratitude. After the fall of France, it was through his personal intervention that my name was added to the list of artists and scientists who, in danger of being captured by the Nazis, were given emergency visas to the United States.

After my miraculous rescue I went to Princeton to thank Einstein and I remember vividly my first impression. Instead of a frail scientist I saw a deep-chested man with a resonant voice and a hearty laugh. The long hair, which in some photographs gave him the look of an old woman, framed his marvellous face with a kind of leonine mane. He wore slacks, a grey sweater with a fountain pen stuck in its collar, black leather shoes, and no socks.

On my third visit I had the courage to ask him why he did not wear any socks. His secretary, Miss Dukas, who overheard me, said, "The professor never wears socks. Even when he was invited by Mr. Roosevelt to the White House, he did not wear any socks." I looked with surprise at Professor Einstein.

He smiled and said, "When I was young I found out that the big toe always ended up by making a hole in the sock. So I stopped wearing socks." As slight as this remark was, it made an indelible impression on me. This detail seemed symbolic of Einstein's absolute and total independence of thought. It was this independence that gave him the courage when he was an unknown twenty-six-year-old patent clerk to publish a scientific paper which overthrew all the axioms held sacrosanct by the greatest physicists of his time.

The question of how to capture the essence of such a man in a portrait filled me with apprehension. Finally, in 1947, I had the courage to bring on one of my visits my Halsman camera and a few floodlights. After tea, I asked for permission to set up my lights in Einstein's study. The professor sat down and started peacefully working on his mathematical calculations. I took a few pictures. Ordinarily, Einstein did not like photographers, whom he called *Lichtaffen* (light monkeys). But he cooperated because I was his guest and, after all, he had helped to rescue me.

Suddenly, looking into my camera, he started talking. He spoke about his despair that his formula $E = mc^2$ and his letter to President Roosevelt had made the atomic bomb possible, that his scientific search had resulted in the death of so many human beings. "Have you read," he asked, "that powerful voices in the United States are demanding that the bombs be dropped on Russia now, before the Russians have the time to perfect their own?" With my entire being I felt how much this infinitely good and compassionate man was suffering from the knowledge that he had helped to put in the hands of politicians a monstrous weapon of devastation and death.

He grew silent. His eyes had a look of immense sadness. There was a question and a reproach in them.

The spell of this moment almost paralysed me. Then, with an effort, I released the shutter of my camera. Einstein looked up, and I asked him, "So you don't believe that there will ever be peace?"

"No," he answered, "as long as there will be man, there will be wars."

The Doctrine of the Sword

MAHATMA GANDHI

When one thinks of power, authority, influence, and the forces that promote change in society, violence and coercion are often inevitable factors in the equation. But nonviolent resistance has been a proven source of power. Mahatma Gandhi (1869–1948) and Martin Luther King, Jr. (1929–1968) each practiced it as a creed essential to the success of a free India in 1948 and an integrated America in 1968. It is indeed ironic that both men were shot to death by assassins. The following selection contains excerpts from the writings of Mahatma Gandhi. They give the essence of his philosophy of nonviolence.

I do believe that, where there is only a choice between cowardice and violence, I would advise violence. Thus when my eldest son asked me what he should have done, had he been present when I was almost fatally assaulted in 1908, whether he should have run away and seen me killed or whether he should have used his physical force which he could and wanted to use, and defended me, I told him that it was his duty to defend me even by using violence. Hence it was that I took part in the Boer War, the so-called Zulu Rebellion and the late war [World War I]. Hence also do I advocate training in arms for those who believe in the method of violence. I would rather have India resort to arms in order to defend her honour than that she should, in a cowardly manner, become or remain a helpless witness to her own dishonour.

But I believe that non-violence is infinitely superior to violence, forgiveness is more manly than punishment. Forgiveness adorns a soldier. But abstinence is forgiveness only when there is the power to punish; it is meaningless when it pretends to proceed from a helpless creature . . . But I do not believe India to be helpless. I do not believe myself to be a helpless creature. Only I want to use India's and my strength for a better purpose.

"The Doctrine of the Sword" is from Ronald Duncan, ed., *Selected Writings of Mahatma Gandhi* (London: Faber & Faber, Ltd., 1951), pp. 53–54, 56, 58, 60, 66. Reprinted by permission of the Navajaivan Trust.

Let me not be misunderstood. Strength does not come from physical capacity. It comes from an indomitable will . . . I am not a visionary. I claim to be a practical idealist. The religion of non-violence is not meant merely for the *rishis* [holy men] and saints. It is meant for the common people as well. *Non-violence* is the law of our species as violence is the law of the brute. The spirit lies dormant in the brute, and he knows no law but that of physical might. The dignity of man requires obedience to a higher law—to the strength of the spirit.

I have therefore ventured to place before India the ancient law of self-sacrifice. . . . The *rishis*, who discovered the law of non-violence in the midst of violence, were greater geniuses than Newton. They were themselves greater warriors than Wellington. Having themselves known the use of arms, they realized their uselessness, and taught a weary world that its salvation lay not through violence but through non-violence.

Non-violence in its dynamic condition means conscious suffering. It does not mean meek submission to the will of the evil-doer, but it means the pitting of one's whole soul against the will of the tyrant. Working under this law of our being it is possible for a single individual to defy the whole might of an unjust empire to save his honour, his religion, his soul, and lay the foundation for that empire's fall or its regeneration. . . .

The next point, that of *ahimsa* [non-violence], is more abstruse. My conception of *ahimsa* impels me always to dissociate myself from almost every one of the activities I am engaged in. My soul refuses to be satisfied so long as it is a helpless witness of a single wrong or a single misery. But it is not possible for me—a weak, frail, miserable being—to mend every wrong or to hold myself free of blame for all the wrong I see. The spirit in me pulls one way, the flesh in me pulls in the opposite direction. There is freedom from the action of these two forces, but that freedom is attainable only by slow and painful stages. I can attain freedom not only by a mechanical refusal to act, but only by intelligent action in a detached manner. This struggle resolves itself into an incessant crucifixion of the flesh so that the spirit may become entirely free. . . .

I have not the capacity for preaching universal non-violence to the country. I preach, therefore, non-violence restricted strictly to the purpose of winning our freedom [India's freedom from British rule] and therefore perhaps for preaching the regulation of international relations by non-violent means. But my incapacity must not be mistaken for that of the doctrine of non-violence. I see it with my intellect in all its effulgence. My heart grasps it. But I have not yet the attainments of preaching universal non-violence with effect. I am not advanced enough for the great task. I have yet anger within me, I have yet [a] duality in me. I can regulate my passions, I keep them under subjection, but before I can preach universal non-violence with effect, I must be wholly free from passions. I must be wholly incapable of sin. Let the revolutionary pray with and for me that I may soon become that. But meanwhile let him take with me the one step to it which I see as clearly as daylight, i.e. to win India's freedom with strictly non-violent means. And then you and I shall have a disciplined, intelligent educated police force that would keep order within and fight raiders from without, if by that time I or someone else does not show a better way of dealing with either. . . .

Not to believe in the possibility of permanent peace is to disbelieve in godliness of human nature. Methods hitherto adopted have failed because rock-bottom sincerity on the part of those who have striven has been lacking. Not that they have realized this lack. Peace is unattainable by part performance of conditions, even as chemical combination is impossible without complete fulfilment of conditions of attainment thereof. If recognized leaders of mankind who have control over engines of destruction were wholly to renounce their use with full knowledge of implications, permanent peace can be obtained. This is clearly impossible without the great powers of the earth renouncing their imperialistic designs. This again seems impossible without these great nations ceasing to believe in soul-destroying competition and to desire to multiply wants and therefore increase their material possessions. It is my conviction that the root of the evil is want of a living faith in a living God. It is a first-class human tragedy that peoples of the earth who claim to believe in the message of Jesus whom they describe as the Prince of Peace show little of that belief in actual practice. It is painful to see sincere Christians . . . limiting the scope of Jesus's message to select individuals. I have been taught from my child-hood, and I have tested the truth by experience, that primary virtues of mankind are possible of cultivation by the meanest of the human species. It is this undoubted universal possibility that distinguishes the human from the rest of God's creation. If even one great nation were unconditionally to perform the supreme act of renunciation, many of us would see in our lifetime visible peace established on earth.

Poverty and Mercy

DOROTHY DAY

One of the most widespread problems of the twentieth century is not modern at all. Poverty has been a motivating force for revolution and historical change for centuries. Yet in the modern world, because of technological advances in communication, the plight of the poor can be revealed with greater accuracy and less abstraction. Class divisions have always been a part of individual societies, but now world divisions have become more evident. The wealth of "First World" countries, such as the United States, Great Britain, and France, are more readily compared to the developing Third World nations in Latin America and Africa. Relief organizations, such as the Peace Corps, Save the Children and CARE have struggled with international poverty for years.

"Poverty and Mercy" is from Robert Ellsberg, ed., *By Little and By Little: The Selected Writings of Dorothy Day* (New York: Alfred A. Knopf, 1983), pp. 93–94, 109–111.

*Independent support has also come from popular rock musicians and enter-
tainers, who have garnered funds through "Live Aid" concerts to relieve
Ethiopian famine victims and to protest South African apartheid policy. Still,
true progress in this sphere does not come from "flash" awareness, but rather
through a long-term commitment to helping others on an individual basis.*

*One of the most influential advocates of social reform in the twentieth
century was Dorothy Day (1897–1980). A founder of the Catholic Worker
movement in 1936, Day established over fifty Houses of Hospitality and
farming communes across the United States where the hungry are fed and the
homeless welcomed. She espoused a life of voluntary poverty and for years
administered to the destitute on Manhattan's Lower East Side, working "little
by little" to restore their dignity and self-respect. A self-proclaimed anarchist
and pacifist, Dorothy Day offers in her writings an ecumenical solution to a
world problem.*

"And There Remained Only the Very Poor" (1940)

[The above quotation] were the words contained in a news account of the
evacuation of Paris. But they apply to New York in the summer. The poor
cannot get away. There is always a residue of the destitute which remains in
the city like mud in a drained pond. You see them in the parks, you see
them lying on the sidewalk in broad daylight along the Bowery, that street
of forgotten men. You see them drifting about the city, from one end to the
other.

They come to us in droves: eight hundred every morning on the coffee
line; one hundred and twenty-five for lunch and again for supper. It is an
informal crowd at noon. They start gathering in the yard, men who have
passed the word along to other transients, homeless ones, that perhaps
there is food to be had. Many days the soup runs short and then there is
only coffee and cake (thanks to Macy's, which gives us their leftovers every
morning).

Many days go by with no money coming in at all. Right now our
telephone is shut off, but the man in the candy store next door calls us to
his phone for messages. Today we expect the gas and electricity to go.
What to do? We can borrow a few oil stoves and continue to cook and feed
those who come. Vegetables are contributed, soup bones, fish. But we must
buy the coffee, sugar, milk, and bread. As long as we are trusted the bills
continue to mount. Even the printer is letting us go to press with $995
owing this summer.

And there is the children's camp on Staten Island, donated by a friend.
It holds eight children—forty can be cared for during the summer—and
they can spend their days on the beach and sleep at night to the rustle of
wind in the maples around the camp. The most beautiful sound in the
world is the sound of little waves on a hot beach. And the sweetest sight is
Viola, aged four, who lives on Grand Street in a six-flight walk-up, one of
eight children, who is playing in the sand and waves on the beach these

days. Or perhaps it is Rosemary and Barbara, Italian and Negro, with their arms around each other's necks as they pose for a picture on the shore.

There is poverty and hunger and war in the world. And we prepare for more war. There is desperate suffering with no prospect of relief. But we would be contributing to the misery and desperation of the world if we failed to rejoice in the sun, the moon, and the stars, in the rivers which surround this island on which we live, in the cool breezes of the bay, in what food we have and in the benefactors God sends.

The heat wave which is a misery to some is to us a joy. We remember the bitter cold of the winter, and those who have to sleep under the stars nestle into the warmth of the hot pavements.

Our greatest misery is the poverty which gnaws at our vitals, an agony to the families in our midst. And the only thing we can do about it is to appeal to you, our readers, begging your help. We are stewards, and we probably manage very badly in trying to take care of all those who come, the desperate, the dispossessed. Like St. Peter, they say, "To whom else shall we go?" and they are our brothers in Christ. They are more than that: they are Christ, appealing to you.

So please help us to keep going. Help these suffering members of the sorrowing Body of Christ.

"Little By Little" (1953)

Poverty is a strange and elusive thing. I have tried to write about it, its joys and its sorrows, for twenty years now; I could probably write about it for another twenty years without conveying what I feel about it as well as I would like. I condemn poverty and I advocate it; poverty is simple and complex at once; it is a social phenomenon and a personal matter. It is a paradox.

St. Francis was "the little poor man" and none was more joyful than he; yet Francis began with tears, with fear and trembling, hiding in a cave from his irate father. He had expropriated some of his father's goods (which he considered his rightful inheritance) in order to repair a church and rectory where he meant to live. It was only later that he came to love Lady Poverty. He took it little by little; it seemed to grow on him. Perhaps kissing the leper was the great step that freed him not only from fastidiousness and a fear of disease but from attachment to worldly goods as well.

Sometimes it takes but one step. We would like to think so. And yet the older I get, the more I see that life is made up of many steps, and they are very small affairs, not giant strides. I have "kissed a leper," not once but twice—consciously—and I cannot say I am much the better for it.

The first time was early one morning on the steps of Precious Blood Church. A woman with cancer of the face was begging (beggars are allowed only in the slums) and when I gave her money (no sacrifice on my part but merely passing on alms which someone had given me) she tried to kiss my hand. The only thing I could do was kiss her dirty old face with the gaping hole in it where an eye and a nose had been. It sounds like a heroic deed but it was not. One gets used to ugliness so quickly. What we avert our eyes from one day is easily borne the next when we have learned a little more about love. Nurses know this, and so do mothers.

Another time I was refusing a bed to a drunken prostitute with a huge, rouged mouth, a nightmare of a mouth. She has been raising a disturbance in the house. I kept remembering how St. Therese said that when you had to refuse anyone anything, you could at least do it so that the person went away a bit happier. I had to deny her a bed but when that woman asked me to kiss her, I did, and it was a loathsome thing, the way she did it. It was scarcely a mark of normal human affection.

We suffer these things and they fade from memory. But daily, hourly, to give up our own possessions and especially to subordinate our own impulses and wishes to others—these are hard, hard things; and I don't think they ever get any easier.

You can strip yourself, you can be stripped, but still you will reach out like an octopus to seek your own comfort, your untroubled time, your ease, your refreshment. It may mean books or music—the gratification of the inner senses—or it may mean food and drink, coffee and cigarettes. The one kind of giving up is not easier than the other. . . .

But the fact remains that every House of Hospitality is full. There is a breadline outside our door, every day, twice a day, two or three hundred strong. Families write us pitifully for help. This is not poverty; this is destitution. . . .

But I am sure that God did not intend that there be so many poor. The class structure is of our making and by our consent, not His, and we must do what we can to change it. So we are urging revolutionary change.

So many sins against the poor cry out to high heaven! One of the most deadly sins is to deprive the laborer of his hire. There is another: to instill in him paltry desires so compulsive that he is willing to sell his liberty and his honor to satisfy them. We are all guilty of concupiscence, but newspapers, radios, television, and battalions of advertising men (woe to that generation!) deliberately stimulate our desires, the satisfaction of which so often means the degradation of the family.

Because of these factors of modern life, the only way we can write about poverty is in terms of ourselves, our own personal responsibility. The message we have been given is the Cross. . . .

On Human Nature (1930)

SIGMUND FREUD

Among the most controversial figures of the twentieth century was the Austrian physician and psychoanalyst Sigmund Freud (1856–1939). Freud sought to apply the critical methods of science to the understanding of the human *unconscious. His research centered on sexuality and the interpretation of dreams in his explanation of human motivation. He portrayed the mind as an area in which the irrational, amoral instincts (*id*) struggled with the restrictive demands of society (*superego*). The ego sought to reconcile these conflicting forces in order to maintain a stable existence. Freud's work stripped humanity of the privacy of its inner nature and led to a revolution in human understanding that has only recently been challenged.*

One of Freud's most revealing works on the antagonisms between the demands of instinct and the restrictions of human society is Civilization and Its Discontents *(1930). In the excerpt below, Freud describes the destructive nature of human beings.*

The element of truth behind all this, which people are so ready to disavow, is that men are not gentle creatures who want to be loved, and who at the most can defend themselves if they are attacked; they are, on the contrary, creatures among whose instinctual endowments is to be reckoned a powerful share of aggressiveness. . . . Anyone who calls to mind the atrocities committed during the racial migrations or the invasions of the Huns, or by the people know as Mongols under Ghengis Khan and Tamerlane, or at the capture of Jerusalem by the pious Crusaders, or even, indeed, the horrors of the recent World War [1914–1918]—anyone who calls these things to mind will have to bow humbly before the truth of this view.

The existence of this inclination to aggression, which we can detect in ourselves and justly assume to be present in others, is the factor which disturbs our relations with our neighbour and which forces civilization into such a high expenditure [of energy]. In consequence of this primary mutual hostility of human beings, civilized society is perpetually threatened with disintegration. The interest of work in common would not hold it together; instinctual passions are stronger than reasonable interests. Civilization has to use its utmost efforts in order to set limits to man's aggressive instincts and to hold the manifestations of them in check. . . . Hence, therefore, the use of methods intended to incite people into identifications and aim-inhibited relationships of love, hence the restriction upon sexual life, and hence too the ideal's commandment to love one's neighbour as oneself—a commandment which is really justified by the fact that nothing else runs so strongly counter to the original nature of man. In spite of every effort, these endeavours of civilization have not so far achieved very much. It hopes to prevent the crudest excesses of brutal violence by itself assuming the right to use violence against criminals, but the law is not able to lay hold of the more cautious and refined manifestations of human aggressiveness. The time comes when each one of us has to give up as illusions the expectations which, in his youth, he pinned upon his fellow-men, and when he may learn how much difficulty and pain has been added to his life by their ill-will. At the same time, it would be unfair to reproach civilization with trying to eliminate strife and competition from human activity. These things are undoubtedly indispensable. But opposition is not necessarily enmity; it is merely misused and made an *occasion* for enmity.

The Communists believe that they have found the path to deliverance from our evils. According to them, man is wholly good and is well-disposed to his neighbour; but the institution of private property has corrupted his nature. The ownership of private wealth gives the individual power, and with it the temptation to ill-treat his neighbour; while the man who is excluded from possession is bound to rebel in hostility against his oppressor. If private property were abolished, all wealth held in common, and everyone allowed to share in the enjoyment of it, ill-will and hostility would disappear among men. Since everyone's needs would be satisfied, no one would have any reason to regard another as his enemy; all would willingly undertake the work that was necessary. I have no concern with any economic criticisms of the communist system; I cannot enquire into whether the abolition of private property is expedient or advantageous. But I am able to recognize that the psychological premises on which the system is based are an untenable illusion. In abolishing private property we deprive the human illusion. In abolishing private property we deprive the human love of aggression of one of its instruments, certainly a strong one, though certainly not the strongest; but we have in no way altered the differences in power and influence which are misused by aggressiveness, nor have we altered anything in its nature. Aggressiveness was not created by property. It reigned almost without limit in primitive times, when property was still very scanty, and it already shows itself in the nursery almost before property has given up its primal, anal form; it forms the basis of every relation of affection and love among people. . . . If we do away with personal rights over material wealth, there still remains prerogative in the field of sexual relationships, which is bound to become the source of the strongest dislike and the most violent hostility among men who in other respects are on an equal footing. If we were to remove this factor, too, by allowing complete freedom of sexual life and thus abolishing the family, the germ-cell of civilization, we cannot, it is true, easily foresee what new paths the development of civilization could take; but one thing we can expect, and that is that this indestructible feature of human nature will follow it there. . . .

The fateful question for the human species seems to me to be whether and to what extent their cultural development will succeed in mastering the disturbance of their communal life by the human instinct of aggression and self-destruction. It may be that in this respect precisely the present time deserves a special interest. Men have gained control over the forces of nature to such an extent that with their help they would have no difficulty in exterminating one another to the last man. They know this, and hence comes a large part of their current unrest, their unhappiness and their mood of anxiety. . . .

The Responsibility of the Individual (1956)

JEAN-PAUL SARTRE

Existentialism has been an important philosophical movement in the twentieth century. Its premier spokesman, Jean-Paul Sartre, in his book Being and Nothingness, *contends that human beings are condemned to be free and that with freedom comes responsibility for one's choices and actions. Such responsibility for war, life, and death is a burden that cannot be shirked and is not easily borne.*

The essential consequence of our earlier remarks is that man being condemned to be free carries the weight of the whole world on his shoulders; he is responsible for the world and for himself as a way of being. . . . Thus there are no *accidents* in a life. . . . If I am mobilized in a war, this war is *my* war; it is in my image and I deserve it. I deserve it first because I could always get out of it by suicide or by desperation; these ultimate possibilities are those which must always be present for us when there is a question of envisaging a situation. For lack of getting out of it, I have *chosen* it. This can be due to inertia, to cowardice in the face of public opinion, or because I prefer certain other values to the value of the refusal to join in the war (the good opinion of my relatives, the honor of my family, *etc.*). Anyway you look at it, it is a matter of a choice. This choice will be repeated later on again and again without a break until the end of the war. . . . Thus, totally free, undistinguishable from the period for which I have chosen to be the meaning, as profoundly responsible for the war as if I had myself declared it, unable to live without integrating it in *my* situation, engaging myself in it wholly and stamping it with my seal, *I must be without remorse or regrets as I am without excuse; for from the instant of my upsurge into being, I carry the weight of the world by myself alone without anything or any person being able to lighten it.*

The Second Sex (1949)

SIMONE DE BEAUVOIR

In 1949, four years after the end of World War II, there appeared two books that sought to examine the subordinate position of women in Western society. Both Simone de Beauvoir and Margaret Mead believed that in a troubled and changing world, society was neglecting the individual and collective resources of women. But their approaches and conclusions differed widely.

Simone de Beauvoir (1908–1986) saw the condition of women in existential terms, as polarized in their relationships with the male sex: man had established his dominance as the One, with woman relegated to status as the Other. In her book The Second Sex *she argued that woman could overcome her inferiority by breaking away from an identity viewed only in relation to man and by asserting her individuality as a creative and responsive being in her own right. By taking charge of her own existence and becoming active like man, she would be able to transcend her "otherness" and establish her unique place in society.*

A man would never get the notion of writing a book on the peculiar situation of the human male. But if I wish to define myself, I must first of all say: "I am a woman"; on this truth must be based all further discussion. A man never begins by presenting himself as an individual of a certain sex; it goes without saying that he is a man. The terms *masculine* and *feminine* are used symmetrically only as a matter of form, as on legal papers. In actuality the relation of the two sexes is not quite like that of two electrical poles, for man represents both the positive and the neutral, as is indicated by the common use of *man* to designate human beings in general; whereas woman represents only the negative, defined by limiting criteria, without reciprocity. In the midst of an abstract discussion it is vexing to hear a man say: "You think thus and so because you are a woman"; but I know that my only defense is to reply: "I think thus and so because it is true," thereby removing my subjective self from the argument. It would be out of the question to reply: "And you think the contrary because you are a man," for it is understood that the fact of being a man is no peculiarity. A man is in the right in being a man; it is the woman who is in the wrong. It amounts to this: just as for the ancients there was an absolute vertical with reference to which the oblique was defined, so there is an absolute human type, the masculine. Woman has ovaries, a uterus; these peculiarities imprison her in her subjectivity, circumscribe her within the limits of her own nature. It is often said that she thinks with her glands. Man superbly ignores the fact that his anatomy also includes glands, such as the testicles, and that they secrete hormones. He thinks of his body as a direct and normal connection with the world, which he believes he apprehends objectively, whereas he regards the body of woman as a hindrance, a prison, weighed down by everything peculiar to it. "The female is a female by virtue of a certain *lack* of qualities," said Aristotle; "we should regard the female nature as afflicted with a natural defectiveness." And St. Thomas [Aquinas] for his part pronounced woman to be an "imperfect man," an "incidental" being. This is symbolized in Genesis where Eve is depicted as made from what Bossuet called "a supernumerary bone" of Adam.

Thus humanity is male and man defines woman not in herself but as relative to him; she is not regarded as an autonomous being. . . . She is simply what man decrees; thus she is called "the sex," by which is meant that she appears essentially to the male as a sexual being. For him she is sex—absolute sex, no less. She is defined and differentiated with reference to man and not he with reference to her; she is the incidental, the inessential as opposed to the essential. He is the Subject, he is the Absolute—she is the Other. . . .

There are, to be sure, other cases in which a certain category has been able to dominate another completely for a time. Very often this privilege depends upon inequality of numbers—the majority imposes its rule upon the minority or persecutes it. But women are not a minority, like the American Negroes or the Jews; there are as many women as men on earth. Again, the two groups concerned have often been originally independent; they may have been formerly unaware of each other's existence, or perhaps they recognized each other's autonomy. But a historical event has resulted in the subjugation of the weaker by the stronger. The scattering of the Jews, the introduction of slavery into America, the conquests of imperialism are examples in point. In these cases the oppressed retained at least the memory of former days; they possessed in common a past, a tradition, sometimes a religion or a culture. . . . Throughout history [women] have always been subordinated to men, and hence their dependency is not the result of a historical event or a social change—it was not something that *occurred.* The reason why otherness in this case seems to be an absolute is in part that it lacks the contingent or incidental nature of historical facts. A condition brought about at a certain time can be abolished at some other time . . . ; but it might seem that a natural condition is beyond the possibility of change. In truth, however, the nature of things is no more immutably given, once for all, than is historical reality. If woman seems to be the inessential which never becomes the essential, it is because she herself fails to bring about this change. Proletarians say "We"; Negroes also. Regarding themselves as subjects, they transform the bourgeois, the whites, into "others." But women do not say "We," except at some congress of feminists or similar formal demonstration; men say "women," and women use the same word in referring to themselves. They do not authentically assume a subjective attitude. . . . But the women's effort has never been anything more than a symbolic agitation. They have gained only what men have been willing to grant; they have taken nothing, they have only received.

The reason for this is that women lack concrete means for organizing themselves into a unit which can stand face to face with the correlative unit. They have no past, no history, no religion of their own; and they have no such solidarity of work and interest as that of the proletariat. They are not even promiscuously herded together in the way that creates community feeling among the American Negroes, the ghetto Jews, the workers of Saint-Denis, or the factory hands of Renault. They live dispersed among the males, attached through residence, housework, economic condition, and social standing to certain men—fathers or husbands—more firmly than they are to other women. . . . The bond that unites her to her oppressors is not comparable to any other. The division of the sexes is a biological fact, not an event in human history. . . . The couple is a fundamental unity with its two halves riveted together, and the cleavage of society along the line of sex is impossible. Here is to be found the basic trait of woman: she is the Other in a totality of which the two components are necessary to one another. . . .

Now, woman has always been man's dependent, if not his slave; the two sexes have never shared the world in equality. And even today woman is heavily handicapped, though her situation is beginning to change. Almost nowhere is her legal status the same as man's, and frequently it is much to her disadvantage. . . . In the economic sphere men and women can almost be said to make up two castes; other things being equal, the former hold the better jobs, get higher wages, and have more opportunity for success than their new competitors. In industry and politics men have a great many more positions and they monopolize the most important posts. In addition to all this, they enjoy a traditional prestige that the education of children tends in every way to support, for the present enshrines the past—and in the past all history has been made by men. At the present time, when women are beginning to take part in the affairs of the world, it is still a world that belongs to men—they have no doubt of it at all and women have scarcely any. To decline to be the Other, to refuse to be a party to the deal—this would be for women to renounce all the advantages conferred upon them by their alliance with the superior caste. Man-the-sovereign will provide woman-the-liege with material protection and will undertake the moral justification of her existence; thus she can evade at once both the economic risk and the metaphysical risk of a liberty in which ends and aims must be contrived without assistance. Indeed, along with the ethical urge of each individual to affirm his subjective existence, there is also the temptation to forgo liberty and become a thing. This is an inauspicious road, for he who takes it—passive, lost, ruined—becomes henceforth the creature of another's will, frustrated in his transcendence and deprived of every value. But it is an easy road; on it one avoids the strain involved in undertaking an authentic existence. . . . How is it that this world has always belonged to the men and that things have begun to change only recently? Is this change a good thing? Will it bring about an equal sharing of the world between men and women?

Male and Female (1949)

MARGARET MEAD

Simone de Beauvoir's impassioned analysis of the subordinate position of women throughout history stands in striking contrast to the arguments of American anthropologist Margaret Mead, whose compilation of lectures ap-

peared in 1949 as Male and Female: A Study of the Sexes in a Changing World. *Mead, whose studies of the cultures of the Pacific islands engendered academic respect and popular acclaim, was later critical of Beauvoir for failing to acknowledge women's contributions as mothers. She disagreed with Beauvoir's glorification of male characteristics and argued for a necessary interplay of unique female and male "gifts" that were essential for the continuity and progress of civilization.*

The differences between the two sexes is one of the important conditions upon which we have built the many varieties of human culture that give human beings dignity and stature. In every known society, mankind has elaborated the biological division of labour into forms often very remotely related to the original biological differences that provided the original clues. . . .

But we always find the patterning. We know of no culture that has said, articulately, that there is no difference between men and women except in the way that they contribute to the creation of the next generation; that otherwise in all respects they are simply human beings with varying gifts, no one of which can be exclusively assigned to either sex. We find no culture in which it has been thought that all identified traits—stupidity and brilliance, beauty and ugliness, friendliness and hostility, initiative and responsiveness, courage and patience and industry—are merely human traits. However differently the traits have been assigned, some to one sex, some to the other, and some to both, however arbitrary the assignment must be seen to be, . . . it has always been there in every society of which we have any knowledge.

So in the twentieth century, as we try to re-assess our human resources, and by taking thought to add even a jot or a tittle to the stature of our fuller humanity, we are faced with a most bewildering and confusing array of apparently contradictory evidence about sex differences. We may well ask: Are they important? Do real differences exist, in addition to the obvious anatomical and physical ones—but just as biologically based—that may be masked by the learnings appropriate to any given society, but which will nevertheless be there? Will such differences run through all of men's and all of women's behaviour? Must we expect, for instance, that a brave girl may be very brave but will never have the same kind of courage as a brave boy, and that the man who works all day at a monotonous task may learn to produce far more than any woman in his society, but he will do it at a higher price to himself? Are such differences real, and *must* we take them into account? Because men and women have always in all societies built a great superstructure of socially defined sex differences that obviously cannot be true for all humanity—or the people just over the mountain should not be able to do it all in the exactly opposite fashion—must *some* such superstructures be built? We have here two different questions: Are we dealing not with a *must* that we dare not flout because it is rooted so deep in our biological mammalian nature that to flout it means individual and social disease? Or with a *must* that, although deeply rooted, still is so very socially convenient and so well tried that it would be uneconomical to flout it—a *must* which says, for example, that it is easier to get children born and bred if we stylize the behaviour of the sexes very differently, teaching them to walk and dress and act in contrasting ways and to specialize in different kinds of work? But there is still the third possibility. Are not sex differences exceedingly valuable, one of the resources of our human nature that every society has used but no society has as yet begun to use to the full?

We live in an age when every inquiry must be judged in terms of urgency. Are such questions about the roles and the possible roles of the sexes academic, peripheral to the central problems of our times? Are such discussions querulous fiddling while Rome burns? I think they are not. Upon the growing accuracy with which we are able to judge our limitations and our potentialities, as human beings and in particular as human societies, will depend the survival of our civilization, which we now have the means to destroy. Never before in history has mankind had such momentous choices placed in its hands. . . .

As a civilization becomes complex, human life is defined in individual terms as well as in the service of the race, and the great structures of law and government, religion and art and science, become something highly valued for themselves. Practiced by men, they become indicators of masculine humanity, and men take great pride in these achievements. To the extent that women are barred from them, women become less human. An illiterate woman is no less human than an illiterate man. As long as few men write and most men cannot, a woman may suffer no loss in her sense of herself. But when writing becomes almost universal—access to books, increased precision of thought, possibilities of communication—then if women cannot learn to write because they are women, they lose in stature, and the whole subtle process begins by which the wholeness of both sexes is undermined. When the women's sense of loss of participation is compensated for by other forms of power, by the iron will of the mother-in-law who has been the docile, home-bound wife . . . then the equilibrating pattern may take the form of covert distortions of human relationships that may persist over centuries. . . . Whatever the compensatory adjustment within the society, women's belief in their own power to contribute directly to human culture will be subtly and deeply impaired, and men's isolation, either covertly threatened or openly attacked, in a world that they have built alone will increase. . . .

Once it is possible to say it is as important to take women's gifts and make them available to both men and women, in transmittable form, as it was to take men's gifts and make the civilization built upon them available to both men and women, we shall have enriched our society. . . . The mother who must learn that the infant who was but an hour ago a part of her body is now a different individual, with its own hungers and its own needs, and that if she listens to her own body to interpret the child, the child will die, is schooled in an irreplaceable school. As she learns to attend to that different individual, she develops a special way of thinking and feeling about human beings. We can leave these special learnings at the present level, or convert them into a more elaborate part of our civilization. Already the men and women who are working together in the human sciences are finding the greatly increased understanding that comes from the way in which their insights complement each other. We are learning that we pay different prices for our insights: for instance, to understand the way a culture socializes children a man must return in imagination to childhood, but a woman has also another and different path, to learn to understand the mothers of these children. Yet both are necessary, and the skill of one sex gives only a partial answer. We can build a whole society only by using both the gifts special to each sex and those shared by both sexes—by using the gifts of the whole of humanity. . . . Only by recognizing that each change in human society must be made by those who carry in every cell of their bodies the very reason why the change is necessary can we school our hearts to the patience to build truly and well, recognizing that it is not only the price, but also the glory, of our humanity that civilization must be built by human beings.

Toward the Twenty-first Century and a Philosophy of History

The autopsy of history is that all great nations commit suicide.

—Arnold Toynbee

Perhaps one of the greatest controversies of the twentieth century has revolved around a comparison of the relative virtues and vices of "bourgeois capitalism" and communism. There is an obvious difference in Marxism as an ideology and theory of social organization, and as practiced by Lenin and corrupted by Stalin. The controversy is made all the more difficult because of confusions in terminology and the distortions of propaganda utilized to win the hearts and minds of various populations. Most of the last half of the twentieth century has been spent in political and military competition between these two spheres in the Cold War of spies and speeches, and more dangerously in Korea and Vietnam.

With the failure of communism to produce the utopia that Marx advocated as inevitable, his ideology has come under increasing attack. In the first selection, Tim Koranda, president of the East/West Alliance, gave his assessment in a speech to the Symposium on World Economic Development. It is followed by Mikhail Gorbachev's call to assess Marxism in a broadened context.

The God That Failed History: "Marx Was Wrong" (1990)

TIM KORANDA

Last June [1989], Francis Fukuyama published a provocative essay in the *National Interest* magazine entitled, "The End of History?" arguing that bourgeois democracy is the telos of political life: the final archetype in man's long march from primitive society to modern society. The article proved prophetic in light of subsequent events in East Berlin, Eastern Europe, and now the Soviet Union. These events have left Marxist historians alienated from the product of their labors. How is it that a communist society—that dictatorship of the proletariat—can revolt and become democratic and capitalist? The question so intrigued me that I decided to do what Marx would have done: re-read history for its paradigms.

According to Marx's materialist conception of history, societies pass through four formative stages on their way to becoming communist: asiatic, ancient, feudal and bourgeois capitalist.

The asiatic stage is a highly organized tribal state characterized by an absence of private property; the ancient, a slave-owning society; the feudal, a rent-based society defined by ownership of land; and the bourgeois capitalist, a society of shareholders and workers.

The history of the East European countries never fit the Marxist paradigm since communism was largely imposed from without. And as historians often point out, Russia and China don't measure up either because neither evolved from feudalism into capitalism on the way to becoming communist. Even today, the U.S.S.R. and China are forty and eighty percent agrarian, respectively.

Marxists learned to live with these contradictions in much the same way a neurotic learns to live with his conflicts. But despite firmly-held beliefs in the face of contrary fact, Marxists now face a crisis of confidence as events conspire to destroy the paradigm.

Marxist history differs from other deterministic systems in its assumption that history is non-cyclical. Marx said that history never moves backwards, and that all its conquests are final and irrevocable. The asiatic society is to be replaced by the ancient; the ancient would give way to the medieval; feudalism was to break down into capitalism. And finally, capitalism was to be swept away by communism. But Marx's reading of history was never true to history. In the West, feudalism wasn't replaced by capitalism. It was replaced by a non-marxist communism.

During the medieval era, walled towns co-existed with landed estates, the former offering escaped serfs and yeoman the promise of a better life.

"The God That Failed History" is from Tim Koranda, speech delivered before the Symposium on World Economic Development, New York, New York, on May 15, 1990. Contained in *Vital Speeches of the Day*, October 15, 1990, pp. 19–21. Reprinted by permission.

Trade guilds, which defined the economic life of the towns, were brotherhoods—collective associations of workers in the same trade that shared profits and spurned competition. There were guilds of goldsmiths and silversmiths, of butchers and bakers, doctors and tailors, hatters and glovers, and of fishmongers and shoemakers. . . .

The guilds, however, were a necessary transition from a feudal to a capitalist society. Merchant guilds such as the Commenda, the Hansa and the Merchant Adventurers, had first-hand experience cultivating overseas markets and cheap sources of raw materials. This broadened the markets that the guilds served but also helped undermine the structure of society. . . .

Change was necessary. Capitalism demanded too much of the guilds. Encumbered by regulation and Christian ideas of brotherhood, they had trouble adjusting to the world they had helped create. Their communistic structure impeded efficiency and their insularity ruled out raising outside capital. By the mid-15th century these communist organizations evolved into "chartered and regulated companies" which traded in "joint stock," allowing outsiders to buy in. This was the beginning of capitalism.

Therefore, Marx was wrong. Communism, guild style, was the precursor of capitalism in the West and not the other way around. And that's precisely what happened in Eastern Europe and is happening in the Soviet Union. Communism was the guild phase—an important step toward capitalist democracy, a transition to more efficient economic organization.

Before communism, Eastern Europe had been underdeveloped. Capital accumulation was extremely low. This lack of accumulation was largely due to large estates continuing wasteful consumption patterns. The principal economic activity—farming—provided very meager savings. And instead of being invested in fixed capital, the savings were earmarked for usurious consumer loans. . . .

The communist takeover after World War II helped steward the region's core capital, providing an exogenous transition from a feudal to a communist society. Now, with the arrival of democracy and capitalism, the paradigm is complete.

Over the past forty years, the East European countries have mastered industrial processes that evolved over one hundred fifty years in the West. Today, Belgrade, Budapest and Prague are manufacturing everything from small motors to men's suits, and finding ready markets in the West. . . . The move to capitalism will bring about greater efficiencies as markets determine the allocation of the nation's resources.

A similar pattern is apparent in Russia. Long before Gorbachev, Peter the Great [seventeenth and eighteenth centuries] made an heroic attempt to modernize the country by establishing new industries and converting small workshops into large scale manufactories. . . . Factories mushroomed during Peter's reign, but demand remained flat prompting his successors to abandon the modernization scheme. Peter the Great attempted the wholesale conversion of a feudal state into a modern capitalistic state. But that conversion is only possible now, after several decades of communist rule. Even though the Soviets renounced the use of foreign capital for industrial development, they desired a high rate of industrial growth and paid for it largely from the earning of agriculture. The collectivization of farms provided the seed money, so to speak, for large scale industry and mass production. The transition to private ownership and entrepreneurship is now all but certain.

The pattern in China is more bewildering. . . . The great achievement of communism in China was not so much in industrialization as in wiping out the corruption and extortion that robbed basic industries of capital. Ironically, recent Chinese attempts to modernize the country through economic incentives have only produced a class of wealthy farmer. But the guild phase of communism—the transition stage—may be taking root right now in the form of joint ventures with foreign companies. Most of the venture partners have now returned to China after last spring's violence. And while democracy may be the only way to avoid more violence and the probable flight of capital, China's leaders are reluctant democrats.

The Chinese will likely arrive at capitalism in a way that again repeals the laws of Marxist history: by revolution against communism. One could say that the only thing they have to lose are their chains.

"The Ideology of Socialism Is Not a Textbook" (1990)
MIKHAIL GORBACHEV

The ideology of socialism [understood as communism] is not a textbook where everything is compartmentalized by chapters, paragraphs, rules and principles. It will shape up together with socialism itself, as we will facilitate the development of a well-fed, civilized, spiritually rich, free and happy country, as we come to embrace universal human values again not as something alien from the class point of view, but as normal for man. These values have been worked out throughout centuries and millennia. What their neglect has brought us is well known.

The ideology of socialism will shape up as the country gets integrated into the general progress of civilization. It is for this reason that new thinking, which is being accepted in the world as our new internationalism, bringing together rather than splitting the world into confronting camps, underlies the widest possible framework for shaping it.

We inherit from Marx, Engels, and Lenin the top methodology, the dialectical way of thinking, on which we will draw in theory and practice. But we will not allow everything created by the classics to be reduced into just another short course, which some people seem to regret judging by

" 'The Ideology of Socialism Is Not a Textbook' " is from Mikhail Gorbachev, speech delivered at the 28th Communist Party Congress, Moscow, U.S.S.R., on July 10, 1990. Contained in *Vital Speeches of the Day*, August 15, 1990, p. 646.

some speeches. This will not come to pass. It will kill perestroika and society.

It struck me that no sooner had a speaker mounted this rostrum, trying to put the problems of our day in a philosophical context and to look at our work in this context, as apathy could be felt in the hall and the clampdown started. But how have we grown accustomed to simple and clear formulas: "to be or not to be," "down with or not down with?" Let us think. We are, after all, a party which lays claim to being the vanguard of society. Given the current level of intellectual work, the sluggishness and our attitude to intellectual work, we will never become the vanguard force and lose even what we have today.

"The Divine Spark of Creative Power Is Still Alive in Us" (1946)
ARNOLD TOYNBEE

As we near the end of the twentieth century, the task of assessing our place in history becomes a vital concern. History has purpose in helping us understand where we are on the road to progress or decline. One of the most important individuals to break from the confines of specialized history and seek a broader perspective regarding the continuity of civilization was Arnold Toynbee (1889–1975). In his masterpiece, A Study of History *(1934–1961), Toynbee examined the rise and fall of twenty-six civilizations in the course of human history. He concluded that they rose by responding successfully to challenges that had been placed before them. Civilizations declined when their leadership could no longer respond creatively to the demands of nationalism, militarism, and the tyranny of a despotic minority. Toynbee did not regard the decline of civilizations as inevitable and explains his ideas in the following excerpt.*

What, then, causes the breakdowns of civilizations? Before applying our own method, which involves the marshalling of relevant concrete facts of history, we had better pass in review certain solutions of the problem which soar higher in search of their evidence and rely for proof either on unprovable dogmas or else on things outside the sphere of human history. . . .

[In earlier chapters, we] disposed of three deterministic explanations of the breakdowns of civilizations: the theory that they are due to the "running down" of the "clockwork" of the Universe or to the senescence of the Earth; the theory that a civilization, like a living organism, has a life-span determined by the biological laws of its nature; and the theory that the breakdowns are due to a deterioration in the quality of the individuals participating in a civilization, as a result of their pedigrees' accumulating too long a tale of "civilized" ancestors. We have still to consider one further hypothesis, generally referred to as the cyclical theory of history. . . .

Does reason constrain us to believe . . . in a cyclic movement of human history? Have we not, in the course of this Study, ourselves given encouragement to such a supposition? What of those movements of Yin and Yang, Challenge and Response, Withdrawal and Return . . . which we have elucidated? Are they not variations on the trite theme that "History repeats itself"? Certainly, in the movement of all these forces that weave the web of human history, there is an obvious element of recurrence. Yet the shuttle which shoots backwards and forwards across the loom of Time in a perpetual to-and-fro is all this time ringing into existence a tapestry in which there is manifestly a developing design and not simply an endless repetition of the same pattern. This, too, we have seen again and again. . . . This harmony of two diverse movements—a major irreversible movement which is born on the wings of a minor repetitive movement—is perhaps the essence of what we mean by rhythm; and we can discern this play of forces not only in . . . modern machinery, but likewise in the organic rhythm of life. . . .

This is a message of encouragement for us children of the Western Civilization as we drift today alone, with none but stricken civilizations around us. It may be that Death the Leveller will lay icy hand on our civilization also. . . . The dead civilizations are not dead by fate, or "in the course of nature," and therefore our living civilization is not doomed inexorably in advance to "join the majority" of its species. Though sixteen civilizations may have perished already to our knowledge, and nine others may be now at the point of death, we—the twenty-sixth—are not compelled to submit the riddle of our fate to the blind arbitrament of statistics. The divine spark of creative power is still alive in us, and, if we have the grace to kindle it into flame, then the stars in their courses cannot defeat our efforts to attain the goal of human endeavor.

The Synthesis of Humanity (1959)

PIERRE TEILHARD DE CHARDIN

Not all twentieth-century philosophy is pessimistic and cut from the mold of existentialism. Pierre Teilhard de Chardin (1881–1955) was a Jesuit father and paleontologist who theorized that man is constantly evolving, mentally and socially, toward a final spiritual unity. He believed that science and religion were two of the essential disciplines of discovery and was concerned that they had always been competing forces. Teilhard advocated the union of science and religion in order to gain a true perspective of the human epic. He is decidedly optimistic in his assessment.

We are, at this very moment, passing through an age of *transition.* . . . To us, in our brief span of life, falls the honour and good fortune of coinciding with critical change. . . . In these confused and restless zones in which present blends with future in a world of upheaval, we stand face to face with all the grandeur, the unprecedented grandeur, of the phenomenon of man. Here if anywhere, now if ever, have we, more legitimately than any of our predecessors, the right to think that we can measure the importance and detect the direction of the process of hominisation. Let us look critically and try to decipher the particular form of mind which is coming to birth in the womb of the earth today. . . .

So far we have certainly allowed our race [the human race] to develop at random, and we have given too little thought to the question of what medical and moral factors *must replace the crude forces of natural selection* should we suppress them. In the course of the coming centuries it is indispensable that a nobly human form of eugenics, on a standard worthy of our personalities, should be discovered and developed.

Eugenics applied to individuals leads to eugenics applied to society. . . . Points involved are: the distribution of the resources of the globe; the control of the trek towards unpopulated areas; the optimum use of the powers set free by mechanization; the physiology of nations and races; geo-economy, geopolitics, geo-demography; the organisation of research developing into a reasoned organisation of the earth. Whether we like it or not, all the signs and all our needs converge in the same direction. We need and are irresistibly being led to create, by means of and beyond all physics, all biology and all psychology, *a science of human energetics.*

It is in the course of that creation, already obscurely begun, that science, by being led to concentrate on man, will find itself increasingly face to face with religion.

To outward appearance, the modern world was born of an antireligious movement: man becoming self-sufficient and reason supplanting belief. Our generation and the two that preceded it have heard little but talk of the conflict between science and faith; indeed, it seemed at one moment a foregone conclusion that the former was destined to take the place of the latter.

But, inasmuch as the tension is prolonged, the conflict visibly seems to need to be resolved in terms of an entirely different form of equilibrium—not in elimination, nor duality, but in synthesis. After close on two centuries of passionate struggles, neither science nor faith has succeeded in discrediting its adversary. On the contrary, it becomes obvious that neither can develop normally without the other. And the reason is simple: the same life animates both. Neither in its impetus nor its achievements can science go to its limits without becoming tinged with mysticism and charged with faith. . . .

In short, as soon as science outgrows the analytic investigations which constitute its lower and preliminary stages, and passes on to synthesis— synthesis which naturally culminates in the realisation of some superior state of humanity—it is at once led to foresee and place its stakes on the future. . . .

Thus . . . the nineteenth century [was] not wrong to speak of a Religion of Science. Their mistake was not to see that their cult of humanity implied the reintegration, in a renewed form, of those very spiritual forces they claimed to be getting rid of. . . . Taking advantage of the immense duration it has still to live, mankind has enormous possibilities before it.

Civilization and Memory: The Elderly as Keepers of the Flame (1990)

STEPHEN BERTMAN

Because of advancements in medical technology and attention to public health care through governmental programs and private initiative, our population is living longer. The concerns of the elderly increasingly occupy a primary position on legislative agendas and in the public view. Traditionally, the elderly have been regarded as the repositories of wisdom and experience. In a speech to the Gerontological Society of America, Stephen Bertman, professor of classics at the University of Windsor, offered his views about the changing roles of the elderly in a modern technological society where short-term memory is everything and computers store and retrieve the information of generations.

The most sacred place in ancient Rome was the Temple of Vesta in the Roman Forum. Vesta was the goddess of the hearth-fire that burned in every home. Maintained by generations of priestesses, an eternal flame inside the temple symbolized the centrality of the family in Roman life and the binding power of tradition.

However progressive Roman civilization became, its validity was forever measured by the extent to which it remained faithful to the traditions of the past, the *mores maiorum*, or ancestral ways. To the extent that Roman civilization deviated from those ways, to that extent was its viability diminished. The importance of guidance from elders was enshrined in the institution of the Roman Senate, a name derived from the Latin word for old person, or *senex*.

"Civilization and Memory" is from Stephen Bertman (The University of Windsor, Windsor, Ontario, N 9B 3P4, Canada), speech delivered to the 43rd Annual Scientific Meeting of the Gerontological Society of America, Boston, Massachusetts, on November 18, 1990. Contained in *Vital Speeches of the Day*, January 1, 1991, pp. 185–186. Reprinted by permission of the author.

Nevertheless, time itself and the accelerating force of social change distanced the Romans not only from the past but from the moral imperatives of that past. Both the Senate and the elderly were eventually deauthoritized. Vesta's flame sputtered and the Empire fell.

The elderly of every era are the biologic embodiment of the past tense. To the extent that past is devalued, to that extent also will the elderly be devalued and deemed socially irrelevant. In the world of the future, the elderly will seem more and more irrelevant—even to themselves—as they continue to lose touch with the rapidly shifting dimensions and contours of the landscape they come to inhabit. Traditionally, elder citizens have been regarded as the living repositories of ancestral wisdom. Three factors, however, will conspire to strip the elderly of such credentials in the future: the accelerating obsolescence of past knowledge, the expanding accumulation of self-justifying data, and the propagation of dehumanized instruments to access facts.

Once valued as guides for a long journey, the elderly will become the trivialized guardians of an empty suitcase—the impotent, grown-up version of the culturally illiterate younger generation of today. As a class the elderly will constitute the social equivalent of the Alzheimer's victim: ironically oblivious to the past at the very time when their collective store of memories should be the greatest.

Time levels all. Denied their special role as defenders of age-old tradition, the old will increasingly ape the young. In the future cult of the NOW, short-term memory will replace long-term as antiquated experience slips down the slick memory-chute to oblivion. In the society of the future, where history itself will be an anachronism, few moral traditions will survive. This is not to deny that the elderly may form a political constituency in the future, united by a commonality of experience, temperament, and need. Nor is it to deny that, by virtue of their longevity and numbers, they will play an increasing role in the governing of America. But any discussion of potential gerontocracy must take into account the *content* of their role, not merely their presence on the stage.

If the elderly cease to stand for traditional values, what *will* they stand for? And if the elderly cease to remember where the Temple of Vesta stands, who then will maintain tradition's fire? . . .

What if the old have forgotten what to teach? And what if the young do not know what to learn? Then civilization itself is in peril. Were our culture to be left with its external trappings only—the glare of military power and the glitter of material wealth—it would not have satisfied the essential conditions that every civilization must fulfill in order to endure. More than a body, every civilization needs a heart. But more than a heart, every civilization needs a memory.

No civilization can exist for long if it is conscious only of the present. It must draw its nourishment instead from two other sources: its dreams for the future and the remembered experiences and dreams of the past.

If there is to be a gerontocracy, then let it be a gerontocracy of wise guardians who reverence not only life, but time, not a gerontocracy of aerobic ghosts dancing in rhythmic frenzy to songs whose words they have long since forgotten.

CHRONOLOGY: Our Contemporary World: The Progress of Civilization

February 1945	Yalta Conference between Churchill, Roosevelt, and Stalin decides on four occupation zones in Germany and the prosecution of war criminals; it prepares an Allied Control Council to run Germany on the basis of "complete disarmament, demilitarization, and dismemberment."
June 1945	Charter of the United Nations signed.
July 1945	Potsdam Conference between Churchill, Truman, and Stalin finalizes agreement on the administration of Germany and the territorial adjustments in Eastern Europe.
August 6–9, 1945	The U.S. drops atomic bombs on Hiroshima and Nagasaki in an atempt to bring a speedy conclusion to World War II.
March 6, 1946	Churchill makes "Iron Curtain" speech at Fulton, Missouri: "From Stettin in the Baltic to Trieste in the Adriatic, an Iron Curtain has descended upon the Continent."
March 1947	In a message to Congress, President Truman outlines the Truman Doctrine, which effectively commits the United States to intervene against Communist or Communist-backed movements in Europe and elsewhere.
June 1947	George Marshall, American secretary of state, calls for a European recovery program (Marshall Plan) supported by American aid.
1948–1949	Soviets impose a complete blockade of traffic into Berlin. Successful airlift of supplies into Berlin continues for nearly one year until blockade is lifted.
April 1949	Creation of NATO (North Atlantic Treaty Organization), a defensive alliance, which pledges mutual military assistance.
September 1951	First Soviet atomic bomb exploded.
March 1953	Death of Stalin. Khrushchev confirmed as First Secretary of the Communist Party (September).
February 1956	Khrushchev attacks the abuses of the Stalin era at the Communist Twentieth Party Congress.
October–November 1956	General strike and street demonstrations in Budapest. Soviets intervene, depose Nagy, and crush the uprising.
1957	Treaty of Rome establishes European Economic Community (EEC, or the "Common Market").

April 1961	First manned Soviet space flight.
August 1961	Berlin Wall constructed to prevent flight from East to West Berlin.
October 1961	Program of Twenty-second Communist Party. Congress advocates further "de-Stalinization."
October 1962	Cuban Missile Crisis after Soviet Union attempts to construct ballistic missile bases in Cuba. Imposition of naval "quarantine" by the United States forces the Soviet Union to back down in the face of the threat of nuclear war.
October 1964	Leonid Brezhnev replaces Khrushchev as General Secretary of the Communist Party.
August 1968	The Soviet Union and other Warsaw Pact forces invade Czechoslovakia and end the "Prague Spring" liberation movement. Czech leaders are forced to agree to reimposition of censorship, centralized Communist control, military occupation, and abandonment of closer links with the West.
May 26, 1972	President Nixon visits Moscow. Strategic Arms Limitation Treaty (SALT 1) signed limiting antiballistic missile systems.
February 1974	Dissident writer and Nobel laureate, Alexander Solzhenitsyn deported from Soviet Union.
October 1975	Soviet physicist and dissident Andrei Sakharov awarded Nobel Peace Prize.
1979	Margaret Thatcher leads Conservative Party to victory in Great Britain and becomes first woman Prime Minister. Stays in office until 1990.
December 1979	Soviet invasion of Afghanistan. United States imposes a grain embargo on Soviet Union.
1980	François Mitterrand, Socialist Party candidate, is elected President of France.
January 1980	Andrei Sakharov sentenced to internal exile in Gorky.
July–September 1980	Widespread strikes among Polish workers led by Lech Walesa at Gdansk result in published demands for free trade unions. New Solidarity unions recognized and reforms on wages and working hours agreed upon.
December 1981	Martial law declared in Poland. Leading members of Solidarity are arrested and the organization banned.
1982	Helmut Kohl becomes West German Chancellor.

November 1982	Death of Brezhnev. Succession of short-lived Soviet leaders: Andropov (d. 1984) and Chernenko (d. 1985).
1985	Mikhail Gorbachev becomes General Secretary of the Communist Party of the Soviet Union.
1988	Development of Gorbachev's concepts of perestroika and glasnost. New constitution adopted in Soviet Union, which permits openly contested elections. Soviet withdrawal from Afghanistan. European Economic Community agrees to work toward free trade zone by 1992.
1989	Revolutionary movements throughout Eastern Europe result in fall of Communist regimes in Hungary, Czechoslovakia, Romania, Bulgaria, and East Germany. Berlin Wall opened in November and thousands of East Berliners cross into the West.
1990	Gorbachev calls for the end of the Communist Party's monopoly on political power in the Soviet Union. Reunification of Germany.
June 1991	Boris Yeltsin elected President of Russian Republic in general election. Open competition with Gorbachev for future political direction of Soviet Union.
August 1991	Gorbachev survives an abortive coup attempt by conservative members of his advisory cabinet. Boris Yeltsin's prestige grows as a result of his defiant public stand during the uprising. Gorbachev resigns as General Secretary of Communist party with his authority in question and the party in disarray. The Baltic states of Estonia, Latvia, and Lithuania achieve independence from the Soviet Union. Future of the U.S.S.R. as a political entity is in doubt as several republics declare their intention to secede from the union.

STUDY QUESTIONS

Section I: Political and Technological Developments

1. Do you think that President Truman was justified in his use of the atomic bomb on Hiroshima and Nagasaki? Are Churchill's arguments in support of this decision convincing? The Baruch Plan was the first comprehensive package for the control of atomic energy. Is this a responsible document? Why? Does it make Truman's use of "The Bomb" easier to accept?

2. The first and only time nuclear weapons have been directed against human beings occurred in 1945. For those born after this date, can the terror of that event long ago maintain our allegiance toward arms control, or must we have an example of an atomic explosion every generation or so in order to promote the seriousness of negotiation? Will people forget the

horrors of Hiroshima the further they are removed by time from the experience?

3. What did Stalin mean in his speech of February 1946 by the phrase "Soviet victory"? What policy was Churchill advocating in his "Iron Curtain" speech? Was he pessimistic or optimistic about the possibility of war?

4. In his book *Why War?* (Paris, 1933), the great physicist Albert Einstein wrote, "Mankind can only gain protection against the danger of unimaginable destruction and wanton annihilation if a supranational organization has alone the authority to produce or possess [nuclear] weapons . . . and the legal right and duty to solve all the conflicts which in the past have led to war." What is your reaction to this opinion? To what extent are organizations like the United Nations and Amnesty International useful and effective? Would it make a difference if they did not exist? Why has there been a renewal of confidence in the values and effectiveness of the United Nations in recent years?

5. Note the assessment of George Kennan ("X") in his article, "The Sources of Soviet Conduct." According to Kennan, what measures should the United States have taken in 1947 to combat international communism? Compare the mentality of this article with the selection entitled "How to Spot a Communist." Select what you consider the most effective and most ridiculous arguments from this source. How does vocabulary, logic, and religion easily give away the communist? Do you find any hypocrisy in this document?

6. According to Theodore White, why is communism successful and what are its weaknesses? What are the main points about capitalism and communism that Khrushchev stressed in his speech to the 22nd Communist Party Congress? After analysis of this document, do you agree or disagree with White's assessment of communism?

7. What are the specific criticisms of Sakharov and Solzhenitsyn in their 1974 dissents against the policies of the Soviet Union? Have these problems been resolved by perestroika and glasnost under the leadership of Mikhail Gorbachev? What did Secretary of State George Shultz say about progress in his 1983 speech on American foreign policy? Was the cooperative relationship between the Soviet Union and the United States achieved by the "tough stance" of the Reagan administration, or by the overtures and new policies of Gorbachev? To what extent has there been true progress between the "superpowers"? Is the Cold War really over?

8. How does Mikhail Gorbachev in his various speeches define the concept of perestroika? Why does he refuse to renounce the values of socialism (communism) and in fact determine that its fate is "inseparable from the success of perestroika"? In 1989, Gorbachev described the Communist party as "society's consolidating and vanguard force." How will the party become the political vanguard of society? Did Gorbachev's view of the party's responsibilities change any in his 1990 speech on "political pluralism"? Compare Gorbachev's 1990 speech on the Soviet Federation and

the ethnic issue with the assessment of R. I. Kosolapov in 1982. In light of this comparison and recent developments, how do you evaluate Kosolapov's account? In your opinion, what is the most demanding problem that the Soviet Union faces in the future? Ethnic division, political restructuring, economic instability, or dictatorship?

9. How does Chancellor Helmut Kohl view the impact of a "new" reunited Germany on Europe? What "lessons of history" has Germany learned? What does Kohl mean when noting that "federalism is our real goal for Europe as a whole"? Do you think Kohl is realistic in his assumptions?

10. According to Rainer Gut, what is the primary objective of a single, internal market for the European Community? How does the EC plan to accomplish its goals, what difficulties do European countries face, and what impact will this economic reorganization have on the United States? Can you visualize the implications of an integrated, international economic market?

11. Some have suggested that the future of Europe will be closely linked to the developing economic interests of the Soviet Union or Japan. What is Rainer Gut's reply to this concern? Now note Gorbachev's speech, "A Common European Home." What are the main points of his argument? Should the United States fear the "nightmare vision" of a Europe united under Soviet hegemony?

12. Both François Mitterrand of France and Vaclav Havel of Czechoslovakia offer philosophical perspectives on unity and the progress of Europe. Both appear optimistic. What do they consider to be the foundations of their optimism? What perspective has been gained over time that Mitterrand can now say, "an era of hope is opening up for mankind"? What does Havel mean by his phrase "Consciousness precedes Being"? What does his statement that "history has accelerated" imply?

13. Explore some of the moral questions that arise from medical research. When you replace someone's internal organs, do you change his or her very being? Do the potentials of genetic engineering bother you? Scientists have developed the birth control pill, made possible test tube babies, and are investigating the possibilities of cryogenic preservation. Are these valid areas of scientific research, or are these steps toward the creation of "Frankenstein's monster"?

14. What are some of Robert Gray's main points in his speech on the war against AIDS? What action should be taken and who should lead the way? Do you agree or disagree with his assessment? How important is "moral authority" in the fight against AIDS?

15. David Linowes in his speech on the Information Age raises several important questions about the future. What areas will undergo the greatest impact? Do you agree with his concern about a new kind of colonialism? Do you find the premise that computers might be able to acquire "wisdom" disturbing? Is wisdom, by its very nature, a uniquely human trait?

16. According to Sherry Turkle, how does the computer threaten the very idea of "self?" In what way is the mind machine? In what ways are humans

unique and different from computers? Are humans "feeling computers" or "emotional machines"? How is the computer philosophically becoming both taboo and fascination?

17. Senator Sam Ervin remarked in 1978 that "each time we give up a bit of information about ourselves to the government, we give up some of our freedom. . . . When the government knows all our secrets, we stand naked before official power." Do you agree with him? In the interests of progress, must we stand "partially clothed," if not "naked," before official power?

Section II: Social and Spiritual Dimensions

18. Note Francis Parkman's arguments against women's suffrage carefully. Which ones could be applied to any political, social, religious, or ethnic group that strives for equal status with an incumbent authority? Which of his arguments do you find most specious? the most well-founded and persuasive? Do you agree with his statement that "progress, to be genuine, must be in accord with natural law"? Or do you support the quotation by Shulamith Firestone at the beginning of this section entitled, "The Women's Movement"?

19. What is the scientific evidence for arguing the general inferiority of women, as presented by George Romanes in his article about the mental differences between men and women? How does Romanes damn women with "faint praise"?

20. According to Virginia Woolf, why is the "looking-glass vision" of supreme importance in history? Do you believe, as she wrote, that it is useless to compare the worth of charwomen and lawyers in society? Why? How would you define the "feminine mystique?" Why did women, as Betty Friedan noted, "go home again" in the 1950s? What is the main point of Gloria Steinem's parody entitled "If Men Could Menstruate"? Do you think she's correct in her assessment of male and female power relationships?

21. Does the United Nations Declaration of Women's Rights (1967) seem like a radical document to you? Compare its pronouncements with the assessments of Francis Parkman or George Romanes. To what extent has there been progress in the establishment of women's rights in the twentieth century? Is the U.N. declaration just an idealistic statement that does not reflect the practical situation throughout the world? How do you explain the failure of the Equal Rights Amendment to secure passage in the United States? What are the main problems that Joan Kenner addresses in her speech, "Women in the Marketplace"? Do you think hers is a fair assessment of current realities in the 1990s? Must women adopt male attributes in order to succeed in modern society? What does Simone de Beauvoir say about this?

22. According to Mahatma Gandhi, is violence always to be avoided? What did he mean when he said, "I am a practical idealist"? How difficult is it to

achieve nonviolence? If one must struggle to obtain a nonviolent attitude, does this mean that violence is a dominant characteristic of human nature? Do you think that Albert Einstein was correct in his assessment that "As long as there will be man, there will be wars"?

23. Carefully note Jimmy Carter's arguments on the connection between human rights and foreign policy. Can foreign policy effectively be conducted on this basis? Or do you subscribe to the Machiavellian notion that all nations primarily work toward their own self-interest with little concern for "higher principles" of international cooperation. Therefore, will progress on a human scale always be a secondary concern, if still a desired byproduct, to national self-interest?

24. According to Archbishop Desmond Tutu in 1983, what was the "strategy" of the white Nationalist government toward blacks in South Africa? How does Tutu use religion as a base of appeal? After reading the 1990 speech by F. W. de Klerk, do you think the situation in South Africa has changed radically? What are his specific solutions for the future? Does Nelson Mandela accept the government at its word? What is Mandela's agenda for the future of South Africa?

25. Is racism an inherent aspect of human nature, or is it an aberration that must be taught and cultivated through education and societal reaffirmation? To what extent has the United States progressed in its race relations?

26. What was Sigmund Freud's view of human nature? Do you agree with this view? Compare Freud's ideas with the attitudes of Dorothy Day, and Mahatma Gandhi. Is humanity disposed more toward respecting life and granting mercy or toward aggression?

27. According to Jean-Paul Sartre, why are there no "accidents" in life? Why has existentialism often been called a "depressing philosophy"? If being "free" is usually considered an advantageous human condition, why does the existentialist believe that one is "condemned to be free"?

28. What does Simone de Beauvoir mean by the "otherness" of women? How do women transcend this "otherness" in order to establish a unique place in society? Do you agree with her ideas? Are women still considered the "second sex"? Compare Margaret Mead's thesis with that of Simone de Beauvoir. Are her ideas and suggestions more persuasive than Beauvoir's?

29. According to Tim Koranda's speech, why was Marx wrong? How does Koranda see the development of history and the role of communism? Are you convinced that Marx's interpretation of historical economic development was wrong? How does Gorbachev defend the efficacy of communism? What does he mean by the sentence "The ideology of socialism is not a textbook"?

30. How would you best describe Toynbee's cyclical theory of history? What does he mean by an "organic rhythm of life"? Toynbee decries Oswald Spengler's assertion that civilization is biological in nature and thus is born, matures, ages, and finally dies, just like human beings. Does this theory seem logical and convincing, or do you share Toynbee's doubts?

Must every civilization respond to challenges in order to survive? Without a crisis or challenge to harden and energize a civilization, will it die of its own inertia? How important is creativity to the survival of a civilization?

31. How would you define the concepts of eugenics and energetics as used by Pierre Teilhard de Chardin in the selection "The Synthesis of Humanity"? Do you agree that neither religion nor science can develop normally without the other? How important are spiritual elements not only to the progress of civilization, but to its very survival?

32. What are the three factors that Stephen Bertman maintains will conspire to strip the elderly of their credentials as the repository of wisdom? Explain them carefully. Will short-term memory replace long-term memory in importance? Has that already happened? What ramifications does that have on the future? What will be the role of the elderly in the future, if not to "maintain traditions' fire"?

33. Although the twentieth century has been termed a "secular age," religion has played a significant role throughout the period. Compare the contributions of Pope John XIII ("Pacem in Terris"), Desmond Tutu ("Blacks Will Be Free Whatever You Do or Don't Do"), Dorothy Day ("Poverty and Mercy"), Pierre Teilhard de Chardin ("The Synthesis of Humanity") and Robert Gray ("The War Against AIDS"). Is there a thematic thread that binds these documents? What is the role of organized religion in contemporary society?

34. After you have read through this chapter on the contemporary world, what are your impressions? How do you define the concept "progress," and what seems to be its key ingredient? Is it love, God, or the unfettered researches and discoveries of pure science? Is nonviolence a practical alternative to violence? What will form the basis of humanity's advancement or destruction in the future? Will we continue to live in a world dominated by the dichotomy of progress and holocaust? How much have we progressed on a political, social, and humanitarian scale since the beginning of the twentieth century?